WILLIAM
SHAKESPEARE

Oxford University Press, Amen House, London E.C.4

GLASGOW NEW YORK TORONTO MELBOURNE WELLINGTON
BOMBAY CALCUTTA MADRAS KARACHI LAHORE DACCA
CAPE TOWN SALISBURY NAIROBI IBADAN ACCRA
KUALA LUMPUR HONG KONG

FIRST EDITION 1930
REPRINTED LITHOGRAPHICALLY IN GREAT BRITAIN
AT THE UNIVERSITY PRESS, OXFORD
FROM SHEETS OF THE FIRST EDITION
1951, 1963

PLATE I

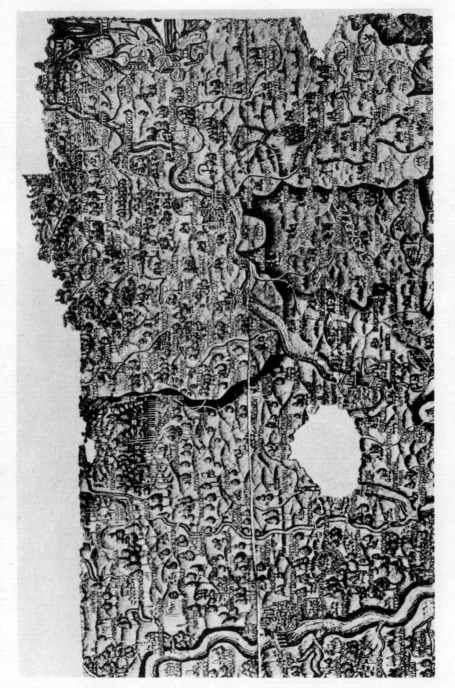

SOUTH WARWICKSHIRE AND NEIGHBOURHOOD

WILLIAM
SHAKESPEARE

A STUDY OF FACTS AND PROBLEMS

BY

E. K. CHAMBERS

VOL. I

'Ο κόσμος σκηνή· ὁ βίος πάροδος·
ἦλθες, εἶδες, ἀπῆλθες
FRAGM. DEMOCRITI

OXFORD
AT THE CLARENDON PRESS

To
N. C.

PREFACE

IN these pages I return, *diversa per aequora vectus*, to the point from which I started in the last century. I then set out to write of Shakespeare, and of the English stage as a background for Shakespeare; and this has been throughout my theme, although I have not found it possible to use quite that brevity of words which the confident surmise of youth anticipated. My remaining purpose is threefold. The present volumes complete the design of *The Elizabethan Stage* by a treatment of its central figure, for which in that book I had no space proportionate to his significance. I collect the scanty biographical *data* from records and tradition, and endeavour to submit them to the tests of a reasonable analysis. And thirdly, I attempt to evaluate the results of bibliographical and historical study in relation to the canon of the plays, and to form a considered opinion upon the nature of the texts in which Shakespeare's work is preserved to us. In so doing, I am led to a confirmation of the doubts expressed in my British Academy lecture of 1924 on *The Disintegration of Shakespeare*, as to the validity of certain drifts of speculation, which tend to minimize at once the originality of that work and the purity of its transmission. I am not so much perturbed as some of my critics seem to think that I ought to be, by finding that my conclusions do not differ essentially from those which have long formed part of the critical tradition. That is itself the outcome of study through many generations by men of diverse tempers, starting from diverse standpoints. They have no doubt left something for modern scholarship to contribute, especially as regards the causes of major textual variations. But I do not think that revolutionary results really emerge from the closer examination of contemporary plays, or of theatrical conditions, or of the psychology of misprints. Shakespeare, as a dramatist, remains something more than the life-tenant of a literary entail.

I have been on well-trodden paths, and my debt to others is heavy: among the earlier writers to Malone, Halliwell-Phillipps, and Dowden beyond the rest; and among my own contemporaries above all to Dr. W. W. Greg, whose published studies I cite on page after page, and upon whose generosity in counsel and information I have constantly drawn during the progress of this book. I have learnt much also from those accomplished bibliographers, Professor A. W. Pollard and Dr. R. B. McKerrow, and from Professor J. Dover Wilson, perhaps most where he most stimulated me to reaction. I have had help on various points from many others, to all of whom my thanks are due: Miss Eleanore Boswell, Miss M. St. Clare Byrne, Dr. H. H. E. Craster, Mr. F. H. Cripps-Day, Mr. P. J. Dobell, Mr. F. S. Ferguson, the Rev. W. G. D. Fletcher, the Rev. E. I. Fripp, Professor E. G. Gardner, Mr. S. Gibson, Mr. M. S. Giuseppi, Father W. Godfrey, the Hon. Henry Hannen, Miss M. Dormer Harris, the late Dr. J. W. Horrocks, Sir Mark Hunter, the Rev. P. J. Latham, Mr. E. T. Leeds, Dr. J. G. Milne, Professor G. C. Moore Smith, Professor D. Nichol Smith, Professor Allardyce Nicoll, Mr. A. M. Oliver, Mr. S. C. Ratcliff, Mr. V. B. Redstone, Miss M. Sellers, Mr. Percy Simpson, Mr. K. Sisam, Professor C. J. Sisson, the late Professor E. A. Sonnenschein, Mr. A. E. Stamp, the Rev. W. Stanhope-Lovell, Mr. A. H. Thomas, Mr. F. C. Wellstood, Dr. C. T. Hagberg Wright. To the Pierpont Morgan Library of New York I owe permission to use the Holgate manuscript of Francis Beaumont's poem.

At the end of my pilgrimage I have yet older memories to set down. The unfailing sympathy, encouragement

and patience of my wife have been my mainstay throughout. To her, Artemis of the Ways, these volumes, like
their predecessors, are dedicated.

 οὐ πολλὴ δ᾽ ἡ χάρις, ἀλλ᾽ ὁσίη.

And I should indeed be an ingrate if I did not now recall
the succession of those who have done so much, one after
another, for the presentation of my work at the Clarendon
Press. They have among them borne with my script and
my divagations for well over a quarter of a century; and
those who survive must share my feeling of relief, if not
its intermingled regret, that the last of many chapters is
now closed.

E. K. C.

EYNSHAM, *July* 1930.

CONTENTS

VOLUME I

VOLUME II

CONTENTS

LIST OF ILLUSTRATIONS
VOLUME I

LIST OF ILLUSTRATIONS

VOLUME II

CHAPTER I

SHAKESPEARE'S ORIGIN

[*Bibliographical Note.* Most of the comprehensive treatises upon Shakespeare and the editions of the plays (ch. ix) deal with his personal biography side by side with his career as a dramatist. The *Lives* by S. Lee (1898, 1925) and J. Q. Adams (1923) are full in this respect. Many documents collected by Malone and his predecessors are to be found in the revised *Life* of the *Variorum Shakespeare* (1821), ii, and its appendixes. Some additions were made by Collier and others, but more by Halliwell-Phillipps in his *Lives* of 1848 and 1853, which are still of value, and in a number of smaller works, often issued in limited editions and now rare. Most, but not all, of these were brought together in his *Outlines of the Life of Shakespeare* which was often enlarged and took its final form in the seventh edition of 1887. Since his time the chief new discoveries have been those of C. W. Wallace, mostly published in *Nebraska University Studies*, v, x (1905, 1910). Selections of documents are in D. H. Lambert, *Cartae Shakespeareanae* (1904), and T. Brooke, *Shakespeare of Stratford* (1926). The papers at Stratford are calendared in F. C. Wellstood, *Catalogue of the Books, Manuscripts, etc. in Shakespeare's Birthplace* (1925). I give the most important documents and extracts from others, as far as possible from originals or facsimiles, with references to some minor dissertations, in *Appendix A*. These are supplemented by the contemporary allusions in *Appendix B* and the traditions in *Appendix C*.

Books of primarily biographical interest are J. Hunter, *New Illustrations of Sh.* (1845); G. R. French, *Shakespeareana Genealogica* (1869); J. P. Yeatman, *The Gentle Sh.* (1896; 1904, with additions); C. C. Stopes, *Sh.'s Family* (1901), *Sh.'s Warwickshire Contemporaries* (1907), *Sh.'s Environment* (1914, 1918), *Sh.'s Industry* (1916); C. I. Elton, *William Sh. His Family and Friends* (1904); J. W. Gray, *Sh.'s Marriage and Departure from Stratford* (1905); A. Gray, *A Chapter in the Early Life of Sh.* (1926); J. S. Smart, *Sh. Truth and Tradition* (1928).

There is no adequate history of Stratford-on-Avon. Dugdale's *Antiquities of Warwickshire* (1656; ed. W. Thomas, 1718) is valuable on the origins. The *Victoria History* covers the college, gild, and school, but has not yet reached the parochial volumes. The Corporation archives are voluminous. H.P. provided a *Descriptive Calendar* (1863) and printed *Extracts from the Council Books* (1864), *Extracts from the Subsidy Rolls* (1864), *Extracts from the Vestry Book* (1865), *The Chamberlains' Accounts, 1590–97* (1866), *Extracts from the Chamberlains' Accounts* (1866–7), *Extracts from the Registry of the Court of Record* (1867). These are being largely replaced by R. Savage and E. I. Fripp, *Minutes and Accounts of the Corporation and other Records* (1921–9, *Dugdale Society*, 4 vols. to 1592 issued). R. Savage has printed the *Parish Registers* (1897–1905, *Parish Register Soc.*) and G. Arbuthnot the *Vestry Minute Book* (1899). J. H.

B

Bloom's *Shakespeare's Church* (1902) is unsatisfactory. He has also edited the *Register of the Gild of Holy Cross* (1907). Other special studies are R. B. Wheler, *Historical Account of the Birthplace* (1824, 1863); G. Arbuthnot, *Guide to the Collegiate Church* (c. 1895); H. E. Forrest, *The Old Houses of S. A.* (1925). Early summary accounts are R. B. Wheler, *History and Antiquities of S. A.* (1806), and J. R. Wise, *Sh.'s Birthplace and its Neighbourhood* (1861); more recent S. Lee, *S. A. from the Earliest Times to the Death of Sh.* (1885, 1907), and E. I. Fripp, *Sh.'s Stratford* (1928). The surrounding neighbourhood is described in E. I. Fripp, *Sh.'s Haunts near Stratford* (1929); earlier guide-books are C. J. Ribton-Turner, *Sh.'s Land* (1893); B. C. A. Windle, *Sh.'s Country* (1899); W. S. Brassington, *Sh.'s Homeland* (1903).

Practically all the available information about John Sh. is collected in H.P.'s *Outlines*. Traditions of the poet's Stratford life are discussed in C. F. Green, *The Legend of Sh.'s Crab-Tree* (1857, 1862); C. H. Bracebridge, *Sh. no Deer-Stealer* (1862); his grammar school in a *Tercentenary Volume* (1853); by A. F. Leach in *V.H.* ii. 329, *English Schools at the Reformation* (1896), *Educational Charters and Documents* (1911); and by A. R. Bayley, *Sh.'s Schoolmasters* (10 *N.Q.* viii. 323; 12 *N.Q.* i. 321); J. H. Pollen, *A Sh. Discovery: His School-master afterwards a Jesuit* (1917, *The Month*, cxxx. 317); W. H. Stevenson, *Sh.'s Schoolmaster and Handwriting* (1920, Jan. 8, *T.L.S.*); and its curriculum by T. S. Baynes, *What Sh. Learnt at School* (1894, *Sh. Studies*, 147); F. Watson, *The Curriculum and Text-Books of English Schools in the Seventeenth Century* (1902, *Bibl. Soc. Trans.* vi. 159); S. Blach, *Shs Lateingrammatik* (1908–9, *J.* xliv. 65; xlv. 51); J. E. Sandys, *Education* (*Sh.'s England*, i. 224). More general works on Sh.'s literary acquirements are H. R. D. Anders, *Sh.'s Books* (1904); H. B. Wheatley, *Sh. as a Man of Letters* (1919, *Bibl. Soc. Trans.* xiv. 109); R. Farmer, *Essay on the Learning of Sh.* (1767; *Var.* i. 300); A. H. Cruickshank, *The Classical Attainments of Sh.* (1887, *Noctes Shakespearianae*, 45); P. Stapfer, *Sh. and Classical Antiquity* (1880); J. C. Collins, *Essays and Studies* (1895); R. K. Root, *Classical Mythology in Sh.* (1903); M. W. McCallum, *Sh.'s Roman Plays and their Background* (1910); L. Rick, *Sh. and Ovid* (1919, *J.* lv. 35); E. R. Hooker, *The Relation of Sh. to Montaigne* (1902, *P.M.L.A.* xvii. 312); J. M. Robertson, *Montaigne and Sh.* (1909); G. C. Taylor, *Sh.'s Debt to Montaigne* (1925); C. Wordsworth, *Sh.'s Knowledge and Use of the Bible* (4th ed., 1892); T. Carter, *Sh. and Holy Scripture* (1905); J. A. R. Marriott, *English History in Sh.* (1918); H. Green, *Sh. and the Emblem-Writers* (1870); R. Jente, *Proverbs of Sh.* (1926 *Washington Univ. Studies* xiii. 391). On the specific sources of the plays are: J. Nichols, *Six Old Plays* (1779); K. Simrock and others, *Quellen des Sh.* (1831); J. P. Collier, *Sh.'s Library* (1844; ed. W. C. Hazlitt, 1875); I. Gollancz and others, *Sh. Classics* (1903–13); F. A. Leo, *Four Chapters of North's Plutarch* (1878); A. Vollmer, *Sh. and Plutarch* (1887, *Archiv*, lxxvii. 353; lxxviii. 75, 215); W. W. Skeat, *Sh.'s Plutarch* (1892); R. H. Carr, *Plutarch's Lives* (1906); W. G. Boswell-Stone, *Sh.'s Holinshed* (1896); A. and J. Nicoll, *Holinshed's*

Chronicles as Used in Sh.'s Plays (1927). On Shakespeare's knowledge of
country life are H. Loewe, *Sh. und die Waidmannskunst* (1904, *J.* xl. 51);
D. H. Madden, *The Diary of Master William Silence* (1897); C. Brown,
Sh. and the Horse (1912, *3 Library*, iii. 152); H. N. Ellacombe, *Sh. as an
Angler* (1883), *Plant-Lore and Garden-Craft of Sh.* (3rd ed. 1896); F. G.
Savage, *Flora and Folk-Lore of Sh.* (1923); A. Geikie, *The Birds of Sh.*
(1916). On his medical knowledge are J. C. Bucknill, *Medical Knowledge
of Sh.* (1860), *Mad Folk of Sh.* (1867); J. Moyes, *Medicine and Kindred
Arts in the Plays of Sh.* (1896). On his legal knowledge and conjectured
training as a lawyer are J. Lord Campbell, *Sh.'s Legal Acquirements* (1859);
W. L. Rushton, *Sh. a Lawyer* (1858), *Sh.'s Legal Maxims* (1859, 1907),
Sh.'s Testamentary Language (1869), *Sh. Illustrated by the Lex Scripta*
(1870); J. Kohler, *Sh. vor dem Forum der Jurisprudenz* (1883, 1919);
W. C. Devecmon, *In re Sh.'s Legal Acquirements* (1899); C. Allen, *Notes
on the Sh.-Bacon Question* (1900); G. G. Greenwood, *Sh.'s Law and Latin*
(1916), *Sh.'s Law* (1920); A. Underhill, *Law* (1917, 1926, *Sh.'s England*,
i. 381); D. P. Barton, *Sh.'s Links with the Law* (1929). On other occupations ascribed to Shakespeare are W. J. Thoms, *Was Sh. ever a Soldier?*
(1865, *Three Notelets on Sh.*); W. Blades, *Sh. and Typography* (1872);
W. L. Rushton, *Sh. an Archer* (1897).]

WILLIAM SHAKESPEARE was born of burgess folk, not unlike those whom he depicts in *The Merry Wives of Windsor*.
Stratford-on-Avon, however, had not grown up in the
shadow of a royal castle. It was a provincial market
town, and counted with Henley-in-Arden after the city of
Coventry and the borough of Warwick among the business
centres of Warwickshire. It stood on the north bank of
the Avon, where a ford had once been traversed by a
minor Roman thoroughfare. A medieval wooden bridge
had been replaced at the end of the fifteenth century by
the stone one which still survives. The great western
highway, following the line of Watling Street to Shrewsbury and Chester, passed well to the north through
Coventry. But at Stratford bridge met two lesser roads
from London, one by Oxford and under the Cotswolds,
the other by Banbury and Edgehill; and beyond it ways
radiated through Stratford itself to Warwick, Birming-
ham, Alcester, and Evesham. 'Emporiolum non in-
elegans' is the description of the place in Camden's
Britannia, and Leland, who visited it about 1540, records
that it was 'reasonably well buyldyd of tymbar', with

'two or three very lardge stretes, besyde bake lanes'. Topographers give the name of Arden to Warwickshire north of the Avon and distinguish it as the Woodland from the cultivated champaign of the Feldon to the south. But even on the north bank of the river there were open cornfields, as well as many enclosed pastures, and frequent hamlets tell of early clearings on the fringe of Arden. The lord had his *boscus* at Stratford in the thirteenth century and later a park, but Leland says that little woodland was visible there in his time.

The town of Stratford only occupied a small part of a large parish which bore the same name. This was ten miles in circuit and had 1,500 houseling people in 1546. Mercian kings had made wide grants to the bishops of Worcester, with a 'hundredal' jurisdiction independent of the sheriff over the liberty of Pathlow, for which they held wayside courts at Pathlow itself and at Gilleputs in Stratford. There was a monastery, afterwards discontinued, for the bishop and his household. Much of the dominion, even in Saxon times, had passed from the bishops by devolution to thanes and in other ways, and in the sixteenth-century parish there were several manors. The hamlet of Clopton was held by the family of that name; Luddington by the Conways of Arrow; Drayton by the Petos of Chesterton; Bishopston by the Catesbys of Lapworth and afterwards by the Archers of Tanworth; part of Shottery by the Smiths of Wootton Wawen. But the principal manor still remained with the bishop up to 1549. In this lay the borough itself, the 'Old Town' which divided it from the parish church of Holy Trinity on the southern outskirts, and a considerable stretch of agricultural land in the fields of Old Stratford, Welcombe, and Shottery.[1] The bishop had also the distinct township of Bishop's Hampton, to the east of Stratford. On the south side of the river were the Lucy manor of Charlecote, the Greville manor of Milcote, and the Rainsford manor of Clifford Chambers in Gloucestershire. The hamlet of Bridgetown beyond the bridge was partly in the borough

---

[1] Cf. plan (Plate III).

and partly in Alveston. To the north-east and north-west
of Stratford were the villages of Snitterfield and Aston
Cantlow. They had been 'Warwickslands', lordships of
the dominant families of Beauchamp and Neville, and had
reverted to the crown on attainder. For all these places
Stratford was the natural urban centre.[1]

The borough had come into existence under Bishop
John de Coutances (1195–8), who had laid out part of his
demesne in quarter-acre plots of uniform frontage and
depth. These were held as burgages, practically on a freehold tenure, subject to shilling chief rents, and with rights
of division and disposition by sale or will. A separate
manor court was presided over by the bishop's steward,
but the burgesses probably chose their own bailiff and
sub-bailiffs as executive officers. The court sat twice in
the year, for 'leets' or 'law days' near Easter and Michaelmas. At these officers were appointed, transfers of
burgages were recorded, small civil actions for debt
and the like were heard, by-laws for good order were
made, and breaches of these, with frays and infringements
of the 'assizes' of food and drink and other standards
for the quality of saleable articles, were punished. Side
by side with the manorial jurisdiction had grown up
the organization of the Gild of Holy Cross, which
ministered in many ways to the well-being of the town.
It dated from the thirteenth century. Early in the fifteenth
it absorbed smaller gilds, and thereafter an almost continuous register preserves the admissions of brothers and
sisters, and the payments for the souls of the dead, whose
masses were sung by the priests of its chapel. The
members of the gild were bound to fraternal relations and
to attendance at each others funerals in their Augustinian
hoods. Periodical love-feasts encouraged more mundane
intercourse. The gild had accumulated much property, in
and about Stratford, from pious gifts and legacies. It
helped its poorer members and maintained an almshouse.
A school, which had existed in some form as far back as
1295, was one of its activities. This had an endowment

[1] Cf. map (Plate II).

from Thomas Joliffe for the gratuitous teaching of grammar by one of the priests. The gild buildings, which stood just within the borough, owed their latest form to Sir Hugh Clopton, Lord Mayor of London in 1492. He, too, had built the bridge. The affairs of the gild were in the hands of a Master and Aldermen, with two Proctors as financial officers. It was at the height of its reputation in the middle of the fifteenth century, and attracted members of distinction from far beyond the limits of Stratford. Later it suffered a decline, perhaps due in part to the rise of trade gilds, in which the craftsmen of the town were linked for business purposes. Probably the gild chapel counted for more in the religious life of the borough than the comparatively distant church. This belonged to a college of priests under a warden, which also had acquired much landed property, in addition to the ample tithes of the large parish. Two chapels in the hamlets of Bishopston and Luddington were under its control.

The reign of Edward VI was a period of considerable change for Stratford. The gild and the college were both dissolved under the Chantries Act of 1547, and their revenues went to the crown. Provisional direction was given for the continuance of the school. In 1549 Bishop Nicholas Heath was driven, apparently for inadequate compensation, to transfer his manor, with that of Bishop's Hampton, to John Dudley, Earl of Warwick and afterwards Duke of Northumberland, who aspired to restore the old domination of the Beauchamps and Nevilles in the county. It passed from him in the same year and back to him in 1553 by exchanges with the crown. On his attainder in 1553 Mary granted it to the duchess, and after her death in 1555 to the hospital of the Savoy. But this grant was almost immediately vacated, and the manor remained with the crown until 1562, when Elizabeth gave it to Northumberland's son Ambrose Dudley, now in his turn created Earl of Warwick. On his death in 1590 it again reverted to the crown, but was sold and acquired by Sir Edward Greville of Milcote.[1] Another event of 1553

[1] Cf. App. A, no. xix.

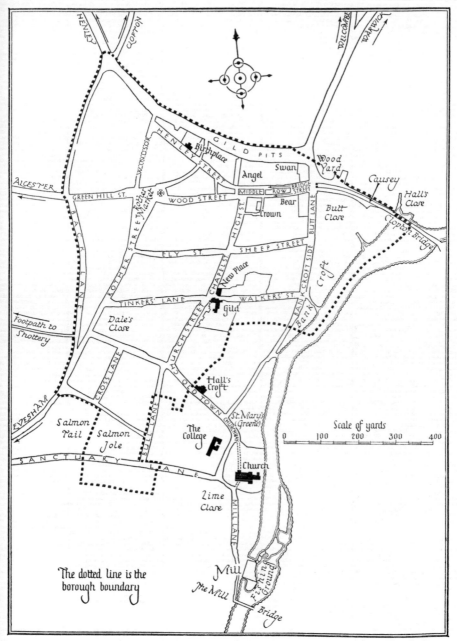

PLATE III

Oxford University Press

TOWN OF STRATFORD-ON-AVON

Based upon the Ordnance Survey Map with the sanction of the Controller of H.M. Stationery Office

had, however, reduced the importance of the manor and
its court in local affairs. The inhabitants, perturbed by
the loss of valuable elements in their civic life, petitioned
for incorporation as a royal borough; and this, presumably
through the influence of Northumberland, then in power,
was accorded by a charter of 28 June 1553. The government of the borough was entrusted to a Bailiff and
a Council of fourteen Aldermen and fourteen Capital
Burgesses, with powers to provide for good order and the
management of corporate property, to fill vacancies in
their number, and to make annual election of the bailiff,
serjeants at the mace, constables, and such other officers
as might prove necessary. The Council was to have the
return to royal writs within the borough, to the exclusion of
the sheriff, and the bailiff to hold crown office as escheator,
coroner, almoner, and clerk of the market. With a chosen
alderman, he was to act as justice of peace. Authority was
given for a weekly market and for two annual fairs, with
a court of pie-powder. There was also to be a court of
record under the bailiff, with jurisdiction in civil causes,
where the amount in dispute was not more than £30. To
meet the municipal expenses, the charter granted the
property of the late gild, worth about £46, and the reversion of a lease of the parish tithes granted by the college,
with the reserved rent of £34.[1] The rest of the college
property remained with the Crown. The funds granted
were charged with the maintenance of the almshouse,
and with salaries for the schoolmaster, the vicar, and his
curate. A general reservation, which afterwards led to
trouble, was made for the rights of the lord of the manor,
and in particular the election of the bailiff was to be subject to his approval, and he was to have the appointment
of the schoolmaster and vicar. For some years from 1553
the records leave it rather difficult to disentangle the
activities of the bailiff and his brethren from those of
the court leet. But soon after a recognition of the charter
by Elizabeth in 1560, the Council was regularly at work,
holding its meetings at 'halls' every month or so in the

[1] Cf. App. A, no. xvii.

buildings of the old gild, making its by-laws, surveying its property, approving leases, ordering the market, the fairs, and the almshouse, and raising small levies for public or charitable purposes to supplement its regular funds.

It had at first a town clerk and afterwards a steward, who assisted the bailiff at the court of record.[1] This, in addition to its jurisdiction between civil litigants, chiefly in cases of debt, took over the imposition of penalties for breaches of by-laws or of the assize. Frays may be assumed to have fallen to the justices of peace. The leet, although shorn of many of its functions, continued to be held. It presumably dealt with matters peculiar to the manor, such as the transfer of burgages. The constables, although chosen by the Council with other officers at Michaelmas, were sworn in at a leet. Disputes arose with the lords of the manor, about toll-corn, about commoners' rights, about the approval of bailiffs. Internal discipline also gave trouble. The aldermen and principal burgesses did not always attend halls regularly, and some of them were inclined to shun the responsibilities of office when their turns came. Towards the end of the century the Council was much occupied with affairs in London.[2] The industries of Stratford were decaying and there had been disastrous fires. Suits were made to the Crown for exemption from subsidies, and for an enlarged charter. One was in fact granted by James in 1610, which extended the boundary of the borough to include the Old Town. The minutes of council meetings are not very full. Rather more illuminating are the accounts of the Chamberlains, who had succeeded the proctors of the gild as financial officers. These were made up annually after each year of office and presented to the Council for audit about Christmas. The chamberlains collected the rents and dues, and kept a detailed record of their expenditure upon salaries, repairs to property, gifts, generally in wine and sugar, to distinguished strangers, and rewards to players. The accounts throw many sidelights on town history and on local personalities. Religious changes for example are

[1] Cf. App. A, no. xvi.   [2] Cf. App. A, nos. xii, xiii.

traceable in payments of 1562–3 for defacing images in
the chapel, and of 1563–4 for taking down the rood-loft,
and in a council order of 1571 for the sale of copes and
vestments.[1]

Stratford has been represented as a dirty and ignorant
town, an unmeet cradle for poetry. There is some want
of historical perspective here. No doubt sanitary science
was in its infancy. But, after all, penalties for the breach of
by-laws, if they are evidence that the by-laws were sometimes broken, are also evidence that they were enforced.
Nor was contemporary London, with the puppy dogs in
its Fleet and its unscoured Moorditch, in much better
case. Stratford had its paved streets and much garden
ground about its houses. It was embosomed in elms, of
which a survey of 1582 records a vast number in .closes
and on the backsides of the burgages.[2] And all around was
fair and open land with parks and dingles and a shining
river. There was much give and take between town and
country-side. The urban industries, weaving, dyeing,
tanning, shoe-making, glove-making, smithing, rope-
making, carpentry, were such as subserve or are fed by
agriculture. Many of the burgesses were also landholders
in the parish or in neighbouring villages. There was much
buying of barley, for the making and sale of malt, which
was a subsidiary occupation of many households.[3] Sheep,
cattle, ducks, and ringed swine ran on the common pasture
called the Bank Croft. Although remote, the town was
not out of touch with a larger civilization. Access to Oxford
was easy, and to London itself, by roads on which carriers
came and went regularly, and the burgesses journeyed on
their public and private business. Nor was it entirely
bookless. Leading townsmen could quote Latin and write
a Latin letter if need be. Critical eyes may have watched
the Whitsun pastoral which David Jones produced in
1583.[4] The Grammar School was probably of good standing. The schoolmaster's salary, which Joliffe fixed at £10,

[1] *M.A.* i. 128, 138; ii. 54.
[2] *M.A.* iii. 105.
[3] Cf. App. A, no. xii.

[4] *M.A.* iii. 137: 'Payd to Davi Jones
and his companye for his pastyme at
Whitsontyde xiij^s iiij^d.'

was increased to £20 by the charter. This was much more than the £12 5s. paid at Warwick or than the amounts usual in Elizabethan grammar schools, outside West-minster, Eton, Winchester, and Shrewsbury. It was better than the emoluments of an Oxford or Cambridge fellowship. And from Oxford or Cambridge came William Smart (1554–65), Fellow of Christ's, John Brownsword (1565–7), a Latin poet of repute, John Acton (1567–9), Walter Roche (1569–71), Fellow of Corpus, Oxford, Simon Hunt (1571–5), afterwards a Jesuit at Douai and English penitentiary at Rome, Thomas Jenkins (1575–9), Fellow of St. John's, Oxford, who came from Warwick, John Cottam (1579–81), and Alexander Aspinall (1581–1624). The actual curriculum of the school is unknown; it was probably based on those planned by Colet for St. Paul's in 1518 and Wolsey for Ipswich in 1529, and not unlike that in force at St. Bees in 1583. Colet required an entrant to be able to 'rede and write Latyn and Eng-lisshe sufficiently, soo that he be able to rede and wryte his owne lessons'.[1] But London had its sufficiency of elementary schools, and the easier standard of Stratford was content if a child was 'fet for the gramer scoll or at the least wyez entred or reddy to enter into ther accydence & princypalles of gramer'.[2] Even the preparation seems at first to have been given by an usher attached to the gram-mar school, whom the chamberlains paid 'for techyng ye chylder'. But by 1604 an independent teacher had for some time taught reading and his wife needlework, 'whereby our young youth is well furthered in reading and the Free School greatly eased of that tedious trouble'.[3] In the grammar school itself there would be little but Latin; the grammar of Colet himself and William Lilly, revised and appointed for use in schools under successive sovereigns; some easy book of phrases, such as the *Sententiae Pueriles* of Leonhard Culmann or the *Pueriles Confabulatiunculae* of Evaldus Gallus; Aesop's *Fables* and the *Moral Distichs* of Cato; Cicero, Sallust, or Caesar, Ovid in abundance, Virgil, perhaps Horace or Terence; pro-

[1] *J.* xliv. 66.   [2] *M.A.* i. 34.   [3] *M.A.* i. 128; iii. xi.

bably some Renaissance writing, the *Bucolica* of Baptista
Spagnolo Mantuanus or the *Zodiacus Vitae* of Marcellus
Palingenius. There is not likely to have been any Greek.
About sixteen a boy was ripe for the University. Sir Hugh
Clopton had left six exhibitions to Oxford and Cambridge;
it is not known whether the Corporation continued them.[1]

Such was the environment of the youthful Shakespeare.
His father, John Shakespeare, was not of native Stratford
stock; there are no Shakespeares in the gild register.
John makes his first appearance in Stratford at a leet
of 29 April 1552, when he was fined one shilling for
having an unauthorized dunghill in Henley St. He may
reasonably be identified with a John Shakespeare of
Snitterfield, who administered the estate of his father
Richard in 1561.[2] Richard had held land on two manors
at Snitterfield, in part as tenant to Robert Arden of Wilmcote in Aston Cantlow. He is traceable there from 1528–
9, and may possibly have come from Hampton Corley in
Budbrooke. But his ultimate origin has eluded research.
When grants of arms to John Shakespeare were applied
for, the heralds recited ancestral service to Henry VII
and a reward of lands in Warwickshire. No confirm-
ing record has been found. Shakespeares were thick
on the ground in sixteenth-century Warwickshire, particularly in the Woodland about Wroxall and Rowington
to the north of Stratford.[3] A Richard Shakespeare was
in fact bailiff of Wroxall manor in 1534, but his after-
history is known, and excludes a suggested identity with
Richard of Snitterfield. Other affiliations have been tried
in vain. There was some cousinship between the poet and
a family of Greene in Warwick, which may one day yield
a clue. John Shakespeare, as administrator to his father, is
called *agricola* or husbandman. Later his brother Henry
is found holding land at Snitterfield, where he died, much
indebted, in 1596. Other documents call John a yeoman.
Technically a yeoman was a freeholder of land to the
annual value of fifty shillings, but the description was
often applied to any well-to-do man short of a gentleman.

[1] Leach 243.　　　　[2] Cf. App. A, no. ii.　　　　[3] Cf. App. E.

A more precise designation is that of 'glover' or 'whittawer'. A whittawer cured and whitened the soft skins
which were the material of the glover's craft. There can
be little doubt that John Shakespeare combined these occupations, and was a freeman of the Mystery of the
Glovers, Whittawers and Collarmakers, which was one of
the Stratford trade gilds. It does not weigh for much
against the contemporary use of these terms that John
Aubrey called him a butcher in 1681, and that Nicholas
Rowe, who made the first attempt at a systematic biography of the poet in 1709, called him a wool-dealer.[1]
Likely enough, he had subordinate activities; he is mentioned as selling both barley and timber. It is possible
that he is the John Shakespeare who was tenant of Ingon
meadow in Bishop's Hampton about 1570. He is clearly
distinct from a John Shakespeare of Clifford Chambers,
traceable there from 1560 to his death in 1610, and from
a second John Shakespeare of Stratford, a corvizer who
dwelt in the town from 1586 to about 1595, and whose
progeny early biographers confused with his.[2] The poet's
father married Mary Arden, daughter of that Robert from
whom the grandfather had held land. He was of the
ancient house of the Ardens of Park Hall, although the
precise degree of relationship is uncertain.[3] Mary was a
co-heiress in a small way. Robert left her some land in
Wilmcote called Asbies by his will of 1556, and had
probably already settled other property there upon her.
She was also entitled to a share in a reversionary interest
of his Snitterfield estate.[4] The marriage must have taken
place between the date of the will and 15 September
1558, when a daughter Joan was christened at Stratford.
She must have died early. There followed Margaret
(c. 1562, b. 1563), William (c. 26 April 1564), Gilbert
(c. 1566), a second Joan (c. 1569), Anne (c. 1571, b.
1579), Richard (c. 1574), and Edmund (c. 1580). The

[1] App. C, nos. xiii, xxv. The wool-
dealer tradition established itself at
Stratford; cf. App. A, no. iii; App. C,
nos. xlvi, liv.

[2] Cf. App. A, no. i (a), (e).
[3] Cf. App. A, no. ii.
[4] Cf. App. A, no. iv.

actual day of William's birth is unknown. A belief that
it was April 23, on which day he died in 1616, seems to
rest on an eighteenth-century blunder.[1] In 1556 John
Shakespeare bought two houses, one in Henley St. and
one in Greenhill St. In 1575 he bought two other houses,
the locality of which is not specified. In 1590 he owned
two contiguous houses in Henley St. Of these the
westernmost is now called the 'Birthplace' and the eastern-
most the 'Woolshop'. But this tradition does not go back
beyond the middle of the eighteenth century. Certainly
the 'Woolshop' was the purchase of 1556. But whether
John was living in the 'Birthplace' in 1552, or whether
he was then living as a tenant in the 'Woolshop', and
bought the 'Birthplace' in 1575, has not been established.[2]
    However this may be, the purchases suggest that John
Shakespeare prospered in business. And he became
prominent in municipal life.[3] Between 1557 and 1561 he
appears as juror, constable, and 'affeeror' or assessor of
fines at the court leet, and was himself again fined for
leaving his gutter dirty and for not making presentments
as ale-taster before the court of record. In 1561 and
1562 he was chosen as one of the chamberlains, and it is
perhaps evidence of his financial capacity that he acted,
quite exceptionally, as deputy to the chamberlains of
the next two years. Probably he was already a capital
burgess by 1561, although his name first appears in a list
of 1564. His subscriptions to the relief of the poor during
that year of plague-time are liberal. In 1565 he was
chosen an alderman, and in 1568 reached the top of
civic ambition as bailiff. In view of contemporary
habits, it is no proof of inability to write that he was
accustomed to authenticate documents by a mark, which
was sometimes a cross and sometimes a pair of glover's
dividers.[4] But it is unfortunate, because it leaves us ignorant as to how he spelt his name. The town-clerk, a
constant scribe, makes it 'Shakspeyr' with great regularity;

[1] Cf. App. A, no. i (a).   [4] C. Sisson, *Marks as Signatures*
[2] Cf. App. A, no. iii.   (1928, 4 *Library*, ix. 22), is sceptical.
[3] Cf. *M.A. passim*.

but some twenty variants are found in Stratford documents.[1] After a customary interval John, like other ex-
bailiffs, was again justice of the peace as chief alderman
in 1571. A few years later there are indications of a
decline in his fortunes. Throughout his career there had
been suits by and against him for small sums in the court
of record. These, however, appear to have been part of
the ordinary routine of business transactions as conducted
in Stratford. An occasional appearance in the High Courts
involved larger sums. In 1571 John proceeded against
Richard Quiney, the son of an old colleague Adrian
Quiney, for £50. In 1573 he had himself to meet the
claim of Henry Higford, a former steward of Stratford,
for £30. He failed to appear and a warrant for his arrest,
and if not found, outlawry, was issued. He was still in
a position to spend £40 on house property in 1575. But
at the beginning of 1577 he suddenly discontinued attendance at the 'halls' of the Corporation, and never again
appeared, except on one or two special occasions. In the
following year he was excused from a levy for the relief
of the poor, and rated at an exceptionally low amount for
the expenses of the musters, which still remained unpaid
in 1579. His wife's inheritance was disposed of. The small
reversion in Snitterfield was sold for £4. Asbies was let
at a nominal rent, probably in consideration of a sum down.
The other Wilmcote holding was mortgaged to Mary's
brother-in-law Edmund Lambert for £40, to be repaid at
Michaelmas 1580. It was not repaid. John Shakespeare
afterwards claimed that he had tendered payment, and
that it was refused because he still owed other sums to
Lambert. This he does not seem to have established. He
also maintained that Lambert's son John, to whom possession passed in 1587, agreed to buy the property outright
from the Shakespeares and their son William, and failed
to keep his agreement. This John Lambert denied.
There was litigation in 1589 and again in 1597, but the
property proved irrecoverable.[2] A singular incident of
1580 still lacks an explanation. John Shakespeare and one

---

[1] Cf. App. E, no. iii.   [2] App. A, no. iv.

John Audley, a hat-maker of Nottingham, were bound
over in the Court of Queen's Bench to give security against
a breach of the peace. They failed to answer to their
recognizances and incurred substantial fines. That of
Shakespeare amounted to £20 for his own default and £20
more as surety for Audley.[1] In 1587 an entanglement
with the affairs of his brother Henry seems to have added
to his embarrassment. And in the same year the patience
of the Corporation was exhausted, and a new alderman
was appointed in his place, 'for that Mᵣ Shaxspere dothe
not come to the halles when they be warned nor hathe not
done of longe tyme'.[2] Further court of record suits
suggest that he was still engaged in business. On 25
September 1592 he was included in a list of persons at
Stratford 'hearetofore presented for not comminge moneth-
lie to the churche accordinge to hir Majesties lawes'; and
to his name and those of eight others is appended the
note, 'It is sayd that these laste nine coom not to churche
for feare of process for debtte'.[3] As arrest for debt could
be made on Sundays in the sixteenth century, the explanation seems, in the light of John Shakespeare's career since
1577, extremely probable. But the notion of a religious
romance in the drab life of a town councillor has proved
too much for his biographers, and much ingenuity has
been spent in interpreting what little is known of John's
personal and official life on the theory that he was in fact
a recusant. The theorists differ, however, as to whether
he was a Catholic or a nonconforming Puritan, and I do
not think that there is much to support either contention.
So far as the recusancy returns of 1592 are concerned, the
position is clear. They had nothing to do, as has been
suggested by a confusion of dates, with the anti-Puritan
legislation of 1593. In 1591 England was expecting a
renewed Spanish attempt at invasion, and county com-
missions were issued and announced by proclamations of

---

[1] *M.A.* iii. 68, from *Coram Rege Roll, Anglia* 20ᵇ, 21ᵃ, Trin. 22 Eliz.

[2] *M.A.* iii. 170.

[3] *S.P.D. Eliz.* ccxliii. 76; *Greville Papers* (Warwick Castle) 2662; texts in

M.A. iv. 148, 159. Stopes, *Cont.* 31, suggests that this was the corvizer (cf. vol. ii, p. 3) of whose religion, as of his debts, we know nothing.

October 18.[1] The instructions to the commissioners are known. They were to collect the names of those who did not attend church, not to 'press any persons to answer to any questions of their conscience for matters of religion', but if they found wilful recusants, to examine them as to their allegiance to the Queen, their devotion to the Pope or the King of Spain, and any maintenance of Jesuits or seminary priests. Clearly Catholics alone, and not Puritans, were in danger. Beyond the return itself, the only document which may bear upon John Shakespeare's religion is the devotional will or *testamentum animae* found in the roof of one of his Henley St. houses in the eighteenth century.[2] I do not think that this is a forgery, but if the John Shakespeare who made it was the poet's father, it probably dates from his early life, and carries little evidence as to his religious position under Elizabeth. Of his personality there may be some genuine reminiscence in a seventeenth-century report of how a visitor, as to whose identity there must be some blunder, found in his shop 'a merry cheeked old man that said "Will was a good honest fellow, but he durst have cracked a jest with him at any time"'.[3] Although no longer a member of the Corporation, John was called upon to advise them on some difficulties with the lord of the manor in 1601. And on September 8 of that year he was buried. No will or administration is known, but of all the property which passed through his hands, only the Henley St. houses are found in those of the poet.

Of William Shakespeare's own early days there is but little on record; and it is no part of my object to compete with those gifted writers who have drawn upon their acquaintance with Stratford and with the plays for the material of an imaginative reconstruction. We are told by Rowe, presumably on the authority of inquiries made by Thomas Betterton at Stratford, that his father bred

---

[1] *Procll.* 837, 839; Dasent, xxii. 138, 174, 181, 205, 211, 227, 245, 316, 324, 325, 336, 340, 342, 365, 369, 406, 427, 543; xxiii. 163, 188, 191; Strype, *Annals* (1824), iv. 78; St. G. K. Hyland, *A Century of Persecution* (1920), 196, 407.

[2] Cf. App. F, no. vi.

[3] App. C, no. vii.

him at a free school, but withdrew him owing to 'the
narrowness of his circumstances, and the want of his
assistance at home'.[1] There is no reason to reject this,
which agrees with what we know of John's financial
history, or to look for a free school other than that of
Stratford itself. It is unfortunate that no early lists of
pupils are preserved there. Rowe's words suggest a somewhat premature withdrawal. From Stratford also comes
the earlier report of one Dowdall (1693) that the poet had
run away from apprenticeship to a butcher.[2] He does not
say that his master was also his father. But the story
shows that Aubrey was not alone in his belief as to John
Shakespeare's occupation, which he confirms by saying
that William followed his father's trade and 'when he
kill'd a calfe, he would doe it in a high style, and make a
speech'.[3] Perhaps this really points to some early exercise
of mimic talent. 'Killing a calf' seems to have been an
item in the repertory of wandering entertainers.[4] Rowe
also learnt of Shakespeare's early marriage and departure
from Stratford as a result of deer-stealing. The documents concerning the marriage involve a puzzle.[5] It took
place towards the end of 1582, not in the parish church
of Stratford, or in any of the numerous likely churches
whose registers have been searched; possibly in the chapel
at Luddington, where an entry is said to have been seen
before the register was destroyed. A licence for it was
issued from the episcopal registry at Worcester on November 27, and a bond to hold the bishop harmless was given
by two sureties on the following day. The procedure was
regular enough, and carries no suggestion of family disapproval. But the register of licences gives the bride's
name as Anne Whateley of Temple Grafton and the bond
as Anne Hathwey of Stratford. Once more, romantic

---

[1] App. C, no. xxv.
[2] App. C, no. xviii.
[3] App. C, no. xiii.
[4] Collier, i. 90, from *Account* of Princess Mary for Christmas 1521, 'Itm pd. to a man at Wyndesore, for kylling of a calffe before my ladys

grace behynde a clothe'. J. Raine, *Priory of Finchale* (Surtees Soc.), ccccxli, cites a 'droll performance' called 'killing the calf' by an eigh-teenth-century entertainer.
[5] App. A, no. v.

biography has scented a mystery. The probable solution is that the bond, as an original document, is correct, and that the clerk who made up the register blundered. Rowe, who certainly never heard of the bond, knew the name as Hathaway. There were several Hathaways in the parish of Stratford, and Anne's parentage is not quite clear. She may have been of Luddington, but more likely of Shottery, where one Richard Hathaway, of a family which bore the *alias* of Gardner, occupied the tenement of Hewland, now known as Anne Hathaway's cottage, and in 1581 left money to a daughter Agnes, then unmarried. That Agnes and Anne, in common usage although not in strict law, were regarded as forms of the same name is unquestionable. If there was any element of haste or secrecy in the affair, it may have been due to the fact that Anne was already with child. A kindly sentiment has pleaded the possible existence of a pre-contract amounting to a civil marriage. A daughter Susanna was baptized on 26 May 1583, and followed by twins, Hamnet and Judith, on 2 February 1585. Guesses at godparents are idle where common names, such as Shakespeare's own, are concerned. But those of the twins, which are unusual, point to Hamnet or Hamlet Sadler, a baker of Stratford, and his wife Judith.

The story of deer-stealing has been the subject of much controversy. Rowe's account has the independent confirmation of some earlier jottings by Richard Davies who became rector of Sapperton in Gloucestershire in 1695.[1] Probably, like Rowe, he drew upon local gossip. Rowe says that the exploit was in the park of Sir Thomas Lucy of Charlecote, that in revenge for prosecution by Lucy Shakespeare made a ballad upon him, and that as a result of further prosecution he was obliged to leave Stratford. Davies says that he was whipped and imprisoned by Lucy, and that in revenge he depicted Lucy as a justice with 'three lowses rampant for his arms'. There is an obvious reference here to *Merry Wives of Windsor*, i. 1, in which Justice Shallow complains that Falstaff has beaten his

---

[1] App. C, nos. xv, xxv.

men, killed his deer, and broken open his lodge, and threatens to make a Star Chamber matter of it as a riot. He is said to bear a 'dozen white luces' in his coat, and Sir Hugh Evans makes the jest on louses. The Lucy family had held Charlecote since the twelfth century, and bore the arms *Vair, three luces hauriant argent*.[1] The Sir Thomas of Shakespeare's day was a prominent justice of peace, and represented Warwickshire in the parliaments of 1571 and 1584–5.[2] It has been held that the whole story is nothing but a myth which has grown up about the passage in the *Merry Wives of Windsor* itself. But I do not think that, so far as the essential feature is concerned, we are called upon to reject it. Deer-stealing was a common practice enough, and was regarded as a venial frolic, even for young men of higher standing than Shakespeare's. Details are another matter. Lucy cannot have whipped Shakespeare, if he proceeded under the ruling game law of 1563, in which the only penalty prescribed was imprisonment. Possibly, if the affair could be regarded as a riot, it might bear a more serious complexion. Nor does Lucy appear to have had a 'park', in the legal sense, at Charlecote. At his death in 1600 he had only a free-warren. It is true that the learned lawyer Sir Edward Coke included roe-deer, but not fallow deer, among beasts of warren, and although other authorities appear to dissent, it was certainly so decided in 1339.[3] It is also true that the Act of 1563 appears to give protection to deer in any enclosure then existing, whether it was a legally enclosed park or not, and the free-warren at Charlecote may well have come under this provision. If the deer was not in

---

[1] The coat is repeated in four quarterings, making a dozen luces, on a Lucy tomb at Warwick (Dugdale, 348).

[2] He led a Committee (4 Mar. 1585) for considering a Bill for the preservation of game and grain, which did not become law, but he was replaced on a later Committee, and there is no reason to assume that he was an active promoter of the Bill, which, indeed, seems to have been concerned with pheasants and partridges, not deer (S. D'Ewes, *Journals of Parliaments*, 321, 327, 363, 366, 369, 373, 374).

[3] G. J. Turner, *Select Pleas of the Forest* (1901), x, from decision of King's Bench, 'Caprioli sunt bestiae de warenna et non de foresta eo quod fugant alias feras de foresta'.

an enclosure protected by the game law, any foray upon
it would have been no more than a trespass, to be remedied
by civil action, and neither whipping nor imprisonment
would have been possible. Rowe, however, only speaks
of prosecution, and of a ballad, which may have amounted
to a criminal libel. A single stanza, claimed as the opening
of this ballad and containing the jest on lousiness, came
into the hands both of William Oldys and of Edward
Capell in the eighteenth century, with a history ascribing
it to information derived from inhabitants of Stratford by
a Mr. Jones who died in 1703.[1] If so, it represents a
third tradition as old as those of Davies and Rowe. A
complete version produced in 1790 by John Jordan, an
out-at-elbows poet and guide for strangers in Stratford,
was probably not beyond his own capacities for fabrication.[2] There is, however, yet another alleged fragment of
the ballad, in a different metre, said on very poor authority
to have been picked up at Stratford about 1690 by the
Cambridge professor Joshua Barnes.[3] Its jest on deer
horns carries the familiar Elizabethan insinuation of
cuckoldry against Lucy, whose monument to his wife at
Charlecote lauds her domestic virtues. Obviously the
fragments are inconsistent, and neither is likely to be
genuine. But some weight must be attached to the fourfold testimony through Davies, Rowe, Jones, and Barnes
to a tradition of the deer-stealing as alive at Stratford
about the end of the seventeenth century. There is later
embroidery which need not be taken seriously.[4] A writer
in the *Biographia Britannica* (1763) ascribes Shakespeare's
release from imprisonment to the intervention of Elizabeth; another in 1862, professedly on the authority of
records at Charlecote, to the Earl of Leicester, who died in
1588, but to a pique of whom against Lucy the inspiration
of the *Merry Wives of Windsor* is none the less attributed.
Towards the end of the eighteenth century, perhaps owing
to the discovery that there was no park at Charlecote, the

[1] App. C, nos. xxxiv, xliv.
[2] App. C, no. xlvi.
[3] App. C, no. xvi.

[4] App. C, nos. xli, xlvi, xlix, li, liv,
lvii, lviii.

story was transferred to the neighbouring park of Fulbrook. This, however, had been disparked by 1557, was not in the hands of the Lucy family during Shakespeare's boyhood, but was bought by them in 1615 and subsequently re-emparked. Some hit at Sir Thomas is probably involved in the *Merry Wives of Windsor* passage. But it would not be a justifiable inference that the presentment of Justice Shallow as a whole, especially in *Henry IV*, is in any way meant to be a 'portrait' of the worthy justice. Such portraiture seems, to me at least, quite alien from the method of Shakespeare's art. A belief, once established, that a distinguished citizen of Stratford had enjoyed a wildish youth, may have encouraged the later tales of Shakespeare's drinking exploits, for which no origin other than the inventiveness of innkeepers need be sought.[1]

We cannot give any precise date to the *Hegira*. A story current at Stratford in 1818 that the venison was stolen to grace the marriage feast is obviously part of the embroidery. Children can be baptized but not begotten without a father, and it is reasonable to suppose that Shakespeare was still in Stratford during 1584.[2] We do not know whether his wife was at any time the companion of his absence. There is no record of her in London, and none in Stratford until after the purchase of New Place. But the boy Hamnet was buried at Stratford on 11 August 1596. On the other hand it is no proof of Shakespeare's continuance in Stratford that according to his father's allegation he concurred in the offer to sell the Wilmcote property to John Lambert about 1587.[3] This seems to have been only an oral transaction, and wherever William was, there is no reason to suppose that he was beyond communication with his family. The words of Rowe's deer-stealing narrative and of Dowdall's parallel story of an escape from apprenticeship imply a migration direct

[1] App. C, nos. xl, xlvi.
[2] James Yates, servingman, in *The Holde of Humilitie*, 17, printed with his *Castell of Courtesie* (1582), has colourless *Verses written at the Departure of his friende W. S. When he went to Dwell at London*. W. S. was a 'Will', but the date is too early, and there are indications in the book which suggest a Suffolk author.
[3] App. A, no. iv.

to London. But these can hardly be pressed. We have no certainty of Shakespeare's presence in London before 1592, when a scoffing notice by Robert Greene shows that he was already an actor and had already begun to write plays.[1] This is no doubt consistent with some earlier sojourn, which may have been of no long duration. A supposed earlier allusion to him as 'Willy' in Spenser's *Tears of the Muses* (1591) is now, I think, universally rejected.[2] We have therefore a very considerable hiatus in his history, extending over a maximum of eight years from 1584 to 1592, to take into account; and it is obvious that many things may have occupied this interval, of which we are ignorant. Tradition, apart from some statements as to his introduction into theatrical life, has done little to fill the gap. It was the actor William Beeston who told Aubrey that he had been a schoolmaster in the country.[3] Beeston's memory might well go back to Shakespeare's own lifetime, and the statement is not in itself incredible. The course at Stratford, even if not curtailed, would hardly have qualified him to take charge of a grammar school; but his post may have been no more than that of an usher or an *abecedarius*. Nor need we suppose that his studies, even in the classics, terminated with his school-days. The most direct contemporary evidence is that of Ben Jonson, who ascribed to him but 'small Latin, and less Greek', writing naturally enough from the standpoint of his own considerable scholarship.[4] There has been much argument on this subject from the time of Richard Farmer's *Essay on the Learning of Shakespeare* (1767), and much enumeration of the books, ancient and modern, erudite and popular, which may, directly or indirectly, have contributed material to his plays. The inferences have not always been discreet. The attempt, for example, of Professor Churton Collins to establish a familiarity with the Greek tragedians rests largely upon analogies of thought and expression which may have had a natural origin out of analogous situations. A saner

[1] App. B, no. iii; cf. p. 58.   [3] App. C, no. xiii.
[2] App. B, no. i.   [4] App. B, no. xxii.

judgement is that of Professor Henry Jackson, who after a careful survey of the evidence found no exceptional learning, but merely an example of a familiarity with classical themes, more widespread in Elizabethan days than in our own, and not indicative of anything beyond a grammar-school education.[1] One may reasonably assume that at all times Shakespeare read whatever books, original or translated, came in his way. It has been asked where he found them in the absence of public libraries. Did he borrow from the Earl of Southampton, or from Jonson or from Camden, or did he merely turn over their leaves on the stationers' stalls? These are foolish questions, to which I propose no answers. We do not know what library he had of his own. Many volumes bear his signatures, and they are mostly forgeries. Some claim has been made for an Aldine *Metamorphoses* of 1502, for a translated Montaigne of 1603, and for a translated Plutarch of 1612.[2] Sceptics point out that he named no books in his will; there was no reason why he should, unless he wished to dispose of them apart from his other chattels. As with Shakespeare's general learning, so with his law. His writing abounds in legal terminology, closely woven into the structure of his metaphor. Here, again, the knowledge is extensive rather than exact. It is shared by other dramatists. Our litigious ancestors had a familiarity with legal processes, from which we are happily exempt. But many have thought that Shakespeare must have had some professional experience of a lawyer's office, although this was not the final opinion of the much-quoted Lord Campbell; and there are those who will tell you by which Stratford attorney he was employed. This is only one instance of the willingness of conjecture to step in where no record has trod. On similar grounds Shakespeare has been represented as an apothecary and a student of medicine. That he was a soldier rests on a confusion with one of many William Shakespeares at Rowington; and that he

[1] *Was Shakespeare of Stratford the Author of Shakespeare's Plays and Poems?* in R. St. J. Parry, *Henry*   *Jackson O.M.* (1926).
[2] Cf. p. 506.

was a printer on the fact that Richard Field, who issued his poems, came from Stratford. In a sense, these conflicting theories refute each other. However acquired, a ready touch over a wide space of human experience was characteristic of Shakespeare. For some of this experience we need look no farther than Stratford itself; the early acquaintance with hunting and angling and fowling; the keenly noted observation of rural life, mingling oddly with the fabulous natural history which contemporary literature inherited from the medieval bestiaries. For the rest, we cannot tell where it was garnered. But we are entitled to assume a roving and apperceptive mind, conversant in some way with many men and manners, and gifted with that felicity in the selection and application of varied knowledge, which is one of the secrets of genius. What has perhaps puzzled readers most is the courtesy of Shakespeare; his easy movement in the give and take of social intercourse among persons of good breeding. We have not, indeed, to think of the well-to-do inhabitants of Stratford as boors; but the courtesy of a provincial town is not quite the courtesy of a Portia. Probably the true explanation is that, once more, it is a matter of apperceptiveness, of a temper alive, not only to facts, but to human values. A recent writer has suggested, with no support either from records or from probability, that Shakespeare did not grow up at Stratford at all, but was carried off in childhood to learn both his courtesy and his Latin, like Drayton, as a page in the household of Sir Henry Goodere of Polesworth near Coventry.[1] No such guess is needed, nor can a similar one reasonably be based on a statement of a not very reliable writer that Fulke Greville, Lord Brooke, the son of Sir Fulke Greville, of Beauchamp's Court, Alcester, claimed to have been the 'master' of both Shakespeare and Ben Jonson. Greville was a patron of poets, but there is nothing to show to what period the claim, if it was made, related.[2]

A sprinkling of Shakespeares in the southern Cotswolds

---

[1] A. Gray, *A Chapter in the Early Life of Shakespeare* (1926).   [2] App. C, no. x.

and a 'tradition' cited in 1848 of a residence by the poet at Dursley have led to the supposition that he may there have found a temporary refuge. Justice Shallow is asked to countenance William Visor of Woncote against Clement Perkes of the hill; and it is pointed out that a Vizard was bailiff at Dursley in 1612, and that neighbouring families of Vizard of Woncot or Woodmancote and Perkes of Stinchcombe Hill long survived.[1] The conjunction of names might be more than a coincidence. But Perkes itself was a common name in Warwickshire and Worcestershire as well as in Gloucestershire, and in fact a Clement Perkes was born at Fladbury, Worcestershire, in 1568. Many Shakespearean names occur in Stratford documents. On most little stress can be laid. It is intriguing to find a Fluellen and a Bardolfe in the same list of recusants as Shakespeare's father, although Shakespeare knew Bardolfe as the title of a nobleman, and a Stephen Sly of Stratford[2] to match the Christopher and Stephen Sly of *The Taming of the Shrew*, although 'Slie' and 'Don Christo Vary' were already given by the source-play of *A Shrew*. Christopher Sly, however, calls himself of Burton Heath, presumably Barton-on-the-Heath, where the Lamberts dwelt; and Marian Hacket, the fat ale-wife of Wincot, must belong to the Wincot which lies partly in Clifford Chambers and partly in Quinton, where a Sara Hacket was baptized in 1591.[3] It is perhaps only a fancy that Clement Swallow, who sued John Shakespeare for debt in 1559, may have contributed with Sir Thomas Lucy to the making of Justice Shallow of Clement's Inn.[4] It seems to have been a Restoration stage-tradition that a ghost scene in *Hamlet* was inspired by a charnel-house in Stratford churchyard; one would have thought the setting more appropriate to the grave-digger scene.[5] Possibly the drowning of a Katherine Hamlet at Tiddington on the Avon in 1579 may have given a hint for Ophelia's end.[6]

[1] Madden, 86, 372.
[2] H.P. ii. 296, says 'Christopher' in error.
[3] Cf. App. C, no. viii.
[4] 10 *N.Q.* x. 286.
[5] App. C, no. xxi.
[6] *M.A.* iii. 50.

All this amounts to very little. Whatever imprint Shakespeare's Warwickshire contemporaries may have left upon his imagination inevitably eludes us. The main fact in his earlier career is still that unexplored hiatus, and who shall say what adventures, material and spiritual, six or eight crowded Elizabethan years may have brought him. It is no use guessing. As in so many other historical investigations, after all the careful scrutiny of clues and all the patient balancing of possibilities, the last word for a self-respecting scholarship can only be that of nescience.

> 'Ah, what a dusty answer gets the soul,
> When hot for certainties in this our life!'

CHAPTER II
THE STAGE IN 1592

[*Bibliographical Note*. The earlier part of this chapter is based on the discussions in *The Mediaeval Stage* (1903) and *The Elizabethan Stage* (1923). In the latter part I have attempted to track more closely the downfall of Queen Elizabeth's company from 1588, and to restate my conjectures as to the relations of the companies of the Lord Admiral, Lord Strange, the Earl of Pembroke, and the Earl of Sussex during 1589–94 in the light of criticisms of *The Elizabethan Stage* by W. W. Greg in *R.E.S.* i. 97, 257, and of the revival of an older view as to the origin of Strange's men in T. W. Baldwin, *The Organisation and Personnel of the Shakespearean Company* (1927). Most of the records of London and provincial performances from 1588 are in Appendix D. Those for the Queen's and Sussex's men must be supplemented from J. T. Murray, *English Dramatic Companies* (1910), subject to some corrections and additions from sources named in *Eliz. Stage*, ii. 1 and the *Bibl. Note* to Appendix D.]

I HAVE elsewhere described, with such elaboration of detail as the envious wallet of time would allow, the gradual establishment of a habit of dramatic representation in this country; tracing its analogies to certain mimetic elements in the customs of the folk, its remarkable emergence in the ritual of a church traditionally hostile to the *histriones*, its relations to outstanding features of medieval society, to the communal celebrations of religious and trade gilds, to the *ludi* of courtly halls, to the varied repertory of the wandering minstrels. And I have endeavoured to show how the medieval passed into the Tudor stage; how humanism brought a new interest in the drama as an instrument of literary and moral education and even of theological and political controversy; how a special class of minstrels, the servants of the Crown or of noble lords, made acting an economic profession and built the permanent London theatres; and how the theatres, buttressed on one hand by a paying public and on the other by court patronage, held their own against puritan opposition, until the Tudor polity itself went under in the civil and religious dissensions of the seventeenth century.

Any intelligible study, however, of the life and work of

the playwright Shakespeare must have its own prelude in
a retrospect of the state of theatrical affairs, as they stood
at the opening of the last Elizabethan decade, when that
playwright made his first appearance. The story may begin with the year 1583, which was something of a turning-
point in the history of the playing companies. In that year
Edmund Tilney, the Master of the Revels, was called
upon by Sir Francis Walsingham, the Secretary of State,
to select a body of players for the direct service of the
Queen. Probably Walsingham was acting in the illness of
the Lord Chamberlain, the Earl of Sussex, within whose
department the oversight of court revels properly fell.
The Queen's men were taken from the most important
of the existing companies, those of the Earl of Sussex
himself, of the Earls of Leicester and Oxford, possibly of
the Earl of Derby and Henry Lord Hunsdon. All these
had made recent appearances at court. They received the
rank of Grooms of the Royal Chamber, probably without
fee, and were entitled to wear the royal livery and badge.
The reasons for the appointment must be matter for conjecture. An old royal company of interlude players, inherited from the Queen's father and grandfather, had been
allowed to die out some years before. In a sense the new
men took their place. But it was not the practice of
the economical Elizabeth to multiply household officers
merely as appanages. And it may be suspected that the
departure of 1583 was an incident in the endeavour of
the government to assert a direct control of the London
stage against the claims of the City corporation. If so, it
was not the only such incident. A power to regulate public
entertainments within their area belonged to the traditional
privileges of the City, as of other incorporated towns.
Moreover, a proclamation issued early in Elizabeth's own
reign, on 16 May 1559, had specifically imposed upon
mayors of towns, as upon justices of peace elsewhere, the
duty of licensing plays, and had instructed them to dis-
allow such as handled 'matters of religion or of the
gouernaunce of the estate of the common weale'. Obviously many of the circumstances of plays were proper

matter for local control. A local authority was best qualified to fix suitable times and places, and to take precautions
against disorder, structural dangers, and infection. The
plan would work well enough, so long as the authority was
reasonable, and did not, as is sometimes the temptation
of licensing authorities, try to convert a power of regulation into a power of suppression. Whether mayors and
justices were equally well qualified to act as censors of
the subject-matter of plays may be doubted; and even if
qualified, they might not always see eye to eye with the
central government. In any case the City of London had
not, from the point of view of Elizabeth's government,
proved altogether reasonable. The Queen required plays
for her Christmas 'solace' at court; and, in order that these
might be economically provided, it was desirable that the
players should have an opportunity of making their living
through public performances. The Corporation was composed of heads of households and employers of labour,
who found that plays distracted their servants and apprentices from business and occasionally led to disorder.
Moreover they were not uninfluenced by a growing
puritan sentiment, which was hostile to plays in the abstract as contrary to the word of God, and found them in
the concrete, even if they did not touch upon religion and
state, full of ribaldry and wantonness. There had been
friction for some years before 1583. The Privy Council
had made more than one attempt to persuade the City to
delegate the licensing to independent persons, no doubt
such as would be acceptable to the Privy Council itself.
This had been refused, and a hint of the royal prerogative
had been given in a patent to the Earl of Leicester's men
in 1574, which gave them authority to perform, in London
and elsewhere, such plays as had been allowed by the
Master of the Revels. The City responded in the same
year with a complete code of play-regulations for their
area. These need not have been oppressive, if not applied
oppressively. But the players probably had their mis-
givings; and they contributed perhaps more than the
Privy Council itself to the defeat of the City, by setting up

theatres just outside its boundaries, where they came under the control of county justices, less active and interfering than the mayor and his brethren. It was not a complete remedy. In summer the apprentices flocked to the plays even farther from their masters' doors, but in winter the comparative inaccessibility of the new houses made recourse to the City inn-yards still inevitable. Meanwhile the puritan sentiment grew, and a spate of controversial sermons and treatises lifted the City into an attitude of complete opposition to the stage. Short epidemics of plague, during which the Privy Council and the City were agreed that plays must be inhibited, brought a complication. It proved easier to get restraints established than to get them withdrawn when the plague was over. In 1581 the patience of the Privy Council was exhausted, and the precedent of 1574 was followed and extended in a new commission to the Master of the Revels, giving him a general power over the whole country, not merely to license individual plays, but to 'order and reforme, auctorise and put down' all plays, players, and playmakers 'together with their playing places'. The powers of justices and mayors under the proclamation of 1559, as well as the ancient privileges of the Corporations, could thus, where necessary, be overruled. No doubt the Master of the Revels, while carrying out the wishes of the Privy Council as to a general toleration for the players and as to censorship, would still normally leave details of times and places to local control. Perhaps, in exasperation, the City now committed a tactical blunder. An order was sent to the gilds, requiring all freemen to forbid the attendance of their 'sarvants, apprentices, journemen, or children' at plays, whether within or without London. It was a *brutum fulmen*, which could not possibly be made effective, particularly beyond the liberties. But the City would not accept defeat, and it was probably during 1582 that, in defiance of the Master of the Revels and his commission, an ordinance was passed, replacing the regulations of 1574 by a simple prohibition of plays within the area. The establishment of a company with the status and dig-

nity of royal servants may reasonably be regarded as a
counter-move on the side of the government. The City
was overawed to the extent of appointing two inn-yards
for the Queen's men in the winter of 1583. In the following year they again proved recalcitrant. The players
brought their case before the Privy Council, and there was
an elaborate exchange of arguments and proposals, as to
which no formal decision is upon record. But it is clear
from events that the City were defeated. They had obtained
a small concession in a standing prohibition of plays on
Sundays. But on the main issue they had to submit to the
power of the royal prerogative, and to content themselves
with showing cause for restraints of plays as often as possible, and pressing for the extension of such restraints to
the Middlesex and Surrey suburbs.

The Queen's men remained the dominant London company for several years after 1583. They did regular
service at court during each Christmas season, according
to an old routine, in plays carefully chosen by the Revels
officers and rehearsed before the Master. Seventeen plays
are credited to them for the five winters from 1583-4 to
1587-8. It may have been a subsidiary object of their
formation to reduce the number of companies which the
City was called upon to tolerate. If so, it was partly
counteracted by the fact that the Queen's men proved
strong enough to occupy more than one playhouse. There
was a protest against this in the negotiations of 1584, and
it may explain an arrangement by which the Curtain was
taken for a term of seven years from Michaelmas 1585
as an 'easer' to the Theatre.[1] But the relations between
companies and playhouses during this period are very
obscure. James Burbadge, the owner of the Theatre, who
had been a member of Leicester's company, was not
chosen for the Queen's, and seems to have entered the
service of Lord Hunsdon. Certainly, however, the
Queen's made some use of the Theatre, and some use of
various inn-yards during the winter. And in the hot days
of summer a section of them, or perhaps the whole com-

[1] *Nebraska Univ. Studies,* xiii. 125.

pany if plague was sporadic, travelled the provinces, where
their livery generally secured them exceptionally liberal
rewards. The older companies, robbed of their best men,
became insignificant. Derby's disappear from the records;
Leicester's, Sussex's, Oxford's, and Hunsdon's survived in
the provinces. There were occasional visits to London.
One play was given at court by Leicester's, one by a new
company under the Lord Admiral, Lord Howard of
Effingham, and one by the same men in combination with
those of Hunsdon, who had become Lord Chamberlain in
1585. There were also several performances of 'activities',
vaulting and tumbling, led by one John Symons, whose
patron seems to have been generally Lord Strange, but in
one year the Earl of Oxford. The chief rivals of the
Queen's men at court were, however, the boy players.
They were to some extent a survival. In the earlier Tudor
dramatic annals the great choirs of St. Paul's and the
Chapel Royal had been at least as conspicuous as the
professional companies. In 1576 a playhouse had been
constructed in an old building of the Dominican priory at
Blackfriars, and this seems to have been occupied about
1583 by boys drawn from both these choirs, together with
others from the private chapel of the Earl of Oxford. The
boys followed the classic and literary tradition which
humanism had brought into the drama, and their Masters
employed academic scholars, such as George Peele and
John Lyly. No doubt this served them better at court,
than with the general London public. Lyly seems to have
been the moving spirit of the Blackfriars combination, and
soon after it broke down in 1585, he began a new series
of plays for Paul's. The Queen's men, on the other hand,
probably contented themselves with pieces of more old-
fashioned and popular types. To this period may belong
the early chronicle histories of *The Famous Victories of
Henry the Fifth* and *The True Tragedy of Richard the Third*.
The titles of the lost *Phillyda and Choryn* and *Felix and
Philiomena* carry more suggestion of literary influence.
But evidently the Queen's relied largely on the pens of
their own members. One of these was Robert Wilson.

He is described in 1581 as capable of writing a 'librum aliquem brevem, novum, iucundum, venustum, lepidum, hilarem, scurrosum, nebulosum, rabulosum, et omnimodis carnificiis, latrociniis et lenociniis refertum'. His extant plays are of the nature of 'moralities'. Another was Richard Tarlton, of part of whose *Seven Deadly Sins* a 'plot' or tiring-house outline is preserved. It shows an attempt at utilizing classical themes. But Tarlton's considerable reputation was evidently in the main that of a joyous jester and buffoon.

The death of Tarlton in September 1588 probably shattered the fortunes of the Queen's men; and with it begins a very difficult phase of company history. Matters were complicated through the controversy aroused in 1589 by the anti-ecclesiastical tracts published under the name of Martin Marprelate. In this both the Queen's men and the Paul's boys took part, possibly at the instigation of Richard Bancroft, afterwards Bishop of London. If so, Bancroft's action was officially disapproved, and the players suffered. The Paul's company was suppressed. The Queen's was not, but was probably required to leave London for a time. '*Vetus Comedia* hath been long in the country', says a pamphlet of October 20. It will be as well to track the Queen's men to their end. Wilson had apparently left the company before Tarlton's death, and among its leaders were now John Laneham and John Dutton, two of the original members, and John Dutton's brother Laurence. Moreover, John Symons had entered the Queen's service, possibly bringing with him some or all of Strange's troop of acrobats. This had presumably taken place before 14 August 1588, when 'the Quenes plaiers' and 'the Quenes men that were tumblers' were rewarded together at Bath.[1] How far Symons maintained an organization independent of the older company it is impossible to say, in view of the habit of dividing forces, which evidently still continued. The travels of 1588 were prolonged until the end of the year, and extended as far

[1] Wardle 111, from *Account* from c. Whitsun 1588 to c. Whitsun 1589, 'given to the Quenes plaiers the xiiij^{th} daie of August xvij.s, more given by Mr Mayour to the Quenes men that were tumblers x.s'.

north as Lancashire, where Queen's men were at the Earl of Derby's house of New Park on October 16. The next day came 'Mr Dutton'. He was probably John Dutton of Dutton in Cheshire, but the actor Duttons may have been kinsmen of that house. On November 6 Queen's men were at Leicester, on December 10 at Norwich, on December 17 at Ipswich, evidently returning London-wards. There were Queen's plays at court on 26 December 1588 and 9 February 1589, and an entry in the Revels Accounts of a pair of hose for 'Symmons the Tumbler' suggests that he contributed 'activities'.[1] The travels of 1589 were long and widespread; the Marprelate episode was no doubt a factor. The movements of more than one group seem to be involved. A tour started at Maidstone in January, and went by a southern circuit through Canter-bury (c. Feb. 2), Dover, Winchester (Mar. 10), Glouces-ter (Apr. 17), Leicester (May 20). Here the reward was to 'others moe of her Mayestyes playars', distinct therefore from the 'certen of her Maiests playars' whose reward for 6 November 1588 appears in the same account. It may have been this or another group who are found moving northwards on an eastern circuit, at Ipswich (May 22), Aldeburgh (May 30), and Norwich (June 3). And either from Leicester or from Norwich Queen's men made their way into the north. They were at Lathom in Lancashire, another of Lord Derby's houses, on July 12 and 13. Then track is rather lost of them. But they are more likely to have stayed in the north than to have returned to London, since Queen's men were again visit-ing Lord Derby, this time at Knowsley in Lancashire, on September 11 to 13, and on September 22 Lord Scrope wrote to the English ambassador in Scotland that they had been for ten days in Carlisle. He had sought them out from 'the furthest parte of Langkeshire', on hearing that King James wished them to visit Scotland, and they had

---

[1] I abandon the conjecture (*Eliz. Stage*, ii. 119) that Simons was tem-porarily with the Admiral's. It is true that the Chamber Account ascribes (App. D) 'activities' to them and not to the Queen's, but it does not follow that the Queen's gave none, and they already had tumblers at Bath (cf. *supra*) on 14 August 1588.

returned to Carlisle, where they had evidently already
been. Perhaps they never visited Scotland, as a projected
royal wedding was deferred. These dates show that it must
have been a second or third group who started an autumn
tour, again on the southern circuit, through Maidstone
(Aug. 2), Canterbury, Dover, Winchester (September), and
Bath (November). Less precisely dated visits to Coventry,
Oxford, and Reading may belong to either of these tours,
or even to the winter of 1588, but the Nottingham accounts for 1588–9 clinch the argument for the duplication
of companies, by recording separate payments to 'Symons
and his companie beinge the Quenes players' and to 'the
Quenes players, the two Duttons and others'. By the
Christmas of 1589 the Queen's must have purged their
summer's offence, since they played at court, under John
Dutton and Laneham, on December 26 and March 1.
There is no mention of Symons, or of 'activities' by the
Queen's. The provincial visits of 1590 are mainly undated.
We may conjecture a summer tour, by Ipswich to Norwich
(Apr. 22), then perhaps by Leicester and Nottingham to
Knowsley (June 25–6) where 'Mr Dutton' was again a
visitor, thence through Shrewsbury (July 24), Bridgnorth
and Ludlow (July), and home by Coventry and Oxford.
An autumn tour may have included Faversham, Canterbury (Aug. 10), Winchester, Marlborough, Exeter,
Gloucester, and Leicester (Oct. 30). And that Symons was
a participant in the summer tour may perhaps be inferred
from the numerous records of 'activities'. At Ipswich the
reward was for 'the Torkey Tumblers', at Norwich for
'the Quenes men, when the Turke wente vpon Roppes at
Newhall', at Leicester for 'certen playars, playinge uppon
ropes at the Crosse Keyes', at Bridgnorth for 'the Quenes
players at the dancing on the rop', at Coventry for 'the
Queenes players and the Turk'. From Shrewsbury we have
a fuller account of the rope-dancing by 'the Queen's
Majesty's players and tumblers', and here the Turk becomes an 'Hongarian'.[1] The Christmas of 1590 seems to

---

[1] Owen and Blakeway, *Hist. of   in 1 Shropshire Arch. Soc. Trans.* iii.
Shrewsbury, i. 385; W. A. Leighton   318, from *Taylor MS.*

give new evidence of division. Two separate warrants were issued on 7 March 1591; one to the Duttons for four plays from December 26 to February 14; the other to Laneham for a single play on January 1.[1] And on the day after Laneham's performance a group of Queen's men was already starting at Maidstone for the southern circuit. It can be tracked through Faversham, Canterbury (Jan. 11), Dover, Southampton (Feb. 14), Winchester, Bath, Gloucester, perhaps Shrewsbury, Coventry (Mar. 24), and Oxford. And at Southampton, Gloucester, and Coventry, probably already at Faversham, it was working in combination with the Earl of Sussex's men.[2] By May it had crossed to the eastern counties, and here it was possibly reinforced by a second group, for at Ipswich rewards were paid to 'the Quenes players' on May 15 and to 'another company of the Quenes players' on May 28. The two groups may have gone on together to Norwich (June 23), where they pass out of sight. Meanwhile, as in 1590, a fresh tour set out on the familiar round by Maidstone (May 28), Faversham (June 2), Southampton (June 29), Winchester, and Bath. At Southampton 'Mr Dutton' is noted as the leader. Then the records fail, but Queen's men visited the Earl of Rutland at Winkburn in Notts on August 18, and were at Coventry both on August 24 and October 20, coming and going, maybe, from the marches or the north. The Shrewsbury visit may belong here. They were only called upon for one court play, on 26 December 1591, but they are not traceable on the road again until March 30 at Canterbury. An allusion in Nashe's *Summer's Last Will and Testament* suggests that at some time in 1592 a Queen's 'vice' was to be seen at the Theatre. Several tours are again probable during this year, but one can only definitely link dates for Ipswich (May 1), Norwich (May 27), and Leicester (June 10); then Southampton (Aug. 3) and Bath (Aug. 22); then Cambridge (c. Sept. 1) and Aldeburgh (Oct. 11), where the Queen's were rewarded 'at the same time' with Lord Morley's men; and

---

[1] *Eliz. Stage*, iv. 163.

[2] The Faversham entry says Essex's, but I suspect an error.

finally Canterbury (Nov. 17) and Southampton (Nov. 26). But they were also at some time during 1591–2 at Maidstone, Rochester, Winchester, Gloucester, Stratford-on-Avon, Coventry, Worcester, Nottingham, and again at Aldeburgh. At Cambridge they got into trouble with the University authorities, who feared infection from the plague then raging in London, and 'one Dutton' is again mentioned as their leader.[1] A letter from the Vice-Chamberlain in December indicates that they would be prevented by the plague from playing at court, and in fact they did not play, although other companies did.[2] Their provincial records for 1593 are comparatively few; the plague had made visitors from London unwelcome in the country. A tour seems to have started in a new direction by Oxford (Feb. 25). Queen's men were at Leicester (June 20), York (September), and Norwich (Oct. 18), and at some time in 1592–3 at Ipswich, Maidstone, Plymouth, Coventry, and Stratford-on-Avon.[3] They made their last appearance at court on 6 January 1594, and an attempt to maintain a footing in London is indicated by a season which they began, with their old associates of 1591, the Earl of Sussex's men, at the Rose or perhaps Newington Butts on April 1. It only lasted eight days. Henslowe's diary records a reconstruction on May 8, 'when they broke and went into the contrey to playe';[4] and for the rest of the reign they are merely a provincial company. No more is heard of the Duttons, or of Laneham.[5] How long the relations of Symons with the Queen's, whatever they were, lasted is uncertain. But there were still 'tumblers that went on the Ropes' at Coventry in 1592–3, and 'a wagon in the pageant for the Turke' at Gloucester in 1594–5. These notices do not specifically name the Queen's.

There is, of course, a strong element of conjecture in all this mapping of travels, and the disclosure of new

[1] *M.S.C.* i. 190.
[2] *M.S.C.* i. 198.
[3] A Southampton visit ascribed by Murray, ii. 399, to August 1593 really belongs to August 1594.
[4] Henslowe ii. 277.
[5] A forged reference to him is in the MS. of *Sir Thomas More* (cf. p. 512).

records may easily supplement or modify its details. But I think it is clear that, from the death of Tarlton onwards, the Queen's men were gradually losing their hold of London. Their court performances only number eleven for 1588–94 against the seventeen for 1583–8. In the country their livery served them better. But they had to split their forces, to join up with stray companions of the road, and to diversify their entertainments with acrobatic tricks. They were reverting to the hand-to-mouth existence of the medieval minstrels. It is perhaps significant that in 1592 the City took advantage of the situation to suggest that public plays were no longer necessary, and that the Queen's service might be adequately provided for by 'the privat exercise of hir Maiesties own players in convenient place'. They approached Archbishop Whitgift, and the cynical ecclesiastic advised them to bribe the Master of the Revels. But the money was not forthcoming, and other players took the place of the Queen's. The disorganization of the hitherto dominant company was, indeed, an obvious opportunity for new men. Two companies come to the front. One is the Lord Admiral's; the other Lord Strange's. The Lord Admiral's have the clearer origin. In 1583 a provincial company of the Earl of Worcester's men included Robert Browne, James Tunstall, Edward Alleyn, Richard Jones, and Edward Browne. The last notice of Worcester's men is in March 1585, the first of the Admiral's in June 1585; and the connexions in which some of these names recur later make it a safe conjecture that, when Lord Howard became Lord Admiral in 1585, some or all of Worcester's men entered his service. The Admiral's played at court, both independently and in conjunction with Lord Hunsdon's, in the winter of 1585–6. They travelled in 1586, were in London by January 1587, but not at court, travelled again in 1587, and returned to London by November. About November 16 they were unfortunate enough to kill a woman and a child during a shooting scene, which must have been the execution of the Governor of Babylon in 2 *Tamburlaine*, v. 1. They now disappear from the provincial records until 1588–9, when a visit to Cambridge is recorded. Possibly they found retirement discreet; possibly they merely gave up travelling. They were at court on 29 December 1588 and 11 February 1589 with plays, and also with 'feates of activity and tumblinge'. Symons had no monopoly of these. About this time there was probably some reconstruction of the company, for on 3 January 1589 Edward Alleyn purchased from Richard Jones his share of a stock of play-books and apparel which the two had held jointly with John Alleyn and Robert Browne. John Alleyn was a brother of Edward. He is described as 'servant' to the Admiral in 1589. Other purchases of theatrical apparel by the Alleyns took place between 1589 and 1591, and to two of these James Tunstall was a witness. It is possible that Robert Browne was also bought out, since he was at Leyden in October 1590, and was accompanied by Jones on a second foreign expedition in February 1592. Conceivably their companions, John Bradstreet and Thomas Sackville, may also have been Admiral's men, but there is no proof of it.

The origin of Strange's men is a more difficult problem. It is natural, at first sight, to regard them as a development from their lord's earlier players of 'activities'; and this, indeed, they may to some extent have been. Symons did not necessarily take the whole troop with him when he joined the Queen's. A reward was paid to Strange's at Coventry during the year ending on All Saints' Day 1588, but this may have been either before or after Symons's departure. Something is known of the pre-history of four men who were ultimately members of or associated with the later company. John Heminges is stated in his grant of arms to have been a servant of Queen Elizabeth, presumably as an actor. He is not, however, in a list, perhaps not quite complete, of 30 June 1588. William Kempe was almost certainly the 'Will, my Lord of Lester's jesting plaier', mentioned in a letter from Utrecht of 24 March 1586. A performance half dramatic, half acrobatic, of *The Forces of Hercules* was given before Leicester at Utrecht on April 23, and in August and September

'Wilhelm Kempe, instrumentist' was at the Danish court of Helsingör. Here too were George Bryan and Thomas Pope, with three other 'instrumentister och springere', Thomas Stevens, Thomas King, and Robert Percy, of whom there is no English record. A sixth, Thomas Bull, killed one of his fellows in a brawl, and presumably met his own end as a result.[1] The five, but not Kempe, went on to Dresden and were there until 17 July 1587. This is doubtless the 'company of English comedians' which Heywood says that Leicester commended to the King of Denmark.[2] Their less dramatic acquirements were naturally prominent abroad. It does not of course follow that these comedians, except perhaps Kempe, had anything to do with Leicester's own long-lived English company. The Earl may have picked them up on the Continent itself. Thomas Bull, at least, had already paid a visit to Denmark in 1579–80.[3] Moreover, Leicester's men were playing at court and elsewhere in England during the period of the continental travels. They went on appearing in the provinces up to and after the Earl's death on 4 September 1588, and if a Faversham record of 1589–90 can be trusted, they were not even then disbanded.[4] Possibly they continued for a time in the service of the Countess, who had in fact similarly retained the company of her first husband, the Earl of Essex, for some years after his death. There is not therefore much support for the theory that Leicester's men passed in a body to Strange. It has been recently revived by Professor Baldwin, who thinks that the continental travellers of 1586–7 were not Leicester's players but his musicians, and that on their return they amalgamated with his players under the patronage of Strange. Leicester no doubt had musicians, who were at Oxford in 1585–6, possibly before he went abroad.[5]

[1] J. L. E. Dreyer in *T.L.S.* for 21 January 1926, citing C. Thrane, *Fra Hofviolernes Tid* (1908); V. C. Ravn, *Engelsker Instrumenter* (1870).

[2] *Eliz. Stage*, iv. 52. [3] *Ibid.* ii. 272.

[4] The accounts were in a bad condition when J. M. Cowper (*1 R. Hist.*

Soc. Trans. i. 218) extracted the entry (c. 1869). I have not been able to consult them.

[5] Boas, *Sh. and the Universities*, 19. Baldwin, 76, confuses them with the players and musicians of Edward Lord Dudley, who were at Coventry (Mur-

I do not think that the evidence allows us to say more than that as early as 10 June 1592 Kempe, who had probably been a Leicester's man, had joined either Strange's or, as will be seen, the Admiral's;[1] and that, at some time before 1590–1, Bryan and Pope, who had been on the Continent, had done the same. There are too many possibilities for confidence. Hunsdon's, who disappear after 1589–90, may have contributed an element, as well as the Queen's and Strange's tumblers. And some or all of the continental company may have taken service on their return with Leicester's brother, the Earl of Warwick, or may even have been his men before they went abroad. Warwick's tumblers were at Bath in 1587–8, just about the time of the return, and Warwick's players at Ipswich in 1592. The real patron must then have been the Countess, since Warwick died on 20 February 1590, and left no heir.

Strange's were not at court for the 1588–9 season. But on the following November 5 both they and the Admiral's were playing in the City. Perhaps one or both companies had failed to take warning from the fate of the Queen's and to keep their tongues off Martin Marprelate, for the Lord Mayor made an attempt to suppress plays, on the ground that Tilney 'did utterly mislike the same'. The Admiral's submitted, but Strange's showed contempt and performed at the Cross Keys, with the result that some of them found themselves in prison. 'Admiral's' are named as at court during the following winter, giving a play on 28 December 1589 and 'activities' on 3 March 1590. 'Strange's' are not, nor are any provincial visits ascribed to them during 1590. 'Admiral's', however, did an autumn tour, perhaps by Ipswich, Maidstone, Winchester, Marlborough (July 25), Gloucester (Sept. 17), Coventry, and Oxford.[2] In the following winter there were plays at James Burbadge's house, the Theatre, and here events occurred about which John Alleyn was afterwards called

---

ray, ii. 238) in 1582–3. There is of course nothing in his point that five men were at Dresden and that the same 'talismanic' number are in the patent to Leicester's men of 1574. Leicester had

six men in 1572 (*Eliz. Stage*, ii. 86).

[1] He was in *A Knack to Know a Knave.*

[2] Possibly some of these visits may have been late in 1589. There were two to Ipswich.

upon to give evidence in a Chancery case.[1] The dispute was between Burbadge and one Mrs. Brayne, who claimed a share in the profits of the house, and charged Burbadge with contempt of court in disregarding an order which she considered to be in her favour. She paid several visits to the Theatre to demand her rights. One of these was in November 1590, and a deposition by John Alleyn on 6 February 1592 suggests that it was on this occasion that James Burbadge spoke words of contempt, and his youngest son Richard beat one of Mrs. Brayne's supporters about the legs with a broomstick. Alleyn claims that he 'did as a servaunt wishe the said James Burbage to have a conscience in the matter'. Burbadge, however, said that 'yf ther wer xx contempts and as many iniunccions he wold withstand them all'. And then Alleyn goes on to relate that 'when this deponent about viij daies after came to him for certen money which he deteyned from this deponent and his fellowes, of some of the dyvydent money betwene him & them, growinge also by the vse of the said Theater, he denyed to pay the same. He this deponent told him that belike he ment to deale with them, as he did with the poor wydowe, meaning the now complainant, wishing him he wold not do so, for yf he did, they wold compleyne to ther lorde & M^r the lord Admyrall, and then he in a rage, litle reuerencing his honour & estate, sayd by a great othe, that he cared not for iij of the best lordes of them all.' Alleyn was, however, called upon to make a second deposition in reply to interrogatories on behalf of Burbadge, in which he was pressed as to the date of these events, and on 6 May 1592 he said that they took place 'about a yere past'. The words about the Admiral were spoken in the 'attyring house' in the presence of James Tunstall. I think that we must take this as Alleyn's most considered dating, and treat the tenure of the Theatre by the Admiral's as lasting to at least about May 1591. The court records for the winter of 1590–1 are on the face of them rather odd. The Privy Council

---

[1] Cf. *Eliz. Stage*, ii. 389. The depositions cited are printed by C. W. Wallace in *Nebraska University Studies*, xiii. 1.

Register notes the issue of a warrant for plays and 'activities' on December 27 and February 16 by the 'Admiral's'; the *Chamber Accounts* show payments for these days to 'George Ottewell and his companye the Lord Straunge his players'. It is difficult to resist the inference that the two companies whose names are thus treated in official documents as equivalent had in fact appeared at court together. And if so they had probably been 'exercising' their court plays together in public performances, under an arrangement with James Burbadge which put the Theatre at their disposal. They may also have had the Curtain, since the lawsuit already cited tells us that it still served as an 'easer' for the Theatre. But the relations with Burbadge indicated by John Alleyn's evidence could hardly fail to bring any such arrangement to an end. Provincial notices suggest an autumn tour of 'Admiral's' men in 1591, closely resembling that of 1590, by Southampton, Winchester, Bath, Gloucester, and Oxford. 'Strange's' seem also to have been at Bath. And there is some reason to suppose that by the summer of 1591 a new London head-quarters had already been found at Philip Henslowe's Rose on the Bankside. The Alleyn papers at Dulwich contain an order by the Privy Council withdrawing a previous one which had restrained 'Strange's' men from playing there and had enjoined them to play three days a week at Newington Butts. With it are petitions from the company and from Henslowe and the Thames watermen asking for the concession. Unfortunately neither order is recorded in the Privy Council Register, and the documents themselves are undated. The players' petition, however, was written 'nowe in this longe vacation'. It recites that 'oure companie is greate, and thearbie our chardge intollerable, in travellinge the countrie, and the contynuance thereof wilbe a meane to bringe us to division and seperacion'. Henslowe's petition begs that he may have leave 'to have playinge in his saide howse duringe such tyme as others have'. It does not look, therefore, as if there had been any general inhibition of plays. This seems to point to 1591 rather than to 1592, the only other possible year. In 1592 there was such a general inhibition on June 23, and it was to last to Michaelmas, and therefore through the 'longe vacation'. If I am right in supposing that 'Strange's' as well as the 'Admiral's' had broken with James Burbadge in the spring of 1591, it seems necessary to refer to some earlier date two tiring-house 'plots' or book-keeper's outlines of plays, since both of them show Richard Burbadge as a performer, and he is not likely to have gone with the companies when they left his father.[1] One, now at Dulwich, is of *The Second Part of the Seven Deadly Sins.* It gives an almost complete cast, which includes, as players of male characters, Mr. Brian, Mr. Phillipps, Mr. Pope, R. Burbadg, R. Cowley, John Duke, Ro. Pallant, J. Holland, John Sincler, Tho. Goodale, W. Sly, Harry, Kitt, and Vincent; and as players of women, T. Belt, Saunder, Nick, R. Go., Will, and Ned. Two speakers and some others, probably mute, have no names assigned; the speakers, who are presenters, may have already been cast in a plot for the first part. The other plot, also probably once at Dulwich, is of *The Dead Man's Fortune.* Unluckily, it is not completely cast. The actors named are Robert Lee, Darlowe, 'b. Samme', and Burbage, who possibly played a messenger, but more probably a substantial part. To the inferences to be drawn from these plots I shall return.

No less than six court plays are credited to 'Strange's' during the winter of 1591–2, on December 27 and 28, January 1 and 9, and February 6 and 8; none to the 'Admiral's'. The Queen's and Sussex's also appeared, once each, and a little-known company of the Earl of Hertford's men. On February 19 Henslowe begins a daily record for 'Strange's' which lasts to June 23. Then came the inhibition provoked by some recent disorders, probably arising from an agitation (cf. p. 511) against alien artisans in London; and before its termination at Michaelmas plague had broken out. 'Strange's' were at Canterbury by July 13, and are also traceable at Gloucester, Coventry,

---

[1] Dr. Greg is revising the texts of *Henslowe Papers*, 127, for his *Dramatic Documents.*

Cambridge, and Oxford (Oct. 6). Notices of 'Admiral's' men during this year are scanty. There is a possible one at Aldeburgh and a certain one at Ipswich on August 7. But here the Admiral's were not alone. The payment is apparently a joint one to the Earl of Derby's and to the Lord Admiral's players. By Derby's I think we must assume Strange's to be here meant. The Earl does not seem to have had a company after 1583. Strange's men would naturally have worn the Stanley badge, and a mistake is intelligible.[1] Late in the year, on December 19, 'Admiral's' men were at Leicester. The plague, however, lulled a little about Christmas, and plays at court became possible. Two were given by a company which at this juncture makes a rather surprising first appearance in dramatic annals, that of the Earl of Pembroke, and three by 'Strange's'. These men also got another month's season with Henslowe. But fresh plague led to a fresh inhibition on 28 January 1593, and on January 31 or February 1 the season ended. 'Admiral's' men were already on the road as far afield as Shrewsbury on February 3. Apparently they were weak in numbers, for at York (April) they were performing with a company described as Lord Morden's, possibly an error for Lord Morley's; at Newcastle (May) certainly with Lord Morley's; at Ipswich with Lord Stafford's. Their name appears alone at Norwich and Coventry. 'Strange's' seem to have remained idle for a time, perhaps hoping for the plague to subside. Edward Alleyn was at Chelmsford with companions on May 2, and a record of 'Strange's' at Sudbury in 1592–3 may perhaps identify them. On May 6 a special travelling warrant was issued by the Privy Council in favour of 'the bearers hereof, Edward Allen, servaunt to the right honorable the Lord Highe Admiral, William Kempe, Thomas Pope, John Heminges, Augustine Phillipes and Georg Brian, being al one companie, servauntes to our verie good Lord the Lord Strainge'. It is a little uncertain

---

[1] A recusant list of 1592 (Bowden, *Religion of Shakespeare*, 79) includes a priest, who 'uses to travel in a blue coat with the eagle and child on his sleeve'.

whether or not the 'being al one companie' is meant to cover Alleyn; in any case he was maintaining some personal relation to the Admiral. For a tour which followed, and in which Alleyn took part, his correspondence enables us to eke out the provincial records; and to learn that members of the company not named in the warrant were Richard Cowley, a boy of Alleyn's called John Pyk, and a 'Mr Douton', who is less likely to be one of the Duttons, than Thomas Downton, who was later an Admiral's man. The route was by Maidstone, Southampton, Bath, Bristol (Aug. 1), Shrewsbury, Leicester, and Coventry (Dec. 2). Alleyn, writing from Bristol, contemplated visits to Chester and York, and a return to London about All Saints' Day. Possibly the prolonged plague caused a change of purpose. The letters show that the company was travelling as 'Strange's'. It is Derby's at Leicester and Coventry, but on September 25 Strange had succeeded to the earldom. At Shrewsbury the payment was to 'my l. Stranges and my l. Admyralls players'. Probably the two tours crossed here. The 'Admiral's' appear to have gone on to Bath and to have found fresh associates in Lord Norris's men. Again an error for Morley's is possible.

Two other companies of interest to us were also on the road in 1593. One was Sussex's, who like 'Strange's' obtained on April 29 a special travelling warrant from the Privy Council. They went far afield, to Sudbury, Ipswich, York (August), Newcastle (September), and Winchester (Dec. 7). The other was Pembroke's, the new court aspirants of the preceding Christmas. They made for their Lord's quarters in the Welsh marches, covering Rye, Bath, Ludlow, Bewdley, Shrewsbury, York (June), Coventry, Leicester, Ipswich. At Bath the careful chamberlains record a receipt of two shillings for a bow that Pembroke's men had broken. It is an allegory, for soon Pembroke's were themselves broken. There are no precise dates, and it is possible, although not very likely, that some of the visits may belong to the end of 1592. But that Pembroke's were in the provinces during 1593 we learn from a letter of September 28 in that year from Henslowe

PLATE IV

FERDINANDO EARL OF DERBY

to Alleyn. They had by then, he says, been at home for
five or six weeks, because they could not save their charges
with travel, and had been obliged to pawn their apparel.

The only company at court for the Christmas of 1593–4
was the Queen's. But there was a short cessation of plague,
and Henslowe's book records a short season from December 26 to February 6 by Sussex's men. This had been
purely a provincial company from 1585 up to its appearance at court on 2 January 1592. But we found it working
with a travelling group of Queen's men in 1591, and after
a fresh outbreak of plague and a consequent inhibition on
February 3, this relation was now renewed in a second
short season with Henslowe from 1 to 9 April 1594.
Meanwhile 'Derby's' men were at King's Lynn, Ipswich
(May 8), and Southampton (c. May 15) where in their
turn they had combined with Morley's. The Earl had in
fact died in the north on April 16, and although this does
not appear to have been known at Southampton, when the
company reached Winchester on May 16 they were
described as the Countess of Derby's. 'Admiral's' men
were with Henslowe from May 14 to 16. The plague was
now really over, and a reorganization of the companies
became possible. Already on May 10 and again on June 1
the City were considering some 'cause' concerning plays
recommended to them by the Countess of Warwick.[1] It
is just conceivable that she had contemplated maintaining
a London company. If so, nothing came of it. On June 5
a company of Chamberlain's men is heard of for the first
time since 1588–9. It was playing with Admiral's men,
probably on alternate days, for Henslowe at Newington
Butts. The arrangement seems only to have lasted
until June 15. The companies then parted, and to the end
of the reign shared the supremacy of the London stage.
On October 8 Lord Hunsdon was negotiating with the
City for the housing of 'my nowe companie' at the Cross
Keys.[2] Most of the men named as 'Strange's' on 6 May

[1] The first record is in *Eliz. Stage*,
iv. 315; the second has been recently
found by Miss A. J. Mill, and will
shortly be printed in *M.S.C.*
[2] *Eliz. Stage*, iv. 316.

1593, William Kempe, Thomas Pope, John Heminges, Augustine Phillips, and George Bryan, became Chamberlain's men. So did others of whom we have heard, Richard Burbadge, Richard Cowley, John Duke, William Sly, John Sincler. Edward Alleyn, on the other hand, continued or resumed his service with Charles Howard, the Lord Admiral, and with him went Richard Jones, now back from the Continent, James Tunstall, and Thomas Downton. John Alleyn is not traceable as a player after 1591. There is some slight evidence connecting George Ottewell or Attewell with the Queen's in 1595.

This complicated chronicle raises some problems which are perhaps beyond solution. What was the precise nature of the association between the Admiral's and Strange's men, and what period did it cover? My impression is that the court documents of 1590–1 enable us to put its beginning not later than 1590, and that from that year to 1594 it amounted to an amalgamation. It may have begun a little earlier, with the expulsion from the City in November 1589. It is of course only for 1590–1 that the identity at court of the 'Admiral's' and 'Strange's' is demonstrated, but the reputation of Edward Alleyn about 1592 renders it almost incredible that he was never called upon to appear before the Queen between 1590–1 and 1594–5; and if he did so appear, it can only have been as a 'Strange's' man in 1591–2 and 1592–3. In these years 'Strange's' are at least as predominant at court as the Queen's men had been in their day. In 1593 there is the clearest evidence that Alleyn, although retaining a personal status as a servant of the Admiral, was travelling as a 'Strange's' man. I take it that the Admiral's, weakened by the loss of Jones and Browne, and perhaps later of John Alleyn, were numerically a subordinate element in the amalgamation. Possibly only Edward Alleyn and James Tunstall were left of the nucleus which came from Lord Worcester's service. Obviously the personal gifts, histrionic and financial, of Edward made him the effective manager of the company. I think it best to call it 'the Alleyn company'. Officially, in Lon-

PLATE V

EDWARD ALLEYN

don at least, it seems to have been known as 'Strange's'.
The provinces are another matter. The records of 1590
and also, but for an isolated visit of 'Strange's' to Bath,
those of 1591 are for the 'Admiral's'. Both names are used
in 1592 and 1593, and during these years probably two
groups were travelling. There are distant records for 'Admiral's' at dates when 'Strange's' cannot have been far
from London. Sometimes the paths of the tours intersect,
and the groups play together. This is not in itself proof
of corporate unity, since both groups also play on occasion
with outside companies, such as Morley's. I interpret the
facts as follows. At the beginning of the amalgamation,
the best of the old Admiral's and Strange's men remained
continuously in London. But at certain seasons a group,
perhaps largely composed of hired men, was sent on tour.
One may guess at either James Tunstall or George Ottewell as the leader. The arrangement is closely analogous
to that of the Queen's men during the same period.
Probably Queen's men could always pass in the provinces
as Queen's men. I do not know what evidence of identity
travelling royal servants had to carry with them. Noble-
men's players certainly required a warrant from their lord.
Probably the amalgamated company still held the Admiral's warrant, as well as Lord Strange's, and could use
this for a travelling group. The London group, at the
time of the petition of 1591 or 1592, were a 'greate' company, and feared 'division and separation' if they travelled.
They had the example of the decaying Queen's men before
them. But plague drove them to form a second travelling
group, and I think it also drove them to still further
'division and separation'. The sudden appearance in a
time of plague of Pembroke's men, only to be extinguished
after a brief career, is perhaps best to be explained as a
budding off from the great amalgamation. A third travelling warrant was thus secured. Again, either Ottewell
or Tunstall, neither of whom is named in the travelling
warrant for 'Strange's', may have taken charge. Probably
some play-books, formerly in use by the Alleyn company,
were handed over as an outfit for the new venture, and in-

cluded *Titus Andronicus*, not necessarily in the extant version, and *2, 3 Henry VI*. The stage-directions to the latter preserve the names of five actors, Gabriel, Humfrey, Sinklo, John Holland, and Bevis. The first two names, not very usual, may point to Gabriel Spencer and Humfrey Jeffes, of whom we have later record. All five may have been written into the books either before or after the transfer to Pembroke's, and the only one who can be shown to have gone with that company is Bevis, who is traceable in a gag found only in the reported version of *2 Henry VI* as given by them.[1] Holland and Sincler are in the 'plot' of *Seven Deadly Sins* already described. It is even conceivable that the names may have been added by the Chamberlain's on a revival, although Sincler alone of the five men is known to have passed to them. If so it must have been an early one, since Spencer and Jeffes were with the later Admiral's by 1597. In any case the Chamberlain's revived the plays before 1599 and left the names standing.[2] If they then used the original prompt-book, Sincler may have taken his old part, and the other names may have been allowed to pass as character-names. There is nothing to suggest that Pembroke's, once constituted, did not form a distinct company. Henslowe's letter of September 1593 suggests that they were financially independent. But indeed we know nothing of the financial conditions under which the amalgamation itself worked. The fate of Pembroke's after September 1593 is obscure. I formerly thought that there was an unbridged interval of three or four years before a company of the same name reappeared in 1597.[3] But visits traced at Ipswich on 7 April 1595 and in 1595–6, and at Oxford in 1595–6, may point to some continuity of existence.[4] It may be significant that Gabriel Spencer and probably Humfrey Jeffes belonged to the Pembroke's company of 1597.

An earlier statement of these views has met with some

---

[1] Cf. p. 288.   [2] Cf. p. 289.   *sities*, 20. The Ipswich notices, found
[3] *Eliz. Stage*, ii. 131.   by Mr. V. B. Redstone, will be printed
[4] Boas, *Shakespeare and the Univer-* in *M.S.C.*

demur from Dr. Greg, than whom no scholar is better acquainted with the evidence or brings more acute powers of criticism to its analysis.[1] The main point at issue is as to the date at which the amalgamation, which Dr. Greg prefers to call an alliance, began. He notes that in the Burbadge lawsuit John Alleyn spoke of the Admiral as the 'lord' of the players at the Theatre, and that the only names mentioned are those of Alleyn himself and of Tunstall, both previously Admiral's men. And he thinks that, although the Admiral's and Strange's gave joint performances at court during 1590–1, they remained independent away from the court; that the Admiral's used the Theatre and Strange's the Curtain; that James Burbadge had some control of both houses; that Richard Burbadge played indifferently for both companies; and that a closer association between them only began at the Rose in 1591. I doubt whether there is sufficient material for any confident decision between these conflicting hypotheses. I will therefore only comment that I know no other contemporary example of an actor playing concurrently for two companies; and that there is an *a priori* probability that the joint performance of plays at court had been preceded by joint 'exercise' in public. It is true, however, that in 1611–12 the King's and Queen's men, certainly distinct companies, seem to have combined for two plays at court.[2] The date of the amalgamation is not without importance, since it bears on the interpretation of the plots. These, from the presence of Richard Burbadge, should be earlier than the breach with his father. On Dr. Greg's theory each must represent the self-contained *personnel* of one of the constituent companies of the later amalgamation. If so, he is probably right in assigning the *Deadly Sins* to Strange's, whom he assumes to have been at the Curtain, while the Admiral's were at the Theatre. The cast in this plot is nearly complete, and it does not include Edward or John Alleyn or Tunstall from the Admiral's. It is true that two important parts, those of Henry VI and Lydgate, are not cast, and two of these

[1] *R.E.S.* i. 257.   [2] Cf. App. D.

actors might have filled them. Dr. Greg suggests that they
were filled by Heminges and Kempe. Neither part, however, looks like such a jesting part as Kempe would
naturally have taken. There is, as it happens, a 'Will
foole' in the plot, but it was taken by John Duke. Moreover, if this was a play of 1590–1, one would expect
George Ottewell, the court payee for that year, to have
appeared in it, and one of the vacant parts should on any
theory have been his. It weighs, I think, a little against
Dr. Greg's view that the plot, which in that view belongs
to a performance with which Alleyn was not concerned,
was found at Dulwich. This he puts down to an 'accident'
during the later amalgamation. The *Dead Man's Fortune*
plot, on the other hand, Dr. Greg ascribes to the Admiral's
at the Theatre. I am not sure that this follows very rigidly,
even from his own premises. Besides Burbadge's, only
three names of minor actors occur. They are not in the
Deadly Sins plot, but might have taken the uncast Sins.
One of them, Robert Lee, had a business transaction
with John Alleyn and Thomas Goodale in 1593 (cf. p. 513),
which proves nothing as to his origin, and recurs in the
next century as a Queen Anne's man. No one of them
is found in the later Admiral's company, unless 'b. Samme'
is Samuel Rowley. On my theory, which puts the amalgamation earlier than the parting with the Burbadges, it
is not possible to say more of the plots than that they
represent performances either by the Admiral's or by
Strange's or by the Alleyn company, and that they carry
no evidence as to which members of that company, as we
find it in 1593, had originally been Admiral's and which
Strange's men. We are left without any ground for assuming that the formation of the Chamberlain's and the
later Admiral's men in 1594 represents a segregation of
elements which had already been distinct before the amalgamation. And we cannot tell at what dates, by 1592 and
1593 respectively, Kempe and Heminges had joined one
of the companies concerned.

Finally, something must be said of the surviving
dramatic texts which can be related to the companies

operative in 1583–94. During the greater part of the period
only a few were printed. The vicissitudes of the Chapel
probably account for Lyly's *Sappho and Phaon* (1584)
and *Campaspe* (1584) and Peele's *Arraignment of Paris*
(1584); the suppression of Paul's certainly does for Lyly's
Endymion (1591), *Galathea* (1592), and *Midas* (1592).
From the Queen's came *The Troublesome Reign of King John*
(1591) and presumably Wilson's *Three Lords and Three
Ladies of London* (1590); from the Admiral's *Tamburlaine*
(1590). *The Spanish Tragedy* (S. R. 1592) had been played
by Alleyn's company at the Rose just before its publication,
although, like *Arden of Faversham* (1592) and *Soliman and
Perseda* (S. R. 1592), it was printed without any indication
of its origin. New conditions were evidently brought
about by the reactions of the plague upon theatrical
finance and organization. From the close of 1592 to
the spring of 1595 about thirty plays, certainly or
probably from the companies of 1583–94, were registered
or printed. Most of these are extant in contemporary
prints; some only in prints of rather later date; some not
at all. A few were probably rescued by the companies;
thus the Admiral's *Dr. Faustus* (1604) and *Jew of Malta*
(1633) were re-entered on the register before their ultimate publication; and so was *King Leir* (1605) which
had been played by Sussex's and/or the Queen's for Henslowe in 1594. Several plays, again, carry no evidence of
their company. Title-pages or register entries ascribe to
the Queen's *Friar Bacon and Friar Bungay* (1594), *True
Tragedy of Richard III* (1594), *Selimus* (1594), *Old Wive's
Tale* (1595), *Famous Victories of Henry the Fifth* (1598,
S. R. 1594), *Clyomon and Clamydes* (1599), and the lost
Valentine and Orson (S. R. 1595 and 1600). We can probably add Wilson's *Cobbler's Prophecy* (1594), and possibly
James IV (1598, S. R. 1594) in which John Adams, traceable as a Queen's man in 1588 but not in any company
thereafter, seems to have been an actor. To the 'Admiral's'
belonged *Orlando Furioso* (1594), *Wounds of Civil War*
(1594), *Battle of Alcazar* (1594), *Two Angry Women
of Abingdon* (1599), and *Massacre at Paris* (n. d.); to

'Strange's' *Fair Em* (n. d.), to 'Ned Allen and his Companie' *A Knack to Know a Knave* (1594). From these companies probably also came *A Looking Glass for London and England* (1594), played by 'Strange's' at the Rose in 1592. To Pembroke's are ascribed *Edward II* (1594), *Taming of a Shrew* (1594), and *2 Contention of York and Lancaster* (1595). Presumably *1 Contention* (1594) had a similar origin. To Sussex's are ascribed *George a Greene* (1599, S. R. 1599) and *Titus Andronicus* (1594). But the title-page of *Titus Andronicus* is exceptionally full, and claims performance of the play by Derby's, Pembroke's, and Sussex's. The evidence from a single name on a title-page must not be pressed too far. It is probably that of the last company which performed the play before it was printed. But this was not necessarily the company for which it was written. Play 'books' might be sold, either by a company as a whole, or by individual actors to whom they had fallen on a division of a joint stock. In some such way we must suppose that the Alleyn company acquired the Queen's play of *Seven Deadly Sins*; possibly also the *Looking Glass*, since this, like *James IV*, seems at one time to have had John Adams in its cast. A company, again, might obtain permission to perform a play, of which the 'book' was not their own property. *Bacon and Bungay* bears the name of the Queen's. They had played it, alone or with Sussex's, at one of Henslowe's houses in 1594. And in the same season had been played *Jew of Malta*, *Ranger's Comedy*, and *King Leir*. But Strange's had already played both *Bacon and Bungay* and *Jew of Malta* at the Rose, and both *Jew of Malta* and *Ranger's Comedy* certainly remained in the hands of the later Admiral's men. Probably, therefore, the Queen's and/or Sussex's only gave these three plays under some arrangement with Alleyn. To whom *Leir* belonged we cannot say. On the other hand, I do not think that performance by a company of a play already printed is proof at this period of ownership by that company before publication, although it is obvious that the possession of parts and properties would facilitate a revival. A definite protection of acting rights in published plays by the Lord Chamberlain seems to have been a seventeenth-century development. Alleyn's company had not, therefore, necessarily possessed *Edward I* (1593), which the later Admiral's possibly revived; nor do I think that the Chamberlain's had any special rights in *Titus Andronicus*, *A Shrew*, *Famous Victories*, *Troublesome Reign*, *Leir*, or *Mucedorus*. If so, a company could not very well sell a play both to another company and to a bookseller. It is likely that the booksellers did not get all their 1593–5 stock in the same way. The ruin of the Queen's and Pembroke's may have led to the dispersal of their repertories in bulk or of the shares of disbanded individuals. *Titus Andronicus* probably passed from Pembroke's to Sussex's and *2, 3 Henry VI* from Pembroke's to the Chamberlain's. Even solvent companies may have parted with plays to meet temporary financial needs, or because they had become obsolete. In particular, versions adapted to the reduced *personnel* of travelling groups may not have been thought suitable for the London theatres. And some of the printed texts appear to rest, not upon tiring-house 'books', but upon surreptitious sales by actors or book-keepers of versions reconstructed from memory.

The fragmentary nature of the evidence makes a dramatic history of the period extremely difficult. The work of even the best-known writers is uncertain in extent and chronology, and much of it has come down in mutilated form. Marlowe's authorship of *Tamburlaine* is a matter of inference; it is only by an accident that we know the *Spanish Tragedy* to be Kyd's. Some at least of the anonymous plays are probably due to untraced pens. No satisfactory attribution of so remarkable a piece as *Arden of Faversham* has been arrived at. We know that Thomas Watson was an active playwright, but nothing passes under his name. Henslowe was paymaster in the later 'nineties to many penmen whose earlier careers are obscure. Henry Porter, for example, is now known to have been at work by 1589.[1] One may venture the suggestion that the rise of Alleyn was due, not only to his own powers

[1] H. C. Hart, *3 Hen. VI* (Arden), xlii.

as an actor, but also to his early employment of better dramatists than the Queen's could boast. All of Marlowe's known work, except *Dido* and possibly *Edward II*, seems to have been for companies with which he was associated. The *Spanish Tragedy* may have been written for him; if not, he made use of it later. Peele, Lodge, Greene, Porter, all contributed to his repertory. He carried on the tradition of the literary drama, which Spenser mistakenly believed to have perished with Lyly. I do not doubt that the Queen's, in their post-Tarlton days, attempted to follow suit. It is only an impression that they put their money on Greene as against Marlowe. I do not suggest that Marlowe, or Greene, or any other writer not himself an actor, was tied to a particular company. We know that Greene's university education did not prevent him from selling *Orlando Furioso* first to the Queen's, and then, when the Queen's were in the country, to the Admiral's.

CHAPTER III
SHAKESPEARE AND HIS COMPANY

[*Bibliographical Note.* I have dealt fully with the Chamberlain's-King's men and their theatres in chh. xiii, xv, xvi, and xvii of *The Elizabethan Stage* (1923). Later books of importance are T. W. Baldwin, *The Organization and Personnel of the Shakespearean Company* (1927); G. Hubbard, *On the Site of the Globe Playhouse of Sh.* (1923); W. W. Braines, *The Site of the Globe Playhouse, Southwark* (2nd ed. 1924). Some theatrical documents are collected and discussed in Appendix A, nos. vii, viii, and Appendix D. The books of wider range noted for ch. i are relevant for this chapter also. On Shakespeare's conjectured travels are K. Elze, *Shs muthmassliche Reisen.*(1873, *J.* viii. 46; *Essays*, 254); Th. Elze, *Italienische Skizzen zu Sh.* (1878–80, *J.* xiii. 137; xiv. 156; xv. 230), *Venezianische Skizzen zu Sh.* (1899); G. Sarrazin, *Sh. in Mantua?* (1894, *J.* xxix. 249), *Neue italienische Skizzen zu Sh.* (1895–1906, *J.* xxxi. 165; xxxvi. 95; xxxix. 62; xlii. 179), *Sh. in Mailand?* (1910, *J.* xlvi. 114); E. Köppel, *War Sh. in Italien?* (1899, *J.* xxxv. 122); W. Keller, *Zu Shs italienischer Reise* (1899, *J.* xxxv. 260); E. Sullivan, *Sh. and the Waterways of North Italy* (1908, *Nineteenth Century*, lxiv. 215), *Sh. and Italy* (1918, *ibid.*, lxxxiii. 138, 323); J. S. Smart, *Sh.'s Italian Names* (1916, *M.L.R.* xi. 339); J. Stefansson, *Sh. at Elsinore* (1896, *Contemporary Review*, lxix. 20); H. Logeman, *Sh. te Helsingör* (1904, *Mélanges Paul Fredericy*); W. J. Lawrence, *Was Sh. ever in Ireland?* (1906, *J.* xlii. 65). Shakespeare's personal relations to other writers are discussed in R. Simpson, *The School of Sh.* (1878); J. H. Penniman, *The War of the Theatres* (1897); R. A. Small, *The Stage Quarrel between Ben Jonson and the So-called Poetasters* (1899); G. Sarrazin, *Nym and Ben Jonson* (1904, *J.* xl. 213); G. G. Greenwood, *Ben Jonson and Sh.* (1921); A. Gray, *How Sh. 'Purged' Jonson* (1928); A. Acheson, *Sh. and the Rival Poet* (1903), *Mistress Davenant* (1913), *Sh.'s Lost Years in London* (1920), *Sh.'s Sonnet Story* (1922); J. M. Robertson, *Sh. and Chapman* (1917). Theories as to his 'topical' handling of contemporary history, and in particular the lives of James I and the Earl of Essex, must be sought in the literature of the plays (ch. ix), especially *Mid. N. Dr.*, *Rich. II*, *Hen. V*, *Ham.*, *Oth.*, *Macb.*, *K. Lear*, *Timon*, *Temp.*, and of the Sonnets (ch. xi). C. C. Stopes has written *The Life of Henry, Third Earl of Southampton* (1922). There is none of the Earl of Pembroke, beyond the *D.N.B.* Conflicting views on Sh.'s religion may be found in J. Carter, *Sh. Puritan and Recusant* (1897), and H. S. Bowden, *The Religion of Sh.* (1899). A pleasant estimate of his character is that of H. C. Beeching, *The Benefit of the Doubt* (1916, *Sh. Homage*, 120).]

THE intricacies of the last chapter have at least shown that 1592 to 1594 were years of theatrical disorganization. It is during this period of hasty seasons broken by plague, of the setting up and ruin of ephemeral companies, that Shakespeare first emerges as player and playwright. Robert Greene, from his squalid death-bed on 3 September 1592, left a literary testament. It foreshadows the end of an epoch, that of the domination of the stage by University pens. Greene's eclipse was shortly to be followed by that of Marlowe on 30 May 1593. But Marlowe and two others, probably Peele and either Nashe or Lodge, were the objects of Greene's address *To those Gentlemen his Quondam Acquaintance, that spend their wits in making plaies*.[1] It is a bitter attack upon the companies, who have been beholden to him for the lines they have spoken and have now deserted him. They will desert his friends likewise, since they have now a writer of their own.

Yes trust them not: for there is an upstart Crow, beautified with our feathers, that with his *Tygers hart wrapt in a Players hide*, supposes he is as well able to bombast out a blanke verse as the best of you: and beeing an absolute *Johannes fac totum*, is in his owne conceit the onely Shake-scene in a countrey.

The invective was printed in *Greene's Groats-worth of Wit*, shortly after the author's death, and Henry Chettle, who prepared it for the press, made something of an apology for it in his own *Kind-Harts Dreame*, itself registered before the end of 1592.[2] The letter had been 'written to divers play-makers' and was 'offensively by one or two of them taken'. With neither of these was Chettle acquainted when he worked on the *Groats-worth*, and with one of them he does not desire to be. But he thinks that he might well have moderated the reference to the other.

That I did not, I am as sory as if the originall fault had beene my fault, because my selfe have seene his demeanor no lesse civill than he exelent in the qualitie he professes: Besides, divers of worship have reported his uprightnes of dealing which argues his honesty, and his facetious grace in writting, that aprooves his Art.

It is probable that the first play-maker here referred to is

---

[1] App. B, no. iii.   [2] App. B, no. iv.

Marlowe and the second Shakespeare, although this implies some looseness in Chettle's language, since Greene's letter was obviously not written to Shakespeare. But there is nothing in the letter as we have it which could be offensive to any play-maker except Marlowe, who is spoken of as an atheist and Machiavellian, and Shakespeare, who is openly attacked. The others, presumably Peele and Nashe, 'young Iuuenall, that byting Satyrist, that lastlie with mee together writ a Comedie', are handled in a more friendly spirit. However this may be, Greene's letter in itself is sufficient to show that by September 1592 Shakespeare was both a player and a maker of plays. And it is a fair inference from Greene's tone that he was only just taking rank as a serious rival to the University men. How far back are we to put the beginnings of his dramaturgy? Probably as far as 1591, if he is responsible, as their inclusion in F1 suggests, for *2, 3 Henry VI*. Greene's letter parodies a line from *3 Henry VI*, which must therefore itself have existed as early as 1592. The relation of these parts to *1 Henry VI*, produced by Alleyn's company on 3 March 1592, is best explained by regarding them as earlier productions of the same company, and since they were not being played in 1592, they had presumably been laid aside. As, moreover, the supplementary play is likely to have followed after no long interval, we may conjecturally put them in 1591. That, then, is the earliest year to which there is ground for ascribing any dramatic work by Shakespeare that we know of. And even as a player his career may not have begun long before 1592. It is a mere fantasy that he was enlisted by Leicester's men on a visit to Stratford-on-Avon in 1586–7; and Professor Baldwin's conjecture that he may have then begun a seven-year period of formal apprenticeship in a company rests upon a complete misapprehension of the nature of theatrical training.[1] Tradition tells us, through the mouth of Dowdall (1693), that Shakespeare 'was received into the playhouse as a serviture', and through that of Rowe (1709) that he was 'at

[1] Malone in *Var.* ii. 166; Baldwin, 286; cf. vol. ii, p. 82.

first in a very mean rank'.[1] Both imply a direct transference from Stratford, which I take to be a foreshortening
of events; and both probably mean the same thing, that
he was at first a hired man and not a sharer, which is likely
enough.[2] Malone (1780, 1790) had heard from the stage
that he was originally employed as a prompter's attendant
or call-boy, but the statement is dropped from his revised
Life. It commends itself to Professor Baldwin.[3] A story
not given by Rowe, but apparently known to him and
originally derived from Sir William Davenant, tells how
before Shakespeare became an actor he occupied himself
in taking charge of horses at the playhouse door, and
showed dexterity in the employment.[4] For what it is
worth, the story points to the Theatre or Curtain, as these
were the only houses reached by horseback. Both were in
the hands of Alleyn's company or its component elements
in 1590–1, and this company may well have seen his first
beginnings, alike as actor and as writer. He is not, however, traceable in the cast of the *Seven Deadly Sins* about
1590, unless we arbitrarily assume that he took one of the
unascribed parts. The 'Will' of that cast was a boy, who
took a woman's part.[5]

After Greene's outburst of 1592, Shakespeare's position
becomes shadowy again, up to the regrouping of the companies in 1594. We certainly cannot have any assurance
that he was with Alleyn's company during their wander-
ings. He is not named in the warrant of 6 May 1593,
which probably gives only sharers, or in Alleyn's correspondence. He may have been with Pembroke's, if that
was formed by a division of Alleyn's company, or with the
group which travelled as the Admiral's, or even with Sussex's.[6] Or he may for a time have dropped acting, and
become an unattached playwright. The only plays that
can very well be assigned to this period are *Richard III*,
Titus Andronicus, and *Comedy of Errors*. Of these *Richard*

---

[1] App. C, nos. xviii, xxv.
[2] Cf. vol. ii, p. 80.
[3] App. C, no. xlviii; cf. Baldwin, 293.

[4] App. C, nos. xxxvi, xxxviii, xlii.
[5] Cf. p. 44.
[6] Cf. App. D for the performances of the companies in 1592–4.

III is certainly a continuation of *2, 3 Henry VI*. It is not in Henslowe's list of performances by the Alleyn company, but it seems clear that *2, 3 Henry VI* must have passed to Pembroke's, and *Richard III* may have been done for them. Perhaps it reappears as the *Buckingham* given by Sussex's men in 1593–4, although the name would also fit a play on Henry the Eighth. The title-page of *Titus Andronicus* suggests that it was played successively by Alleyn's company, Pembroke's, and Sussex's, and any touches put to it by Shakespeare might have been for either, the last most plausibly, of these. *The Comedy of Errors* may have been 'the Gelyous comodey' produced by the Alleyn company on 5 January 1593, but about this I am far from certain. It is at any rate possible, however, that Shakespeare may have been writing for three companies during 1592–4. Much research has been devoted to a conjecture that he spent part of this period in northern Italy. It is certainly true that when the plague was over he began a series of plays with Italian settings, which were something of a new departure in English drama; that to a modern imagination, itself steeped in Italian sentiment, he seems to have been remarkably successful in giving a local colouring and atmosphere to these; and even that he shows familiarity with some minute points of local topography. But the evidence is inconclusive, in view of what he may have learnt through books and the visits of others, or through converse with some of the many Italians resident in London. Supposed travels, now or at another time, to Ireland or to Denmark, are even more speculative. One is on safer ground in pointing out that the plague years gave opportunity for the development of literary ambitions outside the range of the drama, which took shape in the narrative poems of *Venus and Adonis* (1593) and *Lucrece* (1594). Each was dedicated with an elaborate epistle to Henry Wriothesley, Earl of Southampton, a young nobleman of Catholic antecedents, who was just beginning to make a figure at court. A super-subtle criticism detects a great advance in the poet's intimacy with his patron between the two addresses, which I am bound to say is not apparent to me. In the first Shakespeare offers 'the first heire of my inuention', that is, his first published work, and will 'take aduantage of all idle houres, till I haue honoured you with some grauer labour'. In the second, 'What I haue done is yours, what I haue to doe is yours, being part in all I haue, deuoted yours.' Each is subscribed 'in all dutie'. The phrasing in both cases seems to fall well within the normal scope of dedicatory formulas. Not many idle hours would have been at Shakespeare's disposal, had he done all the revisionary work and early drafts or fragments of plays, with which some writers credit his pupil pen; and if such theories were sound, which I do not believe, we should certainly have to antedate 1591 for the beginning of his dramatic career.[1] If one can trust the apparent testimony of *Willobie his Avisa*, he had at any rate sufficient leisure, in or shortly before 1594, for an unsuccessful love affair.[2]

An Elizabethan patron was expected to put his hand in his pocket. Rowe tells us that Shakespeare met with 'many great and uncommon marks of favour and friendship' from Southampton, and on Davenant's authority that the Earl 'at one time, gave him a thousand pounds, to enable him to go through with a purchase which he heard he had a mind to'.[3] The sum named is quite incredible. The aggregate of Shakespeare's known purchases in real estate and tithes throughout his life does not reach £1,000. Probably a cipher has been added to the figures during the transmission of the story; and some such amount as £100 Shakespeare may have spent on acquiring a share in the Lord Chamberlain's company, when it was formed during 1594. There is no ground for supposing that he was the William Shakespeare who had enough spare cash to lend one John Clayton £7 in May 1592, and had to sue for it in 1600.[4] At any rate Shakespeare comes before us on 15 March 1595 with an assured theatrical status as a payee on behalf of the Chamberlain's men for plays given at court in the winter of 1594, and therefore doubtless a sharer

[1] Cf. ch. vii.
[2] Cf. p. 569.
[3] App. C, no. xxv.
[4] App. A, no. vi.

in the company.[1] The Chamberlain's men, as we have
seen, established themselves, like the Admiral's men who
were destined to become their principal rivals, on the
break-up of the Alleyn combination in the spring of 1594.
Ferdinando Earl of Derby died on April 16. On May 16
men under the protection of his widow were playing at
Winchester, and 'Admiral's' men were playing for Henslowe in London. Very shortly afterwards the patronage
of the Lord Chamberlain, Henry Lord Hunsdon, must
have been obtained. But the parting with Alleyn may not
yet have been quite complete, since on June 5 Henslowe
began to record performances by 'my Lord Admeralle
men & my Lorde Chamberlen men' at Newington Butts.[2]
The plays given included *Titus Andronicus*, *Hamlet*, and
Taming of A Shrew. It may be that *A Shrew* was already
The Shrew, but the *Hamlet* was certainly not Shakespeare's. Probably this arrangement terminated on June
15, when Henslowe drew a line across the page of accounts, after which these three plays no longer appear.[3]
Thenceforward the two companies may be taken to have
been quite distinct. The Chamberlain's were at Marlborough about September.[4] On October 8 Lord Hunsdon
was negotiating with the Lord Mayor for the use by 'my
nowe companie' of the Cross Keys inn for the winter
season.[5] It is best to assume that as a business organization the Chamberlain's company, unable to rely on financial support from Alleyn, made a fresh start, and that its
capital was contributed by the sharers. No doubt there
was some apportionment of the 'books' belonging to the
old combination, and in some way all those for Shakespeare's earlier plays, including any which had been performed by Pembroke's or Sussex's, seem to have passed
into the hands of the Chamberlain's. *Titus Andronicus*,
however, was already in print. The membership of the
new company included the five men who had been named
with Alleyn in the warrant for 'Strange's' of 6 May 1593.

[1] Cf. vol. ii, p. 319.
[2] Cf. App. D.
[3] Greg, *Henslowe*, ii. 84.
[4] For all their provincial appearances cf. App. D.
[5] *Eliz. Stage*, iv. 316.

They were William Kempe, Thomas Pope, John Heminges, Augustine Phillips, and George Bryan. It also included Shakespeare and Richard Burbadge, who became its leading actor. Its history, first under the designation of the Chamberlain's men, and then under that of the King's men, is continuous throughout Shakespeare's career, and there is nothing to show that he ever wrote for any other company. It became dominant at court, giving thirty-two performances during Elizabeth's reign to twenty by the Admiral's and thirteen by other companies.[1] And during this period its run of prosperity seems to have been substantially unbroken.[2] Plague only threatened once, for a short period in 1596.[3] In the same year there was a hitch, owing to the death of Lord Hunsdon, and the appointment as Lord Chamberlain of William Lord Cobham, who was less favourable to the stage than his predecessor, and under whom the Corporation secured the exclusion of players from the City inns, while the inhabitants of Blackfriars successfully protested against the opening of the new house which James Burbadge may be presumed to have planned for the use of his son and his son's fellows. Curiously enough, one of the protestants was the new Lord Hunsdon, formerly Sir George Carey, and now the patron of the company.[4] But when he himself became Lord Chamberlain on 17 March 1597, his players had once more the advantage of an official protector. They had of course to face the restraint of 28 July 1597, when offence was given by *The Isle of Dogs*, for which they were not responsible, and in August and September they undertook their only prolonged provincial tour between 1594 and the end of the reign.[5] But they stood to gain by the settlement at the end of the restraint, under which only two companies were to be tolerated, and although a Privy Council order of 22 June 1600 limited each company to two performances a week, it is clear

---

[1] *Eliz. Stage*, iv. 164.

[2] A fuller history of the company than I have here room for is in *Eliz. Stage*, ii. 192.

[3] *Eliz. Stage*, iv. 319.

[4] *Ibid.*

[5] Visits to Cambridge and Ipswich may belong either to the autumn of 1594 or to 1595.

PLATE VI

(*a*) GEORGE LORD HUNSDON

(*b*) HENRY LORD HUNSDON

THE LORDS CHAMBERLAIN

that the restriction was not long enforced. On the other hand they had to face fresh competition from the revival of the boy companies in 1599 and 1600, which for a time hit them pretty hard, and from the toleration of a third company of men in 1602.[1] Some ruffles there were from time to time with the censorship. *Richard II* was printed in 1597 without the abdication scene, which had probably been thought unsuitable for an Elizabethan public. Falstaff had to be substituted for Oldcastle in *Henry IV* and Broome for Brooke in *Merry Wives of Windsor*. Brooke was the family name of the Lords Cobham, who also claimed an hereditary interest in Sir John Oldcastle. In 1598 there were complaints in Scotland that 'the comedians of London should scorn the king and the people of this land in their play'.[2] We do not know that these comedians were the Chamberlain's men. The Scots are hardly treated in *Edward III*, printed in 1596, which may be theirs, and it is conceivable that the absence of the Captain Jamy episode (iii. 2. 69–153) from the 1600 quarto of *Henry V* may be due to censorship, although other explanations are also possible. There is no sign, however, that these incidents brought any trouble upon the company. It is even more remarkable that they suffered nothing on account of the performance of *Richard II*, which they gave at the behest of some of the followers of the Earl of Essex, as a prelude to his misguided outbreak of 8 February 1601.[3] Elizabeth grumbled at the popularity of the play, but showed no resentment against the poet or the players. It may be that during 1600–1 they were absent for a short time from London. There are no certain provincial notices of them, but there is a possible one at Oxford, and the title-page of the Q1 of *Hamlet* records that it had been played at Oxford and Cambridge and elsewhere, as well as in London itself, before it was published in 1603. But it is not clear that the journeying, if it took place, was due to *Richard II*, and the company was at court on 24 February 1601, only a fortnight after the Essex affair, and again as usual during the following Christmas. Perhaps we may

[1] *Eliz. Stage*, i. 298, 380; iv. 321–34.   [2] *Eliz. Stage*, i. 323.   [3] App. D.

credit Elizabeth's leniency, at least in part, to her personal liking for Shakespeare's art. Of this we are informed both by Ben Jonson's lines and by the tradition of her impatience to see Falstaff in love. The alleged interchange of royal courtesies over her dropped glove, when the poet was enacting a king upon the stage, must, I fear, be abandoned.[1] No doubt the Tudor lady had moods in which she was capable of scourging those whom she most favoured. But the Lord Chamberlain was never far from the royal chair. The Hunsdons, father and son, were Elizabeth's nearest cousins and her close personal adherents. Of all the court, they could least be suspected of sympathy with seditious tendencies. It was easy enough to slip in a word to save honest men from the consequences of their indiscretions. After all, the company had only been a cat's-paw for the conspirators. It is impossible to suppose that Shakespeare, in writing *Richard II*, deliberately intended to suggest the analogy between Richard and the queen, which from a matter of jest at court became an instrument of serious intrigue. The play is one of a series of studies in abstract kingship, which culminate not in the *coup d'état* of Henry Bolingbroke, but in the coming to his own of Henry of Monmouth, a legitimate king both by right of birth and as a typical representative of the English nation. That while portraying Henry's kingship Shakespeare became a little doubtful about the ultimate fineness of his humanity, does not affect the main dramatic issue. The political philosophy of the plays, from *Sir Thomas More*, perhaps, to Ulysses, always lays its stress on degree, order, and unity. Imaginative biography, bent on its search for the topical, delights to represent Shakespeare as obsessed by the career of Essex and making that picturesque and second-rate personality the theme of play after play. His is the unstable mind of Hamlet, and Burghley, whom Essex hated, becomes his foil in Polonius. His is the ill-requited generosity of Timon, deserted by Ventidius as Essex was deserted by Bacon. Along such a way of thinking, Essex may also become Henry Boling-

[1] App. C, no. lvi.

broke, or Henry of Monmouth, for all the difference
between them, according to taste. There are, however,
conflicting speculations. For some, Hamlet is not Essex
but James, or both Essex and James, and the adventures
of Mary of Scots and Bothwell, under the guise of Lord
and Lady Macbeth, were chosen for the delectation of
Mary's son. And the minor personages of the time, seen
by us, not as their contemporaries saw them, but ill-
focused through the fragmentary revelations of private
papers, must all be brought into the picture. Most of
these cobwebs are too flimsy to bear touching. One cannot be expected to argue whether Lord Buckhurst was or
was not Sir Toby Belch.[1] I do not myself believe that,
apart from some passages of obvious satire in comic scenes,
there is much of the topical in Shakespeare, whose mind
normally moved upon quite another plane of relation to
life. What little there is, probably remains for the most
part irrecoverable. Of course he had to build up his
characters, consciously or subconsciously, and with the
help of traditional stage types, from the qualities of men
and women he had known, or had read of in books. There
was no other material for him or any other dramatist. But
this is a very different process from the making of portraits. For topics of political controversy, in particular,
there was no room in the Elizabethan theatre, although
the position was somewhat altered under the laxer and less
popular administration of James. You could beat the
patriotic drum against the Spaniards, of course. You
could flout the Scots, at least under cover of an historical
play. Even here there might be a risk, as the wind of
diplomacy veered. But you could not ventilate the griev-
ances of the subject, of which indeed there were few except
the monopolies, or touch upon ecclesiastical affairs, or
champion the conflicting views of Essex and Burghley as to
bringing the war to an end, or above all meddle with the
dangerous *arcana* of the succession problem. Least of all
could you do this, if you were in a company which, since
the Queen's men were never in London, had practically

[1] *T.L.S.* for 28 March 1929.

become an official part of the royal household with a privileged and remunerative position, the preservation of which depended entirely on the avoidance of offence. I do not know what the topical theorists suppose that the censorship was about. They have a dilemma to face. Either the portraits must have been so veiled as to be unrecognizable, alike to the naked Elizabethan eye and through the microscope of modern research. Or alternatively the playwright would have tasted the Marshalsea and the players would have gone to pad the hoof in the provinces.

Essex had a popularity which failed him lamentably when the critical moment came; and of this there is an echo in a chorus to *Henry V*. The theorists, however, assume that Shakespeare was linked to his fortunes through their common friendship for Southampton, whom Essex led to his ruin. And the disaster is sometimes held to account for the critical attitude to society which becomes apparent in *Hamlet*. How far Shakespeare's relations with Southampton outlasted the early dedications is very uncertain. The only external fact which might connect them is a letter of 1599 from Lady Southampton to her husband in Ireland, in which she jests on the birth of a son to Sir John Falstaff and Dame Pintpot.[1] It is most unlikely that by Sir John Falstaff she meant Shakespeare himself. There are the *Sonnets*, and Southampton has been very generally accepted as the friend to whom, over a long period of years, many of these were written. I am quite sceptical about it. The identity of the friend may have eluded us. But if we are to find him in a known patron of Shakespeare, some at least of the facts point to William Lord Herbert, afterwards Earl of Pembroke, rather than to Southampton. The earlier supporters of this identification did not get all the evidence.[2] And although Southampton was still alive when the First Folio was published, it was to Pembroke and his brother that Heminges and Condell dedicated it. If Shakespeare was indeed writing for the company of Pembroke's father in 1592–3,

[1] App. B, no. xviii.   [2] Cf. p. 566.

he may already have been in touch with the Herberts, and a projected marriage in 1595 between the son and Elizabeth Carey, granddaughter of the first and daughter of the second Lord Hunsdon, would be an adequate explanation for the earliest sonnets. Elizabeth Carey ultimately married Sir Thomas Berkeley, and it is quite possible that *Midsummer-Night's Dream* celebrated the occasion. It is reasonable to assume that the services of players to the lords of their companies were not merely nominal.

The only fellow-poet to whom Shakespeare directly refers in his plays is Marlowe: [1]

> Dead shepherd, now I find thy saw of might,
> Whoever loved, that loved not at first sight?

His relations to others have been the subject of much wild writing. Probably nobody now believes that Greene's attack of 1592 was only the last shot of a five-year pamphlet campaign, or that Shakespeare was the Post-hast of *Histrio-mastix*, or that Ben Jonson pursued him with malignity, and made him the Poet-Ape of his epigrams.[2] These fancies have long gone to the limbo of critical aberrations. And with them should go Mr. Acheson's theory of a continuous duel between Shakespeare and Chapman from *Sir Thomas More*, in which he supposes Shakespeare to have revised Chapman's work, to *Troilus and Cressida*.[3] Some jesting at Chapman there may be in *Love's Labour's Lost*, and if he was the rival poet of the *Sonnets*, which is not assured, Shakespeare treated him there with a courtesy touched by irony. But Mr. Acheson's attempt to trace a prolonged give and take of offence and retort between the writings of the two men is singularly far-fetched. There is more material to go upon with Ben Jonson.[4] Rowe (1709) had heard that the poets were 'profess'd friends', and that the acquaintance between them began with 'a remarkable piece of humanity and good nature', when

---

[1] *As You Like It*, iii. 5. 81.

[2] Simpson, ii. 11, 339; W. Gifford in Jonson's *Works* (ed. Cunningham), 1. lxxxi; cf. *Epig.* lvi.

[3] A. Acheson, *Sh. and the Rival Poet* (1903), &c.; F. L. Schoell and

A. Acheson, *Sh., Chapman and S.T.M.* (*Revue Anglo-Américaine*, iii. 428, 514).

[4] Cf. App. B, no. xxii; App. C, nos. iii, vi, vii.

Shakespeare commended a play of Jonson's to the consideration of his company.[1] One would gladly think that Shakespeare is the Virgil of Jonson's *Poetaster*.

> That, which he hath writ,
> Is with such judgement, labour'd, and distill'd
> Through all the needful uses of our lives,
> That could a man remember but his lines,
> He should not touch at any serious point,
> But he might breathe his spirit out of him.

I do not in fact think that Virgil was any one but Virgil, or that Shakespeare was the 'so happy a Genius' who collaborated in the lost first version of *Sejanus*. Jonson's considered judgement of Shakespeare is to be found in his First Folio lines and in his later *Timber*. It shows both admiration for the poet and affection for the man. It does not detract from the genuineness of the admiration that it was not uncritical. Jonson had a critical mind, and Shakespeare's way of writing did not altogether answer to his theory of what dramatic structure should be. Therefore he told Drummond that Shakespeare 'wanted Arte'. He censured a line in *Julius Caesar*, which Shakespeare apparently altered. He disliked the solutions of continuity in the action of *Henry V*. He thought that some of the incidents in the *Tempest* and *Winter's Tale* made 'nature afraid', and that *Pericles* was a 'mouldy tale', which in some respects it was. Perhaps he found 'horror' in *Macbeth*. All this is legitimate criticism by one poet of another. And if Jonson smiled at Shakespeare's 'small Latine, and lesse Greeke', his judgement chimes precisely with the reference, so full of admiration and discriminating kindliness, in the recently recovered lines of Francis Beaumont: [2]

> Here I would let slip,
> If I had any in me, scholarship,
> And from all learning keep these lines as clear,
> As Shakespeare's best are, which our heirs shall hear
> Preachers apt to their auditors to show
> How far sometimes a mortal man may go
> By the dim light of Nature.

[1] App. C, no. xxv.   [2] App. B, no. xliv.

In private talk Jonson may have adopted a more slighting
tone towards his friend's erudition. He is said thus to
have incurred the resentment of John Hales. But if he
chaffed Shakespeare's assumption of a motto in *E.M.O.*
he became in return, according to repute, the mark for
Shakespeare's epigrams. Friends need not spare each
other, writing in the same tavern, and over the same quart
pot. Is Jonson in Shakespeare's plays? About 1599 he
became involved in the *Poetomachia*.[1] This started as a
quarrel between him and Marston, and there is no reason
to suppose that Shakespeare's was one of the 'petulant
stiles' with which Jonson complained that for three years
he had been provoked on every stage. But while he was
preparing his *Poetaster* (1601) against Marston, he seems
to have learnt of the intended production by the Chamberlain's men of Dekker's *Satiromastix*. Dekker, therefore, as
well as Marston, appears in *Poetaster*, together with a
company of players, whose personalities are treated in no
friendly spirit. There are doubtless some hits at the
Chamberlain's men here. Professor Baldwin, with much
ingenuity and little to go upon, has endeavoured to distribute the parts.[2] But even he does not find Shakespeare,
and if Jonson made any allusion to Shakespeare in this
controversy, it can only be in the *Apologetical Dialogue*
written after the appearance of *Satiromastix* later in 1601.
Here, after defending his 'taxation' of some of the players,
he adds:

> Onely amongst them, I am sorry for
> Some better natures, by the rest so drawne,
> To run in that vile line.

A contemporary notice does, however, connect Shakespeare's name with the *Poetomachia*. In *3 Parnassus*, a
Cambridge play, probably produced in the winter of
1601–2, William Kempe, talking of academic writers, is
made to say,

> 'Why heres our fellow Shakespeare puts them all downe, ay and
> Ben Jonson too. O that Ben Jonson is a pestilent fellow, he

---

[1] *Eliz. Stage*, i. 381; iii. 293, 365, 428.   [2] Baldwin 232.

brought up Horace giving the Poets a pill, but our fellow Shakespeare hath given him a purge that made him beray his credit.' [1]

The 'pill' is in *Poetaster*; the 'purge' has been sought in
various plays of Shakespeare. It is often taken to be the
description of Ajax in *Troilus and Cressida*, i. 2. 19, which
seems unnecessarily elaborate for its place, refers to
'humours', and has not much relation to the character of
Ajax as depicted in the play. Professor Sarrazin argued
at length for Nym in *Henry V* and *Merry Wives of Windsor*,
and the suggestion has been revived by Sir Arthur Quiller-
Couch.[2] Mr. Arthur Gray has recently suggested the
censorious and libertine Jaques of *As You Like It*.[3] I dare
say there may be glances at Jonson in all of these, particularly in Nym, who rarely speaks in *Henry V*, and never
in *Merry Wives of Windsor*, without using the word
'humour'. But I do not think that any one of them was
the 'purge'. All the plays concerned, except *Troilus and
Cressida*, are too early in date, since the writer of *3 Parnassus* clearly regarded the 'purge' as an answer to the
'pill'. Probably the 'purge' was *Satiromastix* itself. Horace
is promised one in i. 2. 294, although there is none of a
literal kind in the play. The Cambridge writer may have
thought that Shakespeare was responsible for it, since he
introduces Kempe as a fellow of Burbadge and Shakespeare, although Kempe had left the Chamberlain's men
in 1599, and Danter, who was long dead, as a printer.

Shakespeare's success as a playwright appears to have
terminated all other literary ambitions. His free handling
of the dramatic form gave him ample scope for a wide
variety of poetic expression. The narrative poems, if we
may judge by the frequency of allusions to them and the
number of reprints, won an early and lasting popularity.
But they had no successors. The only occasional verses
which bear Shakespeare's signature are the set on *The
Turtle and Phoenix*, contributed to a volume in honour of

[1] App. B, no. xx; cf. *Eliz. Stage*,
v. 38.
[2] *J.* xl (1904), 213; *Merry Wives
of Windsor* (ed. Quiller-Couch and
Wilson), xxxi.
[3] A. Gray, *How Sh. 'Purged' Jonson* (1928).

one Sir John Salisbury in 1601. No dirge for Elizabeth or paean for James came from his pen. He stood aloof from the practice of commendatory writing, with which most of his contemporaries vaunted each other's wares. Professor Minto thought that he found him in a sonnet by 'Phaeton' prefixed to John Florio's *Second Fruits* of 1591. It is of merit, but does not compel a recognition of Shakespearean authorship, and in any case antedates *Venus and Adonis*.[1] If any of his lyrics are among the anonymous work of the song-books, they were probably written for the stage. The few pieces ascribed to him in manuscript anthologies, like those in *The Passionate Pilgrim*, carry little authority. The authenticity of *A Lover's Complaint*, printed with the *Sonnets*, is gravely doubted.[2] The *Sonnets* themselves are an exception. They continue the poetic impulse of the early work, and their composition covers a period of three years and more, probably from 1595 to 1599 or 1600. One must suppose that some at least of them were originally intended for publication. How else could the immortality in verse promised to the poet's friend be secured? Shakespeare was known to Meres as a sonneteer in 1598. But unless a volume of 1602 has been lost, the *Sonnets* remained in manuscript to 1609, when they were printed without any token of oversight by the author. To whomsoever written, William Herbert, or Henry Wriothesley, or an unknown, or a group of unknowns, the *Sonnets* give us glimpses of a soul-side of Shakespeare imperfectly revealed by the plays. A perturbed spirit is behind the quiet mask. Here is a record of misplaced and thwarted affections, of imperfections and disabilities, inseparable perhaps from an undesired way of life, which clog a mind conscious enough of its own power. Shakespeare, the myriad-minded, is

> Desiring this man's art and that man's scope.

He is tired of life before his time, conscious of 'tann'd antiquity' in the full tide of years, brooding on the decay of beauty and the passing of friends, letting his imagination

[1] Cf. p. 555.   [2] Cf. p. 550.

play freely around thoughts of death. One must not take too literally a way of writing which has some elements of traditional convention in it, or attempt to construct a complete personality from the transient utterances of individual moods. But when all such allowance is made, there is some disharmony between the tone of the *Sonnets* and that of the vivid comedies, abundant in their rendering of the surface of things, which were contemporary with them. They lead up more naturally to the questionings of *Hamlet* and to the distasted essays in disillusion which followed.

A reasonable measure of worldly prosperity came to Shakespeare. We do not know that he ever let go altogether of Stratford. The boy Hamnet died in 1596. Sentiment would trace a reflection of the event in the sympathetic treatment of Arthur in *King John*, which chronology at least does not forbid. The two daughters, Susanna and Judith, remained. There had been no more children. About 1596 Shakespeare may have begun to pick up the broken threads of family life. His father survived to 1601. No will or administration is known, but it is evident that the Henley St. houses, all that was left of John's property, came into his son's hands, subject no doubt to a life-interest for the widow.[1] Probably it was the poet's money which financed an unsuccessful attempt of 1597 to recover the lost Arden inheritance at Wilmcote, as well as an application to the Heralds' Office in 1596 for a grant of family arms, which John had contemplated and dropped when he was bailiff of Stratford in 1568–9.[2] The grant was duly made, and the arms *Or on a bend sable a spear of the first steeled argent*, with a falcon bearing a spear as the crest, adorn the poet's monument. In 1599 there was a second application for leave to impale the arms of Arden, but if this grant too was made, neither Shakespeare nor his descendants appear to have availed themselves of it. The responsible heralds incurred some criticism for assigning arms to a person of base degree, and defended themselves by reciting John's substantial position and civic dignities. In 1597 Shakespeare established himself in his

---

[1] App. A, nos. iii, xxiv.   [2] App. A, nos. ii, iv.

native town through the purchase, for £60 if the sum
named in the fine can be trusted, of the substantial freehold house of New Place.[1] This stood opposite the Gild
Chapel, at the angle formed by Chapel St. and Chapel
Lane, and had a large garden. It had been built at the
end of the fifteenth century by Sir Hugh Clopton, and had
passed by purchase through other hands. There was a
curious hitch in the transaction with Shakespeare. William
Underhill, the vendor, was poisoned by his son Fulke, and
Shakespeare had to secure warranty through a fresh fine
with another son Hercules, to whom the felon's estate had
been granted. About 1540 New Place was described as 'a
praty howse of brike and tymbar'. But in 1549 it was out
of repair, and that Shakespeare may have had to put it in
order is suggested by the sale of a load of stone from him
or his father to the Stratford corporation in 1598. In the
same year he had in Stratford a store of ten quarters of
malt, a commodity in which the well-to-do inhabitants of
the town largely dealt, somewhat to the impoverishment
of their neighbours in a time of dearth.[2] In 1598 also the
correspondence of Richard Quiney of Stratford shows
Shakespeare in friendly relations with a fellow-townsman,
who applied to him for a loan to meet expenses in London,
and at the same time in search of an investment.[3] Oldys
has a stage tradition that he drew Falstaff from a land-
owner who had refused to sell to him.[4] He ultimately, in
1602, bought for £320 from the local family of Combe
a freehold property in the open manorial fields of Old
Stratford, extending to a hundred and seven acres of
arable land, with twenty acres of pasture and rights of
common.[5] This he probably let for tillage by the existing tenant occupiers. And in the same year he acquired,
for the use of his gardener, one may suppose, a cottage in
Chapel Lane, which was copyhold of the manor of Rowington.[6] He cannot as yet have dwelt much at New Place,
although he is not known to have leased it. In London

---

[1] App. A, no. xi.   [4] App. C, no. xxxiv.
[2] App. A, no. xii.   [5] App. A, no. xiv.
[3] App. A, no. xiii.   [6] App. A, no. xv.

he is traceable in 1597 as living in St. Helen's, Bishops-
gate, where, like other poets, he neglected to pay his taxes.
But by the end of 1599 he had moved to the liberty of the
Clink on the Surrey Bankside.[1] In both places he would
have been in close proximity to his playhouse, at first the
Theatre or Curtain, then the Globe.

So Shakespeare stood, when Elizabeth made way for
James. He too, no less than his predecessor, was 'taken',
according to Ben Jonson, with the flights of the 'Swan of
Avon'; and there is no reason to doubt that Shakespeare
remained a *persona grata* after the change of reign. Several
of his older plays were chosen to appear with new ones at
the court performances of 1604–5. I am not so sure as
was Sir Sidney Lee that the letter, said to have been once
at Wilton, in which Lady Pembroke invited the king to see
a representation of *As You Like It* in 1603, is to be put down
as mythical. It certainly cannot now be found, but its
existence was recorded by a competent historian in 1865.[2]
An anonymous writer about 1709 speaks of an 'amicable'
letter, already also lost, but once in Sir William Davenant's
hands, from James to the poet himself.[3] Commentators
have not refrained from guessing that it was in acknowledgement of the honour paid to the new royal house in
Macbeth.

The *status* of the former Lord Chamberlain's men suffered no diminution under James. On the contrary it was
enhanced. They now became King's men and sworn
officers of the royal household as Grooms of the Chamber
in ordinary without fee.[4] Here the oversight of them still
rested with the Lord Chamberlain, no longer Lord Hunsdon, who retired early in the reign and died shortly after,
but successively Thomas Howard, Earl of Suffolk (1603–
14), Robert Carr, Earl of Somerset (1614–15), and
William Herbert, Earl of Pembroke (1615–26). The
appointment did not entail any regular household duties,
other than those of players. But there was an exception in
August 1604, when grooms were needed to attend the

[1] App. A, no. ix.
[2] App. D, *s.a.* 1603.
[3] App. C, nos. xxvii, xxxiv.
[4] *Eliz. Stage*, i. 311.

PLATE VII

RICHARD BURBADGE

Constable of Castile, who came as an ambassador from Spain, and Shakespeare with eleven fellows waited in their red liveries during the peace negotiations. They acted now under the authority of a royal patent, which entitled them to appear both in London and in any city, university, or other town throughout the realm.[1] We have no great certainty as to the playhouses used by the Chamberlain's men at the beginning of their career.[2] They had the Theatre in 1596 and probably from 1594, and they may also have occupied city inns during the winter until that practice was stopped in 1596. In 1598 they were at the Curtain. The Theatre in fact was in bad repair, and after long disputes between the Burbadges and the ground landlord, its timbers were pulled down and carried to the Bankside. Here in the course of 1599 was opened the Globe. This is the house named in the patent to the King's men, and it remained in their possession throughout. In 1608 they acquired the lease of the Blackfriars, and this they began to occupy in the autumn of 1609. Being a roofed house, it was more convenient for winter performances than the Globe, which it seems to have gradually displaced as the head-quarters of the company. The court performances under James were more frequent than had suited the economical disposition of Elizabeth, and during 1603–16 a hundred and seventy-seven fell to the lot of the King's men. This was far more than half the total number given.[3] But there were difficulties to be faced. The rivalry of the boys was continued by other young aspirants, and there were now generally four and sometimes five companies playing in London. Even the King's men themselves did not steer quite clear of troubles with the censor, and there was a restraint in 1608, for which they were not responsible, but which threatened a permanent suppression, and had to be bought off at considerable expense. More serious, however, was the effect

---

[1] This would overrule the bar of 1593 against performances in the universities of Oxford and Cambridge (*Eliz. Stage*, ii. 113; Dasent xxiv. 427; *M.S.C.* i. 200) if it had been maintained;

cf. *T.L.S.* for 21 Feb. to 2 May 1929.

[2] Cf. *Eliz. Stage*, chh. xiii, xvi, xvii, for a more detailed history of the company and its houses.

[3] Cf. App. D, *passim*.

of plague. The epidemic, from which London had been practically free for a decade, broke out again in 1603. The theatres had been closed in March, when Elizabeth's illness became dangerous, and hopes of a season on the arrival of James in May were frustrated. The King's men had to travel. The plague had subsided by the next spring, and the theatres were opened on April 9. The rest of the year was free from infection, but there were recrudescences in each of the next three summers, and a worse visitation in that of 1608, which lasted to nearly the end of 1609. It is probable that plays were more or less automatically suspended, at first when the weekly deaths from plague reached thirty, and from 1608 when they reached forty over a rather wider area. On this basis there would have been closures during the greater part of October to December 1605, July to December 1606, July to November 1607, and from the end of July 1608 to the end of November 1609.[1] During all five years the King's men travelled. Theatrical profits must have been badly hit, in spite of special royal subsidies to the company, in 1603–4 for their 'maintenance and relief', and in 1608–9 and 1609–10 to enable them to undertake 'private practice' for the King's service at Christmas.[2] Possibly this did not exclude the admission of spectators to one of the 'private' theatres. The Whitefriars seems to have been available in 1608–9, although we do not know that the King's men occupied it. In 1609–10 they had the Blackfriars. After 1609 there was no serious plague until 1625. But there was generally a little travelling in the summer.

The company, in the strict sense, consisted of 'sharers', who were bound together by some deed of association, and divided the profits, after setting aside the proportion allocated to the owners of the playhouse, and meeting the current expenses.[3] But there were also hired servants, some of whom may have been primarily actors, while others were musicians, and others again stage attendants.

[1] *Eliz. Stage*, iv. 345; F. P. Wilson, *The Plague in Shakespeare's London* (1927).

[2] *Eliz. Stage*, iv. 168, 175, 176.

[3] Cf. App. A, no. vii, and *Eliz. Stage*, ch. xi.

PLATE VIII

WILLIAM SLY

We hear of the stage-keeper, the tireman, and the book-keeper or prompter, who was an important personage.[1] Probably all, except the book-keeper, were available upon occasion to take minor parts. There were also boys, who took the female parts. They seem to have been bound, perhaps for three years, to individual sharers, who undertook to give them training.[2] The names of only a few of the hired men and boys have come down to us, but of the sharers it seems possible, from patents and other official documents, from wills, and from actor-lists printed with plays, to construct a fairly continuous chronicle for the period of Shakespeare's career.[3] The First Folio itself gives us the names of twenty-six 'Principall Actors in all these Playes', and as twenty-four of them certainly became sharers, it is likely that they all did. Discrepancies with other records, however, make it difficult to regard the order of this list as that of seniority in the company. The patent of 1603 shows eight sharers, William Shakespeare, Richard Burbadge, John Heminges, Augustine Phillips, Henry Condell, William Sly, Richard Cowley, and Robert Armin. There are nine names in the patent, but Lawrence Fletcher, who heads the list, had already been 'comediane serviture' to James in Scotland, and it is probable that his position was only honorific, and that, although appointed a groom of the chamber, he did not become a sharer. Shakespeare and Burbadge stand first in the Folio list, and are followed by Heminges, Phillips, William Kempe, Thomas Pope, and George Bryan. These five had been of Alleyn's company. We do not know the number of sharers in the Chamberlain's company; it may already have been eight. Cowley was a sharer by 1601. On the other hand Kempe, Pope, and Bryan had dropped out by 1603. Bryan was then an ordinary groom of the chamber with household duties. Kempe left the company early in 1599 and was replaced then or a little later by Armin.[4]

---

[1] Cf. p. 105; vol. ii, p. 80.
[2] Cf. vol. ii, p. 82.
[3] Cf. vol. ii, p. 71.
[4] T. W. Baldwin, *Shakespeare's*

Jester (*M.L.N.* xxxix. 447), suggests that, as 'Clonnico de Curtanio' is on the t.ps. of two pamphlets of 1600 to be ascribed to Armin (*Eliz. Stage*, iii.

The dates at which Condell and Sly became sharers are uncertain; they were 'principal comedians' in 1598. So were Christopher Beeston and John Duke. But these are not in the Folio list, and by 1602 they and Kempe, who had travelled in the interval, had joined the Earl of Worcester's men. They may never have become sharers of the Chamberlain's. Conceivably they did, but left as a result of some disagreement, which also led to the omission of their names from the Folio list.[1] The patent of 1603, therefore, seems to represent the company much as it had stood in the later Elizabethan days and to a great extent from 1594 onwards. Its terms leave room for the admission of fresh 'associates', who were doubtless sworn of the Chamber as they joined. In the summer of 1604 the number of grooms was increased to twelve. This is still the number in a patent of 1619; by 1625 one more had been added. Two of the new places of 1604 were probably filled by John Lowin and Alexander Cooke, who were already principal actors in 1603. I conjecture that the third fell to Samuel Crosse, of whom nothing is known outside the Folio list. He probably died almost at once and was replaced by Nicholas Tooley; one must expect early deaths in plague-time. The death of Phillips in 1605 left room for Samuel Gilburne; the deaths of Sly and Fletcher in 1608 for William Ostler and John Underwood. About the same time William Eccleston and possibly Nathan Field were with the company, but not at this date as sharers, since they are soon found elsewhere, and rejoined the King's as sharers later. Of Gilburne no more is heard. Cooke and Ostler died in 1614, Armin in 1615, Shakespeare in 1616, and Cowley in 1619. Gilburne was probably succeeded, not later than 1611, by Robert Gough, and the other five respectively by Eccleston, Robert Benfield, John Shank, Field, and Richard Robinson. The patent of 1619 gives the names thus arrived at,

300), he must have been there with some other company after the Chamberlain's left for the Globe in 1599. But the pamphlets are unregistered, and one at least seems to have been written in 1599.

[1] Cf. vol. ii, p. 79. Is it possible that they sold the company's plays?

PLATE IX

JOHN LOWIN

and here Burbadge, Heminges, and Condell are the only survivors of the old Chamberlain's men. And while it was passing through its stages, Burbadge, long the histrionic mainstay of the company, died. His place was taken by Joseph Taylor, and that of Field, who died in 1619–20, by John Rice. His is the last name in the Folio list. It is clear that the company was recruited in two ways; partly by taking in some of its own hired men and boys, partly by enlisting the most talented actors available from outside, some of whom had been trained as boys in the private theatres. Armin, Lowin, Ostler, Underwood, Eccleston, Benfield, Shank, Field, and Taylor all came from other companies. Gilburne, Robinson, and Rice had been boys with the King's; Gough, Tooley, and Cooke either boys or hired men. It is possible that these three and also Condell and Beeston were with the Alleyn company, as Sly, Cowley, and Duke certainly were, although not as sharers. The cast of *Seven Deadly Sins* has a Harry and a Kit, and a Ro. Go., a Nick, and a Saunder, who were boys. But it is not safe to rely very much upon personal names.[1]

A distinction must be drawn amongst the sharers themselves. Some of them were also 'housekeepers', having acquired an interest in the ownership of the Globe or the Blackfriars or of both houses. One of these was Shakespeare. When the Globe was built in 1599, Burbadge and his brother Cuthbert, who seem to have had an option on the site from the ground landlord, kept a half-interest for themselves and portioned the other half among Shakespeare, Phillips, Pope, Heminges, and Kempe. The housekeepers were responsible, perhaps for the erection, and certainly for the maintenance, of the fabric, and divided the proportion of takings paid over by the body of sharers as rent. Similarly when a lease of the Blackfriars was surrendered to Burbadge by the Queen's Revels in 1608, he made new ones, under which Shakespeare, Heminges, Condell, and Sly each received an interest. Both at the Globe and the Blackfriars the holdings were redistributed from time to time, as housekeepers went out

[1] Cf. p. 44.

or it was desired to admit additional ones, and conse-
quently the value of Shakespeare's interests fluctuated.
We do not know how long he retained them. The
tenancies were 'in common', and therefore alienable to
persons who were not members of the company. But they
do not seem to have passed under his will, and therefore
he may have parted with them before his death; that of
the Globe very likely in 1613, when the fire made a heavy
expenditure on rebuilding inevitable.[1]

Analysis of Shakespeare's plays, with an eye to the possibilities of doubling parts, shows that, as indeed might
have been taken for granted, they were within the compass
of the company.[2] The practice of doubling certainly
existed; it is not necessary to assume that it was always
carried to the full extent theoretically feasible, or on the
other hand that every regular actor in the company performed in every play. The number of persons described
in London parish registers as players suggests that there
must always have been some 'resting', who could be called
upon for occasional jobs, if need arose. From three to five
boys would normally have been sufficient for the female
parts; some special arrangement may have been required
for *Midsummer-Night's Dream* and *Merry Wives of Windsor*. When the company was travelling, there would be
advantages in keeping down the *personnel*, but of course
the less heavily parted plays could be chosen. Some texts,
however, show indications of cuts, with the apparent
object of reducing the cast.[3] Professor Baldwin has some
ingenious speculations as to the 'lines' or types of part
provided for each of the principal men and boy actors.
I think that they are vitiated by a misconception as to the
nature of theatrical apprenticeship, by a chronology which
I believe to be erroneous, and still more perhaps by the
complete absence of any data adequate to support so
elaborate a superstructure. The printed actor-lists, of
which there are none for Shakespeare's plays, rarely allot
parts. The ascriptions of Restoration writers naturally
relate to the Caroline period. Thus John Downes tells us

[1] Cf. App. A, no. vii.   [2] Cf. vol. ii, p. 86.   [3] Cf. pp. 229, 235.

PLATE X

NATHAN FIELD

that Taylor acted Hamlet and Lowin Henry VIII and that both had their instructions from Shakespeare himself. This cannot be true of Taylor, who only joined the company after Shakespeare's death. It might be of Lowin, but Falstaff, which James Wright gives him, was certainly not his from the beginning. Burbadge was doubtless the leading actor in his lifetime. We know that he did Richard III, Lear, Othello, 'young Hamlett', 'ould Heironymoe', probably in *The Spanish Tragedy*, Ferdinand in *The Duchess of Malfi*, and this list, together with the general descriptions of him, suggests a versatility which is characteristic of 'repertory' companies and makes any assignment of 'lines' very problematic. Lowin probably became Burbadge's chief support in later days. The Fool was a familiar figure in every theatre, and we can trace the succession of Kempe, Armin, and Shank, and even note a change of method, when Kempe's serving-men fools gave place to Armin's court fools. Pope is spoken of as a clown. Heminges seems to have followed Phillips as the business manager of the company. He is described as 'stuttering' in 1613 and appears in no actor-list after 1611. The will of Phillips suggests that he was primarily a musician. So may have been Cowley, whose name is not in the actor-lists at all, although stage-directions show that he played Verges to Kempe's Dogberry. He had appeared as a musician in *Seven Deadly Sins*. It is likely enough that the boys were paired, to give a contrast of tall and short, dark and fair, lively and tender among the women. We must assume that Shakespeare, as a practical playwright, had some regard in plotting his plays to the material available for their interpretation. But I cannot believe with Professor Baldwin that he meticulously fitted the ages and complexions of his characters to those of their intended representatives. Here the argument as to a practical playwright tells the other way. He would know that a repertory meant the periodical revival of plays, with changes in the cast and changes of age. And he would not be unfamiliar with the uses of 'make-up'. As to Shakespeare's own acting, we have little to go upon, except late and rather conflicting hints through stage tradition. He 'did act exceedingly well' says Aubrey. But Rowe got the impression that he was no 'extraordinary' actor, and that 'the top of his performance was the Ghost in his own *Hamlet*'. A story, dubious in its details, describes him as playing the very minor part of Adam in *As You Like It*.[1] Chettle, desiring to be courteous, reported him as 'exelent in the qualitie he professes', and 'qualitie' is a term more than once applied to the occupation of an actor. Davies of Hereford speaks of his kingly parts.[2] It is hazardous to infer that he played the king in Peele's *Edward I* from the lines (761–2):

> Shake thy speres in honour of his name,
> Vnder whose roialtie thou wearst the same.

We may gather from *Richard III* and again from *Hamlet* that he was interested in the technique of his profession, and perhaps from the *Sonnets* that he found its practice irksome.[3] He, too, drops out of the actor-lists after *E.M.I.* (1598) and *Sejanus* (1603), and it may be that after a time his plays, together, perhaps, with the oversight of their production, were accepted as a sufficient return for his share in the company. If so, he presumably did not get any special payment for them, although at an earlier date he may, as Oldys apparently learnt, have received £5 for *Hamlet*. I feel sure that Sir Sidney Lee has much over-estimated his theatrical income at more than £700. The evidence is complicated, but I do not see how, as sharer and housekeeper, he can ever have earned more, even in the best years, than about £200. This of course would make him quite well-to-do by Jacobean standards.[4]

We may think, then, of Shakespeare, early in the reign of James, as still making his head-quarters in London, but more free than of old for occasional sojourn in Stratford. Here he brought small actions in the Court of Record against one Phillip Rogers for the value of malt supplied and for a money debt in 1604, and against one John Addenbroke and his surety Thomas Horneby for a money

---

[1] App. C, nos. xiii, xxv, xxxiv, xliv.   [3] Cf. p. 560.
[2] App. B, no. xxvii.   [4] Cf. App. A, no. vii.

debt in 1608–9.[1] And here he added to his investments
in 1605 by purchasing for £440 the lease of a parcel of
local tithes which had once belonged to the Stratford college.[2] Malone thought he had evidence, not now forthcoming, that Shakespeare's London abode was still on the
Southwark Bankside in 1608.[3] Professor Wallace, however, discovered a lawsuit which showed that in 1604 he
was lodging in the house of Christopher Mountjoy, a
Huguenot tire-maker, in Cripplegate ward, and became involved in the family affairs of his landlord.[4] Some information obtained by Aubrey from the actor William Beeston,
a son of Christopher, indicates that at some time he also
lived in Shoreditch.[5] Aubrey tells also of annual visits to
Stratford, of the humour of Dogberry picked up from a
constable at Grendon, which was in fact out of the road,
and of lodging in Oxford at the house of John Davenant,
a vintner who kept a tavern afterwards known as the
Crown. This must have been much later than the days of
Dogberry. Davenant is not known to have had the tavern
before 1613, although he may have had it in 1601. A tavern
was not normally a place for the reception of travellers, and
if Shakespeare did not really lodge at the adjoining Cross
inn, which seems also to have been at one time in Davenant's
hands, he must have been a private guest. The house
still stands in the Cornmarket St., and we may, if we like,
fancy Shakespeare occupying a room in which some interesting mural decoration of the sixteenth century has recently
been uncovered.[6] A gloss on the story, over which Aubrey
hesitated, made Shakespeare the father of Sir William
Davenant, born in 1606. It has not much authority and
may owe something to Davenant's willingness to be suspected of more than a literary affiliation to the greater poet.[7]

The temper of *Hamlet* and *Troilus and Cressida* leads
up, naturally enough, to the long unrolling of the Jacobean
tragedies. These are not without evidence of mental strain

---

[1] App. A, no. xvi.
[2] App. A, no. xvii.
[3] App. A, no. ix.
[4] App. A, no. x.

[5] App. C, no. xiii.
[6] Cf. Plate XVI.
[7] Cf. p. 573.

and sometimes exhaustion. Shakespeare's spirit must have been nearly submerged in *Lear*, and although the wave passed, and he rose to his height of poetic expression in *Antony and Cleopatra*, I think that he went under in the unfinished *Timon of Athens*. The chronology of the plays becomes difficult at this point, and it is therefore frankly a conjecture that an attempt at *Timon of Athens* early in 1608 was followed by a serious illness, which may have been a nervous breakdown, and on the other hand may have been merely the plague. Later in the year Shakespeare came to his part of *Pericles* with a new outlook. In any case the transition from the tragedies to the romances is not an evolution but a revolution. There has been some mental process such as the psychology of religion would call a conversion. Obviously the philosophy of the tragedies is not a Christian philosophy, and in a sense that of the romances is.[1] Richard Davies, a Gloucestershire clergyman of the end of the seventeenth century, stated that Shakespeare 'dyed a papist'.[2] He may or may not have been misinformed, but I am not so certain as was Sir Sidney Lee that we can, without more ado, 'dismiss as idle gossip the irresponsible report', or that it 'admits of no question' that Shakespeare 'was to the last a conforming member of the Church of England'.[3] How did Sir Sidney know that Davies was irresponsible or a gossip? What little is recorded of him suggests that he was a man of scholarly attainments. It was by no means unusual for a seventeenth-century Catholic to be buried in his parish church.[4]

It was perhaps about this time that Shakespeare's thoughts began to turn to New Place as a permanent habitation. If so, he deferred his purpose for a time, since his cousin Thomas Greene, the town clerk of Stratford, who appears to have been living in the house, noted in connexion with a transaction of 1609 that he had found he could stay there for another year.[5] We may put therefore in 1610 the beginning of Shakespeare's final years

[1] Cf. *Sh.: a Survey*, 229, 241, 275, 284, 290, 307.
[2] App. C, no. xv.
[3] Lee, 487.
[4] *Stratford Register*, s.a. 1606, 1611, 1613.
[5] App. A, no. xi.

at his native Stratford, spent, according to Rowe, 'as all men of good sense will wish theirs may be, in ease, retirement and the conversation of his friends'. Even at Stratford time had brought some changes. His elder daughter Susanna had married John Hall, a local physician of some note, in 1607, and had herself a daughter Elizabeth. His younger daughter Judith was still unmarried. His mother had died in 1608. His brother Edmund had, like himself, become an actor in London, although not, so far as we know, in his company, and his death in 1607 had followed that of a base-born son. Two other brothers, Gilbert and Richard, were still alive in Stratford, and died, apparently unmarried, in 1612 and 1613 respectively. His sister Joan had married William Hart, a hatter, and had three sons.[1] Shakespeare's breach with London was not a complete one. He still wrote his plays for the King's men. But the intervals between them became longer, and in 1613, when the wedding of the Princess Elizabeth meant a period of theatrical pressure, he seems to have fallen back upon some kind of collaboration with the younger pen of John Fletcher. After 1613 he wrote no more. Occasionally he visited his old haunts. He was in London on 11 May 1612, when he made a deposition in Christopher Mountjoy's lawsuit, and showed a rather imperfect memory of events which had taken place eight years before.[2] He was there in March 1613, when he designed an *impresa* for Burbadge to paint, and for Francis Earl of Rutland to parade at the annual Accession tilt.[3] He was there on 17 November 1614, when Thomas Greene discussed Stratford business with him and his son-in-law Hall.[4] And it was in London property that during 1613 he made his last investment, buying for £140 and immediately mortgaging for nearly half its value an old building in the Blackfriars, which had once been a gate-house to a lodging for the Prior of the Dominicans, and at later dates a head-quarters of Catholic intrigue.[5]

---

[1] App. A, no. i.
[2] App. A, no. x.
[3] App. A, no. xxii.
[4] App. A, no. xix.
[5] App. A, no. xxiii.

But our imaginative setting for the last days of Shakespeare must be the open fields and cool water-meadows
and woodland of Stratford, and the great garden of New
Place, where the mulberries he had planted were yet
young. He seems to have taken no part in municipal
affairs. He made his contribution to the expenses of pro-
moting a Bill for the better repair of highways, and gave
hospitality to a preacher of one of the annual sermons
founded by pious legacies.[1] Tradition and his will show
that he lived upon friendly terms, not only with the leading
citizens, but with well-to-do gentry of the town and its
neighbourhood.[2] Prominent among these were a family
of Combes.[3] Thomas Combe, whose grandfather had
been a spoiler of the monasteries and his father apparently a Catholic, occupied the mansion of the dissolved
college. He had died in 1609 and left two young sons.
Upon his brother John, who was a rich money-lender,
Shakespeare is credited by repute with exercising his epi-
grammatic wit. If so, a legacy which he received under
John's will of 1613 shows that kindly relations endured.
In 1614 young William Combe, who was a freeholder at
Welcombe on the Stratford manor, was drawn into a
scheme for enclosing some of the open fields, and a controversy arose, which disturbed the peace of Stratford for
some years. Shakespeare had himself no rights of common
in the area affected, but both he as a tithe-holder and the
Corporation, who owned the reversion of the tithes, might
suffer loss, if the enclosure led to the conversion of arable
land into pasture. So far as Shakespeare was concerned,
an agreement for indemnification was made, and he seems
to have taken no further interest in the matter.[4] If he had
troubles in these years, they were concerned with his
daughters. Susanna Hall in 1613 had to bring an action
in the ecclesiastical court for the protection of her character
from a slander of incontinence.[5] Judith, on 10 February
1616, married Thomas Quiney, and the ceremony, which

---

[1] App. A, nos. xx, xxi.
[2] App. A, no. xxiv; App. C, nos.
xxv, lv.
[3] App. A, no. xviii.
[4] App. A, no. xix.
[5] App. A, no. i.

took place in a season prohibited by canon law, led to the subsequent excommunication of the pair.[1] By the time the sentence was pronounced, the poet may have been already dead. John Ward tells that 'Shakespear, Drayton, and Ben Jhonson, had a merry meeting, and itt seems drank too hard, for Shakespear died of a feavour there contracted'. There is no reason to reject this report. Ward had been a student of medicine, and became vicar of Stratford in 1662.[2] Drayton is known to have been in the habit of spending his vacations at 'the Muses' quiet port' of Clifford Chambers near Stratford, where dwelt Sir Henry Rainsford, whose wife Anne had been Drayton's Idea.[3] Attempts have been made to determine the precise nature of Shakespeare's medical history, mainly upon the basis of tremors in the signatures to his will.[4] But the diagnoses of doctors are even less reliable when the patient is not before them than when he is. The will itself was probably drafted in January 1616, but interlineated and partly rewritten later, and finally signed, without the formality of a fair copy, on 25 March.[5] There are small bequests to the poor, to various Stratfordians, and to Shakespeare's 'fellows' Burbadge, Heminges, and Condell, who are to buy rings. Thomas Combe, the brother of William, is to have Shakespeare's sword. The widow, amply provided for by legal dower on the Stratford property, although that on the Blackfriars house had been barred, gets the second best bed by an interlineation. Joan Hart is to occupy her present house, which was one of those in Henley St., for life, and to have £20 and the poet's wearing apparel. Each of her three sons gets £5. Subject to certain contingencies, Judith Quiney is to have a marriage portion of £150, and another £150 later. She is also to have a silver and gilt bowl. The rest of the plate is for Elizabeth Hall; the other chattels and the leases for her parents. The real property in Stratford and London is entailed successively upon Susanna and her heirs male, Elizabeth and

[1] *Ibid.*
[2] App. C, no. ix.
[3] O. Elton, *Michael Drayton*, 10, 128.
[4] Cf. p. 507.
[5] App. A, no. xxiv.

her heirs male, Judith and her heirs male, with remainder to the poet's right heirs.

Death took place on April 23. The little that was mortal of Shakespeare lies under the chancel of Stratford church. A doggerel curse on the stone above, locally believed to be from his own pen, has fortunately prevented exhumation. From the chancel wall a bust by Gheerart Janssen watches quietly. Above is the coat of arms; below a laudatory inscription. The face is full and heavy, with a dome-like head; the modelling may have been from a mask. The present colouring dates from the middle of the nineteenth century, and as for some time before that the bust was whitewashed, it cannot be relied upon.[1] The engraving by Martin Droeshout in the First Folio gives no more attractive presentment, and none of the innumerable portraits which pass as Shakespeare's carry any guarantee of authenticity.[2] Aubrey asserts that the poet was 'a handsome well shap't man: very good company, and of a very readie and pleasant smooth witt'. There is no other reference to his personal appearance, but sufficient testimony to his manners. Rowe had gathered that he was held in esteem for his 'exceeding candor and good nature', but may be only echoing Ben Jonson, who wrote in verse of 'my gentle Shakespeare' and in prose described him as 'honest, and of an open, and free nature'. We cannot, I think, ascribe to Shakespeare that rigid propriety of sexual conduct, the absence of which in more modern poets it has too often been the duty of their family biographers to conceal. The indications of the *Sonnets* and perhaps *Willobie his Avisa*, John Manningham's contemporary talk of a more ephemeral intrigue, the gossip about Mistress Davenant, do not leave an impression of complete fidelity to Anne Hathaway.[3] But as to the normal sobriety of his life we may be content to accept the report of William Beeston to Aubrey that 'he was not a company keeper' and that he 'wouldnt be debauched, & if invited

[1] App. A, no. xxv; cf. Plates XXII, XXIII.
[2] Cf. vol. ii, p. 240, and Plates
XXVI, XXVII.
[3] Cf. pp. 560, 569, and App. B, no. xxiv.

to, writ, he was in paine'.[1] The hope, apparent in Shakespeare's will, of founding a family was not destined to
fulfilment.[2] Susanna Hall had no sons. Elizabeth Hall,
who married successively Thomas Nash of Stratford and
John, afterwards Sir John, Bernard of Abington in
Northamptonshire, had no children. Judith Quiney had,
but the last died in 1639. Shortly afterwards steps were
taken to terminate the entail. Lady Bernard left the
Henley St. houses to the Harts in 1670, and the last
remnants of Shakespeare's property were sold by a distant
kinsman as her residuary legatee after Sir John's death
in 1674. There are no existing descendants of Shakespeare.

[1] App. C, no. xiii.   [2] App. A, no. xxiv.

CHAPTER IV

THE BOOK OF THE PLAY

[*Bibliographical Note*. A list of manuscripts of plays datable up to 1616 is in *Eliz. Stage*, iv. 404. Many of these represent court or academic plays for amateur performance, or purely literary compositions, or translations, or are too fragmentary or of too early date to throw light upon the practice of the professional companies. The *Malone Society Reprints* include admirable type-facsimiles, edited with full palaeographical descriptions by W. W. Greg or under his supervision, of Munday's *John a Kent and John a Cumber* (1923, ed. M. St. C. Byrne from *Mostyn*, now *Huntington MS*.), *Sir Thomas More* (1911, ed. W. W. Greg from *Harl. MS.* 7368), *The Second Maiden's Tragedy* (1909, ed. W. W. Greg from *Lansd. MS.* 807), *The Welsh Embassador* (1920, ed. H. Littledale and W. W. Greg from *Phillipps MS.* 8719, now in Cardiff Public Library), Massinger's *Believe as You List* (1927, ed. C. J. Sisson from *Egerton MS.* 2828), *Edmond Ironside* (1927, ed. E. Boswell from *Egerton MS.* 1994), *The Parliament of Love* (1928, ed. K. M. Lea from *Dyce MS.* 39), *Richard II* or *Thomas of Woodstock* (1929, ed. W. P. Frijlinck from *Egerton MS.* 1994). Similar in character is *Sir John Van Olden Barnavelt* (1922, ed. W. P. Frijlinck from *Addl. MS.* 18653). There are also photographic facsimiles of *John a Kent* (1912), *Sir Thomas More* (1910), and *Believe as You List* (1907) in J. S. Farmer's *Tudor Facsimile Texts*. Two of the above plays are drawn from the collection of William Cartwright the younger (ob. 1687), in *Egerton MS.* 1994. This is described by F. S. Boas in *Shakespeare and the Universities* (1923), 96. It contains twelve other plays, besides a mask, several of which are in hand for *M.S.R.* Three represent plays also extant in early prints, *Nero* (1624), Fletcher's *Elder Brother* (1637), Daborne's *Poor Man's Comfort* (1655; cf. *Eliz. Stage*, iii. 271). One, *Calisto* or *The Escapes of Jupiter*, is put together from Heywood's *Golden Age* (1611) and *Silver Age* (1613), and is described by W. W. Greg in *Anglica* (1925), ii. 212. Four are available in more or less modernized texts, *Dick of Devonshire* and *The Lady Mother* (1883, ed. A. H. Bullen in *O.E. Plays*, ii), *Charlemagne* or *The Distracted Emperor* (1884, *ibid.* iii; 1920, ed. F. L. Schoell; cf. *Eliz. Stage*, iv. 5), Heywood's *The Captives* (1885, *ibid.* iv; 1921, ed. A. C. Judson), as well as *1 Richard II* (1899, ed. W. Keller, *J.* xxxv. 3; cf. *Eliz. Stage*, iv. 42). *The Fatal Marriage* or *A Second Lucreatya*, *The Two Noble Ladies*, *Loves Changelinges Change*, and *The Lanchinge of the Mary* or *The Seamans Honest Wife* are unprinted, but the last is very fully studied by Boas. The manuscripts of Beaumont and Fletcher's *Honest Man's Fortune* (*Dyce MS.* 9) and *Bonduca* (*Addl. MS.* 36758) and of Middleton's *The Witch* (*Malone MS.* 12) are described by W. W. Greg (4 *Library*, vi. 148); that of Beaumont and Fletcher's *The Humourous Lieutenant* (*Lord Harlech's MS.*), here called *Demetrius and Enanthe*, by F. P. Wilson (*ibid.* vii. 194); the five of Middleton's *Game of Chess* in R. C. Bald's edition (1929). The account of *The Faithful Friends* (*Dyce MS.* 10) in E. H. C. Oliphant, *Beaumont and Fletcher*, 526, needs revision. Manuscripts of Middleton's *Mayor of Quinborough* and Beaumont and Fletcher's *Beggar's Bush* require description. The latter is said by F. Marcham, *The King's Office of the Revels* (1925), 6, to be in a hand like that of *The Witch*. The late manuscripts of *Hen. IV*, *Twelfth Night*, and *Merry Wives of W.* are noted in ch. ix. Valuable dissertations on the nature of the manuscripts are W. W. Greg, *Prompt Copies*, *Private Transcripts*, *and the Play-House Scrivener* (1925, 4 *Library*, vi. 148); C. J. Sisson, *Bibliographical Aspects of some Stuart Dramatic Manuscripts* (1925, *R.E.S.* i. 421); F. P. Wilson, *Ralph Crane, Scrivener to the King's Players* (1926, 4 *Library*, vii. 194); W. J. Lawrence, *Early Prompt Books and What they Reveal* (1927, *Pre-Restoration Studies*).

The relations of the Master of the Revels to the stage are described in *Eliz. Stage*, chh. iii, x, and xxii, and the working of the Jacobean and Caroline censorship may be further studied in V. C. Gildersleeve, *Government Regulation of the English Drama* (1908), F. S. Boas, *Shakespeare and the Universities* (1923), E. M. Albright, *Dramatic Publication in England, 1580–1640* (1927), S. R. Gardiner, *The Political Element in Massinger* (1875–6, *N.S.S. Trans.* 314), T. S. Graves, *Some Allusions to Religious and Political Plays* (1912, *M.P.* ix. 545), *The Political Use of the Stage during the Reign of James I* (1914, *Anglia*, xxxviii. 137). The handwritings of the Masters are in W. W. Greg, *English Literary Autographs*, i (1925), xxx. The fragments of Sir Henry Herbert's *Office Book* are collected from Malone (*Variorum*, iii) and G. Chalmers, *Supplemental Apology* (1799), in J. Q. Adams, *The Dramatic Records of Sir Henry Herbert* (1917). A few additional ones are given from books annotated by Malone in W. J. Lawrence, *New Facts from Sir Henry Herbert's Office Book* (1923, Nov. 29, *T.L.S.*), and by F. P. Wilson (4 *Library*, vii. 209). Adams also reprints many of the papers collected by Herbert for his Restoration lawsuits, as given from *Addl. MS.* 19256 in H.P., *A Collection of Ancient Documents Respecting the Office of the Master of the Revels* (1870). The end of Herbert's career is traced in A. Nicoll, *History of Restoration Drama* (ed. 2, 1928), and L. Hotson, *The Commonwealth and Restoration Stage* (1928). There is much on the book-keeper and his fellows in T. W. Baldwin, *The Organization and Personnel of the Shakespearean Company* (1927). W. W. Greg collected the 'plots' in *Henslowe Papers* (1907) and is re-editing them in his coming *Dramatic Documents from the Elizabethan Playhouses*. He discussed the conclusions to be drawn from them in *The Evidence of Theatrical Plots for the History of the Elizabethan Stage* (1925, *R.E.S.* i. 257). He also printed the 'part' of Orlando in *Henslowe Papers*, and edited it fully, in a parallel-text with the corresponding passages of the 1594 Quarto of *Orlando Furioso*, in *Two Elizabethan Stage Abridgements* (1923).]

SHAKESPEARE may be read, to profit and delight, in the barest of unannotated texts, and the plays may be taken

in any order. Nor does their power to evoke mirth and
emotion fail upon the stage, even through such distant ap-
proximation to Elizabethan methods of presentment as the
habits of modern producers and modern actors impose. But
that bare unannotated text is already a reconstruction, due
to generations of scholars, working by patient comparison
and less patient conjecture upon the discrepant and often
dubious versions handed down from the seventeenth century. And the unquiet spirit of criticism is still urgent with
questions, for which the conscientious student will feel his
obligation to attempt answers. These are the problems of
transmission, of authenticity, of revision, of chronology.
How far can the reconstructed text, after all, be accepted as
a faithful rendering of the form in which Shakespeare left
the plays? Was he the sole author of what passes under
his name, or is his work, through adaptation or collaboration, entangled in the traditional canon with that of other
men? Did he himself alter or rewrite what he at first
composed? Can we arrange the plays in an order of time,
and so arrive at some nearer knowledge of the development of a personality, left obscure by the colourless facts
of biographical record, the fragmentary notices of contemporaries, the doubtful stories of a younger age, and the
enigmatic self-revelation of the *Sonnets*? The four problems are closely interwoven, and their solution can best be
approached through some consideration of the conditions
under which Elizabethan plays were prepared for the
stage and passed into print.

The material available, although it is fairly abundant,
has to be pieced together from many sources; and if it is
occasionally necessary to draw upon Caroline, rather than
Elizabethan or Jacobean, evidence, it must be borne in
mind that the occupations, alike of actor and of printer,
were hereditary and conservative, and that, while allowance must be made for changes in detail, the death of
Shakespeare did not constitute a break in traditions which
seem to have been fairly continuous from the middle of
the sixteenth century to the closing of the theatres in
1642. The plays of the earlier professional companies, so

far as we can judge, came mainly from the pens of the actors themselves, and did not as a rule get into print. The independent playwrights appear in the course of the 'eighties, when the University wits were turning to popular literature as a refuge from the scanty and uncertain rewards of patronage. Thereafter they were the chief sources of supply, although the older practice was not entirely abandoned, and was in particular continued by Shakespeare for the Chamberlain's and King's men and by Thomas Heywood for Worcester's and Queen Anne's. Both were actor-playwrights, holding shares in individual companies and writing for these alone. The literary playwrights, on the other hand, were free lances, finding no doubt their ordinary markets in accustomed quarters, but not tied to these, except, as in the cases of Henry Porter and Henry Chettle, under some temporary pressure of economic disadvantage.[1] Their relation to the boy companies may have been slightly different, since here they are sometimes found as members of the syndicates by which the companies were financed and controlled.[2] The records kept by Philip Henslowe throw light upon the procedure followed in the purchase of new plays from poets by the companies for whom he was the agent.[3] Jonson submits a 'plot' of a play, but never writes it. It is taken up by Chapman, who sends in two acts, and apparently no more. 'We haue heard their books and lyke yt' writes an Admiral's man to Henslowe, directing payment to the authors. Another notifies, 'I haue hard fyue shetes of a playe & I dow not doute but it wyll be a verye good playe'; Henslowe is to take 'the papers' into his own hands, as the authors have promised to finish it by Easter. A play of Richard Hathway's falls through. He is to 'haue his papars agayne' and to give security for the amount he has received. Robert Daborne enters into a bond to write a play by a given date, but his 'papers' come in slowly, and some of them are 'not so fayr written all as I could wish'.

---

[1] *Eliz. Stage*, i. 374.
[2] *Ibid.* i. 378.
[3] *Ibid.* i. 373; ii. 161, 167, 252; iii. 194; Greg, *Henslowe Papers*, 49, 55, 56, 65–84.

He is ready to read instalments to Alleyn, and the whole play to the company when it is ready. When pressed for the last scene of another play, he writes, 'I send you the foule sheet & ye fayr I was wrighting as y^r man can testify'. He 'will not fayle to write this fayr and perfit the book'. Evidently the companies watched closely the progress of the plays which they commissioned. And the system of instalments was often applied to the payments as well as to the delivery of sheets. An 'earnest' was generally given at an early stage; there might be further advances later; and a payment 'in full' was made when the work was complete. The total amounts paid ranged from £4 to £10 10s. towards the end of the sixteenth century. About 1613 Daborne was getting from £10 to £20, and boasted that the King's men would give him £25. A successful play might bring the author a gratuity, and a second or third night's 'benefit' seems to have become customary in the seventeenth century.[1] The plays were carefully preserved by the companies, and represented a considerable capital value as part of their 'stock'. If a company was disbanded, they were divided among the 'sharers', and old plays thus got upon the market. Alleyn seems to have acquired plays of the original Admiral's men in 1589, and he and other actors are found selling old plays to the later Admiral's at £2 each.[2]

The author's 'papers', which figure so largely in Henslowe's correspondence, come before us again in the epistle to the First Folio. 'Wee haue scarse receiued from him a blot in his papers', say Heminges and Condell, in commendation of their dead fellow's facility. Another term appears on the title-page, which describes the plays as 'Published according to the True Originall Copies', and in the head-title, where they are 'Truely set forth, according to their first Originall'. This recurs in Humphrey Moseley's epistle to the first Beaumont and Fletcher Folio of 1647. He claims to give 'the Originalls from such as received them from the *Authours* themselves', and says that the readers would appreciate his difficulties if

---

[1] *Eliz. Stage*, i. 373.　　　　　[2] *Ibid.* i. 372; ii. 165, 167, 179.

they 'knew into how many hands the Originalls were dispersed'. And he explains more fully:

When these *Comedies* and *Tragedies* were presented on the Stage,
the *Actours* omitted some *Scenes* and Passages (with the *Authour's*
consent) as occasion led them; and when private friends desir'd a
Copy, they then (and justly too) transcribed what they *Acted*. But
now you have both All that was *Acted,* and all that was not; even
the perfect full Originalls without the least mutilation; So that
were the *Authours* living (and sure they can never dye) they themselves would challenge neither more nor lesse then what is here
published.'

This term 'original' is of common use in the records of
the medieval stage, and there it seems to represent the
authoritative copy of a play by which the performances
were governed, and to replace the earlier *Ordo* of the
liturgical drama. It often appears in some such form as
'regenall', and it is difficult to resist the conviction that
in the mind of medieval writers it was connected with
regere.[1] Moseley does not use it in the medieval sense.
It is perhaps so used when we learn that the Master of the
Revels reallowed an old play, 'the originall being lost'.[2]
But it is clear that the ordinary Elizabethan term for an
authoritative stage-copy was simply 'the book'.[3] This
appears in the titles of play-manuscripts, and Dr. Greg
points out that from these it sometimes made its way into
titles as recorded in the Stationers' Register.[4] Certainly the
'book' was not in all respects identical with the 'original'
as handed in by the author. Moseley indicates that passages were omitted. But 'cuts' were only one feature of the
adaptation which the 'original', even of a writer familiar
with stage conditions, might require in order to make it
a safe and adequate guide to actual performance. And

---

[1] *Mediaeval Stage*, ii. 143.
[2] Herbert 30.
[3] Modern writers often call the
'stage-copy' the 'prompt-copy', and
no doubt this was one of its uses; cf.
p. 121. The earliest use of the term
'prompt-book' in *O.E.D.* is of 1809,
and probably the modern prompt-

book described by H. Granville-
Barker in *R.E.S.* iv (1928), 233, as
'begun at rehearsals' and containing
notes of 'interpretation as well as
mechanism' is an elaborated type.
[4] *4 Library*, vii. 384; cf. the S. R.
entries for *Mer. of Ven.* and *Per.*

indeed, although Moseley may have restored 'cut' passages, it is clear from his texts that apart from these he was often printing from 'books' which had undergone such adaptation. We may distinguish various kinds of adaptation. The author's intentions, as indicated in his original, might have to be accommodated to the stage-structure, properties, and actors of a given theatre at a given date, as well as to the time available for representation, and perhaps to the taste of a given audience. But, also, the expression of these intentions in the manuscript might itself require some correction; speeches might be wrongly distributed, or stage-directions insufficient. A stage-copy must be precise. Further, before a play could be presented, it had to receive the allowance of a censor, by an endorsement on the stage-copy, and this might entail the alteration of passages likely to be objectionable to the censor, or in fact disapproved of by him. It is necessary to consider the operation of the agencies through which such adaptation was carried out and their effect upon the 'book'.

I have already devoted much space to the question of Elizabethan stage-censorship, and need not repeat the whole story here.[1] The main agent was throughout the Master of the Revels, a Household official, working under the direction of the Lord Chamberlain, or in matters of higher importance under that of the Privy Council, the High Commission, or even the sovereign. His original functions included the review of plays given at court. Tentatively under a patent for Leicester's men in 1574, more directly under a commission issued to him in 1581, and effectively, as overruling a claim to censorship by the London corporation, about 1589, they came to cover all plays given in public. A special arrangement for the Queen's Revels in 1604 proved unsatisfactory, and was not of long duration. The requirement of the Master's endorsement 'at the latter end of the said booke they doe play' is already recorded in 1584. An *Act to Restraine Abuses of Players*, which had effect from 27 May 1606, forbade the jesting or profane use in plays of 'the holy Name of

---

[1] *Eliz. Stage*, i. 71–105, 223, 269–307, 317–28; ii. 48–54, 221; iii. 168–70, 191.

God or of Christ Jesus, or of the Holy Ghoste or of the Trinitie'; and although the Master is not specifically referred to, he naturally kept an eye on its observance.[1] From about 1607 onwards he seems also to have acted as licenser for the printing of plays, on behalf of the High Commission. Edmund Tilney was Master from 1579 to his death on 20 August 1610. But under James he had a deputy in his nephew Sir George Buck, who held a reversion of the post and became his successor. Buck lived to 20 September 1623, but by 29 March 1622 he was mad, and Sir John Astley or Ashley, who in his turn held a reversion, was sworn in as Master. He did not officiate long. On 20 July 1623 he granted a deputation, for a consideration of £150 a year, to Henry Herbert, brother of Lord Herbert of Cherbury and of the poet George Herbert, and kinsman of William Herbert, Earl of Pembroke, then Lord Chamberlain.[2] Herbert was knighted and accepted by the king as Master on August 7.[3] Technically he long remained a mere deputy, but on 25 August 1629, he obtained a reversion, with one Simon Thelwall, for their joint lives. A prior reversion had been granted to Ben Jonson on 5 October 1621.[4] But Ashley outlived him, and from Ashley's death on 13 January 1641 Herbert held the Mastership in his own right. His duties lapsed at the closing of the theatres, and although he resumed them at the Restoration, it was only to incur serious embarrassment owing to the conflicting rights granted by Charles II to the patentees of the leading theatres. He died on 27 April 1673. Simon Thelwall was still alive in 1662, but does not appear at any time to have acted as Master. One William Blagrave collected fees for Herbert, and licensed a play as his deputy in 1635.[5]

---

[1] Text in *Eliz. Stage*, iv. 338.

[2] Cunningham xlix, from enrolment of indenture in Audit Office.

[3] R. Warner, *Epistolary Curiosities*, 3.

[4] *Works*, i. 237, from *Patent Roll*.

[5] Boas, *Sh. and the Universities*, 98. Blagrave was a lessee of Salisbury Court in 1629 and payee in 1635 for court plays given by the King's Revels from there (Adams, *Sh. Playhouses*, 369; *L.C.* v. 134, p. 39. The pedigree in *Harl. Soc.* lxv. 83 does not show him a son of Thomas Blagrave, the Elizabethan Clerk of the Revels. He might be a grandson. I take this opportunity

Another deputy, Thomas Herbert, allowed the printing of a play in 1637.[1] It is during Herbert's administration that we get the clearest view of the working of the censorship. He kept an Office Book, which seems also to have contained a few initial entries by Sir John Ashley. This was left at Herbert's death in his house at Ribbesford in Worcestershire. It was used by Malone in 1789 and by Chalmers before 1799. It was then in bad condition and has since disappeared. A statement of Halliwell-Phillipps in 1880 that it was in the possession of the Earl of Powis cannot be verified.[2] The extracts, however, made by Malone and Chalmers, although certainly not complete, enable us to get a fair notion of Herbert's activities; and further light is thrown upon them by a collection of papers relating to his post-Restoration controversies.[3] The Office Book contained dated entries of plays or alterations of plays and of other entertainments licensed for performance by Herbert, and of plays and masks given under his supervision at court.[4] Here, too, he recorded such events as inhibitions for plague and the setting up of new theatres and companies. Only a few entries of licences for printing are among the extracts, and the publications concerned are generally not plays. Possibly, therefore, the citations of licences by Herbert and other Masters in the Stationers' Register normally refer to their licences for performance, and these were regarded as covering printing. Herbert is careful to note the fees he received, and the supplementary exactions in the way of 'benefits' and payments for 'Lenten dispensations' which he levied upon the companies. His brother, Lord Herbert of Cherbury, tells us that he made a great fortune out of court employment. But his losses after the Restoration were considerable. More interesting in the present inquiry is a group of entries showing the disallowances which he felt called upon to make. The

of correcting the statement in *Eliz. Stage*, i. 99, that Thomas Blagrave lived to the end of Elizabeth's reign. He was buried at St. James's, Clerkenwell, on 21 July 1590 (*Harl. Soc. Registers*, xvii. 41).

[1] Arber, iv. 376.
[2] W. W. Greg in *Gentleman's Magazine*, ccc (1906), 72.
[3] *Addl. MS.* 19256; cf. *Bibl. Note*.
[4] For Herbert's notices of Shakespearean revivals, cf. App. D.

object of censorship, says one of the post-Restoration
memoranda, 'is, that all prophaneness, oathes, ribaldry,
and matters reflecting vpon piety and the present governe-
ment may bee obliterated, before there bee any action in
a publique Theatre'.[1] Possible interventions by players in
civil or foreign politics called for constant vigilance. Herbert 'reforms' *The Duchess of Suffolk*, which was full of
'dangerous matter'. He refuses to allow a play of Massinger's, which we can identify as an early form of *Believe
as You List*, because it too had 'dangerous matter, as the
deposing of Sebastian king of Portugal by Philip the
Second, and ther being a peace sworen twixte the kings
of England and Spayne'.[2] Another play of Massinger's,
The King and the Subject, he only passes, with 'reformations' and under an altered name, on express warrant from
the king, who had read the book at Newmarket and
marked a passage 'This is too insolent, and to bee changed'.
In 1640 William Beeston is committed to the Marshalsea
for giving a play without licence. 'The play I cald for, and,
forbidding the playinge of it, keepe the booke, because it
had relation to the passages of the K.s journey into the
Northe, and was complaynd of by his M.[tye] to mee, with
commande to punishe the offenders.' Other disallowances
were due to the Aristophanic satire of prominent personages. 'Abusive matter' in *The Widow's Prize* is reformed. Shirley's *The Ball* must be purged from its
personation of 'lords and others of the court'. Inigo Jones
is protected against *The Tale of the Tub* and 'M[r] Sewster'
against *The City Shuffler*. A care for piety requires the
committal of a broker 'for lending a church-robe with the
names of Jesus upon it, to the players in Salisbury Court,
to present a Flamen, a priest of the heathens'. Herbert
was alive to profanity, and even, odd as it appears to us
after reading the Caroline drama, to indecency. *The
Plantation of Virginia* can only be tolerated, 'the profane-
ness to be left out'. *The Tamer Tamed* is stayed and
'purgd of oaths, prophaness, and ribaldrye'. A play received from Mr. Kirke is burnt by Herbert, after taking

[1] Herbert 125.   [2] Cf. p. 110.

his fee, 'for the ribaldry and offense that was in it'. Even *Winter's Tale* is not allowed without an assurance that there is 'nothing profane added or reformed'. On the other hand, Shirley's *The Young Admiral* receives a special commendation for its freedom from 'oaths, prophaness, or obsceanes'. As to profanity, Herbert sometimes went too far. His reformation of Davenant's *The Wits* resulted in a protest to the king, and the king called Herbert into the window of his withdrawing chamber, and with great courtesy overruled him. Whereupon Herbert noted in the Office Book, 'The kinge is pleased to take *faith, death, slight,* for asseverations, and no oaths, to which I doe humbly submit as my masters judgment; but, under favour, conceive them to be oaths, and enter them here, to declare my opinion and submission.' On the other hand, Herbert's vigilance sometimes failed him. It is true that, when Jonson's *The Magnetic Lady* came before the High Commission, he was absolved of blame. Presumably the players had foisted in something objectionable which he had not allowed. But we know from sources other than the Office Book that early in his career he was called to account for licensing a distinctly political play in Middleton's *Game at Chess*.[1] Professor Gardiner, moreover, has shown that some of Massinger's extant plays do in fact contain obvious political matter. Possibly Herbert had a blind eye for Massinger. They were both adherents of the Earl of Pembroke, whose politics were often in opposition to those of the Duke of Buckingham.

Herbert, of course, was only just in office before the First Folio was published. But his objections to political matter can be abundantly paralleled from the earlier history of the stage, and some protection had been given to persons of importance as far back as 1601.[2] A tendency to criticism of society in general, and of the frailties of gallants and ladies in particular, was, however, a growing

---

[1] Cf. p. 125. James recalled 'a commandment and restraint given against the representing of any modern Christian kings in those stage-plays'. The date of this is unknown, but may be 1604, when *Gowry* gave offence (*Eliz. Stage,* i. 327).

[2] *Eliz. Stage,* iv. 332.

feature of the seventeenth-century drama. Heywood, in his *Apology for Actors*, says: [1]

Now, to speake of some abuse lately crept into the quality, as an inveighing against the state, the court, the law, the citty, and their governements, with the particularizing of private men's humors (yet alive) noble-men and others, I know it distastes many; neither do I in any way approve it, nor dare I by any meanes excuse it.

Similarly John Chamberlain writes to Dudley Carleton in 1620: [2]

Our pulpits ring continually of the insolence and impudence of women; and to help forward, the players have likewise taken them to task; and so to the ballads and ballad-singers; so that they can come nowhere but their ears tingle.

An inevitable sequel drew the irony of Ben Jonson in *Bartholomew Fair*: [3]

It is finally agreed, by the foresaid hearers, and *spectators*, that they neyther in themselues conceale, nor suffer by them to be concealed any *State-decipherer*, or politique *Picklocke* of the *Scene*, so solemnly ridiculous, as to search out, who was meant by the *Ginger-bread-woman*, who by the *Hobby-horse-man*, who by the *Costard-monger*, nay, who by their *Wares*. Or that will pretend to affirme (on his owne *inspired ignorance*) what *Mirror of Magistrates* is meant by the *Iustice*, what *great Lady* by the *Pigge-woman*, what *conceal'd States-man*, by the *Seller of Mouse-trappes*, and so of the rest. But that such person, or persons so found, be left discouered to the mercy of the *Author*, as a forfeiture to the *Stage*, and your laughter, aforesaid. As also, such as shall so desperately, or ambitiously, play the foole by his place aforesaid, to challenge the *Author* of scurrilitie, because the language some where savours of *Smithfield*, the Booth, and the Pig-broath, or of prophaneness, because a *Mad-man* cryes, *God quit you*, or *blesse you*.

Piety had been emphasized by the *Act of Abuses*. This can

[1] Heywood, *Apology*, 61. The date is probably 1607 or 1608. Cf. *Eliz. Stage*, iv. 250.

[2] Birch, *James*, ii. 200.

[3] *Ind.* 140. Cf. the apologetical dialogue to *Poetaster* and the prologue to *Epicoene*:

They make a libell, which he made a play.

Earlier criticism of informers, not necessarily concerned with plays, is cited by Albright 198 from Nashe, *Works*, i. 260; ii. 182; iii. 213.

hardly be set down to the personal predilections of James, who 'would make a great deale too bold with God in his passion, both in cursing and swearing, and one straine higher verging on blasphemie'.[1] Possibly it was a relic of a more general *Bill for Reformation of the Common Sin of Swearing and Blasphemy*, which was passed, not with unanimity, by the House of Commons in 1604, but did not become law.[2] In any case the personal austerity of Herbert pressed its very limited provisions rather far. That he regarded it as his duty to tighten up a rather lax administration is clear from his elaborate entry of 21 October 1633 in the case of *The Tamer Tamed*. This was an old play, and in dealing with it he took occasion to lay down that old plays as well as new must be submitted for his allowance, 'since they may be full of offensive things against church and state; ye rather that in former time the poetts tooke greater liberty than is allowed them by mee'. He made two other requirements. One was that 'The players ought not to study their parts till I have allowed of the booke'; the other that 'The Master ought to have copies of their new playes left with him, that he may be able to shew what he hath allowed or disallowed'. It is not perhaps quite clear whether this was entirely new doctrine of 1633, or the revival of an older practice which had been allowed to lapse. Some old plays had been submitted to Herbert before 1633. In a few cases they had undergone alteration. Most of the rest had been licensed by Sir George Buck. The allowed books of two at least of these, *Winter's Tale* and *The Honest Man's Fortune*, were missing, and that of *Jugurth* had been 'burnt, with his other books'. This was a Fortune play, and the burning might have been at the destruction of that theatre by fire in 1621, when in fact the play-books were lost.[3] It has been thought that books of the King's men might have perished similarly at the fire of 1613. But *Winter's Tale* had been revived since then, and the original *Honest Man's Fortune* seems to have turned up in time for the Folio of

---

[1] A. Welldon, *The Court and Character of King James (Secret History,* ii. 9).

[2] Cf. p. 238.

[3] *Eliz. Stage,* ii. 442.

1647. Moreover, Herbert also reallowed two old books of Buck's time for Prince Charles's men at the Red Bull and the Lady Elizabeth's at the Cockpit, and we can hardly assume unrecorded fires at their houses. It is possible, therefore, that Buck had been in the habit of keeping 'fair copies' of plays submitted to him, and that it was these which were burnt.

When Herbert had done his worst for *The Tamer Tamed* on 21 October 1633, he returned it to the King's men, with an endorsement 'directed to Knight, their book-keeper', of which he recorded a copy.

Mr Knight,
In many things you have saved mee labour; yet wher your judg-ment or penn fayld you, I have made boulde to use mine. Purge ther parts, as I have the booke. And I hope every hearer and player will thinke that I have done God good servise, and the quality no wronge; who hath no greater enemies than oaths, prophaness, and publique ribaldrye, whch for the future I doe absolutely forbid to bee presented unto mee in any playbooke, as you will answer it at your perill.

It was 'of Knight' that he received a fee for *The Magnetic Lady* on 12 October 1632. In allowing *The Launching of the Mary* for another company on 27 June 1633 he wrote, 'I command your Bookeeper to present me with a fairer copy herafter'.[1] It is unfortunate that we know so little about the men who were employed as stage book-keepers. A protection of 27 December 1624 for twenty-one 'musitions and other necessary attendantes', clearly including hired actors, employed by the King's men, gives the names of Edward and Anthony Knight.[2] One or other was presumably the book-keeper of 1633. Neither is in a later protection of 12 January 1637.[3] John Taylor, the water poet, tells in a story of Thomas Vincent, who was 'a book-keeper and prompter at the Globe playhouse'.[4]

[1] Boas, *Sh. and the Universities*, 184. Adams (Herbert 35) prints 'faire', which recalls the new require-ment of 1633. But Herbert also noted of a play in 1624 that it was 'not of a legible hand'.

[2] Herbert 74.
[3] *L.C.* v. 134, p. 142.
[4] *Taylor's Feast* (1638) in *Third Col-lections* of Spenser Soc. 70; cf. Baldwin 124.

It involves John Singer, the Admiral's man, who left acting in 1603, and was probably dead by 1607. This may be the same Vincent who appears in the 'plot' of *Seven Deadly Sins*.[1] According to Cavalier scandal, Hugh Peters, the Independent divine, had been a book-holder at the Red Bull.[2] After the Restoration, John Downes was 'book-keeper and prompter' at Lincoln's Inn Fields.[3] Many references to the book-keeper, book-holder, or prompter can be collected.[4] They do not tell us, as could be wished, where he was posted in the theatre. Obviously he must have been able both to make himself audible at the front of the stage, and to communicate with the tiring-house behind. The allusion in *Cynthia's Revels* suggests that he was in the tiring-house itself, but this, or even a place between the hangings and the stage-wall, seems rather far back. One would be glad to believe with Mr. Granville-Barker that he may have used a grated opening which Mr. Lawrence conjectures to have existed on the

---

[1] Cf. p. 44.

[2] Hotson 15.

[3] *Roscius Anglicanus* (1708), A2.

[4] John Palsgrave, *Lesclarcissement de la Langue Francoyse* (1530), 199, 'Boke bearer in a ploye, prottocolle'; John Higgins, *Nomenclator* (1585), 501, 'He that telleth the players their part when they are out and have forgotten, the prompter or bookeholder'; *Spanish Tragedy* (c. 1589), iv. 4. 9, 'Heere, brother, you shall be the booke-keeper: This is the argument of that they shew'; *Summer's Last Will and Testament* (1592), 1813, 'You might haue writ in the margent of your play-booke, Let there be a fewe rushes laide in the place where *Backwinter* shall tumble, for feare of raying his cloathes: or set downe, Enter *Backwinter*, with his boy bringing a brush after him, to take off the dust if need require. But you will ne're haue any ward-robe wit while you liue. I pray you holde the booke well, we be not *non plus* in the latter end of the play'; *Rom. & Jul.* (1595), i. 4. 7, 'Nor no without-book prologue, faintly spoke After the prompter, for our entrance'; *Cynthia's Revels* (1601) ind. 158, 'We are not so officiously befriended by him, as to have his presence in the Tiring-house, to prompt us aloud, stampe at the Booke-holder, sweare for our Properties, cursse the poore Tire-man, rayle the Musique out of tune'; *Oth.* (1604), i. 2. 83, 'Were it my cue to fight, I should have known it Without a prompter'; *Every Woman in her Humour* (1603–8), 'He would swear like an Elephant, and stamp and stare (God blesse us) like a play-house book-keeper when the actors misse their entrance'; *Maid in the Mill* (1623), ii. 2, 'They are out of their parts sure, It may be 'Tis the Book-holders fault: I'll go see'; *Lady Alimony* (c. 1630–40), i. 2, 'He has been book-holder to my revels for decades of years . . . Be sure that you hold not your book at too much distance. The actors, poor lapwings, are but pen-feathered; and once out, out for ever'.

ground-floor near one of the stage-doors, and Mr. Granville-Barker himself thinks may have survived in a little
latticed and curtained window, now or formerly cut in the
prompt side 'tormentor' in every theatre.[1] This would be
convenient enough, especially if, as seems possible, there
were doors set more forward than the back wall.[2] But Mr.
Lawrence's grounds for his conjecture are not strong.[3] No
doubt it was one of the functions of the book-keeper
Knight in 1633 to prompt. But he had others. He prepared the 'book' for the Master of the Revels and the
'parts' for the actors. The protection of 1624 names a
John Rhodes, taken by Professor Baldwin to have been,
before Knight, book-keeper to the King's men. He
might be a musician who died in 1636, but more likely
the 'Mr Rhodes, a bookseller, being wardrobe-keeper
formerly (as I am informed) to King Charles the First's
company of commedians in the Blackfriars', to whom
Thomas Betterton was apprenticed.[4] This John Rhodes
was born about 1606 and was free of the Draper's Company. He became a bookseller in Little Britain (1628,
1641) and St. Martin-in-the-Fields (1656). But he did
not give up the stage. He was arrested by the Lord
Chamberlain on a dispute with a Prince's man (1632) and
for selling the King's men's plays (1639). He was then of
the Fortune. In 1644 he kept the Cockpit, and in 1660
had a lease of this house, where he maintained Betterton
and others as players, ultimately becoming a stroller.[5]
I doubt whether we can assume that a 'wardrobe-keeper'

[1] R.E.S. iv. 234.

[2] Eliz. Stage, iii. 84, 100.

[3] Physical Conditions of the Elizabethan Public Playhouses, 67. The
'grate' in 2 Antonio and Mellida, ii. 2.
127, was quite clearly not at a door,
but at a vault below the stage (cf.
ii. 1. 44; iv. 1. 271; v. 1. 1). The
setting of Eastward Hoe (v. 3. 6; v. 5.
160) is uncertain and probably abnormal (Eliz. Stage, iii. 149). Moreover these are both 'private' theatre
plays. There is certainly action at a
ground-floor window near a door in
Woman's Prize, iii. 5, and Humourous

Lieutenant, iv. 4, 16, but these were
not necessarily side-doors. They might
be before the alcove, where any desired
frontage (Eliz. Stage, iii. 83) could be
arranged.

[4] Downes, Roscius Anglicanus, 17.

[5] Baldwin 128; McKerrow, Dic-
tionary, 227; A. H. Johnson, Drapers'
Company, iv. 155; Nicoll 270-9;
Hotson 90, 99, 197, 205, 216; B. M.
Wagner, John Rhodes and Ignoramus
(R.E.S. v. 43). G. E. Bentley in
P.M.L.A. xliv. 817; L.C. v. 132,
p. 310; 134, p. 345. Greg (R.E.S. vi.
359) shows him in H. M. Fortune (1625).

is the same as a 'book-keeper'. He is more likely to be the same as the 'tireman', whom we find employed by the Admiral's and Worcester's men, as well as in the private theatres.[1] But the passage in *Cynthia's Revels* shows that the book-holder was distinct from the tireman. Moreover, the tireman was available as a 'super', which the book-holder could not be. The book-holder was also distinct from the stage-keeper, since the pair, represented of course by actors, converse in the induction to *Bartholomew Fair*. On the other hand, the tireman and the stage-keeper might, for all we know, be the same. The tireman brings on stools and in a private theatre lights; the stage-keeper brings on chairs.[2] Who was responsible for communicating the book-holder's calls for actors, properties, and machines? He must have had some help. Malone made and withdrew a conjecture that this was Shakespeare's first duty as a 'servitor' or 'necessary attendant'.[3]

Some light is thrown upon the habits of censors and book-keepers, as well as upon those of authors and scribes, by a study of the few extant manuscripts of plays belonging to the professional companies which have been preserved.[4] Nine of these have been reproduced in typefacsimiles, with full descriptions and annotations by palaeographical experts and photographic facsimiles of sample pages. Of three full photographic facsimiles are also available. *John a Kent* is in the hand of Anthony Munday, and has his autograph signature at the end. A second hand has made some theatrical alterations. A date '— Decembris 1596' is probably in a third, and may have been appended to a memorandum lost through the mutilation

[1] *Eliz. Stage*, i. 371; ii. 149, 226, 541.

[2] *Sir John Van Olden Barnavelt*, 2584 (s.d.), '2 Chaires S^tr: [M]^r Bir.'. Probably Bir. is the actor George Birch. The editor does not interpret S^tr, and says that the reading is doubtful; 'it is possible that g^tr (i.e. *gatherer*) may be meant'. No doubt gatherers were occasionally used as 'supers' (*Eliz. Stage*, i. 371). But to

me S^tr suggests stage-keeper. Stagekeepers appear as 'supers' in the MSS. of *The Captives* and *The Two Noble Ladies*, and apparently a company, to whom these belonged, had more than one (Boas 103). On the academic stage the stage-keepers were stewards (G. C. Moore-Smith, *College Plays*, 46).

[3] App. C, no. xlviii.

[4] Cf. *Bibliographical Note*.

of the final leaf. The play itself may be of much earlier
date. The company is unknown. *Sir Thomas More* raises
a Shakespearean problem, and is more fully dealt with
elsewhere.[1] This, too, is in the hand of Munday. It has
been submitted for censorship to Tilney, who has made
and required alterations. No 'allowance' is endorsed. The
original scenes have been partially cancelled, and new or
rewritten ones added on inserted leaves or on strips pasted
over old matter. These are in five hands, known as A, B,
C, D, E. Hand D has been claimed as Shakespeare's.
Hand A is Chettle's and E Dekker's. Hand B remains
unknown, but may conceivably be Heywood's. Hand C
is that of a stage-reviser. He transcribes and fits in additions, but probably contributes none himself. And he
makes corrections and alterations, both in the original
scenes and in the additions, particularly D's. *John a Kent*
and *S.T.M.* must at some time have been preserved together. The same leaf of a vellum manuscript has been
used to make covers for them, and the title on each cover
is apparently in C's hand. A 'V thomas Thomas' on that
of *John a Kent* is an unassignable scribble. But the second
hand of that manuscript may be C's. He also wrote the
plots of *Seven Deadly Sins* and *Fortune's Tennis*.[2] *The
Second Maiden's Tragedy* is in the hand of a professional
scribe. He inserted some small additions on slips, and
there are corrections in a second hand, probably the
author's, and stage-directions in a third. There are also
a few corrections by Sir George Buck, whose allowance
of the play 'with the reformations' is endorsed. Some
conjectural ascriptions of authorship, which follow, are of
much later date.[3] The play belonged to the King's men.
Sir John Van Olden Barnavelt is also in a professional hand,
identified by Mr. F. P. Wilson with that of Ralph Crane,
who claims in his *Workes of Mercy* (1621) to have had
employment for his pen from the King's men. He seems
to have acted as a stage-reviser, making alterations and
additions, and not merely as a scribe. The history of the
play is known. It was produced in August 1619, prohibited

[1] Cf. p. 499.   [2] Cf. p. 124.   [3] *Eliz. Stage*, iv. 45.

by the Bishop of London, but finally sanctioned. The company was the King's.[1] The authorship has been conjecturally ascribed to Fletcher and Massinger. It is possible, therefore, that the manuscript represents a version revised to meet criticism. One cancel leaf and two additional slips, in the scribe's hand, have been inserted. Some passages, however, are marked by the censor, and one of these is initialled G[eorge] B[uck]. There is no allowance endorsed. *The Welsh Embassador* seems to be wholly in one hand, although the punctuation has been corrected and some marginal additions made after the text was written. The chronology of a prophecy suggests a date about 1623. The same main hand, probably that of a scribe, recurs in *The Parliament of Love,* and the condition of the manuscripts indicates that they have been preserved together. Both may have been written for the Lady Elizabeth's men, for whom Herbert licensed the *Parliament* on 3 November 1624. This also has some corrections, of a literary character. An endorsed allowance has evidently been cut away. *Believe as You List* was disallowed by Herbert on 11 January 1631 and allowed for the King's men, according to the Office Book, on May 7. The manuscript is in Massinger's hand. He has evidently revised the play in the interval, partly transcribing and partly rewriting the original text. Some names left standing in error show that the plot has been ingeniously transferred from Sebastian of Portugal to Antiochus of Syria. A second writer, evidently a stage-reviser, has made a few alterations and appended a prologue and an epilogue in an English hand, and has added other alterations, a title on a wrapper, and a list of properties in an Italian hand. Only one passage, unfortunately mutilated in the manuscript, was 'reformed' by Herbert, whose allowance, here dated May 6, is endorsed. The stage-reviser was also the scribe of *The Honest Man's Fortune and Bonduca,* but Professor Baldwin's inference that he was John Rhodes can only be regarded as extremely hazardous.[2] The

---

[1] Gildersleeve 114, from *S.P.Dom. Jac. I,* cx. 18, 37.
[2] Cf. pp. 111, 125.

manuscripts of *Edmond Ironside* and *Thomas of Woodstock*
may belong, as the composition of the plays more clearly
does, to the sixteenth century. The main hand of each
is probably that of a professional scribe, with stage corrections and additions of different dates and in more than
one hand, which point to seventeenth-century revivals.
Edmond Ironside carries no evidence of submission to the
Master of the Revels. *Thomas of Woodstock* seems to have
been marked by him, and a lost final leaf may have borne
an allowance.

A few other manuscripts, although not fully reproduced, have received some expert examination. *The Honest
Man's Fortune* is one of the transcripts allowed by Herbert
for the King's men in place of lost 'books', and has his
endorsement of 8 February 1624, and a few 'reformations'.
Another hand has made a few alterations for stage purposes. At the end is written what may be a mere scribble,
but may be the signature 'Jhon' of the main scribe.[1]
The Faithful Friends is in the hand of a scribe. There
are corrections and alterations in more than one
hand. One seems to have been concerned to meet the
views of a censor, but no allowance is endorsed. An inserted scene has been ascribed without justification to the
hand of Massinger. The company is unknown and the
date uncertain, but probably not earlier than 1621.[2]
Edmond Ironside and *Thomas of Woodstock* come from a
collection of fifteen pieces, probably made by the younger
William Cartwright, who had been an actor in the King's
Revels company of 1629–37.[3] He became a bookseller
during the Civil War, and may have obtained plays from
various sources. Several plays of the collection are linked
by revising hands and actor-names, but too obscurely to

[1] *Eliz. Stage*, iii. 227; A. Dyce, *Beaumont and Fletcher*, iii. 331; C. J. Sisson in *R.E.S.* i. 422 and *Believe as You List*, xvi; W. W. Greg in *4 Library*, vi. 150; cf. p. 107.

[2] *Eliz. Stage*, iii. 232; A. Dyce, *Beaumont and Fletcher*, iv. 199; C. J. Sisson in *R.E.S.* i. 427; E. H. C.

Oliphant, *Beaumont and Fletcher*, 360, 526; W. W. Greg in *4 Library* ix. 207.

[3] F. S. Boas, *Sh. and the Univer-sities*, 107; E. Boswell, *Young Mr. Cartwright* (1929, *M.L.R.* xxiv. 125); cf. *Bibl. Note*.

determine a common stage-history for them. Some of
the actors are found among the Revels company in 1635.
The Two Noble Ladies was played by an ephemeral
Revels company in 1622–3. *The Captives* was licensed
for the Lady Elizabeth's by Herbert in 1624. *The Lady
Mother* has an endorsed licence of 15 October 1635 by
William Blagrave. An allusion to a 'boy at the Whyte-
fryers' suggests that it belonged to the Revels company, who
were at Salisbury Court in 1635. Herbert himself endorsed *The Launching of the Mary* with a licence on 27 June
1633, but made considerable 'reformations'. This manuscript and that of *The Captives* appear to be in the hands
of the authors; those of *The Lady Mother* and *Dick of
Devonshire* are probably, and that of *The Poor Man's
Comfort* certainly, in those of scribes.[1] *The Escapes of
Jupiter* is in Heywood's hand, and represents a revision
in one play of his own *Golden* and *Silver Ages*. Some
broken lines and other irregularities are the result. The
direction 'A song Iff you will' shows that the author had
the stage in mind. The Dering manuscript of *Henry IV*
and those of *Merry Wives of Windsor* and *Twelfth Night*
formerly owned by Halliwell-Phillipps probably rest on
the printed texts. They may have been prepared for use
in performances, but they have not been subjected to
recent expert examination. In that of *Twelfth Night* the
names of characters were marked at points where the
actors were needed to be ready.

All the manuscripts so far considered were intended to
serve a theatrical purpose. They have many features in
common, but the earlier ones suggest that a distinctively
theatrical style was a matter of gradual development.[2] The
fully reproduced plays are all written on both sides of folio
paper, in fairly even columns, with wide side-margins.
The number of lines to a page varies considerably, as between play and play, and sometimes within a play. The

---

[1] Boas, *Sh. and the Universities*,
169; W. W. Greg, *English Literary
Autographs*, I. xiii, xxii, xxx, and in
Anglica, ii. 212.

[2] *Thomas of Woodstock* was issued
in *M.S.R.* after the following account
was written.

paper has sometimes been lightly folded before use, to facilitate alignment. Prose and long verse lines often extend into the right margin. The original stage-directions are either centred, or placed in a margin. This is most usually the right margin, as in prints. But sometimes entrances are kept by themselves in the left margin. Marginal directions are often enclosed, wholly or partly, by rules, or marked off from the text by a dash or virgule, or brackets. In *Barnavelt* an inverted virgule in the left margin seems to call attention to them. The speeches are separated by rules of varying length. In *Ironside*, they are an addition, and only continue through part of the play. The speech-prefixes are placed in the left margin. The names are given in full in *John a Kent*, and generally in *Believe* and *Ironside*. In the other plays they are more often abbreviated and followed by a colon or full stop. *Ironside* sometimes adds a virgule. The main script is always English, although it may have an admixture of Italianized forms. But personal names and foreign words are normally, although far from consistently, written in Italian script. This is used also, in *Barnavelt* and *2 M.T.*, for some other important words. The practice with regard to stage-directions and speech-prefixes varies. English script is normal for both in *John a Kent* and *Ironside*, although the latter often substitutes Italian. In *S.T.M.* the stage-directions are English. The prefixes are irregular; the generic names tend to be English, and the personal names Italian. In most of the other plays Italian is normal, both for directions and prefixes. *Believe* is exceptional, in that Massinger makes no use of Italian script for any purpose. The writing, of authors, as well as professional scribes, is generally careful and legible. Heywood's hand in *Captives*, as elsewhere, is bad. The initial letters of verse lines are minuscule, with some admixture of majuscule in *John a Kent*, *S.T.M.*, and *Ironside*. Massinger generally begins a fresh sentence within a line by a minuscule, but this is abnormal. Abbreviations are employed, mainly for very common words. The ampersand is used sparsely in *John a Kent*, *2 M.T.*, and *Barnavelt*, and more often in *Welsh Embassador, Parliament of Love*, and *Believe*; the ę in *Ironside, 2 M.T., Welsh Embassador*, and *Parliament of Love*; and old conventional signs for -us in *Ironside* and for -que in *Believe*. In *2 M.T.* such signs survive as mere flourishes. The amount of punctuation varies. There is hardly any in *Ironside, Welsh Embassador*, and *Parliament of Love*; it is light in *Believe*, heavy in *John a Kent*, adequate in the rest. The period ends complete and self-contained sentences; the colon clauses, but also, rather more freely than in modern writing, sentences linked in sense to what follows. The semicolon is rare in the earlier plays, probably more common than the colon in *Believe*. In *John a Kent* and *S.T.M.* a colon often suggests a pause, longer than the sense would justify, at the end of the penultimate line of a speech. Normally there is a tendency to omit stops at the ends of lines. In *2 M.T.* a turned comma is used as an exclamation mark, and is difficult to distinguish from the interrogation mark. In *S.T.M., Ironside*, and *Welsh Embassador*, a heavy stop is sometimes replaced or supplemented by a virgule. A dash is preferred in *2 M.T.*, which also uses the dash freely at changes of address and speech-ends. Round brackets serve as parentheses, to enclose vocatives and explanatory phrases. They are rare in the earlier plays, but tend to become excessive, from a merely literary point of view, later. Passages intended for omission are generally indicated by a vertical line down the left margin. It may or may not have a short arm-piece between the lines at top and bottom, turning it into a bracket. Sometimes they are, concurrently or alternatively, scored over with vertical, diagonal, or horizontal lines. For the most part, they remain legible. Small corrections, if not made *currente calamo*, are interlineated, often but not always with a caret mark. For longer additions or alterations two methods are available. They may be written in the right margin. Here there is room for from one to four verse lines, placed at full length and at right angles to the main text.[1] Sometimes, however, the writing is parallel to the text, and then

---

[1] *John a Kent*, 152; *Barnavelt*, 724, 2334.

verse lines have to be divided, and look like prose.[1] Alternatively, the writing may be upon separate pieces of paper.
These, if complete leaves, are inserted between the original
leaves.[2] If mere slips, they are fastened over these.[3] The
exact place at which they are to be read in may be indicated
by a hand, asterisk, or similar sign, or by a 'cue'. Small
crosses in the left margin seem to be indications, generally
by the censor, that particular lines require alteration or at
least reconsideration.

The censor's dealings with the manuscripts are consistent with our other records of his activities. Six of the
plays bear or bore his allowance at the end, in three cases
with warnings for the observance of his 'reformations'.
Barnavelt, on the other hand, although it has been before
him, has no allowance. I think we must infer that a
further submission would have been necessary. And
surely this would have been so with *Sir Thomas More*, if
the revision had ever been completed. It is hardly possible to hold with Dr. Greg, that Tilney's note at the
beginning was even 'a very conditional licence'. It must
be added that in some of the six and also in some other
plays there are passages which, although not clearly
marked in the censor's own hand, seem to have been
altered in order to obviate his objections. It is of course
not always possible, unless there is a recognizable difference of ink, to say to whom a mere deletion should be
ascribed. The censor's main preoccupation is naturally
with politics. *Believe as You List* had undergone such
careful revision that there was practically nothing left for
him to do. *Barnavelt*, too, may have already been revised.
The original version may have laid more stress on Barnavelt's Arminianism than the Bishop of London could approve. But in the later one Sir George Buck found that
the Prince of Orange, as in effect a foreign sovereign, was
'too much presented', and required a not very effective

---

[1] *S.T.M.* 610, 638, 647; 2 *M.T.*   *Faithful Friends*, iv. 4.
2260; *Barnavelt*, 1028, 1063, 1106.   [3] *S.T.M.* Additions III, V; 2 *M.T.*
   [2] *S.T.M.* Additions I, II, IV, VI;   238, 248, 1700, 1724, 2188; *Launching
Barnavelt*, 763, 1403, 1536, 2919;   *of the Mary.*

toning down of passages which criticized or barely named
him, or exalted his opponent.[1] One of these might perhaps have been taken to be an indirect reflection upon
James.[2] In *Sir Thomas More* Tilney was mainly concerned
to eliminate any encouragement to contemporary agitation against French and Dutch settlers in London. But
More's reasons for resigning the Lord Chancellorship
must also be 'all altered', although one would have thought
that the original author had left them obscure enough.
The Launching of the Mary offended, because of allusions
to a Dutch injustice towards English subjects in Amboyna
and to increases in the English navy and munitions of war,
at a moment when Charles desired to show a fair face
towards Holland, in order to cover his veering in the
direction of a Spanish alliance. Attacks on Catholics and
on a 'vicious vicar' must go out, presumably to avoid
offence to Henrietta Maria and to the ecclesiastics. But
the censor will also curb the licence of dramatists in
criticizing social abuses. That, in view of the proclivities
of James, a wicked king in *The Faithful Friends* had better
not have a favourite, was perhaps obvious enough, even
before the play was submitted. But both in *The Second
Maiden's Tragedy* and *The Honest Man's Fortune* there is a
constant excision, not merely of reflections upon kings and
their ministers, but of allusions to the follies of gallants,
the lusts of women, and the corruptions of lawyers and
officials, which shows a growing sensitiveness in high
places.[3] Milton was not perhaps much concerned to
defend the pens of dramatists, who too often made capital
of what they professed to condemn. But the time for the
protest of the *Areopagitica* was coming. The *Act of Abuses*
itself probably left little real profanity for the Master of the
Revels to tackle. Herbert seems to have thought Buck lax,
and indeed some increase of rigidity is apparent. In *The
Second Maiden's Tragedy*, 'Troth' and 'Faith' are allowed
to stand, while 'Life' is meticulously cut out. In *The*

---

[1] *Barnavelt*, 36, 51, 281, 679, 724,
2284.
[2] *Ibid.* 2434.

[3] Many of the deletion-marks in
the MSS. of *F.F.* and *H.M.F.* are unnoted in Dyce's edition.

Launching of the Mary, according to Dr. Boas, both 'Yfaith' and 'Troth', as well as ' 'Slife' are banned, together with 'every religious reference or expression, however inno- cent'. A comparison of the manuscript of *The Honest Man's Fortune* with the Folio texts of the play proves rather interesting in this respect. The word 'God' occurs rather often in the text of 1647, which presumably rests upon the author's original. In anticipation of Herbert, the scribe of the manuscript has almost always replaced it by 'Heaven', and the same substitution is even more scrupu- lously carried out in the text of 1679. On the other hand, many minor asseverations, such as 'By my troth', to which Herbert does not here seem to have taken exception, remain in the manuscript, but are represented, together with some coarse but not exactly profane expressions, by dashes in both the printed texts.

It is upon the operations of the stage-reviser that the manuscripts are most illuminating. One may reasonably identify him with the book-keeper, carrying out, maybe, on some points, instructions received from the company or an authoritative member of it. He appears in nearly all the manuscripts, to a varying extent; perhaps most con- spicuously in *Believe as You List.* And the services which he renders are multifarious. In *Welsh Embassador* and *Honest Man's Fortune* he may himself be the scribe. In *Sir Thomas More* he certainly copies additions by divers hands, and fits them to their places in the original text. He may add a title-page or a prologue and epilogue.[1] One would infer from Herbert's Office Book that it was his special function to observe the requirements of the censor- ship. This is less obvious from the manuscripts. Mere deletions, as already noted, are difficult to assign, and sub- stantial 'reformations' seem to be generally the work of the censor himself or of the author. Nor is it clear whether the book-keeper's general overhaul of a play preceded or followed its submission to the Master. Here his object is to bring the manuscript into a state in which it can serve as an effective guide to an actual performance. Authors

---

[1] *J. a K., S.T.M.* (t.ps.); *Believe* (t.p. and prol., epil.).

are not always very practical persons. The book-keeper may have to add missing speech-prefixes or alter erroneous ones.[1] Incidentally, he sometimes revises what he takes, rightly or wrongly, to be oversights in the text itself.[2] He applies deletion-marks to passages which it has been decided to cut. He looks to the intervals by which the action is to be broken. Here the practice of the authors is not uniform. *Sir John Van Olden Barnavelt* and *Believe as You List* are fully divided into acts and scenes. *Second Maiden's Tragedy*, *Welsh Embassador*, and *Parliament of Love* have acts only. So has *John a Kent*, with an indication at the beginning of each act that it is *scena prima*. *Sir Thomas More* and *Edmond Ironside* have no original divisions. The book-keeper does not seem to be interested in scenes; it looks as if they were only literary divisions and of no importance in representation. But he is in acts. He marks them for himself in *Edmond Ironside*; and in *Believe as You List*, while he sometimes cuts out the scene indications, he keeps those for acts, and notes two of them as 'long', evidently thinking of an 'act' as an interval, rather than as a section of a play.[3]

As one might expect, the book-keeper is much concerned with the stage-directions. These are clearly in the main the work of the authors. Unless they are mere substantival, participial, or adverbial *marginalia*, they are generally couched in the indicative mood. Very rarely they are in the imperative.[4] I do not think one need regard the imperative as a special note of the book-keeper. The habits of authors differ, but in the manuscripts the stage-directions tend to be pretty full, perhaps particularly in the earlier plays. The fullest of all are in *Sir Thomas More*. Processional entries, spectacular episodes, and fights are often described with much elaboration. The author has a double purpose to serve by his stage-directions. They are not all strictly necessary for the conduct of an actual per-

---

[1] E.g. *Believe*, 704, 709, 1989, 2023, 2081.

[2] E.g. *S.T.M.* (cf. p. 502); *Believe*, 548, 1493, 1618, 2335.

[3] C. J. Sisson in *Believe*, xxiii.

[4] *J. a K.*, 736, 'look in his glasse'; *E.I.* 955, 'Sound Drum wᵗʰ in'.

formance. They are in part designed to explain the structure of his play to the company and to make clear the way
in which he wishes it to be staged. When his characters
first enter, he often adds to their names indications of their
social status, or of their relationships to other characters,
such as we find in a modern theatre-programme. Sometimes even an important character is left with a mere
generic description and no name at all.[1] He makes notes
of the costumes to be worn and the properties to be
carried.[2] He gives the ordering of his entries. Personages
must come in 'severally' or 'aloofe', and when a number
enter together, he is careful to prescribe a grouping.[3] He
provides for the use of the structural features of the stage;
for 'one door' and 'the other door', for 'discoveries' by the
alcove, for appearances 'above' and 'on the walles'.[4] More
rarely he specifies the locality of a scene.[5] And to a greater
or less degree he gives directions, often in the margin, for
the movements and gestures of the actors; even for their
attitudes and facial expressions.[6] Many of the points with
which he is dealing will of course be settled in the tiring-
room or at the rehearsals, long before the performance

---

[1] E.g. the Tyrant and the Lady
in 2 *M.T.*

[2] E.g. *J. a K.* 214, 'Enter Iohn a
Kent like an aged Hermit', 369, 'one
drest like a Moore, wth a Tun painted
with yellow oker, another with a
Porrenger full of water and a pen in
it', 780, 'Enter an antique queintly
disguysde'; *S.T.M.* 410, 'Enter . . .
Doll in a shirt of Maile, a head piece,
sword and Buckler', 955, 'the Lady
Maioresse in Scarlet'; 2 *M.T.* 1879,
'Enter Gouianus in black, a booke in
his hand, his page carrying a Torche
before hym'; *Barnavelt*, 2810, 'Enter
. . . wth a Coffin & a Gibbett'; *Believe*,
1, 'in philosophers habits', 2322, 'his
head shaude in the habit of a slaue'.

[3] E.g. *J. a K.* 604, 'Enter the
Earle of Chester in his night gowne,
and Shrimpe following aloofe of,
some seruaunts wth him'; *S.T.M.* 104,
'An Arras is drawne, and behinde it

(as in Sessions) sit the L. Maior,
Iustice *Suresbie*, and other Iustices,
Sheriffe Moore and the other Sherife
sitting by, *Smart* is the Plaintife,
Lifter the prisoner at the barre'.

[4] E.g. *J. a K.* 137, 848, *S.T.M.*
1862, *E.I.* 813 (doors); *J. a K.* 780,
798, *S.T.M.* 1 (ends of stage); *S.T.M.*
104 (arras); *Barnavelt*, 1883 (study);
2 *M.T.* 1725 (tomb discovered);
Barnavelt, 2144, *Believe*, 1958, 1983
(above); *Barnavelt*, 887, *E.I.* 872
(walls).

[5] *S.T.M.* 1412, 'as in his house at
Chelsey', 1729, 'as in his chamber in
the Tower'.

[6] E.g. *S.T.M.* 240, 'shrugging
gladly', 1068, 'florishing his dagger',
1237, 'with great reuerence', 1575,
'pondering to him selfe'; 2 *M.T.* 821,
'Enter . . . sadly', 1657, 'Enter . . .
wondrous discontedly'; *E.I.* 512,
'hee shewes his tongue'.

takes place. On the other hand, he is often lacking in precision, particularly with regard to supernumeraries. He asks for 'lords' or 'officers' or 'attendants', and does not specify how many. He may give a deliberate option.[1] Crowds, even when their members are elsewhere specified, come and go under a group designation.[2] Quite important characters may be handled in this vague way.[3] Evidently much is left for the management to dispose as it will or can.

The book-keeper revises the author's directions freely. He is careful to add missing entries. He does not trouble about exits, and many, clearly required by the action, remain unnoted. Actors might be trusted to find their own way off the stage. But it was important that they should enter at the right moment. The author may fail to secure this. It is his tendency to place an entry just before the first speech of the character concerned. The cautious book-keeper sometimes shifts it to an earlier point, so as to allow time for the character to cross the stage.[4] He makes additional notes for the introduction of properties.[5] And he provides much more fully than the author for the musical and other noises to be made behind the stage, often specifying the nature of the movement to be sounded, or the instruments to be used.[6] By the time he has got to work, the play has been cast, and the resources of the theatre wardrobe explored. He can therefore clear up the author's uncertainties, and be explicit as to the number of supernumeraries. He tends to economy, appointing one or two only, where the author would have liked more.[7] And for the same reason he occasionally

---

[1] *S.T.M.* 453, 'Enter three or foure Prentises', 954, 'so many Aldermen as may'; *J. a K.* 1098, 'playing on some instrument'.

[2] E.g. *J. a K.* 334, 'Enter . . . wth his crewe of Clownes', 554, 'wth their Consort', 648, 'his trayne'; *S.T.M.* 411, 'a crewe attending'; 2 *M.T.* 1657, 'nobles afarr of'; *E.I.* 104, 'Enter a Companye of cuntrymen makeinge a noyse'.

[3] *J. a K.* 581, 'the Bridegroomes come foorth'; *Believe*, 1176, 'exevnt Carthaginians'.

[4] *J. a K.*, *Barnavelt*, *Believe* show this feature.

[5] *Barnavelt*, 1184, 1610, 2159, 2810; *Believe*, 1, 301, 1185, 1793, 2367.

[6] *J. a K.*, 2 *M.T.*, *Barnavelt*, *Believe*, *E.I.* show this feature.

[7] *Barnavelt*, 334, 864.

cuts out a small part for which the author has definitely
provided.[1]　When he has to rewrite a stage-direction, he
often abbreviates it, leaving out the descriptive notes of
relationship, costume, and the like, which are by now
superfluous.[2]　There are various indications that the book-
keeper is considering the manuscript as one to be used for
a prompt-copy. He notes the points at which properties
and the like are required. But sometimes he also marks
the points in advance, at which he must call for them to
be made ready in the tiring-room.[3]　Calls for particular
actors, perhaps elsewhere occupied, to be brought to the
door of entry, or for stage attendants to take up the post
assigned to them, are similarly inserted.[4]　It is also noteworthy, that while author's directions are generally in the
right margin, those of the book-keeper are generally in
the left, as if that was the place in which they would most
easily attract attention during a performance.[5]　The exceptionally meticulous book-keeper of *Believe as You List*
seems to have transferred some directions in this way,
when there was no other obvious reason for altering them.
In *Welsh Embassador*, where book-keeper and scribe may
have been one, the original directions are in the left margin.　A similar care for practical convenience must explain
the pains with which the book-keeper of *Believe as You
List* transfers a bit of dialogue relating to a song from the
top of one page to the bottom of another overleaf, so that
it may be all before him at a glance.[6]　Finally, and again

---

[1] *J. a K.* 608, 1295; *Barnavelt*, 231,
333, 459, 601, 820, 1182, 1215, 1817,
2159, 2540; *Believe*, 618.

[2] E.g. *Believe*, 1985, 'Ent: Iaylor
(wth bread & water)' for 'Enter Iaylor,
with browne bread, & a woodden
dishe of water'.

[3] *Believe*, 654, 'Table ready: & .6.
chaires to sett out' (for 732), 982, 'the
great booke: of Accomptes ready'
(for 1115), 2378, 'All the swords
ready' (for 2717 and 2722); *Welsh
Emb.* 1934, 'sett out a Table' (for
1962).

[4] *Believe*, 662, 'Mr Hobs: calld vp'

(for 830), 1824, 'Gascoine: & Hubert
below: ready to open the Trap doore
for Mr Taylor (for 1931), 1877,
'Antiochus ready: vnder the stage'
(for 1931), 1968, 'Harry: Willson: &
Boy ready for the song at ye Arras'
(for 2022), 2823, 'Be ready: y^e .2.
Marchantes: w^m Pen: Curtis: &
Garde' (for 2862). In *Welsh Emb.*
nearly all entries have a marginal 'bee
redy', normally from twenty to thirty
lines before they occur.

[5] *J. a K., S.T.M.,* 2 *M.T., Believe,
E.I.* show this feature.

[6] *Believe*, 2023.

to a varying extent, the casting of a play gets noted in the manuscript. Against the name of a character, the book-keeper writes the name, or more often an abbreviation of the name, of the actor who is to play it. As a rule only the smaller parts are so treated, and often by no means all of these.[1] It is very convenient for the modern scholar, since evidence for the dating of plays, or the assignment of them to the right companies, is thus furnished. But the book-keeper was not thinking of posterity. We must suppose that these notes, too, were made to help him in securing the smoothness of entries, and that he did not trouble to make them when he felt able to trust his memory as to the casting.

The book-keeper does not trouble about the author's marginal directions for action and gesture. If they were valuable, they were probably transferred to the actors' 'parts'. These were important subsidiary documents, to which there are many references.[2] We learn from Herbert that the oversight of their preparation rested with the book-keeper. Unfortunately only one Elizabethan 'part' has survived. This is the part of Orlando, as played by Edward Alleyn, possibly in 1592, in Robert Greene's *Orlando Furioso*. It has been reproduced and carefully studied by Dr. Greg.[3] It is now mutilated, and preserved in separate leaves, without a title. About three-quarters of it survive. According to Dr. Greg's reconstruction, it originally formed a continuous roll, some 17 feet long and 6 inches wide, made up of 14 half-sheets of paper divided lengthways, and pasted together by the narrow ends of these strips. At the heads of some of the strips is written 'Orlando'. The careful script is mainly in an English hand, probably that of a professional scribe. A few contractions are used. Some blanks have been filled in and some corrections made in Alleyn's own hand. The

---

[1] S.T.M. (1 only, in an addition), 2 M.T. (2 only, not minor characters), *Barnavelt* (11), *Believe* (11, with 6 major characters incidentally and 2 stage-hands), *E.I.* (4), *Two Noble Ladies* (5), *Captives* (3), *Thomas of Woodstock* (3), *H.M.F.* (3).

[2] *Eliz. Stage*, ii. 44; iii. 194, and in many plays of Shakespeare.

[3] Cf. *Bibl. Note*.

speeches assigned to the actor are transcribed successively, and separated by long rules, at the end of which are written the closing words, from one to four in number, of the foregoing actor's speech. These are the 'cues', to which also there are many references.[1] Orlando's departures from the stage are sufficiently indicated by further rules and generally an 'exit'. There are some directions in the left margin, for action by Orlando himself, or for fights and other episodes during which he is silent. The verse is occasionally mislined; the initial letter of each line is in minuscule. The punctuation is slight; the comma is a stop of all work; stops are often omitted at the ends of lines; a comma, otherwise superfluous, sometimes marks the so-called *caesura*. Prose is written in lines of irregular length, but with no attempt to let the end of a clause be also the end of a line.

The conduct of a performance involved, besides the parts, certain other subsidiary documents. The most important was the 'plot', a skeleton outline of the action, with notes of entrances and exits, and of the properties and noises required. The plot was written in double columns, mounted on a sheet of paste-board, and pierced with a square hole to fit a peg. Seven plots, some only fragmentary, are known, and of six the manuscripts survive. All have been reproduced, and studied in the minutest detail, by Dr. Greg.[2] Those of *The Dead Man's Fortune* and *The Second Part of the Seven Deadly Sins* were probably used by Strange's men and the Admiral's, separately or in combination, about 1590; those of *Frederick and Basilea*, *The Second Part of Fortune's Tennis*, *Troilus and Cressida*, *The Battle of Alcazar*, and *The First Part of Tamar Cam* by the Admiral's during 1597–1602. *The Deadly Sins* and *Fortune's Tennis* are in the hand of the book-

---

[1] *Eliz. Stage*, ii. 541; iv. 367, and in several plays of Shakespeare. *O.E.D.* rejects a derivation from *queue*, which the arrangement at the end of a rule may have suggested. The French term is *replique*. In early texts the word often appears as 'Q', 'q', 'q.', '.q.', 'qu'. Seventeenth-century writers derived it from *qualis* or *quando*. The latter seems more plausible, but probably in its Italian use. In Locatelli's *Scenari* (cf. p. 493) each episode is ended by an 'in q⁰', introducing the next.   [2] Cf. *Bibl. Note*.

keeper concerned with *Sir Thomas More.* In the plots, as
in some of the play manuscripts, the names of actors are
appended to those of the personages whom they represented. But they are more fully given, amounting in most
cases to a complete or nearly complete cast for the play.
Dr. Greg has pointed out that the phrasing of the descriptions of action often recalls that of the stage-directions
supplied by authors, and suggests that the plots were
abstracted from prompt-copies. They have their own
characteristic in the frequent linking of successive entries
by the words 'To them'.[1] They differ rather curiously
from the extant play manuscripts in that more attention
seems to be paid to scene-division, than to act-division.
The scenes are always carefully separated by rules. In
Dead Man's Fortune crosses placed upon some of them,
together with accompanying directions for music, indicate
act-divisions. Elsewhere there is no special sign for these,
although they can sometimes be inferred from the incidence of dumb-shows, choruses, or the interventions of
presenters. As in the plays, exits are often disregarded.
We do not know exactly where the plots were hung; perhaps rather in the centre of the tiring-house, for the
general use of the company, than at the prompter's
corner, since he had a duplicate of the material at his
disposal. A title—'The Booke and Platt of the Second
part of The 7 deadly Sinns'—suggests that, when not in
use, book and plot were preserved together. Less important than the plots were what we may call the 'scrolls'.
These were copies of letters and the like, written out on
separate pieces of paper, to be read by the appropriate
actor, who was thus saved from having to commit them to
memory. Their existence may be gathered from a schedule
of them appended by the book-keeper to *Believe as You
List.* Verses read by Orlando do not appear in his 'part'.[2]

One general remark on the theatrical manuscripts will
help in a subsequent discussion. While they are sometimes in the hand of the author and sometimes in that of
the book-keeper or another scribe, it is clear that the same

---

[1] I find this formula in *J. a K.* 368.   [2] *Orlando Furioso*, 648.

copy might serve both as the official 'book' endorsed by the Master of the Revels, and as a working stage-copy, probably an actual 'prompt-copy', for the ordering of performances. And in *Believe as You List* and *Launching of the Mary*, at least, we have evidence that this copy might be the author's own original.

Besides the theatrical manuscripts there are extant a few others of a different type. They are careful and sometimes even calligraphic transcripts, evidently intended for private reading. Some have dedicatory epistles to patrons. Those which have been fully described are all rather late. *Bonduca* is in the hand of the book-keeper of *Believe as You List*, but Dr. Greg says that it has 'none of the usual stigmas of the prompt copy'. Similar manuscripts were prepared by Ralph Crane, the scribe of *Sir John Barnavelt*. Of these *The Witch* has an epistle, also in Crane's hand, from Middleton to Thomas Holmes. *The Humourous Lieutenant* is dedicated by Crane himself to Sir Kenelm Digby, and dated 27 November 1625. Of *The Game at Chess* he made two copies. One has no epistle; the other, which is an abridged version, has one to Thomas Hammond, in Middleton's own hand. Here the entries are massed at the beginning of each scene, as in some Shakespearean texts.[1] The play had been suppressed for rather audacious political references in 1624, and was naturally dear to collectors.[2] Three other copies exist, for which Crane was not responsible. One is wholly, another partly, in Middleton's hand. Naturally manuscripts of this class do not tell us much about theatrical conditions. But there is an interesting note in *Bonduca*. When the transcript came to be made, part of the necessary material was missing, and the book-keeper wrote in apology:

> The occasion, why these are wanting here, the booke where by it was first Acted from is lost: and this hath beene transcribd from the fowle papers of the Authors wch were founde.

Unfortunately, he does not say whether the 'fowle papers' were preserved at the theatre or in the hands of the author or his representatives.

---

[1] Cf. p. 154.   [2] *M.S.C.* i. 379; Bald 159; B. M. Wagner in *P.M.L.A.* xliv. 827.

CHAPTER V

THE QUARTOS AND THE FIRST FOLIO

[*Bibliographical Note*. I dealt fully with the general history of Elizabethan publishing in ch. xxii of *The Elizabethan Stage* (1923) and need not repeat the list of books and dissertations there given. Of recent additions, the most comprehensive is E. M. Albright, *Dramatic Publication in England, 1580–1640* (1927). The review by W. W. Greg in *R.E.S.* iv (1928), 91, will show that it requires handling with some caution. It has itself a full bibliography. Other contributions are A. W. Pollard, *The Stationers' Company's Records* (1926, 4 *Library*, vi. 348); W. W. Greg, *Some Notes on the Stationers' Register* (1927, 4 *Library*, vii. 376), *The Decrees and Ordinances of the Stationers' Company, 1576–1602* (1928, 4 *Library*, viii. 395); E. Kuhl, *The Stationers' Company and Censorship* (1929, 4 *Library*, ix. 388). Fresh light may be expected from the text of the Decrees and Ordinances, excluded from Arber's edition of the *Stationers' Registers*, but now under preparation by W. W. Greg for the Bibliographical Society. A full bibliography of early drama from the same hand is also still expected.

On the Shakespearean prints themselves the fundamental work is A. W. Pollard, *Shakespeare Folios and Quartos* (1909). It is supplemented for the Quartos by A. W. Pollard and H. C. Bartlett, *A Census of Shakespeare's Plays in Quarto* (1916); by H. R. Plomer, *The Printers of Shakespeare's Plays and Poems* (1906, 2 *Library*, vii. 149); H. Farr, *Notes on Shakespeare's Printers and Publishers* (1923, 4 *Library*, iii. 225). The literature of the First Folio is considerable. S. Lee prefixed an elaborate introduction to the Clarendon Press *Facsimile* (1902) and added *A Census of Extant Copies with Some Account of their History and Condition*. To this he made additions in 2 *Library*, vii (1906), 113, and in *A Survey of First Folios* contributed to *Studies in the First Folio* (1924, Shakespeare Association). Others are made by R. M. Smith and H. S. Leach in *Lehigh University Publications*, i (1927). An example of special interest is described in F. Madan, G. M. R. Turbutt, and S. Gibson, *The Original Bodleian Copy of The First Folio of Shakespeare* (1905). The Shakespeare Association volume of 1924 also includes, besides papers elsewhere named, an *Introduction* by I. Gollancz, and a study of *The First Folio and its Publishers* by W. W. Greg, which supplements his *The Bibliographical History of the First Folio* (1903, 2 *Library*, iv. 258). Other dissertations are J. Q. Adams, *Timon of Athens and the Irregularities in the First Folio* (1908, *J.E.G.P.* vii. 53); W. Keller, *Shakespeares literarisches Testament* (1916, *E.S.* l. 1), *Die Anordnung von Shakespeares Dramen in der ersten Folio-Ausgabe* (1920, *J.* lvi. 90); R. C. Rhodes, *Shakespeare's First Folio* (1923); F. P. Wilson, *The Jaggards and the First Folio of Shakespeare* (1925, Nov. 5, 12, *T.L.S.*); E. E. Willoughby, *An Interruption in the*

Printing of F1 (1928, 4 *Library*, ix. 262). C. A. Smith discusses *The Chief Differences between the First and Second Folios of Shakespeare* (1901, *E.S.* xxx. 1).

The Quartos of 1619 are studied from various angles in A. Wagner, *Eine Sammlung von Sh.-Quartos in Deutschland* (1902, *Anglia*, xxv. 518); A. W. Pollard, *Sh. in the Remainder Market* (1906, June 2, *Academy*), *Sh. Ff and Qq* (1909), *On the Supposed False Dates in Shn. Qq* (1910–11, 3 *Library*, i. 46; ii. 101), *Sh.'s Fight with the Pirates* (1917, 1920); W. W. Greg, *On Certain False Dates in Shn. Qq* (1908, 2 *Library*, ix. 113, 381); S. Lee and others (1908, May 9 to 1909, Jan. 30, *Athenæum*); W. Jaggard, *False Dates in Shn. Qq* (1909, 2 *Library*, x. 208); A. H. Huth, *On the Supposed False Dates in Shn. Qq* (1910, 3 *Library*, i. 36); W. J. Neidig, *The Sh. Qq of 1619* (1910, *M.P.* viii. 145), *False Dates on Sh. Qq* (1910, *Century Mag.*, 912).

A. W. Pollard's theory of the surreptitious or 'Bad' Quartos is set out in his *Folios and Quartos* and *Shakespeare's Fight*, and elaborated (cf. ch. vii), with the help of J. D. Wilson, in *The 'Stolne and Surreptitious' Shn. Texts* (1919, Jan. 9, 16, March 13, Aug. 7, 14, *T.L.S.*, with discussion, Aug. 21, 28), and by Wilson in *The Copy for Hamlet, 1603, and the Hamlet Transcript, 1593* (1918). The 'shorthand' theory and the systems of shorthand on which it is based are discussed in M. Levy, *Sh. and Shorthand* (1884), *William Sh. and Timothy Bright* (1910); C. Dewischeit, *Sh. und die Anfänge der englischen Stenographie* (1897), *Sh. und die Stenographie* (1898, *J.* xxxiv. 170); O. Pape, *Über die Entstehung der Q1 von Shs Rich. III* (1906); A. Seeberger, *Zur Enstehung der Q des 1 Jeronimo* (1908, *Arch. f. Stenographie*, lix. 236, 257); W. J. Carlton, *Timothe Bright Doctor of Physicke* (1911); P. Friedrich, *Timothy Bright's Characterie* (1914, *Arch. f. Schriftkunde*, i. 88); A. Schöttner, *Über die mutmassliche Stenographische Entstehung der Q1 von Shs R.J.* (1918); H. T. Price, *The Text of Hen. V* (1920); H. Roloff, *Zu Ford's Neudruck von Bright's Stenographiesystem 'Characterie' 1588* (1922, *Archiv*, cxliii. 47); M. Förster, *Zum Jubiläum der Sh.-Folio* (1924, *Z. f. Bücherfreunde*, N. F. xvi. 53). I have not seen W. Kraner, *Die Entstehung der ersten Q von Shs Hen. V* (1923). A study of the 'memorization' theory must start from W. W. Greg's edition of Q1 of *Merry Wives of W.* (1910) and his *Bad Quartos Outside Sh.* (1919, 3 *Library*, x. 193) and *Two Elizabethan Stage Abridgements: Alcazar and Orlando* (1923). L. B. Wright has an interesting *Note on Dramatic Piracy* (1928, *M.L.N.* xliii. 256).

A classification of the 'Good' texts must rest largely on the collations in the *Cambridge Shakespeare*. Parallel-texts and the analyses by P. A. Daniel and others in the *Shakespeare Quarto Facsimiles* and by J. D. Wilson in the *New Shakespeare* are valuable. Dissertations bearing on the subject are A. W. Pollard and J. D. Wilson, *What Follows if Some of the Good Q Editions of Sh.'s Plays were Printed from his Autograph MSS.?* (1920, *Bibl. Soc. Trans.* xv. 136, in summary); A. W. Pollard, *The Foundations of Sh.'s Text* (1923, *Brit. Acad.*); J. D. Wilson, *The Task of Heminge and Condell* (1924, *Sh. Ass. Studies*, 53); P. Simpson, *The Bibliographical*

Study of Sh. (1923, *Proc. Oxford Bibl. Soc.* i. 19); B. A. P. van Dam, *Textual Criticism of Sh.'s Plays* (1925, *English Studies*, vi. 97); W. W. Greg, *Principles of Emendation in Sh.* (1928, *Brit. Acad.*)]

MUCH has been written about the regulation of the London book-trade. It is not necessary to repeat here the story of its beginnings in the characteristic Tudor desire to control the expression of opinions hostile to the established order of things, from time to time, in church and state.[1] Earlier procedure had been regularized, before any play of Shakespeare could come in question, by an Order in the Star Chamber of 23 June 1586.[2] This provided for limiting the number of printers and of their presses, and put the licensing of books in the hands of the Archbishop of Canterbury and Bishop of London. It was in fact delegated to correctors, most of whom were episcopal chaplains or prebendaries of St. Paul's. On the business side, the detailed administration was in the hands of the Company of Stationers, who in their turn were subject to the linked supervision of the Privy Council and the ecclesiastical Court of High Commission. All the London booksellers, some 250 in number with their journeymen, and the great majority of the twenty or so printers, many of whom exercised the double trade, were freemen of the Company. Elected officers, a Master, two Wardens, and a Court of Assistants, governed its affairs. Most of our knowledge of the system is due to the well-preserved records of the Company. A few of these, as yet unpublished, may still give fresh light. The most important document is the Register, by the entry of his 'copy' in which a stationer might secure the sole right of selling a book, other than such as were held by the Company itself or by the crown printer, or by individuals, who were not always freemen of the Company, under privileges granted by letters patent. The privileges, however, did not affect plays; small affairs commercially, and generally handled by the less important stationers. The Company imposed severe penalties upon breaches of copyright. A great many plays were never entered in the Register at all, for

[1] Cf. *Eliz. Stage*, ch. xxii.   [2] Arber, ii. 807; extract in *Eliz. Stage*, iv. 303.

reasons which remain obscure. In some cases a desire to save the sixpenny fee on entry may have operated; in others the manuscript may have been illegitimately obtained, although it is not clear how far, if at all, the Company concerned itself with such matters.[1] An unentered book presumably carried no copyright. But transfers of books from one stationer to another were also registered, and it seems that such a transfer might secure copyright, even when there had been no original entry. Sometimes stationers went out of business without disposing of their copyrights, and in such cases the books became derelict, and available for reprinting by others.[2] Whether copyright also lapsed, when a book had been entered, but never published, is uncertain. In theory, it must be supposed that the Company were expected not to enter a book without seeing the allowance of the licenser upon the manuscript or a print. Practice did not always follow theory, where insignificant or obviously safe publications were concerned. But in 1599 special instructions were given by the archbishop and bishop 'that noe playes be printed excepte they bee allowed by suche as haue aucthoritye';[3] and thereafter in making entries, the Company's clerk generally recited the name of the licenser by whom, in addition to a warden, the authority was given, or added a note that printing was not to take place until proper authority was obtained. Presumably such conditional entries gave provisional protection to the copyright.[4] The entries suggest that about 1607 an arrangement was made by which the Master of the Revels normally acted as the official for licensing plays.[5] It is possible that, if the manuscript produced already bore the Master's allowance for

[1] Cf. *Eliz. Stage*, iii. 176.

[2] Sometimes (Arber, v. l) the Court required a fee of 6*d*. in the £ for the benefit of poor stationers.

[3] Arber, iii. 677; *Eliz. Stage*, iii. 168.

[4] *Eliz. Stage*, iii. 169; cf. p. 146.

[5] The first licence by the Master was perhaps a joint one with an ordinary episcopal licenser, noted in the record of a transfer of 21 Nov. 1606 (Arber, iii. 333). He licensed sixteen alone in Apr.–Oct. 1607. Rhodes 29 suggests that these had been held up by a dispute as to procedure. But eight of the plays represent the repertory of Paul's thrown on the market by their closure in the latter part of 1606 (*Eliz. Stage*, ii. 22; iv. 390).

acting, no further reference to him was necessary.[1] After Sir John Ashley became Master of the Revels in 1622, a letter was sent by the Lord Chamberlain to the Company concerning the licensing of plays, and was read to the master printers.[2] Some further restrictions on the entry of plays belonging to the acting companies will be discussed later.[3] It must not be assumed that, because a play was not registered for copyright, it had not been licensed.

The publication of Shakespearean plays, in separate issues known as the Quartos, was first approached by a group of publishers, among whom shifting business relations seem to have existed, and some of whose proceedings, from a literary and probably also from a commercial point of view, were discreditable. John Danter, a printer, registered and published *Titus Andronicus* in 1594, and entrusted it for sale to Edward White and Thomas Millington. In the same year Millington registered and published *2 Henry VI*, describing it as the first part of *The Contention of York and Lancaster*, and followed it in 1595, apparently on the strength of the same registration, with *3 Henry VI*, as *The True Tragedy of Richard Duke of York*. In 1597 Danter published *Romeo and Juliet* without registration. In 1600 Millington, now conjoined with John Busby, published *Henry V.* This again was unregistered, but copyright was established by a transfer in the same year to Thomas Pavier. In 1602 Busby registered *Merry Wives of Windsor* and transferred it on the same day to Arthur Johnson, who at once published it. Finally, also in 1602, Millington transferred to Pavier, 'saluo iure cuiuscunque', not only *The Contention*, now

[1] Herbert, 105, 112, notes that Buck licensed *A King and No King* 'to be Acted in 1611, and the same to be printed', but it is not quite clear whether these were two licences or one.

[2] Noted by Malone from the Stationers' Company's *Court Book*, C. 76, in his annotated *Shakespeare* (1790), i. 2. 132 (*Bodl. Malone*, 1046). Arber, v. lv, says that an entry in the Stationers' Register without licence led to an order to the Clerk 'at the instigation of Sir Henry Herbert' not to enter 'plays, tragedies, tragic comedies, or pastorals' without the authority of the Master of the Revels. This was apparently after the Restoration.

[3] Cf. p. 135.

described as the first and second parts of *Henry VI*, but also *Titus Andronicus*. This had been Danter's, but Danter, who had been more than once in trouble with the Company for infringing privileges, was now dead, and possibly Edward White, who had reissued the play in 1600, and Millington were able to claim it under the arrangement by which they sold it. The 'saluo iure cuius-cunque' must have been a reservation for the interest of White, who reissued it again in 1611. So much for this group. With the exception of *Titus Andronicus*, all their plays appeared in extremely bad texts, the nature of which will presently require examination.[1] Meanwhile, other publishers had got to work with better texts. Cuthbert Burby published *Love's Labour's Lost* in 1598 and *Romeo and Juliet* in 1599. This, which is described on its title-page as 'newly corrected, augmented, and amended', was evidently meant to replace Danter's text, and as *Love's Labour's Lost* bears a similar description, it is extremely likely that of this too there had been an earlier bad version. Danter, having failed to register, could be ignored; it is not so clear why Burby himself did not register either play. A more substantial contribution than Burby's was that of Andrew Wise, who duly registered and published *Richard II* (1597), *Richard III* (1597), and *1 Henry IV* (1598) by himself, and somewhat later *2 Henry IV* (1600) and *Much Ado About Nothing* (1600) in conjunction with William Aspley. He transferred the first three to Matthew Law in 1603, and is not heard of again. No doubt the other two remained with Aspley. *Midsummer-Night's Dream* was registered and published by Thomas Fisher in 1600. Of him, too, nothing is known after 1601. Probably the book became derelict. Some doubt hangs about the activities of James Roberts, a printer who had acquired by marriage in 1593 a special right of printing bills for players.[2] In 1598 he registered *Merchant of Venice*, subject to an unusually worded condition that he should first obtain licence from the Lord Chamberlain. No publication by him is known, but in 1600 he transferred the play

---

[1] Cf. p. 156.   [2] *Eliz. Stage*, ii. 548; McKerrow, *Dict.* 229.

to Thomas Heyes, for whom he then printed it. In 1602
he registered *Hamlet*. This was published in the next year
by Nicholas Ling and John Trundell. The printer was not
Roberts, but Valentine Simmes. The text was a bad one,
much like those already noted. A good one, claiming on
its title-page to be 'according to the true and perfect
Coppie', was substituted in 1604. The publisher was
again Ling, acting alone, and now Roberts was the printer.
In 1607 Ling acquired Burby's copyrights of *Love's
Labour's Lost* and *Romeo and Juliet*, and transferred
them, together with *Hamlet*, to John Smethwick. An
unregistered transfer of *Hamlet* from Roberts to Ling
must be assumed. In 1603 Roberts registered *Troilus and
Cressida*, after the exceptional procedure of a 'full court'
held by the Company, and with the proviso that 'sufficient
aucthority' must be obtained. He never published the
play.

By the end of Elizabeth's reign, therefore, fifteen
Shakespearean texts had appeared. Of these six, and
probably seven (*2, 3 Henry VI, Romeo and Juliet, Henry V,
Merry Wives of Windsor, Hamlet, Love's Labour's Lost?*),
were originally in bad texts, although of two and probably
three (*Romeo and Juliet, Hamlet, Love's Labour's Lost?*)
good ones were substituted. Of eight (*Titus Andronicus,
Richard II, Richard III, 1, 2 Henry IV, Much Ado About
Nothing, Midsummer-Night's Dream, Merchant of Venice*)
the original texts were good. A note in the Register suggests that at one time the publication of *As You Like It*,
as well as *Troilus and Cressida*, had been contemplated.[1]
But these, with *Comedy of Errors, Taming of the Shrew, Two
Gentlemen of Verona, John, Julius Caesar, Twelfth Night*, and
All's Well That Ends Well, probably all of Elizabethan
date, remained unprinted. There was little more fresh
publication before the time of the First Folio. In 1607
Busby and Nathaniel Butter registered *King Lear* and
Butter published it in 1608. Edward Blount registered
both *Anthony and Cleopatra* and *Pericles* in 1608. He pub-
lished neither of them. But *Pericles* was published in the

[1] Cf. p. 145.

next year by Henry Gosson, to whom no transfer is recorded. *King Lear* and *Pericles* cannot be called good texts, although they are not of the same type as the bad texts of the early publishers.[1] Busby had been one of these, and both he and Butter were concerned with plays of Heywood, to the publication of which the author took exception.[2] In 1609 Richard Bonian and Henry Walley registered and published a good text of *Troilus and Cressida*, with the unusual feature, in Shakespearean quartos, of an epistle, in which they complained of the unwillingness of 'the grand possessors' to allow publication. Either the earlier registration by Roberts had been overlooked, or his copyright had lapsed through failure to publish before he left business about 1608. Finally, on the eve of the First Folio, Thomas Walkley registered *Othello* in 1621 and published it in 1622.

Meanwhile several of the plays had been reprinted from time to time, notably those in the hands of Law (*Richard II, Richard III, 1 Henry IV*) and Smethwick (*Romeo and Juliet, Hamlet*). A scene omitted from the Elizabethan editions of *Richard II* was added in 1608. With this exception, there is not much to be said about the reprints. The distribution of them may be a measure either of the popularity of the plays or of the energy of the copyright-owners.[3] There was, however, one reprinting enterprise, the nature of which it has been left to the acuteness of recent bibliographers to establish. Examples have been preserved together, in half a dozen different collections, of ten plays which have certain features in common. They are rather taller than most Quartos, and their imprints are exceptionally short. They are as follows:

2, 3 Henry VI (*The Whole Contention betweene . . . Lancaster and Yorke*). Printed at London, for T. P.
Pericles. Printed for T. P. 1619.
A Yorkshire Tragedy. Printed for T. P. 1619.
Merry Wives of Windsor. Printed for Arthur Johnson, 1619.
Merchant of Venice. Printed by J. Roberts, 1600.

[1] Cf. p. 154.
[2] Cf. p. 47.
[3] A table of pre-1623 Quartos is in App. G.

King Lear. Printed for Nathaniel Butter 1608.
Henry V. Printed for T. P. 1608.
1 Sir John Oldcastle. London printed for T. P. 1600.
Midsummer-Night's Dream. Printed by Iames Roberts, 1600.

The Contention and *Pericles* have continuous signatures and were clearly designed for issue together. It will be observed that two of the plays are not Shakespeare's. Both had been registered and published by Thomas Pavier; *Sir John Oldcastle* in 1600 and *A Yorkshire Tragedy* in 1608. The latter, but not the former, which was in fact written by Drayton and others for the Admiral's men as an answer to *Henry IV*, Pavier had at the time ascribed to Shakespeare.[1] Successive investigations by Professor Pollard, Dr. Greg, and Mr. Niedig have demonstrated that, in spite of the apparent variation in the dates, all the ten reprints really appeared in 1619. They came from the press of William Jaggard, the publisher, in 1599, of *The Passionate Pilgrim*.[2] Only the heads of the complicated bibliographical evidence, by which this conclusion is reached, can be given here. The type used for *Merchant of Venice* differs from that of the same size used by Roberts, who is not likely to have had a duplicate fount not traceable in any other book printed by him. It was used by Jaggard. The ten plays are all linked by the watermarks on their paper, and the ordinary life of a 'make' of paper was too short to allow of the assumption that one used in 1600 could still be available in 1619. Paper with similar watermarks was used by Jaggard, both before and after the latter date. Still more convincing grounds are to be found in the title-pages. The date-numerals are of a large size, not found elsewhere before 1610. All the plays, with one exception, bear the same printer's device (McKerrow 283) of three flowers on a stalk with the motto *Heb Ddieu heb ddim*. This is not known to have been used by Roberts, but was used by Jaggard, both before and after 1619. The *Midsummer-Night's Dream* bears another (McKerrow 136), the arms of Geneva, with the motto *Post Tenebras Lux*. This was once used by Roberts, but also by Jaggard

[1] Cf. p. 535.   [2] Cf. p. 547.

before 1619. Finally, it has been shown, by accurate measurements and by recurrent flaws in the letters, that the lower parts of all the title-pages, except that of *Midsummer-Night's Dream*, must have been printed off from the same setting of type, which remained undistributed, while the actual titles were altered above it. The arguments as to dating seem to me conclusive. The other aspects of the transaction leave more room for conjecture. William Jaggard succeeded to the printing business of James Roberts about 1608, and by 1617 had associated in it his son Isaac Jaggard, whose imprint is on a book of that year.[1] The reprinting of 1619 was no doubt done in concert with Pavier who owned the copyright of five of the plays, and whose friendship with Jaggard may be inferred from the fact that the latter named him as overseer in his will.[2] Presumably licence was obtained from Johnson for the use of *Merry Wives of Windsor*, and from Butter for that of *King Lear*. Of the other three, *Midsummer-Night's Dream* was probably derelict, and *Merchant of Venice* may have been believed to be so. Blount's registration of *Pericles* had already been overlooked, and there is nothing to show that Gosson had any copyright. The shortened imprints suggest that the title-pages were originally meant for half-titles in a comprehensive volume, which would naturally begin with a general and more explicit title-page. So far, there is nothing which points to any deliberate trade irregularity. On the other hand, the absence of continuous signatures after *Pericles* and the obsolete dates '1600' and '1608' seem to bear witness to departures from the original purpose. And the most plausible explanation of at least one of these departures is, I think, to be found in an intervention by the King's men. It was nothing to Pavier and Jaggard that they were reprinting bad texts and ascribing to Shakespeare plays that were not his. Perhaps Shakespeare's fellows viewed

---

[1] Heywood's *A Woman Killed with Kindness*. It is interesting to note that W. Jaggard had (cf. vol. ii, p. 365) a Warwickshire Shakespeare as an apprentice.

[2] Greg, *Emendation*, 41, 45, notes that in *Contention* and *Hen. V* (both Pavier's) the texts of 1619 show some unexplained anticipations of F1.

such proceedings with less equanimity. On 3 May 1619 a letter was addressed by the Lord Chamberlain to the Stationers' Company directing that none of the King's men's plays should be printed 'without some of their consents'. Its exact terms are not preserved. But they appear to be recited in a later letter of similar import written on 10 June 1637 by Philip Earl of Pembroke, then Lord Chamberlain, and brother of William Earl of Pembroke, who was Lord Chamberlain in 1619. It had been represented to Earl Philip's brother that by the printing of plays of the King's men 'not only they themselves had much prejudice, but the books much corruption, to the injury and disgrace of the authors', and the Stationers' Company had been advised 'to take notice thereof, and to take order for the stay of any further impression of any of the playes or interludes of his majesties servants without their consents'.[1] It is certain that in the language of the printing trade the term 'impression' covered a reprint as well as a first publication. We do not know how far Pavier and Jaggard had gone before this bombshell fell. They

[1] Earl William's letter is recorded by Malone under the date 1619 alone from the Stationers' Company's *Court Book*, C. f. 55ᵇ, in his annotated *Shakespeare* (1790), i. 2. 132 (*Bodl. Malone*, 1046). Earl Philip's is printed in full from *P.R.O. Ld. Chamberlain's Records*, V. 95, f. 178, in *Variorum*, iii. 160. He adds: 'I am informed that some copies of playes belonging to the king and queenes servants, the players, and purchased by them at dear rates, having been lately stollen or gotten from them by indirect means, are now attempted to be printed; which, if it should be suffered, would directly tend to their apparent detriment and prejudice, and to the disenabling them to do their majesties service: for prevention and redresse whereof, it is desired that order be given and entered by the master and wardens of the company of printers and stationers, that if any playes be already entered, or shall hereafter be brought unto the hall to be entered for printing, that notice thereof be given to the king and queenes servants, the players, and an enquiry made of them to whom they do belong; and that none bee suffered to be printed untill the assent of their majesties' said servants be made appear to the Master and Wardens of the company of printers and stationers, by some certificate in writing under the hands of John Lowen, and Joseph Taylor, for the kings servants, and of Christopher Beeston for the king and queenes young company, or of such other persons as shall from time to time have the direction of these companies.' A confirmation of 7 August 1641 by Robert Earl of Essex, then Lord Chamberlain, for the King's men, is printed from *P.R.O. Ld. Chamberlain's Records*, V. 135, p. 135, in *M.S.C.* i. 364. It contains a list of sixty plays belonging to the company, none of which were yet in print.

may have issued all the ten plays. It is perhaps more likely that they had already abandoned the continuous signatures and perhaps the idea of a comprehensive volume, had separately issued those dated '1619', and had the rest ready in print. If so, rather than sacrifice their material, they took the rather hazardous course of altering the dates on these to agree with those of the last impressions, so that they might pass as not new at all.[1] The explanation is not wholly satisfactory, since it would have been safer to substitute fresh title-pages more exactly agreeing in detail with the old ones. But it seems to be the best available.[2] It is true that *Henry V* is given the date 1608 and that the last impression now extant is of 1602. It is also true that the extant *Midsummer-Night's Dream* of 1600 does not bear the name of its printer, and that that printer is not likely to have been Roberts. It is conceivable, in both cases, that an edition, known to Jaggard, may have disappeared. But it is also possible that the '1608' for *Henry V* may be due to a failure to alter the lower part of the type, as it had stood for *King Lear*. The affair of 1619 had one other repercussion. *Merchant of Venice* was not derelict after all. Thomas Heyes had left it to his son Laurence. He was then a boy, but he now put in a claim, and *Merchant of Venice* was adjudged to him in a full court on 8 July 1619. It remains to add that no further reprints in fact appeared, before the Commonwealth put an end to the Lord Chamberlain's authority, of any of the bad or unauthentic texts, except in so far as *Pericles*, of which the history is throughout obscure, can be reckoned as one of these.

Whatever the events of 1619, they can have left no enduring malice between the King's men and the Jaggards, since it was again from their press that the collection of Shakespeare's plays known as the First Folio came,

[1] McKerrow, 203, notes a probable similar antedating of an edition of Heywood's *Love's Mistress*.

[2] Neidig thinks that the *Mer. of Ven.* t.p. was printed before that of *Merry Wives of W.*, which would throw my explanation out. Greg approves his technical argument; if it is sound, it is difficult to see why '1619' was allowed to appear on *Merry Wives of W.*, unless by a sheer oversight.

with the active co-operation of Heminges and Condell, in 1623. This contained eighteen of the nineteen plays already published in Quarto. *Pericles* was omitted. Good texts of *2, 3 Henry VI, Henry V,* and *Merry Wives of Windsor* appeared for the first time. Eighteen plays were added, and of these sixteen were covered by the following registration entry:[1]

8o Nouembris 1623.

Mr Blounte Isaak Jaggard. Entred for their Copie vnder the hands of Mr Doctor Worrall and Mr Cole, warden, Mr William Shakspeers Comedyes Histories, and Tragedyes soe manie of the said Copies as are not formerly entred to other men. vizt. Comedyes. The Tempest. The two gentlemen of Verona. Measure for Measure. The Comedy of Errors. As you Like it. All's well that ends well. Twelft night. The winters tale. Histories. The thirde parte of Henry the sixt. Henry the eight. Coriolanus. Timon of Athens. Julius Caesar. Tragedies. Mackbeth. Anthonie and Cleopatra. Cymbeline.

The licenser was here not the Master of the Revels, but one of the episcopal delegates, Thomas Worrall, a prebendary of St. Paul's.[2] The title-page of the Folio runs:

Mr. William Shakespeares Comedies, Histories, & Tragedies Published according to the True Originall Copies. [*Portrait, signed* Martin Droeshout sculpsit London] London. Printed by Isaac Iaggard, and Ed. Blount. 1623.

There is a head-title:

The Workes of William Shakespeare, containing all his Comedies, Histories and Tragedies: Truely set forth, according to their first Originall.

By 8 November 1623 Isaac Jaggard had succeeded his father, who was dead before November 4.[3] The book, however, apart from its title-page and preliminary matter,

---

[1] Arber, iv. 107. A facsimile is in *F1 Studies* xix. A 'G. S.' in the margin is modern and may stand for 'Gulielmus Shakespeare' or 'George Steevens'.

[2] W. W. Greg in *4 Library,* vii. 381.

[3] *Bibl. Soc. Trans.* xiv (1919), 194; F. P. Wilson in *T.L.S.* 5, 12 Nov. 1925.

must have been printed during William Jaggard's life-time, since his name is in the colophon, which runs:

Printed at the Charges of W. Jaggard, Ed. Blount, I. Smith-weeke, and W. Aspley, 1623.

The first evidence of actual publication is the binding of a copy for the Bodleian on 17 February 1624. It may be assumed to have taken place in 1623, as the date indicates. It can hardly have preceded registration, in spite of the inscription 'Ex dono Willelmi Iaggard Typographi. A°. 1623' on the copy once belonging to the herald Augustine Vincent. This is in Vincent's hand, not Jaggard's, and may only commemorate a lifetime promise. It has been shown that the date of '1622', said to have been found on a single example, is a fabrication.[1] But that earlier publication was at first contemplated is shown by a Frankfort list of books published between the marts of April and October 1622, which includes the entry 'Playes, written by M. William Shakespeare, all in one volume, printed by Isaack Iaggard, in fol.'.[2] Mr. Willoughby has an ingenious argument, based on recurrent flaws in a tail-piece, which makes it probable that printing began as far back as 1621, and was suspended at an early stage in the composition of the histories, owing to the pressure of other work which there is reason for thinking that the Jaggards were regarding as urgent towards the end of that year.[3] If so, the initiation of the enterprise may have followed pretty closely upon the abandonment of that of 1619.

The colophon shows that publication was undertaken by a syndicate of stationers. Edward Blount and Isaac Jaggard held the new copyrights. The play described in the Register as 'The thirde part of Henry the sixte' is clearly *1 Henry VI*. The transfer of the *Contention*

[1] Lee, *Introd. to Facs.* xxxii; *Census,* 24.

[2] F. P. Wilson (1925, Nov. 5, *T.L.S.*) from *Catalogus Universalis pro Nundinis Francofurtensibus.* There are other English books in this list, which did not appear before 1623, and the *Catalogus* for Oct. 1623–Apr. 1624 has the corresponding entry 'Master William Shakespeares workes, printed for Edward Blount, in fol.'.

[3] *4 Library,* ix. 262. The actor-list (cf. vol. ii, p. 78) also points to 1621.

in 1602 had made *2, 3 Henry VI* the first and second parts, as viewed by the trade. Jaggard had no earlier copyrights. Blount, who was not a printer as the title-page suggests, but a publisher of better standing than most of those who concerned themselves with Shakespeare's plays, may have forgotten that he had already registered *Anthony and Cleopatra*, together with the absent *Pericles*, in 1608. But possibly his right had lapsed through failure to publish, or the object of the re-entry was to give Jaggard an interest. Smethwick contributed *Romeo and Juliet, Love's Labour's Lost*, and *Hamlet*, and Aspley *Much Ado About Nothing* and *2 Henry IV*. The syndicate could use the derelict *Midsummer-Night's Dream*. But for other plays already in print they must have made arrangements with outside owners of copyrights; with Pavier for *Titus Andronicus, 2, 3 Henry VI*, and *Henry V*; perhaps with White also for *Titus Andronicus*; with Law for *Richard II, Richard III*, and *1 Henry IV*; with Heyes for *Merchant of Venice*; with Johnson for *Merry Wives of Windsor*; with Butter for *King Lear*; with Bonian and Walley for *Troilus and Cressida*; and with Walkley for *Othello*. Walkley, indeed, publishing after the Lord Chamberlain's letter of 1619, may himself have had no more than a conditional assent to his use of the play from the King's men. Two of the added plays, which are not in the registration entry, remain to be accounted for. The *Taming of the Shrew* and *King John* must have been allowed to pass as reprints of the old plays, *The Taming of A Shrew* and *The Troublesome Reign of John, King of England*, on which they were founded. *A Shrew* had been registered and published by Peter Short in 1594, and sold for him by Burby. Dr. Greg thinks that Humfrey Lownes, who married Short's widow, might have claimed it. But Burby had transferred it to Ling in 1607 and from Ling it had passed to Smethwick. *The Troublesome Reign* had been successively issued by Sampson Clarke, John Helme, and Thomas Dewes. It had never been registered, and there seems to have been no copyright. We are left to speculate why *Pericles* was excluded. Pavier appears to have had as good a claim to it as any one, except perhaps Blount himself. At any rate, his widow transferred his 'right in Shakesperes plaies or any of them' to Edward Brewster and Robert Bird in 1626, and Bird transferred *Pericles* to Richard Cotes in 1630. It can hardly be that a more satisfactory text than that of the Quarto was not available, for there were revivals in 1619 and 1631.[1] No doubt it was known to be only in part Shakespeare's, but *Henry VIII*, which was in like case, to say nothing of some earlier plays, whose history may have been forgotten, were not excluded. *The Two Noble Kinsmen*, however, was, and was published in Quarto, as by Fletcher and Shakespeare, in 1634.

The Folio is arranged in three separately paginated sections, for comedies, histories, and tragedies respectively. *Troilus and Cressida* and *Cymbeline* rank as tragedies. The histories are in chronological order, but there may have been some half-hearted attempt to put comedies and tragedies not previously printed at the beginnings and ends of their sections. There are no half-title-pages for the sections or for the individual plays. No sufficient reason has been shown for supposing that the three sections were set up concurrently, or that any presses other than those of the Jaggards were normally used. The types and most of the ornaments recur in other books printed by them. There are 908 pages in all, of which a few are blank. Misprints, both in the pagination and in the signatures, complicate the collation.[2] Some of these, and others in the text, were corrected during the course of the printing, and are not found in all examples.[3] Minor irregularities have affected the treatment of *2 Henry IV* and *Winter's Tale*.[4] Something more important must have happened in the case of *Troilus and Cressida*. Apparently the original intention was to put it in the middle of the tragedies, but the printing was suspended, and at the last moment, possibly after the preliminary matter had been

---

[1] Cf. App. D.

[2] Pollard, *F. Q.* 108, gives one, together with many bibliographical details not necessary here. E. E. Willoughby adds others in *R.E.S.* iv. 323; v. 198, and *4 Library*, ix. 385.

[3] Cf. p. 174.

[4] Cf. pp. 380, 488.

printed, it was inserted at the beginning of that section.[1] Some hitch in the negotiations for the copyright may have arisen. The preliminary matter itself is differently ordered in different examples. But Professor Pollard has shown, upon the evidence of signatures, conjunct leaves, and the presence and absence of watermarks, that the intended order was probably that found in the Grenville copy in the British Museum. This gives (*a*) verses to the reader, on the portrait, by Ben Jonson; (*b*) the title-page and portrait on an inserted leaf; (*c*) an epistle to the Earls of Pembroke and Montgomery, by Heminges and Condell; (*d*) an epistle to the readers, by the same; (*e*) commendatory verses by Ben Jonson and Hugh Holland; (*f*) a 'Catalogue' of the plays, from which *Troilus and Cressida* is omitted; (*g*) commendatory verses by Leonard Digges and an unknown I. M.; (*h*) a head-title and 'The Names of the Principall Actors in all these Playes'.[2] The portrait is found in more than one state.[3] Steevens called attention to some parallels between the epistle to the readers and the works of Ben Jonson, and suggested that he wrote part of it and revised the rest. Professor Pollard offers an alternative in Blount, who showed some literary facility in epistles to his editions of Marlowe's *Hero and Leander* (1598) and Lyly's *Sixe Court Comedies* (1632). Jonson's claim seems to me on the whole the better.[4] The research of Sir Sidney Lee has located over 180 extant examples of the First Folio, of which only fourteen are in a perfect state of preservation. As a rule, leaves have gone at the beginning and end. The Grenville example in the British Museum is as good as any. The largest known measures $13\frac{3}{8} \times 8\frac{3}{4}$ inches. The only example of which a continuous history can be traced is now in the collection of Mr. H. C. Folger. It was originally bought in 1628 by William Sheldon of Weston in Warwickshire. The example owned by the

---

[1] Cf. p. 441.

[2] McKerrow, 262, suggests that confusion may have been caused by folding the sheet containing (*g*) and (*h*) the wrong way round, and that possibly they should come, in reverse order, between (*d*) and (*e*). This would put all the commendatory verses together.

[3] Cf. vol. ii, p. 240, and Plates XXVI, XXVII.

[4] The epistles and commendatory verses are in App. B, nos. l–liii.

Bodleian in 1624 was sold when the Third Folio appeared in 1663, and has recently been recovered. Various guesses have been made as to the probable size of the edition; Dr. Greg points out that a sale of less than 1,000 copies would hardly have repaid the publishers, unless the Earls of Pembroke and Montgomery showed munificence.[1] Jaggard's interest in Shakespeare's plays was transferred by his widow to Thomas and Richard Cotes about 19 June 1627, and Blount's to Robert Allot on 16 November 1630.[2] The Second Folio was printed by Thomas Cotes for Allot, Smethwick, Aspley, Richard Hawkins, and Richard Meighen in 1632. Hawkins had acquired the copyright of *Othello* and Meighen that of *Merry Wives of Windsor*. The Third Folio was printed for Philip Chetwinde, who had married Allot's widow, in 1663, and to a second issue of 1664 were appended reprints of *Pericles* and of the 'apocryphal' *London Prodigal, Thomas Lord Cromwell, 1 Sir John Oldcastle, Puritan, Yorkshire Tragedy,* and *Locrine*.[3] The Fourth Folio was printed for a syndicate of booksellers in 1685. These later Folios and the post-1623 Quartos are of little value for textual criticism.

Upon the nature of the copy which reached the publishers, first for the Quartos and afterwards for the First Folio, the amount of authority to be attached to the traditional texts, as representative of what Shakespeare actually wrote, must in the last resort depend. I have already cited the claim of the First Folio, on its title-page and in its head-title, that its plays are derived from the author's 'originals'.[4] And this receives some expansion in the epistle to the readers, where Heminges and Condell profess—

so to haue publish'd them, as where (before) you were abus'd with diuerse stolne, and surreptitious copies, maimed, and deformed by the frauds and stealthes of iniurious impostors, that expos'd

---

[1] The price of the Folio may have been about £1 and that of a Quarto about 6*d.*, but the question is obscure; cf. McKerrow, 133.

[2] Arber, iv. 182, 243.
[3] Cf. ch. x.
[4] Cf. p. 96.

them: euen those, are now offer'd to your view cur'd, and perfect of their limbes; and all the rest, absolute in their numbers, as he conceiued them.

An epistle, like a title-page, is an advertisement, rather than an affidavit. But while a desire to exalt the merit of the Folio is apparent, it would be unreasonable to ignore altogether the stress laid upon the fidelity of the texts to the original intentions of the author. The eighteenth-century editors, impressed by corruptions and signs of stage manipulation, took the statement of Heminges and Condell rather lightly. Johnson in 1765 wrote of the plays:

They were immediately copied for the actors, and multiplied by transcript after transcript, vitiated by the blunders of the penman, or changed by the affectation of the player; perhaps enlarged to introduce a jest or mutilated to shorten the representation; and printed at last without the concurrence of the author, without the consent of the proprietor, from compilations made by chance or by stealth out of the separate parts written for the theatre: and thus thrust into the world surreptitiously and hastily, they suffered another depravation from the ignorance of the printers, as every man who knows the state of the press in that age will readily conceive.

Modern research, based upon a closer evaluation of the texts themselves, a wider knowledge of the methods of players and printers, and in particular a study of the manuscripts described in Chapter IV, has brought many qualifications to this judgement. But the doctrine of multiplied transcripts has died hard, and it was still possible for Sir Sidney Lee to maintain in 1925, as regards the Quartos, that 'the publication of separate plays was deemed by theatrical shareholders, and even by dramatists, injurious to their interests', and that 'as a rule, the publisher seems to have bought of an actor one of the copies of the play which it was necessary for the manager to provide for the company'; and as regards the Folio, that 'external and internal evidence renders it highly improbable that Shakespeare's autographs were at the printer's disposal', that the existing theatrical manuscripts were destroyed at the Globe fire in 1613, that the library was 'replenished' from transcripts in the private possession of actors or from 'fair copies' which had been presented to friends and patrons, and that these were the foundation of the new texts of 1623.[1] There are several statements here which invite comment. It is true that there are many indications of a desire on the part of acting companies to control the transmission of plays to the press. They are most frequent, as it happens, in the case of the Chamberlain's and King's men. They begin with Roberts's entry of *Merchant of Venice* in 1597, made conditional on a licence from the Lord Chamberlain. This certainly suggests that the company were using the influence of their patron to protect themselves against publishers who had not come to terms with them. And perhaps a similar inference is to be drawn from the following memoranda, which appear on a spare page of the *Stationers' Register*.[2]

My lord chamberlens mens plaies Entred
viz.

27 May 1600   A moral of clothe breches and veluet hose
To master
Robertes
27 May   Allarum to London
To hym.

4 Augusti

As you like yt, a booke ⎤
Henry the ffift, a booke │
Every man in his humour, a booke ⎬ to be staied
The Commedie of muche A doo about │
nothing a booke ⎦

Of the four 'staied' plays, *Every Man In His Humour* and *Much Ado About Nothing* were regularly registered later in August 1600 and published in good texts. There was no Quarto of *As You Like It*. But the stay, whatever its nature, did not prevent the appearance in 1600 of a bad text of *Henry V* or the acknowledgement of copyright when it was transferred on August 14 of that year. Professor

---

[1] Lee, 100, 548, 559.
[2] Arber, iii. 37. The marginal notes refer to Roberts's entries (Arber, iii. 161), both of which were subject to

'further aucthoritie'. *A Larum for London* was printed in 1602 (*Eliz. Stage*, iv. 1). No edition of *Clothe Breches* is known.

Pollard thinks that the Chamberlain's men, perhaps un-
willing to invoke their patron too often, fell back upon a
plan of employing Roberts to make conditional blocking
entries, which were not to be acted upon, but would keep
out other publishers, and that Blount's entries of 1608
were meant to serve a similar purpose.[1] If so, the plan
was not particularly successful, since it did not stop the
bad texts of *Hamlet* and *Pericles*, or of *Merry Wives of
Windsor* which Roberts did not enter, or prevent Bonian
and Walley from publishing *Troilus and Cressida* in spite
of the opposition of the 'grand possessors'. I agree with
Professor Pollard that there is no reason to regard the
operations of Roberts as fraudulent. But that he was an
agent of the players seems to me very disputable. The
terms of the *Merchant of Venice* entry do not suggest that
they were relying on him. That his other entries, except
in the case of *Hamlet*, were conditional, is hardly relevant.
They are not, like that for *Merchant of Venice*, distinguishable in form from many entries by other publishers, in
which the further authority required was pretty clearly the
allowance of an episcopal licenser.[2] Moreover an uncon-
ditional entry would have served Professor Pollard's assumed purpose just as well. Roberts was a printer, and his
object in making the entries may well have been to transfer
them to another stationer in return for the printing rights.
Perhaps it was not always attained. But he did print
Merchant of Venice for Heyes in 1600, if not earlier; and
although he did not print Q1 of *Hamlet*, he did print Q2
for Ling in 1604. And we must surely assume that the
copyrights of Heyes and Ling, acknowledged later, were
derived by transfer from Roberts. One way or another,
the King's men seem to have been successful in safe-
guarding most of their Shakespearean plays during the
reign of James, and from 1619 onwards they had, as has
already been shown, protections from successive Lords
Chamberlain.[3] Whether other companies shared these
before 1637 is uncertain. But they had the same problem

---

[1] Pollard, *S. F.* 36, 42.   [2] *Eliz. Stage*, iii. 169.
[3] Cf. p. 135.

to face, and did their best to protect themselves. We find
the Admiral's in 1600 giving the printer 40*s*. 'to staye the
printing of Patient Gresell'. The agreement of the King's
Revels syndicate in 1608 contains a clause forbidding the
individual partners to print the play-books. Heywood, in
the epistle to his *English Traveller* of 1633, tells us that
some of his plays 'are still retained in the hands of some
Actors, who thinke it against their peculiar profit to haue
them come in print'.¹ He is no doubt referring mainly to
Christopher Beeston, who held most of the plays of Queen
Anne's men, for whom Heywood had written. The statement in the First Folio that some 'surreptitious' plays did
get into print can also be confirmed from Heywood.² In
the epistle to his *Rape of Lucrece* (1608), he takes credit
for not being one of those who 'have used a double sale
of their labours, first to the Stage, and after to the presse',
and says that he now only prints because 'some of my
plaies have (unknown to me, and without any of my
direction) accidentally come into the Printers handes and
therfore so corrupt and mangled (copied onely by the eare)
that I have bene as unable to knowe them, as ashamde to
challenge them'. So, too, in a late prologue for a revival of
his *If You Know not Me, You Know Nobody*, he 'taxeth the
most corrupted copy now imprinted, which was published
without his consent', by Nathaniel Butter in 1605, and
says that—

Some by stenography drew
The plot: put it in print: (scarce one word trew:)

Various reasons have been offered for the reluctance of the
players to allow printing. Perhaps they thought, as some
managers are said still to think, that the competition of a
book would diminish their takings.³ It is often held that
what they feared was the appropriation of their plays for
acting by other companies. About this I am rather sceptical. It is, of course, impossible to hold, with Miss Albright, that there was a common law stage-right, which
would have prevented appropriation.⁴ A common law

---

¹ *Eliz. Stage*, ii. 64; iii. 183, 292, 319.   ³ McKerrow, 143.
² *Ibid.* iii. 342, 344.   ⁴ Albright, 217.

right, laid down by no court, cannot be improvised for argumentative ends. A recorded action for a wrongly withheld 'book' in *Downton* v. *Slater* was merely for the value of the corporeal book and for damages arising from its detention, and in fact the court only awarded the value of the book.[1] But it is reasonable to suppose that there was some comity among the London companies in the matter.[2] Very likely this would not cover plays acted by a company which had dropped out of the London theatres. Shakespeare seems to have been able to use the old *Troublesome Reign of John*, *Famous Victories of Henry V*, and *King Leir*, two certainly and the third probably Queen's plays, and the old *Taming of A Shrew*, a Pembroke's play, at any rate as sources. The company which originally produced *The Spanish Tragedy* is unknown. The Admiral's revived it with 'adicyons' in 1602. But the Chamberlain's must also have played it, and probably about the same time, since the authentic version of the elegy on Burbadge names 'ould Heironymoe' as one of his parts, and in *3 Parnassus* he is represented as trying a novice in it.[3] It is even possible that the edition of 1602 may contain the version of the Chamberlain's and not the Admiral's men. For invasion by one company of the legitimate repertory of another there is very little evidence. I do not think that the case of *The Malcontent* can be so accounted. It was originally a Blackfriars play, but was given also by the King's men, with 'additions', including an induction, in which comes this dialogue:

Sly. . . . I would know how you came by this play.

Condell. Faith, sir, the book was lost; and because 'twas pity so good a play should be lost, we found it and play it.

Sly. I wonder you would play it, another company having interest in it.

Condell. Why not Malevole in folio with us, as Jeronimo in decimo-sexto with them? They taught us a name for our play; we call it *One for Another*.

---

[1] *Eliz. Stage*, ii. 157.

[2] Greg suggests (*R.E.S.* iv. 96) that provincial companies may have made up their repertories from prints, but if they did, I am not sure that it would hurt the London companies very much.

[3] *Eliz. Stage*, ii. 309.

Surely this is chaff; one does not advertise a real theft in an induction. I take it that the King's and the Queen's Revels shared *The Malcontent* by arrangement, just as the King's and Paul's shared *Satiromastix*.[1] But of course a mere comity leaves room for abuses, and ultimately the Household officers stepped in to protect stage-rights as well as printing-rights. Heminges paid Sir Henry Herbert £5 in 1627 'to forbid the playing of Shakespeare's plays to the Red Bull company', and the Lord Chamberlain in 1639 issued a mandate to rival companies not to 'intermeddle' with William Beeston's repertory at the Cockpit.[2] One of the plays named in this is Beaumont and Fletcher's *Father's own Son*, which was in fact printed in the same year, under the alternative title of *Monsieur Thomas*, as 'Acted at the Private House in Blacke Fryers', where the King's men must have given it. Miss Albright thinks that these documents merely record arbitrations on disputes as to acting-rights, which arose when players changed companies.[3] But whether this is so or not, they had authority behind them. If we set nervousness as to stage-rights aside, the attitude of the players towards printing remains completely intelligible. It was mainly determined by financial considerations. They had a valuable property in their manuscripts, and they did not intend, either that these should be used except when it was convenient to them, or that the purchase money paid by the stationers should pass into other hands. This may not have been much. The fee for a pamphlet—and a play would rank as no more—is said to have been about £2.[4] But it was some offset against the £6 or £10 which the author had received. Philip Herbert's letter of 1637, carefully read, seems to put the whole matter on a financial

[1] *Eliz. Stage*, iii. 293, 431. *Jeronimo* here is probably *The First Part of Ieronimo* (*Eliz. Stage*, iv. 22), perhaps written for the Chamberlain's as an introduction to *Span. Trag.*, but printed in 1605 in a corrupt and probably 'reported' form, which suggests performances by boys.

[2] Herbert, 64; *Var.* iii. 159. The order of 1639 is in *P.R.O. Ld. Chamberlain's Records*, V. 134, p. 337, and has 'Cockpitt Playes appropried' in the margin; cf. *M.S.C.* i. 364.

[3] Albright, 230.

[4] Pollard, *S.F.* 24.

basis. The players had bought 'at dear rates'. They
would have 'detriment and prejudice' if their plays were
'stolen', and His Majesty's service would suffer, which
was Herbert's reason for intervention. The fluctuations in
the output of printed plays also suggest the prevalence of
economic considerations. It was greatest in 1594 when the
companies were in straits owing to the plague; in 1600,
when the Chamberlain's and Admiral's had had to face
the cost of new theatres; in 1607 when the stock of the
ruined King's Revels came on the market. Apart from
the bad texts, there is really no *a priori* reason to suppose
that copy for the Elizabethan Quartos of Shakespeare
reached the stationers in any other way than through a
normal process of sale by the companies. Let us credit
these with a higher motive in the desire to replace the bad
texts of *Love's Labour's Lost, Romeo and Juliet,* and *Hamlet*
by more commendable versions. Whether Shakespeare
himself had anything to say in the matter, we cannot tell.
But the prefatory epistles by other authors, which accompany so many plays, suggest that some concession had to
be made by the companies to literary ambition, and provide further evidence in favour of regular publication.[1] It
is true that a large proportion of these were plays from the
boys' companies, where the authors may have had some
share of control.[2] It is true, also, that the authors themselves sometimes complain that their hands were forced by
the fear of unsupervised printing.[3] But this was largely a
convention, inherited from the courtiers, who affected to
write for their friends alone.

I have been elaborate about the relation of the companies to the publishers because, if Sir Sidney Lee were
right, the textual authority of the Quartos would be seriously diminished. His theory that the Folio texts were
derived from copies belonging to actors or private persons
and collected after the fire at the Globe depreciates these
in their turn. But here it is possible to be more brief.
There is no proof that any manuscripts were destroyed at

[1] Albright, 205, gives a partial list.   [3] *Ibid.* iii. 344, 441; Albright, 208–
[2] *Eliz. Stage,* i. 378.   13.

the Globe fire. The numerous accounts of this say nothing
about them. For what they are worth, one tells us that
the silken flag was burnt, and another that 'nothing did
perish but wood and straw and a few forsaken cloaks'.
Very likely this means no more than that no lives were
lost. Sir Sidney cites as his sole evidence the fact, which is
recorded, that at the Fortune fire in 1621 the Palsgrave's
men lost their play-books.[1] But to argue thus, without any
regard for the rules of logic, from the known separable
accidents of one case to the unknown separable accidents
of another, is not permissible. The books of the King's men
may quite well have been saved, or, as has often been suggested, they may have been at the Blackfriars. The 'allowed' book of *Winter's Tale*, that of *Honest Man's Fortune*,
and the stage-copy of *Bonduca* were all at one time or other
missing. The two latter must have been recovered before
the Beaumont and Fletcher Folio of 1647 was printed, and
when a transcript of *Bonduca* was wanted, it was supplied,
not from the sources indicated by Sir Sidney, but from the
author's 'foule papers'.[2] And certainly the loss of *Winter's
Tale* can hardly have been due to the fire, as a revival in
1618 and possibly another in 1619–20 had intervened.
The study of the extant theatrical manuscripts, a small
sample indeed out of the many hundreds that must have
been written, gives no support to Sir Sidney's statement
that it was 'necessary' for the manager to provide copies
for the company. *A priori*, one might perhaps have expected that the author's original would have been laid up
for ultimate reference in the theatre archives, and transcripts made for submission to the Master of the Revels
and for the use of the prompter. It is clear that in fact
the original itself sometimes became both the 'allowed'
copy and the prompt-copy. The individual actors needed
no copies except their 'parts'. On the other hand, the
manuscripts give hardly less support to the notion of 'continuous copy', which dominates the reconstructions of
Professor Wilson; the notion, that is, of 'the long-lived
manuscript in the tiring-house wardrobe, periodically

---

[1] *Eliz. Stage,* ii. 419, 442.   [2] Cf. p. 125.

taken out for a revival and as often worked upon by fresh hands, abridged and expanded, recast to fit the capabilities of new performers, brightened with current topical allusions, written up to date to suit new tastes in poetic diction'.[1] Certainly transcripts were used for prompt-copies as well as originals; and indeed it stands to reason that the more a book-keeper had annotated a manuscript with the names of supernumeraries and other jottings for use in one series of representations, the more advantage there would be in making a transcript at a revival. A prompt-copy had above all things to be clear and easy to consult at a glance. We do not, for example, find substituted names of fresh supernumeraries in the extant manuscripts. The same consideration would point to transcription in the event of substantial textual revision, in so far as that ever took place.[2] When Massinger had to recast *Believe as You List*, he wrote out the old matter with the new; and the textual *marginalia* and slipped insertions which we do find in the manuscripts are, with one exception, of very limited extent. The exception is *Sir Thomas More*, and on a generalization from this obscure and probably abnormal case the doctrine of continuous copy is mainly founded. Professor Wilson's point that transcription would cost time and money cannot weigh much against obvious convenience; and it is safer to allow for the possibility that there may have been a good deal of it in the theatres, even if the career of Ralph Crane does not give us a glimpse of that recently banned ghost, the stage scrivener. On the other hand, there is no reason whatever why some, both of the Quarto and the Folio texts, should not have been set up from Shakespeare's autographs; and a use of these for the Folio is the natural interpretation both of the epistle to the readers and of the stress laid on originals in the title-page and head-title. It would be taking the language too literally to argue that transcripts were in no case substituted, and where there are parallel texts, we are often driven by their disagreement to conclude that one or other, if not both, must be

---

[1] *Disintegration of Shakespeare*, 18; cf. Wilson, *Temp.* xxxiii, 79.   [2] Cf. ch. vii.

derived from such a source. In any case it would be pressing Heminges and Condell too hard to infer that the originals had been completely purged from the results of after-touching. Both in Folio and in Quarto texts, it is often possible to find traces of musical or spectacular elaboration, or of the book-keeper establishing his prompt-copy. In mere stage-directions it is difficult, where there is only one text, to distinguish his hand from that of an author writing, as Shakespeare wrote, in full knowledge of stage conditions, although a modification may sometimes be suspected from the form of the wording or from a duplication of substance. Where there are two texts, the book-keeper may show himself in additional notes for music or other noises, in divergence from the author's details, and perhaps most unmistakably in 'cuts'.[1] One cannot even altogether exclude the possibility of occasional recourse to a transcript made not as a prompt-copy, but expressly for the printer, or for the satisfaction of a private owner. Most of the extant examples of private manu-scripts, however, may be late, and the reference to them in the Beaumont and Fletcher Folio of 1647 certainly is.[2] They may not have become usual before 1619, when the Lord Chamberlain's protection made the multiplication of copies less risky.

One other possibility must be considered. Malone's theory of the construction of copy for the printers from actors' 'parts' has received some recent favour, notably from Professor Wilson.[3] A loss of prompt-copy, through fire or other cause, is generally assumed, together with reliance upon a 'plot' to help in the reconstruction. A generation obsessed by machinery calls the method 'as-sembling'. One would suppose, however, that both parts and plot, if preserved, would be kept with the prompt-copy, and that the loss of one would mean the loss of all. Certainly the 'book' and 'plot' of *Seven Deadly Sins* were at one time kept together.[4] The case for assembling is

[1] Cf. p. 235.   [2] Cf. p. 125.
[3] He is supported by Rhodes, 96.
W. J. Lawrence dissents in *Assembled*

Texts in the First Folio (1922, Jan. 12, *T.L.S.*).
[4] Cf. p. 124.

primarily based upon the Folio texts of *Two Gentlemen of Verona* and *Merry Wives of Windsor*. These have a common feature in the complete or almost complete absence of stage-directions, except for an initial entry for each scene, in which all the characters taking part in that scene are named, more or less in the order of their appearance.[1] Somewhat, but not quite analogous, is *Winter's Tale*. Here are the same comprehensive initial entries, except in two scenes (iv. 3; v. 2), but in some cases the successively entering characters or groups of characters are marked off from each other by colons. Moreover, there are some later stage-directions, including some repetitions of entries already given.[2] On the theory the initial entries are taken from plots. These could of course provide them. It is not the case, however, that either the extant plots or the one extant part, that of Orlando, are without stage-directions other than entries; nor do the texts in question use the characteristic phrase 'to them' with which the plots link their entries. Professor Wilson uses three subsidiary arguments in support of assembling. One is the freedom of *Two Gentlemen of Verona* from textual difficulties, since a part must be made clear, even if the prompt-copy is confused; although he is not at a loss for an explanation when the text of *Merry Wives of Windsor* turns out to be far from lacking in textual difficulties. The text of Orlando's part is by no means always clear. The second is the printing of prose in capitalized lines of varying length, rather like verse, which is certainly curious, and which he thinks may have been a practice in writing out parts.[3] The third is the appearance of gag, or what Professor Wilson thinks may be gag, but whether gag would get into parts, and on the other hand would not get into prompt-copy, I am not sure. Professor Wilson also finds assembling in *As You Like It* and *Measure for Measure*, which have not grouped entries, but have a paucity of stage-directions,

---

[1] I am not sure that the entries in *Two Gent. of Ver.* iv. 2 and *Merry Wives of W.* v. 5 strictly follow the order of appearance.

[2] Rhodes, 99, gives the facts very inaccurately.

[3] Cf. p. 181.

and on special grounds in *Comedy of Errors* and *Merchant of Venice*.[1] There would be no substance in these cases, unless a practice of assembling could be better established elsewhere. I do not think that assembling is inconceivable, as a last resort for recovering a text, when no original or foul papers or transcript was available. But surely it would be a very laborious and difficult business. Cues, at any rate in *Orlando*, do not give the names of the speakers, and they often consist only of a word or two, which might occur at more than one speech-ending. All would perhaps go well in dialogue between a couple of speakers, but if many were concerned, the book-keeper would be confronted with a considerable puzzle, as he peered in search of the cue-words from one to another of half a dozen rolls or strips cut from rolls on the table before him. I should expect to find in a text so produced two kinds of error, of which examples have not in fact been brought forward. One would be a false sequence of speeches and another the accidental inclusion of cues in the following lines. An alternative explanation of the grouped entries is to be found, as pointed out by Dr. Greg, in the influence of the 'classical' method of scene-division adopted by Ben Jonson and some other playwrights. Here each new grouping of characters begins a new scene, and the names of the characters head it. Whether the adaptation of this arrangement to *Two Gentlemen of Verona* and *Merry Wives of Windsor* and in part to *Winter's Tale* was due, as Dr. Greg thinks, to a printer's devil, or to a freak of the author, must be matter for conjecture.[2]

The possibilities left open make it necessary to consider the origin of the printers' copy for each play as a separate problem, in the light of such literary, scenic, and bibliographical indications as it may yield. A summary treatment, inevitably based to a large extent on the work of others, is alone feasible in such a book as this, but in the upshot, some classification of the texts may be attempted.[3]

---

[1] Cf. ch. ix.
[2] Greg, *Merry Wives of W*. xvi; cf. p. 125 and *Eliz. Stage*, iii. 200.
[3] Cf. the discussions of individual plays in ch. ix.

An isolated group is formed by the corrupt editions of the early publishers, *2, 3 Henry VI* (the *Contention*), *Romeo and Juliet* (Q1), *Henry V*, *Hamlet* (Q1), *Merry Wives of Windsor*. Professor Pollard has conveniently designated these as 'Bad Quartos'. They differ in detail, and each presents features of special difficulty. But they have in common a measure of textual corruption, far beyond anything which a combination of bad transcription and bad printing could explain. Many passages are only intelligible in the light of the better texts which followed. There are constant omissions leaving *lacunae* in the sense, constant paraphrases, constant inversions of the order of sentences, and dislocations in the sequence of dialogue and episodes. The metre is bungled; verse lines are wrongly divided; prose is printed as verse and verse as prose. The diction betrays a substitution of synonyms or loose verbal equivalents or of variant inflections, for the wording intended by the author. The total effect is one of perversion and vulgarization. To emend is futile; it is incredible that Shakespeare should have written or the Chamberlain's men presented such texts.[1] It cannot be doubted that these are primarily the versions which Heminges and Condell stigmatized as 'surreptitious'. Whether a surreptitious origin is indicated by the circumstances of publication seems less clear. There was due registration of *2 Henry VI*, which may perhaps be taken to have covered *3 Henry VI*, and of *Merry Wives of Windsor* and *Hamlet*, but the transactions between stationers as to *Merry Wives of Windsor* and *Hamlet* look rather unusual, and copyright for *Romeo and Juliet* and *Henry V* was only established through transfers. The omission of the publisher's address from the imprint of *Romeo and Juliet* is also exceptional, but one can hardly suppose that the authorities would not know where to find Danter, and books whose promoters really feared pursuit were apt to bear such addresses as 'Middleburg' or 'ouersea in Europe', or to have no imprint at all.[2] Certain

---

[1] Hubbard's 'edition' of the Q1 of *Ham.* shows the futility.

[2] The 'at a place, not farre from a Place' of *An Almond for a Parrat* (Nashe, iii. 339) and the 'at the signe of the crab tree cudgell in thwack-coate lane' of *Pappe with an hatchet* (Lyly, iii. 393) are burlesques.

other features of some or all of the bad texts suggest that the copy for them was obtained, not by transcription from originals, but from stage performances by some process of reporting. There are errors which may be due to mishearing, although these are not unlike some which are made by printers and transcribers.[1] There are unmetrical ejaculations and connective words, such as actors introduce to accompany their gestures and demonstrate their indifference to the blank verse. There are bits of gag. The confusion tends to be greatest in bustling episodes or in the rapid interchange of dialogue between a number of speakers. In *Romeo and Juliet* and *Hamlet* there are stage-directions which look like the attempts of a spectator to describe the action seen on the stage. In *Hamlet*, conversely, bits of action seem to have been translated into dialogue. One naturally asks what kind of reporter can have been at work. A note-taker in the audience would almost inevitably have attracted attention. Moreover, there is one singular feature, apparent in all the texts except *Henry V*, which by itself seems to exclude such a note-taker. The dislocation of matter extends to the incorporation in scenes of phrases which really belong to earlier scenes or even to later scenes. A long interval may separate these from their rightful positions. Such 'anticipations and recollections' imply a reporter who has throughout some knowledge of the play as a whole, and point to a process, not of direct note-taking, but of reproduction from memory. The exhaustive analyses by Dr. Greg of *Merry Wives of Windsor* and of the analogous case of *Orlando Furioso* have explored the possibilities of memorization as a method of textual transmission, and have shown them to be fully equal to the production of such results as the bad Quartos exhibit.[2] Speculation remains open as to the status and identities of the reporters. Obviously the members of the company which had performed a play would have better opportunities of becoming roughly familiar with its course and wording than would

[1] Cf. p. 180.
[2] Albright, 311, gives parallels from

the practice of the seventeenth-century Spanish stage.

mere spectators, even after repeated visits. The precise method may not have been the same in all cases. Dr. Greg inclines to think that *Orlando* was collectively reported by a group of actors, each in his turn dictating his part, and that the primary object was to reproduce a lost prompt-copy, rather than to furnish material for the printers.[1] This theory implies conditions which could hardly apply to the Chamberlain's men's plays. Sometimes certain scenes are better reported than the rest and are linked by a common character, that of Marcellus in *Hamlet*, that of the Host in *Merry Wives of Windsor*. Naturally the actors of these characters have incurred suspicion of treachery. It is a hardly tenable view that it would be possible to prevent individual actors from obtaining, at performances or rehearsals, knowledge of scenes during which they were not themselves on the stage or waiting their calls at the stage-door. But no doubt they would be most successful in rendering dialogue in which they had shared. Where there is no such outstanding character, I have thought it possible that the reporter may have been a prompter. And in some cases there is reason to think that the help of a written 'part' (*3 Henry VI*; *Hamlet*) or of a 'plot' (*2, 3 Henry VI*) may have been available. A report does not, except perhaps in *Henry V*, wholly account for the differences between the bad and the good texts. The performances reported or later performances represented by a prompt-copy may have been subject to variations in scenic detail or by cuts. There have been changes in nomenclature of characters in *Hamlet* and *Merry Wives of Windsor*. A little rewriting of bits of *2, 3 Henry VI* is not unlikely. Most of the bad Quartos contain passages of non-Shakespearean verse which amount to rather more than the ordinary padding of the reporter. This has led to a theory that the texts underlying them were not the completed work of Shakespeare, but earlier versions

---

[1] Fynes Moryson (*Eliz. Stage*, i. 343) describes the travelling companies on the Continent as 'pronowncing peeces and patches of English playes'. L. B. Wright (*M.L.N.* xliii. 256) gives examples of plays reproduced from parts and memory for performance in the eighteenth century.

of the plays by other hands, only partially revised by him.[1]
There are, however, two other possibilities to be considered. In the first place, a lapse of memory may have
been remedied by sheer faking; and for this we need not
call in a hack playwright, since many actors, as Henslowe's
records show us, were capable of putting together a play
at need. In the second place, the vagrant memory of the
reporter did not stop short at its 'anticipations and recollections' of scenes of a play other than that under reproduction. It went so far as to bring in matter from alien plays.
This is clearly to be traced in 2 *Henry VI*, *Merry Wives of
Windsor*, and *Hamlet*, and in view of the number of plays
now lost with which every actor and book-keeper must
have been familiar, who shall say what limit is to be set
to borrowings of this nature? I do not know that it is
possible to say for what exact purpose the reporting of a
play was undertaken. The amount which a bookseller
would pay for 'copy' is not likely to have been very
tempting. Dr. Greg is, I believe, inclined to think that
the primary object was to enable a company to perform
a play, the 'book' of which they had parted with or
never possessed. But a company which performed a
play without having the allowance of the Master of the
Revels endorsed on the 'book' would be running a risk.[2]
I do not say that it was one which a provincial company
in straits would never take. Perhaps these were the 'peeces
and patches of English playes' performed abroad, and
were sold to the stationers when the companies came
home, as useless in this country.

The counter-theory to reporting from memorization is
reporting by shorthand. This art was in its infancy during
the sixteenth century. The first system since Roman
times appeared, after some private experiments of his own,
in Timothy Bright's *Characterie, an Arte of shorte, swift
and Secrete writing by Character* (1588).[3] It was a very
cumbrous one. Each letter had a symbol, but except in

[1] Cf. p. 226.
[2] *Eliz. Stage*, ii. 222.
[3] A reprint by J. H. Ford (1888) is
shown by Roloff to be inaccurate.

spelling out proper names, these were mainly used as parts of more complex symbols or 'characters', representing complete words. The characters were short bars, placed in various positions and modified at either end by angular or curved hooks. There were 570 of them, and to them corresponded a vocabulary of 570 words, the characters for which the scribe had to learn by heart. But a character might stand not only for a 'primitive' word, such as a noun, but also for its 'derivatives', such as verbs and adjectives, and for all inflexions both of the primitive and the derivatives. The discrimination was left to the intelligence of the note-taker and the transcriber, with the help in a few cases of diacritical marks in the form of one or more dots disposed around the characters. Further, a character might also stand, by what Bright called the 'consenting' or 'dissenting' method, either for an equivalent to its proper word or for a word of opposite sense; and in these cases the note-taker was expected to write the symbol for the initial letter of the word really intended to the right or left of the character, as the case might be. Finally, the student was instructed that unless the very express words were necessary, the sense only need be taken with the character; that is to say, he might omit words and employ paraphrases. It is clear that a use, and in particular a bungling use, of this system might produce some of the features of our bad texts; the paraphrases, the confusion of inflexions, above all the substituted equivalents. A diacritical mark is easily omitted, or neglected in transcription. It might explain the omission of out-of-the-way words, for which even the consenting and dissenting methods made no provision. It would not, unless the bungling was very exceptional, explain the numerous cases in which Bright's vocabulary gives a simple character for the right word and the reporter substitutes the wrong one. And it would not, any more than any other process of direct note-taking, explain the anticipations and recollections at all. A more subjective impression is that the system was altogether too cumbrous to be applied to anything so difficult as a play.

There are examples of its use in reporting sermons. But the regular, even if impassioned, utterance of a preacher, with the reporter sitting in a strategical position among a quiet audience, is one thing. The give and take of several speakers, in the hubbub of a theatre, complicated by the need for noting speech-prefixes and the fear of detection, is quite another. It is fair to admit that German students of stenography, on the other hand, believe that the thing could be done and was done, although I do not know whether they have put their view to the test of practical experiment.

Peter Bales in *The Writing Schoolmaster* (1590) and *The Arte of Brachygraphy* (1597) has a system very much like Bright's.[1] Something more workable seems to emerge in John Willis's *Art of Stenography* (1602). This is too late for any of the bad texts under discussion, but it is earlier than Heywood's complaint of 'stenography', or than any recorded allusion to 'brachygraphy' in the theatres.[2] Bright does not use either term. That there was at some time reporting of plays by some kind of shorthand we must take from Heywood. His *If You Know not Me, you Know Nobody*, is not a good text, but it is not as bad as the memorized bad texts of Shakespeare. Possibly the method of Willis was fairly efficient. It has not, so far as I know, yet received the expert examination in relation to play-texts which has been devoted to that of Bright. Professor Pollard suggests that the recovered scene of *Richard II*, as it appears, badly mislined and showing *lacunae*, in the Q3 of 1608, may be due to shorthand.[3] This may very possibly also be a factor in *King Lear* (1608) and *Pericles* (1609). Both have long continuous passages of verse printed as prose, and in *King Lear* these, although

---

[1] I have not seen his *New Years Gift for England. The Art of New Brachygraphy* (1600). The only copy is in the Bibliothèque Nationale.

[2] Sir G. Buck, *Third Vniversitie of England* (1612), 'They which know it [brachygraphy] can readily take a Sermon, Oration, Play, or any long speech, as they are spoke, dictated, acted and uttered in the instant.' It is a trial and not a play that is in question in Webster, *The Devil's Law Case* (c. 1620), iv. 2. 28, 'Doe you heare, Officers? You must take speciall care, that you let in no Brachigraphy men, to take notes.' For Heywood, cf. p. 147.

[3] Pollard, *Rich. II*, 64.

fairly adequate textually, are almost entirely punctuated by commas. They look to me like the result of shorthand notes well taken, but not properly worked upon at the stage of transcription. Punctuation and metre are of course always the weak points of a report. It is perhaps relevant that all these texts are very much of the date of Heywood's complaint.

There are fourteen plays for which we have parallel Quarto and Folio texts. They include at least two, *Romeo and Juliet* and *Hamlet*, for which the Quartos had replaced reported ones. *Love's Labour's Lost* may be a third. All the fourteen Quartos may reasonably claim Professor Pollard's epithet 'Good', in contradistinction to the six admittedly 'Bad' ones. They are not all of equal merit, and Heminges and Condell would probably have claimed that *Troilus and Cressida* and *King Lear*, if not also *Othello*, fell within the category of 'stolne and surreptitious' texts. There is no reason to suppose that the eleven others were not issued with the assent of the company. It is the existence of parallel texts in these fourteen cases which gives us our closest insight into the nature of the copy which reached the printers. I discuss the relations of the texts in chapter ix, so far as is possible within the limits of brief disquisitions and without the opportunities for tabulation and illustration which an editing of the plays would afford. Here I can only set out summary conclusions. Of the fourteen Quartos, I take *King Lear* to rest upon a report, *Richard III* upon a theatrical transcript of a cut version, and *Troilus and Cressida* and *Othello* also upon transcripts, which may, however, have been made for private collectors, and not for stage purposes. *Othello*, but not *Troilus and Cressida*, again represents a cut version. *Love's Labour's Lost* and *Romeo and Juliet* may rest in the main on originals, but it is possible that the former and probable that the latter was in part set up on a corrected example of a bad Quarto, and if so, an element of transcription is involved. The text of *Romeo and Juliet* is not good enough to exclude the possibility of more extensive transcription. The other eight may all be from originals. *Titus Androni-*

cus is not very likely to have been in Shakespeare's hand throughout. The rest—*Richard II, 1, 2 Henry IV, Midsummer-Night's Dream, Merchant of Venice, Much Ado About Nothing, Hamlet*—all might have been. I do not think that it is possible to say more than this in any case. The probability is highest for *Hamlet*, since the Q version shows no signs of adaptation for the stage, and it is therefore difficult to see why a transcript, at any rate for theatrical purposes, should ever have been made. Stage-directions of the type which suggest an author's hand might of course be preserved by a transcriber.[1] So too, although with less justification, might duplications of matter, such as we find in *Love's Labour's Lost* and *Romeo and Juliet*, as well as in *Midsummer-Night's Dream*. Nor can I attach much importance to the presence of abnormal spellings, analogous to those in the part of *Sir Thomas More* claimed for Shakespeare. These, too, might survive a transcriber, since *ex hypothesi* they must have survived a compositor. Could we be sure that Shakespeare's hand is in *Sir Thomas More*, the recurrence of the spellings in some of the Quartos would be consistent with his hand being also in the copy for these. It would not be proof, for we could not in any event take it for granted that he had a monopoly of such spellings. At the same time, we know that originals, as well as transcripts, were used for stage 'books'; and there is no reason to assume that transcripts were made without need.[2] *Hamlet* is apart, but although all the other six texts in question bear the evidence of intrusive actor-names or of cuts and other stage alterations, that their manuscripts had been used as prompt copies, there is nothing which could not be provided for on the originals, at the most with the help of an additional leaf for *Midsummer-Night's Dream* and an appended slip for *Merchant of Venice*. Transcripts, for anything that we can trace, would be quite superfluous.

From a comparison of the fourteen Good Quarto texts with their Folio counterparts two generalizations emerge. The first is that, in spite of the apparent wholesale re-

[1] Cf. pp. 118, 201.   [2] Cf. pp. 124, 151.

pudiation of the Quartos by Heminges and Condell, nearly all the Folio texts were in fact set up from examples of the Quartos. As a rule, the Quarto used was the latest that had been issued. The evidence for this consists partly in a general resemblance of orthographical and typographical detail, and partly in the repetition of obvious errors. It is at its strongest where the errors have been introduced in Quartos later than the first. It is less conclusive where there is only one Quarto, and a possibility remains that the common errors may derive from a common manuscript source. It has indeed been doubted whether Quartos were used for *2 Henry IV* and *Troilus and Cressida*, although I think that in *Troilus and Cressida* the argument from general resemblance is strong. The only certain exceptions are *Othello* and *Hamlet*. The Quarto (1622) of *Othello* indeed may hardly have been in existence when the copy for the Folio was prepared. Here the texts are independent, but clearly represent the same original, with cuts in the Quarto and accidental omissions in the Folio. In *Hamlet*, on the other hand, the Folio gives a cut version, in which theatrical alterations have been made. The second generalization is that most and probably all of the reprinted texts have undergone some modification beyond what can be attributed to the compositors. Even where there is no general textual divergence, there is theatrical alteration. Passages are cut or added; stage-directions and speech-prefixes are revised; actor-names, which must be due to the bookkeeper, make their appearance.[1] Invariably there seems to be some elimination, often very slight, of profanity, as a result of the *Act of Abuses* of 1606. I shall discuss this later on, and give reasons for supposing that its objective was theatrical rather than literary.[2] The total amount of departure from the Quarto basis varies considerably. There is very little in *Romeo and Juliet*, *Love's Labour's Lost*, *Midsummer-Night's Dream*, *Merchant of Venice*, *Much Ado About Nothing*, and *1 Henry IV*, and in these it may be regarded as wholly theatrical. To *Titus Andronicus* a whole

[1] Cf. p. 122.   [2] Cf. p. 238.

scene, possibly of late origin, has been added. In *Richard II* cuts have been restored and the scene which was recovered by a bungling reporter for Q4 is regularly printed. But in this play textual differences also begin to occur. There is a reversion to some readings of Q1 departed from by its successors. The changes in *2 Henry IV* also include the restoration of cuts, but although numerous, they are again mainly theatrical. Textual divergence, however, is persistent in *Richard III*, *Troilus and Cressida*, and *King Lear*, in all of which we get independent versions of a common original, analogous to those of *Othello*. In these cases at least we must assume that the Quarto used as a basis was altered from a theatrical manuscript which was regarded as authoritative. It does not, of course, follow that the alteration was always complete and accurate. The question arises as to whether the Quartos used for the Folio had been specially prepared to provide its copy, or had been originally altered for use as prompt-copies. Dr. Greg pertinently asks for more evidence that printed texts were ever, in ordinary circumstances, so used. I know of none, although a closer acquaintance than mine with late Jacobean and Caroline stage-history might perhaps furnish it. It is obvious that the substitution of a print for a manuscript would mean a gain in legibility for the book-keeper. But if this were the motive, one would expect an early Quarto, rather than a late one, to be used. Moreover, while the book-keeper's own alterations for revivals could as easily be made on a print as on a manuscript, the gain in legibility would largely disappear if such substantial variants as we find in *Richard III*, *Troilus and Cressida*, and *King Lear* had to be incorporated. Other probabilities are rather conflicting. On the one hand, it is difficult to see why a transcriber, deliberately preparing a Quarto for the press, should take in those actor-names which a compositor might very easily preserve through inadvertence, if he found them in a prompt-copy. On the other, the sporadic nature of the elimination of profanity is rather inexplicable on the assumption that the texts were primarily meant for theatrical purposes. I must leave it at that.

There is less to be said about the eighteen plays for which the only texts are in the Folio, and the four for which the only alternative is a bad Quarto. There is no obvious reason why most of them should not have been set up from originals. That of *1 Henry VI* is not likely to have been for the most part in Shakespeare's hand. Both this and *2, 3 Henry VI* may contain some scenes of comparatively late date. There are probably some theatrical interpolations in *As You Like It* and *Cymbeline*, and perhaps *Tempest*, and both interpolations and cuts in *Macbeth*. An original ending may have gone from *Taming of the Shrew*. On the other hand, I do not suppose that *Timon of Athens* was ever staged. The known history of *Winter's Tale* makes it likely that it was printed from a transcript, and this is confirmed by some typographical features. The badness of the text in *Measure for Measure* and *All's Well* suggests that here too transcripts may have intervened. I have already considered the theories which ascribe *Winter's Tale*, *Two Gentlemen of Verona*, and *Merry Wives of Windsor* to 'assembling'. The plausibility is greatest in the case of *Two Gentlemen of Verona*.[1]

We come back to the claim of Heminges and Condell and the Folio publishers to have given the plays 'according to the True Originall Copies' and 'absolute in their numbers, as he conceiued them'. It is clear that this cannot be quite literally pressed. It may reasonably be admitted that genuine pains were taken, according to the standard of the times, to secure reliable texts. The bad Quartos were quite properly disregarded. The labour spent on glossing good Quartos from manuscripts must have been considerable. We could wish that First Quartos and not later ones had been chosen, but perhaps Heminges and Condell were not so familiar as we are with the progressive deterioration of successive reprints. Doubtless the use of transcripts was sometimes inevitable; we know that the original of *Winter's Tale* was lost. Perhaps we could hardly expect that interpolations should have been removed; still less that they should have been placed in

[1] Cf. pp. 153, 329.

square brackets. Some hint might have been given of the occasional presence of non-Shakespearean scenes. A fuller text of *Macbeth* would have been welcome; that of *Romeo and Juliet* could probably have been improved. Something must have gone wrong with the directions for the treatment of cuts, as a result of which *Richard II* and *King Lear* show *lacunae* in the Folio which are not in the corresponding Quartos. The greatest lapse is of course the complete failure to make any use of the full Second Quarto of *Hamlet*.

CHAPTER VI

PLAYS IN THE PRINTING-HOUSE

[*Bibliographical Note*. Much of the writing on Shakespeare's publishers (cf. *Bibl. Note* to ch. v) deals also with his printers. R. B. McKerrow, *An Introduction to Bibliography for Literary Students* (1927), gives an admirable survey of Elizabethan printing-house methods. Special studies by the same writer are *The Use of the Galley in Elizabethan Printing* (1921, 4 *Library*, ii. 97) and *Elizabethan Printers and the Composition of Reprints* (1925, 4 *Library*, v. 357). Other valuable dissertations are B. A. P. van Dam and C. Stoffel, *Chapters on English Printing, Prosody and Pronunciation* (1902); W. W. Greg, *The First Edition of Ben Jonson's E.M.O.* (1920, 4 *Library*, i. 153), *An Elizabethan Printer and his Copy* (1923, 4 *Library*, iv. 102), *Massinger's Autograph Corrections* (1923, 1924, 4 *Library*, iv. 207; v. 59), *The Riddle of Jonson's Chronology* (1926, 4 *Library*, vi. 340), and P. Simpson, *Proof-Reading by English Authors of the Sixteenth and Seventeenth Centuries* (1928, *Proc. Oxford Bibl. Soc.* ii. 5).

The special problems of the relation of Shakespearean texts to Shakespearean 'copy' are dealt with by A. W. Pollard, *King Richard II. A New Quarto* (1916); in the discussions of *Sir Thomas More* (cf. p. 499); by J. D. Wilson in the *Textual Introduction* (1921) to *Temp.* (*New Shakespeare*) and *Spellings and Misprints in Q2 of Ham.* (1924, *Essays and Studies*, x. 36); and by W. Blades, *Common Typographical Errors, with especial Reference to the Text of Shakespeare* (1872, Jan. 27, *Athenæum*); B. A. P. van Dam, *William Sh.: Prosody and Text* (1900), *The Text of Sh.'s Ham.* (1924), *Textual Criticism of Sh.'s Plays* (1925, *English Studies*, vi. 97); L. Kellner, *Restoring Sh.* (1925), on which W. W. Greg's review (*R.E.S.* i. 463) should be read.

Useful works of general reference are E. A. Abbott, *A Shn. Grammar* (1869); W. Viëtor, *Sh.'s Pronunciation* (1906); W. Franz, *Sh.-Grammatik* (3rd ed. 1924); H. C. Wyld, *History of Modern Colloquial English* (3rd ed. 1925). Elizabethan script is analysed in the books on *S.T.M.* and in that of Kellner, and by H. Jenkinson, *English Current Writing and Early Printing* (1915, *Bibl. Soc. Trans.* xiii. 273), *The Later Court Hands in England* (1927); M. St. C. Byrne, *Elizabethan Handwriting for Beginners* (1925, *R.E.S.* i. 198); R. B. McKerrow, *The Capital Letters in Elizabethan Handwriting* (1927, *R.E.S.* iii. 28). W. W. Greg's *English Literary Autographs* (1925, 1928, in progress) give examples of many Elizabethan hands. On Orthography are A. Lummert, *Die Orthographie der F1 der Shn. Dramen* (1883); T. Satchell, *The Spelling of F1* (1920, June 3, *T.L.S.*); A. W. Pollard, *The Variant Settings in 2 Hen. IV and their Spellings* (1920, Oct. 21, *T.L.S.*), *Elizabethan Spelling as a Literary and Bibliographical Clue* (1923, 4 *Library*, iv. 1); M. St. C. Byrne, *A. Munday's Spelling as a Literary Clue* (1923, 4 *Library*, iv. 9), *Thomas Churchyard's Spelling* (1924, 4 *Library*, v. 243);

W. Marschall, *Shs Orthographie* (1927, *Anglia*, li. 307). On Elisions
are W. E. Farnham, *Colloquial Contractions in Beaumont, Fletcher,
Massinger and Sh. as a Test of Authorship* (1916, *P.M.L.A.* xxxi.
326); J. D. Wilson, *A Note on Elisions in the Faerie Queene* (1920,
M.L.R. xv. 409). M. A. Bayfield, *A Study of Shakespeare's Versification*
(1920), represents an extreme theory as to the treatment of elisions by the
printers, which may be compared with that equally extreme in Van Dam's
writings. A correspondence on the subject is in *T.L.S.* (1920, Sept.–Dec.).
On Punctuation are P. Simpson, *Shn. Punctuation* (1911); R. M. Alden,
The Punctuation of Sh.'s Printers (1924, *P.M.L.A.* xxxix. 557); C. C.
Fries, *Shn. Punctuation* (1925, *Michigan Studies in Sh., Milton and
Donne*); H. Jenkinson, *Notes on the Study of English Punctuation of the
Sixteenth Century* (1926, *R.E.S.* ii. 152); J. Isaacs, *A Note on Dramatic
Punctuation* (1926, *R.E.S.* ii. 461); E. M. Simpson, *A Note on Donne's
Punctuation* (1928, *R.E.S.* iv. 295). The structure of Acts and Scenes is
discussed by T. S. Graves, *The Act-Time in Elizabethan Theatres* (1915,
S.P. xii. 103); M. Hunter, *Act- and Scene-Division in the Plays of Sh.*
(1926, *R.E.S.* ii. 295); J. D. Wilson, *Act- and Scene-Divisions in the Plays
of Sh.* (1927, *R.E.S.* iii. 385), *They Sleepe all the Act* (1928, *R.E.S.* iv.
191); W. J. Lawrence, *Act-Intervals in Early Shn. Performances* (1928,
R.E.S. iv. 78); W. W. Greg, *Act-Divisions in Sh.* (1928, *R.E.S.* iv. 152).]

THE printers of Shakespeare's plays, other than Danter,
Roberts, and the Jaggards, may be taken to have been employed by the publishers who owned the copyrights. Of
those concerned with the first editions, the most prominent
are Valentine Simmes, who did *Richard II, Richard III,
2 Henry IV, Much Ado About Nothing,* and the bad
Hamlet, and Thomas Creede, who did the bad *2, 3
Henry VI, Henry V,* and *Merry Wives of Windsor,* and the
good Q2 of *Romeo and Juliet.* William White did *Love's
Labour's Lost* and *Pericles,* Peter Short did *1 Henry IV,*
George Eld *Troilus and Cressida,* and Nicholas Okes
Othello. The printers of three plays are not named on the
title-pages, and can only be guessed at on the doubtful
evidence of the ornaments used. The bad *Hamlet* is thus
assigned to Simmes and *King Lear* to Okes or to George and
Lionel Snowden whose business he acquired about 1608.
Midsummer-Night's Dream remains doubtful. The orna-
ments suggest Richard Bradock rather than Roberts, but
Edward Allde is also a possibility.[1] The best work is that

---

[1] Cf. p. 356. The ornaments recur
in the editions of Marlowe's *Ed
ward II,* printed by Bradock, but
a printer's ornaments are not so distinctive as his 'devices'.

of Simmes, the worst that of Eld. Simmes, who was often in trouble for trade disorders, had been an apprentice to Henry Bynneman, a good printer according to Elizabethan standards, which were not high. Creede put good workmanship into some of his books, but his plays are nothing to boast of. One would gladly know more of these men and of their journeymen and apprentices, on whose equipment of intelligence, experience, sobriety, and attention much of the quality of Shakespearean texts depends. A practice of dividing work between different printing-houses does not seem to have affected the Quartos, except possibly Q1 of *Romeo and Juliet*, where the character of the setting-up changes half-way through the play.[1]

The technique of Elizabethan printing has been carefully studied by Dr. McKerrow, who finds that there was little advance in essentials between 1500 and 1800, and is able therefore to draw upon the descriptions in Joseph Moxon's *Mechanick Exercises* (1683). The main points from Dr. McKerrow's lucid and detailed account will serve as preliminary to a consideration of printing-house errors. It is necessary to distinguish between the functions of the compositor, the pressman, and the corrector. These may not, indeed, in a small establishment, have been separate individuals. In particular, although the earlier printers, especially those concerned with classical texts, employed competent scholars as correctors, it may be suspected that pamphlets and plays often had no supervisor but the master-printer himself. Irregularities in the make-up of a book may sometimes be due to the concurrent employment of more than one compositor or pressman on different parts of it.[2] Probably there was little preliminary examination to ensure that the copy for the Quartos was complete and in order. It was handed, with directions as to the size of paper and type required, to the compositor, who fixed it in a stand on the desk or table at which he worked. A theory that it was dictated to him is now

---

[1] Cf. p. 339.   [2] McKerrow 128; cf. pp. 141, 339.

generally abandoned.[1] There is little support for it, beyond a tradition first recorded in the eighteenth century,
that the practice, which would have been both incon-
venient and expensive, was followed at Basle, and a few
very singular 'auditory' errors, of which one or two suggest the incorporation of guttural noises or instructions
coming from a reader. It is of course possible that dictation may have occasionally been resorted to when the light
was bad. Before the compositor were also ranged trays or
'cases', divided into compartments to hold the types.
These were separately cast on metal bodies, with the
letters or other symbols in relief on their upper faces.
Moxon shows a pair of cases, as used together in his time.
The lower case holds the small letters, with the odd exception of 'k', the punctuation marks, and the 'spaces', which
had no reliefs; and the sizes of its main compartments are
varied in proportion to the frequency with which each
type is likely to be needed. The upper case, sloped at an
angle above the lower one, holds the capitals, the numerals,
and the more rarely used symbols. An Elizabethan
printer, however, made considerable use of italic type, and
either the arrangement of his cases must have been somewhat different to Moxon's, or he must have had access to
additional ones for this purpose. In his left hand the
compositor held the 'composing-stick', a short tray capable
of holding six or eight lines of type, and adjustable to the
required length of line. He memorized a line or so of
matter from the copy before him, and with his right hand
picked out the types from the cases in due order, and
transferred them to the stick, putting the faces upside-
down, since the outlines of the reliefs would be reversed
in printing-off. Between the words he set spaces. If his
matter did not fit a line, he 'justified' it by varying the
width of the spaces, but for this he had less need than
a modern compositor, since he could also modify the
spelling.[2] When the stick was full, he slipped the contents
into a larger tray or 'galley', which held just sufficient type

---

[1] McKerrow 241; Pollard, *Rich. II*, 34; Albright 326.   [2] Cf. p. 186.

for a page, and when this was full, he laid it aside for the pressman.

At the stage of actual printing, the page-blocks of type were removed from the galleys, and placed in frames or 'chases', each of which took enough pages to occupy one side of a sheet of paper. These constituted a 'forme'. There was an outer forme for one side of the sheet, and an inner forme for the other, and the blocks were so arranged that, when the sheet was folded, the pages would follow each other in the proper order. Plays had not, as a rule, pagination numbers, but a clue to the order was provided by setting-up the first word of each page as a 'catchword' at the foot of that preceding it. Similarly the first page of each sheet bore a letter at the foot as a 'signature', and the signatures ran in an alphabetical series. If four blocks of type were printed on each side of a sheet and it was folded twice it became a 'quarto' sheet of four leaves and eight pages. The signatures of a quarto were generally repeated with differentiating numbers on the first pages of the second and third leaves. An 'octavo' sheet was folded three times and had eight leaves and sixteen pages.[1] A 'folio' sheet was folded once only and had two leaves and four pages. But folio sheets were generally placed within each other in 'gatherings' of three sheets, six leaves and twelve pages. The first three leaves of such a gathering had a common signature letter, with a differentiating number. The chase was packed between the blocks of type with larger spaces or 'furniture', corresponding to the margins of the pages when the sheet was folded, and firmly 'locked up' by wedges or 'quoins'. It was then placed on the bed of the press. This slid backwards and forwards, and to its front was hinged a frame or 'tympan', holding two sheets of parchment with padding between them, on which the sheet of paper to be printed was laid. The type was inked with pads or 'balls' of cotton or hair covered with leather and fixed at the ends of short sticks. The ink did not reach the small spaces, but as it inevitably got upon the furniture of the chase, a

---

[1] The Q1 of *3 Hen. VI*, although classed with the Quartos, is really an Octavo.

second frame or 'frisket', hinged in its turn to the free
end of the tympan, held a protective sheet of paper, in
which rectangular spaces, corresponding to the positions
of the blocks of type, had been cut. The frisket was
turned over the sheet on the tympan, and both frisket and
tympan were turned over the chase. The bed of the press
was then slid back under a screw, which brought down
over tympan, frisket, paper, and chase a heavy wooden
board or platen, and effected an impression of the inked
type on the paper. Each sheet, of course, required two
impressions, one for each side, before it could be folded,
and had to be laid across a string to dry between them.
All the copies of each sheet were printed on one side,
before the other side was taken in hand. When the printing was complete, the type was 'distributed', probably by
the compositor, who put a few lines into his left hand, took
out a word or two at a time in his right, read them, shook
the types apart, and dropped them into their compartments in the cases.

Press-correction must often have been a very casual
business. There is plenty of evidence that authors could,
as now, see 'proofs', and even for the use, by the Jaggards
and others, of 'reviewes', or as we call them 'revises'.[1]
The modern slip-proofs, specially printed in 'long' galleys,
had not, however, come into use, and what the author got
would be an ordinary sheet, in which, if one side only had
yet been printed, the pages would not be continuous. As
a rule authors seem to have been expected to visit the
printing-house daily, for the purpose of making their corrections; and they sometimes apologize for errors, on the
ground that they could not do this. But there are cases
in which proofs were sent out by messenger. Jonson, no
doubt, saw proofs. There is nothing to indicate that
Shakespeare did, and in view of the number and character
of the errors in the Quartos, it is unlikely. Nor can we
suppose that, even if the copy was supplied rather by his
company than by himself, any other member of it took the

---

[1] McKerrow 65, 205; Albright 348; P. Simpson in *Trans. Oxford Bibl. Soc.* ii (1928), 5.

responsibility. Whether the Folio had any editor is a rather more complicated question.[1] Failing an author to 'oversee' the work, all rested with the press-corrector, and his operations were often perfunctory. Presumably he ought to have read the proof with the copy, or had the latter read to him, as was the practice in Moxon's day. But frequent erroneous corrections show that, even in reprints, he was apt to proceed by guess-work. Nor does it seem that printing-off was suspended until the proof had been considered. Different examples of the same edition of a play often exhibit variant readings. Occasionally this may be due to the accidental displacement and wrong replacement of type.[2] But many variants can only be explained on the assumption that corrections were made at a late stage, and that the incorrect sheets already printed were not scrapped, but used indiscriminately with the corrected ones when the book was put together. Different examples, therefore, may contain incorrect and corrected sheets in various combinations, and indeed one side of a sheet may have been corrected and not the other. This makes the work of a modern editor extremely arduous.

The title-page and other preliminaries, such as epistles by an author or publisher, were generally printed, at any rate in first editions, after the body of the book. The 'A' signatures might be reserved for them, or special signatures, such as asterisks, used. The title-page itself does not bear a signature. It is of the nature of an advertisement, and separate copies were struck off as hand-bills. Nashe complains that his *Pierce Penniless* bore a 'tedious Mountebanks Oration to the Reader'.[3] Title-pages were probably prepared in the printing-house. This accounts for the frequent laudatory terms and the elaborate descriptive titles, which are not always accurate. The Welsh parson of *Merry Wives of Windsor* appears as 'Syr Hugh the Welch Knight', and the Marina of *Pericles* as Mariana. The author's own wording is more likely to be found in a head-title at the beginning of the text. Advertisement

[1] Cf. p. 198.   [2] Cf. p. 176.   [3] *Works* (ed. McKerrow), i. 153.

may also be traced in the mention of court performances
(*Love's Labour's Lost*, *King Lear*), and in the claims, sometimes but not always justified, of reprints to be 'corrected'
or 'augmented'. The engraved emblematic or other 'device'
of the printer or publisher or some ornamental design
often follows the title. At the foot of the title-page is the
'imprint', which generally gives the name of the printer,
of the publisher 'for' whom the book was printed, if distinct from the printer, and the publisher's address. Sometimes the printer's name is omitted, or only indicated by
initials. And sometimes the address is that of a stationer,
who had not himself financed the book, but was selling it
on commission.[1] Imprints may show variants when two
stationers were publishing jointly. In early books the
imprint was at the end of the text in a 'colophon', but
colophons are rare in plays.[2] To the imprint is usually
appended the date of publication. Dr. Greg thinks that
plays were dated according to the calendar year beginning
on January 1, and not according to the year beginning on
March 25, which was generally followed both in private
letters and in official documents, including the *Stationers'
Register*.[3] A second 'issue' of an edition, from the original
stock of sheets, may have a new title-page on an inserted
leaf or 'cancel' replacing the old one, and a serious error
in the text, discovered late, may be similarly corrected.[4]
It is uncertain whether, after printing, copy was restored
to the owner, or destroyed as printing-house waste. If
the Chamberlain's men sent their 'allowed' copies to the
printers, they must, one thinks, have recovered them for
their own protection in case of a revival. Only two bits
of used copy are known, and they are not plays. One is
a fragment of Hooker's *Ecclesiastical Polity* (1597), printed
by John Windet. It has author's corrections, which have
been observed in the print, although additional ones seem
afterwards to have been made.[5] The other is the greater

---

[1] W. W. Greg in *Studies*, 130.

[2] McKerrow 95.

[3] *Studies*, 154, and *The Riddle of Jonson's Chronology* (1926, 4 *Library*, vi. 340).

[4] Cf. pp. 349, 380, 438.

[5] *Bodl. Addl. MS.* C. 165; cf. P. Simpson (*Oxford Bibl. Soc. Trans.* ii. 20).

part of Sir John Harington's translation (1591) of Ariosto's *Orlando Furioso*, printed by Richard Field.[1] Here also the print shows that the author made many alterations in proof. There are some special directions to the printer on the copy, and the printer himself has added symbols indicating where fresh pages should begin, and in one case where a particular ornament should be inserted. Such supervision is likely to have been more careful in Field's office than in those of inferior printers. This manuscript was probably returned to the author, many of whose papers are preserved.

The errors of printers must be looked at both qualitatively and quantitatively. The causes of misprints are various. Some may be called mechanical, some psychological. Mechanical errors may arise at several stages. Type may drop out of the stick or an ill-locked chase, or be pulled out by the inking balls, and be put back in the wrong order, even if loose type lying on the floor is not picked up instead. The paper on the frisket may be unevenly cut or may shift, and prevent the type at the ends of lines from printing. A space-type may project and leave an impression. A letter may be badly cast or broken, and its impression may look like that of some other letter. Thus a broken 'e' may be indistinguishable from a 'c'. But the most prolific source of mechanical error is what is known as 'foul case'; that is, the presence of types in the wrong compartment, either because they have slipped from an overfull compartment into that below it, or more usually because they have been wrongly distributed. Many 'literal' misprints, which make no sense, may have this origin. Whether the very common but not textually important substitution of a 'turned n' for a 'u' or vice versa is due to foul case seems doubtful.[2]

Most misprints, however, are psychological, and arise during composition, which must be taken to include the subsequent carrying out of corrections. They may be

---

[1] *B.M. Addl. MS.* 18920; cf. W. W. Greg, *An Elizabethan Printer and his Copy* (1923, 4 *Library*, iv. 102).

[2] McKerrow 255; Greg in *R.E.S* i. 466.

further classified as due to failures either of vision, or of attention, or of memory, or of automatism, or of judgement. The classification is a rough one, since human faculties are not isolated. In particular, want of attention is to some extent a factor in all misprints, and may itself be the result either of stupidity or carelessness or self-confidence or haste or fatigue or drink or talkativeness or absorption in alien ideas. Similar misprints may result from different causes, and further many errors such as compositors make are also made by transcribers, and some even by authors in writing down their thoughts, so that, especially when transcription may have intervened, it is not always possible to be sure where the fault lies. The methods of transcribers have not been so closely investigated as those of printers. The manuscript of Alleyn's part of Orlando shows an example of careful transcription for the theatre.[1] But one may perhaps assume that a transcriber would often be less of a trained expert than a compositor, and would be more likely to alter passages which he found difficult to read or understand.[2]

A failure of vision means, of course, a misreading of the copy. Professor Wilson tells us:

It is a cardinal principle of critical bibliography that when anything is wrong with the text, the blame should be laid rather on the 'copy' than on the compositor.[3]

It may be doubted whether critical bibliography has any cardinal principle, other than the obvious one that every effect has a cause, and that the distribution of ink-marks on pieces of paper is no exception to the rule. However that may be, there are certainly competent bibliographers who do not accept Professor Wilson's principle. Thus Professor Pollard writes of

the ease with which errors were introduced in the process of printing and the extreme danger of assuming that the faultiness of a printed text involves a corresponding faultiness in the manuscript which it follows.[4]

[1] Greg, *Abridgements*, 271.   [3] Wilson, *Temp*. xl.
[2] Cf. pp. 440, 460.   [4] Pollard, *Rich. II*, 38.

And Dr. Greg says:

It must now be abundantly evident that other causes besides misreading are at work in the production of misprints; indeed, that these other causes are probably more widely operative than errors of the eye. Nothing could in fact be more misleading than the dogma that 'Misprints must be accounted for by the Handwriting'.[1]

The antithesis of 'copy' and 'compositor' is, indeed, in itself misleading; what we are concerned with is the relation between the compositor and his copy. But the manuscripts described in chapter iv are as a rule well written, and it is reasonable to suppose that, in Elizabethan times as now, the best workmen were set to handle the most difficult material. Moreover, there are abundant errors in reprints, where the complications of manuscript copy had not to be faced. Nevertheless failure of vision is a factor in misprinting, and Professor Wilson has furnished valuable analyses of the types of 'literal' error to which it might lead. His basis is primarily the hand of D in *Sir Thomas More*, and this, whether Shakespeare's or not, is at any rate a very normal Elizabethan hand, not unlike his, and at the same time such as any transcriber might employ. We have to envisage an 'English' hand, in which most of the letter-forms differed from those of the 'Italian' hands now followed, which were then only just beginning to come into popular use. Some intermixture of Italian forms there may have been, and some differentiation, probably very incomplete, of foreign words, proper names, speech-prefixes, and perhaps stage-directions by Italian script.[2] Normally an italic fount of type provides a corresponding differentiation in print. The use of capitals for the word 'God' in *Merchant of Venice* (Qq), ii. 2. 75, is exceptional. Abnormal spellings in the copy might lead to misunderstanding.[3] Or again it might show contracted forms, although these do not seem very frequent in theatrical manuscripts.[4] A 'p', with a loop to indicate the omission of letters, is easily misread, and a ę looks much like an 'e', although it

<hr>

[1] *R.E.S.* i. 472.   [2] Cf. p. 113.   [3] Cf. p. 187.   [4] Cf. p. 113.

stands for 's' or 'es'. The commonest confusions in reproducing an 'English' hand are due to the similarities
between 'e' and 'd', between 'e' and 'o', between 'a' and
'o', between 'c' and 't', and among 'm', 'n', 'u', 'w', 'c',
'r', 'i' (if undotted), and a particular form of 'a', all of which
are or, unless very carefully formed, may be constructed
of short downward strokes or 'minims'. It is clear, however, from Professor Kellner's tables of misprints that
there may be transmutation between almost any pair of
letters, even where the production of a veritable word
seems to exclude the probability of a cause, such as 'foul
case', alternative to an error of vision. Obviously, long-
tailed and long-stemmed letters are only likely to replace
others with similar features. But letters, individually distinct, may none the less be confused when they appear in
combination. Many misprints involve more than one
wrong letter within the same word; an initial error once
made often tends to persist and to help in the misinter-
pretation of its context. Beyond this, an inexperienced
reader of manuscript will get a word wrong, by contenting
himself with a mere general impression of it, without
following the outlines of the letters at all. Possibly a tired
or careless compositor might do the same, although it
would be contrary to his training. It is a blunder which
one would rather expect from a transcriber. Failure of
vision may also be responsible for the misdividing of
words. A word is split into two, or two words are merged
in one. Of course the 'hand' of a manuscript is often a
contributing factor in visual errors. A writer may easily
degrade the rather elaborate forms of the 'English' letters.
Concave and convex curves may not be properly discriminated. The 'i's may be undotted. Tops of letters
which should be closed may be left open. The minims
may be superfluous or deficient. The spacing may be bad.
Linking strokes may be made between words, or omitted
between the letters of words.

   Failures of attention cause many errors. The compositor, misled perhaps by the recurrence of the same
word at the ends of neighbouring lines or clauses, starts

at the wrong point in memorizing a bit of copy, and leaves out a line or even a considerable passage. The parallel texts reveal some serious mutilations of this nature.[1] On the other hand, cancelled matter, such as a duplicate version, is sometimes inserted, through the neglect of a deletion mark.[2] Single words and letters are often omitted. When this is due to overlooking a repetition of them in the copy, it is called haplography. Words and letters are also unduly repeated, and that is called dittography. A whole line may be repeated, perhaps at the turn of a page. The order of letters, words, and lines may be dislocated, either through an initial error or through a careless attempt to correct one.

Some of the most subtle and baffling misprints probably arise from failures of memory. The compositor reads more of his copy at once than his memory is able to carry, and reproduces it inaccurately. Thus, too, transpositions may occur. Prefixes and word-endings get altered. Much more considerable perversions may take place. The subconscious mind, through some association, substitutes for the right word an equivalent word, or even a contrasting word. If the compositor's apprehension of read matter works through auditory rather than visual representations, the substituted word may be one similar, not in sense, but in sound. Such results are much like those which the loose memories of actors and reporters also yield.[3] Or again, a past word, just leaving the threshold of consciousness, may be echoed, or a coming word, just entering it, may be anticipated. Authors themselves are very prone in writing to the same trick. Parallel texts often reveal the existence of memory errors; in the absence of these they may well remain 'cruces'. The human mind is a fallible instrument. There is further a kind of muscular memory due to habit. The compositor's reaching out for type becomes automatic. If he is tired, the automatism may fail, and he may take a type from the wrong compartment. Here is a third origin, besides foul case and the confusion of outlines, for literal misprints and erroneous spacing.

[1] Cf. pp. 440, 459, 467.   [2] Cf. pp. 231, 235.   [3] Cf. p. 157.

Finally, the compositor may fail in judgement where there is, or where he thinks there is, anything in his copy which requires regulating. He may mistake a parenthesis-bracket for a deletion mark.[1] He may insert a marginal addition at the wrong point. He may misinterpret an ambiguous contraction. He may expand an abbreviated speech-prefix incorrectly. He may attach a speech-prefix, written rather high or low, to the wrong line. He may incorporate a speech-prefix or a stage-direction in the text. He may, perhaps excusably, retain a book-keeper's note of an actor's name or other warning.[2] Errors of judgement must play some part in the complex phenomena of mis-lineation. Blank verse is often wrongly divided, and more-over verse is often printed as prose, and prose, perhaps less often, as verse. Again Professor Wilson must be quoted:[3]

If there is one lesson to be learnt from a bibliographical study of the Good Quartos, it is that compositors had no means of distin-guishing between prose and verse except by line-division in their copy.

This dogma, too, needs some qualification. It may be assumed that, in an age when there was much popular poetry, and a compositor was constantly setting-up both prose and verse, he acquired some knowledge of scansion. Normally he was called upon to capitalize the beginnings of verse lines and not those of prose lines, although both, unless Shakespearean manuscripts were unlike the extant manuscripts, began with minuscules in his copy. No doubt he often followed the lineation of the copy, but certainly he sometimes used his intelligence to regulate it according to what he believed to be the author's intention; and either method might bring him out. The confusion of prose and verse in the bad Quartos belongs to the reporter's muddled paraphrasing. But it is also a feature of good texts, particularly in scenes in which Shakespeare's rapid transitions between verse and prose are frequent, and which are sometimes complicated by the habit which

---

[1] Cf. p. 197.   [2] Cf. p. 237.   [3] Wilson, *Ham.* 50.

Shakespeare shares with many other writers of letting his
prose fall into blank verse rhythms. For example, Pistol's
intrusions of bombastic verse into prose scenes regularly
appear as prose in the Quarto *2 Henry IV* and the Folio
Henry V and *Merry Wives of Windsor*. Shakespeare cannot
have written them so. There are many other instances.
Professor Wilson is apt to regard the transitions as evidence of rewriting, and to treat misprinted verse as due
to irregular arrangement in a margin.[1] But the transitions
themselves are often of high literary value, and give no
reason to suppose that they are not deliberate. It is difficult not to attribute .the misprinting to failures of the
compositor's judgement. In other cases, where he has not
the same ground for confusion, a blind following of the
copy becomes more plausible. A marginal insertion might
be written parallel with the main text, and in half-lines for
lack of space. There are such insertions in extant manuscripts, and others where the lines are at full length and
at right angles to the text.[2] Or again, as Professor Wilson
has himself suggested, a writer, near the end of passage
or scene, and also near the foot of a page, might crowd his
matter and write two or three lines continuously. *Sir
Thomas More* furnishes an example.[3] Either of these arrangements might result in the setting-up of short passages of
verse as prose. But some other cause is required to account
for the long passages so misprinted in the Quarto of *King
Lear*. There are many of them and the text throughout
the play varies much from that of the Folio. I conjecture
that they are the notes of a shorthand reporter, which he
has taken down with approximate fidelity, but has not felt
able, or has not troubled, to arrange as verse. There is
some confirmation of this in the fact that they are almost
entirely punctuated with commas. *Pericles* has some
similar passages, especially in Acts iii–v, but they are
better punctuated. On the other hand, the admittedly bad
Quartos of *Hamlet*, *Henry V*, and *Merry Wives of Windsor*
have much more prose, capitalized and in irregular lengths
like those of verse, than we can well ascribe to the com-

[1] Cf. p. 233.   [2] Cf. p. 114.   [3] Cf. p. 510.

positor. Professor Wilson, who finds the same feature in
A Shrew, the Quarto *Richard III*, and the Folio *Merry
Wives of Windsor*—he might have added the *Famous
Victories*—thinks that the arrangement may represent the
practice of some company, which liked to have its parts
written so.[1] The Folio *Merry Wives of Windsor* and
Richard III passages seem to me cases of ordinary mis-
judgement. The *Merry Wives of Windsor* irregularities are
trifling, and there is only one prose scene in *Richard III*,
which might easily upset the compositor.[2] In the other
plays concerned there is a more or less marked tendency
for the lengths to coincide with grammatical clauses. Perhaps parts might be written so, to facilitate memorizing,
although the scanty prose in the Orlando part, while
somewhat irregularly written, does not follow the clause-
structure. I have noticed three rather similar bits of prose
arrangement in the Folio, which come at the bottoms of
pages, and may have been deliberately spaced out to cover
some error discovered in a passage of composition which
had progressed too far to make regular resetting practicable.[3] Blank verse, even when printed as such, is often
wrongly divided. Again a marginal insertion may sometimes be responsible.[4] In the bad Quartos an initial omission throws the reporter out, and the verse runs wrongly
but plausibly, as verse sometimes will, from a medial
pause of one line to one in the next, until another error
or the end of a speech recovers it. In the better texts, a
compositor may be similarly misled by an omission, perhaps due to a cut. In some of the later plays, such as
Antony and Cleopatra and *Coriolanus*, it is noticeable that
mislineation particularly affects the beginnings and ends
of speeches. And here it looks like a result of misjudge-
ment working upon irregularities in the copy. In the
later plays Shakespeare tended more and more to end a
speech and begin a new one in the middle of a line. The

---

[1] Wilson, *Ham.* 51.

[2] *Merry Wives of W.* ii. 1. 20–32, 121–3; iii. 3. 87–92; *Rich. III*, i. 4. 101–56.

[3] *Ham.* ii. 2. 211–18; *As You Like*

It, ii. 6; iii. 4. 1–15. Dr. McKerrow tells me that he too would attribute these examples of irregularity to the compositor rather than the 'copy'.

[4] Cf. e.g. pp. 360, 481.

half-lines should no doubt have been written out separately. But it may be suspected that in Shakespearean copy they were in fact often written continuously with the foregoing or subsequent lines. The compositor sometimes followed the copy and sometimes tried unsuccessfully to adjust the context. Finally, a single verse line is often split and printed in two half-lines. In the Folio, this is generally due to the narrow space available in the columns. It becomes almost normal in the opening lines of speeches, where speech-prefixes have to be accommodated, and compositors acquired a habit of splitting these lines, even where it was not absolutely necessary. Mr. Simpson suggests that other lines were deliberately split, to indicate a substantial pause in utterance.[1] This may very likely be so. There is often a change of subject or address, or a gesture or interval for reflection is conceivable. My treatment of mislineation is necessarily tentative. The whole subject needs more investigation than it has yet received or can receive here.

It is difficult to measure the amount of divergence from Shakespeare's originals caused by misprinting, even where alternative versions are available. The general standard of typographical accuracy was not high, and is likely to have been at its lowest in such books as plays, especially if they were not 'overseen' by the authors.[2] The proportion of emendations adopted by modern editors is no safe guide, since the adoption is often superfluous, and on the other hand parallel texts disclose misprints which no editor would suspect and omissions which no emendation could recover. These may also exist in the single texts. For what it is worth, Dr. Furness calculated, without taking account of 'stage-directions, metrical division of lines, mere punctuation, and immoment changes of spelling', that the Cambridge editors adopted 60 emendations in the 3,064 lines of the single Folio text of *Antony and Cleopatra*. The Globe edition obelizes about 130 lines as corrupt and incapable of emendation, or as bearing witness

---

[1] Simpson, *Punctuation*, 69; cf. p. 459.

[2] Albright 356 cites contemporary complaints and apologies by printers.

to *lacunae*, in the plays and poems as a whole.[1] Dr. Greg
thinks that, in view of the clearness of extant theatrical
manuscripts and the probability that the best compositors
were put upon manuscript copy, we may expect the errors
of first editions to have been 'of the same order of mag-
nitude' as those appearing in reprints.[2] The accuracy of
reprints we can measure, since each Quarto at least seems
to have been normally set up from its immediate predecessor, with some conjectural corrections, but without
further reference to copy. The continuance of old misprints is itself one proof of this. Professor Pollard has
traced the process of degeneration in the five Quartos of
Richard II.[3] He assumes, for the purposes of the analysis,
the authority of the Cambridge text, and lists divergences
from it by way of the omission, transposition, addition, and
substitution of words and letters, but not errors in 'line-
arrangement, speakers, spelling, and punctuation', or a
few others which he considers 'negligible'. On this calculation Qq2–5 between them make 214 errors which were
not in Q1. Their contributions vary from the 123 of Q2
to the 18 of Q4. The Folio, reprinting from the Quarto
of *Much Ado About Nothing*, introduces 122 errors.[4] On
the other hand, Q2 of Jonson's *Every Man Out of his
Humour* is an almost exact reprint of Q1.[5] Jonson, however, 'oversaw' his own plays with extreme care. A little
direct evidence as to first editions is furnished by some
manuscript alterations made by Massinger in prints of his
plays. In a presentation copy of *The Duke of Milan*, of
which he does not seem to have seen proofs, he corrected
33 errors and overlooked perhaps a dozen more. In a
collection of eight plays he made between 200 and 300
corrections, many of them merely in punctuation. Some
had already been made during printing in variant examples.
Of course he may have introduced a few afterthoughts.[6]
The conclusions to be drawn as to the purity of the Shakespearean texts will differ for the pessimist and the optimist.

[1] Pollard, *F.Q.* 129.
[2] Greg, *Abridgements*, 271.
[3] Pollard, *Rich. II*, 38.

[4] Wilson, *Much Ado*, 154.
[5] Greg in *4 Library*, i. 153.
[6] Greg, *ibid.* iv. 207; v. 59.

The influence of the printing-house upon the texts is not confined to verbal misprints and mislineation. Probably from the beginning, certainly in some of the re-printed Quartos, and more markedly in the Folio, there is a small amount of conjectural emendation intended to remove errors or presumed errors in the copy. Thus the later Quartos of *Richard II*, while accumulating misprints, also correct 25 out of 69 slips in Q1. There are some puzzling changes in the *Henry V* and the *2, 3 Henry VI* of 1619, which may even point to a source of amelioration more authoritative than conjecture. On the other hand, there are certain subsidiary matters, in which we have to recognize the probability of considerable departures from the originals. The most important of these are orthography, elision, punctuation, and capitalization. Orthography in the sixteenth century was in a state of transition and indeed of chaos. Private letters, even when written by well-educated men and women, show an extreme of individualism. Grammarians, such as Richard Mulcaster, put forward systems on more or less scientific lines, but the modern standard spelling, as it gradually established itself during the seventeenth century, took its own way, without much regard for science.[1] Printed books display a uniformity much greater than that of popular usage, but within the limits of this there was still room for a great deal of variation. Many vowel-sounds could be represented either by a single vowel, a double vowel, or a diphthong. A mute 'e' could be added or omitted at will. The 'y' was convertible with 'i' and with 'ie'. The variation affected the length of words, and it has already been pointed out that compositors made use of it in 'justifying' their lines.[2] This would not much affect blank verse, except in the Folio, where the double columns cramped the space. Individual compositors had probably their own tendencies.[3]   It is

---

[1] R. Mulcaster, *Elementarie* (1582, ed. E. T. Campagnac, 1925), chh. xvi–xxiv, with a table of spellings (ch. xxv).

[2] Cf. p. 171. William Salesbury, *Plain Introduction teaching how to pronounce . . . Welch* (1567), complains of the mute 'e', but adds, 'the Printers in consideration for the iustifying of the lynes, as it is sayde of the makers to make vp the ryme, must be borne wythall'.

[3] T. Satchell (1920, June 3, *T.L.S.*)

clear that they were not normally expected to follow the spellings of their copy, and indeed to do so would largely increase the time taken in setting-up, and therefore the cost. Field's treatment of Harington's *Ariosto* furnishes good evidence, since Harington was in many respects particular about the printing. Of 136 variants from the modern standard Field normalizes 84, alters but leaves variant 29, and keeps 23. He adds 8 variants.[1] Similarly some habitual spellings found in the manuscripts of Gabriel Harvey do not appear in his printed work.[2] It is true that others by Anthony Munday and Thomas Churchyard do sometimes so appear.[3] Possibly an author, as now, could get his eccentricities respected if he made a point of it. But in any case one must not suppose that a compositor was always on his guard against the influence of his copy. He would be likely enough to follow it in an unusual word, or one which obviously represents a deliberate mispronunciation by Fluellen or another, or even elsewhere through inadvertence. And in fact 'occasional' abnormal spellings are common enough, and may sometimes represent an author's spellings slipping through. There are a good many abnormal spellings in the controverted addition to *Sir Thomas More*, and some of these or of similar types recur in Shakespearean Quartos. Professor Wilson gives some valuable lists.[4] Of such things one writer could rarely have had a monopoly. Moreover, a compositor might himself have abnormal spellings at the back of his mind. Some at least of those relied upon by Professor Wilson to link Shakespeare with *Sir Thomas More* are to be found in texts not at all likely to have been set up from originals or even transcripts of these.[5]

seems to show that two compositors, with different tendencies, worked on *Macbeth*.

[1] 4 *Library*, iv. 110.
[2] McKerrow 247.
[3] M. St. C. Byrne in 4 *Library*, iv. 9; v. 243.
[4] *Sh. Hand*, 132; *Spellings and Misprints in the Second Quarto of Hamlet*

(*Essays and Studies of the English Association*, x. 36).

[5] Thus *a leuen* or *a leauen* (for *eleven*) is not ónly in S.T.M. and in *Mer. of Ven.*, *Love's Lab. Lost*, and *Ham.* (Q2), but also in *Troil. & Cres.* (Q1), and in the reported *Rom. & Jul.* (Q1). This also has *hudwinckt*, *twinckle*, *incke*, *senceles*, *darkenes*,

Elisions are important in that they affect the metre, since the presence or absence of them means the difference between disyllabic and trisyllabic feet.[1] Dr. McKerrow suggests that it was the business of the actors to know how to speak verse, and that possibly the author, no more than the compositor, would take much pains about the textual form, so that we may 'exercise our own judgement in its interpretation'.[2] Shakespeare's measure of confidence in the actors is shown by Hamlet's warning to them to speak 'trippingly on the tongue', which can only mean not to slur the trisyllables.[3] Dr. McKerrow's doctrine is a comfortable one for editors, but highly dangerous. It would justify Dr. Van Dam in adding innumerable elisions of his own and reducing the text of *Hamlet* to a strictly decasyllabic basis. And it would justify Mr. Bayfield in his constant disregard of apostrophes in the interests of trisyllabic rhythm. The methods are equally perverse. No doubt Spenser's frequent apostrophes show that he clung to the decasyllable.[4] But dramatic blank verse may reasonably approach nearer to the manner of common speech than epic. Shakespeare certainly used both elisions and trisyllabic feet, and distributed them with a growing delicacy of ear. The ingenuous Mr. Bayfield, after arguing at length that the elisions were foisted in by transcribers and printers, arrived at the afterthought that they were probably legitimate but only indicated a light pronunciation of syllables. For this he conceived himself to find support in Jonson's use of apostrophes. Jonson, however, knew perfectly well that an apostrophe normally meant the 'rejecting' of a vowel.[5] Professor Pollard believes that elided syllables 'should almost always be pronounced, but so lightly as not to interfere with the rhythm of the verse'.[6] I have something of the same feeling myself. One retains some consciousness of the elided

---

singlenes, chaples, likenes, drudg, stopp, bin (been), and other spellings regarded by Wilson as 'significant'.

[1] Cf. p. 262.
[2] McKerrow 250.
[3] *Ham.* iii. 2. 1.

[4] J. D. Wilson, *A Note on Elisions in the Faerie Queene* (*M.L.R.* xv. 409).
[5] Jonson, *English Grammar*, ii. 1; cf. Herford-Simpson, ii. 428.
[6] Pollard, *Rich. II*, 75.

sound, but it does not amount to a metrical syllable. This is, however, a subtlety which we cannot expect typography to recognize. It is true that, in the poems of Spenser and Donne, in Jonson's plays with some frequency, and occasionally in the later Shakespearean Quartos and the Folio, we get a fully printed word followed by an apostrophe.[1] This probably indicates not an elision, but merely a light pronunciation of what is still a syllable. It was an abnormal device, which has not endured. Ordinarily an apostrophe means an elision.[2] But often there is no apostrophe, and the elision is indicated merely by the omission of a vowel, or by its transference to the end of a word.[3] Often there is an accompanying consonantal modification.[4] An elided word may be merged with the next.[5] The elision of pronouns yields some special forms.[6] The prefixes of nouns and verbs may be dropped without an apostrophe. A rather minute examination of the elisions in the Q1 of *Merchant of Venice* leaves the impression that in that text at least the copy was followed with some fidelity. Its elisions and trisyllables generally supply a satisfactory rhythm. One or two are clearly wrong, and a score or so of others may be doubtful. But even if these are misprints, the proportion is not a high one. Other First Quartos, even good ones, may very possibly be less correct. And certainly there is a tendency in reprints, and notably in the Folio, to alter readings in the direction of eliminating trisyllabic feet.[7] One cannot, therefore, feel much confidence in the elisions of plays which are only preserved in

[1] Bayfield 300; Herford-Simpson, ii. 430; Wilson in *M.L.R.* xv. 412. The Folio has *to' th'* (*Ant. & Cleo.* ii. 1. 11; ii. 2. 25) and Q1 of *Oth.* i. 1. 67, *carry' et.*

[2] Jonson says 'though it many times, through the negligence of writers and printers, is quite omitted'.

[3] e.g. in *Mer. of Ven.*, *ashamde, tride, eyde, stolne.*

[4] e.g. *worshipt, vnlockt, drest, crost, falne, tane, waft.*

[5] e.g. *thafternoon, thinteriour, tyn-trap.* This is also found in *S.T.M.* There is a discussion in *T.L.S.* (1924, Aug. 21–Oct. 16) around the emendation of *the eft* for *theft* in *Love's Lab. Lost,* iv. 3. 336.

[6] e.g. *tis, twill, thowlt, ist, Ile, yle, theyle, weele, youle, ant, ont, ons, ith, yfaith.* I do not find *Im* or *I'm* in *Mer. of Ven. I am* easily runs into a trisyllabic foot.

[7] Many examples are in Bayfield 52 *sqq.*

the Folio.[1] On the other hand, consonantal elision becomes more prominent in the later plays, and this may perhaps indicate a change in Shakespeare's own habit.[2] The appearance of elisions in prose, where they have no metrical value, is rather puzzling. They often suggest a colloquial utterance, but are not used with any uniformity.[3] They may have come naturally to a pen accustomed to use them freely in verse.

Punctuation affords a difficult and much controverted problem. That of Elizabethan manuscripts is unprincipled and generally scanty. Harington's, in his translation of Ariosto, is mechanical and pays little regard to the sense. His printer used great freedom in regulating it.[4] Dr. McKerrow is no doubt right in thinking that any rules which existed are more likely to have been observed in the printing-houses than elsewhere.[5] Such rules had been formulated by Aldus Manutius in 1561, on principles which do not differ essentially from modern usage; and these may have introduced the semicolon, the function of which is still imperfectly established in our texts.[6] It is not recognized by such of the sixteenth-century grammarians as discuss punctuation at all.[7] But even in the printing-houses there can have been little consistency of practice. The punctuation of the Quartos varies very much, and in some it is extremely bad. The Folio, when reprinting, makes many alterations, generally in the direction of heavier stopping. Clearly different minds have been at work, and as clearly it is impossible to ascribe to Shakespeare much of what we find. This did not deter

---

[1] The tendency of the F printer sometimes leads him to put *'t* where the metre clearly requires *it*.

[2] The commonest are in such combinations as *o' th'* and *i' th'*, but I find *i' th' reare' our Birth* (*Wint. Tale*, iv. 4. 592) and *at' Pallace* (*Wint. Tale*, iv. 4. 731), where whole words go. In *Mer. of Ven. ever* and *never* become *ere* and *nere*, but *even* is not elided, except once, in the odd form *in* (iii. 5. 24).

[3] Cf. Bayfield 262 *sqq.*

[4] *4 Library*, iv. 115.

[5] McKerrow 250.

[6] *Interpungendi Ratio* in *Orthographiae Ratio* (Venice, 1561), 52; cf. H. Jenkinson in *R.E.S.* ii. 152.

[7] John Hart, *A Methode or comfortable beginning for all vnlearned* (1570); R. Mulcaster, *Elementarie* (1582), ch. xxi; [G. Puttenham?] *Arte of English Poesie* (1589), ii. 5.

Professor Wilson from writing at the outset of his editorial work on Shakespeare:

The old texts were prompt-copy, more akin to operatic score than to modern literary drama. This explains the ungrammatical punctuation which, hitherto neglected or despised by editors, is now recognized as of the highest dramatic importance. The stops, brackets, capital letters in the Folio and Quartos are in fact stage-directions, in shorthand. They tell the actor when to pause and for how long, they guide his intonation, they indicate the emphatic word, often enough they indicate 'stage-business'.[1]

This principle, so far as stops are concerned, Professor Wilson regarded as a 'discovery' of Mr. Simpson's *Shakespearian Punctuation* (1911). He departs from it considerably in his detailed treatment of some individual plays. Thus in *Much Ado About Nothing* he discerns Shakespeare's careful punctuation mainly in set speeches, and elsewhere a light punctuation 'largely supplied by the compositor, who found little guidance in his copy'. And in *Love's Labour's Lost* he thinks that we get, again with some exceptions, a punctuation 'not only frequently absurd but greatly overweighted throughout, especially in the matter of full-stops'. The 'operatic score' has receded into the background. No doubt in the interval Professor Wilson has been influenced by a new study of Professor Pollard's theory, as set out in his *Shakespeare's Fight with the Pirates* and his edition of *Richard II*. This also assumes that Shakespeare was normally a rapid writer, who did not trouble about punctuation, but occasionally became more careful, when he wanted a speech delivered in a particular way, and that the printers, while perhaps adopting his stops when there were any, were obliged to do the best they could for themselves when there were not. As to Shakespeare's main habit, Professor Pollard may very likely be right. If he wrote the scene claimed for him in *Sir Thomas More*, the inadequate punctuation of that would be a confirmation.[2] The belief in his occasional interven-

---

[1] *Temp.* xxix, xxxvii. Professor Wilson disfigures his own text by introducing a new punctuation, largely composed of dots and dashes, like a feminine novel.

[2] Cf. p. 510.

tion to control the actors is more open to dispute. This also is at least in part derived from Mr. Simpson's investigation, the object of which was to show that 'English punctuation has radically changed in the last hundred years', and that, while modern punctuation attempts to be logical, 'the earlier system was mainly rhythmical'.[1] Even if it were so, it would hardly bear out Professor Wilson's initial pronouncement, since Mr. Simpson was primarily analysing the punctuation of the Folio. This is largely its own, and we surely cannot suppose that its compositors, or indeed those of the Quartos, were undertaking the task of providing shorthand stage-directions. Mr. Simpson himself appears to be now content with Professor Pollard's view, although some phrases in his original statement were open to misconstruction on this point.[2] His main theory has had to stand the fire of much criticism, some of it ill-conceived. The term 'rhythmical' was not altogether a happy one, since it suggested a habit of regularly punctuating the end of every line, or each of those mid-line pauses which the Elizabethans and some modern metrists inaccurately call 'caesuras'. Such a habit is apparent in some contemporary printed verse, but not to any great extent in the Shakespearean texts.[3] On the contrary, stops, which would have been required in prose, are often omitted at line-ends; and this is intelligible, since an 'end-stopped' line by itself entails a pause quite equal to that of a comma. Professor Pollard's 'dramatic' expresses the meaning better, and perhaps 'rhetorical' is better still. When Mr. Simpson calls his collection of Folio uses a 'system', he is putting it rather high. He contents himself with bringing together positive instances, and does not pay much attention to negative ones; and even then he has to acknowledge alternative uses. There are three ways, for example, of treating the vocative, and five ways of treating the break in an uncompleted sentence. Nevertheless, the collection is an illuminating one. It is a more fundamental criticism that the antithesis between a logical punctuation and a rhetorical punctuation is not really

---

[1] Simpson 8.   [2] *Proc. Oxford Bibl. Soc.* i. 39.   [3] Cf. however, p. 123.

sound. All punctuation has elements both of logic and of rhetoric. It has its origin in spoken utterance. Mr. Simpson points out that 'distinction', which was an Elizabethan term for a 'stop', was used by classical grammarians in the sense of a 'pause'.[1] For the matter of that, a 'stop' also means a 'pause'. Pauses are primarily for taking breath in speech. On the other hand, the terms for individual stops, 'period', 'colon', and 'comma', indicate in the language of the grammarians, not pauses, but sentences or parts of sentences.[2] The Elizabethans were conscious of the spoken aspect of pronunciation. Mr. Simpson quite rightly quotes Mulcaster and Heywood to show this.[3] But Mulcaster and Heywood could not have said anything different, if they had had modern usage before them. In spoken utterance, however, the main pauses for breath come at the syntactical junctures which determine the logical structure. Were it not so, the utterance would be unintelligible. And if a written language uses stops, these naturally follow suit. The primary dominance of logic, however, still leaves a great deal of room for rhetorical variation of effect. Pauses can be lengthened or shortened, or additional ones introduced. Thus we may indicate the solemnity of emphasis, the affected hesitation which awakes attention, the rapidity of impassioned appeal. Stops can be similarly manipulated. Modern usage does not here differ essentially from Elizabethan usage. We divide sentences by full-stops, sometimes inserting a conjunction when the sentences are logically related. We link independent but closely related clauses within a sentence by semicolons, some of us also by colons, or like Professor Wilson by commas. We link co-ordinate clauses and phrases and attach subordinate clauses and phrases by

[1] *Ibid.* i. 36.

[2] Fries 80 cites Aristotle, Cicero, and Quintilian on the point.

[3] Mulcaster, *Elementarie*, ch. xxi, 'This title of distinction reacheth verie far, bycause it conteineth all those characts, and their vses, which I call before signifying, but not sounding which help verie much, naie all in all to the right and tunable vttering of our words and sentences.' Heywood, *Apology*, c3ᵛ, says that academic plays taught a student 'to speak well, and with iudgement, to obserue his comma's, colons, & full poynts, his parentheses, his breathing spaces, and distinctions'.

commas or semicolons, or without stops. And these variations depend, not only on the length of the sentences, clauses, and phrases, but also upon deliberate rhetorical purpose. The divergence of the Folio from modern usage, which Mr. Simpson's examples illustrate, is in detail rather than in principle. Much of it is merely a matter of the use of symbols. A colon is put where we should put a full-stop, or where we should put a comma. The difference is in the value attached to the colon, not in the length of pause intended. A comma is often put where we should put a semicolon. Clearly the use of the semicolon was not yet fully appreciated. Mr. Simpson has a list of independent clauses linked by commas, but the actual length of pause required in utterance varies considerably.[1] A more free use of semicolons would have made a finer rhetorical differentiation practicable. The colon is independently used, not only as now to introduce a quotation, but also, indifferently with the interrogation mark, to supply the want of an exclamation mark. There are differences to be observed also in the distribution of commas. Professor Pollard says that the Elizabethan usage was nearer to normal speech than ours, which 'balances comma by comma with a logic intolerable in talk'. I do not altogether agree. Modern usage has some superfluous commas, marking off vocatives and imperatives and very short clauses and phrases. But often, if a pause is required for intelligibility at the end of such a clause or phrase, one is required at the beginning also; and the Folio habit of omitting an initial comma in such cases does not make for good utterance. What, however, strikes one most about the Folio is the frequent excess of its commas. They come, for example, according to Mr. Simpson, at the end of a composite subject, or again between an accusative and a dative. Frequently, and in a most irritating way, they supplement a conjunction in linking nouns, verbs, and adjectives, which have a common position in a sentence. But surely, as so used, they are logical or grammatical, rather than rhetorical,

[1] Simpson 16.

devices. You do not want a rhetorical pause in such lines
as—[1]

> The Cowslips tall, her pensioners bee,

or—

> I could haue giuen my Vnkles Grace, a flout,

or—

> Your brother, and his louer haue embrac'd;

or—

> Th' extrauagant, and erring Spirit, hyes

This last line has two commas, one superfluous and the
other clearly wrong. And indeed the constant intrusion
of a comma directly between subject and predicate is one
of the most disturbing features in the Folio punctuation.[2]
Here, and in commas between object and complement,
and in similar intrusions of colons and even full-stops, Mr.
Simpson often discerns a rhetorical purpose. It may sometimes be there. There are parallel cases in the works of
Donne, who seems to have punctuated more carefully than
most of his contemporaries.[3] And there is no reason why
the Elizabethans should not have handled the possibilities
inherent in the system of punctuation rather more freely
than we do. This would not constitute it a different
system. But I cannot believe that any intention of Shakespeare is represented by the second stop in the line from
Hamlet quoted above or by

> To each of you, one faire and vertuous Mistris;
> Fall when loue please, marry to each but one.[4]

Curiously enough, the Restoration found the punctuation
bequeathed to it inadequate in just what Mr. Simpson
regards as its distinguishing characteristic. In 1665 John
Evelyn proposed that the Royal Society should invent
some 'new Periods and Accents, to assist, inspirit, and
modifie the Pronunciation of Sentences, & to stand as
markes beforehand how the voice & tone is to be govern'd;
as in reciting of Playes, reading of Verses, &c. for the

---

[1] *Mid. N. Dr.* ii. 1. 10; *Rich. III,*
ii. 4. 24; *Meas. for Meas.* i. 4. 40;
Ham. i. 1. 154.
[2] It recurs in the badly printed
Sonnets.
[3] Grierson, *Poems of Donne,* II.
cxxii; E. M. Simpson in *R.E.S.* iv. 295.
[4] *All's Well,* ii. 3. 63.

varying the tone of the voyce, and affections, &c'.[1] Fortunately nothing came of it. In one respect, indeed, we are ourselves more rhetorical than the Elizabethans. They made little use of the dash; an unpleasing device which, as in this sentence, I try to avoid. Where there are possible rhetorical stops in the Shakespearean texts, the general character of the punctuation must make us hesitate before ascribing them with any confidence to Shakespeare himself. There are obvious exceptions in such passages as Pistol's gabble while he eats the leek or the pace of Margaret's tongue in *Much Ado About Nothing*.[2] Here the compositor may have preserved an intention of the author, as he sporadically preserved dialectic pronunciation. Clearly it is so with Quince's prologue.[3]

The parenthesis is on rather a different footing. It is not properly a punctuation mark, and primarily it encloses something which breaks the run of the sentence; an aside, a qualification, an afterthought. Here it may be regarded as rhetorical, and a change of intonation may be appropriate.[4] But the use of it gets much extension in the Shakespearean texts, and brackets merely replace commas, to enclose vocatives, exclamations, short appositions, adjectival or adverbial phrases, and the like. They also introduce quotations. Professor Wilson thinks that in Q2 of *Hamlet* they generally imply 'some kind of mental or spiritual disturbance'. There are only thirteen examples, and most of them are quite colourless.[5] One may therefore suspect a misapplied subtlety, when Professor Wilson quotes—

My fathers spirit (in armes) all is not well,

and adds that 'the brackets simply vibrate with the tones

[1] Cf. J. Isaacs in *R.E.S.* ii. 462.

[2] *Hen. V*, v. 1. 49; *Much Ado*, iii. 4. 93.

[3] *Mid. N. Dr.* v. 1. 119, 'He hath rid his prologue like a rough colt; he knows not the stop'.

[4] Mulcaster, *Elementarie*, ch. xxi, 'Parenthesis is expressed by two half circles, which in writing enclose some perfit branch, as not mere impertinent, so not fullie coincident to the sentence, which it breaketh, and in reading warneth vs, that the words inclosed by them, ar to be pronounced with a lower & quikker voice, then the words either before or after them.'

[5] In i. 5. 170–8 the brackets exceptionally include a divagation of nine lines.

of mystery and amazement'. And when he finds 'a wild hysterical chuckle' in Q1's—

> (My tables) meet it is I set it down,

it is we who chuckle with the reporter.[1] The frequency of brackets varies. There are only thirteen pairs in *Merchant of Venice* and forty-four in *Midsummer-Night's Dream*. In both cases the Folio, reprinting, follows the Quartos, which looks as if the printers were normally guided by their copy in this respect. On the other hand, in *1 Henry IV*, the Folio doubles the seventeen examples of the Quarto. Brackets are exceptionally common in *Winter's Tale*; there are even brackets within brackets. They seem to have become mere flourishes, and may confirm the conjecture that *Winter's Tale* was printed from a calligraphic transcript. The Quarto of *Othello* omits two lines, which in the Folio are bracketed.[2] Did a transcriber take the brackets for deletion-marks? Inverted commas occasionally seem to call attention to gnomic passages. Probably they came from copy. They are occasionally to be found in printed books of non-dramatic poetry, as well as in plays.[3] I do not see why the reporter could not have introduced them into the Q1 of *Hamlet*.[4] We may assume that the printers capitalized the beginnings of sentences, including some which follow a colon or semicolon, and of verse-lines, when they did not happen to be short of capital type.[5] Individual words, mainly but not wholly nouns, also receive capitals. Very likely some of these are due to the author. The use is comparatively sparing in the Quartos, being commonest in titles and designations, names of classes of mankind, and personifications. The Folio considerably extends it, often capitalizing the names of animals, plants, and other natural objects, and of craft products. But there is no uniformity anywhere. Of course many of the words are important, but it is rather an

---

[1] Wilson, *Ham.* 9.
[2] *Oth.* i. 2. 65; 3. 63. If Q1 of *K. Lear* is reported, its omission of i. 1. 50–1 cannot be similarly explained.
[3] They are common, e.g. in Sir John Davies, *Nosce Teipsum* (1599).
[4] Wilson, *Ham.* 11.
[5] Cf. p. 370.

exaggeration to speak of 'emphasis-capitals'. A 'slight exaltation of tone' is often fanciful, even apart from conventions like 'Lord', 'Madam', and 'Sir'.[1] The frequent capitalization of C may be due to a scribal distaste for the insignificant minuscule, and that of M to the resemblance of the majuscule and minuscule forms.[2] Italics are used, both in the Quartos and the Folio, for proper names, but not quite systematically, and for speech-prefixes. The Folio regularly uses them for stage-directions throughout.[3] This is also the commonest practice in the Quartos. But sometimes the body of a stage-direction is in roman type and only the names or some of them in italics, and sometimes this arrangement is reversed. The variant methods may appear side by side in the same Quarto. It is notably so in Q1 of *Merchant of Venice*. Broadly these uses of italics answer to those of Italian script in theatrical manuscripts, but the printers may well have done some regularization.[4] There is an exceptional appearance of italics for ordinary dialogue both in Q1 and Q2 of *Romeo and Juliet*. They are also used normally for songs, letters, inscriptions, and the like. These were read from scrolls on the stage, but the scrolls were presumably extracted, like parts, from the originals. In the texts it is not always clear by whom matter is read. It may merely have some such heading as 'A letter', without a speech-prefix. And if it is inserted in a speech, and a comment by the speaker follows, there is sometimes a second speech-prefix for the comment. This is so in Q2 of *Hamlet*, which is not likely to rest on a stage-copy. There is therefore no reason to think with Professor Wilson that elsewhere the same arrangement shows that a scroll formed part of the copy.[5]

It has been held that the Folio received, from Heminges

---

[1] Simpson 103; Pollard, *Sh. F.* 93, *Rich. II*, 30, 71.

[2] Cf. McKerrow in *R.E.S.* iii. 29.

[3] Some stage-directions in *Temp.* ii. 2, iv. 1, v. 1, *Two Gent. of Ver.* ii. 5, 6, 7, and *Merry Wives of W.* i. 1, ii. 1, 2 have the names in roman type; there may be other exceptions.

[4] Jonson's MS. *Mask of Queens*, Dr. Greg tells me, like a non-dramatic MS. noted by McKerrow 251, has words underlined, as if for italicization.

[5] *Ham.* ii. 2. 125; iv. 6. 32; 7. 50; cf. Wilson, *Mer. of Ven.* 96.

and Condell, or Ben Jonson, or Edward Blount, or another, some sort of editing beyond what a printing-house would naturally supply. The evidence is not very strong. The process of sophistication, already noticed in the orthography and in the smoothing out of metre with the help of elisions, is perhaps also traceable here and there in the diction. There may be some tendency to eliminate dialectic, colloquial, or merely unusual words and archaic inflexions. The use of 'a' for 'he', 'of' or 'on' seems to meet with particular disapproval. Even puns are misunderstood or disliked. Trifling grammatical solecisms in moods and cases are removed. Adverbial adjectives give way to adverbs. There are substitutions of 'thou' for 'you' and of 'mine' for 'my' and of 'my' for 'mine' before a vowel or consonant respectively. I have noticed about a score of possible examples in *Merchant of Venice*.[1] There are others in Professor Pollard's lists of variants for *Richard II*, in Professor Wilson's for *Much Ado About Nothing*, and in Dr. Van Dam's for *Hamlet*, although here a transcript has doubtless intervened. It is not at all clear that we need look beyond the compositors. Indeed, the interchanges, especially between 'my' and 'mine', are not always in the same direction. Nor is it clear that the sophistication is deliberate; it may be merely due to subconscious misprinting.[2] One way or another, those of our texts which rest on the Folio alone are probably somewhat farther from Shakespeare's originals than the others. In the Quartos, except partially for *Othello*, and for some typographical devices in *Pericles* and part of the bad edition of *Romeo and Juliet*, the plays are not divided by acts and scenes. This is the commonest arrangement in prints

---

[1] *Mer. of Ven.* i. 2. 7 small ⟨ meane (pun), 18 then be ⟨ then to be, 25 whom ⟨ who, 47 afraid ⟨ afeard, 55 to be ⟨ be, 69 should ⟨ shall, i. 3. 123 should ⟨ can, 152 it pleaseth ⟨ pleaseth, ii. 9. 7 thou ⟨ you, iii. 1. 32 fledg'd ⟨ flidge (a good dialect word), iii. 2. 93 makes ⟨ maketh, 160 nothing ⟨ something (pun), iii. 4. 50 cosins hand ⟨ cosin, hands, iv. 1. 22 exacts't ⟨ exacts, 77 fretted ⟨ fretten, 123 soale ⟨ soule (pun), 142 endlesse ⟨ curelesse, 258 should ⟨ doe, 290 whom ⟨ who, 334 thee ⟨ you, 379 Gods sake ⟨ God-sake, v. 1. 209 mine honour ⟨ my honour, 233 my bedfellow ⟨ mine bedfellow.

[2] Cf. p. 180.

of plays belonging to the public theatres.[1] The Folio introduces such divisions, but very incompletely. Each play begins with the heading *Actus primus, Scena prima*, or in three cases *Actus primus* alone. The typography suggests that headings, with their enclosing rules, were set-up for blocks of plays, and transferred successively from one to another of them.[2] Seventeen plays are also fully divided by acts and scenes throughout, two imperfectly by acts and scenes, eleven by acts alone, while six remain undivided. These variations cannot be correlated at all exactly, either with the chronological order of the plays, or with Professor Pollard's theory that special care was spent upon those disinterred for the Folio. It is perhaps noteworthy that the four latest written plays are all fully divided, and that of the eight earlier plays of which revivals during 1610–23 are traceable, five are fully and three partially divided.[3] It is therefore at least possible that, while the division was imperfectly carried out, the information for it came from the theatre. Professor Wilson's conjecture that the King's men came to pay more attention to act-intervals after they occupied the Blackfriars in 1609 is an attractive one.[4] The curious stage-direction at the end of act iii of *Midsummer-Night's Dream* —'They sleepe all the Act'—is an addition of the Folio. Here 'Act' means the act-interval. Mr. Lawrence's argument that the parody, if it is one, of the device in *Histriomastix* iii. 299 shows the act-interval to be of old standing is inconclusive, since *Histriomastix* itself may have received an addition before the print of 1610.[5] *The Malcontent* shows that long act-intervals were not in use at the Globe in 1604.[6] It does not follow that there were no breaks at all. Shakespeare himself uses the terms 'act' and 'scene'

---

[1] *Eliz. Stage*, iii. 199; W. W. Greg in *R.E.S.* iv. 152.

[2] E. E. Willoughby in *R.E.S.* iv. 323.

[3] Cf. 5. The plays are *1, 2 Hen. IV*, *Much Ado*, *Jul. Caes.*, *Ham.*, *Twelfth Night*, *Oth.*, *Macb.*

[4] *R.E.S.* iii. 385.

[5] Lawrence in *R.E.S.* iv. 78; cf.

Wilson (iv. 191).

[6] *Ind.* 89, on the additions made 'to entertain a little more time, and to abridge the not received custom of music in our theatre'. But 'abridge' is not found in the sense of 'bridge over', and only means 'shorten'; cf. *Eliz. Stage*, iii. 125, 132.

rather indifferently, and with no clear technical significance. On the other hand, the evidence of the plots and
the extant manuscripts seems to show that some account
was taken both of act and scene divisions in the public
theatres generally, and there is no obvious reason to suppose that the Globe was an exception.[1] A scene division,
no doubt, need not have implied more than a momentary
pause in the continuity of a performance. Whatever their
origin, the Folio divisions can hardly be correct, or at least
Shakespeare's, in *1 Henry VI*, *Comedy of Errors*, *Taming of
the Shrew*, *King John*, and *Henry V*. Modern editors have
frequently altered the scene divisions unnecessarily, introducing a new scene where there is no change of time or
locality, or even a real clearance of the stage, but only a
shift of action from the outer stage to the alcove or gallery,
or a fresh 'excursion' in a battle.[2] The Folio supplies lists
of 'actors', that is, of *Dramatis Personae*, for six plays, with
indications of 'The Scene' for two of them. The object
may be to fill up blank pages or half-pages. Professor
Pollard traces editing in another feature of some of the
special Folio plays. There is, he thinks, a 'substitution of
literary for theatrical stage-directions, i.e. of notes helping
a reader to understand the play for memoranda reminding
the prompter and actors of what had to be done'.[3] I once
accepted this view, but have now come to regard it as
extremely dubious.[4] Certainly the directions of the *Tempest*, *Henry VIII*, *Timon of Athens*, and *Coriolanus* are unusually elaborate; but they are not more so, although they
are more elegant, than those of *2, 3 Henry VI*; and these
cannot be editorial, since they are substantially reproduced,
perhaps through the medium of a plot, in the reported
Contention. Of course the descriptive directions in some
other 'reported' texts are not comparable.[5] I believe the
stage-directions throughout the plays to be substantially
Shakespeare's. They were no doubt modified by the additions, eliminations, and alterations of the book-keeper, and

[1] Cf. pp. 118, 124.
[2] M. Hunter in *R.E.S.* ii. 296.
[3] *Sh. F.Q.* 125.
[4] *Eliz. Stage*, iii. 196.
[5] Cf. p. 157.

to this point I shall have to return.[1] But in origin they seem to me to be the suggestive notes to the management of an author familiar with theatrical conditions, rather than the authoritative instructions of the management to the prompter and actors. Looking at the matter chronologically, I conceive Shakespeare to have begun by writing stage-directions rather fully. When he settled down with the Chamberlain's men, and thereafter during the greater part of his career, they became comparatively slight. He was on the spot and was able to take his share in planning and rehearsing productions. In the late plays named above they are full again. It is an ingenious and probable suggestion by Professor Wilson that these plays may have been written in the country, for production during his absence.[2] *The Tempest* and *Henry VIII*, in particular, are full of spectacular episodes, for which the dialogue by itself would be an inadequate guide. Descriptive touches are natural here. But throughout the plays the general character of the directions is the same. They show familiarity with the technical resources of the theatre. And they contain notes for incidental action on the stage. But they also include others for apparel and the use of properties, for the grouping of entries, even for the bearing of the actors. Sometimes they indicate the relationship of characters; sometimes the scope of a scene, and very rarely its locality.[3] Thus they deal with points many of which had to be considered and settled in the tiring-house, long before the opening of performances. The suggestive element is especially noteworthy in directions which leave for later decision such details as the number of supernumeraries to be employed in a scene. These are precisely the features which we find in the directions written by the main hands in extant play-manuscripts, and which are freely altered by the book-keepers there.[4] I think they are to be discerned

[1] Cf. p. 236.

[2] Wilson, *Temp.* 80: *Coriol.* facs. I do not suppose *Timon* to have been actually produced, and presumably many of the *Hen. VIII* stage-directions are not Shakespeare's.

[3] *2 Hen. IV* (Q), iv. 1. 1. 'Enter . . . within the forrest of Gaultree'; *Hen. V* (F), iii. 1. 1, 'Scaling Ladders at Harflew'.

[4] Cf. p. 118.

in the four late plays, as well as in the earlier ones.[1] It is not inconsistent with what we may suspect of Shakespeare's temperament that many of his directions are written in an off-hand manner. The characters are designated, now by individual, now by generic names.[2] When a group which has been once seen, returns, it often gets a summary description. Here again the extant manuscripts provide parallels, as well as for the frequent omission of entries and exits. The book-keeper should have supplied the former, if not the latter.[3] Sometimes the Folio and even the reprinted Quartos do, but only, one supposes, by inference from the text. I have an impression that Shakespeare sometimes wrote the initial direction to a scene before he had thought out the dialogue, and sometimes, as a result, left the name of a character standing there for whom, after all, he had provided no speech.[4] There is a casual aspect, also, about the speech-prefixes. They are often much abbreviated, and not consistently in the same form. Lords and servants may be differentiated only by a '1', '2', '3'. Dr. McKerrow thinks that the

[1] e.g. *Coriol.* i. 1. 227 'Enter a Messenger hastily', 231 'with other Senatours', i. 3. 1 'Volumnia and Virgilia, mother and wife to Marcius', i. 4. 1 'as before the City Corialus', 30 'Marcius Cursing', i. 6. 1 'Cominius as it were in retire', i. 9. 1 'Martius, with his Arme in a Scarfe', ii. 2. 1 'Officers, to lay Cushions, as it were, in the Capitoll', 41 'Enter the Patricians, and the Tribunes of the People, Lictors before them: Coriolanus, Menenius, Cominius the Consul: Scicinius and Brutus take their places by themselues: Coriolanus stands', iii. 1. 1 'all the Gentry', 181 'a rabble of Plebeians', 186 'They all bustle about Coriolanus', iv. 1. 1 'the young Nobility of Rome', iv. 4. 1 'Coriolanus in meane Apparrell, Disguisd, and muffled', iv. 6. 20 'three or foure Citizens', 128 'a Troope of Citizens', v. 2. 1 'to the Watch or Guard', v. 3. 182 'Holds her by the hand silent', v. 6. 9 '3 or 4 Conspirators'; and for

theatrical structure i. 1. 47 'Showts within', i. 4. 13 'on the Walles', i. 8. 1 'at seueral doores', v. 5. 1 'passing ouer the Stage'; *Temp.* ii. 1. 1 'Enter ... and others', iii. 3. 1 'Enter ... &c', 17 'seuerall strange shapes ... inuiting the King, &c. to eate', 53 'with a quient deuice', iv. 1. 139 'certaine Reapers (properly habited)'—not a description, but a warning to have 'wardrobe wit'—194 'Ariell, loaden with glistering apparell, &c.'; and for theatrical structure, i. 1. 63 'A confused noyse within', iii. 2. 48 'Enter Ariell inuisible' (a stage convention; cf. *Eliz. Stage*, iii. 108), iii. 3. 17 'Prosper on the top (inuisible)'—cf. *1 Hen. VI* for the only parallel to 'the top'—v. 1. 171 'Here Prospero discouers Ferdinand and Miranda'. But v. 1. 255 'Enter Ariell, driuing in Caliban ...' inverts theatrical usage.

[2] Cf. pp. 119, 232.

[3] Cf. p. 120.

[4] Cf. p. 231.

compositors treated the prefixes in their copy freely, tending to unify the use of a form throughout a page.[1] Sometimes a prefix has got attached to the wrong line. If Shakespeare, like the writer of the addition to *Sir Thomas More*, wrote the text first, and added the prefixes afterwards, they may well have occasionally, in spite of speech-rules, been placed too high or too low.[2]

[1] *4 Library*, ii. 102.   [2] Cf. p. 510.

CHAPTER VII
THE PROBLEM OF AUTHENTICITY

[*Bibliographical Note.* I have gone over much of the ground of this chapter in *The Disintegration of Shakespeare* (1924, *British Academy*) and *The Unrest in Shakespearean Studies* (1927, *Nineteenth Century and After*, ci. 255). Dramatic collaboration is discussed in E. N. S. Thompson, *Elizabethan Dramatic Collaboration* (1908, *E.S.* xl. 30); O. L. Hatcher, *Fletcher's Habits of Dramatic Collaboration* (1910, *Anglia*, xxxiii. 219); F. E. Pierce, *The Collaboration of Dekker and Ford* (1912, *Anglia*, xxxvi. 141, 289); L. Wann, *The Collaboration of Beaumont, Fletcher and Massinger* (1916, *Wisconsin Studies*, 147); W. J. Lawrence, *Early Dramatic Collaboration: a Theory* (1927, *Pre-Restoration Studies*, 340); C. Sisson, *Keep the Widow Waking* (1927, 4 *Library*, viii. 39, 233); E. H. C. Oliphant, *Beaumont and Fletcher* (1927), *Collaboration in Eliz. Drama* (1929, *Phil. Q.* viii).

My Disintegration lecture summarizes the earlier theories as to elements of unauthenticity in the Shakespearean canon. For later material I must refer to the *Bibl. Notes* to ch. ix, and notably to J. D. Wilson's views as set out in the *New Shakespeare*. More general treatments are in E. H. C. Oliphant, *Shakespeare's Plays: An Examination* (1908–9, *M.L.R.* iii. 337; iv. 190, 342) and W. Keller, *Sh. als Überarbeiter fremder Dramen* (1922, *J.* lviii. 68). Many, but not all, of J. M. Robertson's studies are in his *Sh. and Chapman* (1917), *The Shakespeare Canon* (1922–30), *Introduction to the Study of the Shakespeare Canon* (1924). Some special points dealt with in this chapter are studied in F. H. Hoffmann, *Über die Beteuerungen in Shs Dramen* (1894); J. M. Manly, *Cuts and Insertions in Sh.'s Plays* (1917, *S.P.* xiv. 123); A. Gaw, *Actors' Names in Basic Shn. Texts* (1925, *P.M.L.A.* xl. 530); W. J. Lawrence, *Sh.'s Lost Characters* (1928, *Sh.'s Workshop*, 39), *A New Shakespearean Test* (*ibid.* 48); R. C. Bald, *Macbeth and the 'Short' Plays* (1928, *R.E.S.* iv. 429).]

THE canon of Shakespeare's plays rests primarily on the authority of title-pages. Thirty-six are included in the First Folio. Quartos, good and bad, of fifteen of these also bear his name; it is not on those of *Titus Andronicus*, *Romeo and Juliet*, or *Henry V*. Quartos also ascribe to him *Pericles* and a share in *Two Noble Kinsmen*, which are not in the Folio. The registration entries of *2 Henry IV* and *King Lear*, which name him, probably themselves rest on the title-pages. There is confirmation for some of the plays in contemporary references. The most important is the list given by Francis Meres in his *Palladis Tamia* of 1598.

This, on the assumption that *Love Labours Won* is an alternative title for *Taming of the Shrew*, contains twelve plays, but not *Henry VI*, which must be early work.[1] John Weever in 1599 speaks of *Romeo and Juliet* and either *Richard II* or *Richard III* as Shakespeare's, Gabriel Harvey in or before 1601 of *Hamlet*, Ben Jonson in 1619 and later of *Julius Caesar* and *Winter's Tale*.[2] The Revels Accounts of 1604–5 assign to him *Measure for Measure, Comedy of Errors*, and *Merchant of Venice*, but leave the *Moor of Venice, Merry Wives of Windsor, Henry V*, and *Love's Labour's Lost* anonymous.[3] This evidence is of a kind which is ordinarily accepted as determining the authorship of early literature. It is better than anything which we have for many of Shakespeare's dramatic contemporaries. *The Spanish Tragedy*, for example, is only attributed to Kyd on the basis of a casual reference by Nashe, and of Marlowe's authorship of *Tamburlaine* there is no direct contemporary record at all.[4] But of course title-pages are capable of rebuttal, on sufficient external or internal grounds shown. Publishers are not always well-informed or even honest. Shakespeare's name is also in the registration entry and on the title-page of *A Yorkshire Tragedy* and on those of *The London Prodigal* and Jaggard's reprint of *Sir John Oldcastle*, and the initials 'W. S.' are on those of *Locrine* (1595), *Thomas Lord Cromwell* (1602), and *The Puritan* (1607); and these six plays, with *Pericles*, were added as his to the Third Folio in 1664. All six can be safely rejected from the canon. But the reason for the appearance of the name may not be the same in all cases. It is conceivable that Shakespeare or another W. S. 'oversaw' the printing of the old court play *Locrine*. Three of the other plays belonged to his company, and the publishers may have been ignorant of their authorship. The same charitable supposition will not cover *The Puritan* or *Sir John Oldcastle*, a distinct play from *Henry IV*, which also sometimes went under that name. The 'W. S.' is similarly found on the Q2 of the *Troublesome Reign*, Shake-

---

[1] App. B, no. xiii.
[2] App. B, nos. xvii, xix, xxii.
[3] App. D.
[4] *Eliz. Stage*, iii. 396, 421.

speare's source-play for *King John*. This never got into
a Folio. Other misascriptions are due to Commonwealth
and Restoration booksellers.[1] The only bit of external
evidence against the authority of the First Folio itself is
the statement of Edward Ravenscroft in 1687 that Shakespeare only touched up *Titus Andronicus*.[2] But the inclusion of an individual play under the comprehensive title
of that collection must not be pressed too far. Heminges
and Condell and their publishers were not attempting a
modern 'critical' edition, and no doubt their methods were
imperfect. It is quite possible that they saw no harm in
including without comment a play which Shakespeare had
only revised, one or two for which he had a collaborator,
and one to which he had contributed little, but which had
long been linked to other 'parts' of an historical series. It
follows, of course, that alien matter may be present in other
plays than *Titus Andronicus*, *Taming of the Shrew*, *Henry
VIII*, and *1 Henry VI*. Contrariwise the possibility that
Shakespeare may have had a hand in some uncollected
plays cannot be wholly disregarded. Nevertheless the
Folio must be regarded as the chief authority for the main
range of Shakespeare's dramatic responsibility, and it requires deference as coming from men who were in the
best position to know the facts. A desire to do justice to
a dead 'fellow' and some care taken in the work are apparent enough in the epistles. Mr. J. M. Robertson, who
attempts to impugn the external evidence for the canon,
tells us that the players ascribed to Shakespeare work that
was not his 'in order to maintain their hold on the copyrights'.[3] They had no publishing copyrights, but were

[1] Cf. ch. x.

[2] Cf. p. 316, and App. C, no. xiv.

[3] *Canon* II. xvii, 'We may pardon
the players for obstinately specifying
as Shakespeare's works—in order to
maintain their hold on the copyrights
about which they are so obviously and
so naturally anxious—a collection of
plays as to which they knew and we
know that much of the writing is not
Shakespeare's at all'; cf. *Introd.* 66, 70,
76, 80-1, 'To father on Shakespeare

every piece in their repertory in which
they had proprietary rights was for
Heminge and Condell a way of maintaining their own interest.' Mr. Robertson protests (*Canon* III. 3) that he
has not charged Heminges and Condell with 'commercial fraud'. It may
be so; I do not know what degree of
misrepresentation in one's own financial interest amounts to commercial
fraud.

protected against stationers before 1623, and certainly an author's name on a print could not help them. If Mr. Robertson means stage-rights, his case might be better.[1] But the corroborative testimony of Meres cannot be disposed of by the repeated assertion that his list was 'derived from the theatre'.[2] We do not know whence he derived it. He was a literary clergyman, resident in London, and evidently interested in writers for the stage, about whom he tells us other things not recorded elsewhere. Many sources of information may have been open to him. His style tends to parallelism, and he balances six comedies of Shakespeare against six tragedies. He does not mention *Henry VI*. It would have upset the balance. But Meres did not complete his university career until 1593, and *Henry VI* may not have been played in London between his arrival and the compilation of his list.

In so far as the authority of the Folio is departed from, it must, except for the isolated case of *Titus Andronicus*, be on grounds of internal and not external evidence. It has often been departed from. A chronicle of the earlier scepticisms need not be set forth here.[3] They rested in part on an imperfect knowledge of the order in which the plays were written, which made the variations of style puzzling, and they were largely modified by the chronological investigations of Malone. Some oracular utterances of Coleridge bridge a gap. Modern essays at disintegrating the canon start from Fleay, whose own theories were ingenious if kaleidoscopic, but who called attention to many features of the texts, both stylistic and bibliographical, which are still receiving study. It is at present held by many students, and with varying degrees of stress on the different issues, that the Quarto and Folio texts have often been altered or abridged by other hands than Shakespeare's; that he revised his plays, with the result that variant texts, and even a single text, may contain fragments of different recensions; that he also revised the

---

[1] Cf. pp. 136, 149.
[2] *Introd.* 19, 59, 62, 65; *Canon* II. 21, 139.

[3] Cf. *The Disintegration of Shakespeare.*

work both of predecessors and contemporaries, whose writing remains entangled with his in the texts. There are certain practices of Elizabethan dramaturgy, which have helped to create a prepossession in favour of such theories. Collaboration and revision are both *verae causae*. Collaboration, rarely found in other forms of contemporary literature, was very common in drama. This can be established on records alone, without regard to the findings of conjecture. It begins with the courtly and legal amateurs of the 'sixties. *Gorboduc, Tancred and Gismund, Jocasta,* and later *Locrine* and *The Misfortunes of Arthur* had all from two to seven collaborators.[1] It is traceable among the University wits. The *Looking Glass* bears the names of Greene and Lodge; *Dido* those of Marlowe and Nashe. Greene, in 1592, addresses a 'young Juvenal, that biting satirist, that lastly with me together writ a Comedy'.[2] Probably we find the practice at its maximum in Henslowe's accounts for the Admiral's and Worcester's men during 1597–1604. Fees were paid for about 130 new plays, and of these well over half were written in collaboration by from two to as many as five hands. Of the more important contributors Webster and Wilson never stood alone, Chettle only in 12 plays out of 44, Dekker in 9 out of 41. An exception is Chapman, all of whose five plays were unaided, but for the use of a plot which Jonson had abandoned.[3] Jonson himself wrote one play alone and shared in three others. We may speculate as to the reasons for a method which cannot have made for good workmanship, and we hardly get beyond speculation. Many of the plays were ephemeral productions. Plays did not have long runs. One which did not draw was quickly discarded, and a new one called for, often at short notice. Even for the court, Munday had to bind himself to furnish a play within a fortnight.[4] The playwrights themselves were needy, and presumably small but frequent returns suited

[1] Cf. p. 536 and *Eliz. Stage*, iii. 320, 348, 456, 514.
[2] *Ibid.* iii. 451.
[3] Cf. Greg's tables in Henslowe, ii.
364. The ascriptions in *Eliz. Stage*, ch. xxiii, differ in some details; the facts are not always clear.
[4] Henslowe, i. 93.

their purses. We have little information as to the men, other than Shakespeare and Jonson, who wrote for the Chamberlain's company. Probably they were the same who wrote for Henslowe. There is no reason to suppose that, as a rule, a playwright, who was not himself an actor, was anything but a free lance. The special arrangements, by which Henslowe tied the impecunious Chettle and Porter to write for the Admiral's only, carry this implication.[1] Jonson wrote two unaided plays for the Chamberlain's, but for his *Sejanus* of 1603 he had a collaborator, whose work, with a compliment, he replaced by his own, before it went to press.[2] There is no recorded parallel to this proceeding, which must be set down to Jonson's conscious pride of artistry. In the seventeenth century we get the familiar and enduring partnership of Beaumont and Fletcher, although certainly Fletcher and probably Beaumont also wrote independently. The contemporary testimony of Sir Aston Cokain informs us that Massinger also had a hand in some of the plays printed as Beaumont and Fletcher's in 1647. Chapman, Jonson, and Marston joined in *Eastward Ho*, and there were various shifting combinations, in which Dekker, Middleton, Rowley, and Webster are conspicuous. In *Eastward Ho* and in the Beaumont and Fletcher plays, the literary difficulties of collaboration are fairly well surmounted. Much has been written as to the way in which labour was divided in joint plays. It is not necessary to assume that the same method was always followed. Presumably an outline was agreed upon and some sort of a *scenario* prepared. Thereafter the actual writing might be distributed according to the interweaving of a plot and sub-plot, of which one might be tragic and the other comic. Or each author might follow up particular characters, which would come to much the same thing. Or one author might start all the main themes, and the rest carry them forward on his lines. There are certainly cases of a rough-and-ready partition by

[1] *Eliz. Stage*, i. 374.
[2] *Ibid.* iii. 368. It has been shown (cf. App. B, no. xxii) that Samuel Sheppard's age makes it impossible for him to have been the collaborator.

acts. Daborne gave Tourneur an act of his *Arraignment of London* to write, and Dekker contributed the first act of *Keep the Widow Waking* and one speech in the last act.[1] There is no evidence at all for anything of the nature of a line-by-line collaboration, which certainly would not have made for expedition.

Clearly there need be no reason for surprise if Shakespeare occasionally had a collaborator. The problem of revision is more complicated. Plays which had been laid aside were often revived. A stock favourite was called a 'get-penny'.[2] I have collected the notices of Shakespearean revivals.[3] The Admiral's men bought old plays in order to reproduce them.[4] When the Chapel resumed their activities in 1600, it was complained that 'the vmbrae, or ghosts of some three or foure playes, departed a dozen yeeres since, haue bin seen walking on your stage heere'.[5] And revival was sometimes accompanied by revision. Even with a familiar play, it was a fairly obvious device to increase the attraction. And sometimes a forgotten play was passed off as new.[6] It may be that higher entrance fees could be charged for a play called new. Revision does not seem to have been regarded as very exalted dramatic work. Dekker speaks of 'a Cobler of Poetrie called a play-patcher', and in Jonson's *Poetaster* Demetrius Fannius, who is probably Dekker himself, is 'a dresser of plaies about the towne, here'.[7] It is difficult to estimate the extent of the practice. Again, it will be best to begin with recorded cases. Conceivably three or four plays marked 'ne' in Henslowe's accounts for 1594–7 may have been revived and not strictly new; the significance of 'ne' is not quite clear. During 1597–1603 the Admiral's men appear to have revived at least 23 old plays. The latter

---

[1] *Henslowe Papers*, 72; C. Sisson in *4 Library*, viii. 243.

[2] *Eliz. Stage*, i. 372.

[3] App. D.

[4] *Eliz. Stage*, ii. 167, 179.

[5] *Ibid.* ii. 43.

[6] Beaumont and Fletcher, *The False One* (c. 1620), prol., 'New Titles warrant not a Play for new'; D. Lupton,

London and the Countrey Carbonadoed and Quartered (1632), 'The players are as crafty with an old play, as bauds with old faces; the one puts on a new fresh colour, the other a new face and name.'

[7] Dekker, *News from Hell* (1606, *Works*, ii. 146); Jonson, *Poetaster*, iii. 4, 367.

must have been popular, since 11 of them have come down to us in print, a quite disproportionate number, in view of the oblivion which has overtaken most of the 300 or so plays named by Henslowe. If one may judge by the fees paid to the poets, only four of the revivals entailed substantial revision and two others small alterations. There were also small alterations to five recent plays, and new prologues and epilogues were written for three revivals.[1] In several cases the plays concerned were being prepared for court, and alterations may have been due to the special scrutiny by the Revels officers required for court performances. The total amount of revision for the Admiral's men during a period of six years was therefore very slight. As to its nature we are not wholly in the dark. Three of the four substantially altered plays are extant. Of *Old Fortunatus* we have only the later text; it seems probable that the original play was in two parts and that the revision compressed them into one. Both *Dr. Faustus* and *The Spanish Tragedy* survive in duplicate versions. The earliest (1604) of *Dr. Faustus* is corrupt, and the textual history of the play is therefore difficult to reconstruct. But it is at least possible to trace, both here and in a later version of 1616, the progressive introduction of farcical prose scenes alien to Marlowe's design.[2] The *Spanish Tragedy* is in somewhat similar case. Some alterations in the version of 1602 amount to the insertion of new scenes into an otherwise unaltered text. It is, however, most improbable that these particular scenes represent the revision for the Admiral's men.[3] There are parallels elsewhere both to the compression of *Fortunatus* and to the expansion of *Faustus* and *The Spanish Tragedy* by added passages. Heywood,

[1] Henslowe, i. 94, 99, 114–16, 124–5, 143, 149, 153, 164–8, 171–3. Dekker altered the old *Tasso's Melancholy* (£4), *Fortunatus* (£9), and *Phaethon* (£2), and did a prologue and epilogue for *Pontius Pilate* (10s.); Chettle altered the old *Vayvode* (£1) and recent *1, 2 Robin Hood* (10s. each), *1, 2 Cardinal Wolsey* (£1 each), and *Friar Rush* (10s.), and did a prologue and epilogue for an unspecified play (5s.); Jonson altered the old *Spanish Tragedy* (£2 and part of £10); Bird and Rowley altered the old *Dr. Faustus* (£4); Middleton did a prologue and epilogue for *Friar Bacon* (5s.).

[2] Cf. P. Simpson in *Essays and Studies*, vii (1921), 143.

[3] Cf. p. 148 and W. W. Greg in M.S.R. reprint, xviii.

at some uncertain date, constructed an *Escapes of Jupiter* out of scenes taken from his series of *Ages*.[1]   An allusion in *Satiromastix* suggests a possible counter-device of expanding one play into two.[2]   *Histriomastix* appears to have been rehandled by the insertion of passages, some long and some short.[3]   Chapman's *Bussy D'Ambois* was touched up, at some unknown date before 1641, possibly to improve its effectiveness on the stage.[4]   Two plays of the King's men, *The Malcontent* and *Mucedorus*, received additional scenes, the former to lengthen the performance, the latter for a revival at court.   The original conclusion of Jonson's *Every Man Out of his Humour* was altered because it had given offence.   It is not certain whether the variants at the beginning and end of the corrupt Q1 of *Philaster* indicate a revision.[5]   No doubt there are later examples, and no doubt, as time went on, a tendency to bring revived plays into accordance with new dramatic fashions is likely enough to have developed.[6]   But Sir Henry Herbert's documents of 1622–42 do not disclose any great change of conditions.   The extracts made by Malone and Chalmers from his Office Book include notices of licences for some 130 plays.   Of these only fifteen were old, and seven of them had been revised.   One was a play of Fletcher's 'corrected' by Shirley; one had undergone 'renewing' and one 'alterations'; four had had one or more scenes added.[7]   There is throughout little evidence, so far as the records go, for any widespread theatrical practice of what may be called stylistic revision, the systematic

---

[1] Greg in *Anglica*, ii. 212.

[2] *Satiromastix*, 980. Horace says that Demetrius Fannius 'cut an innocent Moore i' the middle, to serue him in twice; & when he had done, made Poules-worke of it'.

[3] *Eliz. Stage*, iv. 17.

[4] T. M. Parrott in *M.L.R.* iii. 126.

[5] *Eliz. Stage*, iii. 222, 360, 431; iv. 34.·

[6] Chamberlain writes in 1615 (Birch, *James*, i. 290), 'Our poets' brains and inventions are grown very dry, insomuch that of five new plays there is not one pleases, and therefore they are driven to furbish over their old, which stand them in best stead, and bring them most profit.' Heywood apologizes in 1637 for the out-of-date rhyme of his *Royal King and Loyal Subject*, to which 'strong lines' had come to be preferred.

[7] Herbert may have missed some revivals, although normally (cf. p. 104) he required old plays to be submitted to him, and the extracts we have are not (cf. pp. 93, 100) complete. A list of revivals is in Albright 253.

line-by-line correction or rewriting of old dialogue, either by the original author or by another. Examples of this may be found in Wilmot's recast of *Gismond of Salerne* as *Tancred and Gismund*, and in some of Ben Jonson's re-handling of his own work, notably *Every Man In his Humour*.[1] But these were of the nature of literary rather than theatrical enterprises. The nearest approach to the same sort of thing in a theatrical text is the rewriting of parts of *Sir Thomas More*. It probably came before production, if there was a production. The rewriting of *Believe As You List* for the satisfaction of the censor is, of course, not in point. When, therefore, one finds stylistic revision brought forward again and again, as a con-jectural factor in the literary history of one after another in a series of plays, one is justified in expressing a profound scepticism as to whether the practice, if it existed at all, can have been anything like so universal as the theorists assume. And indeed all the probabilities are against it. The ordinary Elizabethan audience is not likely to have been very critical of style, and it is difficult to see how the process contemplated could have resulted in any increase of drawing power commensurate with the cost and trouble involved. Even if the rewriting could be done on the margins of an existing prompt-copy, which I do not be-lieve, the reviser would have to be paid and new parts made out. These any actors already familiar with the old version would learn with reluctance. Minor alterations or even the addition of scenes would not cause quite the same inconvenience, and no doubt some adaptation to changing conditions of cast, theatre, and audience may be taken for granted. There are, of course, texts which have not come down to us in their original form. Some are reported; some have been interpolated; some have been abridged. Abridgement, like interpolation, is a form of revision, and it may involve consequential adjustment of context. Again we must assume that it would not be lightly undertaken. The motives which prompted it are obscure. It has been held that plays were abridged for court performance.

---

[1] *Eliz. Stage*, iii. 359, 514; Herford-Simpson, i. 358.

There is no obvious reason why this should have been so. Court entertainments often lasted for three hours, and a full-length play of 3,000 lines would not require more.[1] It is true that in Elizabethan, although not in Jacobean days, a mask often followed. For the matter of that, a jig often followed on the public stage.[2] Some of the shorter plays may have originally been written to go with an afterpiece. It has also been held that abridgement was for provincial performance. But again, while we do not know much about provincial conditions, it is a mere assumption that a country audience would want a particularly short entertainment. There is plenty of leisure in the country. It is true that, if a travelling company was a small one, the cutting of superfluous parts and *spectacle* might incidentally lead to shortening. But such companies were often ten or more strong, and probably many London plays could be found to fit them without going to the trouble and expense of extensive adaptation.[3] It is just possible that conditions of lighting tied the London public theatres themselves to shorter performances in the winter than in the summer, and that this may be one explanation of abridgement.[4]

I return to the topic of stylistic revision. Mr. Robertson questions the analogy suggested by the rarity of payments for alterations in the accounts of the Admiral's men; and of course such an analogy is not conclusive. It overlooks, he says:[5]—

the cardinal fact that Shakespeare's company had in him what no other company possessed—a gifted member who could revise for them any play that came into their hands, lending to other men's work new qualities of beauty and strength where he would or could, pruning redundances, and rewriting or planing down Chapmanese rhodomontade.

Mr. Robertson's 'cardinal fact' is neither 'cardinal' nor a

[1] *Eliz. Stage*, i. 225. To the evidence there given may be added *Mid. N. Dr.* v. 1. 32,

    what masques, what dances sh: 'l
      we have,
To wear away this long age of three
    hours

Between our after-supper and bed-time?
[2] *Eliz. Stage*, ii. 551.
[3] *Ibid.* i. 332; cf. W. J. Lawrence in *T.L.S.* (1919, Aug. 21).
[4] *Eliz. Stage*, ii. 543.
[5] *Canon*, iii. 76.

'fact'; it is a conclusion, not a starting-point, and it is a
conclusion from Mr. Robertson's own long series of conjectures. The only fact behind it, other than the interpretation of internal evidence for which it is treated as
axiomatic, is the isolated statement of Ravenscroft about
an exceptional play. I do not altogether reject that statement, but it is not much on which to establish a conception
of Shakespeare's habitual method of work, so divergent
as Mr. Robertson's from what we are told and what we
can gather for ourselves of his temperament. 'His mind
and hand went together; and what he thought, he uttered
with easiness', say Heminges and Condell. 'He flowed
with facility', says Ben Jonson. The last man, one would
suppose, in the absence of rigid proof, to tie himself to the
painful following up and meticulous correction of the
thoughts and words of another. So far as facts go, it is the
Admiral's and not the Chamberlain's company which we
know to have had cobblers of poetry ready to hand, in
Chettle and in Dekker, the 'dresser of plaies' chaffed by
Jonson, who between them did most of the small amount
of revision required.[1] I doubt whether many critics think
with Mr. Robertson that Shakespeare went on dressing
up alien plays well into his mid-career, even if they believe
him to have had a fancy for rewriting his own work. It is,
however, very commonly held that such was the occupation of his apprenticeship. Even this is hardly a certainty.
Two things, besides Ravenscroft's statement, seem to have
contributed to form the notion. One is the long-standing
belief in the derivation of 2, 3 *Henry VI* through a line-by-
line revision of the *Contention*. That support must go,
when it is realized that the *Contention* is a reported text,
and could never have been written as it stands. The other
is the reference to Shakespeare in Robert Greene's address
of 1592 to his fellow dramatists.[2]

Base minded men all three of you, if by my miserie you be not
warnd: for vnto none of you (like mee) sought those burres to

---

[1] Cf. p. 211. It was Dekker also
who altered *Sir John Oldcastle* for
Worcester's men (Henslowe, i. 181).
[2] Cf. App. B, no. iii.

cleaue: those Puppets (I meane) that spake from our mouths, those Anticks garnisht in our colours. Is it not strange, that I, to whom they all haue beene beholding: is it not like that you, to whome they all haue beene beholding, shall (were yee in that case as I am now) bee both at once of them forsaken? Yes trust them not: for there is an vpstart Crow, beautified with our feathers, that with his *Tygers hart wrapt in a Players hyde*, supposes he is as well able to bombast out a blanke verse as the best of you: and beeing an absolute *Iohannes fac totum*, is in his own conceit the onely Shake-scene in a countrey. O that I might intreat your rare wits to be imploied in more profitable courses: & let those Apes imitate your past excellence, and neuer more acquaint them with your admired inuentions.

The phrase 'beautified with our feathers', helped by the parody of *3 Henry VI*, i. 4. 137, has been regarded as a charge of appropriating the plays of Greene and his fellows, and in particular the *Contention*, by rewriting them.[1] With the fall of the *Contention*, this interpretation at once becomes less plausible. And a closer examination of the passage shows that there is really no charge of appropriation at all. It is an attack by a disgruntled poet on the players who have profited by him and now have no further use for his services, and one of whom thinks that he can do everything himself, and is taking the job of writing out of the mouths of better men. There is a charge of imitation at the end, no doubt, but imitation is not rewriting. The 'beautified with our feathers' cannot be dissociated from the 'garnisht in our colours' applied just before to the actors as such, of which it is a mere variation. The line of attack, the use of the feather metaphor, the comparison of an actor to a crow, were none of them new. Nashe wrote in 1589 of gentlemen poets who had 'tricked up a company of taffata fooles with their feathers'.[2] Greene himself in 1590 had made Cicero speak of Roscius as 'proud with *Esops* Crow, being pranct with the glorie of others feathers'.[3] There is a conflation of themes drawn ultimately from Aesop, Martial, and Macrobius, all used

---

[1] R. B., no doubt, so took it, when he echoed the *Groat's-Worth* in his *Greene's Funeralls* (App. B, no. vi).
[2] *Epistle* to *Menaphon*; cf. *Eliz.*
Stage, iv. 234.
[3] *Francescoes Fortunes*; cf. *Eliz. Stage*, iv. 236.

to point the gibes of playwrights against their paymasters.[1]
It was Greene's prospect of further employment, not
his property in what he had already. written, that he
bewailed.

Shakespeare did not as a rule invent his plots; that is to
say, the narratives to which he gave dramatic form. This
we know, because for many plays we have his direct
sources, although for others we may suspect that we have
only more remote sources which reached him in intermediate versions, perhaps themselves dramatic. The
direct sources he handled very freely when they were
romance, and rather less so when they were history. Often,
especially in the histories, he adopted words and phrases
from what lay before him. Shakespeare is not revising
Holinshed and Plutarch, and he is not merely pruning
and planing down *A Shrew*, *The Troublesome Reign*, and
King Leir. He is taking a story, using so much of it as
appeals to his sense of dramatic values, altering what does
not, and giving it literary form through his command of
language. The habit of stylistic revision, if it was his at
all, must be established elsewhere, and on internal, not
external, grounds. The observed use of sources does not
reveal it. The task has been approached from two angles,
that of style itself and that of bibliography. Mr. Robertson is the most prominent of many writers who find dis-
parate styles in the plays of the canon. His conviction of
these leads him to seek 'clues' to other dramatists, whose
work it is historically possible that Shakespeare might
have revised; and after he has framed to his satisfaction
canons of their plays, the conviction is confirmed. Here
are styles consonant to those which he repudiates for
Shakespeare. As a result he transfers the primary responsibility for *Richard III*, *Richard II*, *Henry V*, *Julius
Caesar*, and *Comedy of Errors* to Marlowe, for *Romeo and
Juliet* to Peele, for *Two Gentlemen of Verona* to Greene,
for *Troilus and Cressida*, *All's Well that Ends Well*, and
Measure for Measure to Chapman. There has been much
collaboration between some of these and possibly with Kyd

[1] *Eliz. Stage*, i. 377.

and others. Shakespeare has rehandled all these, some more, some less, 'with a view, first and last, to making them serve the company's ends'. Of the plays as a whole, 'the great majority are simply not of Shakespeare's drafting'.[1] Here, of course, common sense revolts. After all, we have read the plays for ourselves, and have learnt to recognize in them, through all their diversities, a continuous personality, of which style is only one aspect. A single mind and a single hand dominate them. They are the outcome of one man's critical reactions to life, which make the stuff of comedy, and of one man's emotional reactions to life, which make the stuff of tragedy. Something must be wrong with the methods which have led to such devastating conclusions.

Everything indeed is wrong with them. It would be both tedious and unprofitable to follow Mr. Robertson's painstaking investigations in detail, when one's starting-point is a complete rejection of the axioms by which they are governed. And it is perhaps superfluous to stress the remarkable diversity between his reconstructions and those of other students who work, broadly speaking, upon the same lines. The variant distributions of *Julius Caesar* among Marlowe, Shakespeare, Jonson, Beaumont, Chapman, and Drayton furnish a noteworthy example.[2] No doubt a method may be sound, and may be more skilfully applied by one practitioner than by another. But the conflicts do not inspire any great confidence in the critical principles which underlie them. The fundamental error lies in a misconception of the limits within which the discrimination of styles, as applied to the particular subject-matter of the Elizabethan drama, must operate. The percipience of style is a very real quality. It has its origin, I suppose, in the same natural feeling for the value of words and the rise and fall of rhythm, which is the starting-point of literary expression itself; and it may be trained, half-unconsciously, through reading and reflection and comparison into a valuable instrument of criticism. A quasi-intuitive sense is developed. It becomes effective

---

[1] *Canon*, iii. 100, 200.   [2] Cf. p. 398.

in the presence of a writer who has a characteristic style and has room and inclination to give that style free play. It enables one, for instance, to dismiss some of the apocryphal plays ascribed to Shakespeare without more ado. It helps at least to disentangle collaborators, if their styles are sufficiently distinct, and their separate contributions of sufficient length. It must make allowance, of course, for many things; for the gradual evolution of styles, for influences, for experiments, for variations of interest and temper, for the adaptation of manner to subject-matter. It will be at a loss when a writer, as sometimes happens with Shakespeare, is bored, or in haste, or merely careless, and fails to hold his style. Moreover dramatic writing, and Elizabethan dramatic writing in particular, contains many bits of undistinguished joiner's work which may help the action along, but are in themselves colourless. One man might have written them as well as another. The most percipient critic cannot reasonably claim to have acquired a faculty which is fine enough to identify commonplace passages or very short passages. And he will be wise if he refrains, so far as possible, from detecting the small touches of a reviser. Now and then a phrasing seems to stand out in startling distinctness from its context; like the 'poor worm' which 'casts copp'd hills towards heaven' in the normally unShakespearean part of *Pericles*.[1] But even in such cases attributions can rarely be made with conviction. It is said that the ultra-violet rays will reveal over-painting in pictures through different effects upon different pigments. The sense of style does not work like an ultra-violet ray. It must be added that the sense of style is itself ultimately dependent upon external evidence. There is no way of getting at the characteristics of an individual writer, except from work of which his authorship is acknowledged. And if the acquired sense is then used to discredit the canon wholesale, a vicious circle is set up, of which the inevitable result is chaos.

The scholarly mind seeks to confirm its intuition by an analysis of the concrete features of style. A writer forms

[1] *Per.* i. 1. 100.

his own rhetorical habits in the building of lines and the linking of line to line, in the use of exclamation, antithesis, iteration, and cumulation, in the balance of noun against noun and verb against verb. He has his own small mannerisms of locution; his recurrent catch-phrases; his ellipses and inversions; his superfluous auxiliaries; his archaisms, it may be, and grammatical solecisms. These are the more characteristic, because they become unconscious, and are often at first sight unnoticeable. Such things can be observed and tabulated, with due regard to the risk of assuming monopolies in them. It is a matter of degree; one man may prefer 'you' and another 'ye', one ''em' and another 'them', if printers can be persuaded not to interfere. It is so too with rhythm. The normal iambic blank verse is capable of a great deal of variation, both in the structure of individual lines and in the grouping of lines into paragraphs. Stresses can be inverted; additional syllables can be introduced; pauses can come at the ends of lines or can break their flow; rhyme can be employed, sporadically, or with a clinching effect. Alliteration may be obvious or restrained. Writers acquire different habits of verse-manipulation, and many, like Shakespeare, follow different habits at different stages of their development.[1] Many metrical variations can be expressed in statistics, but not all, and not the interplay of variations upon which the resultant rhythmical effect largely depends. Metrical analysis requires ample space, if it is to be significant, since a rhythmical habit is itself varied according to subject-matter, and these variations only average out over long stretches of verse. Comparative figures for complete plays, perhaps for complete acts, may be of value, but not for single scenes and still less for single speeches. The method has proved useful in dividing the results of collaboration. The rhythm of Shakespeare's later verse, for example, differs markedly from that of Fletcher's; less so from that of Beaumont's or of Massinger's. Naturally each writer has also his individual range of thought, of dramatic situations, of imagery, of allusion, of vocabulary.

[1] Cf. ch. viii.

But here there is much give and take, and there is nothing more dangerous than the attempt to determine authorship by the citation of parallels. Authors repeat their predecessors; their successors repeat them; they repeat themselves. Shakespeare's self-repetitions are innumerable. They are commonest between plays of approximately the same date, but common also between plays remote in time, especially when analogous themes recur. His younger contemporaries also repeat themselves freely and they repeat him just as freely. Parallels, therefore, are always open to a double interpretation, if chronology and lack of ascription permit; they may be from one pen or from two. It could hardly be otherwise. All literature is full of parallels, but especially the literature of the Elizabethans, because they had a far more restricted tradition behind them than the moderns, and especially the literature of the dramatic writers, because they were men of the theatre. Even if they were not actors themselves, they lived in a world of representations and rehearsals, and their minds were filled with auditory images of spoken words, which naturally came to the surface when they wrote. Parallels are of all degrees; they descend from elaborate passages involving a combination of common elements, through dramatic motives, similes and metaphors, historical and mythological allusions, special collocations of words, mannerisms, down to the mere occurrence of unusual words. They are in fact constantly brought forward by critics as evidence of common authorship. This they rarely can be. Where anonymous work is in question nothing better may be available, but conclusions so formed should at the most be held as possibilities. Probably the most striking parallels are the least evidential; it is the vivid idea or phrase which catches the imagination of another. There is a negative value in comprehensive collections of parallels, however slight, to a doubtful play. If none are found to a given writer, he is not likely to have written it. The converse does not hold true, but it may chime with other evidence. The collections made for *Pericles* and *Henry VIII* confirm distributions of shares arrived at on other grounds. It is, however, difficult, even when a concordance is available, to be sure that a collection is complete.

The history of Shakespeare's writing is one of the gradual development of a characteristic style or series of styles. In its matured flights it is often unmistakable. Its beginnings belong to a period in which the difficulties of style-discrimination are at their maximum. The dramatists of the 'eighties may reasonably be called a school.[1] They have largely a common style and a common vocabulary, which owe much to Spenser, to the Elizabethan translators of the classics, to Seneca and his court imitators. Marlowe is the dominant figure, with Peele, Greene, Lodge, and Nashe as his satellites; Kyd stands a little apart. There is a mass of anonymous work. There were other prolific writers, such as Thomas Watson, of whose plays we know nothing. Probably we should be able to differentiate some of the personalities a little better, if we had reliable canons. Even now, Marlowe's is more distinct than the rest. But there are no such canons. Only from two to seven plays are ascribed to any one man, and of these many have been transmitted in such corrupt texts that they are valueless. The style of non-dramatic work may be compared; the translations of Marlowe, the pamphlets of Greene, the ceremonial poems of Peele. But these only give limited help in judging the handling of dialogued verse. It is illegitimate to follow Mr. Robertson in expanding the canons by adding first one anonymous play, and then on the basis of this another, and then again another. There is no certainty in this process, which mainly rests on parallels, and the chain becomes weaker at every link. This school was Shakespeare's early environment, and his first plays were inevitably in its manner. The influence of Marlowe is discernible until well on in his career. Mr. Robertson, who has all the arts of the debater, except perhaps that of lucidity, abounds in pejorative terms for what he calls the 'Imitation theory'. He represents it as charging Shakespeare with a 'passion for plagiarism', with 'tranced' or 'slavish' mimicry, with 'abject parodies'. If he

[1] Cf. *The Unrest in Shakespearean Studies* (1927, *Nineteenth Century*).

repeated the phrase of a predecessor, he must have been an 'avid copyist' or possessed by an 'overwhelming impulse of apery'. This is only beating the air. Young writers, even when they have done good work, do remain subject to influences, especially if they are of receptive, as well as creative, temperaments. There is no reason why Shakespeare should have been an exception. Very likely there was some deliberate imitation at first of admired models, but the issue is not primarily one of imitation. I have written above of parallels and repetitions. Psychologically, these may mean anything from plagiarism to quite unconscious echoing. A writer's mind is a well of subliminal memory, into which words and images sink, and to the surface of which they arise again, unbidden, in the act of composition.[1] I do not think it would be possible to assert Shakespeare's authorship of 2, 3 *Henry VI* on internal evidence alone. They are school work and full of school echoes. There are many images drawn from country life, which set them a little apart, and may be marks of Shakespeare. Those which recall the sea are also noteworthy. Links of style with the plays to come, especially *Richard III*, are not wanting. Double endings are much more often used to vary the blank verse rhythm than in any of the ascertainable plays of Marlowe and his fellows, and Mr. Robertson does not really meet this point, either by citing the higher proportion of double endings in Marlowe's non-dramatic translation of Lucan, or by the *a priori* argument that towards the end of their careers Marlowe, Kyd, and Greene must all have felt the need of some relief to the monotony of their earlier systems.[2] Metrical evolution is not a *Zeitgeist* which all poets are alike bound to follow. We are not, however, left to internal evidence for 2, 3 *Henry VI*, and there is certainly no such disparity of style as need compel us to abandon the authority of the First Folio. Ravenscroft's testimony puts *Titus Andronicus* upon a rather different footing. It may be

---

[1] Cf. the admirable study of the working of Coleridge's imagination in J. L. Lowes, *The Road to Xanadu* (1927).

[2] *Canon*, ii. 24; *Introd.* 27; cf. p. 260.

that further study of the dramatic style of the 'eighties in relation to its origins will disclose lines of demarcation which are not at present apparent. At present it is tangled country, in which it is not much use to run like a hound through the undergrowth, catching a scent of Marlowe here, and whimpering there at a suspicion of Kyd or Peele. Complicated theories of collaboration and revision cannot be based upon such findings.

Critical bibliography, or applied bibliography, as Professor Pollard prefers to call it, is a valuable and comparatively new instrument of textual research. It begins with the observation of irregularities in the texts which are not capable of being explained by printing-house operations, and ascribes them, reasonably enough, to the condition of the copy brought to the printers. And it finds reasons for this condition in the vicissitudes through which plays may have passed at the theatre itself. It attempts, in fact, to reconstruct their stage-histories. In the hands of its initiators, this process has generally involved the assumption of one or more revisions; revisions by Shakespeare of earlier work, revisions of Shakespeare's work by later adapters, revisions by Shakespeare of his own work; and on occasion, since these are intrepid researchers, who do not quail before intricate conclusions, revisions of all three types successively. All this is not pure bibliography, although bibliographical facts are its starting-point. Historical allusions in the plays are drawn upon to furnish support for suggestions of double or treble dating. Judgements of style are also involved, and incur the hazards of style-discrimination already considered, although these are diminished when it is only a question of comparison between the phases of Shakespeare's own style, the general course of which is fairly well established. I must not be taken as implying that the judgements are always sound; they seem sometimes to rest upon work which is not fully characteristic. There are some anticipations of the bibliographical method in the unsystematic writings of Fleay. But it came to the front in two notable papers by Professors Pollard and Wilson on The 'Stolne and Surreptitious'

Shakespearian Texts.[1] These are the bad Quartos of *Romeo and Juliet*, *Henry V*, *Merry Wives of Windsor*, and *Hamlet*, and the papers offer a common theory as to their origin. A factor of reporting by a pirate actor is admitted. But this is held not to explain all the facts. It is supposed that the pirate could only report scenes to which he had special access. Moreover, there are obvious cuts; there is non-Shakespearean, as well as Shakespearean matter, especially towards the end of each play; and there are 'bibliographical links' between the bad and good texts, in identical misprints, punctuation, spelling, capitals, and lineation, which imply 'some kind of organic connexion' between the manuscripts used. The theory is that the plays existed in non-Shakespearean versions before 1593; that by that year Shakespeare had made a beginning with the revision of them all; that from the manuscripts in this condition abridged transcripts were 'hastily' taken for the provincial tour of 'Strange's' men which began in May 1593; that Shakespeare subsequently retouched and completed his revisions on the original manuscripts; and that when these were performed, the bad Quartos were printed from the transcripts, which had been brought by the pirate actor into 'some kind of conformity' with the final versions. These papers were followed by separate studies of *Romeo and Juliet*, *Henry V*, and *Merry Wives of Windsor*, and had been anticipated in a more elaborate dissertation by Professor Wilson on *Hamlet*.[2] Here the same theory was developed, except that Shakespeare was eliminated from the earlier revision of *Merry Wives of Windsor*, and a revision of *Hamlet*, anterior to his, by one or more dramatists for an unknown company was introduced. There is much in the theory which I do not find it possible to accept. I do not think that the hypothesis of a memorizing reporter, who could do a little 'faking', is inadequate to account for the bad Quartos.[3] I do not accept the evidence for an early *Merry Wives of Windsor* or for traces of early

[1] *T.L.S.* (9 and 16 Jan. 1919).
[2] *Ibid.* (13 Mar., 7, 14 Aug. 1919); Wilson, *The Copy for Hamlet*, 1603, *and the Hamlet Transcript*, 1593 (1918).
[3] Cf. p. 157.

dates in the others. My imagination boggles at the picture of Shakespeare concurrently revising three or four
different plays. The 'bibliographical links' are, I believe,
confined to *Romeo and Juliet* and *Hamlet*, and they seem
to me to point most naturally to some use made of the bad
Quartos in setting-up the good ones. Here, indeed, is a
particularly weak point in the theory. The transcripts,
to accord with it, must have been, as Professor Wilson
admits, 'meticulous', and what Elizabethan transcriber,
working 'rapidly', is likely to have been meticulous about
spelling, punctuation, and capitals? Two prepossessions
appear to have had great influence upon the theorists. One
is that of Shakespeare as essentially a 'play-patcher', for
which I have endeavoured to show that there is little
foundation. The other is that of 'continuous copy', which
I suspect to be nothing but an illegitimate generalization
from the anomalous case of *Sir Thomas More*, aided by
a notion that the cautious and economical companies
wanted above all things to avoid the multiplication of
transcripts, although they did not, if the views of Professors Pollard and Wilson are sound, take any care to keep
them out of the hands of pirates when they were made. In
order to fit Professor Wilson's reconstruction, Shakespeare's two revisions of *Hamlet*, if not also that of the
anterior dramatists, must all have been done on the manuscript of the original play, and this must still have existed
in 1604, and have served as copy for the Second Quarto.
Newly written sheets may have replaced part of it, but on
part the old matter must still have been standing, scored
out and transformed by the superimposed results of at
least two rehandlings on its margins and on appended
slips. There is no room for a fair copy, because the 'bibliographical links' between the two Quartos have to be
preserved. Yet the Second Quarto does not show any
obvious signs of the considerable textual disturbance
which one would expect in such circumstances.

Professor Pollard has also made a study of the Yorkist
plays, which may perhaps require reconsideration, if
it is admitted that the texts of *The Contention* are re-

ported.[1] Professor Wilson has dealt bibliographically with
most of the comedies in full-dress editions. Here, too, the
doctrine of 'continuous copy' is apparent, although many of
the reconstructions involve transcripts at some stage or
other. There are few plays which are not suspected, sometimes on the faintest of indications, of having originated in
the rehandling of old dramatic material. Part of this material
is here and there supposed to have been retained.[2] Fairly
drastic adaptations by later hands are inferred.[3] But perhaps the most noteworthy feature of the treatment is its
frequent resort to hypotheses of self-revision.[4] Even if
one is unconvinced by Professor Wilson's reconstructions,
one must be impressed by the alertness of his mind, the
keenness of his observation, and the ingenuity with which
he fits the details of complicated theories together. He has
certainly called attention to many points which require
explanation. I think that he often overlooks the possibility
of alternative explanations. Still more I think that he and
I take different views of Shakespeare's temperament. I am
prepared to accept some very poor work as Shakespeare's.
He must have been subject to moods, which were not all
compatible with concentration on what he was writing.
During a considerable period he was under the shadow of
some preoccupation or disillusionment, the cause of which
remains obscure; and the life and subtlety of his style
suffered. But throughout he was often careless, and often
perfunctory. He composed easily, and his artistic conscience did not impel him to be scrupulous in avoiding
inconsistencies of time, action, and characterization. No
doubt he was aware how very easily dropped threads pass
unnoticed on the stage. I do not suppose that he had a
very high opinion of the intelligence of his audiences.
I am not essaying here a complete appreciation of Professor Wilson's contribution to Shakespearean scholarship.
Much of it, especially on the strictly textual side, is ad-

[1] *T.L.S.* (19, 26 Sept. 1918).
[2] *Com. of Err., Tam. of Shrew, Mer. of Ven., Merry Wives of W.*
[3] *Two Gent. of Ver., Meas. for Meas.*

[4] *Love's Lab. Lost, Mid. N. Dr., Mer. of Ven., As You Like It, Much Ado, Temp.*

mirable. Some of his views on major problems have been
referred to,[1] and others, directly concerned with revision, now demand consideration. I will begin with
'cuts'. We know that cutting was a theatrical practice,
since authors themselves have told us so.[2] That Shakespeare's plays were not immune is shown both by the
condition of the bad Quartos and by some of the omissions
in parallel-text plays, for which cuts are the most plausible
explanation.[3] The latter are not extensive; they do not
amount to the replacement of a three-hour play by a two-
hour play.[4] Two or three hundred lines go, to prevent
normal limits from being exceeded, or merely to prevent
particular scenes or speeches from dragging. Probably
Hamlet was always too long for performance as a whole.
Shakespeare may have been more intent upon his poetry,
than upon getting it over the stage-rails. One hopes that
he remained unperturbed when some of his best lines were
sacrificed. Cutting may be suspected also in plays for
which we have not parallel-texts. The very short *Macbeth*
possibly represents a substantial abridgement. In Professor
Wilson's reconstructions abridgement appears as a factor
subsidiary to revision.[5] Old motives have been omitted or
given less importance in order that new ones may be
introduced, and traces of the process remain. Among
these he is apt to cite the presence of short lines. These
may very well in some cases indicate cuts, especially when
they are abrupt or harsh, or are accompanied by textual
disturbance or some *hiatus* in the sense. But a great many
of those called in aid by Professor Wilson do not present these features, and more plausible reasons can be
found for them. Shakespeare made constant use of short
lines for exclamations and interjections, for formulas of

---

[1] Cf. pp. 153, 181, 187, 191, 198.

[2] *Eliz. Stage*, iii. 192. W. J. Law-rence (*T.L.S.* 21 Aug. 1919) adds R. Brome, *The Antipodes* (1640), 'You shall find in this Booke more than was presented on the stage, and left out of the Presentation for superfluous length

(as some of the Players pretended).'

[3] *Rich. III* (Q), *Tit. Andr.* (Q), *Rich. II* (F), *2 Hen. IV* (Q), *Ham.* (F), *Oth.* (Q), *K. Lear* (F).

[4] Cf. p. 214.

[5] *Two Gent. of Ver.*, *Much Ado*, *Meas. for Meas.*, *Temp.*

welcome and dismissal, and for changes of address. To a growing extent he tended to end his speeches in mid-line. The beginning of the next speech does not always complete the line. Short lines occur also in mid-speech, and often with fine rhythmical effect. There is a pause for meditation or gesture, or for reversion to the business in hand. The cadence of a broken line seems to have pleased Shakespeare's ear. Professor Wilson knows all this very well, but these are alternatives which he commonly disregards when he is hot on the scent of a revision. He finds further evidence for abridgement in the dropped threads, and particularly in 'ghosts' who appear once and do not recur, and in personages to whom reference is made, but who do not appear at all. He supposes that these must have been given more prominence in lost scenes. The 'kitchen vestal' Nell in *Comedy of Errors* is a ghost, whom 'the young Shakespeare must surely have felt an almost irresistible temptation to make something more of than has come down to us'.[1] It is difficult to take such a priorisms very seriously. Every dramatist has to resist the temptation to over-elaborate his minor characters. They serve the purpose of an episode and vanish. A good example of a personage, whom we should naturally have looked to see but do not, is Petruchio's cousin Ferdinand in *Taming of the Shrew*.[2] Petruchio, when he gets home, sends for Ferdinand to make Katharina's acquaintance, and he never comes. Perhaps the audience were not exactly on the tip-toe of expectation for him, but it is a badly dropped thread, all the same. In the *Tempest*, the Duke of Milan's 'brave son' is said to have been seen in the wreck.[3] He does not appear with the other rescued travellers, and there is no lamentation for him. An introduction of Maudlin Lafeu would seem obvious in the last scene of *All's Well that Ends Well*, but she remains absent.[4] In these and in countless other cases, I think we have a deliberate dramatic device. Persons and incidents are alluded to, but kept out of the action. The effect is

---

[1] Wilson, *Com. of Err.* 76.   [3] *Temp.* i. 2. 438.
[2] *Tam. of Shrew*, iv. 1. 154.   [4] *All's Well*, v. 3.

one of solidity, as if life were passing on all the time behind the stage. Characters, again, are sometimes named in initial stage-directions, but have no share in the dialogue. Violenta enters with Diana in a scene of *All's Well that Ends Well*, and is forgotten throughout.[1] Juliet is unexpectedly dumb on her first appearance in *Measure for Measure*.[2] We must of course allow for mutes, especially in court or processional scenes. But sometimes the silence is clearly unnatural. Leonato is accompanied by 'Innogen his wife' at the beginning of *Much Ado About Nothing*.[3] She recurs in one later scene, but has not a word throughout the play. A lady, whose daughter is successively betrothed, defamed, repudiated before the altar, taken for dead, and restored to life, ought not to be a mute. It is not motherly. Abridgement is a possible explanation. But did Shakespeare sometimes write down initial entries before he had thought out the dialogue, and omit through carelessness to correct them by eliminating characters for whom he had found nothing to say, and ought to have found something to say, if they were to be on the stage at all?

To establish abridgement would not of itself serve to establish any further revision. Professor Wilson has been successful in pointing to mislineations which can be best explained as due to the incorporation in the text of passages irregularly written in margins, or in one case on an appended slip with a catchword.[4] These may well be later additions. Some of them only amount to interpolations of clowning or *spectacle*. The most notable are in the last act of *Midsummer-Night's Dream*, and that act has, I think, been revised. Many other mislineations, to which he would assign a similar origin, may be better put down to different causes, such as the printer's confusion between prose and verse.[5] There are textual duplications also, where one may agree with him in thinking that corrected and uncorrected versions have been left standing together, through the absence or disregard of deletion marks.[6] This

---

[1] *Ibid*. iii. 5.
[2] *Meas. for Meas*. i. 2. 120.
[3] *Much Ado*, i. 1. 1; ii. 1. 1. Some modern editions omit her.

[4] Wilson, *Mer. of Ven*. 106.
[5] Cf. p. 181.
[6] Wilson, *Love's Lab. Lost*, 107.

indicates revision, no doubt, in a sense, but by no means
necessarily the wholesale revision of a play. The alterations may be mere afterthoughts at the time of original
composition. We cannot, on this hypothesis, take quite
literally the statement of Heminges and Condell that they
had scarce received a blot in Shakespeare's papers. It
would be absurd to take it quite literally. But it certainly
does not suggest any constant habit of self-revision. Another feature upon which Professor Wilson frequently
relies is the variation of nomenclature. In so far as this is
merely a matter of spelling, whether in text, stage-directions or speech-prefixes, little importance can be attached
to it. The orthographic vagueness of the Elizabethans
reaches its maximum with proper names. The same name
will have different spellings in a single letter or other document. Some men do not even spell their own names
consistently; it seems that Shakespeare did not.[1] The
most one can say is that, if one spelling is habitually used
in one batch of scenes and another in a second batch, the
two batches are not likely to have been written at the same
sitting. But Professor Wilson is more concerned with the
variations in stage-directions and speech-prefixes between
personal and descriptive or 'generic' names, and he has
evolved a theory that generic names 'may be taken as clues
suggesting revision'. He even goes so far as to conjecture
that Dogberry and Verges may be designated as Constable and Headborough in a scene of *Much Ado About
Nothing* because these, of all names, Shakespeare 'could
not be bothered' to remember.[2] I do not believe a word
of it. Such variations occur in nearly every play. Professor Wilson sometimes weaves them into his argument,
and sometimes leaves them unnoticed. He lets Abner
by and spots Melchizedek. Any attempt at a uniform
application of his theory would indeed land him in chaos.
Probably Shakespeare wrote Dogberry and Verges when
he was conscientious before dinner, and Constable and
Headborough when he was relaxed afterwards. It did not
matter. He was not following the precise tradition of the

[1] Cf. p. 506.   [2] Wilson, *Love's Lab. Lost,* 112; *Much Ado,* 96.

literary drama. The personal and the generic names would be alike intelligible to the players and their book-keeper. Similar variations are to be found in play manuscripts and 'plots', and here too we get summary notes for the return of groups, although it is with 'something of a gasp' that Professor Wilson comes in *Love's Labour's Lost* upon the 'bald' direction 'Enter the Ladyes'.[1] Revision, according to Professor Wilson, sometimes took the form of rewriting verse scenes in prose, and of this traces remain in the presence of lines still recognizable as verse. 'Verse-fossils' he calls them. I do not think that these rhythms have any such significance. They are a constant feature of Shakespeare's prose. They are most frequent in the comedies of his mid-career, such as *As You Like It* and *Twelfth Night*. But there are many also in *Coriolanus* and *Winter's Tale*, and no play is altogether without them. Often they form single line speeches, and here it may be uncertain whether prose or verse is intended. But they also occur sporadically in the middle of speeches, and sometimes in groups. Professor Wilson is far from noticing them all. The number might be much increased if, with Professor A. E. Morgan, one took into account not only regular decasyllabic rhythms, but others which could be carried as such in a blank verse passage by substituting a verse intonation for a prose one and allowing for tri-syllabic feet.[2] These, however, when they come in a prose passage, do not really read as anything but prose. A dramatic value is sometimes involved. The rhythm corresponds to a rise in the emotional scale of utterance. It is often so in single lines of *As You Like It*. And Shakespeare was not unconscious of the device. Orlando enters in a prose scene with 'Good day and happiness, dear Rosalind', and Jaques departs with the comment, 'Nay, then, God be wi' you, an you talk in blank verse'.[3] More generally, a writer, who makes habitual transitions between prose and verse, may naturally have had the instinct

---

[1] Wilson, *Love's Lab. Lost*, 113; cf. p. 119.

[2] A. E. Morgan, *Some Problems of* *Sh.'s Henry IV* (1924).

[3] *As You Like It*, iv. 1. 30.

that the use of a rather rhythmical type of prose served to
bridge the line of demarcation. But the feature is not at
all one peculiar to Shakespeare. Verse rhythms are common enough in prose of all kinds. The most austere
modern taste, based on eighteenth-century models, tends
to reject them from ordinary straightforward discourse.
But they are freely used in imaginative writing, especially
to give a final grace to a period. Landor has them and
Walter Pater. Stevenson is fond of them. Ruskin ends a
decorative passage of *The Crown of Wild Olive* with one
decasyllabic and two octosyllabic rhythms. There are no
doubt places in Shakespeare where, with what Professor
Wilson calls 'a little innocent faking', several prose lines
together could be turned into blank verse. The rhythms
here may be a little overdone, but I do not feel that,
without the faking, they are so obtrusive as to necessitate
a theory of revision.[1] Professor Pollard, who has noticed
the same characteristic of the middle comedies, realizes
the difficulty of crowding Shakespeare's early years with
too many first versions of plays, but thinks that he may have
written some fragmentary scenes in verse, laid them aside,
and utilized them for the prose of later plays.[2] The suggestion is one which there is evidence neither to confirm
nor to refute.

Internal evidence makes it necessary to accompany a
general acceptance of the traditional Shakespearean canon
with certain qualifications, which may be set out in summary form.[3] Collaboration must be admitted in *Henry VIII*
and probably in *Taming of the Shrew*, as well as in the
uncanonical *Pericles* and *Two Noble Kinsmen*, and possibly in *Edward III*. Of replacement of the work of a
collaborator, which figures in some of the speculations of
Fleay, and was presumably suggested by Ben Jonson's
treatment of *Sejanus*, there is no sign.[4] Apart from the
touching-up of *Titus Andronicus*, which rests primarily on
external evidence, and the insertion of two late scenes into

[1] Wilson, *As You Like It*, 94; cf. my
comment in *Year's Work*, vii. 125.
[2] Pollard, *Foundations*, 14, and in

[4] *Library*, v. 374.
[3] For details, cf. ch. ix.
[4] Fleay, *L.W.* 180, 204; cf. p. 210.

the heterogeneous structure of *1 Henry VI*, there is nothing substantial which points to the dressing-up of alien plays. Some afterthoughts written into *Love's Labour's Lost*, *Romeo and Juliet*, *Julius Caesar*, and *Troilus and Cressida*, are revealed by failures to delete the original wordings. Mislineations in *The Shrew* and *Timon of Athens* may indicate others. But such alterations are no proof of complete rewriting, and for this the evidence is of the scantiest. An exception may be made for *Midsummer-Night's Dream*, which looks as if it had been converted from a wedding entertainment into a play for the public stage, by some changes in the last act and the provision of an alternative ending. Some passages in *2, 3 Henry VI* may owe their origin to a revival. We know, again on external evidence, that a line not now found in *Julius Caesar* met with criticism from Jonson. It would be absurd to lay down categorically that there has been no touching-up anywhere else. But that the great majority of the plays are Shakespeare's from beginning to end, and that, broadly speaking, when he had once written them, he left them alone, I feel little doubt. These are propositions which, so far, disintegrating criticism has entirely failed to shake.

That most of the texts have undergone some adaptation for theatrical purposes is obvious. Here, again, I do not believe in any substantial rewriting. There has clearly been some shortening, and although the existence of alternative versions sometimes makes it possible to restore the omitted passages, this is not so for all the plays. Whether Shakespeare himself exercised any discretion as to the cuts we cannot tell; they are not all equally judicious. A few interpolations can also be traced; bits of *spectacle*, a growing feature of the seventeenth-century stage, in *As You Like It*, *Cymbeline*, *Tempest*, and notably *Macbeth*; bits of clowning in *Merchant of Venice*, *Hamlet*, *King Lear*, and possibly *Othello*.[1] It is not always certain that the songs used

---

[1] Cf., however, Gildon's tradition (App. C, no. xxi) as to Shakespeare's responsibility for incongruous clowning in *Othello*. Sheer gag, of which the bad Qq show evidence, would presumably not get into the prompt-book, unless it was exceptionally successful.

were Shakespeare's own. Altered stage-directions tell of
casting decisions and of the activities of the book-keeper in
giving effect to these and in clearing up uncertainties. The
methods followed are already familiar to us in the theatrical
manuscripts.[1] Again the parallel texts come to our aid.
The Folio directions for *1 Henry IV* almost exactly repeat
those of the Quarto. In *2 Henry IV* the basis is the same,
but there has been a minute revision, which indicates a
careful study of the text. Many directions are shortened
by the omission of notes for apparel and the like. Errors
are corrected, although a few new ones are made. Overlooked entries are marked. Indefinite numbers are replaced by specific ones. Superfluous supernumeraries are
eliminated. The same features are apparent in the Folio
versions of *Hamlet*, *Othello*, and *King Lear*, and to a lesser
extent in other plays. The speech-prefixes may be checked,
and the musical notes altered or varied. Mr. Lawrence
thinks that the King's men did not use cornets until they
acquired the Blackfriars and took on the musical tradition
of that house. If he is right, the appearance of cornets in
a Folio stage-direction would be evidence of production
or revival in or after 1609. Such a revival would not of
course necessarily imply textual revision, as Mr. Lawrence
assumes.[2] Even where there are no parallel texts, the hand
of the book-keeper may be suspected in directions so
worded as to suggest a gloss or to leave a duplication.[3] It
is not necessary to ascribe to him the placing of entries in
advance of lines spoken by the entrants; or references to
properties familiar in the tiring-house but not to the
audience, such as 'Enter Piramus with the Asse head'; or
technicalities such as 'for' in the sense of 'disguised as'.[4]

---

[1] Cf. p. 118.

[2] W. J. Lawrence, *Sh.'s Workshop*,
48. Lawrence doubts whether a similar significance attaches to the mention
of hautbois; cf. *T.L.S.* (1929, June 13,
July 18, 25).

[3] *Com. of Err.* iv. 4. 43, 'Enter . . .
a Schoolemaster, call'd Pinch'; 149,
'Runne all out', duplicating 150, 'Exe-
unt omnes, as fast as may be, frighted';

v. 1. 190, 'Enter . . . E. Dromio of
Ephesus'; *Mer. of Ven.* ii. 5. 1,
'Enter Iewe and his man that was the
Clowne'; *As You Like It*, ii. 4. 1,
'Enter . . . Clowne, alias Touchstone';
Much Ado, ii. 1. 1, 'Enter Leonato, his
brother, . . . and Beatrice his neece,
and a kinsman', with similar examples
at ii. 1. 89, 218; iii. 4. 1; iii. 5. 1.

[4] *Mid. N. Dr.* iii. 1. 106 (F); *As You*

An actor-author, thinking in terms of the theatre, might quite well so write. Nor are imperative directions certainly the book-keeper's, although the form would be natural for him.[1] I do not think that warnings for the preparation of properties in advance occur in the canonical plays. They do in *Two Noble Kinsmen*. But the book-keeper is clearly revealed in several places where the printer has preserved the name of an actor written beside or in substitution for that of the character which he played.[2] Generally this occurs in stage-directions, and the analogy of the theatrical manuscripts rules out the alternative explanation of Professor Gaw, who finds here the mind of Shakespeare unconsciously identifying the part with the personality of its representative.[3] The case is perhaps not so simple where, as in *Much Ado About Nothing*, the actor-names run through a series of speech-prefixes. But probably Shakespeare wrote inadequate prefixes, in the form of mere numerals, and the book-keeper glossed them. A guard must be kept against the attempts of Fleay and others to find the names of actors in those assigned textually to servants and other members of crowds.[4] The book-keeper could have no occasion to trouble about textual names, and the author, writing in advance of casting, would certainly not know to whom such small parts would be given.

Traces of the censorship must also be expected in the texts. They are not very numerous. The Chamberlain's and King's men were, of all companies, in the closest relation to the court through their patrons, and the least likely to run counter to authority, except by inadvertence. An episode capable of political misrepresentation was removed

Like It, ii. 4. 1, 'Enter Rosaline for Ganimed, Celia for Aliena'; *Dead Man's Fortune*, plot 12, 'Exit Eschines and enter for Bell veille'.

[1] His 'Ring the bell' seems to have got into the text of *Macb.* ii. 3. 85. I do not know that we need ascribe the frequent 'Knocke' to him. In fact we do not know whether knocking was done by an in-coming actor or by a stage-hand.

[2] Cf. chh. ix, x (2, 3 *Hen. VI*, *Tam. of Shrew*, *Rom. & Jul.*, *Mid. N. Dr.*, 2 *Hen. IV*, *Hen. V*, *Much Ado*, *All's Well*, *T.N.K.*).

[3] A. Gaw, *Actors' Names in Basic Shakespearean Texts* (*P.M.L.A.* xl. 530); cf. p. 122.

[4] Fleay, *L.W.* 265; Wilson, *Tam. of Shrew*, 118.

from *Richard II* before it was printed, and restored in
Jacobean editions. Possibly two passages, at which Anne
of Denmark might be likely to take offence, were similarly
removed from *Hamlet*. These point to press censorship,
rather than stage censorship. Indiscreet nomenclature
has been reformed in *Henry IV* and *Merry Wives of Windsor*, and possibly in *Hamlet*. A jest on German and Spanish
costume has disappeared from the Folio version of *Much
Ado About Nothing*, and one on a Scottish lord from that of
the *Merchant of Venice*. An intervention of the censor may
also account for the absence of the 'four nations' scene,
with its Captain Jamy, from the reported text of *Henry V*.
We know that James resented the girding at Scotland in
English plays.[1] Conceivably the absence of Shallow's
'dozen white louses' from the reported *Merry Wives of
Windsor* may be no mere accident. There seems to have been
some pruning of social and political criticism in *King Lear*,
which has differently affected the Quarto and the Folio;
of pathological details, with a similar divergence, in *Troilus
and Cressida*; and of an unpatriotic sentiment and some
bits of indelicacy in *2 Henry IV*. All this comes to very
little. The treatment of profanity is something of a
puzzle. Dr. Greg, discussing the oaths in *Merry Wives of
Windsor*, suggests that they may not have been altered
before the text was prepared for press in 1623.[2] This is
possible, but it does not seem to me very probable. The
Act of Abuses survived the wreck of more comprehensive
measures against profanity, which were debated in Parliament during 1604 and 1605–6, but proved controversial
and never got upon the Statute-book.[3] It was of very
limited application. No person may 'in any Stage play,
Interlude, Shewe, Maygame or Pageant jestingly or pro-
phanely speake or use the holy Name of God or of Christ
Jesus or of the Holy Ghoste or of the Trinitie'.[4] I am not

[1] Cf. p. 65.
[2] Greg, *Merry Wives of W.* xxxvi, with a comparative table (liv) for Q and F. Similar tables would be valuable for other plays.
[3] *Commons Journals*, i. 247, 250, 251, 270, 286, 294, 300; *Lords Journals*, ii. 338, 340, 354, 365, 368, 369, 381, 400, 412, 414, 416, 436, 446.
[4] Full text in *Eliz. Stage*, iv. 338.

lawyer enough to know whether the courts were ever called upon to interpret the Act. Presumably it would bar the diminutive oaths in which the divine names are corrupted or implied, but not those by the Virgin, or the saints, or the rood, or the mass, or mere imprecations.[1] Sir Henry Herbert, as we have seen, was inclined to press it hard, and was overruled by Charles I.[2] If the king had been a better etymologist, he would have realized that, while 'Faith' was an asseveration, 'Death' and 'Slight' were, at least in origin, oaths. 'By God's death' is said to have been the favourite oath of Elizabeth.[3] But whatever degrees of profanity the Act covered, it clearly only related to words spoken on the stage, and not to words put into print. One does not see, then, why the publishers of the First Folio should have gone to the pains of expurgation. There is certainly none in the Quarto reprints between 1606 and 1623. Whether there is any evidence for Dr. Greg's suggestion outside Shakespeare, I am unable to say. *The Honest Man's Fortune* was reformed when Herbert re-allowed it in 1625, but printed with its oaths in the Beaumont and Fletcher Folio of 1647, and again reformed for that of 1679. On the whole it looks as if the expurgation of Shakespeare must date from stage revivals of 1606 or later. Whatever its genesis, it is nowhere complete and in most plays quite perfunctory. My notes as to this are far from exhaustive, but perhaps sufficient to give a fair picture. The plays which have suffered most are *1, 2 Henry IV*. Here 'God', 'Lord', 'Jesus', even when seriously used, are generally omitted, or replaced by a substitute. On the other hand, they are sometimes kept, even when profane. 'Christ' remains, but the epithet is dropped from 'christen names'. Of other forms, 'God's body', 'God's light', ''Sblood', and 'Zounds' go, but 'Cock and pie' is kept. So, as a rule is 'Marry', but 'By'r Lady' and 'By

---

[1] Examples of profanity are oaths by God's blood (plud), body, bodykins, bread, lady, lid, liggens, lugges, light, mother, sonties, wounds; God's my life; and the corrupt forms, 'sblood, sdeath, 'sfoot, 'slid, 'slight, 'swounds, Zounds, Gogs wouns, 'cock and pie', by Gis, 'ods heartlings, lifelings, me, my little life, my will, nownes, pillikins, plessed will.

[2] Cf. p. 102.

[3] Speed, *Chronicle*, f. 1200.

the mass', which one would have thought equally outside
the danger of the Act, generally go. Even imprecations
and asseverations are not always spared. Here the treatment is quite inconsistent, since 'Faith', 'By my troth', and
'By this hand', while sometimes altered, are also introduced as substitutes. Similarly, although 'Heaven' normally replaces 'God', there is at least one omission of 'By
heaven'. 'The devil' and even 'Hang yourself' are also
omitted. Two scriptural citations are cancelled.[1] But it
is amusing to notice that Hotspur's advice to his wife to
leave 'in sooth' and swear 'a good mouth-filling oath'
remains unaltered, except for the omission of 'Heart!'.[2]
One is tempted to think that Herbert must have been at
work on *Henry IV*; possibly also on *Othello*, where the
pruning, although less stringent, follows much the same
lines. Elsewhere the asseverations are usually left alone,
and even the revision of oaths proper is lightly taken.
There is a fair amount of it in *Hamlet*. These plays give
a little support to the theory that the expurgation took
place at revivals, since there is some evidence for the
performance of them all during 1606–23. On the other
hand, the same is true of *Much Ado About Nothing* and
Titus Andronicus. But *Much Ado About Nothing* has only
lost a single passage, with four 'Gods' in it, and *Titus
Andronicus* only the word 'Zounds'.[3] Of the other plays
for which good parallel texts are available, alterations are
not infrequent in *Richard II* and *Richard III*, but *Love's
Labour's Lost*, *Midsummer-Night's Dream*, *Romeo and
Juliet*, and *Merchant of Venice* show only one or two apiece.
There is more variation between the Folio and the bad
Quartos of *Henry V* and *Merry Wives of Windsor*, but here
we cannot tell how much profanity the reporters may have
contributed. Fluellen in the one and Sir Hugh Evans and
Doctor Caius in the other are, however, hard swearers,
only equalled by Mrs. Quickly. The commonest feature
throughout is the substitution of 'God' by 'Heaven'. In

[1] *1 Hen. IV*, i. 2. 99; *2 Hen. IV*,
iii. 2. 41.
[2] *1 Hen. IV*, iii. 1. 252.
[3] *Much Ado*, iv. 2. 19–22; *Tit. Andr.*
iv. 2. 71.

Love's Labour's Lost 'Jove' takes its place.[1] 'The dickens' for 'The devil' in *Merry Wives of Windsor* is the earliest known example of that euphemism.[2] For some reason 'Zounds' is an expletive particularly selected for reprobation. Nearly all the plays written after 1606, as well as the earlier *Julius Caesar*, *Troilus and Cressida*, and *King Lear*, have pagan settings, and to swear by heathen deities was safe enough. There are of course a few anachronisms. On the other hand, pagan asseverations, particularly by 'Jove', also appear in plays whose setting is not pagan. Among the later plays *Henry VIII* has still a moderate amount of profanity. How far the early plays, for which we have only Folio texts, have been altered can only be matter for conjecture. In *Twelfth Night*, of which there were certainly late revivals, Sir Toby Belch swears less and more mildly than one would expect, and the use of 'Jove' is common. In *King John* the examples of 'Heaven' markedly outnumber those of 'God'. But it must remain doubtful whether such indications, or the slighter changes in some of the Folio texts already noted, can be taken as evidence of revivals. It certainly cannot be assumed that when Rosalind swears 'by my troth, and in good earnest, and so God mend me, and by all pretty oaths that are not dangerous', she was thinking of the *Act of Abuses*.[3] Quite apart from the use of 'God', profanity was 'dangerous', long before a Jacobean Parliament made it so. On the other hand, with the case of *Much Ado About Nothing* before us, it is equally impossible to assume that the preservation of numerous oaths in the Folio means that there was no late revival. The sporadic nature of the expurgation, where any is traceable, remains perplexing. Professor Wilson suggests that it may have been more completely done in 'parts' than in prompt-copies.[4] But if so, why should it have been done in prompt-copies at all? It is an alternative possibility that marginal expurgations on prompt-copies were not always observed by the printers or perhaps were not thought worth the trouble of carrying to examples of

---

[1] *Love's Lab. Lost*, v. 2. 316.
[2] *Merry Wives of W.* iii. 2. 19.
[3] *As You Like It*, iv. 1. 194.
[4] Wilson, *Love's Lab. Lost*, 190.

the Quartos when these were used as copy for the Folio. It certainly cannot be assumed that, even under the comparatively mild régime of Sir George Buck, there was not more expurgation in the actual representation of revived plays, especially at court, than the state of the Folio texts reveals.

CHAPTER VIII

THE PROBLEM OF CHRONOLOGY

Bibliographical Note. Malone's *Attempt to Ascertain the Order in which the Plays of Shakspeare were Written* first appeared in the 2nd ed. (1778) of the *Works* by Johnson and Steevens. Its final form is in *Variorum*, ii. 288. G. Chalmers accumulated additional 'topical' allusions, many of which were far-fetched, in his *Supplemental Apology* (1799), 266, and others have been detected by later commentators. A collection is in H. P. Stokes, *An Attempt to Determine the Chronological Order of Shakespeare's Plays* (1878). The successive chronologies of F. G. Fleay are in his *Sh. Manual* (1876, 1878), 22, C. M. Ingleby's *Sh. the Man and the Book*, i. (1881), 99 *sqq.*, and his *Life and Work of Sh.* (1886), 175. That of E. Dowden is in his *Shakspere, His Mind and Art* (1875, &c.), and as a table in his *Shakspere Primer* (1877), 56. That of F. J. Furnivall, in its fullest form, is in his *Introduction* to the *Leopold Shakespere* (1877) and in the revision of that, with the help of J. Munro, for the *Century Shakespeare* (1908). Naturally most biographies and systematic commentaries deal with the subject. Among German contributions are W. König, *Ueber den Gang von Shs dichterischer Entwickelung* (1875, *J.* x. 93); H. Conrad (Isaac), *Zu den Shs Sonn.* (1878–9, *Archiv*, lix. 155, 289; lx. 33; lxi. 177, 393; lxii. 1, 129), *Die Son.-Periode in Shs Leben* (1884, *J.* xix. 176), *Die Ham.-Periode in Shs Leben* (1885–6, *Arch.* lxxiii. 163, 371; lxxiv. 45; lxxv. 1, 269), *Shs Selbstbekenntniss* (1897), *Eine neue Methode der chronologischen Sh.-Forschung* (1909, *Germ.-Rom. Monatsschrift*, i. 232, 307); B. T. Sträter, *Die Perioden in Shs dichterischer Entwickelung* (1881–2, *Archiv*, lxv. 153, 383; lxvi. 121, 273; lxvii. 1, 289, 417); G. Sarrazin, *Zur Chronologie von Shs Jugenddramen* (1894, *J.* xxix. 92), *Zur Chronologie von Shs Dichtungen* (1896, *J.* xxxii. 149), *W. Shs Lehrjahre* (1897), *Wortechos bei Sh* (1897–8, *J.* xxxiii. 120; xxxiv. 119), *Aus Shs Meisterwerkstatt* (1906); E. Ekwall, *Die Sh-Chronologie* (1911, *Germ.-Rom. Monatsschrift*, iii. 90).

On vocabulary are R. Simpson, *Sh.'s Once-Used Words* (1874, *N.S.S. Trans.* 115), J. D. Butler, *Once-Used Words in Sh.* (1886, *N.Y. Sh. Soc.*). Tables of such words for individual plays are in the *Henry Irving Shakespeare*. On Sh's. prose are H. Sharpe, *The Prose in Sh.'s Plays* (1885, *N.S.S. Trans.* 523); V. F. Janssen, *Die Prosa in Shs Dramen* (1897); G. Bordukat, *Die Abgrenzung zwischen Vers und Prosa in den Dramen Shs* (1918). The special treatises on metre are given in the *Bibl. Note* to Appendix H. On other stylistic features are G. Kramer, *Ueber Stichomythie und Gleichklang in dem Dramen Shs* (1889); L. Wurth, *Das Wortspiel bei Sh* (1895); F. G. Hubbard, *Repetition and Parallelism in the Earlier Elizabethan Drama* (1905, *P.M.L.A.* xx. 360), *A Type of Blank*

Verse Line Found in the Earlier Elizabethan Drama (1917, *P.M.L.A.* xxxii. 68); W. Hübner, *Der Vergleich bei Sh* (1908); H. Barth, *Das Epitheton in den Dramen des Jungen Sh und seiner Vorgänger* (1914).

Theories about *Love's Labour's Won* are in R. Farmer, *Essay on the Learning of Sh.* (1767, *Var.* i. 314); J. Hunter, *Disquisition on Tp.* (1839, *New Illustrations of Sh.* i. 130, 359); G. L. Craik, *The English of Shakespeare* (1857), 7; A. E. Brae, *Collier, Coleridge and Sh.* (1860); P. A. Daniel, *Q. Facs. of M.A.* (1886), v; R. Boyle, *A.W. and L.L.W.* (1890, *E.S.* xiv. 408); F. v. Westenholz, *Shs L.L.W.* (1902, *Beilage zur Allgemeinen Zeitung*); A. H. Tolman, *Shs L.L.W.* (1904, *Views about Ham.* 243); H. D. Gray, *L.L.L. with a Conjecture as to L.L.W.* (1918).]

A RECOGNITION of the substantial homogeneity of most of the plays simplifies the approach to the problem of chronology, since it makes it reasonable to assume, in the absence of any special ground for suspecting an insertion, that datable allusions have not been added by a reviser, and that the mention of a play by name implies its existence much in the form in which it is preserved to us. It will again be well to attach primary weight to external evidence, and a convenient starting-point is provided by the list of plays in the *Palladis Tamia* of Francis Meres, which was presumably compiled before the registration of that book on 7 September 1598.[1] This at once enables us to segregate a considerable group of comparatively early works. There are six comedies, *Two Gentlemen of Verona, Comedy of Errors, Love's Labour's Lost,* '*Loue labours wonne*', *Midsummer-Night's Dream, Merchant of Venice*; four histories, *Richard II, Richard III, Henry IV, King John*; and two tragedies, *Titus Andronicus* and *Romeo and Juliet*. Meres names them in the order here followed, but it is not necessary to suppose that he paid attention to their respective dates of production. On the other hand, the list is so long as to suggest that it includes all that were known to him, and that it was only by a happy accident that he was able, by treating the histories as tragedies, to balance six of these against six comedies in accordance with his artificial manner of writing. Meres took his M.A. degree at Cambridge in 1591 and by incorporation at Oxford on 10 July 1593. It was probably after that date that he

---

[1] App. B, no. xiii.

came to London, where he was dwelling in Botolph Lane by 1597, and if so, *Henry VI* or any other play not on the stage between 1593 and 1598 may have been unknown to him. His mention of *Henry IV* leaves it uncertain whether he knew both parts, and the identity of *Love Labours Won* must for the present be left aside.

Terminal dates before which production must have occurred can be established for a good many plays. The commonest sources are entries in the *Stationers' Register*, or the title-pages of printed editions. The former give precise dates, the latter years only, which are best taken as calendar years.[1] Twice the Register specifically notices a court performance during the preceding Christmas. The lists of such performances for 1604–5 and 1611–12 give some help. So does the *Diary* of Philip Henslowe. A few performances at the Inns of Court or in public theatres are independently recorded in contemporary documents. And there are a few literary notices, some of which are not capable of very exact dating. Echoes cannot be relied on, but Jonson's quotation of *Julius Caesar* in *E.M.O.*, 'Reason long since is fled to animals, you know', is more than an echo. Only one play carries its own evidence. This is *Henry V*, where a chorus indicates not only a terminal date, but also an initial date, after which the production can be placed. As a rule the initial dates are much less certain than the terminal ones. Henslowe's 'ne's are fixed, but it is only the earliest of Shakespeare's plays with which Henslowe can have been concerned. An account of the Globe fire shows that *Henry VIII* was then a new play. For the rest we can only rely upon the dates at which 'sources' became available, in most cases too remote to be helpful, and upon allusions in the plays themselves to datable historical events. These require handling with great caution. Few are so definite as to be primary evidence; others at the most come in as confirmatory, after a provisional date has been arrived at on safer grounds. We can be pretty sure that the references to Scottish kings of England in *Macbeth* are Jacobean, and if so, the reference

---

[1] Cf. p. 175.

to equivocators in the same play is likely to be to the equivocators of the Gunpowder Plot. We can be a little less sure that the bit about the currish wolf in *Merchant of Venice* reflects the Lopez conspiracy, but if so, a phrase about a coronation may echo that of Henri IV. Yet both equivocation and coronations were common phenomena, to which any dramatist might refer at any date. So, too, were the plague and tempests and even eclipses, although an allusion is fairly plausible in *Midsummer-Night's Dream* to the rather unusual bad weather of 1594–5, which impressed the chroniclers, and an allusion in *King Lear* to the double eclipse of sun and moon in 1605, which was heralded by the astrological prophets. But Shakespeare does not seem to have been greatly given to 'topical' allusions, and the hunt for them becomes dangerous, especially if it is inspired by a desire to link the plays with contemporary literary controversies in which he may have taken but little interest, or with incidents in the chequered careers of the Earls of Southampton and Essex, revealed to us by the ransacking of political archives, but of doubtful familiarity to the Elizabethan populace or its playwrights.[1]

It is, however, possible, on external evidence alone, to draw up a trial-table of primary indications limiting initial and terminal dates for nearly but not quite all of the plays. They are not all equally convincing, but I have excluded a good many others which are less so. I put them in columnar form, the 'initial' indications on the left, the 'terminal' indications on the right. The order, for convenience of reference, is that of my final table.[2]

2 Henry VI.

> Registration (12 March 1594).
> Print (1594).

3 Henry VI.

> Parody by Greene (ob. 3 September 1592).
> Print (1595).

---

[1] Cf. p. 67.   [2] Cf. p. 269.

1 Henry VI.

Production (ne) by Henslowe   Production by Henslowe
(3 March 1592).   (3 March 1592).
                                                         Allusion by Nashe in *Pierce
                                                         Penilesse* (8 August 1592).

Richard III.

Registration (20 October 1597).
Print (1597).

Comedy of Errors.

Performance at Gray's Inn
(28 December 1594).

Titus Andronicus.

Production (ne) by Henslowe   Production by Henslowe
(24 January 1594).   (24 January 1594).
                                                         Registration (6 February 1594).
                                                         Print (1594).

Two Gentlemen of Verona.

Notice by Meres (7 September
1598).

Love's Labour's Lost.

Allusion to Chapman's *Shadow*   Performance at court (Christ-
of Night (1594).   mas 1597–8 at latest).
                                                         Print (1598).

Romeo and Juliet.

Print (1597).

Richard II.

No use in 1st edition of Daniel's   Use in 2nd edition of Daniel's
Civil Wars (1595).   *Civil Wars* (1595).
                                                         Performance for Sir Edward
                                                         Hoby (9 December 1595).
                                                         Registration (29 August 1597).
                                                         Print (1597).

Midsummer-Night's Dream.

Allusion to weather of 1594.   Notice by Meres (7 September
Allusion to baptism of Henry of   1598).
Scotland (30 August 1594).

King John.

Notice by Meres (7 September
1598).

Merchant of Venice.

Allusion to death of Lopez
(7 June 1594).

Use of Gobbo as nickname for
Sir Robert Cecil (27 October
1596).
Registration (22 July 1598).

1 Henry IV.

Registration (25 February
1598).
Print (1598).

2 Henry IV.

Survival of name Oldcastle
(abandoned by 25 February
1598).

Much Ado About Nothing.

No notice by Meres (7 September 1598).

'Stay' in *Stationers' Register*
(4 August 1600).
Registration (23 August 1600).
Print (1600).

Henry V.

Allusion to campaign of Essex
in Ireland (begun 27 March
1599).
No notice by Meres (7 September 1598).

Allusion to campaign of Essex
in Ireland (ended 28 September 1599).

Julius Caesar.

No notice by Meres (7 September 1598).

Performance seen by Thomas
Platter (21 September 1599).
Quotation in Jonson's *E.M.O.*
(1599).
Echo in Weever's *Mirror of
Martyrs* (1599).

As You Like It.

No notice by Meres (7 September 1598).

'Stay' in *Stationers' Register*
(4 August 1600).

Twelfth Night.

Use of Robert Jones's *First Book of Airs* (1600).
No notice by Meres (7 September 1598).

Performance at Middle Temple (2 February 1602).

Hamlet.

Allusion to revival of boy actors (1599).
No notice by Meres (7 September 1598).

Notice by Gabriel Harvey (before 25 February 1601).
Registration (26 July 1602).
Print (1603).

Merry Wives of Windsor.

No notice by Meres (7 September 1598).

Registration (18 January 1602).
Print (1602).

Troilus and Cressida.

Echo in prologue of Jonson's *Poetaster* (1601).
No notice by Meres (7 September 1598).

Registration (7 February 1603).

[Meres names no later plays, but his list is getting too remote to be worth citation.]

Measure for Measure.

Performance at court (26 December 1604).

Othello.

Performance at court (1 November 1604).

King Lear.

Registration of source-play *Leire* (8 May 1605).
Allusions to eclipses (27 September and 2 October 1605).

Performance at court (26 December 1606).
Registration (26 November 1607).
Print (1608).

Macbeth.

Allusion to equivocation of Gunpowder conspirators (Jan.–March 1606).
Allusion to reign of James I (25 March 1603).

Performance seen by Forman (20 April 1611).

Antony and Cleopatra.

> Registration (20 May 1608).

Pericles.

> Performance seen by Venetian
> ambassador (5 January 1606⟨⟩
> 23 November 1608).
> Print of derivative novel (1608).
> Print (1609).

Cymbeline.

> Performance seen by Forman
> (21⟨⟩29 April 1611).

Winter's Tale.

> Performance seen by Forman
> (15 May 1611).
> Performance at court (5 No-
> vember 1611).

Tempest.

> Performance at court (1 No-
> vember 1611).

Henry VIII.

Performance, as 'new' play (29   Performance (29 June 1613).
June 1613).

Two Noble Kinsmen.

Use of dance from mask by Beaumont (20 February 1613).

The table is a mere scaffolding. Four plays, *Taming of
the Shrew, All's Well That Ends Well, Coriolanus,* and *Timon
of Athens,* do not appear in it at all; and for many others,
especially in the Jacobean period, a considerable range of
dating remains open. On the other hand, it provides confirmation of the *Palladis Tamia* list for the early years, except
as regards the *Two Gentlemen of Verona* and *King John.* It
establishes fixed points for *1 Henry VI, Titus Andronicus,
Henry V,* and *Henry VIII;* and fairly narrow limits for
*Much Ado About Nothing, Julius Caesar, Merry Wives of
Windsor, As You Like It, Twelfth Night,* and *Hamlet,* on

the reasonable assumption that if these had existed when
Meres wrote, he would have named them. It points to an
early run of Yorkist histories and a later run of Lancastrian
histories. And it at least suggests several other tentative
groupings. There is a common lyrical quality in *Love's
Labour's Lost*, *Romeo and Juliet*, *Midsummer-Night's
Dream*, and *Richard II*, which are all in Meres's list.
There is a common vein of realistic comedy in *Henry IV*
and the *Merry Wives of Windsor*, which are further linked
by the recurrence of identical characters. There is a common vein of courtly comedy in *As You Like It* and *Twelfth
Night*. Both of these groups must come very near the
end of the sixteenth century. *Julius Caesar*, *Hamlet*, and
Troilus and Cressida again must all be late Elizabethan
tragedies, and *Othello* seems to begin a series of Jacobean
tragedies, to which *King Lear*, *Macbeth*, and *Antony and
Cleopatra*, coming in no certain order, belong. Finally *Cymbeline*, *Winter's Tale*, and *Tempest*, which emerge in rapid
succession at the tail-end of the list, have again a common
quality of romantic tragi-comedy, which makes it probable
that they were not far apart in origin. These are not all
equally valid inferences, since some of them rest, not so
much upon positive indications, as upon the absence of
earlier indications. But if they are provisionally accepted
and the plays studied in accordance with the time-order
of the groups, it is possible to arrive at an outline conception of Shakespeare's development, as regards both dramatic temper and the use of language, which in its turn
makes a starting-point for further progress. This is not
a book of aesthetic criticism, and I do not propose to
retrace an argument which has been already worked out
by many writers. Instead I will draw upon the admirable
treatment of Professor Dowden. He distinguishes four
stages in Shakespeare's career, which he calls respectively
'In the workshop', 'In the world', 'Out of the depths', and
'On the heights'. The first is the period of 'dramatic
apprenticeship and experiment', the second that of the
later historical plays and the mirthful and joyous comedies,
the third that of grave or bitter comedies and of the great

tragedies, the fourth that of 'the romantic plays, which are at once grave and glad, serene and beautiful poems'. He has a corresponding 'impression' of changes in diction.

In the earliest plays the language is sometimes as it were a dress put upon the thought—a dress ornamented with superfluous care; the idea is at times hardly sufficient to fill out the language in which it is put; in the middle plays (*Julius Caesar* serves as an example) there seems a perfect balance and equality between the thought and its expression. In the latest plays this balance is disturbed by the preponderance or excess of the ideas over the means of giving them utterance. The sentences are close-packed; 'there are rapid and abrupt turnings of thought, so quick that language can hardly follow fast enough; impatient activity of intellect and fancy, which, having once disclosed an idea, cannot wait to work it orderly out'; 'the language is sometimes alive with imagery'.[1]

Of course Professor Dowden has a great deal more to say about Shakespeare's mental and stylistic history than this; I have only given so much as I think can be justified from a grouping of the plays on external evidence alone. A full literary and psychological analysis can only follow and not precede the establishment of a chronology. And in the meantime we are bound to a circular process. A preliminary dating sets up impressions of temper and style, and the definition of these helps to elaborate the dating. This is inevitable, once we depart from the external evidence. The chronology can only become a complex hypothesis, pieced together from materials not in themselves conclusive, and depending for its acceptance on the success with which it combines convergent and reconciles conflicting probabilities. General impressions, such as Professor Dowden formulates, make it at once possible to give some expansion to the groups already realized. *Two Gentlemen of Verona* finds its natural affinities with the experimental plays, *King John* with the later histories, *All's Well That Ends Well* with *Measure for Measure*, *Coriolanus*

[1] Dowden, *Shakespeare Primer*, 37, 47. My own feeling is that the balance of thought and expression is recovered in the magnificent phrasing of *Antony and Cleopatra*; and that in the romances too, the intricate weaving of clauses is a closely fitting vesture for the involutions and qualifications of the ideas.

and *Timon of Athens* with the Jacobean tragedies, *Pericles* with the romances. *Merchant of Venice* and *Much Ado About Nothing* approximate, perhaps rather less closely, to the joyous comedies.

Obviously the mere grouping of plays is only the first stage of the chronological problem. There remain the more difficult tasks of determining an order of succession within the groups and between the members of over-lapping groups, and of fitting this order into the time allowed by the span of Shakespeare's dramatic career. Here it is legitimate to make some cautious use of minor topical allusions and echoes forwards and backwards, which were rejected as not sufficiently convincing to fur-nish primary evidence. An attempt is made to assemble these, play by play, elsewhere.[1] The cumulative results can at the most only support conclusions of higher or lower degrees of probability. The main effort of recent scholarship has been to supplement external evidence by a closer analysis of style, and to establish chronological 'tests' analogous to those which have already been dis-cussed as determinative of authorship.[2] The outcome is not without value, although a doubt must be expressed at the outset whether it is ever possible to determine an order for work of more or less level date upon stylistic considera-tions alone. The style of every writer has its intelligible development, no doubt. But it is not always a matter of smooth progression. Subject-matter has its reaction upon style. During all the first half of Shakespeare's career, he moves more freely in comedy than in history. Moreover, allowance has to be made for the influence of moods and for deliberate experiment. The resultant leaps forward and set-backs become apparent when a chronological order is already known, but may be very misleading as material from which to reconstruct one. Certainly particular aspects of style can be singled out and studied in isolation, and by such a process the general impression of charac-teristic style and of its phases is naturally both strengthened and refined. There is the aspect of structure, for example,

[1] Cf. ch. ix.   [2] Cf. p. 220.

in the types of character employed and the choice of dramatic situations. One may note that in the earlier plays comic relief is often afforded by the use of a lout and that in the later plays a court fool takes his place; or again that a rather artificial balancing between pairs of young men or young women tends to disappear after the experimental stage. On the other hand, such features are not always purely stylistic; they depend in part on the nature of the story adapted for the plot, and probably in part also on the succession of actors available. Nor are they all significant of period. The favourite device of concealed identity runs through the plays from beginning to end. One may take, again, Shakespeare's imagery, and compare its range at different periods. No doubt similes and metaphors from country sights and sounds prevail in his earliest and perhaps his latest plays and those from urban life in his middle plays, although it must not be forgotten that the unconscious memory is a reservoir, giving up from its store things both new and old. There are aspects of diction too, to be observed; an early habit of ringing the changes upon some particular word, a later habit of coining new words, and so forth. All such investigations make for a closer and more confident grouping of plays, but they do not really help us to get beyond the grouping.

I do not think that anything different can be said of the particular features of style out of which it has in fact been attempted to construct 'tests'. Of these there are three: parallels, vocabulary, metre. The parallel test is the invention of the late Professor Conrad.[1] He proposed to determine the time-relation of plays, not on the basis of conspicuous parallels, but by enumerating all the parallels, both of thought and sentiment, which he regarded as the more significant, and of verbal expression, between each pair of plays, and forging a chronological chain in which each play would be linked on either side with those to which its parallels were most frequent. Professor Conrad, so far as I know, never published his full enumeration. A sample prepared for *Twelfth Night* was very far from

[1] *G.R.M.* i. 232.

complete.[1] And it is difficult to see how completeness could be secured. Verbal parallels can no doubt be traced by the patient exploitation of a concordance. But what scholar can claim the gifts of observation and memory required to assemble out of thirty-six plays all the parallels of thought and sentiment for which verbal clues are lacking? Even if an exhaustive enumeration were available, it could not be stated in statistical terms. The units would not be convertible counters. They might be anything from mere repetitions of commonplaces to significant passages pointing to some kind of association of ideas between the passages concerned. There is no valid criterion for demarcation of the two categories. Moreover, when an association of ideas exists, it may be due to some other cause than a common date of origin. It may arise from a similarity of situation, or a revival may have recalled old work to Shakespeare's mind. Broadly speaking, it is probably true that parallels are most frequent between contemporaneous plays. But this, again, does not take us beyond grouping. To some extent the same criticisms apply to Professor Sarrazin's vocabulary test; but not wholly, because recurrent words are much more nearly convertible counters than parallels of thought and phrase, and Professor Sarrazin limits his field to what he calls 'dislegomena' and 'trislegomena', that is, words only used twice or thrice by Shakespeare.[2] In other respects his method is much like Professor Conrad's. The words listed include many rare or invented words, and also some which are not unusual, and the incidence of which is determined by the need for expressing the ideas which they connote. The latter are hardly significant. Once more, the recurrences are commonest in plays of more or less the same date, although by no means confined to these. And once more we do not get beyond grouping.

A great deal of work has been done upon what are roughly called 'verse' or 'metrical' tests. Differences in the handling of blank verse afford units which readily

---

[1] *J.* xxxi. 177; cf. Sarrazin's criticism in *J.* xxxii. 163.

[2] *J.* xxxiii. 120; xxxiv. 119.

lend themselves to statistical treatment. Variations in the length of lines, in the number of syllables carried by lines, in the value given to unstressed vowels, in the distribution of stresses and pauses, can all be enumerated and tabulated.[1] The extent of departure from the blank verse form by the introduction of prose and rhyme can also be measured. An intermixture of mediums is characteristic of Shakespeare from an early stage. Only about two-thirds of the hundred thousand lines or so occupied by the plays are in blank verse. The modification of blank verse itself is on the whole progressive. It culminates in the Jacobean tragedies, and in some of the more excited scenes of these, where transitions between prose and verse are also common, the blank verse norm hardly remains recognizable. These metrical phenomena first attracted attention in the middle of the eighteenth century, when Richard Roderick noted the frequency of inverted first-foot stresses and 'redundant' final syllables as characteristic of *Henry VIII*. Little use of them was made as a guide to chronology by Malone, except that he took a high proportion of rhyme as being a sign of early work.[2] The study was resumed nearly a hundred years after its initiation, notably in an essay by Charles Bathurst, in which the gradual changes in Shakespeare's manner, as regards both the employment of redundant final syllables and the coincidence of rhythmical pauses with line-endings, were well brought out. Much of the earliest work of the New Shakspere Society was also devoted to the subject. The chief contributor was F. G. Fleay. He was primarily concerned with 'tests' of authorship rather than of chronology. But he prepared a table, based upon the Globe text, in which he enumerated for each play the total lines, those of blank verse, prose, and rhyme, the abnormally short and long lines, and the redundant syllables, which he called 'double endings'. This was reprinted, with little alteration, in his *Shakespeare Manual* of 1876. Such a table, accurately done, would have been of great value as a basis for statistical

---

[1] I give what seem to me the most useful tables in Appendix H.   [2] *Var.* ii. 327.

analysis. Unfortunately Fleay's was extremely inaccurate, as may be seen from the fact that his totals often do not add up to anything like the Globe lines and sometimes diverge to the extent of hundreds. It is not very creditable to modern scholarship that these figures have been constantly reproduced down to Professor Tucker Brooke's *Shakespeare of Stratford* in 1926. Fleay in fact revised them, and printed new tables in C. M. Ingleby's *Shakespeare the Man and the Book* of 1881. Here he made some slight alterations in the basis, gave details for each scene, as well as for each play, and claimed to have 'detected several errors' in the earlier version. The new figures are, however, still very far from accurate.[1] Other students, both English and German, now took up the investigation, and made an advance upon Fleay's methods by relating their results in percentage form to the total number of blank-verse lines in each play, and thereby making a statistical comparison between play and play possible. Professor König, for example, thus dealt with several 'tests' in his *Der Vers in Shaksperes Dramen* of 1888. In more recent years a number of new tests have been worked out by Professor Conrad. Neither of these scholars gives the counts from which his tables of proportions are calculated, and Professor Conrad's tables do not cover all the plays. Counts are supplied, however, in the dissertations, written under his influence, of Dr. Kerrl on *King John* and *Julius Caesar* and of Dr. Norpoth on *Two Gentlemen of Verona*, and for important features the lines counted are cited and sometimes even quoted. This is, of course, the better method, as it facilitates checking, and makes it feasible to estimate the personal equation of the investigator.

Some survey of the ground covered and of the difficulties to be faced may be attempted. There are no percentage tables for the distribution of prose, and probably none would be helpful. It is used throughout the plays, except in two or three of the histories, and appears to have no chronological significance. If it is commonest in the second period, the reason is that comedies, to which it is

---

[1] Cf. vol. ii, p. 406.

particularly appropriate, then come most thickly. *Merry Wives of Windsor* is almost entirely, and *2 Henry IV*, *Much Ado About Nothing*, *As You Like It*, *Twelfth Night*, and *All's Well That Ends Well* are predominantly, in prose. *Hamlet* has a great deal; *Julius Caesar*, not far removed in date, less than almost any other play. *King Lear*, *Coriolanus*, and *Winter's Tale* have much more than their respective neighbours *Macbeth*, *Antony and Cleopatra*, and the *Tempest*. In scenes where prose and verse are mingled, it is not always easy to say whether a short sentence should be treated as prose or truncated verse, or whether a rhythmic phrase in a prose environment is intended to be metrical or not.[1] Counts will differ according to the judgement of the counters on these points. For rhyme, Professor König gives percentages of rhymed decasyllabic lines to all lines, and Professor Conrad percentages of all rhymed lines to blank-verse lines. Probably alternate rhymes and certainly sonnets, songs, other short rhymes, and doggerel rhymes should be kept apart from the ordinary heroic couplets, since they are generally introduced for special purposes. Professor Heuser gives independent figures for heroic couplets. Doggerel, except for a few lines, some of which may be of doubtful authenticity, is only found in quite early plays. From the point of view of chronology, continuous passages of rhymed dialogue should be distinguished from sporadic couplets. The former rarely appear after *Twelfth Night*, and as a rule with some deliberate intention, such as the enunciation of sententious comment by choric elders. The latter are used throughout, but with diminishing frequency towards the end, as 'tags' to clinch long or significant speeches, or the final speeches of scenes. Here again counts may differ through uncertainty as to whether sporadic rhymes are intended as such, or are merely accidental.

Chronologically, the departures from blank verse are of less importance than the variations within the blank-verse *cadre* itself. And among these again there is not much to be said about the abnormally short or long lines. Like all

[1] Cf. p. 233.

irregularities, they tend to increase, and reach a maximum in the Jacobean tragedies. But there is no even progression. *Richard III* and *Richard II* alike show a considerable excess of both over many plays which follow them. The actual numbers have probably been perverted both by printers' errors and by the editorial rearrangement of lines, and some at least of the short lines may be the result of cuts.[1] Some writers distinguish between Alexandrines with six marked stresses and other lines which they treat as five-foot lines carrying two redundant syllables after the final feet. This seems to me unnecessary, since an ordinary five-footer often has no marked stress in the final foot. Professor Conrad has a percentage table for all six-footers, but the smallness of the total number deprives it of value.[2] In calculating metrical variations generally, six-footers are best grouped with five-footers as normal blank verse.

Variations of stress have not so far received much study. The investigation is a difficult one, because there is often much uncertainty as to where stress is intended to fall. The stress in disyllabic words and at least the main stress in longer words is fairly fixed, although in some words the Elizabethan was not quite the same as the modern usage. But monosyllables can be stressed or unstressed, according to a rhythmic intention. Actually, of course, there are degrees of stress, and upon this much of the finer modulation of verse depends. But for metrical analysis, one can hardly get beyond the distinction of relatively stressed and relatively unstressed syllables. The normal iambic line consists of five feet, in each of which an unstressed is followed by a stressed syllable. A continuous succession of such lines is rare in Shakespeare. There are many 'pyrrhic' feet in which both syllables are unstressed, and some 'spondaic' in which both are stressed. Here we get level stress. There are also 'trochaic' feet, in which the stressed syllable precedes the unstressed syllable, instead of following it. Here we get inverted stress. Shakespeare made progressive use of level stress, and up to the end of the

---

[1] Cf. p. 229.   [2] Conrad, *Macbeth*, xxviii; cf. p. 266.

tragedies of inverted stress, as part of a general instinct to vary the iambic norm. Inverted stress is already frequent in Marlowe, chiefly in the first feet of lines, since trochees come most naturally after pauses. Shakespeare, as naturally, introduced them after his mid-line pauses, and occasionally elsewhere, although fifth-foot trochees remain exceptional throughout. Professor Conrad gives some figures as to these and as to trochees after the mid-line pause, and also as to what he calls 'Doppeljamben'.[1] But these are no more than particular cases of level stress, in which a pyrrhic is followed by a spondee. I do not attach much weight to these figures, since I find myself constantly at variance with the scansion of foreign observers and doubt whether they fully appreciate the incidence of English stress. In reading Shakespeare, I feel that there is a great deal of level stress, and that in many lines there are very few strong stresses. These features may vary at different periods, but the subject still wants working out. How far the actors emphasized stress, where it was optional, we cannot say. Polonius commended the 'good accent' of a highly stressed speech; but he was no judge.[2]

The most easily recognized type of syllabic variation is the use of the 'redundant' final syllables demonstrated by Bathurst. They make what are called 'feminine' or 'double' or 'hendecasyllabic' endings. As a rule they are the unstressed final syllables of words, but include an increasing number of personal pronouns and even other unstressed monosyllables. Fletcher often employs stressed monosyllables, but Shakespeare very rarely. Percentage tables are given by Professors König, Hertzberg, and Conrad. Their results do not quite agree. Professor König includes not only the ordinary double endings, which he calls 'klingende', but also, as 'gleitende', the final feet of those six-foot lines, which do not form regular Alexandrines. And he excludes not only final syllables in -ed, -est, and -en, where these are capable of elision, but also those of a number of words, such as 'heaven', 'devil',

---

[1] Conrad, *Macbeth*, xxix, xxxv.   [2] *Ham.* ii. 2. 489.

'spirit', 'prayer', 'fire', 'hour', 'power', and the like, which can be pronounced either as monosyllables or disyllables. This he does on the ground that the monosyllabic pronunciation is predominant, although not invariable, when such a word comes in the middle of a line.   My own feeling is that at the end of a line, where the line-break leaves room for an open utterance, the effect is disyllabic.   One cannot here, I think, rely upon differences of spelling as a guide, since forms in -*ier*, -*ire* and in -*ower*, -*owre* rhyme together in the poems.[1]   On the other hand, I do not feel that word-endings in -*ion* and -*ious*, although these are also sometimes treated as disyllabic in the mid-verse at any rate of the earlier plays, make double endings.   And so too with -*ed* and -*est*.   But clearly there is the possibility of divergent computations.   Double endings are not always the result of an instinct for metrical variation.   Sometimes they are due to the need for accommodating a refractory personal name within a line.   Sometimes they emphasize a ringing of the changes upon words.   The large number of them in *King John*, i. 1, as compared with the rest of the play, comes from the recurrence of 'father', 'mother', and 'brother'.   And it is curious to notice how often 'money' and 'dinner' make double endings in the *Comedy of Errors*.   Moreover, double endings are not felt by Shakespeare to be equally appropriate to all kinds of subject-matter.   They are more frequent both in excited dialogue and soliloquy and in the give and take of social conversation, than in meditative or imaginative passages, or in continuous narrative, or in grave oratory.[2]   Redundant syllables also occur before a mid-line pause, and Professor Conrad gives a percentage table for these; but they never become numerous.[3]   More important is the 'resolution' of feet by the insertion of additional unstressed syllables, whereby iambs become anapaests and trochees dactyls.   These trisyllabic feet add much to the grace and flexibility of blank-verse rhythm, and a careful enumera-

---

[1] W. Viëtor, *Shakespeare's Pronunciation*, i. 154, 264.

[2] Cf. E. Abbott in *N.S.S. Trans.*

(1874), 75; Mayor, 174; D. L. Chambers, 44.

[3] Conrad, *Macbeth*, xxvii.

tion would probably show that Shakespeare made a progressive and at times considerable use of them. Here,
too, Professor Conrad has a table, for anapaests alone,
which are by far the greater number.[1] I mistrust it, because foreign students have a habit of treating as 'slurred'
or elided many syllables which I should certainly sound,
although lightly. The proportion of feet counted as trisyllabic is thus much reduced.

Variations in stresses and syllables affect the internal
structure of lines. But the linking of line to line is also
capable of variation. In the blank verse which Shakespeare inherited, the pauses almost invariably coincided
with breaks between the lines. It was 'end-stopped' verse.
There was a juxtaposition of clauses, principal and subordinate, each occupying its full line, and it was by a succession of such lines that Marlowe built up his rolling
periods. Shakespeare escaped from the tyranny of the
'drumming decasyllabon' by altering the incidence of
pausation and introducing shorter clauses; and this was
the main factor in the conversion of blank verse into a
plastic medium, which both came nearer to the run of
ordinary speech, and furnished a sensitive instrument for
registering the rise and fall of emotion and following the
turns of an intricate thought. The sense, in Milton's
words, was now 'variously drawn out from one line to
another'. Statements that Shakespeare substituted the
verse paragraph or the rhythmic phrase for the line as
the unit of composition require some qualification. Just
as the iambic norm of the individual line remains recognizable through the overlay of resolved feet and level or
inverted stresses, so the recurrence of equivalent units,
while modified by the manipulation of pauses, is not forgotten. Such recurrence is of the essence of verse. The
form still controls the patterns which it comes to support.
An obvious element in pause-variation is a reduction in
the number of end-stopped lines. There are overflows of
sense from one line to another. Some scholars speak of
enjambements, or of 'run-on' or *offene* lines. Where over-

[1] Conrad, *Macbeth*, xxix.

flows occur, there can be no marked pause at the breaks between the lines. I agree with Dr. Bradley that a slight impression of pause always survives, but it is reduced to a minimum. The definition and valuation of overflows have been the subject of many discussions, and it cannot be said that there is any agreed basis. It is usually accepted that to constitute an overflow the sense of a single clause and the voice must run on together. But here are involved both the objective criterion of grammar, which analyses the sense, and the subjective criterion of elocutionary feeling, which rules the voice, is largely individual, and sometimes disregards grammar. Attempts have been made to rely for statistical purposes wholly upon the objective or wholly upon the subjective criterion. I think that the elocutionary feeling must have the last word. But there is clearly a large class of necessary overflows, in which the voice and the sense can hardly help coinciding. They occur when the line-break directly divides parts of a single clause placed in their logical order; a subject and the verb of its predicate, the elements of a compound subject, a noun and its epithet adjective, a preposition and the noun it precedes, a verb and its direct or indirect objective, an auxiliary and a main verb, a relative or conjunction and the rest of the subordinate clause which it introduces. There are other cases in which there is still some running-on of the sense and no room for a marked pause, but in which more account may be taken of the line-break. An inversion of order diminishes the connexion between the divided parts of the clause. Or a vocative or short adverbial or adjectival qualification intervenes between one of these and the break. Or what is divided off may itself be such a qualification. Or a dependent noun clause may be divided from its governing verb. Or the division may come between co-ordinate words occupying the same position in the clause. The treatment of such cases as overflows is largely optional. It is a matter of degree. The length of the divided-off member becomes a factor. Overflow is encouraged by a mid-line pause shortly before the break and discouraged by a stress on the final syllable. In

the following passage from the *Tempest*, I have marked
with one and two asterisks the lines in which overflow
seems to me respectively optional and necessary, and of
the former, in a solemn invocation, I should only be sure of
taking as overflows the second, fourth, eleventh, twelfth,
and fourteenth, should reject the third and seventeenth,
and should feel doubtful about the seventh, thirteenth, and
sixteenth.   I might, indeed, accept them at one reading
and reject them at another.[1]

      Ye elves of hills, brooks, standing lakes and groves,
*   And ye that on the sands with printless foot
*   Do chase the ebbing Neptune and do fly him
*   When he comes back; you demi-puppets that
      By moonshine do the green sour ringlets make,
** Whereof the ewe not bites, and you whose pastime
*   Is to make midnight mushrooms, that rejoice
      To hear the solemn curfew; by whose aid,
** Weak masters though ye be, I have bedimmed
      The noontide sun, call'd forth the mutinous winds,
*   And 'twixt the green sea and the azured vault
*   Set roaring war: to the dread rattling thunder
*   Have I given fire and rifted Jove's stout oak
*   With his own bolt; the strong-based promontory
** Have I made shake and by the spurs pluck'd up
*   The pine and cedar: graves at my command
*   Have waked their sleepers, oped, and let 'em forth
      By my so potent art.

I believe that my conception of an overflow and certainly
of a necessary overflow is more restricted than those upon
which Professors König and Conrad have based tables.
Professor Conrad's percentages are the lower of the two.
I find that Professor D. L. Chambers and Dr. Bradley
also regard Professor König's net as cast too wide. He
claims, however, only to include *schroffe* overflows, where
the metrical pause is overridden, and not *milde* ones,
where some account is taken of it. Professor Conrad's
leichte overflows seem intended to be the equivalent of
Professor König's *schroffe*, and his *schwere* overflows the

[1] *Temp.* v. 1. 33–50.

equivalent of the 'light' and 'weak' endings studied by
Professor J. K. Ingram. These are unstressed final monosyllables. The light endings, upon which Professor Ingram thinks that the voice can very slightly dwell, are
mainly pronouns and auxiliaries. The weak endings, which
he thinks essentially proclitic, are prepositions and con-
junctions. There are few of either class, and the weak
endings only appear in the latest plays. Both represent,
I think, nothing more than extreme cases of necessary
overflows. A calculation of overflows is not by itself a
complete measure of pause-variation. There are some of
them, even necessary overflows, in pre-Shakespearean
blank verse. But they do not much affect the character
of the rhythm, because when the sense passes the line-
break, it generally runs on, not to a mid-line pause, but
to the end of the next line. Shakespeare's mid-line pauses
grow in number. To the end there are more of them in
broken dialogue, than in long speeches. Their incidence
is greatest after the second and third feet. Pauses after
the first or before the fifth foot, or even in the middle of
these, are a comparatively late feature. One aspect of the
development is a tendency to end a speech in mid-line.
Professors Pulling and König have tables for such endings, relating their percentages to the number of speeches,
of which Professor Pulling gives a count. Professor Conrad's table for divided lines is not on the same basis, since
the line in which a speech ends is often not taken up by
the next speaker, but remains short. There has not been
much systematic study of internal mid-line pauses, although
their importance was long ago pointed out by Spedding.[1] Drs. Kerrl and Norpoth count the pauses which
require more than a comma to punctuate them in the
special plays they study, and relate those in mid-line to
the total number. Possibly a table showing the proportion
of lines containing such strong pauses to the total lines
would be a better guide. I have attempted to construct
a rough one.[2] The distribution of lighter pauses, of
course, also affects the rhythm, but these it is less easy

---

[1] *N.S.S. Trans.* (1874), 26.   [2] App. H, Table V.

to be sure of. In any case one is dependent upon the punctuation of modern editors, which may not always faithfully represent Shakespeare's intention.[1]

Professor Conrad has a few miscellaneous tables. One of these attempts to represent the proportion of irregular to regular lines; and by an irregular line he means one which contains two trochees or two of his 'Doppeljamben', or a trochee elsewhere than in the first foot or after a mid-line pause, or one of the few anapaests he allows, or a one-syllable foot. It is a rather arbitrary distinction. Another table is for 'amphibious sections', the cases in which a half-line serves both as the end of one full line and the beginning of the next. Others bear upon pronunciation rather than upon metre, and show the gradual disuse of the unelided word-ending in -ed.[2]

The verse-tests are by no means all of equal value, and much caution is required in drawing inferences from them. In the first place the variations occur discontinuously, and the law of averages must be respected. The greater the number of variations, and the greater the number of opportunities for variation, the more reliable an average figure, such as a percentage, is likely to be. In the present investigation, the measure of opportunities for variation is generally the number of lines, sometimes the number of speeches, taken into account. Percentages for total plays are therefore far more comparable than those for single acts; those for individual scenes or shorter passages have little meaning, because they do not leave room for the discontinuities to average out. Some passages in a play may show a continuous or nearly continuous series of overflows or double endings; in others there may be none over a considerable stretch. It is futile to point out that the former show an exceptionally high percentage of the variations, and to use this as an argument in favour of a diversity of authorship or a diversity of date. Mr. Robertson's handling of metrical evidence is much open to this criticism. For the same reason, one must look with suspicion upon the attempts of Professor Conrad and his

[1] Cf. p. 190.   [2] Conrad, *Macbeth*, xxviii, xxx.

followers to establish intervals between the composition
of different acts of plays upon metrical grounds, and to
isolate particular passages as metrically of later date than
the rest. Even where complete plays are in question, the
metrical tables are very likely to be misleading as to those
in which the total amount of blank verse is small. Similarly, comparative figures are of little value, when the
variations upon which they are based are only of rare
occurrence. Accident may be too great a factor in these
to make averaging reliable. Such are six-foot lines, extra
syllables before mid-line pauses, anapaests as reckoned by
Professor Conrad, light and weak endings. Nor must
importance be given to small percentage fluctuations.
The Conradist tables are expressed in per-mills instead of
per-cents. This obscures the issue. In a play of 3,000
lines, three occurrences of a variation make the difference of
a whole unit in the per-millage. Even where percentages
are used, they should be rounded off, and not calculated
to decimals, which give an appearance of scientific precision far from justified by the nature of the material.

A second caution is that variations which become part
of the unconscious or subconscious instinct of a writer are
more likely to be significant of a chronological development than those which involve deliberation. Fleay, like
Malone, was impressed by the abundance of rhyme in
some of the early plays, and assumed that the proportion
of rhyme was a measure of earliness. He went so far as to
make *Midsummer-Night's Dream* the first of the comedies,
and others have given the same position to *Love's Labour's
Lost*. But no man can substitute rhyming for blank-verse
dialogue without realizing what he is doing, and it is most
reasonable to suppose that at some date Shakespeare decided to make a deliberate experiment in lyrical drama.
A very natural stimulus would be afforded by his experience of lyrical work in the narrative poems. The actual
percentage of rhyme in the plays affected by such an
experiment is of no importance. There seems to have been
a notion that rhyme was a characteristic of the pre-
Shakespearean drama, which Shakespeare gradually dis-

carded. It is true that mid-Elizabethan popular plays were written in various forms of doggerel. These, and not heroic couplets, were the 'iygging vaines of riming mother wits', which Marlowe repudiated. There is little use of the heroic metre in the plays of Shakespeare's immediate predecessors. Marlowe has only a few sporadic couplets, including some curious ones in which a line of blank verse interrupts the rhyme. Kyd's *Spanish Tragedy* has one continuous scene, and there are some passages in Greene's *James IV*, in Greene and Lodge's *Looking-Glass*, and in scenes of *1 Henry VI*, which may not be Shakespeare's. There is more in the anonymous *Selimus*, and by Peele, mainly in *Arraignment of Paris*. But this is a court play for boys, and so, if it is of early date at all, is the anonymous *Maid's Metamorphosis*, which only uses heroics. Substantially, the medium of Shakespeare's models was blank verse. The rhyme of the lyric plays represents a fresh start and not a looking backwards. And it seems to bear some relation to a feature in his use of double endings. The growth of these does not follow a very smooth curve at any point. But it is particularly noticeable that, while he begins with a fairly high proportion, there is a marked drop, not only for the lyric plays, but also for *King John* and *1 Henry IV*, which must follow them pretty closely. Heroics themselves, of course, have rare double endings. But it looks as if the constant recurrence of final stress, which is normally entailed by English rhyme, had reacted upon the manner of Shakespeare's blank verse. And the sudden rise in the percentage for *2 Henry IV* can only suggest that here too there is an element of deliberate purpose. Conscious variation of metre is further illustrated by prologues and epilogues, by inserted plays and masks, and by the characteristic bombast of Pistol. These are meant to contrast with the ordinary dialogue, and should be left out of account in computing the variations of its blank verse.

Probably the variations that most easily become unconscious are those of pausation. But here a third caution must be observed. A test, to be reliable, must be uniformly applied throughout, and this is difficult, unless it is objective; rests, that is to say, upon units which can be identified and enumerated with certainty. But we have seen that the overflow test is extremely subjective; much depends upon the personal equation of the enumerator. It may be thought that this does not much matter, so long as the enumerator is the same throughout, since only one personal equation can be in question. It is not really so. Nothing can be more difficult, as any one who has dealt with large batches of literary examination papers will know, than to maintain a continuous subjective standard through a long series of qualitative judgements. Even Rhadamanthus has his moods. And there is the effect of environment to be reckoned with. The same man may very well be impressed by an overflow in a play comparatively free from them, which he would certainly pass over where they come more thickly.

In view of all the uncertainties attaching to the metrical tests, I do not believe that any one of them or any combination of them can be taken as authoritative in determining the succession of plays which come near to each other in date; and I have chiefly used them as controls for the indications of external evidence. In the following table I have attempted to bring together the results of chapter ix and to fit them into the facts of Shakespeare's dramatic career as given in chapter iii. There is much of conjecture, even as regards the order, and still more as regards the ascriptions to particular years. These are partly arranged to provide a fairly even flow of production when plague and other inhibitions did not interrupt it. It is on the whole more practicable to take theatrical seasons, roughly from early autumn to the following summer, rather than calendar years, as a basis. I assume some slackening towards the end of Shakespeare's career, and do not treat literally Ward's statement that he supplied his company with two plays a year.[1]

---

[1] Cf. App. C, no. ix.

1590–1.

2 Henry VI.
3 Henry VI.

1591–2.

1 Henry VI.

1592–3.

Richard III.
Comedy of Errors.

1593–4.

Titus Andronicus.
Taming of the Shrew.

1594–5.

Two Gentlemen of Verona.
Love's Labour's Lost.
Romeo and Juliet.

1595–6.

Richard II.
Midsummer-Night's Dream.

1596–7.

King John.
Merchant of Venice.

1597–8.

1 Henry IV.
2 Henry IV.

1598–9.

Much Ado About Nothing.
Henry V.

1599–1600.

Julius Caesar.
As You Like It.
Twelfth Night.

1600–1.

Hamlet.
Merry Wives of Windsor.

1601–2.

Troilus and Cressida.

1602–3.

All's Well That Ends Well.

1603–4.

———

1604–5.

Measure for Measure.
Othello.

1605–6.

King Lear.
Macbeth.

1606–7.

Antony and Cleopatra.

1607–8.

Coriolanus.
Timon of Athens.

1608–9.

Pericles.

1609–10.

Cymbeline.

1610–11.

Winter's Tale.

1611–12.

Tempest.

1612–13.

Henry VIII.
Two Noble Kinsmen.

Something may be added about the main points of difficulty. The first is as to the position of *Taming of the Shrew*. It has often been put nearer to 1598 than to 1594, because of the resemblance of its provincial environment to that of *2 Henry IV*. The neighbourhood of Stratford

must, however, always have been within the scope of
Shakespeare's memory. The problem is complicated by
that of identifying the *Love Labours Won* of Meres's
list. It is most natural to take this as an alternative title
for some extant play. Such alternative titles, which may
sometimes be no more than unofficial descriptions, are not
uncommon, although the only ones which have got into
the prints of the plays are *The Contention of York and
Lancaster* for *2, 3 Henry VI* and *What You Will* for
Twelfth Night. But elsewhere we get, certainly or probably, *Robin Goodfellow* for *Midsummer-Night's Dream*, *Oldcastle*, *Falstaff* and *Hotspur* for *Henry IV*, *Benedicte
and Betteris* for *Much Ado About Nothing*, *Malvolio* for
Twelfth Night, *All is True* for *Henry VIII*.[1] Claims have
been made for the equation of *Love Labours Won*
with *Love's Labour's Lost*, *Midsummer-Night's Dream*,
Twelfth Night, *Much Ado About Nothing*, *All's Well That
Ends Well*, *Tempest*, and *Taming of the Shrew* itself. The
two first may be at once dismissed; they assume that
Meres meant to attach a second title to the entries which
follow and precede that of *Love Labours Won*, and
this his wording makes impossible. There is little to go
upon, except the implications of the title itself, and the
possibility of finding a play of early date not otherwise
named by Meres. The titles of Shakespeare's comedies
have rarely any significance; *As You Like It* and *What
You Will* are floutingly vague. Almost any love comedy
might bear the title in question; it is least appropriate to
Much Ado About Nothing, which is, however, on the border
of Meres's range, and might fall within it. The wit-
combats between Benedick and Beatrice, resembling those
between Berowne and Rosaline in *Love's Labour's Lost*,
have been called in aid, and the references which the two
plays have in common to Cupid as the god of love and to
Hercules, who no doubt performed labours. Similarly, it
is pointed out that the resemblance of twins is a motive
common to *Twelfth Night* and the *Comedy of Errors*. But
is it not more likely that an interval would have been

[1] Cf. vol. i, pp. 329, 343, 344, 346, 347, 382.

allowed to expire before such situations were repeated?
The 'labours' found in *The Tempest* are Ferdinand's
athletic wrestlings with the logs. There is really no reason
for assuming an early version of *Twelfth Night* or of *The
Tempest*. It is upon the assumption of such a version that
the case for *All's Well That Ends Well* has been defended,
and this also I reject. A suggestion of an old as well as
a new title might indeed be found in 'All is well ended, if
this suit be won', and in Helena's statement just before
that Bertram is 'doubly won'. *Taming of the Shrew* also
has several references to winning, although more obviously
the winning of Petruchio's wager than of his wife's love.[1]
If we set aside *Much Ado About Nothing* as too remote in
theme from the title, *Taming of the Shrew* is the only
comedy which, as it stands, could fill a gap in Meres's
list. And the stylistic evidence, so far as one can judge it
through the uncertainty as to the extent of Shakespeare's
authorship, is in favour of a quite early date. With some
hesitation I have put *Merry Wives of Windsor* at a little
distance from the other Falstaff plays, and I think that this
is justified by the borrowing from *Hamlet* in a report
which must rest on early performances, since the ob-
noxious name Brooke still survived. And if an explanation
is necessary for the continuance of light-hearted comedy
after the period of gloom had begun, the need to obey a
royal behest may supply it. The time-relation of *King Lear*
and *Macbeth* is not very clear. The verse-tests, as shown by
Dr. Bradley, confirm the priority I have given to *King Lear*,
but I cannot put much confidence in their application to
a play like *Macbeth*, which can hardly be in its original
form. Nor am I at all clear about the dating of *Timon of
Athens*. This Dr. Bradley would place between *King Lear*
and *Macbeth*, partly because of the resemblance of its temper
to that of *King Lear*, and partly again on metrical grounds.[2]
But an unfinished play is even less likely than an abridged

---

[1] *All's Well*, v. 3. 315, 336; *Tam.
of Shrew*, iv. 5. 23; v. 2. 69, 112, 116,
186. But the winning of love's labour
connotes an unsuccessful suit in *Two
Gent. of Ver.* i. 1. 32,

If haply won, perhaps a hapless gain;
If lost, why then a grievous labour
won.
[2] Bradley, 443, 470.

play to answer to the metrical tests, and it would be hard
to find room for *Timon of Athens* in the already rather
full year 1605–6. I agree as to the temper. Both *King
Lear* and *Timon of Athens* seem to show symptoms of mental
disturbance. But mental disturbance may come in waves.
It may very likely only be a whimsy of my own that during
the attempt at *Timon of Athens* a wave broke, that an illness
followed, and that when it passed, the breach between the
tragic and the romantic period was complete.

CHAPTER IX

PLAYS OF THE FIRST FOLIO

[*Bibliographical Note*. Facsimiles of F1 were edited by H. Staunton (1866), H. P. (1876), and S. Lee (1902, Cl. Press), and a series of all four Folios was issued (Methuen) in 1904–10. A series of single plays, edited by J. D. Wilson, is in progress. For many purposes the very accurate reprint by L. Booth (1862–4) will serve. The *Shakespeare Quarto Facsimiles* (1880–9, 43 vols.), supervised by F. J. Furnivall, replace the lithographic series (1862–71, 48 vols.) done by E. W. Ashbee for H.P. But the photographic reproduction is not always satisfactory. Only the more important of the critical editions can here be named. Many of them underwent reprints and revisions, and a list of these and of other editions of less critical significance is in W. Jaggard, *Shakespeare Bibliography* (1911), 494. The best eighteenth-century work is surveyed in T. R. Lounsbury, *The First Editors of Sh.* (1906); H. B. Wheatley, *Sh's. Editors* (1916, *Bibl. Soc. Trans.* xiv. 145); A. Nicoll, *The Editors of Sh. from F1 to Malone* (1924, *Studies in F1*, 157); D. Nichol Smith, *Sh. in the Eighteenth Century* (1928). The first edition was that of Nicholas Rowe (1709, 6 vols.). It was followed by those of Alexander Pope (1723–5, 6 vols.); Lewis Theobald (1733, 7 vols.), who had criticized Pope in his *Sh. Restored* (1726); Sir Thomas Hanmer (1743–4, 6 vols.); William Warburton (1747, 8 vols.); Edward Capell (1767–8, 10 vols.), who added separate *Notes and Various Readings*, of which vol. i appeared in 1774, and was withdrawn, to be reprinted in 1779 and reissued in 1783, with additions printed in 1780, and a vol. iii, not directly concerned with the plays, called *The School of Shakespeare*. Capell had been preceded by Samuel Johnson, whose first edition (1765, 8 vols.) underwent a series of revisions. The first (1773, 10 vols.), but for a little help from Johnson himself, was by George Steevens, who had already published his *Twenty of the Plays of Shakespeare* (1766, 4 vols.) from Quartos. The second (1778, 10 vols.) was also by Steevens, not, as is sometimes said, by Isaac Reed. Edmund Malone contributed to it his first *Attempt to Ascertain the Order in which the Plays of Shakespeare were Written*, and added a *Supplement* (1780, 2 vols.) with notes, the first draft of his *History of the Stage*, and the poems and doubtful plays. To this he issued an *Appendix* (1783). The third revision was by Isaac Reed (1785, 10 vols.). The fourth was again by Steevens (1793, 15 vols.), and the fifth (1803, 21 vols.) and sixth (1813, 21 vols.) by Reed. A few notes given by Malone to the edition of 1785, and critical of Steevens, led to an enduring feud, and Malone's *Dissertation on the Three Parts of Henry VI* (1787) was followed by an independent edition (1790, 10 vols.). A revision occupied Malone to his death in 1812, and was published, so far as complete, by the younger James Boswell (1821, 21 vols.). The booksellers have chosen to call the 1803 and 1813 editions of Johnson and Steevens the *First* and *Second Variorum Shakespeares*, and the 1821 edition of Malone, although of different origin, the *Third Variorum*. This does, however, incorporate many prefaces and notes of Malone's predecessors, and may be regarded as the final word of eighteenth-century scholarship on Shakespeare. Of the earlier nineteenth-century editions may be noted those of S. W. Singer (1826), C. Knight (1838 ?–43), J. P. Collier (1842–4, revised 1858), G. C. Verplanck (1847, N.Y.), H. N. Hudson (1852–7, Boston, revised 1881), J. O. Halliwell [-Phillipps] (1853–65, *Folio*), N. Delius (1854–65, Elberfeld), A. Dyce (1857, revised 1864–7), R. G. White (1857–66, Boston), H. Staunton (1858–60). But another term was reached in the *Cambridge* edition of W. G. Clark, J. Glover, and W. Aldis Wright (1863–6, 9 vols., revised by Wright, 1891–3), with minute collations, which are still the basis of textual study, although modern scholarship looks for a closer genetic analysis of the relations between the texts. This is in part supplied by the introductions of F. J. Furnivall, P. A. Daniel, and others to the *Sh. Q. Facsimiles*. The conception of a parallel-text edition by J. Appleton Morgan and others (1886–1906, *Bankside*, N.Y., 22 vols.) is better than its execution. More scientific parallel-texts for individual plays are noted separately. The most useful current edition for general commentary is the *Arden* (1899–1924, 39 vols.) under the successive general editorship of W. J. Craig and R. H. Case, but the volumes, by various hands, are also of various merit. The *New Variorum* edition (1871–1928, 19 plays issued) by H. H. Furness and his son of like name, is overloaded with dead matter, and the earlier volumes pass out of date more rapidly than the later ones are added. Other editions of note are by F. A. Marshall and others (1887–90, *Henry Irving*, 8 vols.), I. Gollancz (1894–6, *Temple*, 40 vols.), C. H. Herford (1899, *Eversley*, 10 vols.), A. H. Bullen (1904–7, *Stratford Town*, 10 vols.). The *Yale* edition (1918–28, 40 vols.) is by various American hands. The *New* edition of A. T. Quiller Couch and J. D. Wilson (1921–30, 13 plays issued) is good on textual criticism and interesting but speculative on textual history. It is unfortunate that many editions, attractive to readers, systematically follow the Folio text for all plays. A text in Elizabethan spelling is still a *desideratum*. The *Old Spelling* edition of F. J. Furnivall, W. G. Boswell-Stone, and F. W. Clarke (1907–12, 17 plays issued) remains incomplete. Much valuable commentary is also to be found in grouped editions of selected plays for students, the *Clarendon Press* by W. G. Clark and W. A. Wright, the *Pitt Press* by A. W. Verity, an unnamed series (Clar. Press) by G. S. Gordon, and the *Falcon* and *Warwick* editions by various hands. The latter are cited under the plays concerned. Of single-volume texts, the standard is the *Globe* (1864) by W. G. Clark and W. A. Wright, not so much for its readings, which are sometimes open to question, as for its line-numeration, which is generally used for references. Some original errors in this were tabulated in *N.S.S. Transactions* (1880–6) 3†, and appear to have been corrected in later issues. This numeration is

preserved in the *Eversley* edition, from which, in view of its greater convenience to the eyesight, my references are taken. Other single-volume
editions are by W. J. Craig (1892, *Oxford*), W. A. Neilson (1906, *Cambridge, U.S.A.*).

I have given for each play a list of monographs and other dissertations,
especially recent ones. These lists must not be taken as exhaustive. They
exclude papers of aesthetic discussion, and probably some others of value,
unknown to me, in foreign periodicals. They include some which I have
not consulted, particularly on sources. I give these to supplement my own
very slight treatment of *Quellenforschung*.]

I, II, III. HENRY THE SIXTH

[S.R. 1594.] xij° Marcij. Thomas Myllington. Entred for
his copie vnder the handes of bothe the wardens a booke
intituled, the firste parte of the Contention of the twoo
famous houses of York and Lancaster with the deathe of
the good Duke Humfrey and the banishement and Deathe
of the Duke of Suffolk and the tragicall ende of the prowd
Cardinall of Winchester, with the notable rebellion of
Jack Cade and the Duke of Yorkes ffirste clayme vnto
the Crowne vj^d (Arber, ii. 646).

[Q1. 1594.] The First part of the Contention betwixt
the two famous Houses of Yorke and Lancaster, with the
death of the good Duke Humphrey: And the banishment and death of the Duke of Suffolke, and the Tragicall
end of the proud Cardinall of Winchester, with the notable
Rebellion of Iacke Cade: And the Duke of Yorkes first
claime vnto the Crowne. [Creede's device (McKerrow
299).] London. Printed by Thomas Creed, for Thomas
Millington, and are to be sold at his shop vnder Saint
Peters Church in Cornwall. 1594. [*Head-title, part in caps.*]
The First Part of the Contention of the two famous Houses
of Yorke & Lancaster, with the death of the good Duke
Humphrey. [*Running-title*] The first part of the conten-
tion of the two famous Houses, of Yorke and Lancaster.
[*As Colophon*, device and imprint repeated.]

[Q1. 1595.] The true Tragedie of Richard Duke of Yorke,
and the death of good King Henrie the Sixt, with the
whole contention betweene the two Houses Lancaster and

Yorke, as it was sundrie times acted by the Right Honourable the Earle of Pembrooke his seruants. [Millington's
device (McKerrow 302).] Printed at London by P⟨eter⟩
S⟨hort⟩ for Thomas Millington, and are to be sold at his
shoppe vnder Saint Peters Church in Cornwal. 1595.
[*Head-title*, under ornament with Stationers' arms] The
true Tragedie of Richard Duke of Yorke, and the good
King Henry the Sixt. [*Running-title*] The Tragedie of
Richard D. of Yorke, and Henrie the sixt.

[In 8°, not 4to.]

Facsimiles. C. Praetorius (1889, *Sh. Q.* xxxvii, ed. F. J. Furnivall;
1891, *Sh. Q.* xxxviii, ed. T. Tyler).

Reprints. J. O. Halliwell (1843, *Sh. Soc.*); W. C. Hazlitt (1875,
Sh's. Library, v. 379; vi. 1); W. A. Wright (*Cambridge Sh.* ix.
507).

[Q2. 1600.] The First part of the Contention betwixt the
two famous houses of Yorke and Lancaster, with the death
of the good Duke Humphrey: And the banishment and
death of the Duke of Suffolke, and the Tragical end of
the prowd Cardinall of Winchester, with the notable
Rebellion of Iacke Cade: And the Duke of Yorkes first
clayme to the Crowne. [Simmes's device (McKerrow 142).]
London Printed by Valentine Simmes for Thomas Millington, and are to be solde at his shop vnder S. Peters
church in Cornewall. 1600. [*Head-title*] The first part of
the Contention of the two famous Houses of Yorke and
Lancaster, with the death of the good Duke Humphrey.
[*Running-title*] The first part of the contention of the two
famous houses, of Yorke and Lancaster.

[An alleged issue printed for Millington by W. W. in 1600 rests
only on a MS. t.p. prefixed, together with one reproducing the
Simmes's imprint, to one of Malone's examples (*Bodl. Mal.* 36),
which has lost its printed t.p. Probably Malone was guessing.]

[Q2. 1600.] The True Tragedie of Richarde Duke of
Yorke, and the death of good King Henrie the sixt: With
the whole contention betweene the two Houses, Lancaster
and Yorke; as it was sundry times acted by the Right
Honourable the Earle of Pembrooke his seruantes. [Orna-

ment] Printed at Londou ⟨*sic*⟩ by W⟨illiam⟩ W⟨hite⟩ for
Thomas Millington, and are to be sold at his shoppe
vnder Saint Peters Church in Cornewall. 1600. [*Head-
title.*] The True Tragedie Of Richard Duke Of Yorke,
And The Good King Henrie The Sixt. [*Running-
title*] The Tragedie of Richard D. of Yorke, and Henrie
the Sixt.

[S.R. 1602.] 19 Aprilis . . . Thomas Pavier. Entred for
his copies by assignement from Thomas Millington these
bookes folowinge, Saluo Jure cuiuscunque viz. . . . The
firste and Second parte of Henry the vj^t ij bookes xij^d . . .
Entred by warrant vnder master Setons hand (Arber, iii.
204).

[Q3. 1619.] The Whole Contention betweene the two
Famous Houses, Lancaster and Yorke. With the Tragicall
ends of the good Duke Humfrey, Richard Duke of Yorke,
and King Henrie the sixt. Diuided into two Parts: And
newly corrected and enlarged. Written by William
Shakespeare, Gent. [W. Jaggard's device (McKerrow
283).] Printed at London, for T⟨homas⟩ P⟨avier⟩. [A2
Head-title] The first part of the Contention of the two
Famous Houses of Yorke and Lancaster, with the death
of the good Duke Humfrey. [I *Head-title*, under ornament with royal arms] The Second Part. Containing
the Tragedie of Richard Duke of Yorke, and the good
King Henrie the Sixt. [*Running-title, for both parts*]
The contention of the two famous Houses of Yorke
and Lancaster.

[Datable by continuity of signatures with those of *Pericles* (1619).]
Facsimile. C. Praetorius (1886, *Sh. Q.* xxiii, xxiv, ed. F. J.
Furnivall).

[S.R. 1623.] Mr William Shakspeers Comedyes Histories, and Tragedyes soe manie of the said Copies as are
not formerly entred to other men. vizt . . . The thirde
parte of Henry ye Sixt . . .

[For full entry, cf. p. 138. This must be *1 Henry VI*. There
is no original entry of *3 Henry VI*, but the transfer of 1602 must
have been relied upon.]

[F1. 1623.] [*Catalogue*] The First part of King Henry the Sixt. . . . The Second part of King Hen. the Sixt. . . . The Third part of King Henry the Sixt. [*Histories*, pp. 96–172, sign. k2ᵛ–q4ᵛ. *Head-titles*] The first Part of Henry the Sixt. . . The second Part of Henry the Sixt, with the death of the Good Duke Humfrey. . . The third Part of Henry the Sixt, with the death of the Duke of Yorke. [*Running-titles*] The first Part of Henry the Sixt. . . The second Part of Henry the Sixt. . . The third Part of King Henry the Sixt.

[*1 Henry VI*. Acts and scc. 1, and in iii and iv all scc. marked (altered in modern eds.) *2,3 Henry VI*. Act i, sc. 1 marked for each.]

Parallel-Texts. [*2 Henry VI*] C. W. Thomas; [*3 Henry VI*] A. Morgan (1892, *Bankside*, xix, xx).

Modern Editions. H. C. Hart (1909, *1 Henry VI*; 1909, *2 Henry VI*; 1910, 1925, *3 Henry VI*; *Arden*); C. F. T. Brooke (1918–23, *Yale*).

Dissertations. E. Malone, *Dissertation on H. VI* (1787, repr. *Var.* xviii. 553); C. Knight, *Essay on H. VI and R. III* (1838?–43, *Pict. Sh.* vii. 399); R. G. White, *On the Authorship of H. VI* (1859, repr. *Sh.* vii. 403); F. G. Fleay, *Who Wrote H. VI?* (1875, *Macmillan's*); J. Lee, *The Authorship of 2, 3 H. VI and their Originals* (1876, *N.S.S. Trans.* 219); N. Delius, *Zur Kritik der Doppeltexte des Sh's. 2, 3 H. VI* (1880, *J.* xv. 211; *Abl.* ii. 95); J. B. Hennemann, *The Episodes in 1 H. VI* (1900, *P.M.L.A.* xv. 290); W. J. Courthope, *On the Authenticity of Some of the Early Plays Assigned to Sh.* (1903, *H.E.P.* iv. 455); K. Schmidt, *Margareta von Anjou vor und bei Sh.* (1906); H. Conrad, *Entstehung des 2, 3 H. VI* (1909, *Z. f. franz. und engl. Unterricht*, viii. 481); C. F. Tucker Brooke, *The Authorship of 2, 3 H. VI* (1912, *Trans. Connecticut Acad.* xvii. 141); P. Seyferth, *In welchem Verhältnis Steht 2 H. VI zu Cont. und 3 H. VI zu True Trag.?* (1916, *Anglia*, xl. 323); H. D. Gray, *The Purport of Sh.'s Contribution to 1 H. VI* (1917, *P.M.L.A.* xxxii. 367); A. W. Pollard, *The York and Lancaster Plays in the Sh. Folio* (1918, Sept. 19, 26, *T.L.S.*); E. v. Schaubert, *Drayton's Anteil an 2, 3 H. VI* (1920); P. Alexander, *2 H. VI and the Copy for Cont. and 3 H. VI and True Trag.* (1924, Oct. 9, Nov. 13, *T.L.S.*), *Sh.'s H. VI and R. III* (1929); C. L. Kingsford, *Fifteenth Century History in Sh.'s Plays* (1925, *Prejudice and Promise in Fifteenth Century England*, i); I. Gourvitch, *Drayton and H. VI* (1926, *N.Q.* cli. 201, 219, 239, 257); A. Gaw, *The Origin and Development of 1 H. VI* (1926, *Univ. South Carolina Studies*, i); E. K. Chambers, *The Relation of Cont. to 2, 3 Hen. VI* (1926, *Proc. Oxford Bibl. Soc.* ii. 1, in summary'), *Actors' Gag in Elizabethan Plays* (1928, Mar. 8, *T.L.S.*).

(a) 2, 3 Henry VI.

The tradition of scholarship from the time of Malone has, with occasional dissent, regarded *The Contention* (Q) as an original two-part play, afterwards revised as 2, 3 *Henry VI* (F). I formerly accepted this view,[1] but a recent study, suggested by Alexander's papers and Greg's work on *Merry Wives of Windsor* and *Orlando Furioso*, has convinced me that it is wrong. Q and F compare as follows. The main structure, in plot, order of episodes, distribution of characters, even succession of speakers, is, subject to certain *lacunae* and dislocations, the same. Q is in both parts the shorter by about a third, and omits a good deal of the best poetry in F. The purport of what is left agrees, but the differences of phrasing are very notable; especially in 2 *Henry VI*, where Q throughout diverges far more from F than in 3 *Henry VI*. Misprints in both texts must of course be allowed for. Sometimes the speeches are identical. Sometimes the identity is only broken by the introduction of equivalent words, variant inflexions, variant minor parts of speech, variations in the order of words. In these passages there is often not much to choose between the two versions from a literary point of view. Sometimes, again, the versions are little more than paraphrases of each other, with an occasional phrase in common, and sometimes complete paraphrases. There are passages in Q which look like mosaics of scraps from F. Prose in Q may represent verse in F. A Q line often appears in an earlier or even later speech or scene or even part of F, and may be repeated there in Q. Thus in 2 *Hen. VI*, iii. 49 of Q is from ii. 3. 29; vi. 55 from i. 1. 254; x. 14–15 from iii. 1. 69–71; in 3 *Hen. VI*, v. 52–3 from i. 2. 33–4; x. 30–1 from v. 3. 1–2; xii. 107 from v. 7. 22; xxiii. 19–21 from iv. 8. 60–1; also in 2 *Hen. VI*, ix. 118 from 3 *Hen. VI*, i. 4. 102; xxii. 64 from 3 *Hen. VI*, ii. 5. 135.[2] Metrically, Q is inferior to F; it has more harshly irregular lines and many collocations of ten syllables,

---

1 *Eliz. Stage*, ii. 130, 200; *Sh., a Survey*, 4.
2 I cite the lineation of the *Sh. Quarto Facsimiles*.

which pay no regard to stress. The pronunciation of individual words is more archaic in Q than in F. The lineation of Q constantly goes astray, and this often seems due to the omission of F words or to the presence of superfluous 'connective' phrases (cf. p. 157) not in F, after which the verse lines follow regularly but are wrongly divided, until a broken line or a fresh error leads to recovery. Broadly speaking, Q is often halting and barbarous, where F is logical and rhythmical.

Much of this can be explained and has been explained on the theory that a reviser took an old play in hand, wrote it up almost speech by speech, smoothed out metrical irregularities and obsolete pronunciations, replaced prose by verse, expanded throughout, added many poetical passages, but at the same time took pains to use every shred of the old text which could be made to suit his purpose, either in its original or in an altered position. Against this theory there are two *a priori* objections. Firstly, there is no evidence (cf. p. 213) for any such practice of meticulous stylistic revision in the Elizabethan theatre. Secondly, who could ever have written such a text as Q, which in some places shows the hand of a competent dramatist, and in others is too bad for the veriest stage hack, to say nothing of the competent dramatists to whom it has been ascribed? It must anyhow have undergone corruption, and in fact the stylistic differences from F can be explained just as well by the corruption of a memorizing reporter (cf. p. 157) as by revision. Many of the features of Q, indeed, recur in the 'bad' Qq of *Hamlet*, *Romeo and Juliet*, *Merry Wives of Windsor*, and *Henry V*, where also a reporter seems to be wholly or in part responsible. Moreover, a report is the best explanation of the mislineations, as due to 'connective' phrases picked up from the mouths of actors, of certain historical confusions which appear in the Q text, and one at least of which cannot have been due to the plotter of the play, and perhaps of numerous 'auditory' errors, although the compositor may (cf. p. 180) be responsible for some of these. And it is the only satisfactory explanation of the transference of lines, often from later passages of the text, which a reviser is not likely to have studied in advance, but which the imperfect memory of a reporter, having already his knowledge of the whole play, may well have dislocated. The same imperfect memory will account for the unevenness of the reporter's work. Sometimes he attained fair precision. Often he forgot lines to the detriment of sense, grammar, and dramatic effect; often he misplaced lines or speeches; often he was only able to recover broken phrases; often he was driven to piece out a general recollection of purport with poor verse or prose of his own. As to who the reporter is likely to have been, there is room for difference of opinion. A shorthand writer (cf. p. 159) would not transfer remote lines. Alexander conjectures for 2 *Henry VI* an actor who had played Suffolk and Cade, perhaps with the aid of a fragmentary transcript, and for 3 *Henry VI* an actor who had played Warwick and Clifford, perhaps with the aid of 'parts'. I do not see any evidence for a fragmentary transcript, or know why any such document should come into existence. Conceivably the reporter had the short 'part' of the Citizen.[1] But I doubt whether the characters named by Alexander are so much better rendered than the rest throughout, as to point to actors. On the whole I am inclined to suggest that the reporter was a book-keeper, who would be in a good position to get a general but inexact knowledge of the whole course of a play which he had often prompted. Perhaps he did 3 *Henry VI* better than 2 *Henry VI* because it had been more recently on the stage. And I think he may have retained a 'plot', which would not help him for the dialogue, but would for the ordering of the scenes, and for the stage-directions. These, in both F and Q, are exceptionally full and descriptive, with many notes on the purport of scenes, the relation of characters, grouping, apparel, properties, and both at entries and in the margin for action and the address of speeches. They differ by omissions and additions and in details. But they have clearly a common origin. The longest is identical in the two texts.[2] The hand of an

---

[1] 2 *Hen. VI*, iv. 5.   [2] 2 *Hen. VI*, ii. 3. 59.

author is discernible, especially in part 2, in vagueness as to numbers and the like, left to the discretion of the management. The directions of F might well be the author's, perhaps expanded by a book-keeper; those of Q an adaptation for a 'plot'. Q, but not F, has the common 'plot' formula for the entry of characters 'to' each other.[1] Musical notes and a few directions in the imperative mood suggest that both sets were primarily for the guidance of stage action rather than a reader.

In two scenes, however, of part 2 (i. 4; iii. 2) a different staging appears to be contemplated by Q and F, and this is not the only indication that the intervention of a reporter does not by itself completely account for the relation of the versions. The basis of Q must have been a production for which the original text had been cut. Two or three short episodes may have been omitted. Sections of long speeches in F, which should have been the easiest to remember, have disappeared without leaving any traces upon Q. The object of the cutting is not quite clear. Probably a reduction in the time required for presentation was alone in view; there is no reduction in the number of actors needed for the most crowded scenes. It is not, of course, possible to say how much of the difference in length between F and Q is due to cuts, and how much to the reporter's lapses. The method of the cuts is interesting. Much of the poetry goes out, the similes, the classical allusions; all the Latin. This is noticeable even in short *lacunae*, which one would otherwise put down to the reporter. There is a process of vulgarization. If there was an adaptation by cutting for the stage, a few differences in the order of speeches and episodes may also be due to adaptation, rather than to the reporter. There is one pretty clear case. In part 3, iv. 6 has been cut, but a bit about Henry Tudor, too interesting to an Elizabethan audience to be lost, has been salvaged by attaching it to iv. 8.

A few passages in both parts, while written in fairly good blank verse, are not in F or so unlike those in F as to require some buttressing of the 'report' theory. I do not suppose

[1] *2 Hen. VI*, ii. 3. 1; *3 Hen. VI*, v. 6. 1.

that the same explanation is applicable to them all. One or two scenes in F (cf. *infra*) may have been rewritten after the Q production. Similarly, some highly coloured Q lines in i. 4 of part 2 may have been removed when the staging of that scene was altered. There are other special Q passages, which are so featureless that perhaps they may reasonably be ascribed to the reporter. But there are two which betray the singular fact that his capricious memory has not stopped short of bringing in lines from another play altogether. He takes his vii. 10 and ix. 134–6 of *2 Henry VI* from Marlowe's *Edward II* 2651, 965–6. On the other hand, *Massacre of Paris* 952–3, 1376–9, are probably themselves taken from *3 Hen. VI*, v. 3. 1–2 and *3 Hen. VI*, ii. 1. 68–9.[1] There are similar transfers in the reported Qq of *Hamlet* and *Merry Wives of Windsor* (*q.v.*). And if a play known to us has been so drawn upon, other comparatively striking Q lines may belong to plays not known.[2] Finally, Q probably incorporates some small theatrical interpolations and gags. Occasionally the mention of a place-name at the end of a scene helps the audience to locate a coming scene. The Cade episodes of Q chiefly differ from those of F by an unusual amount of dislocation and several gags. Such are the knighting of Dick Butcher (*2 Hen. VI*, Q xiii. 77) and others (xviii. 17–21, 71–7) less decent.

Discussions of authorship have been much complicated by the revision theory. Most of those who have found the hands of Marlowe, Kyd, Peele, Greene, Lodge, and Nashe, as well as of Shakespeare, in the plays, have held it, and have been dispensed by it from putting their theories to the test of indicating where one hand ended and another began. A partial exception is Fleay, who recognized the surreptitious character of Q, and in 1886 modified an earlier view by assigning *3 Henry VI* substantially to Marlowe, and dividing *2 Henry VI* between Greene (i. 1), Peele (most of i. 2–ii. 4), Kyd (ii. 1. 59–153), Marlowe (i. 3. 45–103; iii. 1–iv. 1), and Lodge (iv. 2–v. 3).

---

[1] Cf. Greg in *M.S.R. Massacre*, viii.

[2] E.g. xxi. 52–4, inserted after *2 Hen. VI*, v. 1. 70.

Shakespeare he only brought in about 1600, as revising *2 Henry VI* considerably and *3 Henry VI* slightly. In 1591 he substituted Drayton as reviser. Von Schaubert also finds Drayton in several scenes, but this has been sufficiently refuted by Gourvitch. The external evidence of F and the 1619 title-page of course tells substantially for Shakespeare. Meres does not name the plays as Shakespeare's in 1598, but while the presence of a name in his list has great weight, the absence of one has much less. There may, moreover, have been no revival between his coming to London and the compilation of his list. The plays, as they stand, are loosely constructed, especially part 2. The Cade scenes are naturally differentiated by their comic subject-matter. Clifford's speech in *2 Hen. VI*, v. 2. 31–65, seems to me clearly of later style than the rest. It is certainly Shakespearean, although the unfortunate Miss Lee, pressed by Furnivall to be precise in her attributions, gave it to Marlowe, in spite of the internal pausation. The pastoral of *3 Hen. VI*, ii. 5, may also be later Shakespeare, although not so late. Otherwise I find no obvious sutures either of style or structure. The careless substitution of Elinor, Elianor and Nell for Margaret as the Queen's name in *2 Hen. VI*, iii. 2, is odd, and would be odd on any theory of authorship. Pollard, a revisionist, thinks that the character of Richard has undergone transformation; that he was originally conceived by Marlowe as a valiant hunchback, and afterwards altered by another writer, with a prospective *Richard III* play in his mind, into an ambitious hypocrite. And he supposes the Q version of the soliloquy in *3 Hen. VI*, iii. 2. 124–95, to be an afterthought indicating this change of intention, and inconsistent with the rest of his presentment in Q until almost the last scene, where it is clearly being linked up with the coming *Richard III*. On the assumption that F is the original text, this view can hardly stand. Richard only takes hold of the play, naturally enough, after his father's death, but his ultimate character is already apparent in ii. 1. 41–2; iii. 2. 1–117; iv. 1. 83, 124–6. And he is still valiant at the end of *Richard III*. If, as I hold, *Richard III* is Shakespeare's, the continuity of Richard's character is strong ground for his authorship of *3 Henry VI*. The internal evidence of style I find difficult to handle. I do not think that we have adequate *criteria* for distinguishing with any assurance from the style of his contemporaries that of a young writer still under their influence. Most of the rhetorical features of *Richard III* are also to be found in *3 Henry VI*, but less continuously, among straightforward spaces of unornamented writing. The same is true, perhaps in a minor degree, of *2 Henry VI*. I do not see anything improbable in the stylistic development which the historical succession of the plays suggests. The large proportion of feminine endings in both parts tells for Shakespeare. Certainly there are many parallels of vocabulary and phrase to the work of other men, notably that of Marlowe and Peele; many also to Shakespeare's own plays and poems. But I think weight must be given to the numerous similes and metaphors from natural history and country life, some of them literary, but others testifying to direct observation. I do not find these in any of the contemporaries who have been called in question. They are very common in *Venus and Adonis* and *Lucrece*. On the other hand, there are scraps of Latin, and many classical allusions. *Richard III* has not the erudition and not much natural history, except for the purposes of vituperation. Did Shakespeare take warning from the extent to which both features were 'cut' by the actors in adapting *2, 3 Henry VI*?

Greene's *Groatsworth of Wit* parodies *3 Hen. VI*, i. 4. 137. This does not in my view give us any information about the authorship of the line, but is certainly not inconsistent with Shakespeare's. But it shows that the play, and naturally also *2 Henry VI*, were in existence before Greene's death on 3 September 1592. As the theatres had probably been closed since June 23, we may put them a little farther back. The title-page of the Q of *3 Henry VI* makes it a play of Pembroke's men. Of these there is no trace before the winter of 1592–3, and some other company may have been the original producers. The plays are not in Henslowe's list of 1592 for 'Strange's' men, and if theirs (cf. *infra*) can hardly be later than 1591. The stage-directions of *3 Hen. VI*, i. 2. 48; iii. 1. 1, have 'Gabriel' for a messenger and 'Sinklo' and 'Humfrey' for two keepers. These are probably the actors Gabriel Spencer, John Sincler, and Humphrey Jeffes. There is a similar substitution in the stage-directions to *2 Hen. VI*, iv. 2. 1. Here among Cade's followers are 'Beuis' and 'Iohn Holland'. They are not named in the text, although editors have chosen to take thence the Christian name of 'George' for Bevis. But John Holland, like John Sincler, is an actor in the cast (cf. p. 44) for *2 Seven Deadly Sins*, as played by Strange's or the Admiral's or the Alleyn company about 1590. Spencer and Jeffes are not in that cast. Of Bevis I know nothing, but probably he too was a minor actor. In *2 Hen. VI*, ii. 3. 92, the Armourer says, 'therefore, Peter, have at thee with a downright blow!', and Q adds, 'as Bevys of South-hampton fell upon Askapart'. Surely Bevis played the Armourer as well as a rebel, and this is a bit of his gag. These names, interesting as they are, prove rather elusive, when one attempts to draw any inference from them as to the original ownership of *2, 3 Henry VI*. All the five actors may have been together in the Alleyn company; and again all of them may have passed from that to Pembroke's in 1592. That Bevis was in Pembroke's we can be sure, since his gag comes from a reported performance by them. Neither he nor Holland is heard of later. Sincler probably joined the Chamberlain's men in 1594, as he is in *Taming of the Shrew*, and was certainly with them in 1597–8 and in 1604. But Spencer and probably Jeffes were in the Pembroke's company of 1597, and thereafter both were in the Admiral's company. I formerly thought[1] that they might have been Chamberlain's men during 1594–7, but the recent discoveries (cf. p. 50) of evidence for a Pembroke's company in 1595–6 makes this now seem less likely. All that we can say with certainty is that the F texts may rest upon prompt-copy either for the Alleyn company about 1591 or

[1] *Eliz. Stage*, ii. 200.

for the Pembroke company about 1593, and that the Q texts must rest on performances by the Pembroke company about the same time. I suspect that the report was made for sale to the printers after the company broke down in the autumn of 1593. Dr. Greg suggests to me that it may have been made for performances earlier in 1593, and I am content to leave that as a possible alternative. Somehow, the legitimate prompt-copies must have passed, from the Alleyn company on Dr. Greg's theory, or from Pembroke's on mine, to the Chamberlain's, who left the old actor-names standing in them. If Sincler did not change his part, they could pass as character names, or be disregarded, as the original directions and prefixes would be still legible. A revival by the Chamberlain's is pointed to, both by the alterations incorporated in the F text and by the reference in the epilogue of *Henry V* to Henry the Sixth:

> Whose state so many had the managing,
> That they lost France, and made his England bleed:
> Which oft our stage has shown.

It may have been later than the record of Meres. The plays, as revived, seemed old-fashioned to Jonson, but the date of his reference (App. B, no. xxii) is not certain. There is no evidence of a Jacobean revival. The F text shows no changes due to the *Act of Abuses*. I cannot explain a few passages in which Q3 varies the Q1 text in the direction of that of F. Whether derived from a performance, or from the information of the author or the theatre, they hardly justify the 'newly corrected and enlarged' of the title-page.

The historical matter seems to be mainly from Holinshed, but Halle, Fabyan, Grafton, and Stowe may also have been consulted.[1]

(b) *1 Henry VI.*

This is a very different problem. There is no Q. F has again elaborate stage-directions. Those in i often have the unusual opening 'Here'. The scene-division is confined

---

[1] Boswell-Stone, xi. 253.

to iii and iv, and while iv is twice the length of i and ii,
v is a single scene of 108 lines. As F does not divide
2, 3 *Henry VI* into scenes at all, these indications may have
been taken over from heterogeneous 'copy', perhaps in
more than one hand. Moreover, there are certainly several
styles in the play. Various attempts have been made to
disentangle and identify them, but none are quite satisfactory. I group the scenes, as divided in modern editions,
in the following sections: (*a*) i. 1, 3; ii. 5; iii. 1, 4; iv. 1, 4;
v. 1, 4. 94–end; (*b*) i. 2, 4–6; ii. 1–3; iii. 2–3; iv. 7. 33–end;
v. 2, 3. 1–44, 4. 1–93; (*c*) iv. 3, 5, 6, 7. 1–32; (*d*) v. 3.
45–end, 5; (*e*) ii. 4; (*f*) iv. 2. Sections (*a*) and (*b*) contain
the bulk of the play, and are by distinct hands. In (*a*)
the matter is of English politics, the quarrels of Gloucester
and Winchester and of Somerset and York; it looks forward to 2, 3 *Henry VI*, and the style more nearly resembles
theirs than anything else in the play. In (*b*) the matter is
of fighting in France and Joan of Arc. It is in a very
inferior style, with many flat and some absurd lines, much
tautology, and a tendency to drag in learned allusions.
There is room for doubt as to whether a few colourless
passages about Talbot (i. 1. 103–47; iii. 4. 1–27; iv. 1.
9–47; iv. 4) belong to (*a*) or (*b*). But I do not understand
how Pollard and others fail to appreciate the very clear
differentiation between (*a*) and (*b*) during the greater part
of i and ii. And I think that the same hands continue
throughout. Gaw, however, who has made the fullest
study of the play, thinks that the (*b*) matter passed in iii–v
to two fresh hands. This view is largely based upon
differences in the F spelling of proper names, as to which
(cf. p. 232) the Elizabethan practice was very loose.
Certainly 'Gloster' and 'Glocester' appear within a few
lines of each other in a perfectly homogeneous passage of
iii. 1. I cannot therefore attach much importance to the
differences between 'Ioane' and 'Ione', 'Puzel' and 'Pucell',
'Burgundie' and 'Burgonie', merely because they are used
in different scenes. Section (*c*) consists of the Talbot death-
scenes, which are largely in heroic rhyme. They are often
claimed for Shakespeare, but on the whole I think it is

more likely that they are by the author of (*b*), and the
duplication of a tasteless comparison of Talbot and his
son to Daedalus and Icarus favours this. But if so, the
(*b*) man was a better hand at rhyme than at blank verse.
Section (*d*), containing the Suffolk and Margaret scenes,
also points forward to *2, 3 Henry VI*. I think it is by a
third hand. Shakespeare's presence is only clear to me in
(*e*), the Temple garden scene, and (*f*), an unrhymed Talbot
scene leading up to (*c*). These I take to be new scenes,
written in or later than 1594. Probably both replaced scenes
of the original play; almost certainly (*e*) did, as later passages carry on the motive of the roses. Some would add
ii. 5, the scene with Mortimer in the Tower, but this
I take to be the best of the (*a*) scenes. It has very few
double endings, although that is not conclusive against
Shakespeare in a single scene. As to the authorship of the
original play, I feel no assurance. If Shakespeare is in it
at all, it must be in (*a*). The evidence of F is not very
strong here, since clearly by 1623 the piece was regarded
as an integral part of his *Henry VI*. The style of (*a*) might
be a first stage in the development (cf. *supra*) up to *Richard
III*. It is Marlowesque, and might also, as some think, be
Marlowe's. The percentage of double endings (8 %) is
high for Marlowe, and lower than that of *2, 3 Henry VI*.
If, however, as seems likely (cf. *infra*), *1 Henry VI* followed
these, an attribution of (*a*) to Shakespeare is much less
plausible. In any case I do not think it necessary to assume, with Gaw and others, that he 'touched up' the work
of other men in the play, merely because a few lines here
and there are better or more like him than the rest. Hart,
who disregards the distinction between (*a*) and (*b*), finds
Greene predominant in i and ii. This I much mistrust.
The parallels quoted are very slight, and Greene's only
extant history-play, *James IV*, is of a very different type.
If Greene is in the play, (*d*) seems more like him. But
I should be surprised to find him writing for Alleyn's
company after the *Orlando Furioso* swindle,[1] and in the
Groatsworth he seems aloof from his fellow dramatists

---

[1] *Eliz. Stage*, iii. 325.

as well as from the players. Gaw finds Peele in some of the (*b*) scenes, and I see no obvious reason why he should not have written them all, with the Talbot scenes. He uses rhyme in other plays, and the nationalist tone is like him. On the other hand, some of his characteristic mannerisms are not very apparent. Nashe, Lodge, and Kyd have also been speculated upon, and of course Chapman by Robertson.

Nashe, in his *Pierce Penniless*, registered on 8 August 1592, records the triumph on the stage of 'braue *Talbot* (the terror of the French)', whom the spectators beheld 'fresh bleeding'.[1] I do not think that any inference can be drawn for or against his own share in the authorship. But the date helps to identify the play with the 'Harey the vj' produced by Strange's men for Henslowe (App. D) on 3 March 1592. It was 'ne' and probably therefore either actually new, or substantially remodelled. Evidently the death of Talbot was already a prominent feature. Pollard thinks that behind *1 Henry VI*, as we now have it, is an original Joan of Arc play by two hands, altered at a first stage by the insertion of the Talbot death-scenes, and at a later by the garden, tower, and Margaret scenes, as links to an already existing *York and Lancaster*. It may be so. But the rivalry between York and Somerset is wanted in the play itself to explain the abandonment of Talbot (iv. 3, 4). And there are passages in other scenes than those named by Pollard which seem closely linked to *2, 3 Henry VI*; bits about the roses (iii. 4; iv. 1); the disputes of Gloucester and Winchester (i. 1, 3; iii. 1; v. 1), which lead to little here, but seem suggested by the 'ancient bickerings' of *2 Hen. VI*, i. 1. 144, although indeed this might be argued either way as to priority; a passing allusion (i. 1. 39) to the duchess of Gloucester, so prominent in the later play; the prophecies (i. 1. 48; iii. 1. 187; iv. 1. 182; iv. 3. 47) of the choric Bedford, Exeter, and Lucy. It is at least as tenable a theory that the whole thing, except Shakespeare's two later scenes, was put together in 1592, to exploit an earlier theme which had been

[1] Cf. *Eliz. Stage*, iv. 238.

successful. Even so the Admiral's men in 1599, after producing three parts of *The Civil Wars of France*, wound up with an *Introduction to the Civil Wars of France*.[1] A multiplicity of authors is sufficient to account for the odd scening of the 'copy' for F, as well as for the numerous inconsistencies of action in the play, even if some of these authors were not individually careless. Tentatively, therefore, I ascribe *2, 3 Henry VI* to 1591 and *1 Henry VI* to 1592. Presumably *1 Henry VI* shared in the revival indicated by the epilogue to *Henry V*, for which the present ii. 4 and iv. 2 may have been written.

There is an interesting bit of staging in the use of the 'top' in i. 4 and iii. 2,[2] but I do not accept Gaw's elaborate argument to show that this was a new structural feature first invented at the Rose in 1592, or think with him that it was the loft from which the theatre's flag waved and its trumpet was blown. Nothing here could come into the action of a play, in view of the intervention of the projecting 'heavens'. The 'top' must have been over the stage balcony, on a level with the upper row of galleries, as the balcony itself was on a level with the middle row. Halle, Holinshed, and Fabyan seem all to have been drawn upon for the historical matter.[3] The recital of Talbot's dignities in iv. 7 comes from his epitaph at Rouen, of which there are later printed versions in R. Crompton's *Mansion of Magnanimitie* (1599), and R. Broke's *Catalogue and Succession of the . . Earles . . of England* (1619).[4] But travellers went to Rouen, although Essex and his soldiers failed to take it in 1591. The chronology throughout the play is much perverted. Foreshortening was inevitable, since Henry could not well be presented on the stage as a child at the beginning of the play and marriageable at the end.

---

[1] *Eliz. Stage*, ii. 169.
[2] Cf. *ibid*. iii. 98.
[3] Boswell-Stone, xi.
[4] *Ibid*. 233.

IV. RICHARD THE THIRD
[S.R. 1597.] 20 Octobris. Andrewe Wise. Entred for his copie vnder thandes of master Barlowe, and master warden Man. The tragedie of kinge Richard the Third with the death of the Duke of Clarence vj^d (Arber, iii. 93).

[Q1. 1597.] [Ornament] The Tragedy Of King Richard the third. Containing, His treacherous Plots against his brother Clarence: the pittiefull murther of his iunocent ⟨sic⟩ nephewes: his tyrannicall vsurpation: with the whole course of his detested life, and most deserued death. As it hath beene lately Acted by the Right honourable the Lord Chamberlaine his seruants. [Ornament] At London ¶ Printed by Valentine Sims, for Andrew Wise, dwelling in Paules Chuch-yard ⟨sic⟩, at the Signe of the Angell. 1597. [No Head-title. Running-title] The Tragedy of Richard the third.

Facsimiles. W. Griggs (1886, *Sh. Q.* xi, ed. P. A. Daniel); J. S. Farmer (1913, *T.F.T.* from Ashbee).

[Q2. 1598.] The Tragedie of King Richard the third. Conteining his treacherous Plots against his brother Clarence: the pitiful murther of his innocent Nephewes: his tyrannicall vsurpation: with the whole course of his detested life, and most deserued death. As it hath beene lately Acted by the Right honourable the Lord Chamberlaine his seruants. By William Shake-speare. [Creede's device (McKerrow 299)] London Printed by Thomas Creede, for Andrew Wise, dwelling in Paules Church-yard, at the signe of the Angell. 1598. [No Head-title. Running-title] The Tragedie of Richard the third.

[Q3. 1602.] The Tragedie of King Richard the third. Conteining his treacherous Plots against his brother Clarence: the pittifull murther of his innocent Nephewes: his tyrannical vsurpation: with the whole course of his detested life, and most deserued death. As it hath bene lately Acted by the Right Honourable the Lord Chamberlaine his seruants. Newly augmented, By William Shakespeare. [Creedes device (McKerrow 299)] London. Printed by Thomas Creede, for Andrew Wise, dwelling

in Paules Church-yard, at the signe of the Angell. 1602.
[*No Head-title. Running-title*] The Tragedie of Richard
the Third.
[There are no augmentations]
Facsimile. C. Praetorius (1888, *Sh. Q.* xlii, ed. P. A. Daniel).

[S.R. 1603.] 25. Junii Mathew Lawe. Entred for his
copies in full courte Holden this Day. These ffyve copies
followinge ij^s vj^d viz. iij enterludes or playes. The ffirst
is of Richard the .3. . . . all kinges . . all whiche by consent of the Company are sett ouer to him from Andrew
Wyse. (Arber, iii. 239.)

[Q4. 1605.] The Tragedie of King Richard the third.
Conteining his treacherous Plots against his brother
Clarence: the pittifull murther of his innocent Nephewes:
his tyrannicall vsurpation: with the whole course of his
detested life, and most deserued death. As it hath bin
lately Acted by the Right Honourable the Lord Cham-
berlaine his seruants. Newly augmented, By William
Shake-speare. [Creede's device (McKerrow 299)] London,
Printed by Thomas Creede, and are to be sold by Mathew
Lawe, dwelling in Paules Church-yard, at the Signe of the
Foxe, neare S. Austins gate, 1605. [*No Head-title. Running-title*] The Tragedie of Richard the third.

[Q5. 1612.] The Tragedie of King Richard The Third. . . .
As it hath beene lately Acted by the Kings Maiesties
seruants . . . 1612. [Otherwise the same as Q4.]

[Q6. 1622.] The Tragedie Of King Richard The Third.
Contayning his treacherous Plots against his brother
Clarence: The pittifull murder of his innocent Nephewes:
his tyrannicall Vsurpation: with the whole course of his
detested life, and most deserued death. As it hath been
lately Acted by the Kings Maiesties Seruants. Newly
augmented. By William Shake-speare. [Ornament] London, Printed by Thomas Purfoot, and are to be sold by
Mathew Law, dwelling In Pauls Church-yard, at the
Signe of the Foxe, neere S. Austines gate, 1622. [*No Head-
title. Running-title*] The Tragedie of Richard the Third.
Facsimile. C. Praetorius (1889, *Sh. Q.* xliii, ed. P. A. Daniel).

[F1. 1623.] [*Catalogue*] The Life & Death of Richard the Third. [*Histories*, pp. 173–204, sign. q 5–t 2ᵛ. *Head-title*] The Tragedy of Richard the Third: with the Landing of Earle Richmond, and the Battell at Bosworth Field. [*Running-title*] The Life and Death of Richard the Third.

[Acts and scc. marked (altered in modern eds.).]

Later Quartos. 1629 (John Norton, sold by Mathew Lawe); 1634 (John Norton).

Parallel-Text. E. A. Calkins (1891, *Bankside*).

Modern Editions. W. A. Wright (1880, *O.U.P.*); G. Macdonald (1896, *Warwick*); A. H. Thompson (1907, *Arden*); H. H. Furness, jun. (1908, *New Var.*); J. R. Crawford (1927, *Yale*).

[*Dissertations.* W. Oechelhaüser, *Essay über R. III* (1868, *J.* iii. 27; 1894, *Shakespeareana*); N. Delius, *Über den ursprünglichen Text des R. III* (1872, *J.* vii. 124; *Abl.* i. 234); F. G. Fleay, *Who Wrote Hen. VI?* (1875, *Macmillan's*); J. Spedding, *On the Corrected Edition of R. III* (1875, *N.S.S. Trans.* 1); E. H. Pickersgill, *On the Q and the F of R. III* (1875, *N.S.S. Trans.* 77); R. Koppel, *Textkritische Studien über Shs R. III und Lear* (1877); A. Schmidt, *Qq und F. von R. III* (1880, *J.* xv. 301); K. Fischer, *Shs Charakterentwickelung R. III* (2nd ed. 1889); G. B. Churchill, *R. III up to Sh.* (1900); K. Schmidt, *Margareta von Anjou, vor und bei Sh.* (1906); O. Pape, *Über die Entstehung der Q1 von R. III* (1906), *Die Q1 von R. III ein stenographische Raubdruck* (1906, *Arch. f. Stenographie*, lvii. 152, 186, 241); R. A. Law, *R. III, i.* 4 (1912, *P.M.L.A.* xxvii. 117); W. D. Moriarty, *The Bearing on Dramatic Sequence of the Varia in R. III and Lear* (1913, *M.P.* x. 451); O. J. Campbell, *A Dutch Analogue of R. III* (1916, *Wisconsin Studies*, 231); A. W. Pollard, *The York and Lancaster Plays in F1* (1918, Sept. 19, 26, *T.L.S.*); J. M. Robertson, *The Authorship of R. III* (1922, *Sh. Canon*, i. 155); P. Alexander, *Sh.'s H. VI and R. III* (1929).]

Each Q, other than Q5, is reprinted from its immediate predecessor. There are occasional corrections, not involving reference to a manuscript, and a progressive accumulation of errors. Q5 appears sometimes to follow Q4 and sometimes Q3. The use of both, or of a copy made up of sheets from each, has been suggested. It seems also possible that the sheets of Q4 may have been corrected during printing, and some form, not collated, used as copy for Q5. F1 repeats many errors of the later Qq and one of them must have been used to print from; doubtless Q6, as several of these errors are not in the other Qq.

On the other hand, the differences between F1 and all the Qq are so great as to point clearly to alteration of the Q6 basis from a manuscript source. Q1 and F1 must therefore be regarded as distinct texts. The main differences are as follows. F has about 230 lines which are not in Q. Of these about half are in six considerable passages (i. 2. 156–67; ii. 2. 89–100, 123–40; iii. 7. 144–53; iv. 4. 221–34, 288–342). They form parts of long speeches or long sections of dialogue, do not differ in style from the rest of the play, fit in without awkward joints, and in some cases leave the context abrupt or less effective when omitted. The other special F lines form short dispersed passages, often single lines. Q has about forty lines not in F, similarly dispersed, except one passage (iv. 2. 101–19), which again fits well into its context. A few passages show small transpositions of order, and the prose of Clarence's murderers in i. 4. 84–161, most of which is correctly given in F, is capitalized throughout as verse in Q. But in the main the texts agree in arrangement, speech for speech, and even line for line. There is, however, much divergence in phrasing, which, after allowing for numerous misprints in both texts and the influence of Q6 on F1, disappears from iii. 1. 1–157 and from v. 3. 79 onwards. A word of one text is often represented in the other by a synonym or the same word in a different number, case, mood, or tense. Often a word is repeated in Q and another is substituted for the repetition in F. There is some tendency to uniformity in variation. The *which, betwixt, whilst* of Q are several times replaced by *that, between, while,* or *when* in F. The same words are differently ordered within a line. Or the wording of one text is a complete paraphrase of the sense given in the other. A metrically normal ten-syllable line in F often represents one in Q which has one or more extra syllables. Shakespeare, of course, uses trisyllabic feet and six-foot lines, but many of these in Q are harsh, and occasionally the abnormality seems due to the intrusion of an exclamatory or other 'connective' word, such as actors introduce to accompany their gestures. These facts are capable of more than one explanation, and there are

broadly two views as to the relation between Q and F
which they may indicate. It has been held that Q represents the original text of the play, and F a later revision
by Shakespeare or some other hand. And it has been held
that F represents the original text and Q either a revision
for stage purposes or a corrupt report of the play as
staged. It generally goes with the first theory that the
special F passages were added on revision and with the
second that they were 'cut' in representation. I do not
suppose that any very simple formula will explain everything. But substantially I regard the second theory as
sound. In particular the suggested stylistic revision seems
to me out of the question. There has been much inconclusive discussion as to the respective literary merits of
bits of Q and F wording. On balance, I think that F is the
better of the two; and so it might well be on either theory.
But the difference of value, for stage purposes at least, is
negligible. And I cannot reconcile with any reasonable
conception of Shakespeare's methods of work a revision
limited to the smoothing out of metre and the substitution
of equivalent words, without any incorporation of any new
structure or any new ideas. Nor can I think that either
Shakespeare or any one else at the theatre would have
thought it either worth while or practicable to make actors
relearn their parts with an infinity of trivial modifications.
Still less can I, with Pollard, suppose that Shakespeare
revised the F into the Q form.

The history of the text must, I think, be somewhat as
follows. The play, as written by Shakespeare, was slightly
altered for stage purposes. It was shortened by cutting
six long passages. Minor alterations were made to enable
certain scenes (i. 4; ii. 1, 4; iii. 4, 5; v. 1, 2, 3) to be played
with a reduced number of minor parts. Incidentally these
account for a few of the lesser passages omitted in Q, and
in connexion with them some small corrections of nomenclature and topography (i. 3. 333; ii. 1. 7, 66) seem to
have been made in the text. Q1 was based on this stage-
version. I do not think that it was 'surreptitious', in the
sense of being printed without the consent of the Chamber-

lain's men. There is nothing in the circumstances of the
publication to suggest irregularity. Certainly some of the
textual features—omissions, paraphrases, substitution of
equivalent words, incorporation of actor's 'connectives'
—are such as appear in 'reported' plays, and there are
some 'auditory' errors. But the text, and in particular
the lineation, is so much better than that of the accepted
'bad' quartos, as to suggest the use of a transcript from the
original. It must, of course, have been a bad transcript, to
explain the verbal divergences from F. I suggest that it
was specially prepared by the book-keeper for the printer.
Possibly the original was required at the time for representations. The book-keeper adopted the alterations marked
on the original for stage purposes. His transcription,
except for accesses of conscience at iii. 1. 1 and v. 3. 79,
was done carelessly. He was familiar with the play, which
he had prompted, and although he generally checked the
succession of lines, in writing them out he often allowed
himself to follow their purport as he had heard them, thus
vulgarizing the style, and producing in a minor degree the
features of a reported text. An occasional transference by
memory from some other part of the play (ii. 2. 24 from i.
4. 252; iv. 4. 507 from iv. 3. 48; iv. 4. 235 from iv. 4. 398)
is particularly significant. Responsibility for the omission of stray lines the transcriber must perhaps share with
the Q printer. Shakespeare's original remained at the
theatre, marked perhaps for the stage adaptation, but
without further alteration, except the usual perfunctory
excision of some of the profanity for a Jacobean revival.
In 1623 it was made available for the correction of a Q6
as copy for F, with instructions to restore the passages cut
or altered for the stage, but not the oaths. The correction
was not perfectly done, and the result was not perfectly
printed. Among the errors were the omissions of a few Q
lines, including iv. 2. 101–19. Possibly an editor, or no
more than a press-corrector, may have made a few alterations, by conjecture, as printers of the successive Qq had
done, or to bring into conformity with what he regarded
as current usage. A substitution, perhaps only by mis-

print, of 'Pursuing' for 'Ensuing' in ii. 3. 43 has left a trace
in a catch-word. The respective stage-directions of Q and
F are consistent with this view of the relation between
the texts. Those of F are rather more elaborate than is
usual in Shakespearean texts, although less so than those
of *2, 3 Henry VI.* They include some for attiring or the
use of properties, some indicating the scope of an opening
scene, and some in the margin for details of action. These
look to me more like the work of an author familiar with
the stage than of a producer. But a producer may have
added the numerous notes for the use of musical instruments. The directions of Q are clearly related to those of
F, but vary in detail. Generally, but not always, they are
shorter. Thus at iii. 5. 1 F has 'Enter Richard, and Buckingham, in rotten Armour, maruellous ill-fauoured', but
Q merely 'Enter Duke of Glocester and Buckingham in
armour'. I think the transcribing book-keeper has
abridged. It is certainly less likely that an editor of F
added descriptive touches for readers. An exceptionally
literary note is at v. 3. 237, where the first line of
Richmond's speech is followed by the heading 'His Oration to his Souldiers'. But this is in Q as well as F, and
in fact it is F, not Q, which omits at v. 3. 314 the corresponding heading in Richard's speech, 'His Oration to his
army'. Perhaps something should be said of the curious
note 'Newly augmented' on the title-page of Q3. There
are no augmentations. It may be merely a publisher's
lure. I do not think it can be pressed as meaning that
when sheet A, containing the title-page, was printed in
1602, the publisher knew of a recent revision, new passages from which he hoped, but afterwards failed, to get.
He may just as well have contemplated an augmentation
not of the play, but of his book, by adding passages of the
original known to have been omitted from earlier Qq.
The 'new additions' to Q3 of *Richard II* were of such
original matter. It has also been suggested that the words
added in 1602 ought to have appeared in 1597, as an indication that *Richard III* as a whole was Shakespeare's augmentation of an earlier play. This seems to me desperate

'Newly' could not be so used for the first time in 1602, although if it had appeared on an earlier title-page it might have been repeated without alteration.

If a hand other than Shakespeare's is to be found in *Richard III*, it must be upon different grounds. Coleridge once, but not consistently, doubted the genuineness of the play. But the scepticism of some recent writers seems to be traceable to the influence of Fleay, who in 1875 thought that the play was left unfinished by Peele and completed and revised by Shakespeare, in 1881 substituted Marlowe and Peele for Peele, in 1886 substituted Marlowe alone, but did not 'think it possible to separate Shakespeare's work from Marlowe's', and in 1891 added Drayton as a reviser for F. The theory in all its phases is but slightly argued. It is largely a matter of subjective impression. But stress is laid upon variations of nomenclature in text and speech-prefixes as evidence for two hands. Such variations seem to me (cf. p. 232) a constant feature of Shakespeare's work. Pollard thinks the incorrect use of 'Derby' for 'Stanley' in certain scenes evidential. But his two hands are not Marlowe's and Shakespeare's; they are those of Peele, to whom he ascribes at least iii. 1. 1–157, and of a 'dull' man, found also in the *True Tragedy*. Shakespeare, besides revising the F form into the Q form, added the opening soliloquy, with i. 2 and perhaps the Margaret scenes, as audacious and splendid afterthoughts. If I have understood the view rightly, it is difficult to reconcile it with the obvious presence of these passages in the manuscript used for F1. Robertson is a thorough-going sceptic. For him the play is Marlowe's, with 'primary collaboration' by Kyd in certain scenes. Heywood did 'a good deal of later eking out and expanding'. But Shakespeare, 'however much he may have revised, contributes only some six or seven speeches, some of them very short'. The denial of Shakespeare is again based upon subjective impressions that the style and psychology are too 'primitive' to be his, and so different from that of such other plays as Robertson is prepared to allow him, as to exclude a common authorship. There are constant assertions, not convincing to me in detail, that such and such lines cannot be Shakespeare's. There is a theory, which I think quite unfounded (cf. p. 224), that Marlowe is more likely than Shakespeare to have written, at the date of *Richard III*, a play with so large a proportion of double endings. Similarly, it is stylistic impression, with the help of the unreliable 'clues' afforded by echoes, mainly verbal, from other plays, which directs Robertson to his substitutes. There is no attempt to disentangle completely the contributions of Marlowe, Kyd, and Heywood. We are invited to see the hand, now of one, now of another. It is pointed out that Heywood duplicates certain episodes of *Richard III* in *Edward IV*. He is called a 'docile imitator', and it is indeed probable that he is here docilely imitating. I do not myself think (cf. p. 223) that we have any assured criterion for distinguishing on internal grounds between the diction, about 1593, of Shakespeare on the one hand, and those of Marlowe, Peele, and Kyd on the other; and it is therefore unsafe on such grounds to disregard the strong external evidence for his authorship. Nor do I see any adequate reason for assuming two hands. There are 'dull' scenes, but the style is uniform throughout. It is a highly mannered rhetorical style, extravagant in utterance, with many appeals and exclamations. There is much violent and vituperative speech; the word 'blood' runs like a *leit-motif* through the play. Epithets, and sometimes nouns, are piled up, in pairs, with or without a conjunction; in triplets or even greater numbers. Types of line-structure tend to recur. One is based on such a triplet; another is the 'balanced' line, of noun and epithet against noun and epithet. A 'clinching' line at the end of a speech is also common. There are 'cumulative' passages of parallel lines with parisonic beginnings or ending. Words and phrases are repeated for emphasis. There is much 'ringing of the changes' on individual words, between line and line and speech and speech. Sometimes this is progressive, as new words are introduced. Sometimes it takes the form of a bitter pun. There is rhetorical structure, in antithesis, antiphon, stichomythia. Some of it is

ultimately of Senecan origin. All these features occur individually in pre-Shakespearean plays and recur in later
Shakespearean plays, with diminishing frequency. But I
do not think that they are quite so massed and multiplied
elsewhere. I find nothing here which might not be
Shakespeare, at an early stage of development, and while
he is still much under the influence of his predecessors.
Perhaps I should make a qualification. I am not certain
that the extremely ineffective speeches of the ghosts
(v. 3. 118–76) may not be a spectacular theatrical addition.
Certainly the psychology is 'primitive', as compared with
that of later plays. It is in the key and at the distance from
life of melodrama, not tragedy. But its resemblance to that
of Marlowe is not close. The concentrated remorselessness
of Richard recalls him, of course, and so does the choric
Margaret, in his earlier work rather than in *Edward II*,
which must be the nearest in date to *Richard III*. But his
presentation of character offers no parallel to the vivid
analysis of the many-sided Richard, with his grim humour
of introspection, his audacities and levities of speech, his
irony and mock humility, his plausibility and adroitness,
his histrionics and sense of dramatic effect. Nor is Marlowe's the give and take of the dialogue, in which speeches
are not merely juxtaposed but articulated, as the ideas of one
disputant provoke and determine those of the next. It is
a natural and improvised, rather than a prepared,
dialogue.

The play has been variously dated. There are several
contemporary allusions to it and to Burbadge's playing of
Richard (App. B, nos. xiii, xvi, xix, xx, xxiv), but all are
later than Q1, with the possible exception of one by
Weever, which is itself of uncertain date, and may refer
to *Richard II*. Both style and psychology point to an
early period in Shakespeare's work, and the links with
Henry VI suggest that it followed that play after no long
interval. I do not think it inconceivable that it was the
Buckingham performed, not as a new play, by Sussex's
men on 1 Jan. 1594 (App. D). Certainly Buckingham
is not the chief character, but Henslowe was not precise

in his use of titles. The historical facts are almost all from the chronicles of Halle and Holinshed, themselves based mainly on Polydore Vergil's *Anglicae Historiae* (1534) and the *Life* of Richard generally ascribed to Sir Thomas More. Holinshed substantially follows Halle, but each has some special features represented in the play, and probably both were consulted. Possibly a hint or two came from *A Mirror for Magistrates*. It is not very likely that Shakespeare knew Thomas Legge's academic *Richardus Tertius*[1] although both have a wooing scene for Richard. Churchill 497 enumerates many parallels of incident and phrasing, not given by the chronicles, but often very slight, to *The True Tragedy of Richard the Third*,[2] and thinks that Shakespeare used it. Hart points out that in this play, as in *3 Henry VI* and *Richard III*, Richard is given to the use of proverbial expressions. Its date is uncertain. It was registered on 19 June 1594, and printed in the same year as a Queen's play. The text is so bad as to render any inference hazardous. It seems to be a reported text, in which much of the verse has been paraphrased in prose. Even if the play itself was earlier the reporter may have incorporated reminiscences of *Richard III*. Law notes a rather close resemblance between the handling of *Rich. III*, i. 4, and that of sc. xix of *Leir*.[3] This was entered on 14 May 1594, but apparently not printed until 1605, as it was then re-entered. It was played by the Queen's or Sussex's or both, not as a new play, in April 1594, and may therefore be either older or younger than *Richard III*.

There was probably a Jacobean revival of Shakespeare's play, as the oaths are somewhat pruned in F1, but the first seventeenth-century performance on record was at court on 16 Nov. 1633 (App. D). There were rival plays on the theme of *Richard III*. Robert Wilson wrote a second part of *Henry Richmond* for the Admiral's in 1599, and a fragment of its *scenario* is at Dulwich. Jonson at least began a *Richard Crookback* for the same company in 1602 (Greg, *Henslowe*, ii. 207, 222). Heywood's *Pleasant Dialogues and Dramas* (1637), 247, have lines headed 'A young

---

[1] *Eliz. Stage*, iii. 407.   [2] *Ibid*. iv. 43.   [3] *Ibid*. iv. 25.

witty Lad playing the part of Richard the third: at the Red Bull: the Author because hee was interessed in the Play to incourage him, wrot him this Prologue and Epilogue'. This would be a play of Queen Anne's men. To one of these must belong the story in R. Chamberlain's *A New Booke of Mistakes* (1637) of an actor who had to speak the lines,

> My leige, the Duke of Buckingham is tane,
> And Banister is come for his reward.

and by a slip inverted the names. Banister is no character in *Richard III*, but is in the Chronicles, the *True Tragedy*, and the *scenario* of *Henry Richmond*. The first line is identical with Shakespeare's iv. 4. 533, but is of a type which two dramatists might be capable of hammering out independently. The Dutch *De Roode en Witte Roos of Lankaster en Jork* (1651) of Lambert van den Bosch is more likely to have had a source in one of these later plays than in a hypothetical early version of *Richard III*, which it does not appear to resemble, structurally or in language.

V. THE COMEDY OF ERRORS.

[F1. 1623.] [*Catalogue*] The Comedy of Errours. [*Comedies*, pp. 85–100, sign. H 1–I 2ᵛ. *Head-title*] The Comedie of Errors [*Running-title*] as head-title.

[Acts and scc. 1 marked.]
Parallel-Text. A. Morgan (1894, *Bankside*).
Modern Editions. H. Cuningham (1906, *Arden*); A. Quiller-Couch and J. D. Wilson (1922, *C.U.P.*); R. D. French (1926, *Yale*).

[*Dissertations.* H. v. Friesen, *Bemerkungen zu den Altersbestimmungen für einige Stücke von Sh.* (1867, *J.* ii. 37); P. Wiscilenus, *Zwei neuentdeckte Sh.-quellen* (1879, *J.* xiv. 87); H. Isaac, *Shs C.E. und die Menächmen des Plautus* (1883, *Archiv*, lxx. 1); J. Gröne, *Zwei neuentdeckte Quellen zu Shs C.E.* (1894, *J.* xxix. 281); K. Roeder, *Menechmi und Amphitruo im englischen Drama bis zur 1661* (1904); F. Lang, *Shs C.E. in englische Buhnenarbeitung* (1909); W. H. D. Rouse, *The Menaechmi: the Original of Sh's C.E.* (1912, *Sh. Library*); J. M. Robertson, *The Authorship of C.E.* (1923, *Sh. Canon*, ii. 126); E. Gill, *A Comparison of the Characters of C.E. with those in the Menaechmi* (1925, *Texas Studies*, v. 79); A. Gaw, *The Evolution of C.E.* (1926, *P.M.L.A.* xli. 620).

The text is a fair one, with a few mislineations, some of

which are probably due to confusion by the sudden transitions between blank verse, prose, and doggerel in certain scenes. I see no obvious reason why a manuscript by Shakespeare should not have been the basis. Wilson, however, sees one in the absence of such abnormal spellings as he finds in some quartos, and takes to be author's spellings which have escaped the normalization of the printing-house. But whatever positive inference may follow from the presence of such spellings in one text, it is surely impossible to base a negative one upon their absence from another, in which the normalization may have been more vigilant. Wilson's own theory of the *Comedy of Errors* text involves (*a*) dictation to a scribe in the play house from (*b*) players' 'parts', with the aid of a 'plot' for a few brief stage-directions, and (*c*) subsequent expansion by a second scribe imperfectly familiar with the text as it stood in the 'parts', who also touched up the speech-prefixes. For (*a*) he relies upon certain textual errors which might be due to mishearing, but such errors can also be made (cf. p. 180) through the subconscious operations of a compositor's mind. Such a process of 'assembling' as (*b*) contemplates, although not inconceivable, would be attended (cf. p. 155) by serious difficulties. For (*c*) I find no sufficient ground. The stage-directions are mainly of a practical kind; occasionally they contain a note of the relationship of characters, or for attire or properties, or action; occasionally something is left by a 'three or foure' (iv. 4. 109) or 'as fast as may be' (iv. 4. 150) to the discretion of the theatre. I think that they are primarily author's directions. But in places (iv. 4. 43, 149; v. 1. 190) a superfluity or error points to expansion, either in printing F or more likely by the book-keeper, who is probably also responsible for the first speech-prefixes after entrances, which as suggested by Greg, the author seems habitually to have left blank. The substitution of *Juliana* for *Luciana* (iii. 2. 1) both in stage-direction and speech-prefix is probably a mere printer's error. There are variations in the spelling of proper names, in the text as well as the stage-directions and speech-prefixes, which do not seem to me evidence of anything but a want of uniformity in spelling-habits. The speech-prefixes show the tendency to substitute descriptions for personal names, which is common in Shakespeare's plays, and represents, I think (cf. p. 232), an idiosyncrasy of his. They are also much abbreviated. Probably this was also so in the original stage-directions and the book-keeper has expanded them, not always correctly. Thus *Antipholis* appears for *Antipholus* until an occurrence of the name in the text serves as a guide to correction. An off-hand writer, a book-keeper, and a printer seem to me to explain all the facts, without recourse to any process of dictation.

The play (1,777 lines) is Shakespeare's shortest, and was probably meant to precede a mask, jig, or other afterpiece. A few abrupt short lines and passages of textual corruption may point to cuts, not necessarily of great length. But again I cannot follow Wilson in the theory that there has been substantial abridgement, perhaps by the excision of dinner scenes at the Phoenix and the Porpentine, which might have expanded the sketchy characters of the Courtesan, Balthazar, and the kitchen vestal, or in the further suggestion that this abridgement was for a provincial tour. Any shortness of *personnel* would surely have led to cutting out Balthazar altogether. Nor do I think with Wilson that the transitions between blank verse, doggerel, and prose imply any rewriting of verse as prose. The staging of the play is interesting. The stage-direction (v. 1. 10), 'Enter Antipholus and Dromio againe' suggests that the action was continuous throughout and the F division into acts uncalled for, since these characters left the stage at the end of Act iv. There are some unusual stage-directions indicating entries and exits 'from the Courtizans' (iv. 1. 14), 'from the Bay' (iv. 1. 85), 'to the Priorie' (v. 1. 37), 'to the Abbesse' (v. 1. 281). Probably the stage was set in the same way throughout. At the back of the stage three houses or doors represented to the right and left the Priory with some religious emblem over it, and the Courtesan's house with the sign of the Porpentine, and in the centre the house of Antipholus with the sign of the Phoenix. As Wilson points out, Adriana and Luce must here appear 'above' in iii. 1. There is no other action above and none within; all is either at the doors of the houses, or in an open place, often referred to as the 'mart'. The mart scenes were played at the front of the stage, and the side entrances were supposed to lead to the bay and to the town respectively. But while characters sometimes seem to move direct from the mart to the houses. there are also passages which suggest that they go off the stage on the way between these. Such inconsistencies would probably not be much felt in a bustling action.

Ritson suggested that the doggerel was taken over by Shakespeare from an earlier writer, and the same view is held by many recent critics.[1] Some of it is in short passages from the mouths of the Dromios, but most of it in the first part of iii. 1, where several more serious characters share it with them; and this is taken as a scene retained by Shakespeare from a hypothetical earlier form of the play. Why it should have been so retained requires a more satisfactory explanation than it has received. Wilson says that Shakespeare 'thought it good enough to pass muster as it stood'; Gaw that he was so 'inexperienced' that he 'left the scene as hopeless'. I will present the advocates of the retention theory with the fact that the word 'mome' (iii. 1. 32), not used elsewhere by Shakespeare, is a common vituperative term in the drama of Udall's time, and add that it seems to me just as easy to suppose that here and in *Taming of the Shrew* and *Love's Labour's Lost*, where there is also a substantial use of doggerel, Shakespeare was consciously experimenting with an archaistic form for comic effect. There are other stylistic experiments in the play, comic stichomythia, rhyme, and lyric quatrains for the sentimental matter of iii. 2 and iv. 2. Nor can I attach much importance to the suggestion of an old text derived from the Paul's court play of 'The historie of Error' in 1577, perhaps through Sussex's court play of 'A historie of fferrar' in 1583.[2] We know nothing about these plays except their names. Obviously Paul's might have adapted a Plautine play and called it *Error*. But there

---

[1] *Var.* iv. 147.   [2] *Eliz. Stage*, iv. 151, 159.

are many kinds of error. They might also, for example, have produced a moral with Error as a character. A Paul's play is not likely to have proved very suitable for Sussex's men, even if Paul's, who continued active up to 1589, wanted to part with it in 1583. And Sussex's 'fferrar' looks to me very much like 'Ferrara'. I see no reason to suppose that the Revels Clerk made up his accounts from dictation. The kitchen vestal is called Luce in iii. 1. 53 and Nell in iii. 2. 111, and this has been held to confirm the alien origin of the earlier passage. She is also called Dowsabel in iv. 1. 110, but that is a joke. I think that Shakespeare altered his name, either to get his pun on 'an ell' or to avoid confusion with Luciana, and forgot to correct iii. 1. 53. On either supposition he left an inconsistency. There are others in the play. The age of the twins is differently given, unless there is a misprint, by the various indications of i. 1. 125, 133 and v. 1. 309, 326, 400. The goldsmith at iii. 2. 178 has forgotten what he was told about the chain at iii. 1. 117.

The theory of continuous play-copy over a long span of years has proved so exciting as to lead more than one writer to suggest the intervention of yet another hand in an evolution from *Error* to *Errors*. The episodes dealing with the history of Egeon and Æmilia (i. 1 and parts of v. 1) are written in a formal narrative style which contrasts with the more boisterous manner of the greater part of the play. Percentages are valueless in dealing with so small a number of lines, but there are many grammatical overflows, although little pausation within the lines, several examples of the 'balanced' line, and few double endings. A touch or two here and there (i. 1. 32, 64) may come from classical reminiscence. There is no reason why Shakespeare should not have thought a difference of style appropriate to a difference between tragic and comic subject-matter. But Wilson tentatively suggested the hand of Greene, and Gaw would substitute Kyd. I think the passages too weighty for the one and too dignified for the other. Robertson leaves them to Shakespeare, and indeed he leaves little else except the lyrical matter in iii. 2, regarding the play in the main as a comedy by—Marlowe. This view is largely based on stylistic impression, helped out by very slight vocabulary 'clues' and an unfounded theory (cf. p. 224) as to Marlowe's supposed late addiction to double endings. In the absence of any evidence as to Marlowe's manner in comedy, for which Robertson substitutes another hypothesis that he wrote in *A Shrew*, it is difficult to discuss it seriously.

As to date, the first clear record of the play is the performance at Gray's Inn on 28 December 1594. Fleay *L.W.* 178 is of course wrong in supposing that the hit at the barrenness of Scotland (iii. 2. 123) motived the protest of James against the scorning of himself and his people in London plays, since this was not, as he says, in 1595, but in 1598.[1] But the corresponding hit (iii. 2. 126) at France, 'armed and reverted, making war against her heir', takes us a little farther back, as Henri IV became entitled to the crown on 12 August 1589, and the struggle of the League against him was ended by a truce of 19 July 1593. So far as this goes, the *Comedy of Errors* might quite well be 'the gelyous comodey' produced as a new play by 'Strange's' men on 5 January 1593 (App. D). I am not sure that it was not. Jealousy is a sufficiently prominent motive (ii. 2; iii. 1; iv. 2; v. 1) to justify such a description from the inexact pen of Henslowe. On the other hand, it is a prominent motive in many comedies, and there were no further performances of the comedy during the season, unless it was identical with that of *Cosmo*. This would have been unusual. Moreover, there are two apparent echoes of the *Comedy of Errors* which seem to point to an earlier date than 1593. Wilson noted the resemblance to iv. 4. 88–9 of the phrase 'heart and good will, but neuer a ragge of money' in Nashe, *Four Letters Confuted*,[2] registered on 12 January 1593 and published with the imprint '1592', which Greg thinks would not, in a popular pamphlet, mean 1593. Gabriel Harvey's *Foure Letters*, to which Nashe replied, was itself registered on 4 December 1592. The description of a villain in *Arden of Faversham*,

---

[1] *Eliz. Stage*, i. 323.   [2] ed. McKerrow, i. 301.

ii. 1. 51, registered on 3 April 1592 and printed in the same year,[1] links the epithets 'leane faced' and 'hollow eied'. much as they are linked in that of Pinch in v. 1. 237–40. Of course echoes may go either way or have a common origin, but *Arden* has many from contemporary plays, and Nashe, earlier in his chaff of Gabriel Harvey in *Four Letters Confuted* (i. 271) quotes *Spanish Tragedy*, i. 2. 172, and adds '*Memorandum*: I borrowed this sentence out of a Play. The Theater, Poets hall, hath many more such prouerbes to persecute thee with.' If, therefore, Nashe echoed Shakespeare we must put the *Comedy of Errors* back to at least December 1592. A private performance then might be compatible with a public production on the following January 5. But if *Arden* also echoed him, which I think the less certain of the two, we must put the *Comedy* back to at least the spring of 1592. The stylistic development, with its beginnings of lyric comedy in iii. 2, is in favour of the later date, after Shakespeare's work on *Venus and Adonis*. I must leave it at that. There was a revival at court on 28 December 1604 (App. D).

The main source, direct or indirect, is the *Menaechmi* of Plautus, but iii. 1 is probably due to his *Amphitruo*, in which a husband is locked out from his own house while a substitute eats his dinner, and this may also have suggested the addition of twin servants to the twin masters. The *Comedy of Errors* has elaborated and varied the intrigue and added the enveloping tragic action. Possibly the story of Apollonius of Tyre, used for *Pericles* (cf. p. 527) may have given a hint for this. Suggested parallels with Chaucer's *Knight's Tale* and Sidney's *Arcadia* are very slight. A translation of the *Menaechmi* by W⟨illiam⟩ W⟨arner⟩ was registered on 10 June 1594; the only print known is dated 1595. The verbal resemblances of this to the *Comedy of Errors* are trifling, and may well be accidental, but preliminary verses by Warner claim 'much pleasant error'. If Shakespeare used this, it was probably in manuscript, and in fact a printer's preface

---

[1] *Eliz. Stage*, iv. 3.

states that it was one of 'diverse of this Poettes Comedies Englished, for the use and delight of his private friends' by the translator. The *Amphitruo* might have been another. But I see no reason to doubt that Shakespeare could have read Plautus in the original. A puzzle is afforded by the appearance in the earlier stage-directions of the *Comedy of Errors* of the designations Antipholis Erotes (i. 2. 1) and Errotis (ii. 2. 1) for Antipholus of Syracuse, and Antipholis Sereptus (ii. 1. 1) for Antipholus of Ephesus. These look like misprints for Surreptus and Erraticus or Errans, although I do not accept the suggestion that the Plautine name for the Courtesan, Erotium, has contributed. Both in Plautus and in Warner the twins are Menaechmus and Sosicles, but Warner also calls them the Citizen and the Traveller, and the Plautine prologue, which Warner does not translate, speaks of the Citizen as *surreptus*; while in the *Comedy of Errors* the Abbess (v. i. 351) says that 'rude fishermen of Corinth' took Antipholus of Ephesus from her. Possibly, therefore, Shakespeare had access to a Latin text, such as the Plantin edition of 1566, which included the prologue.

VI. TITUS ANDRONICUS.

[S.R. 1594.] vj^{to} die ffebruarii. John Danter. Entred for his Copye vnder thandes of bothe the wardens a booke intituled a Noble Roman Historye of Tytus Andronicus. vj^d. John Danter. Entred also vnto him by warrau$nt from Master Woodcock the ballad thereof. vj^d. (Arber, ii. 644).

[Q1. 1594.] The Most Lamentable Romaine Tragedie of Titus Andronicus: As it was Plaide by the Right Honourable the Earle of Darbie, Earle of Pembrooke, and Earle of Sussex their Seruants. [Danter's device (McKerrow 281)] London, Printed by Iohn Danter, and are to be sold by Edward White & Thomas Millington, at the little North doore of Paules at the signe of the Gunne. 1594. [*Head-title*, under ornament with initials I. D.] The most Lamentable Roman Tragedie of Titus Andronicus: As it was Plaide by the Right Honourable the Earle of Darbie, Earle of Pembrooke, and Earle of Sussex

PLATE XI

HENRY PEACHAM'S ILLUSTRATION OF *TITUS ANDRONICUS*

their Seruants. [*Running-title*] The most Lamentable
Tragedie of Titus Andronicus.

[Collection of H. C. Folger.   Photographs of the t.p. and four other
pages are *Bodl. Malone Adds.*, 48, f. 1.]

[MS. 1595.] *Harley Papers* (Marquis of Bath's MSS. at
Longleat) i. f. 159ᵛ. Calligraphic copy of i. 1. 104–21
(first half of line) and v. 1. 125–44, linked by two and
a half lines not in Qq F. There are slight textual and
many orthographic variants, of which 'haystackes' (v. 1.
133) agrees with F, where Q1 has 'haystalkes' and Q2
and Q3 'haystakes'. At the end is a speech-prefix for
Alarbus, who has no speech in Qq F. Above is a drawing
of Tamora and two sons in supplication to Titus, and
Aaron standing with a sword drawn. In the margin is
'Henricus Peacham Anno mᵒqᵒ 9 qᵒ', and a spare page
is endorsed 'Henrye Peachams Hande 1595'.

Facsimile. E. K. Chambers (1925, 4 *Library*, v. 326; cf. Plate XI).

[Q2. 1600.] The most lamentable Romaine Tragedie of
Titus Andronicus. As it hath sundry times beene playde
by the Right Honourable the Earle of Pembrooke, the
Earle of Darbie, the Earle of Sussex, and the Lorde
Chamberlaine theyr Seruants [Ornament]. At London,
Printed by I⟨ames⟩ R⟨oberts⟩ for Edward White and are
to bee solde at his shoppe, at the little North doore of
Paules, at the signe of the Gun. 1600. [*Head-title*] The
most lamentable Romaine Tragedie of Titus Andronicus:
As it was plaid by the Right Honorable the Earle of
Darbie, Earle of Pembrooke, and Earle of Sussex theyr
Seruants.   [*Running-title*] The most lamentable Tragedie
of Titus Andronicus.

Facsimiles. E. W. Ashbee (1866); C. Praetorius (1886, *Sh. Q.*
xxix, ed. A. Symons).

[S.R. 1602.] 19 Aprilis . . . Thomas Pavier. Entred for
his copies by assignement from Thomas Millington these
bookes folowinge, Saluo Jure cuiuscunque viz . . . A
booke called Titus and Andronicus vjᵈ Entred by warrant
vnder master Setons hand (Arber, iii. 204).

[Q3. 1611.] [Ornament] The most Lamentable Tragedie

of Titus Andronicus. As it hath sundry times beene plaide by the Kings Maiesties Seruants [Allde's device (McKerrow 284)] London, Printed ⟨by Edward Allde for⟩ for Eedward ⟨*sic*⟩ White, and are to be solde at his shoppe, nere the little North dore of Pauls, at the signe of the Gun. 1611. [*Head-* and *Running-titles*, nearly as in Q2.]

[F1. 1623.] [*Catalogue*] Titus Andronicus. [*Tragedies*, pp. 31–52; sign. cc 4–ee 2^v. *Head-title*.] The Lamentable Tragedy of Titus Andronicus. [*Running-title*] The Tragedie of Titus Andronicus.

[Acts i, sc. 1, ii–v marked.]

[S.R. 1624.] 14 Decembris, 1624 Master Pavier John Wright Cutbert: Wright Edward. Wright John Grismond Henry Gosson. Entred for their Copies at a full Court holden 6° Novembris, last, The Copies of the Ballades hereafter perticulerly menconed. Provided that this entrance shall not preiudice any other man that have any Interest to any of them by any former Entrance or otherwise xx^s. ⟨128 titles, including⟩ Titus and Audconmus (Arber, iv. 131).

[S.R. 1626.] 4° August 1626. Edward Brewster Robert Birde Assigned ouer vnto them by Mistress Pavier and Consent of a full Court of Assistantes all the estate right title and Interest which Master Thomas Pavier her late husband had in the Copies here after mencioned . . vizt . . Master Pavier's rights in Shakesperes plaies or any of them. His parte in any sorts of Ballads . . ⟨18 items⟩ . . . Tytus and Andronicus (Arber, iv. 164).

Parallel-Text. A. Morgan (1890, *Bankside*).

Modern Editions. H. B. Baildon (1904, *Arden*); A. M. Witherspoon (1926, *Yale*).

German Version. Eine sehr klägliche Tragœdia von Tito Andronico und der hoffertigen Kayserin (1620, *Engelische Comedien und Tragedien*); repr. W. Creizenach, *Die Schauspiele der Englischen Komödianten* (1889), 1; tr. Cohn 161.

Dutch Version. Jan Vos, *Aran en Titus, of Wraak en Weerwraak* (1641, &c.).

[*Dissertations.* H.P., *Memoranda on* . . . *T.A.* (1879); J. Appleton Morgan in *Shakespeareana*, vi (1888); M. M. A. Schröer, *Über T.A.* (1891); E. Köppel, *T.A.* (1892, *E.S.* xvi. 365); H. Varnhagen, *Zur Vorgeschichte der Fabel von Shs T.A.*(1893,*E.S.*xix.163); G.Sarrazin,*Germanische Heldensage in Sh.'s T.A.* (1896, *Archiv*, xcvii. 373); A. B. Grosart, *Was Robert Greene substantially the Author of T.A.* (1896, *E.S.* xxii. 389); C. Crawford, *The Authenticity of T.A.* (1900, *J.* xxxvi. 109); H. de W. Fuller, *The Sources of T.A.* (1901, *P.M.L.A.* xvi. 1); G. P. Baker, *Tittus and Vespacia and Titus and Ondronicus* (1901, *P.M.L.A.* xvi. 66); J. M. Robertson, *Did Sh. Write T.A.?* (1905, revised 1924, as *Introduction to the Study of the Shakespeare Canon*); W. Keller, *Die neuaufgefundene Q des T.A. von 1594* (1905, *J.* xli. 211); C. J. R. Schreckhas, *Über Enstehungszeit und Verfasser des T.A.* (1906); W. W. Greg, *T.A.* (1908, *Henslowe*, ii. 159), *T.A.* (1919, *M.L.R.* xiv. 322); W. Dibelius, *Zur Stoffgeschichte des T.A.* (1912, *J.* xlviii. 1); H. D. Gray, *The Authorship of T.A.* (1916, *Leland Stanford Jun. Univ. Flügel Memorial Vol.* 114), *T.A. Once More* (1919, *M.L.N.* xxxiv. 214), *The T.A. Problem* (1920, *S.P.* xvii. 126), *Sh.'s Share in T.A.* (1926, *P.Q.* v. 166); C. F. Tucker Brooke, *T.A. and Sh.* (1919, *M.L.N.* xxxiv. 32); T. M. Parrott, *Sh.'s Revision of T.A.* (1919, *M.L.R.* xiv. 16); F. Granger, *Sh. and the Legend of Andronicus* (1920, Apr. 1, *T.L.S.*, followed by discussion); R. C. Rhodes, *Titus and Vespasian* (1924, Apr. 17, *T.L.S.*, followed by discussion); E. K. Chambers, *The First Illustration to Sh.* (1925, *4 Library*, v. 326); E. G. Clark, *Titus and Vespasian* (1926, *M.L.N.* xli. 523); A. K. Gray, *Sh. and T.A.* (1928, *S.P.* xxv. 295); J. S. G. Bolton, *The Authentic Text of T.A.* (1929, *P.M.L.A.* xliv. 765).

Q1 was known in 1691 to Langbaine, who copied 'Essex' in error for 'Sussex' from its title-page. The only copy now known was found in Sweden in 1905. It has not been reprinted, but Keller gives a collation by E. Ljung-gren, which shows that its text was substantially that of Q2, except that Q2 omitted 3½ lines after i. 1. 35, evidently as inconsistent with the action later in the scene, and made a few less intelligible alterations in v. 3. Sub-ject to this, Q2 was printed from Q1, Q3 from Q2, and F1 from Q3, with the addition of iii. 2, which is in none of the Qq. The collation does not show whether in Q1, as in Q2, the speech-prefixes of i. 1. 1–56 and v. 1. 121–4 are, exceptionally, centred. If they are, it may point to excisions during printing-off. The fragment in the *Longleat MS.* is on the whole more likely to be a perversion from Q1 than to rest on an independent text. The Q stage-directions are rather full and suggest an author's hand. They are slightly varied in F, and at the beginning of Act ii F substitutes 'Flourish. Enter Aaron alone' for the 'sound trumpets, manet Moore' of the Qq, which apparently contemplated no act-interval. Possibly the use of *An.* for *Titus* throughout the speech-prefixes of iii. 2 and here alone and the spelling 'Tamira' for 'Tamora' in the text point to a distinct scribal origin for this added scene.

The following *data*, in addition to those given in the bibliographical history, bear on the date and authorship of the play. (*a*) 'Strange's' men produced *Titus and Vespasian* as 'ne' for Henslowe on 11 April 1592 and played it to 25 January 1593; (*b*) Sussex's men produced *Titus Andronicus* as 'ne' for Henslowe on 24 January 1594 and played it to 6 February 1594; (*c*) the Admiral's and/or Chamberlain's men played *Andronicus* for Henslowe on 7 and 14 June 1594 (App. D); (*d*) Jonson in 1614 implied that *Andronicus*, like the *Spanish Tragedy*, had been on the stage 'these fiue and twentie, or thirtie yeeres' (App. B, no. xxii); (*e*) In *A Knack to Know a Knave*, produced by 'Strange's' as 'ne' on 10 June 1592 and registered on 7 January 1594, is the allusion (F2ᵛ):

> As Titus was vnto the Roman Senators,
> When he had made a conquest on the Goths;

(*f*) Meres included *Titus Andronicus* among Shakespeare's plays in 1598 (App. B, no. xiii); (*g*) Ravenscroft in 1687 reports a stage tradition that *Titus Andronicus* was by a 'private author', and Shakespeare 'only gave some master-touches to one or two of the principal parts or characters' (App. C, no. xiv). This is the only bit of external evidence against the authenticity of any play in F1. Partly as a result of it, and partly on stylistic grounds, Shakespeare's original authorship has been very generally doubted from the days of Malone onwards. Dissentients have tended to regard the play as very early work. Most of the doubters have assumed some measure of revision by him, but with no great agreement as to its nature and extent. There have been many attempts to find an alternative author, or alternative authors, amongst dramatists known to us. The latest is that of Robertson, who brings an elaborate and discursive investigation to the conclusion that there have been two, or, if I understand him aright, possibly three collaborations, and that while the final form is due mainly to Peele and partly to Marlowe, both of these, with Kyd and Greene, may have worked at earlier stages. Of course, if anything of this kind has happened, there is no solvent for the amalgam; and all that Robertson can do is to go through the scenes, pointing here to a passage in which he discerns the rhythm of one writer, there to a structural device, or a bit of characterization, or a 'clue' of vocabulary or phrase, which hints at another, and often finding that the clues conflict and that no conclusion is possible. The methods employed inspire me (cf. p. 223) with very little confidence, in view of the amount of 'common form' in plays of the period and the number of little-known writers who may have been at work. In particular 'parallels', whether 'echoes' or not, are insecure evidence. There are many in *Titus Andronicus* to both plays and poems of Shakespeare. Those to Marlowe, Kyd, Greene, and others seem to me slight. But there are many also to Peele, and some, chiefly to his *Edward I* and his poem *The Honour of the Garter*, both printed in 1593, go rather beyond a repeated use of out-of-the-way words or of short collocations of words. As a whole the play does not very strongly remind me of any of Peele's known plays, although I think that he wrote with different degrees of care at different times. It has not the long pedestrian passages so common in *Edward I* and *Alcazar*, or the passages of rhyme with which Peele generally varies his blank verse. The proportion of double endings is about the same as in *1 Henry VI*, appreciably less than that in *2, 3 Henry VI*. Whether the play can be very early work by Shakespeare, at some date before we have any standard for comparison, I cannot say. The subject-matter is imitative, but the actual writing is fairly competent, and does not obviously suggest a beginner. It cannot, as a whole, be Shakespeare's at a date later than *Richard III* and the *Comedy of Errors*.

If, then, one could be sure that the play was really new on 24 January 1594, I should be inclined to accept

Ravenscroft's tradition much as it stands, and to suppose that the author, whether 'private' in the Restoration sense or not was some one unknown to us. He took his notions of plotting from Kyd, and outwent him in his use of realism, of horrors, of mystifications, of maniacal episodes; his notions of character-drawing from Marlowe and outwent him by representing Aaron as obsessed by a lust, not for power through conquest, or gold, or knowledge, but for abstract villainy. He had learnt to write from Peele and others, and made very free use, consciously or unconsciously, of the common stock of diction, and perhaps consciously of *Edward I* and the *Garter*. On this theory the difficulty would really be to lay a finger on any passages which Shakespeare could reasonably be supposed to have contributed. Here, as elsewhere, parallels afford little guidance. The mere out-of-door feeling of such passages as ii. 2. 1–6; ii. 3. 10–29 is not special to him. The touches of closer natural observation in ii. 4. 54; iii. 1. 137; v. 1. 14 are too slight to lay stress upon. The highly coloured descriptions of ii. 1. 1–25; ii. 3. 226–36; ii. 4. 11–57; iii. 1. 220–34—like the rhetoric of iii. 1. 267–79; iv. 2. 87–105—seem of a piece with the play as a whole. The clown of iv. 3. 77–121 compares poorly with Jack Cade. Driven to a choice, one would fall back on a few comparatively dignified and far from showy speeches, such as i. 1. 104–20, 148–56, 187–200; iii. 1. 1–47; iv. 4. 81–93; v. 3. 67–95, 159–71. I feel no confidence about them.

Moreover, there is some reason to suppose that *Titus Andronicus* was not altogether new in 1594. I do not attach much importance in this connexion to the German and Dutch versions of 1620 and 1641. They are late and there were apparently other continental versions; a trace of one, probably related to the source of Vos, is in a German programme of 1699.[1] Fuller has compared them minutely with each other and with *Titus Andronicus*, finds that they have certain common incidents not in *Titus Andronicus*, and on the other hand, that, while all the incidents of *Titus Andronicus* are in one or other of them, some are

[1] *J.* xxiii. 266.

only preserved in the German and the other in the Dutch. He infers that they derive from two distinct English plays, identifies these with the *Titus and Vespasian* and *Titus Andronicus* of Henslowe, and regards the extant *Titus Andronicus* as a conflation of the two. I do not accept the inference. The facts are quite consistent with the natural hypothesis of divergence from a common source in an adaptation of *Titus Andronicus* for continental travel. It is true that in the German version Lucius is renamed Vespasian, which might point to *Titus and Vespasian*. But nearly all the characters are renamed and the Goths turned into Moors, and in this process Vespasian might naturally suggest itself. On the other hand, it is not so clear, on the English evidence alone, that some form of *Titus Andronicus* did not exist before 1594, and if so, that it was not *Titus and Vespasian*. In itself this title of course suggests a play on the siege of Jerusalem, but Strange's men had already a *Jerusalem* in 1592. That Q1 represents the play of 1594 is certain from the mention of Sussex's men on its title-page. The same title-page suggests earlier performances, not of necessity from precisely the same text, by Derby's and Pembroke's, and presumably in this order. We can hardly take Q2, which puts Pembroke's first on its title-page, but not in its head-title, as a better authority on the point than Q1. 'Derby's' in 1594 probably means Alleyn's company, which was 'Strange's' in 1592, when it gave *Titus and Vespasian*. Further, the allusion in *Knack to Know a Knave*, also a 'Strange's' play, points to a knowledge of Titus and the Goths, not Moors, in 1592, and no such combination is known outside *Titus Andronicus*. It may be then, after all, that 'Strange's' did produce a form of *Titus Andronicus* as *Titus and Vespasian* in 1592, and that it was transferred by them to Pembroke's, and by Pembroke's to Sussex's, who revised it as the extant *Titus Andronicus*. The appearance of a *Titus and Vespasian* in a Revels list of plays about 1619 (App. D) gives some confirmation to the view that the titles are equivalent. If we pressed Jonson's rather vague dating, we should have to put the origin of *Titus Andro-*

nicus as far back as 1589, but I do not know that we need
press it. It must be added that the theory of a play written,
or conceivably revised, in 1592, and then revised in 1594,
is not without its own difficulties. It is a short interval for
a play to become out of date in. Henslowe's 'ne', whatever its precise significance, is certainly a mark attached to
a play 'the fyrst tyme yt wasse playde'.[1] Generally it
seems to have been a new play in the full sense. It is probable that it was sometimes a revised play, and possible
that it was sometimes an old play, given by a particular
company for the first time.[2] But there is no clear case of
this last type, and there are several clear cases in which
such a performance was not marked 'ne'. We come back
to authorship. If *Titus Andronicus* was not new in 1594, we
cannot of course say how much revision then took place,
or whether Peele or another, as well as Shakespeare,
helped in it. All that can be assigned to Shakespeare at
that date seems very little to justify a 'ne'. And, again,
if the play was originally written in 1592, and still more
if in 1589, the stylistic case against Shakespeare as an
original writer is weakened, and as the *Garter* poem did
not exist, that for Peele as an original writer is, so far as
the parallels to it have any weight, strengthened. I am
sorry to be so inconclusive, but the complicated *data* are
themselves so. It remains to notice a theory put forward
by Greg. It is this. The play was originally Pembroke's.
They made a variant version for travelling. This did not
include iii. 2. When they were in straits during 1593, the
variant version came into the hands of Sussex's, who played
it for Henslowe, and then allowed it to be printed. The full
version they sold to Alleyn. It was played by 'Derby's,'
and passed to the Chamberlain's, who played it for Henslowe. This version was revised by Shakespeare, which
accounts for the mention by Meres. It was afterwards
burnt in the Globe fire. The King's men replaced it by
a copy of Q3, derived from the variant version, but added
iii. 2, which they were accustomed to play, from memory.
Shakespeare's revision is therefore lost, except in so far

[1] Henslowe, i. 45, 50.   [2] *Ibid.* ii. 148 ; *Eliz. Stage,* ii. 145.

as anything of his may be in iii. 2. This is ingenious, and reconciles Meres with the difficulty of finding Shakespeare's hand in the extant text. But it assumes a considerable concatenation of unusual incidents, and involves the acceptance of the Q2 title-page as against that of Q1 for the order of the performing companies.

There were probably Jacobean revivals. The 'Kings' of the Q3 title-page might merely bring up to date the 'Chamberlains' of Q2. But Jonson's reference of 1614 and the *Titus and Vespasian* record of c. 1619 both suggest that the play held the stage, and F, although retaining 'God', substitutes (iv. 2. 71) 'Out' for 'Zounds', a word which seems to have been especially within the danger of the *Act of Abuses*. If iii. 2 was not added at this or an earlier revival, it must have been in some way recovered from the original text, in which a mark of deletion may have excluded it from Q1. This seems less likely. The scene does not advance the action. The earlier part, no doubt, is not unlike the rest of the play. I have sometimes fancied that the fly episode might be Webster's. I see no clear signs of Shakespeare.

The ballad registered by Danter in 1594 may, in view of the rather complicated ownership disclosed by the S.R. entries of 1624 and 1626, be that printed by A. Mathews for T. Langley in Richard Johnson, *The Golden Garland of Princely Pleasures* (1620), and also in a broadsheet by Edward Wright. If so, it rested on the play as we have it. It was also appended to a chapbook version of the story, undated but printed by C. Dicey at Northampton in the eighteenth century, and described by H.P.,[1] and presumably the same as one noted by Farmer.[2] It claims to be 'newly Translated from the Italian copy printed at Rome', but H.P. says nothing to suggest that it has any other source than *Titus Andronicus*. According to Steevens Painter's *Palace of Pleasure* (1566-7) speaks of the story of Titus as well known, but this must be due to a confusion.[3] There are analogous themes in romance literature

---

[1] *Rarities*, 77; *Memoranda on All's Well, &c.*, 73.

[2] *Var.* xxi. 381.

[3] *Ibid.* xxi. 258; Anders, 266.

of rape and murder by a revengeful Moor and of love relations between a Moor and a European lady, but they do not come very close to the play. The studies of Morgan, Dibelius, and Granger make it likely that an ultimate source existed in some perversion of Byzantine chronicles dealing with the twelfth-century emperor Andronicus Comnenus and the more or less contemporary Thamar, Queen of Georgia.

VII. THE TAMING OF THE SHREW

[S.R. 1594.] Secundo die Maij. Peter Shorte. Entred vnto him for his copie vnder master warden Cawoodes hande, a booke intituled A plesant Conceyted historie called the Tayminge of a Shrowe vj^d (Arber, ii. 648).

[1594.] A Pleasant Conceited Historie, called The taming of a Shrew. As it was sundry times acted by the Right honorable the Earle of Pembrook his seruants. [Short's device (McKerrow 278)] Printed at London by Peter Short and are to be sold by Cutbert Burbie, at his shop at the Royall Exchange. 1594.

Facsimile. C. Praetorius (1886, *Sh. Q.* xv, ed. F. J. Furnivall).

Modern Edition. F. S. Boas (1908).

[1596.] P.S., sold by Cuthbert Burbie.

[S.R. 1607.] 22. Januarij. Master Linge. Entred for his copies by direccon of A Court and with consent of Master Burby vnder his handwrytinge These. iij copies. viz. . . . . The taminge of A Shrewe (Arber, iii. 337).

[1607.] V⟨alentine⟩ S⟨immes⟩ for Nicholas Ling.

[S.R. 1607.] 19. Novembris. John Smythick. Entred for his copies vnder thandes of the wardens. these bookes followinge Whiche dyd belonge to Nicholas Lynge .viz. . . . . 9 The taminge of A Shrewe vj^d (Arber, iii. 365).

[F1. 1623.] [*Catalogue*] The Taming of the Shrew. [*Comedies*, pp. 208–29; sign. S2^v–V1. *Head-title* and *Running-title*] as in *Cat.*

[Acts i. sc. 1, iii, iv. sc. 1, and v marked; altered in modern eds.]

[Q. 1631.] A Wittie and Pleasant Comedie Called The Taming of the Shrew. As it was acted by his Maiesties Seruants at the Blacke Friers and the Globe. Written by Will. Shakespeare [Smethwick's device (McKerrow 376)] Printed by W. S. for Iohn Smethwicke, and are to be sold at his Shop in Saint Dunstones Churchyard vnder the Diall. 1631.

Parallel-text (F. and *A Shrew*).   A. R. Frey (1888, *Bankside*).

Modern Editions. R. W. Bond (1904, 1929, *Arden*); H. T. E. Perry (1921, *Yale*); A. T. Quiller-Couch and J. D. Wilson (1928, *C.U.P.*).

[*Dissertations.* S. Hickson, *T.S.* (1850, *1 N.Q.* i. 345); R. Köhler, *Zu Shs T.S.* (1868, *J.* iii. 397); F. G. Fleay, *On the Authorship of T.S.* (1874, *N.S.S. Trans.* 85; *Sh. Manual*, 175); A, v. Weilen, *Shs Vorspiel zu T.S.* (1884); R. Urbach, *Das Verhältniss des Shs T.S. zu seinen Quellen* (1887); J. Bolte, *Eine Parallele zu Shs T.S.* (1892, *J.* xxvii. 130); A. H. Tolman, *Sh. and T.S. and Sh.'s Love's Labour's Won* (1904, *Views About Hamlet*, 203); E. H. Schomburg, *T.S.* (1904); E. P. Kuhl, *Sh.'s Purpose in Dropping Sly* (1921, *M.L.N.* xxxvi. 321), *The Authorship of T.S.* (1925, *P.M.L.A.* xl. 551); J. M. Robertson, *Marlowe and Comedy* (1923, *Sh. Canon*, ii. 134); P. Alexander, *The Taming of A Shrew* (1926, Sept. 16, *T.L.S.*); F. H. Ashton, *The Revision of the F Text of T.S.* (1927, *P.Q.* vi. 151); B. A. P. van Dam, *A.S. and T.S.* (1928, *English Studies*, x. 97, 161).

The bibliographical *data* up to 1607 relate to *The Taming of A Shrew*,[1] but it is clear that *A Shrew* and *The Shrew* were regarded commercially as the same, and that the copyright acquired by Smethwick in 1607 covered both F1 and the Q of 1631, which was printed from it. F1 has the full author's stage-directions usual in Shakespeare's earlier work. I see no reason to think with Wilson that they were added by a second hand to a dictated transcript. Doubtless, however, the manuscript had been used as stage-copy. There is an obvious addition at *Ind.* i. 1, 'Enter Begger and Hostes, Christophero Sly', which may be due to the book-keeper. At *Ind.* i. 88, the name of the actor Sincklo has been substituted for *Player*. He is known as a hired man of the Chamberlain's company. Other possible actor-names in stage-directions or speech-prefixes are *Nicke* (iii. 1. 82), *Par* (iv. 2. 71), *Fel* (iv. 3. 63), *Peter* (iv. 4. 69). They are not all certain and, unless

[1] *Eliz. Stage*, iv. 48.

Nicke is Nicholas Tooley, we cannot identify them. It is unsafe to assume that this *Nicke* and this *Peter* played the similarly named servants in iv. 1. They are two out of five who appear and speak. There are six others who are named, but do not appear. One of these is Gabriel, whom it is still less safe to take as the actor Gabriel Spencer. These are all textual names, and the book-keeper cannot (cf. p. 237) be responsible for them. Gabriel can never have been cast. The act-divisions of F are not good, and the beginning of Act ii is not marked.

The relation of *A Shrew* to *The Shrew* is a matter of dispute. I adhere to the older view that it was used as a source-play, and think that in basing *The Shrew* upon it Shakespeare had, exceptionally for him, the assistance of a collaborator. I assign to Shakespeare *Ind.* i, ii; ii. 1. 1–38, 115–326; iii. 2. 1–129, 151–254; iv. 1, 3, 5; v. 2. 1–181. Possibly he also contributed to the Petruchio episode in i. 2. 1–116. Some critics give him less than I have done. On my view his share amounts to about three-fifths of the play, and includes all the Sly and Petruchio-Katharina scenes. The other writer is responsible for the sub-plot of Bianca's wooers. I do not know who he was. Lodge, Greene, and Chapman have been suggested on very slight grounds. His work, although not incompetent, is much less vigorous than Shakespeare's. He has many awkward lines, which disregard stress or contain unmanageable trisyllabic feet. He uses double endings in much the same proportion (17%) as Shakespeare (19%). The numerous scraps of Latin and Italian and the doggerel belong to his part. He makes less use than Shakespeare of phrases from *A Shrew*. Kuhl has argued for Shakespeare's sole author-ship, largely on the ground that the characterization, especially of Petruchio, is consistent throughout. He finds the stylistic differences inconclusive. Some of them are, individually, but collectively they are less so, and bear out a general stylistic impression from which I cannot escape. The collaborators may well have agreed upon a common conception of Petruchio.

A Shrew furnished the main structure of both plots,

with their characters and entanglement, and of the induction. Shakespeare in particular follows its details pretty closely, and although his dialogue, as well as that of his collaborator, is new, the recurrence of stray words and phrases and of half a dozen practically identical blank-verse lines (iv. 3. 171–3; v. 2. 114, 130–1) shows that the old text was continuously before him. There is a still closer resemblance in iv. 3, where many points in Grumio's jesting with the tailor are taken over from *A Shrew*. This is not sufficient to justify the suggestion that Shakespeare himself contributed to *A Shrew*, and Sykes has made a fair case for assigning the comic prose of that to Samuel Rowley. The rest of the play is mainly written in pedestrian verse, often neglectful of stress, but this is varied by some highly wrought sections or speeches, full of classical allusions, and much in the manner of Marlowe. Robertson and others have taken them to be Marlowe's, but the parallels to *Tamburlaine* and *Dr. Faustus* collected by Boas leave this hardly possible. Some of these might be mere echoes, but in others from two to four lines are reproduced, exactly or approximately, from Marlowe in a way which must exclude his authorship. Nor does any known dramatist elsewhere use him in this fashion. It looks as if some one, conscious of his own poetic insufficiency, had attempted to heighten his style by deliberate imitation and even plagiarism. He may also have drawn from other plays, learnt or heard on the stage, but not preserved. If this is so, the date of *A Shrew* must remain uncertain. Lines in it seem to be satirized in Greene's *Menaphon* (1589) and Nashe's epistle thereto, but these may be among the borrowings. If the play is as old as 1589, it cannot have been originally written for Pembroke's men. Saunder, who is a player in the induction, probably only bears a character name, as it is textual in the main plot, where Saunder is the prototype of Grumio. In any case he can hardly be the Saunder of the *Seven Deadly Sins* plot (c. 1590), who was then still a boy taking women's parts.

A somewhat different view from mine is put forward by

Herford, who thinks that the conversion of *A Shrew* into *The Shrew* was done by the 'other hand', and that Shakespeare revised him. Similarly Miss Ashton would find traces of revision in the sub-plot. Wilson, who does not (cf. *infra*) regard *A Shrew* as a source, suggests revision by Shakespeare of a hypothetical play, from which he thinks that some clown-dialogue by Nashe may have been preserved. I do not find much evidence of dislocation in F1 to bear out such views. It is a fairly clean text. As Wilson points out, there is a tendency, more marked in some scenes than others, to drop or add small words, which may be that of an incompetent compositor or, as he thinks, a transcriber. Some speech-prefixes (iii. 1. 46–58; iv. 2. 1–8; iv. 4. 5–6) are incorrect or wrongly placed. There is no extensive mislineation. Here and there a few lines are wrongly printed as prose, doggerel, or blank verse respectively. One longer passage (iii. 2. 169–85) is in prose instead of verse throughout, and may have been written in a margin. The 'Enter Peter' at iv. 4. 69, if it does not yield an actor's name, may mean that the Petruchio scene (iv. 5) had been started upon here, and then deferred for the addition of another 41 lines to the sub-plot scene iv. 4. There are some slight inconsistencies of action, such as Petruchio's call (iv. 1. 154) for a 'cousin Ferdinand', who never appears. I see nothing here which a compositor might not produce from careless or hasty copy, which incorporated some afterthoughts, and in which (cf. p. 204) the speech-prefixes had been written later than the text.

The use of a collaborator may in itself point to haste. The play has been variously dated. It is sometimes put about 1598, because Meres does not name it, and the induction has affinities of matter with *Henry IV*. But its metrical features are consistent with 1594, and it may quite well be the *Love Labours Won* of Meres. This is largely an application of the method of exclusions, since there is no other extant comedy, at any rate in its present form, available (cf. p. 272). The title itself might fit almost any sentimental plot. Perhaps the fourfold refer-

ence (v. 2. 69, 112, 116, 186) to Petruchio's winning of
his wager is relevant. The title-page of *A Shrew* shows
that it was played by Pembroke's men, who emerge late
in 1592, and were broken by September 1593.[1] A performance (App. D) for Henslowe on 13 June 1594 was presumably by the Chamberlain's, and Henslowe's 'A Shrowe'
need not prejudice opinion as to which version was then
used. On the whole I think it probable that *A Shrew*
originally belonged to the Alleyn company, that it was
handed by them to Pembroke's in 1592 and recovered in
1593, that it was allocated to the Chamberlain's on the
reconstitution of companies in 1594, and that they rather
hastily based *The Shrew* upon it, sold the old book to the
printers in May, and played the new one in June. About
the exact details of this I should not like to be dogmatic.
Henslowe does not mark the piece 'ne' and it is possible
that the Chamberlain's began by playing *A Shrew* and
revised it a little later in 1594.

A quite distinct theory of the relation between *A Shrew*
and *The Shrew* has been outlined by Alexander[2] and
accepted by Wilson. According to this, *A Shrew* is not
the source of *The Shrew*, but a 'bad Quarto' of it, due to
an attempt of Pembroke's, after owning *The Shrew* and
selling it in 1593, to reproduce it from memory, with the
aid of a good deal of rewriting, and to resume playing it in
the winter of 1593–4. I am quite unable to believe that
A Shrew had any such origin. Its textual relation to *The
Shrew* does not bear any analogy to that of other 'bad
Quartos' to the legitimate texts from which they were
memorized. The nomenclature, which at least a memorizer
can recall, is entirely different. The verbal parallels are
limited to stray phrases, most frequent in the main plot,
for which I believe that Shakespeare picked them up from
A Shrew. He picks up phrases from Holinshed and
North in just the same way. It is true, as shown by Hickson long ago, that some of these phrases have more point
in *The Shrew* than in *A Shrew*. But this might be the
case on either hypothesis, and the *A Shrew* versions are

[1] *Eliz. Stage*, ii. 128; cf. p. 46.   [2] *T.L.S.* for 16 September 1926.

not unintelligible as they stand. Alexander's strongest argument is that the sub-plot of *The Shrew* comes closer than that of *A Shrew* to the ultimate source in Ariosto's *I Suppositi*. This again is true, and I take it that Shakespeare's collaborator made use of *I Suppositi* or its translation in Gascoigne's *Supposes*, as well as of *A Shrew*.[1]

Shakespeare himself probably used no other literary source than *A Shrew*, which had already incorporated widespread story-motives in the 'taming' itself and the transformed drunkard. He worked Warwickshire reminiscences into the induction. Christophero Sly is in *A Shrew*, but Stephen Sly (*Ind*. ii. 95) figures in the enclosures controversy; Marion Hacket, the fat ale-wife of Wincot,[2] came from just over the Gloucestershire border (App. C, no. viii); and Burton Heath[3] is presumably Barton-on-the-Heath, where dwelt Shakespeare's cousins, the Lamberts (App. A, no. iv). A note in the records of the Stationers' Company for 1596 of a suppressed ballad called 'The taminge of a shrewe' is untrustworthy (App. F, no. xi (*l*)).

The 1631 title-page shows that the play held the seventeenth-century stage, and a court performance of 26 November 1633 is on record (App. D). A Jacobean revival may be pointed to by the counterblast in Fletcher's *The Woman's Prize or the Tamer Tamed*, of which, however, the date is very uncertain,[4] and by an allusion in S. Rowlands, *Whole Crew of Kind Gossips* (1609):

> The chiefest Art I have I will bestow
> About a worke cald taming of the Shrow.

The divisions in F are very irregular. A heading for ii has probably been omitted by accident. But v consists of only one scene of 189 lines, and the whole play is rather short. Possibly a final Sly scene has been excised for some reason of staging. There was one in *A Shrew*, and *The Shrew* seems rather incomplete without one.

---

[1] *Eliz. Stage*, iii. 321.
[2] *Ind*. ii. 22.
[3] *Ibid*. ii. 19.

[4] *Eliz. Stage*, iii. 222; Oliphant, *Beaumont and Fletcher*, 151.

VIII. THE TWO GENTLEMEN OF VERONA

[F1. 1623.] [*Catalogue*] The two Gentlemen of Verona. [*Comedies*, pp. 20–38; sign. B 4ᵛ–D 1ᵛ. *Head-title*] The Two Gentlemen of Verona [*Running-title*] The two Gentlemen of Verona. [*At end*] The names of all the Actors.

[Acts and scc. marked. 'The names of all the Actors' at end. Pages 37 and 38 have the running-title for *M.W.* in error.]

Modern Editions. R. W. Bond (1906, *Arden*); A. T. Quiller-Couch and J. D. Wilson (1921, *C.U.P.*); K. Young (1924, *Yale*).

[*Dissertations.* F. G. Fleay, *On the Date and Composition of T.G.* (1874, *N.S.S. Trans.* 287, with comment by F. J. Furnivall); J. Zupitza, *Über die Fabel in Shs T.G.* (1888, *J.* xxiii. 1); H. F. Bründel, *Shs T.G. in englischen Bühnenbearbeitung* (1909); H. Norpoth, *Metrisch-chronologische Untersuchung von Shs T.G.* (1916); J. M. Robertson, *The Authorship of T.G.* (1923, *Sh. Canon*, ii. 1); O. J. Campbell, *T.G. and Italian Comedy* (1925, *Michigan Studies*); T. P. Harrison, *Concerning T.G. and Montemayor's Diana* (1926, *M.L.N.* xli. 251).

The F text is fairly free from misprints and mislineations. All the entries and nearly all the exits within the scenes are unmarked, and there are no stage-directions, except final exits and entries at the beginning of each scene for all its characters in the order, doubtfully correct for iv. 2, of their appearance. Wilson draws the inference that the text was 'assembled' from 'parts' with the aid of a 'plot'. There are considerable difficulties (cf. p. 153) about any theory of 'assembling', but perhaps the case for it is stronger in *Two Gentlemen* than elsewhere. In a few passages prose is printed in irregular capitalized lines. Wilson also thinks that the play has been abbreviated and added to by an adapter. I do not accept the mingling of prose and verse in certain dialogues, or the presence of blank-verse rhythms in prose, or mentions of personages who do not appear, as evidence of this. They are common features (cf. pp. 181, 230–4) of Shakespeare's plays. There may have been some abbreviation. The text is rather short, and some of the scenes (ii. 2; v. 1; v. 3) are summary, and there are a few abrupt short lines and corruptions which may indicate 'cuts'. But I do not think that any scenes or incidents have been omitted. Time is foreshortened here and there, but this easily passes on the stage. Nor do I see the hand of an adapter. There are inconsistencies of action and nomenclature, but these need point to no more than careless original work. Milan, Verona, and Padua are hopelessly confused. Apparently Shakespeare at first meant the main action to be at an emperor's court at Milan; then altered it to a duke's court at Verona, and forgot to make the indications uniform. Verona is nowhere said to be the home of Proteus, Valentine, and Julia; in fact they go from home by sea. Padua (ii. 5. 1) must be a slip, any-how. Wilson suggests that the part of Speed is inter-polated, but it seems inextricable from that of Launce in ii. 5 and iii. 1, and i. 2. 38 shows that Valentine had a page. There is some poor writing towards the end of the play, especially in iv. 1 and in v. 4, which is also bad in senti-ment. But the badness is not necessarily un-Shakespearean.

Robertson thinks that *Two Gentlemen* is a comedy by Greene, and that Shakespeare only altered the opening and inserted or retouched some later passages. He lays stress on the poverty of much of the comic relief and on the end-stopped iambic versification. It is true that the iambic norm is less varied by trochees and pyrrhics than is usual with Shakespeare, and possible that, as a beginner in romantic comedy, he was influenced by Greene, as he certainly was by Lyly. But Greene did not write the play; if for no other reason, because he never used so many double endings.

The date can hardly be fixed with precision. There is no external evidence beyond the mention by Meres in 1598. Two allusions to Hero and Leander (i. 1. 21; iii. 1. 119) are not necessarily later than Marlowe's poem of 1593. Allusions to 'the wars' and travels to dis-cover islands (i. 3. 8), to pestilence (ii. 1. 22), and to the winning and losing of love's labour (i. 1. 32) are even more inconclusive. The 'print' in which Speed found ii. 1. 171–4 has not been traced. The play has affinities of motive, manner, and vocabulary to the *Comedy of Errors*, to *Romeo and Juliet*, *Merchant of Venice*, and others riper than itself, and to some of the *Sonnets*. This, together with the inequality of workmanship, led Fleay to conjecture that it is of two dates. According to one of several forms which his theory took, Shakespeare only finished the play after an interval; according to another it was written about 1591 with a collaborator, whose work Shakespeare replaced by his own in 1595. The notion of a diversity of dates has received some support, but I think that a single date, early in the season of 1594–5, really meets all the conditions, and that the outset of the career of the Chamberlain's men was a not unlikely time for hasty composition. No performance of the play is on record.

The only clear source is the story of Felix and Felismena in Jorge de Montemayor's *Diana Enamorada*. If Shakespeare could not read Spanish, he may have used the translation of Bartholomew Yonge, printed in 1598 but finished sixteen years earlier, or the French translation of Nicolas Collin (1578, 1587), or the play of 'Felix & Philiomena' given at court by the Queen's men in 1585.[1] Montemayor's story is varied and elaborated in *Two Gentlemen*, especially by the introduction of Valentine, and with him the motive of the conflict of love and friendship. Shakespeare is obsessed by this theme in the *Sonnets*, and it is so common in Renaissance literature that slight analogies to *Two Gentlemen* in Lyly's *Euphues* and *Endimion*, Barnabe Rich's *Apollonius and Silla* (cf. p. 407), *Fedele and Fortunio*,[2] and elsewhere become of little importance. There is a rather closer resemblance in the German play of *Julio and Hyppolita*, printed in *Engelische Comedien und Tragedien* (1620). But this is a tragedy, and its relation to *Two Gentlemen* or any possible forerunner is quite uncertain. Campbell notes that many features of *Two Gentlemen* are commonplaces in Italian comedy.

IX. LOVE'S LABOUR'S LOST

[Q 1. 1598.] [Ornament] A Pleasant Conceited Comedie Called, Loues labors lost. As it was presented before her Highnes this last Christmas. Newly corrected and augmented By W. Shakespere. [Ornament] Imprinted

---

[1] *Eliz. Stage*, iv. 160.   [2] *Ibid.* iv. 13.

at London by W⟨illiam⟩ W⟨hite⟩ for Cutbert Burby. 1598. [*No Head-title. Running title*] A pleasant conceited Comedie: called Loues Labor's Lost.

Facsimile. W. Griggs (1880, *Sh. Q.* v, ed. F. J. Furnivall).

[S.R. 1607.] 22 Januarij. Master Linge Entred for his copies by direccon of A Court and with consent of Master Burby vnder his handwrytynge These. iij copies. viz. . . . Loues Labour Loste . . . (Arber, iii. 337).

[S.R. 1607.] 19 Novembris. John Smythick. Entred for his copies vnder thandes of the wardens. these bookes followinge Whiche dyd belonge to Nicholas Lynge. viz. . . . 11 Loues Labour Lost. vj^d . . . (Arber, iii. 365).

[F1. 1623.] [*Catalogue*] Loues Labour lost. [*Comedies*, pp. 122–44; sign. L 1^v–M 6^v. *Head- and Running-titles*] Loues Labour's lost.

[Acts marked, with iv repeated for v.]

[Q2. 1631.] Loues Labours lost. A Wittie And Pleasant Comedie, As it was Acted by his Maiesties Seruants at the Blacke-Friers and the Globe. Written by William Shakespeare. [Smethwick's device (McKerrow 376)] London, Printed by W. S. for Iohn Smethwicke, and are to be sold at his Shop in Saint Dunstones Church-yard vnder the Diall. 1631. [*Head- and Running-titles*] Loues Labour's lost.

Parallel-Text. I. H. Platt (1906, *Bankside*, xxi).

Modern Editions. H. H. Furness (1904, *New Variorum*, xiv); H. C. Hart (1906, *Arden*); H. B. Charlton (1917, *Heath*); A. T. Quiller-Couch and J. D. Wilson (1923, *C.U.P.*); W. L. Cross and C. F. T. Brooke (1925, *Yale*).

[*Dissertations.* S. Lee, *A New Study of L.L.L.* (1880, *Gentleman's Mag.*); F. G. Fleay, *Sh. and Puritanism* (1884, *Anglia*, vii. 223); G. Sarrazin, *Die Entstehungszeit von L.L.L.* (1895, *J.* xxxi. 200); J. de Perott, *Eine spanische Parallele zu L.L.L.* (1908, *J.* xliv. 151); J. Phelps, *Father Parsons in Sh.* (1915, *Archiv*, cxxxiii. 66); H. B. Charlton, *A Disputed Passage in L.L.L.* (1917, *M.L.R.* xii. 279), *A Textual Note on L.L.L.* (1917, *3 Library*, viii. 355), *The Date of L.L.L.* (1918, *M.L.R.* xiii. 257, 387); J. M. Robertson, *L.L.L.* (1917, *Sh. and Chapman*, 107); H. D. Gray, *The Original Version of L.L.L.* (1918); A. Lefranc, *L.L.L.* (1919, *Sous Le Masque de Sh.* ii. 17); A. K. Gray, *The Secret of L.L.L.* (1924, *P.M.L.A.* xxxix. 581); O. J. Campbell, *L.L.L. Re-studied* (1925, *Michigan Studies*); A. R. Bayley, *Or Mons, the hill* (1925, *N.Q.* cxlviii. 399, 417).

Q1 is a badly printed text, with many 'literal' and other errors and blundering punctuation. It preserves a number of abnormal spellings. There are slight variants in the extant examples. F1 was set up from a Q1 in which there may have been others. But the F printer has made many corrections and introduced as many fresh errors, of which Greg gives an interesting analysis in *R.E.S.* i. 471. Wilson shows that the example used had already been altered in the theatre by a revision of the stage-directions and speech-prefixes. Q2 was set up from F. The absence of, an original entry in the Stationers' Register and the 'Newly corrected and augmented' on the title-page of Q1 suggest that it may, like the Q2 of *Romeo and Juliet* where the same conditions recur, have been preceded by a surreptitious print. If so, the title-page is not in itself evidence of anything more than revision of the printing, as distinct from a rewriting of the play. But a rewriting has been suspected on other grounds. Two passages, iv. 3. 296–317 and v. 2. 827–32, are clearly duplicated by what follows in each case, and Wilson is probably right in suggesting that they were marked for deletion and the marks disregarded by the printer. But it is by no means so clear that these changes were made at a rewriting of the play; the cancelled passages can be just as well interpreted as false starts at the time of the original writing. A half-line left in Q before iv. 3. 317, but omitted in modern editions, looks like an abandoned first attempt to amend that line, before the fresh start was made. Similarly, the first line of the rejected Berowne-Rosaline dialogue in v. 2. 827–32 was immediately used to open a Dumaine-Katharine dialogue, and the opening of a new Berowne-Rosaline dialogue deferred to 847. Something has also gone wrong with ii. 1. Here Berowne is clearly meant to be paired with Rosaline throughout, Longaville with Maria, Dumaine with Katharine. But the arrangement is not consistently followed. Possibly Shakespeare has been careless; possibly confusion has arisen through an attempt to set up *Love's Labour's Lost* like *Romeo and Juliet* (q.v.) by correcting a bad Quarto. I do not think that Wilson has given a satisfactory explanation in terms of a rewriting. He finds, however, further evidence of this in (*a*) small typographical variations and dislocations in Q, which are capable of several explanations; (*b*) a supposed difference in the character of the stage-directions in different places, which seems to me imaginary, as the stage-directions are comparatively slight throughout; and (*c*) the use, here of personal, and there of generic, descriptions in stage-directions and speech-prefixes. And he assigns to a first 'draft', more or less altered on revision, i. 1, 2; ii. 1; iii. 1. 69–end; iv. 2, 3; and to a revised version, with traces of the first draft, iii. 1. 1–68; iv. 1; v. The variations of nomenclature, frequent enough in other plays, are more conspicuous in *Love's Labour's Lost* than elsewhere. We get, in full or abbreviation, Navarro and King for Ferdinand, Braggart for Armado, Pedant for Holofernes, Curate for Nathaniel, Wench and Maid for Jaquenetta, Clown for Costard, Constable for Anthony or Dull, and 1, 2, 3 Lady for Maria, Katharine, and Rosaline. Wilson uses some of these; others, which he does not use, do not square with his theory that the use of generic names points to rewriting. But this theory I do not (cf. p. 232) accept. Somewhat exceptional are the variations of Duke for King and Queen for Princess, since these appear in the text, and are inconsistent, except that the Princess apparently becomes Queen of France on her father's death in v. 2, and is thereafter addressed as 'Maiestie' instead of 'Grace'. H. D. Gray has made an independent attempt to trace the lines of a rewriting. He supposes that the original play ended with a complete rejection of the lovers; that Rosaline was transformed from a fair into a swarthy beauty; that Holofernes and Nathaniel were only introduced at the rewriting; and that this explains the difference between the planning and performance of the *Worthies*. The view seems to me quite fantastic. Love-comedies do not end with rejections. Rosaline is throughout white-skinned; only her hair and brows are black; there is a similar difference between the planning and the performance of the play in *Midsummer-Night's Dream*.

Both Wilson and Gray find their new matter mainly at the end. The great length of v. 2 is not, I think, relevant. *Love's Labour's Lost* does not fall into acts. F might have divided better than it did, but probably there were no intervals in the play as originally given. It is possible that, if a 'surreptitious' early Q ever turns up, some of the supposed evidence for revision and other features of the text may prove to be due to an attempt, as in *Romeo and Juliet*, to use a heavily corrected example of that as 'copy' for Q1.

So far as style is concerned, I see no evidence for two dates, and no evidence for a very early date. The versification is extremely adroit, and certainly not that of a beginner. I regard the play as the earliest of the lyrical group which includes *Midsummer-Night's Dream*, *Romeo and Juliet*, and *Richard II*, and I put it in 1595. The variety entertainment at the close links it with *Midsummer-Night's Dream* and the black-browed and black-eyed Rosaline with the *Sonnets*. Nor are the numerous topical and literary allusions inconsistent with this date. The 'Monarcho' (iv. 1. 101) can in any case be a tradition only, as his epitaph in T. Churchyard, *Chance* (1580), shows him then dead. Charlton has traced the 'first and second cause' in duelling (i. 2. 183) to Segar's *Book of Honor and Arms* (1590). The 'dancing horse' (i. 2. 57) of John Banks was travelling from 1591 until long after 1595. There is no reason whatever to suppose that Elizabeth shot a deer with a bow (iv. 1) for the first or the last time at Cowdray in 1591. 'Lord have mercy on us' (v. 2. 419) was a formula used in the plague of 1592–3, but by no means for the first time.[1] There may be a reference in 'saved by merit' as a 'heresy in fair, fit for these days' (iv. 1. 21) to the conversion of Henri IV on 25 July 1593. There must be a reference in 'piercing a hogshead' (iv. 2. 89) to the wit-exchange between Nashe and Gabriel Harvey, begun by Harvey's *Pierce's Supererogation* (1593). If, as seems probable, iv. 3. 346–7 echo Chapman's *Shadow of Night*, that was printed in 1594. The Muscovite mask (v. 2) can have

1 F. P. Wilson, *The Plague in Sh.'s London*, 63.

nothing to do with the wooing of Lady Mary Hastings for the Emperor of Muscovy in 1583, but does reflect an English interest in Russian affairs, and perhaps derives from the similar use of Russian apparel on 6 January 1595 in the Gray's Inn revels which were also adorned by *Comedy of Errors*. Robert Southwell, in prison from 20 June 1592 and executed on 21 February 1595, wrote some lines on eyes (App. B, no. xi) which have been supposed to echo Berowne's disquisition in iv. 3, but it is probable that they are of earlier date. There is an analogy to the jest on 'guerdon' and 'remuneration' (iii. 1. 170) in J. M., *A Health to the Gentlemanly Profession of Servingmen* (S.R. 15 May 1598), sign. I, but nothing to determine priority. Obviously, if *Love's Labour's Lost* was revised, some of these passages may belong to the second version. But I find nothing which is necessarily later than 1595. The jest on Ajax and the lion sitting on a close-stool (v. 2. 579) is based on the arms of Alexander, as given in Gerard Legh, *Accedens of Armorie* (1563, 1591), and is more likely to have given a hint to than taken one from Harington's *Metamorphosis of Ajax* (1596). Shakespeare, if the borrower, would have worked in 'metamorphosis'. There may be other topical allusions in an obviously satirical play over which time has drawn a veil. Many attempts have been made to trace portraits in the exponents of the *Worthies*. Armado has been identified with the Monarcho, Antonio Perez, Lyly, Philip of Spain, and Sir Walter Raleigh; Holofernes with John Florio, Bishop Cooper, Thomas Harriot, Chapman, and one Richard Lloyd, who wrote lines on the Worthies in 1584; Moth with La Mothe-Fénelon, a French ambassador, as far back as 1568–75, and with Nashe; and so forth. Most of this is mere beating the air. As Campbell points out, this underworld of *Love's Labour's Lost* represents the stock masks of Italian comedy, the *capitano* and his *zanni*, the *pedante* or *dottore*, the parasite or *affamato*, the clown, the magistrate. It does not follow that there may not be personal touches in the reproduction of them. Moth, like Nashe by Greene and Meres, is called (iii. 1. 67) a 'juvenal'.

Holofernes gets his name from Rabelais, and Rombus
in Sidney's *May Lady*, an entertainment of about 1578,
is a rather remote analogy.[1] Both Chapman and Gabriel
Harvey may have contributed something to Holofernes, but it is pressing the thing too far to speak of
'portraits'. If the Q reading in iv. 3. 255 'Schoole of
night' is correct, there may be a further allusion to Chapman's *Shadow of Night*, in which learning is called upon
to shun the day, and perhaps also to Sir Walter Raleigh's
alleged 'School of Atheism,' which Chapman seems to
laud in his epistle, although apparently only knowing of
it through Matthew Roydon. But if he was right in
regarding Sir George Carey as a member, there could be
no 'attack' by Shakespeare, since Carey was son of Lord
Hunsdon, and later himself the patron of Shakespeare's
company. No source is known for the main plot. If there
was one, it may have helped to account for the Ferdinand,
Duke, and Queen. No Ferdinand was ever King of
Navarre. But Ferdinand is given (ii. 1. 163) a father
Charles and the dispute as to an inherited debt of 200,000
crowns, for which Ferdinand holds part of Aquitaine,
bears some analogy to financial transactions between a
historic Charles of Navarre and the King of France
about 1425. Probably, however, the visit of the Princess
to Ferdinand rests upon something more recent than
1425, in a visit to Henri IV at Nérac in 1578 by his wife
Marguerite de Valois, a princess of France. They were
separated, and questions of dowry, involving towns in
Aquitaine, were at issue. Marguerite describes the visit
and its festivals in her *Mémoires*. She was accompanied by a
troop of ladies, and temporarily renewed amorous relations
with her husband. The *Mémoires* also tell the pathetic
story of the death, two years before, of Hélène de Tournon,
which seems to be alluded to in v. 2. 13–17. It took place in
Brabant (ii. 1. 114), whither Marguerite went after a visit to
her brother, the Duc d'Alençon (ii. 1. 61) in 1578. Shakespeare can hardly have known all this at first hand. Neither
the *Mémoires* nor the accounts of Henri and Marguerite by

---

[1] *Eliz. Stage*, iii. 491.

Brantôme and others were yet available in print. Unless there was a source-play, some English or French traveller must have been an intermediary. On the other hand, the names of Berowne, Longaville, and Dumaine would be well enough known in England from events of later date. Armand and Charles Gontaut, successive Ducs de Biron, and Henri, Duc de Longueville, were supporters of Henri IV in his wars of 1589–93 for the crown of France. Charles, Duc de Mayenne, was his opponent. He has probably been confused with another supporter, Maréchal D'Aumont.

Love's Labour's Lost suggests a courtly rather than a popular audience. Wilson, who puts his first version in 1593, supposes it played at the Earl of Southampton's house in plague-time. A. K. Gray relates it to the Titchfield visit in the progress of 1591,[1] and thinks that Southampton hoped to hint by the *denouement* at the desirability of a twelve-months' respite before his marriage to Elizabeth Vere. Southampton is the ready *deus ex machina* of Shakespearean speculation. If the title-page of Q1 does not merely repeat an earlier one, the court performance to which it refers must, on Greg's view as to the dates on play title-pages (cf. p. 175), have been in 1597–8. The abrupt ending, 'The words of Mercury are harsh after the songs of Apollo', which was altered in F, looks like the beginning of an epilogue or of a presenter's speech for a following mask. Mercury has nothing to do with what precedes. There was a revival in January 1605 and a performance at Cranborne's house or Southampton's (App. D). F alters 'God' into 'Ioue' in one only (v. 2. 316) of twenty cases. The 1631 title-page shows that the play held the stage after the King's men acquired the Blackfriars.

X. ROMEO AND JULIET

[Q1. 1597.] [Ornament] An Excellent conceited Tragedie of Romeo and Iuliet. As it hath been often (with great applause) plaid publiquely, by the right Honourable the L. of Hunsdon his Seruants. [Danter's device (McKerrow

---

[1] *Eliz. Stage*, iv. 106.

281)] London, Printed by Iohn Danter. 1597 [*Head-title*]
The most excellent Tragedie of Romeo and Iuliet. [*Run-
ning-titles*] The most excellent Tragedie, of Romeo and
Iuliet. (sign. A–D); The excellent Tragedie of Romeo and
Iuliet. (sign. E–K)].

[A different type begins with sign. E at ii. 3. 82, and from the beginning of iii. 5 the text is divided by ornaments, apparently marking off
scenes.]

Facsimile. C. Praetorius (1886, *Sh. Q.* xxv, ed. H. A. Evans).

Reprints. P. A. Daniel (1874, *N.S.S.*); W. A. Wright (1893,
Cambridge Sh. ix. 639).

Modern Edition. F. G. Hubbard (1924, *Wisconsin Univ. Studies*).

[Q2. 1599.] The Most Excellent and lamentable
Tragedie, of Romeo and Iuliet. Newly corrected, augmented, and amended: As it hath bene sundry times
publiquely acted, by the right Honourable the Lord
Chamberlaine his Seruants. [Creede's device (McKerrow
299)] London Printed by Thomas Creede, for Cuthbert
Burby, and are to be sold at his shop neare the Exchange.
1599. [*Head-title*] The Most Excellent and lamentable
Tragedie, of Romeo and Iuliet. [*Running-title*] The most
lamentable Tragedie of Romeo and Iuliet.

Facsimile. C. Praetorius (1886, *Sh. Q.* xxvi, ed. H. A. Evans).

Reprint. P. A. Daniel (1874, *N.S.S.*).

Modern Edition. P. A. Daniel (1875, *N.S.S.*).

[S.R. 1607.] 22 Januarij Master Linge Entred for his
copies by direccon of A Court and with consent of Master
Burby vnder his handwrytinge These .iij copies. viz.
Romeo and Juliett . . . (Arber, iii. 337).

[S.R. 1607.] 19 Novembris John Smythick. Entred for
his copies vnder thandes of the wardens. these bookes
followinge Whiche dyd belonge to Nicholas Lynge. viz. . . .
10 Romeo and Julett vj^d (Arber, iii. 365).

[Q3. 1609.] The Most Excellent and Lamentable
Tragedie, of Romeo and Juliet. As it hath beene sundrie
times publiquely Acted, by the Kings Maiesties Seruants
at the Globe. Newly corrected, augmented and amended:
[Ornament] London Printed for Iohn Smethwick, and

are to be sold at his Shop in Saint Dunstanes Church-
yard, in Fleete streete vnder the Dyall. 1609. [*Head-* and
Running-titles, nearly as in Q2.]

[Q4. n.d.] *Title*, with Smethwick's device of 1612–37
(McKerrow 376), *Head-* and *Running-titles*, nearly as in Q3.
[In some copies 'Written by W. Shake-speare' precedes
'Newly corrected . . .]

Facsimile. C. Praetorius (1887, *Sh. Q.* xxxvi, ed. H. A. Evans).

[F1. 1623.] [*Catalogue*] Romeo and Juliet. [*Tragedies*,
pp. 53–79 (omitting 77–8); sign. ee 3–gg 2, Gg. *Head-*
and *Running-titles*] The Tragedie of Romeo and Iuliet.
[Act i, sc. 1, marked.]

[Q4. 1637.] *Title*, with 'Written by W. Shake-speare',
Head- and *Running-titles*, as in Q3. Printed by R.
Young for John Smethwicke, . . . 1637.

Parallel-Texts. T. Mommsen (1859); P. A. Daniel (1874, *N.S.S.*);
B. R. Field (1889, *Bankside*, v).

German Version. *Romio und Julietta* (Cohn 309, with tr., from
Vienna Hofbibliothek MS. 13107).

Modern Editions. H. H. Furness (1871, 1909, *New Variorum*);
E. Dowden (1900, *Arden*); W. H. Durham (1917, *Yale*).

[*Dissertations*. G. Pace-Sanfelice, *The Original Story of R.J.* (1868);
P. A. Daniel, *Brooke's Romeus and Juliet and Painter's Rhomeo and
Julietta* (1875, *N.S.S.*); K. P. Schulze, *Die Entwickelung der Sage von R.J.*
(1876, *J.* xi. 140), *The Jolly Goshawk* (1878, *J.* xiii. 205); F. G. Fleay
(1877, *Macmillan's Mag.*); T. A. Spalding, *On the First Quarto of R.J.*
(1878, *N.S.S. Trans.* 58); R. Gericke, *R.J. nach Shs MS.* (1879, *J.* xiv.
207); N. Delius, *Brooke's episches und Shs dramatisches Gedicht von R.J.*
(1881, *J.* xvi. 213; *Abl.* ii. 135); K. Lentzner, *Zu R.J.* (1887, *Anglia*, x.
601); E. Dowden, *R.J.* (1888, *Transcripts and Studies*); A. Cohn, *Adrian
Sevin's Bearbeitung der Sage von R.J.* (1889, *J.* xxiv. 122); L. Fränkel,
Untersuchungen zur Entwickelungsgeschichte des Stoffes von R.J. (1890–1,
Z. f. vergleichende Litteraturgeschichte, N.F. iii. 171; iv. 48), *Sh. und
das Tagelied* (1893), *Neue Beiträge zur Geschichte des Stoffes von Shs R.J.*
(1894, *E.S.* xix. 183); L. H. Fischer, *Die Sage von R.J. in deutschen
Prosa-Darstellung des 17 Jahrhunderts* (1890, *J.* xxv. 124); R. Davidsohn
(1903, *Deutsche Rundschau*, cxvii. 419); C. F. McClumpha, *Shs Sonn. und
R.J.* (1904, *J.* xl. 187); H. de W. Fuller, *Romeo and Juliette* (1906,
M.P. iv. 75); W. Smith, *A Comic Version of R.J.* (1909, *M.P.* vii. 217);
M. J. Wolff, *Ein Beitrag zur Gesch. des Stoffes von R.J.* (1909, *Z. f. ver-
gleichende Litteraturgeschichte*, N.F. xvii. 439); S. B. Hemingway, *The*

Relation of M.N.D. to R.J. (1911, *M.L.N.* xxvi. 78); H. D. Gray, *Romeo, Rosaline, and Juliet* (1914, *M.L.N.* xxix. 209); A. Schöttner, *Über die mutmassliche stenographische Entstehung der Q1 von Shs R.J.* (1918); J. D. Wilson and A. W. Pollard, *R.J.* (1919, Aug. 14, *T.L.S.*); R. Fischer, *Quellen zu R.J.* (1922); J. M. Robertson, *R.J.* (1925, *Sh. Canon*, iii. 113); M. P. Tilley, *A Parody of Euphues in R.J.* (1926, *M.L.N.* xli. 1); G. Hjort, *The Good and Bad Qq of R.J. and L.L.L.* (1926, *M.L.R.* xxi. 140); B. A. P. van Dam, *Did Sh. Revise R.J.?* (1927, *Anglia*, li. 39).]

Q1 is one of the bad Quartos (cf. p. 156), but it preserves many readings better than those of Q2, which, although 'Newly corrected, augmented, and amended', contains many errors. The fairly full stage-directions of Q2, with notes for the use of properties, suggest an author's hand supplemented in the theatre, of which there is a clear sign in the substitution (iv. 5. 102) of 'Enter Will Kemp' for 'Enter Peter'. Several entries and exits are unmarked. Q3 is printed from Q2, and F and the undated Q independently from Q3. Each introduces some corrections, apparently from conjecture. As originally set up, *Romeo and Juliet* ended on p. 77 of the *Tragedies*, and *Troilus and Cressida* began over-leaf on p. 78. When *Troilus and Cressida* (q.v.) was for a time withdrawn, the end of *Romeo and Juliet* was reprinted as p. 79 and *Timon of Athens* begun on p. 80 overleaf. The can-celled leaf with pp. 77–8 is accidentally preserved in two examples. The relation of Q1 to Q2 has been the subject of much discussion. Q1 is certainly a 'reported' text, and its derivation from an original more closely resembling Q2 is apparent. Lines necessary to explain the sense of what is left are omitted (i. 1. 115–22; i. 2. 1–3; iii. 2. 45–51; 102–6). Points are lost through alterations of order (i. 1. 19–37; 51–8; i. 2. 38–45). Passages are represented by mere paraphrases, or by scattered lines, with or without connective padding. The reporter tends to break down in bustling scenes, with much action and confused speech. The fight in i. 1. 69–87 is only indicated by a stage-direc-tion, and the stage-directions generally vary from Q2 and often read like descriptions of action seen on the stage. Except a short dialogue of servants in i. 5. 1–17, no episode of Q2 is entirely omitted. There are many small mislineations, and a good deal of irregular metre. Even well-reported passages contain alternatives of syntax or vocabulary to the language in corresponding lines of Q2. Actor's ejaculations are occasionally introduced. There is a gag (ii. 4. 21). Most evidential of a reporter are transpositions of lines and phrases from one place to another (i. 1. 120 to iii. 1. 172; ii. 4. 25 to iii. 1. 104; ii. 6. 21 to ii. 3. 31; iii. 2. 88 to ii. 5. 26; iii. 4. 6–7, 33 to i. 5. 126; v. 1. 64–5 to ii. 5. 5; v. 2. 6–8 to v. 3. 251). The reporter, however, is more competent than some others, and succeeds in working his fragments into a fairly continuous text. The best-done scenes are perhaps i. 1. 88–end; i. 2; i. 3. 1–48; i. 4; i. 5. 18–146; ii. 1–4; iii. 3; iii. 5. 1–59; iv. 1. On the whole the work deteriorates from ii. 6 onwards, and towards the end the divergence from Q2 is considerable. It does not seem possible to identify the reporter. If he was an actor, Capulet, the Nurse, Benvolio occasionally suggest themselves, but no part is consistently well rendered. Conceivably more than one hand has contributed. Several words look like errors of mishearing, but neither these nor the 'equivalents' can be taken (cf. pp. 156–61) as evidence of shorthand.

A report does not account for everything. Very possibly the report is of a text shortened for performance. Q1 has 2,232 lines and Q2 has 3,007. It is hardly possible to distinguish the reporter's omissions from others, but several *lacunae* in long speeches or dialogues may be 'cuts'. Other features of the relation between the texts have been explained on a theory of revision. Such a theory is stated by Wilson and Pollard. Q2 was printed from the author's MS. A transcriber would not, unless 'slavishly faithful', preserve numerous careless slips, and notably a duplication of ii. 3. 1–4 in a passage inserted before the last two lines of ii. 2. Moreover, Q2 'teems with evidences of revision', examples of which are in long passages of verse printed as prose, such as the Queen Mab speech in i. 3. 54–91. This must have been written in a margin without line divisions, or so heavily corrected in a margin that the compositor 'cut the Gordian tangle by resorting to a prose arrangement'. If, then, Q2 was 'derived from' a revised MS., Q1 must be 'derived from' this same MS. 'at an earlier stage of its development'. The evidence for this is in the close typographical resemblance of Q1 and Q2, as regards spelling, punctuation, and the use of capitals and italics, in certain passages, of which ii. 4. 39–46 and iii. 5. 27–31 are examples. Q1 contains 'pre-Shakespearian' passages 'of the Greene-Lodge school'. The MS. was twice handled by Shakespeare. At a first revision he brought Acts i and ii very nearly to their final state, but only rewrote iii–v here and there. At a second revision he altered iii–v less thoroughly, omitting to prefix sonnets, as he had done for i and ii, and leaving the spelling 'Capolet' in place of 'Capulet'. Q1 represents 'an abridged version of Shakespeare's first revision of an older play eked out by what a pirate could remember of the later version'. I do not find this theory satisfactory. The term 'derived from' is vague. Wilson and Pollard cannot mean that the actual MS. partly revised by Shakespeare was first altered by the reporter as copy for Q1 and was then passed back to the theatre, further revised by Shakespeare, and used as copy for Q2. They must mean that what the reporter handled was a transcript; and this is consistent with their general theory (cf. p. 226) that Shakespeare, early in his career, made partial revisions of several old plays, of which abridged transcripts were prepared for provincial performance during the plague of 1592–4. But if so, the typographical resemblance of parts of Q1 and Q2, upon which they rightly lay stress, remains unexplained. Wilson has himself made it probable, in dealing with other plays, that Shakespeare's orthography was individual, and was normalized, with his punctuation, in varying degrees by different printers. How could two printers, one perhaps working from the original, but the other from a transcript, itself certainly not literally true to the original, have produced the typographical resemblance. This, moreover, is not confined to i and ii, but extends to clearly Shakespearean writing later, to which, on the theory, Q1 had only access through the reporter and not from a MS. The resemblance is certainly striking, and the only plausible explanation of it seems to be that some parts at least of Q2 were set up from corrected pages of Q1. To this also point cases (ii. 2. 54; iii. 3. 102) of common mis-lineation in Q1 and Q2. I find a similar view taken by Greg, *Emendation*, 19, 49, and by Hjort and Van Dam. If it is sound, the alterations from Q2 were them-selves transcribed, either in margins or on attached slips and sheets. I do not share the difficulty which Wilson and Pollard feel about this. If the duplication at the end of ii. 2 and beginning of ii. 3 was not due to the transcriber himself, the first version was not necessarily more than a false start by Shakespeare, such as we find in *Love's Labour's Lost*, left undeleted or inadequately deleted. It would not take a particularly 'slavish' transcriber to copy it as it stood. There is another duplication in Q2 of iii. 3. 41. Certainly these are not evidence of a general revision of the play. Nor is the prose for verse of the Queen Mab passage, as this may merely represent cor-rections transcribed on a page of Q1. Prose for verse in Q1 one may generally put down to the reporter. The only other 'long' passage of this kind in Q2 is, I think, i. 3. Here Q2 follows Q1, and both texts have another odd feature which has not been explained. In the dialogue between Lady Capulet and the Nurse, all the Nurse's speeches, but not Lady Capulet's, are italicized in Q1. The italics are carried on in Q2 and extended to one of two speeches omitted by Q1. The Nurse's speeches are also italicized by Q1, although not by Q2, in i. 5, but not in later scenes. One would suppose that the Nurse's 'part', written in Italian script, was available for Q1, but the relation to Q2, although too close to leave room for revision, is not one of identity, and Q1 also italicizes a speech (i. 3. 100–4) by another servant. I do not accept Robertson's suggestion that the lines in question may have been left behind him by a dead contributor to the play, and printed in italics as 'a way of paying a small tribute to his memory'. This is scientific criticism with a vengeance.

On the whole, given the circumstances in which Q1

and Q2 respectively were printed, I do not see sufficient reason for supposing either that Shakespeare retained dialogue from a pre-Shakespearean play, or that he re-wrote his own work. Robertson regards *Romeo and Juliet* as 'a composite play, drafted before Shakespeare by several hands, merely revised and expanded by him in the version preserved in Q1, and further modified by his *and other* hands in the version preserved in Q2'. Even in Q2 he finds much of Peele, whom he thinks the main 'draftsman', and of Marlowe, Greene, and Kyd, although Shakespeare is allowed 'far more, alike of revision and of fresh writing, than he did in Titus'. I do not suppose that Wilson and Pollard would go as far as this, and I do not propose to take it seriously. The whole essay reads like a burlesque of Robertson's own theories upon earlier plays. Certainly there is some non-Shakespearean matter in Q1, especially towards the end. The most consecutive passages are ii. 6; iii. 2. 57–60; iv. 5. 43–64; v. 3. 12–17, and parts of v. 3. 223–67. I do not see that we need look for an author beyond the reporter. If he was an actor, as is probable enough, we know from Henslowe's records that many actors, without becoming habitual playwrights like Shakespeare and Heywood, were able to turn out a play upon occasion; and the style of 'the Greene-Lodge school' is just what such men might be expected to use, after better poets had grown out of it.

As to date, 1591 has been favoured, usually for a 'first version', because the Nurse (i. 3. 35) makes it eleven years since an earthquake, and there was a real earthquake in London in 1580.[1] This is pressing the Nurse's interest in chronology—and Shakespeare's—rather hard. The style of the play is that of the lyrical group, and I should put it in 1595, preferably before *Midsummer-Night's Dream*, as its theme seems to be parodied in that of Pyramus and Thisbe, and its wall (ii. 1, 2) in Snout's wall. This and another point of staging are discussed in *Eliz. Stage*, iii. 94, 98. Weever's mention of Romeo (App. B, no. xix) has been put as early as 1595, but may be as late as 1599.

---

[1] *Eliz. Stage*, iv. 208.

A ballad on the story was registered on 5 August 1596.[1] The plague is recalled (v. 2. 9). The 'first and second cause' (ii. 4. 25) are from Segar's *Book of Honor* (1590). Rosaline (ii. 4. 4, 14) recalls her namesake of *Love's Labour's Lost*. There is a general resemblance of phrase and imagery to much in the *Sonnets*. All this fits well enough with 1595. The company was then the Chamberlain's, but the Q1 title-page uses the designation which it bore when that was printed. We learn from Marston (App. B, no. xv) that the play was at the Curtain about 1598. There is no evidence of a Jacobean revival, beyond two alterations of 'Zounds' (iii. 1. 52, 104) in F, which retains the rest of the profanity.

The theme of escape from marriage through a sleeping-draught is as old as the *Ephesiaca* of Xenophon of Ephesus (4th cent. A. D. ?). It came to Shakespeare through an Italian channel. Masuccio of Salerno told the story, much in its later form, of Sienese lovers in his *Il Novellino* (1476). Luigi da Porto's *Istoria di due Nobili Amanti* (c. 1524) transferred it to Romeo and Giulietta at Verona, and connected it with the noble families of Dante, *Purgatorio*, vi. 106, 'Vieni a veder Montecchi e Cappelletti', although the Cappelletti seem to have been really of Cremona. From Da Porto it passed to the *Infelice Amore* (1553) of G. Bolderi, the *Novelle* (1554) of Matteo Bandello, and the *Hadriana* (1578) of Luigi Groto. It was treated as serious Veronese history by Girolamo de la Corte (1594–6), who followed Bandello in placing it during the rule (c. 1303) of Bartolomeo della Scala. There were various offshoots, including the *Castelvines y Monteses* of the Spanish Lope de Vega. Pierre Boaistuau translated Bandello in the *Histoires Tragiques* (1559), and was in turn translated in William Painter's *Palace of Pleasure* (1565–7), and more freely handled in Arthur Brooke's poem *The Tragicall Historye of Romeus and Juliet* (1562). Of this Bernard Garter's *Two English Lovers* (1563) is an imitation, with other names. A *Roméo et Juliette* by Côme de la Gambe, *dit* Chasteauvieux, was being played in France

---

[1] Arber, iii. 68.

about 1581, but is not preserved.[1] Shakespeare had probably read Painter, and not very successful attempts have been made to show that he used Luigi Groto and Lope de Vega. But substantially his source, so far as we know, was Brooke. Brooke, however, says, 'I saw the same argument lately set foorth on stage with more commendation, then I can looke for: (being there much better set forth then I haue or can dooe)'. He does not tell us whether this play was Latin or English, popular or academic, and we cannot say whether it accounts for any of Shakespeare's divergences from *Romeus and Juliet*. A fragmentary *Romeus et Julietta* in *Sloane MS.* 1775 dates from about 1615.[2] But Brooke's statement has naturally encouraged those who believe that Shakespeare rewrote an earlier play. Fuller has attempted to trace one behind the Dutch *Romeo en Juliette* of J. Struijs (1634), but does not convince me that this had any source other than Boaistuau, who was translated into Dutch by 1618. A *Romeo and Juliet* was played at Nördlingen in 1604 and at Dresden in 1626 and 1646.[3] Robertson unjustifiably assigns to 1626 the MS. of the extant German *Romio und Julietta*, which according to Creizenach, *Schauspiele der Englischen Komödianten*, xli, is shown by dialect and local allusions to have been written in Austria during the second half of the seventeenth century. It is based upon Shakespeare in the Q2 form, since it uses passages (iii. 1. 157–80; v. 3. 12–17) as there given and not in Q1. But it has a preliminary scene in which the Prince reconciles Montague and Capulet, and this, according to Robertson, must go back to England in 1562 when 'the dangers of civil strife are seriously dwelt upon', and 'is inexplicable as a German recast'. I cannot imagine why. The dangers of civil strife have been obvious to all peoples in all ages. There were German renderings of Boaistuau from 1615 onwards.

[1] E. Lanson in *Revue d'Hist. Litt.* x. 199; G. H. White in *N.Q.* cliv. 95.

[2] *Eliz. Stage*, iv. 378.

[3] *Ibid.* ii. 283; Herz 86.

XI. RICHARD THE SECOND

[S.R. 1597.] 29° Augusti. Andrew Wise. Entred for his Copie by appoyntment from master Warden Man, The Tragedye of Richard the Second vj^d (Arber, iii. 89).

[Q1. 1597.] The Tragedie of King Richard the second. As it hath beene publikely acted by the right Honourable the Lorde Chamberlaine his Seruants. [Simmes's device (McKerrow 142)] London Printed by Valentine Simmes for Androw Wise, and are to be sold at his shop in Paules church yard at the signe of the Angel. 1597. [*No head-title. Running-title*] The Tragedie of King Richard the second.

Facsimiles. C. Praetorius (1888, *Sh. Q.* xviii, from Huth, now B.M., copy, ed. W. A. Harrison). W. Griggs (1890, *Sh. Q.* xvii, from Devonshire, now Huntington, copy, ed. P. A. Daniel).

[Q2. 1598.] The Tragedie of King Richard the second. As it hath beene publikely acted by the Right Honourable the Lord Chamberlaine his seruants. By William Shake-speare. [Simmes's device (McKerrow 142)] London Printed by Valentine Simmes for Andrew Wise, and are to be sold at his shop in Paules churchyard at the signe of the Angel. 1598. [*No head-title. Running-title*] The Tragedie of King Richard the Second.

[Q3. 1598.] The Tragedie of King Richard the second. As it hath beene publikely acted by the Right Honourable the Lord Chamberlaine his seruants. By William Shake-speare. [Simmes's device (McKerrow 142)] London Printed by Valentine Simmes, for Andrew Wise, and are to be solde at his shop in Paules churchyard, at the signe of the Angel. 1598. [*No head-title. Running-title*] The Tragedie of King Richard the Second.

[W. A. White collection.]
Facsimile. A. W. Pollard (1916).

[S.R. 1603.] 25 Junij. Mathew Lawe. Entred for his copies in full courte Holden this Day. These ffyve copies folowinge . . . viz iij enterludes or playes . . . The second of Richard the .2. . . . all kinges . . . all whiche by consent

of the Company are sett over to him from Andrew Wyse
(Arber, iii. 239).

[Q4. 1608.] The Tragedie of King Richard the second. As
it hath been publikely acted by the Right Honourable the
Lord Chamberlaine his seruantes. By William Shake-speare.
[White's device (McKerrow 188ᵇ)] London, Printed
by W⟨illiam⟩ W⟨hite⟩ for Matthew Law, and are to be
sold at his shop in Paules Church-yard, at the signe of the
Foxe. 1608. [*No head-title. Running-title*] The Tragedie
of Richard [*or* King Richard] the Second.

[*Cancel t.p. in some copies.*] The Tragedie of King Richard
the Second: With new additions of the Parliament Sceane,
and the deposing of King Richard, As it hath been lately
acted by the Kinges Majesties seruantes, at the Globe.
By William Shake-speare. [White's device (McKerrow
188ᵇ)] At London, Printed by W. W. for Mathew Law,
and are to be sold at his shop in Paules Church-yard, at
the signe of the Foxe. 1608.

Facsimile. C. Praetorius (1888, *Sh. Q.* xix, ed. W. A. Harrison).

[Q5. 1615.] The Tragedie of King Richard the Second:
With new additions of the Parliament Sceane, and the
deposing of King Richard. As it hath been lately acted
by the Kinges Maiesties seruants, at the Globe. By
William Shake-speare [Ornament] At London, Printed
for Mathew Law, and are to be sold at his shop in Paules
Church-yard, at the signe of the Foxe. 1615. [*No
head-title. Running-title*] The Tragedie of Richard the
Second.

[F1. 1623.] [*Catalogue*] The Life & death of Richard the
second. [*Histories*, pp. 23–45, sign. b 6–d 5. *Head-title*] The
life and death of King Richard the Second. [*Running-title*]
The life (Life) and death (Death) of Richard the second.
[Acts and scc. marked.]

[Q6. 1634.] By Iohn Norton.

Facsimile. C. Praetorius (1887, *Sh. Q.* xx, ed. P. A. Daniel).

Parallel-Text. A. Waites (1892, *Bankside*, Q1+F1).

Modern Editions. E. K. Chambers (1891, *Falcon*); C. H. Herford

(1893, *Warwick*); I. B. John (1912, 1925, *Arden*); Ll. M. Buell (1921, *Yale*).

Dissertations. A. Schmidt, *Qq and F von R. II* (1880, *J.* xv. 301); H. R. Plomer, *An Examination of Some Existing Copies of Hayward's King Henrie IV* (1902, 2 *Library*, iii. 13); F. W. Moorman, *Sh.'s History Plays and Daniel's Civile Wars* (1904, *J.* xl. 69); J. M. Robertson, *The Authorship of R. II* (1923, *Sh. Canon*, ii. 45); E. M. Albright, *Sh.'s R. II and the Essex Conspiracy* (1927, *P.M.L.A.* xlii. 686); E. P. Kuhl, *Sh. and Hayward* (1928, *S.P.* xxv. 312).

The interrelation of the texts is minutely examined in Pollard's admirable introduction to Q3. Q1 is a good text, and may very possibly have been printed from the author's manuscripts. Modern editors find on an average one error of wording to a page. Seventeen corrections were made during printing, and the extant examples contain corrected and uncorrected sheets in various combinations. The punctuation is generally careless and inadequate, but becomes more elaborate in set speeches; and here Pollard (cf. p. 191) is inclined to trace the author's hand. A few mislineations are generally due to the merging of short with full lines. I think there may be some textual disturbance in York's speech of ii. 2. 98–122, which reads very unmetrically. A variant spelling of 'Martiall' for 'Marshall' in three out of four cases in i. 3 may have no significance. The stage-directions are of the short type, which now becomes normal in Shakespeare's plays. The later Qq were successively set up from each other, with some correction of errors, and a progressive accumulation of new ones, to which Q2 is the chief contributor. The 'abdication' or 'deposition' scene (iv. 1. 154–318) first appears in Q4; it is in all extant examples, but all have not the cancel title-page calling attention to it. Some omissions and much mislineation, partly due to these, suggest that the copy was derived from a shorthand report. F is shown by the retention of some Q errors to have been set up from a Q. This was probably Q5, but just possibly Q3. Many fresh errors are introduced, and there are some colourless verbal variants, which are probably best ascribed (cf. p. 180) to the subconscious operations of the compositor's mind. But many Q1 readings are also restored, and there are a few corrections, including two on points of historical fact, which are perhaps beyond the normal capacity of a press corrector. Moreover, the stage-directions are elaborated; there is a general substitution of 'Heaven' for 'God'; the 'abdication' scene is properly lined; and the omission of passages amounting to about 50 lines in all (i. 3. 129–33, 239–42, 268–93; iii. 2. 29–32; iv. 1. 52–9) may be due to a desire for shortening or the removal of obscurities. Pollard thinks that the example of Q5 used had been imperfectly collated with one of Q1 altered to serve as prompt-copy.[1]

Some evidence for a date of production in 1595 is furnished by Samuel Daniel's *Civil Wars between Lancaster and York*. This was registered on 11 October 1594. Two editions appeared in 1595, and the second of these contains parallels to *Richard II*, which are not in the first. Obviously both might have preceded the play, but on the whole it seems more likely, especially on the analogy of Daniel's handling of his *Cleopatra* (cf. *Antony and Cleopatra*), that he made these alterations after seeing it. And there is some confirmation of a 1595 date in a letter (App. D) from Sir Edward Hoby, apparently inviting Sir Robert Cecil to a performance of *Richard II* on December 9 of that year. This again is not quite conclusive, as one cannot be certain that the play was new. And although the style and lyrical tone of the scenes in which Richard figures would fit well enough with 1595, there is much poor and bombastic matter, especially in Acts i and v, which recalls the period of *2, 3 Henry VI* and *Richard III*. Certainly Shakespeare is still under the influence of Marlowe in his handling of chronicle-history. Robertson, indeed, boldly claims the whole play as one by Marlowe or by Marlowe and Peele, 'substantially preserved' in an adaptation by Shakespeare. I do not think that such parallels of vocabulary and diction as he produces are in the least capable of proving this; or that there is any clear evidence of Marlowe's hand, as distinct from his influence; or that it is plausible to argue that Marlowe is likely to have made a use of continuous

[1] Cf., however, p. 165.

rhymed dialogue, which is markedly absent from his known plays. Nor do I think that Peele writing poor matter under Marlowe's influence can be discriminated with any assurance on purely internal grounds from Shakespeare writing poor matter under the same influence. The conception of Richard's tragedy, as well as its detailed presentation, seems to me clearly Shakespearean and not Marlowean; and it is safest to assume that in the inferior scenes Shakespeare, completely uninterested in chronicle-history as such, allowed himself to slip into a perfunctory and traditional treatment of all that was not directly concerned with that tragedy. It is quite possible that he had an older source-play before him, and conceivably he may have preserved rather more of a predecessor's phrasing than he did in the almost contemporary *King John*. If so, it probably dealt, perhaps in a first part, with the murder of Thomas, Duke of Gloucester, a knowledge of which seems assumed in the play as it stands. Certainly there were other Elizabethan plays on the reign, besides Shakespeare's. There was the old *Life and Death of Jack Straw*, printed in 1593, but this does not cover the murder.[1] There was the play, sometimes called *Thomas of Woodstock*, preserved in *Egerton MS.* 1994.[2] This, although the manuscript has probably been used for a seventeenth-century revival, seems to be of sixteenth-century composition. It might conceivably be a first part of Shakespeare's source, if he had one. There are some slight verbal resemblances to *Richard II*, and the subject is the death of Gloucester, although this is not treated exactly as we should expect from the references in *Richard II*, since Mowbray is not among the characters. Neither *Jack Straw* nor *Thomas of Woodstock* can be definitely assigned to any company with which Shakespeare was concerned. But we do know from Simon Forman (App. D) that in 1611 the King's men had a *Richard II* other than Shakespeare's, the description of which does not answer to either of them, but which covered Straw's riot, the death of Gloucester, on lines inconsistent with *Richard II*, and a plot of John of Gaunt

---

[1] *Eliz. Stage*, iv. 22.   [2] *Ibid.* iv. 42; cf. p. 111.

to make his son king. Whether it also covered the actual
deposition of Richard is not clear. Perhaps it is even more
likely than *Thomas of Woodstock* to represent the first part
of a source-play used by Shakespeare.

There are many indications of an analogy present to
the Elizabethan political imagination between the reign
of Richard II and that of Elizabeth herself. A letter of Sir
Francis Knollys on 9 January 1578 excuses himself for giving unwelcome counsel to the queen.[1] He will not 'play the
partes of King Richard the Second's men'; will not be a
courtly and unstatesmanlike flatterer. Clearly the phrase
was familiar. Henry Lord Hunsdon similarly wrote at
some date before 1588, 'I never was one of Richard II's
men'.[2] More cryptic is a letter from Raleigh to Robert
Cecil on 6 July 1597, 'I acquaynted my L: generall
⟨Essex⟩ with your letter to mee & your kynd acceptance
of your enterteynemente, hee was also wonderfull merry
att yᵉ consait of Richard the 2. I hope it shall never alter,
& whereof I shalbe most gladd of as the trew way to all
our good, quiett & advancement, and most of all for her
sake whose affaires shall therby fynd better progression.'[3]
All these allusions are of course in perfect loyalty, the
utterances of devoted, if critical, officials. In 1597 Cecil,
Raleigh, and Essex were for once on friendly terms. The
publication of *Richard II*, without the abdication scene,
came shortly after Cecil wrote. In 1598 a disgruntled
Essex drifted into an attitude of political opposition, and
the government became, or professed to become, aware of
an unfriendly parallel drawn between Elizabeth herself
and the deposed Richard.[4] John Hayward's prose history
of *The First Part of the Life and Raigne of King Henrie IIII*
was registered on 9 January 1599 and published with a
dedicatory epistle to Essex, which contained a dangerous
description of him as 'magnus et presenti iudicio et futuri
temporis expectatione'. Apparently Essex took alarm and,
after keeping the book by him for a fortnight, moved the
Archbishop of Canterbury to require the cancellation of the

[1] Wright, ii. 74. [2] Strickland 653.   nenbaum, *Problems*, 209.
[3] Edwards, ii. 169; facs. at Tan-   [4] Cf. vol. ii, p. 323.

epistle. A second edition of the book was suppressed altogether. At the trial of Essex on 5 June 1600 for his proceedings in Ireland, his relation to the book, which the queen had come to regard as seditious, was made one of the charges against him. In July Hayward and Samuel Harsnett, who had given the licence for publication, were called before the Star Chamber; and Hayward was imprisoned. An official note of evidence against Essex compiled at this time lays stress not only on the offending epistle to the book, but also on 'the Erle himself' being so often present at the playing thereof, and with great applause giving countenance and lyking to the same'. A few months later, on 8 February 1601, Essex attempted rebellion. On the day before some of his supporters had gone to the Globe, where they had persuaded Augustine Phillips to revive an old play of Richard II. Evidence of this was given at their arraignment for participation in Essex's treason, and was used with Hayward's book to suggest that the earl, who had some remote claim to the crown through a descent from Thomas of Woodstock, had planned to play the part of Henry Bolingbroke to Elizabeth's Richard. On all this several interesting points arise. In the first place, there can surely be little doubt that the play of 7 February was Shakespeare's. It was given by the Chamberlain's men. A play produced in 1595 and laid aside might well be 'stale', from the theatrical point of view, by 1601. It dealt with the deposing and killing of the king, and although we know from Forman that the company had another play of *Richard II* in 1611, it is on the whole improbable that its subject-matter overlapped with Shakespeare's. That some of the references speak of a play of 'Henry IV' is immaterial. The frequent performances which Essex was accused in 1600 of having attended must of course have been earlier than that of 1601, at which indeed he was not present. They are no doubt those which the Queen spoke of to Lambarde in 1601 as given '40^tie times in open streets and houses'. And they may reasonably be placed about 1595, in view of a statement in some *Directions for Preachers* of 1601 that

Essex had been plotting treason for six or seven years.[1] The deposition scene was evidently given at the 1601 performance. I think it was probably given in 1595 also. That it was part of the original writing is quite clear. The lines immediately preceding it have been altered in Q1 to square with the excision, but this has left without point the Abbot's subsequent comment 'A woeful Pageant haue we here beheld'. Pollard, however, thinks that it may have been cut in representation, partly because the Chamberlain's men thought that there was 'too much Richard' in the play, and partly because of the Pope's bull of deposition in 1596. There was (cf. p. 366) no such bull, and it seems to me more likely that the interest taken by Essex in the play led to some popular application of the theme to current politics, and this in turn to the intervention of the censor, perhaps at the theatre, but more probably when the play came to be printed. That it was written with any seditious intent is of course most unlikely, and indeed only an unreasonably sensitive instinct of suspicion could regard the deposition scene in particular as encouraging resentment against Richard. The Hunsdons, whom the company served, were always loyal supporters of Elizabeth, and in no way entangled with the fortunes of Essex, even if Essex himself can be supposed to have had any notion of aping Henry of Bolingbroke as early as 1595. Nor is Sir Edward Hoby likely to have invited Cecil, of all men, to witness a disloyal play. And Shakespeare's own supposed attachment to Essex is a merely speculative theory. Even in 1601, little blame seems to have fallen upon the Chamberlain's men. A passage in *Hamlet* (q.v.) may imply that they travelled for a time. But they were at court a few days after the trial of Essex and several times in the following winter. Under James, who had an affectionate remembrance of Essex, the deposition scene could safely be printed. The 1608 title-page and the attention paid to the *Act of Abuses* in the F text indicate a Jacobean revival. Probably Shakespeare's was the *Richard II* given at sea (App. D) by Keeling's sailors in

[1] Cheyney, ii. 535.

1607. They are not likely to have used anything but a printed play. There was a revival at the Globe in 1631 (App. D).

The main source of *Richard II* was the *Chronicle* of Holinshed, in the second edition of 1587, since ii. 4. 8 uses a passage not in that of 1577. For a few historical points other chroniclers may have been drawn upon. Two features not in Holinshed, the introduction of Queen Isabel, and the attribution of a soliloquy to Richard just before his murder, are common to *Richard II* and the first edition of Daniel's poem, but the treatment, both of these topics and of the rest of the action, is so different as to make an influence either way unlikely. Miss Albright's suggestion that Shakespeare may have used Hayward's history in manuscript is perverse, in view of the relative dates of the prints. She rests it on a statement by Hayward that he had contemplated handling the subject a dozen years back, and neglects his further statements that he had told no one of this, and only began to write the book a year before it was published. There are parallels, but they may best be explained through use by the historian of the play.

XII. A MIDSUMMER-NIGHT'S DREAM

[S.R. 1600.] 8 Octobris. Thomas Fyssher. Entred for his copie vnder the handes of master Rodes and the Wardens. A booke called A mydsommer nightes Dreame vj^d. (Arber, iii. 174).

[Q1. 1600.] [Ornament] A Midsommer nights dreame. As it hath beene sundry times publickely acted, by the Right honourable, the Lord Chamberlaine his seruants. Written by William Shakespeare. [Fisher's device (McKerrow 321)] ¶ Imprinted at London, for Thomas Fisher, and are to be soulde at his shoppe, at the Signe of the White Hart, in Fleetestreete. 1600. [*Head-title*] A Midsommer Nights Dreame. [*Running-title*] A Midsommer nightes dreame. [The printer may be Allde or Bradock. An elaborate ornament at the end recurs on the t.p. of *Edward II* (1594), and that is linked by its final ornament to *Edward II* (1598), which Bradock printed.]

Facsimile. W. Griggs (1880, *Sh. Q.* iii, ed. J. W. Ebsworth).

[Q2. 1619.] [Ornament.]   A Midsommer nights dreame.
As it hath beene sundry times publikely acted, by the
Right Honourable, the Lord Chamberlaine his seruants.
Written by William Shakespeare. [W. Jaggard's device,
formerly Roberts's (McKerrow 136)]   Printed by Iames
Roberts, 1600. [*Head-title*] A Midsommer Nights
Dreame. [*Running-title*] A Midsommer nights Dreame.
[On the misdating cf. p. 133.]
Facsimile. W. Griggs (1880, *Sh. Q.* iv, ed. J. W. Ebsworth).

[F1. 1623.] [*Catalogue*] Midsommer Nights Dreame.
[*Comedies*, pp. 145–62, sign. N–O 3ᵛ. *Head-title*] A Mid-
sommer Nights Dreame. [*Running-title*] A Midsommer
nights Dreame.
[Acts marked.]
Parallel-Text. W. Reynolds (1890, *Bankside*, Q1 + F1).

Modern Editions. H. H. Furness (1895, *New Variorum*); E. K.
Chambers (1897, *Warwick*); H. Cuningham (1905, *Arden*); W. H.
Durham (1918, *Yale*); A. T. Quiller-Couch and J. D. Wilson
(1924, *C.U.P.*).

Dissertations. J. O. Halliwell-Phillipps, *Introduction to M.N.D.* (1841),
Illustrations of the Fairy Mythology of M.N.D. (1845, Sh. Soc.), *Memoranda
on M.N.D.* (1879); N. J. Halpin, *Oberon's Vision in M.N.D.* (1843, Sh.
Soc.); C. C. Hense, *Shs M.N.D. Erläutert* (1851); K. Elze, *Zum M.N.D.*
(1868, *J.* iii. 150; *Essays*, 30); H. Kurz, *Zum M.N.D.* (1869, *J.* iv. 268);
F. Krauss, *Eine Quelle zu Shs M.N.D.* (1876, *J.* xi. 226); B. ten Brink,
Über den M.N.D. (1878, *J.* xiii. 92); L. E. A. Proescholdt, *On the Sources
of M.N.D.* (1878); A. Schmidt, *Die ältesten Ausgaben des M.N.D.* (1881);
Dr. Finkenbrink, *The Date, Plot and Sources of M.N.D.* (1884); K.
Gaedertz, *Zur Kenntniss der altenglischen Bühne* (1888); E. Flügel,
Pyramys and Tysbe (1889, *Anglia*, xii. 13, 631); G. Hart, *Die Pyramus-
und-Thisbe Saga* (1889–91); A. Würzner, *Die Orthographie der beiden Qq
von Shs M.N.D.* (1893); G. Sarrazin, *Die Abfassungszeit des M.N.D.* (1895,
Archiv, xcv. 291), *Scenarie und Staffage im M.N.D.* (1900, *Archiv*, civ.
67); L. Fränkel, *Vor-Shakespearesches Pyramus und Thisbe-Stück?* (1897,
J. xxxiii. 275); R. Tobler, *Shs M.N.D. und Montemayor's Diana* (1898,
J. xxxiv. 358); W. Vollhardt, *Die Beziehungen der M.N.D. zum italie-
nischen Schäferdrama* (1899); F. von Westenholtz, *Shs Gewonnene Liebes-
müh* (1902, Jan. 14, *Beilage zur Allgemeine Zeitung*); H. Reich, *Der Mann
mit dem Eselskopf* (1904, *J.* xl. 108); F. Sidgwick, *Sources and Analogues of
M.N.D.* (1908, *Sh. Classics*); S. B. Hemingway, *The Relation of M.N.D.
to R.J.* (1911, *M.L.N.* xxvi. 78); E. K. Chambers, *The Occasion of M.N.D.*
(1916, *Sh. Homage*, 154); W. J. Lawrence, *Sh. from a New Angle* (1919,

Studies, viii. 442), *Date of M.N.D.* (1920, Dec. 9, *T.L.S.*), *A Plummet for Bottom's Dream* (1922, *Fortnightly*, cxvii. 833; *Sh.'s Workshop*, 75); A. Lefranc, *Le Réalité dans M.N.D.* (1920, *Mélanges Bernard Bouvier*); E. Rickert, *Political Propaganda and Satire in M.N.D.* (1923, *M.P.* xxi. 53, 133); A. Eichler, *Das Höfbühnenmässige in Shs M.N.D.* (1925, *J.* lxi. 39); H. Spencer, *A Nice Derangement* (1930, *M.L.R.* xxv. 23).

Q1 is a fairly well-printed text, with some abnormal spellings, and may be from the author's manuscript. The stage-directions are not elaborate. Q2 is from Q1, and F1 from Q2, but Wilson's analysis points to the incorporation of notes for a revival. The clearest indication is the stage-direction at v. 1. 128, 'Tawyer with a Trumpet before them'. A division into Acts has been superimposed upon a text written for continuous performance, resulting in the stage-direction at the end of iii, 'They sleepe all the Act', by which is meant the act-interval.

The hymeneal character of the theme has led to the reasonable conjecture that the play was given at a noble wedding, and various writers have suggested the weddings of (1) Robert Earl of Essex and Frances Lady Sidney in April or May 1590, (2) Sir Thomas Heneage and Mary Countess of Southampton on 2 May 1594, (3) William Earl of Derby and Elizabeth Vere at Greenwich on 26 January 1595, (4) Thomas Berkeley and Elizabeth Carey at Blackfriars on 19 February 1596, (5) Henry Earl of Southampton and Elizabeth Vernon about February or August 1598, (6) Henry Lord Herbert and Anne Russell at Blackfriars on 16 June 1600. There is obvious flattery of Queen Elizabeth as the 'fair vestal throned by the west' (ii. 1. 148–68), and a possible allusion to the bride in the 'little western flower' on which Cupid's bolt, harmless against the 'imperial votaress', fell. The imagery of this passage has been regarded as a reminiscence of the entertainment of Elizabeth at Kenilworth in 1575, and more plausibly of that by the Earl of Hertford at Elvetham in 1591,[1] although there is a generic quality about such pageants, and the special feature of 'a mermaid on a dolphin's back' does not belong to either occasion. The

[1] *Eliz. Stage*, i. 122.

flattery does not of course prove that Elizabeth was present at the wedding celebrated by *Midsummer-Night's Dream*, although it is likely enough. She was in fact at weddings (3) and (6), and very possibly at (4), since the bride was her god-daughter, and the grand-daughter of her cousin and Lord Chamberlain. It may be assumed that she was not at (1), (2), and (5), all of which brought the bride-grooms into disfavour, while (5) was in secret, and not likely to have received the publicity of a play. Considera-tions of date also make (1), (5), and (6) improbable, and the effective choice lies between (3) and (4). I have de-scribed the circumstances of these in *Sh. Homage*, 154, but should add that the Derby wedding was certainly at Greenwich, although the Queen seems to have accom-panied the bride to Burghley House a few days later, and a play might have been given at either place.[1] Of the Berkeley wedding, unfortunately, no details are known. The Queen was at Richmond, but could easily have come to Blackfriars by river. The use of the Chamberlain's company would be natural enough on this occasion, since the bride's grandfather and father were its successive patrons; and Sir George Carey's musical establishment (cf. vol. ii, p. 86) could perhaps supply any additional boys needed to impersonate fairies. Some of the Chamber-lain's men had of course formerly been the men of Derby's brother and predecessor, Ferdinando, Earl of Derby. Earl William, however, had a company of his own, although, so far as we know, only a provincial one.[2] A family chronicler tells us that affection between Thomas Berkeley and Elizabeth Carey began in the autumn of 1595. Wil-liam Stanley and Elizabeth Vere might possibly have met at Elvetham in 1591, but a conceivable reflection of that in the 'little western flower' is too slight a clue to lay stress upon. Either wedding would fit such indications of date as the play yields. It belongs to the lyric group of 1594–6. I do not think that the proposed show of Muses mourning for the death of learning in beggary (v. 1. 52) is an allusion to the death of Robert Greene in 1592. It was to be a

---

[1] Cf. *Eliz. Stage*, iv. 109.   [2] *Ibid*. ii. 126.

'satire, keen and critical', which suggests something on the lines of Spenser's *Tears of the Muses*. Greene, although a University man, could hardly stand for a typical representative of learning in such a connexion. If any particular death was in mind, Tasso's, on 30 April 1595, seems more plausible. The bad weather described in ii. 1. 81–117 is probably that which began in March 1594, prevailed during the greater part of that year, and ushered in a long period of corn shortage (cf. App. A, no. xii). The alarm of the clowns (iii. 1. 33) lest that 'fearful wild-fowl' the lion might scare the ladies recalls the abandonment of a projected lion at the baptismal feast of the Scottish Prince Henry on 30 August 1594, *A True Reportarie* of which was registered on 24 October 1594.[1] This allusion, as well as that to the weather, would be more up to date in January 1595 than in February 1596. On the other hand, if Pyramus and Thisbe parody *Romeo and Juliet* (q.v.), *Midsummer-Night's Dream* is likely to be the later play of the two. Moreover, there are allusions (i. 2. 31, 42; v. 1. 47) to the labours of Hercules, and, while this is nothing in itself, the last appears to confuse his fight against the Centaurs with that of Theseus, and may echo the similar confusion in Heywood's *Silver Age*,[2] which again may be the 2 *Hercules* produced by the Admiral's on 23 May 1595.[3] The labours of Hercules, however, had been dramatized before 1592.[4]

There remains the question whether *Midsummer-Night's Dream* is all of even date. In v. 1. 1–84 correctly lined passages alternate with others which are mislined, and I agree with Wilson that the latter probably represent additional matter written without lineation in the margin of the manuscript. They are a little more freely written than the original lines which they supplement. This hardly excludes the possibility that they were afterthoughts at the time of original composition. Wilson, however, also points out that the fairy mask of v. 1. 378–429 and the epilogue of 430–45 look very much like alternative endings to the

---

[1] Arber, ii. 662.
[2] ed. Pearson, iii. 141–4.
[3] *Eliz. Stage*, iii. 344.
[4] *Ibid.* iv. 241.

play. On the whole I think that there has probably been some revision in v. I take the epilogue as the later ending, and conjecture that children used for a mask at the wedding were not available on the public stage; and that possibly some personal allusions to the bride and bridegroom were also replaced by other matter, in order to adapt the play for theatrical use. Others, however, carry the notion of revision a great deal farther. Wilson himself conjectures an original writing in 1592 or earlier and an intermediate revision in 1594, both possibly hymeneal, as well as a final revision, which he believes to have covered the fairy scenes as well as the last act, and to have been for the Southampton wedding of 1598. His case for the first revision rests mainly upon differences of style between the lover scenes and the fairy scenes, which, such as they are, seem to me sufficiently explained by the difference of subject-matter; and that for the revision of the fairy scenes themselves upon the appearance of generic for personal names in the stage-directions and speech-prefixes of certain passages, which also I find unconvincing (cf. p. 232). I have discussed this reconstruction more fully in *M.L.R.* xx. 340. Lawrence thinks that the play was written in 1598 to gratify a popular taste for 'nocturnals', and that 'Phibbus car' (i. 2. 37) is a gird at Dekker's lost *Phaethon* of that year.[1] This hardly seems to need refutation. He assigns a revision to the Herbert wedding of 1600, and takes the death of learning to be the death of Spenser in 1599. But we have an account of the Herbert wedding, which tells of a mask of eight, not nine, Muses, but of no play.[2] Miss Rickert supposes that the play was planned by the Earl of Hertford in 1595, as a political move, encouraged by the Cecils, in support of his son's claim of succession to the crown; that this son is the changeling (ii. 1. 21, 120); that the rival claim of James of Scotland and his offers of marriage to Elizabeth were satirized in Bottom; that Hertford dropped the scheme; and that the play was adapted for the public stage about 1598 by a revision 'by which both the allegory and the satire were

[1] *Ibid.* iii. 302.   [2] *Ibid.* i. 169.

almost obscured'. The notion is worked out with great
ingenuity, and is quite incredible. No doubt plays in deri-
sion of James were given in England;[1] and if the traits
of resemblance noted by Miss Rickert seem rather far-
fetched, much can be done by make-up. But Hertford and
the Cecils could never have conceived that a presentation
in which it is Titania who is enamoured of Bottom, rather
than Bottom of Titania, would make a satire attractive
to Elizabeth. Equally impossible is the assumed adaptation
of the discarded skit for theatrical use, since if the allegory
and satire are there at all, they are not so far 'obscured'
as not to be still apparent, at any rate to Miss Rickert.
    But I am breaking a butterfly. It is an amusing com-
ment that *Midsummer-Night's Dream* was probably one
of the first plays chosen for revival before James, on
1 January 1604. 'We had', writes Dudley Carleton to
John Chamberlain, 'a play of Robin goode-fellow.'[2] F
only expunges a single profanity (v. 1. 326), but it was
probably a later revival than that of 1604 in which Tawyer
(cf. *supra*) played, and there is a curious story (App. D) of
what appears to have been yet another for the Sabbath
delectation of Bishop Williams in 1631. A commonwealth droll of *The Merry Conceited Humours of Bottom the
Weaver* was printed in 1661 and in Francis Kirkman's
Wits, or Sport upon Sport (1672).
    There is no comprehensive source. Shakespeare was
presumably familiar with fairies and with Robin Goodfellow in Warwickshire folk-lore. There is much of Robin
in R. Scot, *Discovery of Witchcraft* (1584), together with
a version of the story, as old as Lucian and Apuleius, of
transformation into an ass. W. Adlington's translation
(1566) of Apuleius was more than once reprinted. There
is no ground, other than forgeries (cf. App. F, no. xi, *n*),
for assuming a sixteenth-century version of *Robin Goodfellow, his Mad Prankes and Merry Jests*, registered on
25 April 1627, or of the ballad of *The Mad Merry Prankes
of Robin Goodfellow*, registered on 23 March 1631. The
nature of a play of The King of Fairies, mentioned by

---

[1] *Eliz. Stage*, i. 323.   [2] *Ibid.* iii. 279.

Nashe in 1589 and Greene in 1592, is unknown.[1] Oberon comes ultimately from the romance of *Huon of Bordeaux*, and an old play with this title was given by Sussex's men in 1593–4 (App. D). Oberon is the fairy king in Greene's *James IV*,[2] and Auberon in the Elvetham entertainment. Here the queen is Aureola, and in a Woodstock entertainment of 1575 Eambia.[3] Ovid, *Met.* iii. 173, but not his translator Golding, uses Titania as a synonym for Diana. In W. Bettie's *Titana and Theseus*, registered on 13 August 1608, she is not a fairy, but a mortal princess. A hint for the love-juice might have been taken from Chaucer, *Merchant's Tale*, 2258, where the fairies are Pluto and Proserpine, or from Montemayor, *Diana Enamorada* (cf. *T.G.*). Chaucer's *Knightes Tale* or North's *Plutarch* (1579) would furnish the Theseus matter, and the *Merchant's Tale*, 2128, happens also to have one of many allusions to the well-known story of Pyramus and Thisbe. A book of 'Perymus and Thesbye' was registered by William Griffith in 1562–3, but is unknown.[4] Nor can statements by Warton, *H.E.P.* iv. 297, and Collier, *Stationers' Registers*, ii. 80, that it was printed for Thomas Hacket, be verified. T. More, *A Dialogue of Comfort against Tribulation* (Tottell, 1553), has an engraved representation of the story on its title-page, which can hardly have been originally designed for that book. It recurs in J. Brende's *History of Quintus Curcius* (Tottell, 1553), according to Gaedertz 25, who traces it to a German engraving of 1526, which he ascribes to Lucas Cranach. There are some verbal resemblances to Shakespeare's treatment in a poem by I. Thomson in Clement Robinson's *Handefull of Pleasant Delites* (1584). A play on the theme by N⟨athaniel?⟩ R⟨ichards?⟩ in *Addl. MS.* 15227, f. 56ᵛ, is of seventeenth-century origin. The repertory of a company, possibly of English actors, at Nördlingen and Rothenburg in 1604, included a *Pyramus and Thisbe*,[5] but Herz 79 shows that the story was well known on the Continent, and had been dramatized in Germany by 1601.

---

[1] *Ibid.* iv. 236, 241.
[2] *Ibid.* iii. 330.
[3] *Ibid.* iii. 402; iv. 66.

[4] Arber, i. 215.
[5] *Eliz. Stage*, ii. 283.

XIII. KING JOHN

[1591.] The Troublesome Raigne of Iohn King of England, with the discouerie of King Richard Cordelions Base sonne (vulgarly named, The Bastard Fawconbridge): also the death of King Iohn at Swinstead Abbey. As it was (sundry times) publikely acted by the Queenes Maiesties Players, in the honourable Citie of London. [Thomas Orwin's device (McKerrow 273)] Imprinted at London for Sampson Clarke, and are to be solde at his shop, on the backeside of the Royall Exchange. 1591. [*Head-title*, under ornament with Stationers' arms and W. D., and *Running-title*] The troublesome Raigne of King Iohn.

[1591.] The Second part of the troublesome Raigne of King Iohn, conteining the death of Arthur Plantaginet, the landing of Lewes, and the poysning of King Iohn at Swinstead Abbey. As it was (sundry times) publikely acted by the Queenes Maiesties Players, in the honourable Citie of London. [Ornament] Imprinted at London for Sampson Clarke, and are to be solde at his shop, on the backeside of the Royall Exchange. 1591. [*Head-title*, under ornament as in Part i] The Second part of the troublesome Raigne of King Iohn, containing the entraunce of Lewes the French Kings sonne: with the poysoning of King Iohn by a Monke. [*Running-title*] The troublesome Raigne of King Iohn.

Facsimiles. C. Praetorius (1888, *Sh. Q.* xl, xli, ed. F. J. Furnivall); J. S. Farmer (1911, *T.F.T.*).

Modern Edition. F. J. Furnivall and J. Munro (1913, *Sh. Classics*).

[1611.] The First and second Part of the troublesome Raigne of John King of England. . . . As they were (sundry times) lately acted by the Queenes Maiesties Players. Written by W. Sh. . . . Valentine Simmes for Iohn Helme . . . 1611.

[Separate head-title for Part ii, but continuous signatures.]

[1622.] The First and second Part of the troublesome Raigne of John King of England. . . . As they were

(sundry times) lately acted. Written by W. Shakespeare.
. . . Aug. Mathewes for Thomas Dewe . . . 1622.

[Separate t.p. for Part ii, but continuous signatures. Dewe seems (Arber, iv. 190) to have had some partnership with John Helme, who died in 1616.]

[1623.] [*Catalogue*] The Life and Death of King John [*Histories*, pp. 1–22; sign. a–b 5ᵛ. *Head-* and *Running-titles*] The life and death of King John.

[Acts and scc. marked, with iv repeated for v (altered in modern editions).]

Parallel-Text. A. Morgan (1892, *Bankside*, xviii).

Modern Editions. F. G. Fleay (1878); G. C. Moore Smith (1900, *Warwick*); I. B. John (1907, *Arden*); H. H. Furness, jun. (1919, *New Variorum*); S. T. Williams (1927, *Yale*).

Dissertations. E. Rose, *Sh. as an Adapter* (1878, *Macmillan's Mag.*); G. H. E. Kopplow, *Shs K.J. und seine Quelle* (1900); G. C. Moore Smith, *Sh's K.J. and the T.R.* (1901, *Furnivall Misc.* 335); A. Kerrl, *Die Metrischen Unterschiede von Shs K.J. und J.C.* (1913); F. Liebermann, *Sh. als Bearbeiter des K.J.* (1921–2, *Archiv*, cxlii. 177; cxliii. 17, 190).

The bibliographical entries up to 1622 relate to the source-play, *The Troublesome Reign of King John*,[1] but the absence of *King John* from the S.R. entry for F1 suggests that, like *Taming of the Shrew*, it was regarded as commercially identical with its predecessor. Sampson Clarke is not traceable as a publisher beyond 1598, and it may be that thereafter *T.R.* was a derelict, and that neither John Helme nor Thomas Dewe could claim copyright against the F stationers. F is fairly well printed, with normal slight stage-directions. There are some variations in the speech-prefixes. 'Actus Secundus' has only 74 lines, at the end of which Constance is left on the stage. But the following iii. 1. 1 gives her a fresh entry. Modern editors attempt to cure this by turning 'Scaena Secunda' of F's 'Actus Primus' into ii and merging F's 'Actus Secundus' in iii. 1. It is not satisfactory. The juncture at iii. 1. 75 is very abrupt, and i in its turn is reduced to 276 lines. Possibly an original ii. 2 has been cut.

---

[1] *Eliz. Stage*, iv. 23.

There is practically no external evidence to fix the date of the play before its mention by Meres in 1598. *T.R.* was available in print by 1591. Basilisco (i. 1. 244) is in *Soliman and Perseda* (c. 1589–92). Little stress can be laid on suggestions that the Lopez plot of 1594 (cf. s.v. *M.V.*) recalled the poisoning of John, that repeated references (ii. 1. 335; v. 1. 17; v. 2. 48; v. 4. 53) to tempests and inundations reflect the weather of the same year (cf. s.v. *M.N.D.*), and that the 'choice of dauntless spirits' in 'English bottoms' (ii. 1. 72) made its appearance at the Cadiz expedition of 1596; perhaps not much more upon a possible echo of the death of Hamnet Shakespeare (August 1596) in Constance's laments for Arthur. The Arden editor speaks of a papal bull of 1596 as making regicide 'meritorious' (iii. 1. 176). He must have misread Malone's reference to the bull of 1570. There was another in 1588, the terms of which are unknown. On internal grounds, however, the winter of 1596–7 is not an unlikely date for the play. It has a general stylistic resemblance to *Richard II*, and is sometimes dated before it, on the ground that Shakespeare would not break the sequence of the Lancastrian tetralogy with another historic play. But *Richard II* belongs to the experiment in lyric drama, which the comparative paucity of rhyme in *King John* shows to have been abandoned, although its aftermath in an abstinence from double endings (cf. p. 268) is shared with *I Henry IV*. There are some fairly close phrasal echoes with *Merchant of Venice*. Kerrl regards i as written some time before the rest, and iii. 2, 3 and iv. 1 as revised considerably later; but this is on the basis (cf. p. 266) of verse-tests, which cannot be safely applied to sections of no more than 276 and 216 blank-verse lines. There are certainly more double endings in i than elsewhere, but this is due to the constant recurrence of the words 'brother', 'mother', 'father' in final positions during the Bastard episode, and this is for emphasis on the theme, rather than for variety of rhythm. There is no evidence of a Jacobean revival. One can hardly suppose with W. W. Lloyd that 'Now these her princes are come home again' (v. 7. 115) refers to the return of Prince Charles and the Duke of Buckingham from Spain in 1623.

The principal source was *T.R.* which is followed pretty closely as regards historical events, the selection of scenes, and even the logical run of many of the dialogues. The writing itself is all new, but Shakespeare must have kept the old book before him. Only one line (v. 4. 42) is in common, but in some 150 places a few words from *T.R.* are picked up and used, by no means always in the same context. Where the structure is altered, there is generally a dramatic intention. There is less comedy. Although *T.R.* is in two parts, *King John* is only shorter by about 300 lines. Shakespeare does not appear to have made any substantial use of chronicles. But some trifling variations from *T.R.* may be due to these. And somehow Shakespeare came to say (iv. 2. 120) that Eleanor died on April 1. That is an historic fact, but was not in any available chronicle. Liebermann suggests that Shakespeare saw it in a calendar at the Earl of Southampton's house of Beaulieu, where Eleanor founded an abbey. But I incline to think, with Moore Smith, that he arrived at it by accident, having noticed April 1 as the date of a meteor, recorded by Holinshed on the same page as the death.

There is nothing to bear out the suggestion of Pope that *T.R.* itself was by Shakespeare and William Rowley.[1] Malone ascribed it to Marlowe. Sykes, *Sidelights on Sh.*, 99, has made out a fair case for Peele, largely on the ground of small recurrent tricks of padding, which are more evidential (cf. p. 221) than echoes. The strong nationalist and anti-papal tone is consistent with Peele. Robertson, *Introduction*, 278, 400, weakens some details of the case, and argues for Marlowe in the stronger passages, finding also some inconclusive 'clues' to Greene and Lodge.

[1] *Var.* xv. 193.

XIV. THE MERCHANT OF VENICE

[S.R. 1598.] xxij° Julij. James Robertes. Entred for his copie vnder the handes of bothe the wardens, a booke of the Marchaunt of Venyce, or otherwise called the Jewe of Venyce, Prouided, that yt bee not prynted by the said James Robertes or anye other whatsoeuer without lycence first had from the Right honorable the lord Chamberlen vj^d (Arber, iii. 122).

[S.R. 1600.] 28 Octobris. Thomas Haies. Entred for his copie under the handes of the Wardens and by Consent of master Robertes. A booke called the booke of the merchant of Venyce vj^d. (Arber, iii. 175).

[Q1. 1600.] The most excellent Historie of the Merchant of Venice. With the extreame crueltie of Shylocke the Iewe towards the sayd Merchant, in cutting a iust pound of his flesh: and the obtayning of Portia by the choyse of three chests. As it hath beene diuers times acted by the Lord Chamberlaine his Seruants. Written by William Shakespeare. [Ornament] At London, Printed by I⟨ames⟩ R⟨oberts⟩ for Thomas Heyes, and are to be sold in Paules Churchyard, at the signe of the Greene Dragon. 1600. [*Head-title*] The comicall History of the Merchant of Venice. [*Running-title*] The comicall Historie of the Merchant of Venice.

[Cited by Cambridge and other eds. as Q2.]

Facsimile. C. Praetorius (1887, *Sh. Q.* xvi, ed. F. J. Furnivall).

[Q2. 1619.] The Excellent History of the Merchant of Venice. With the extreme cruelty of Shylocke the Iew towards the saide Merchant, in cutting a iust pound of his flesh. And the obtaining of Portia, by the choyse of three Caskets. Written by W. Shakespeare. [William Jaggard's device (McKerrow 283)] Printed by J. Roberts, 1600. [*Head-title*, under ornament with royal arms] The Comical History of the Merchant of Venice. [*Running-title*] The Comicall History of the Merchant of Venice.

[Cited by Cambridge and other eds. as Q1. On the misdating cf. p. 133.]

Facsimile. W. Griggs (1880, *Sh. Q.* vii, ed. F. J. Furnivall).

[S.R. 1619.] 8° Julij 1619. Laurence Hayes. Entred for his Copies by Consent of a full Court theis two Copies following which were the Copies of Thomas Haies his fathers vizt. A play Called The Marchant of Venice, . . . (Arber, iii. 651).

[F1. 1623.] [*Catalogue*] The Merchant of Venice. [*Comedies*, pp. 163–84, sign. O 4–Q 2^v. *Head- and Running-titles*] The Merchant of Venice.
[Acts marked.]

[Q3. 1637.] M. P. for Laurence Hayes.
['Actors' names' ⟨Dramatis Personae⟩ on back of t.p.]

[Q4. 1652.] for William Leake.
[Sheets of Q3 reissued.]

[S.R. 1657, Oct. 17.] Transfer from Bridget Hayes and Jane Graisby to William Leake (Eyre, ii. 150).

Parallel-Text. W. Reynolds (1888, *Bankside*, Q1+F1).

Modern Editions. H. H. Furness (1888, *New Variorum*); C. K. Pooler (1905, 1927, *Arden*); W. L. Phelps (1923, *Yale*); A. T. Quiller-Couch and J. D. Wilson (1926, *C.U.P.*).

Dissertations. K. Elze, *Zum M.V.* (1871, *J.* vi. 129; *Essays*, 67); L. Toulmin Smith, *The Bond-Story in M.V.* (1875, *N.S.S. Trans.* 181); S. Lee, *The Original of Shylock* (1880, *Gent. Mag.*), *Elizabethan England and the Jews* (1888, *N.S.S. Trans.* 143); H. Graetz, *Shylock in den Sagen, in den Dramen, und in der Geschichte* (1880); J. Bolte, *Jakob Rosefeldt's Moschus* (1886, *J.* xxi. 187), *Der Jude von Venetien* (1887, *J.* xxii. 189), *Zur Shylockfabel* (1892, *J.* xxvii. 225); W. A. Clouston, *Shylock and his Predecessors* (1887, June 18, Aug. 6, *Academy*); E. Köppel, *M.V.* (1892, *E.S.* xvi. 372); J. W. Hales, *Sh. and the Jews* (1894, *E.H.R.* ix. 652); A. Dimock, *The Conspiracy of Dr. Lopez* (1894, *E.H.R.* ix. 440); E. Mory, *Ms Jude von Malta und Shs M.V.* (1897); R. Eberstadt, *Der Shylockvertrag und sein Urbild* (1908, *J.* xliv. 1); F. Brie, *Zur Entstehung des M.V.* (1913, *J.* xlix. 97); B. A. P. van Dam, *The Text of M.V.* (1927, *Neophilologus*, xiii. 33); A. Tretiak, *M.V. and the Alien Question* (1929, *R.E.S.* v. 402).

Q1 is a good text, and requires very little emendation, so far as the wording goes, except for a few literal misprints. A bad one at iv. 1. 73–4 was corrected while sign. G4 was being printed off and does not appear in all examples. Some departures from Q1 in modern editions are due to the erroneous belief of the Cambridge editors that Q2 was the earlier version. The mislineations are slight, and generally caused by a wrong treatment of short lines. The author's intention as regards elisions seems, as a rule, to be carefully regarded. The punctuation is less good; full stops or colons are occasionally omitted or inserted in error. There are some odd typographical features. A temporary shortage of type may perhaps explain the frequent appearance of lower-case initials at the beginnings of lines. It is difficult to believe, with Van Dam, in an aberration through which the compositor followed the minuscules which he probably found in his copy. There is a variant use of roman and italic types for stage-directions. These are normal. One entry and several exits are left unmarked. A theatrical hand has probably added some definition, glossing, for example (ii. 5. 1), 'Enter Iewe and his man that was' with the final words 'the Clowne'. Lancelot is often 'Clowne' and Shylock 'Jew' in stage-directions and speech-prefixes. Wilson, who generally finds evidence of revision in such variants, here suggests the type-shortage as the cause, but the feature is common (cf. p. 232) in Shakespearean texts. Abbreviated speech-prefixes have led to some confusion among minor characters of similar names. Wilson may be right in thinking that Shakespeare only provided a Solanio and a Salerio, and that a Salarino has emerged from the confusion. The 'Dramatis Personae' of the 1637 Q include Salanio and Salarino, but not Salerio. This may only rest on inference from the stage-directions. There is some irregularity in the use of speech-prefixes before and after letters and inscriptions read (cf. p. 198) from 'scrolls'. I see no clear reason why the copy used for Q1 should not have been in Shakespeare's hand. The features just described seem characteristic of him, and the compositor has passed some abnormal spellings analogous to those (cf. p. 187) in other plays. I do not, therefore, find sufficient evidence for the element of 'assembling' in Wilson's elaborate reconstruction of the textual history of the play. As pointed out by Greg, the phrase 'A booke called the booke of' in the S.R.

entry of 28 October 1600 suggests the use of official copy
from the theatre.[1]

Pollard, *F. and Q.* 98, and Wilson have sufficiently
shown that Q2 and F were set up independently from Q1.
Some misprints have in both cases been corrected and
others made, and in both cases there has been some
attempt at a revision of stage-directions and speech-prefixes, and at conjectural emendation, generally erroneous,
of sense, grammar, metre, and spelling. I do not know
that most of this is beyond a printing-house corrector, and
Jaggard is not very likely to have had access in 1619 to
theatrical manuscripts. But the Q1 used for F probably represented prompt-copy. Musical notes have been
added. Two profanities (i. 2. 121; v. 1. 157) have been
removed, and the substitution (i. 2. 83) of an 'other' for
a 'Scottish' lord points to Jacobean censorship. What is
more puzzling is that some of the Q2 and F alterations
agree, and that a few of these are not very likely to have
been independently arrived at. Possibly the corrector of
F glanced from time to time at a copy of Q2 preserved
in Jaggard's printing-house.

I return to Wilson's reconstruction. This I have discussed more fully in *M.L.R.* xxii. 220. It involves (*a*) the
prompt-book of *The Jew* (*v. infra*); (*b*) several probable
intermediate handlings by various dramatists; (*c*) a revision by Shakespeare early in 1594; (*d*) the addition of a
passage after the execution of Lopez in June 1594;
(*e*) a further revision by Shakespeare at an unknown date;
(*f*) the presumable loss of the prompt-book; (*g*) the transcription by one scribe of the dialogue from players'
'parts', with abbreviated speech-prefixes to form a new
prompt-book; (*h*) the addition of stage-directions by another scribe; (*i*) the insertion of theatrical interpolations.

I agree with Greg and Wilson that v. 1. 34–48 is probably a theatrical interpolation in the interests of the clown,
disclosed by the misplacement of a catchword intended to
connect it with the text. But its existence hardly justifies
the assumption that one (iii. 2. 216) of several indelicacies

---

[1] *4 Library,* vii. 384; cf. p. 97.

is also an interpolation, and still less the treatment by Wilson of iii. 5, with its beautiful laudation of Portia from Jessica's mouth, as a scene in which 'Shakespeare had no hand whatever'. Nor do I find adequate evidence for the supposed double recension by Shakespeare, either in the fact that the mask planned in ii. iv–vi is never given; or in the obscurity as to the cause of Antonio's melancholy, which to me as to Wilson seems sufficiently explained by his prevision of the loss of a friend through marriage; or in the frequent short lines, which are all, except possibly ii. 6. 46, intelligible enough without recourse to the supposition of cuts.

As to the date of the play, there is not much external evidence to go upon. Some reference to the execution of the Jew Roderigo Lopez on 7 June 1594 for the attempted poisoning of Elizabeth and of Don Antonio of Portugal (confused by Lee 134 and others with Antonio Perez) is probable; especially, as Wilson points out, in the Pythagorean description (iv. 1. 134) of Shylock as inhabited by the spirit of a wolf (*lupus*) 'hang'd for human slaughter'.[1] But the analogy of Shylock to Lopez is not very close, and there is obviously little, beyond the name, between the Merchant and Don Antonio. There may also be an allusion (iii. 2. 49) to the coronation of Henri IV on 27 February 1594, although presumably every coronation has its flourish. In any case such allusions are not necessarily quite contemporary. On the other hand, the Gobbo of the play seems likely to have inspired two malicious references by Francis Davison in letters of 1596 to an unnamed enemy of the Earl of Essex, who can only be the hunch-backed Robert Cecil.[2] On October 27 he writes, 'If he be vanquished . . . all the world shall never make me confess, but that bumbasted legs are a better fortification than bulwarks, and St Gobbo a far greater and more omnipotent saint than either St Philip or St Diego'. And on November 10 he writes, evidently with reference to Cecil's appointment as Secretary of State, of 'the late

---

[1] Cf. Donne, *Progress of the Soul*, 401.
[2] T. Birch, *Elizabeth*, ii. 185, 204.

instalment and canonisation of the venerable saint'. If I am right, *Merchant of Venice* can hardly be later than the autumn of 1596, although of course it might have furnished Cecil's nickname some time before. On general grounds of style and links with other plays and the *Sonnets*, the autumn of 1596 is a very probable date for the play, which is certainly more mature than the comedies of 1594–5. There was a revival for the court in the winter of 1604–5 (App. D).

The two main elements of the plot, the bond-motive and the casket-motive, have been traced as old and widespread story themes. So far as the bond-motive is concerned, it is unnecessary to go farther back, in seeking an ultimate source for *Merchant of Venice*, than *Il Pecorone*, iv. 1, of Ser Giovanni of Florence, written c. 1378, but first printed in 1558. This combines the lover and his older friend, the wooing of a lady at Belmont, the friend's bond to a Jew for a pound of flesh, the intervention of the lady dressed as a lawyer, and the ring begged as a fee. It does not bring in the theft of the usurer's daughter, which is, however, found in another bond story, yielding several points of resemblance to Shakespeare's, in Anthony Munday's *Zelauto* (1580). And the test by which the lady is won is other than that of the casket-motive. This may have been substituted from the 66th story of Richard Robinson's version, apparently first printed in 1577, of the *Gesta Romanorum*.[1] Possibly Shakespeare did not himself link the two themes. Stephen Gosson's *Schoole of Abuse* (1579) mentions a '*Iew* . . . showne at the Bull . . . representing the greedinesse of worldly chusers, and bloody mindes of usurers: . . . neither with amorous gesture wounding the eye: nor with slouenly talke hurting the eares of the chast hearers'.[2] We know no more of this play. There may conceivably be an allusion to it in Greene's *Mamillia* (1583), 32, 'He which maketh choyce of bewty without vertue commits as much folly as Critius did, in choosing a golden boxe filled with rotten bones'; and less probably, in view of the date, in a letter (c. 1573)

---

[1] S. J. H. Herrtage, *Early English Versions of the G.R.* xxii.   [2] *Eliz. Stage*, iv. 204.

of Gabriel Harvey to Edmund Spenser, describing himself as 'He that is faste bownde unto the in more obliga-
tions then any marchante in Italy to any Jewe there'.[1]
There is of course nothing to show that *Merchant of Venice*
had any closer relation to the *Jew* than that of theme. As
it stands, it certainly does not justify the ethical commendation of the puritan Gosson. Wilson does not go far
towards establishing a textual continuity between plays
of different companies, fifteen or twenty years asunder,
with several probable intermediate handlings by various
dramatists, by pointing to a Shakespearean inconsistency
as to the number of Portia's wooers, to another as to the
precise political effect which a refusal of justice to Shylock
would have upon the state of Venice, and to the presence
in the play of a scrap of doggerel and some passages of
inferior workmanship. There are traces of euphuism in
i. 2, but so there are elsewhere in Shakespeare.

   Merchant of Venice probably owes something to the *Jew
of Malta*, but nothing to Wager's *Cruel Debtor*[2] or to
Gerontus the Jew and the Mercatore in R. Wilson's *Three
Ladies of London*,[3] or to the bond-story in the ballad of the
Northern Lord.[4] There are some verbal parallels in that of
Gernutus.[5] Whether this is the 'ballad called the vserers
rewarde' registered on 19 June 1594 must be uncertain.[6]
Those in the 95th declamation[7] of *The Orator* (1596), a
translation by L⟨azarus⟩ P⟨iot⟩ from the *Histoires Tragiques* (1588) of Alexandre Vandenbushe or Sylvain, are
very slight, and it is doubtful whether the translation,
which had still to be made when the book was registered
on 15 July 1596, is not later than *Merchant of Venice* itself.[8]
Piot was at one time identified with Anthony Munday,
but H. Thomas, *Spanish and Portuguese Romances of
Chivalry* (1920), has distinguished them. An earlier and
apparently only partial translation of the *Histoires Tragiques* by E. A. was registered on 25 August 1590, but is

[1] *G. Harvey's Letter-Book*, 78.
[2] *Eliz. Stage*, iii. 505; *M.S.C.* i. 315.
[3] *Eliz. Stage*, iii. 515.
[4] Hazlitt, *Sh. Library*, i. 1. 367.
[5] *Ibid.* i. 1. 375.
[6] Arber, ii. 654.
[7] Hazlitt, *Sh. Library*, i. 1. 355.
[8] Arber, iii. 67.

unknown.¹ The names Shylock (cormorant) and Jessica (looker-out) are shown by Gollancz to be of Hebrew origin. Gobbo is traceable as a family name at Titchfield, Hants.²

English actors in Germany, probably the company of John Green, played *The Jew* or *The Jew of Venice* at Passau (1607), Gräz (1608), Halle (1611), and *Joseph the Jew of Venice* at Dresden (1626).³ Possibly this is also the play called at Gräz *A King of Cyprus and a Duke of Venice*, and in part at least the foundation of a later German play by the actor Christopher Blümel (born 1630) of which MSS. are at Vienna and Karlsruhe. This contains elements from both *Merchant of Venice* and *Jew of Malta*, but cannot be called a version of either. A King of Cyprus, a Duke of Venice, a Venetian Jew, called both Barabbas and Josephus, and a French Doctor are among the characters. It must remain uncertain whether the compilation also drew upon Dekker's lost *Jew of Venice*, registered on 9 September 1653,⁴ and whether this bore any relation to the Admiral's play or plays of the *Venetian Comedy* and the *French Doctor* in 1594.⁵ But it is safe to say that no ground has been shown for the suggestion of Fleay, *L. and W.* 30, 197, that *Merchant of Venice* was founded on a *Jew of Venice* written by Dekker c. 1592.

XV, XVI. HENRY THE FOURTH
[Part I]

[S.R. 1598.] xxvᵗᵒ die Februarij. Andrew Wyse. Entred for his Copie vnder thandes of Master Dix: and master Warden Man a booke intituled The historye of Henry the iiijᵗʰ with his battaile of Shrewsburye against Henry Hottspurre of the Northe with the conceipted mirthe of Sir John Ffalstoff vjᵈ (Arber, iii. 105).

[H.P. had (*Rarities*, 19) a fragment (sign. C, 4 leaves) of an edition which he thought earlier than Q1. It is now in the collection of H. C. Folger (Bartlett 25).]

¹ *Ibid.* ii. 560.
² L. G. Thompson in *T.L.S.* 17 Sept. 1925.
³ *Eliz. Stage*, ii. 281.
⁴ *Ibid.* iii. 301.
⁵ Cf. Greg, *Henslowe*, ii. 170.

[Q1. 1598.] The History of Henrie the Fourth; With the battell at Shrewsburie, betweene the King and Lord Henry Percy, surnamed Henrie Hotspur of the North. With the humorous conceits of Sir Iohn Falstalffe. [Short's device (McKerrow 278)] At London, Printed by P⟨eter⟩ S⟨hort⟩ for Andrew Wise, dwelling in Paules Church-yard, at the signe of the Angell 1598. [*Head-title*] The Historie of Henry the fourth. [*Running-title*] The Historie of Henrie the fourth.

Facsimile. W. Griggs (1881, *Sh. Q.* viii, ed. H. A. Evans).

[Q2. 1599.] The History of Henrie the Fourth; With the battell at Shrewsburie, betweene the King and Lord Henry Percy, surnamed Henry Hotspur of the North. With the humorous conceits of Sir Iohn Falstaffe. Newly corrected by W. Shake-speare. [Stafford's device (McKerrow 281)] At London, Printed by S⟨imon⟩ S⟨tafford⟩ for Andrew Wise, dwelling in Paules Church-yard, at the signe of the Angell. 1599. [*Head- and Running-titles*] The Historie of Henry the fourth.

[S.R. 1603.] 25 Junij. Mathew Lawe. Entred for his copie in full courte Holden this Day. These ffyve copies followinge . . . viz iii enterludes or playes . . . The Third of Henry the .4 the first parte. all kinges . . . all whiche by consent of the Company are sett ouer to him from Andrew Wyse (Arber, iii. 239).

[Q3. 1604.] The History of Henrie the fourth, With the battell at Shrewsburie, betweene the King, and Lord Henry Percy, surnamed Henry Hotspur of the North. With the humorous conceits of Sir Iohn Falstaffe. Newly corrected by W. Shake-speare. [Ornament] London Printed by Valentine Simmes, for Mathew Law, and are to be solde at his shop in Paules Churchyard, at the signe of the Fox. 1604. [*Head- and Running-titles*] The Historie of Henry the fourth.

[Q4. 1608.] The History of Henry the Fourth, With the battell at Shrewesburie, betweene the King, and Lord Henry Percy, surnamed Henry Hotspur of the North. With the humorous conceites of Sir Iohn Falstalffe. Newly corrected by W. Shake-speare. [Ornament] London, Printed for Mathew Law, and are to be sold at his shop in Paules Churchyard, neere vnto S. Augustines gate, at the signe of the Foxe. 1608. [*Head-title*] The Historie of Henry the fourth. [*Running-title*] The History of Henrie the fourth.

[Q5. 1613.] The History of Henrie the fourth, With the Battell at Shrewseburie, betweene the King, and Lord Henrie Percy, surnamed Henrie Hotspur of the North. With the humorous conceites of Sir Iohn Falstaffe. Newly corrected by W. Shake-speare. [White's device (McKerrow 188ᵇ)] London, Printed by W⟨illiam⟩ W⟨hite⟩ for Mathew Law, and are to be sold at his shop in Paules Church-yard, neere vnto S. Augustines Gate, at the signe of the Foxe. 1613. [*Head-title*] The Historie of Henrie the fourth. [*Running-title*] The Historie of Henry the fourth.

[Q6. 1622.] T⟨homas⟩ P⟨urfoot⟩ for Mathew Law.

[F1. 1623.] [*Catalogue*] The First part of King Henry the fourth. [*Histories*, pp. 46–73, sign. d 5ᵛ–f 6. *Head-title*] The First Part of Henry the Fourth, with the Life and Death of Henry Sirnamed Hotspur. [*Running-title*] The First Part of King Henry the Fourth.

[Acts and scc. marked.]

[Q7. 1632.] Iohn Norton, sold by William Sheares.

[Q8. 1639.] John Norton, sold by Hugh Perry.

Parallel-Text. W. H. Fleming (1890, *Bankside*).

Modern Editions. R. P. Cowl and A. E. Morgan (1914, 1923, *Arden*); S. B. Hemingway (1917, *Yale*).

[Part II]

[S.R. 1600.] 23 Augusti. Andrew Wyse William Aspley. Entred for their copies vnder the handes of the wardens Two bookes, the one called . . . Thother the second parte of the history of Kinge Henry the iiij^th with the humours of Sir John Falstaff: Wrytten by master Shakespere. xij^d (Arber, iii. 170).

[Q. 1600.] The Second part of Henrie the fourth, con-
tinuing to his death, and coronation of Henrie the fift.
With the humours of sir Iohn Falstaffe, and swaggering
Pistoll. As it hath been sundrie times publikely acted by
the right honourable, the Lord Chamberlaine his seruants.
Written by William Shakespeare. [Ornament] London
Printed by V⟨alentine⟩ S⟨immes⟩ for Andrew Wise, and
William Aspley. 1600. [*Head-title*] The second part
of Henry the fourth, continuing to his death, and coronation of Henry the fift. [*Running-title*] The second part
of Henry the fourth.

[In some examples a cancel sheet E, with six leaves in place of four,
adds iii. 1, originally omitted.]

Facsimile. W. Griggs (1882, *Sh. Q.* ix, ed. H. A. Evans).

[F1. 1623.] [*Catalogue*] The Second part of K. Henry
the fourth. [*Histories*, pp. 74–100 + 2 pp. unnumbered,
sign. f 6ᵛ–gg 8ᵛ. *Head-title*] The Second Part of Henry the
Fourth, Containing his Death: and the Coronation of King
Henry the Fift. [*Running-title*] The second Part of King
Henry the Fourth.

[Acts and scc. marked. 'The Actors Names' at end. Pollard,
F.Q. 136, describes some irregularities in the printing.]

Parallel-Text. W. H. Fleming (1890, *Bankside*).

Modern Editions. S. B. Hemingway (1921, *Yale*); R. P. Cowl
(1923, *Arden*).

[Parts I and II]

Dering MS.

[A compilation, in a seventeenth-century hand, of scenes from Q5
of Part 1 and Q of Part 2, probably for private performance, with
alterations in the hand of Sir Edward Dering (1598–1644) of
Surrenden, Kent, where the MS. was found.]

Edition. J. O. Halliwell-[Phillipps] (1845, *Sh. Soc.*).

Dissertations. J. Gairdner, *Historical Elements in Sh.'s Falstaff* (1873,
Fortnightly); K. Hagena, *Remarks on the Introductory Scene of 2 Hen. IV*
(1878, *N.S.S. Trans.* 347); F. Solly-Flood, *The Story of Prince Henry of
Monmouth and Chief-Justice Gascoign* (1886, 2 R. Hist. Soc. Trans. iii. 47);
G. Sarrazin, *Falstaff, Pistol, Nym und ihre Urbilder* (1902, *Kleine Sh.
Studien*), *Nym und Ben Jonson* (1904, *J.* xl. 212); F. W. Moorman, *Sh.'s
History Plays and Daniel's Civile Wars* (1904, *J.* xl. 69); W. Baeske,
Oldcastle-Falstaff in der englischen Literatur bis zu Sh. (1905); L. W.

Harcourt, *The Two Sir John Falstaffs* (1910, *3 R. Hist. Soc. Trans.* iv. 50);
C. L. Kingsford, *The First English Life of Henry V* (1911); H. Ax, *The
Relation of Sh.'s Hen. IV to Holinshed* (1912); A. W. Pollard, *The Variant
Settings in 2 Hen. IV and their Spellings* (1920, Oct. 21, *T.L.S.*); J.
Monaghan, *Falstaff and his Forbears* (1921, *S.P.* xviii. 353); A. E.
Morgan, *Some Problems of Sh.'s Hen. IV* (1924, *Sh. Ass.*); R. P. Cowl,
Some Literary Allusions in Hen. IV (1925, Mar. 26, *T.L.S.*), *Echoes of Henry
IV in Eliz. Drama* (1925, Oct. 22, *T.L.S.*), *Some Echoes in Eliz. Drama
of Hen. IV* (1926), *Hen. IV and Other Plays: an Experiment with Echoes*
(1927), *Notes on the Text of Hen. IV* (1927), *Sources of the Text of Hen. IV*
(1929); J. E. Morris, *The Date of Hen. IV* (1926, Jan. 28, *T.L.S.*); W. G.
Bowling, *The Wild Prince Hal in Legend and Literature* (1926, *Washington
Univ. Studies*, xiii. 305); R. A. Law, *Structural Unity in the two Parts of
Hen. IV* (1927, *S.P.* xxiv. 223); J. Dawtrey, *The Falstaff Saga* (1927).

The successive Qq and F1 of Part 1 are regularly set
up from each other, with the usual misprints and conjectural alterations. Nothing more than these justifies the
'Newly corrected' of the Q2 title-page. The Cambridge
editors thought that Qq earlier than Q5 were probably
consulted for F1, but the few cases in which F seems to
revert to these are all capable of explanation as conjectures. Profanity has, however, been excised from F1 with
exceptional thoroughness. The normal stage-directions of
Q1 are preserved by F1. Q1 is therefore the sole authority
for the text. This is somewhat rough metrically, owing
partly to the difficulty of manipulating proper names, and
partly to misprints as to elisions and the like, which editors
might perhaps emend more freely than they do.

The Q and F1 of Part 2, on the other hand, although
representing substantially the same text, show much
greater variation in detail. The Q stage-directions are normal,
and some disagreements (i. 1. 1, 34, 161; i. 3. 1; ii. 4. 21;
iv. 3. 27, 81; iv. 4. 1) between stage-directions and text as
to the personages introduced are best explained as the
result of changes of intention by the author during
composition. Thus in i. 1. Lord Bardolf has replaced Sir
John Umfreville through a belated historical correction,
not fully carried out. There are some abnormal spellings,
such as 'Scilens' for 'Silence', which may also (cf. p. 187)
point to the author's hand. The MS. has probably been
used as prompt-copy, since at v. 4. 1 the name of the

actor Sincklo is given to the Beadle whom he played.
When Q was first set up, iii. 1 was omitted, and Pollard's
T.L.S. article minutely analyses the typographical methods
employed in partly resetting sheet E with two additional
leaves to allow of its introduction. Some examples of
Q retain the unrevised sheet. Slighter corrections are also
found in other sheets. The main differences between Q
and F are as follows. There are many small textual
variants. These do not indicate constant subconscious
substitutions, such as some plays (cf. p. 180) exhibit.
Many look like alternative readings of a difficult copy, and
many like sophistications in F of wording and grammar.
Some short lines are perhaps needlessly filled out. Profanity has again been meticulously removed. There are
several passages, aggregating 168 lines, not in Q (i. 1.
166–79, 189–209; i. 3. 21–4, 36–55, 85–108; ii. 3.
23–45; iv. 1. 55–79, 103–39), and as the absence of some
of these leaves *lacunae* in the sense, they may all be taken
as 'cuts' in Q. On the other hand, F omits about forty lines
found in Q. These are mostly short passages not likely to
be cuts. They are probably not all to be explained in the
same way. Some may be due to slips of the F printer, and
others (i. 1. 161; iii. 1. 53–6; iv. 1. 93, 95) to emendation.
But a few suggest that the censorship of profanity has been
extended to passages of indelicacy (ii. 1. 126–7; ii. 2. 26–
30; ii. 4. 159–62; iii. 2. 337–9, 340–3) and in one case
(i. 2. 240–7) anti-patriotic criticism. They are not sufficiently detached from their contexts to be 'gags' in Q. The
F stage-directions and speech-prefixes show, unlike those
of Part 2, careful revising, with close attention to the indications of the text, although with some slips, e.g. the omission of an exit and re-entry at iii. 2. 234, 258. 'Suggestive'
stage-directions and non-speaking personages have been
eliminated and entries unmarked in Q added. It seems
clear that F follows in the main a theatrical manuscript. This
may, indeed, have been the same manuscript which was used
for Q, but if so it had undergone subsequent overhauling
by the book-keeper, and the intention of Q must have been
to observe, and that of F to disregard, the cuts shown upon

it. It is not equally clear that no use was made of Q in printing F. There are several cases of common error, which would at least be consistent with such use. But these, between F and a single Q, have not the evidential value which attaches to common errors between F and the derivative Qq of other plays.

Morgan thinks that, apart from the 'cuts' in the Q of Part 2, both parts have been abridged. His evidence for this consists mainly of short lines. So far as Part 1 is concerned, the explanation is quite superfluous; but Part 2 has some abrupt short lines, left imperfectly corrected by F, in the King's speech at iv. 5. 60–82. However this may be, I cannot (cf. p. 233) accept Morgan's further view that the prose scenes have been rewritten from an earlier metrical version, at the time when Shakespeare substituted Sir John Falstaff as his leading humorist for Sir John Oldcastle. As to the fact of this substitution there can be no doubt. Tradition from as early as about 1625 (App. C, nos. i, iv, v, xxxiv) records it, and it has left traces in the texts. In Part 1, it has left the jesting address 'my old lad of the Castle' (i. 2. 47) pointless, and ii. 2. 115 unmetrical. In Part 2, *Old.* still stands for *Fal* as speech-prefix to i. 2. 137 in Q, and the *Epilogue*, originally short, as the prayer for the Queen left in error by Q at the end of the first paragraph shows, has been extended by two other paragraphs, of which one introduces a dance, and the other an apology, 'Olde-castle died Martyre, and this is not the man'. F completes the revision, by transferring the prayer to the end of the third paragraph. There is an echo in the rival Admiral's play of *1 Sir John Oldcastle*,[1] produced in November 1599, where the prologue has—

> It is no pamperd glutton we present,
> Nor aged Councellor to youthfull sinne,
> . . . . . . Let fair Truth be grac'te,
> Since forg'de inuention former time defac'te.

A reason for the change can readily be found in the fact that Sir John Oldcastle married an ancestress of the Lords

[1] *Eliz. Stage,* iii. 306.

Cobham, who were prominent at the Elizabethan court. It had clearly been made before Part 2 was registered on 25 February 1598, and almost equally clearly not before the play was originally produced, since 'Oldcastle' lingered in popular usage as the name of the character. *Henry IV* must have been the *Sir John Old Castell* with which the Lord Chamberlain entertained an ambassador on 8 March 1600, since the players were his men and not the Admiral's;[1] and it is alluded to in Field's *Amends for Ladies* (1618), iv. 3, as—

> The Play where the fat Knight, hight Old-castle,
> Did tell you truly what his honour was?

There is a similar reference as late as *Hey for Honesty* (1651), iv. 1, and even in an official document (App. D) the play seems to be called *Ould Castel* in 1638. Perhaps, therefore, the Cobham intervention came when *1 Henry IV* was specially reviewed by the Revels officers for court performance.[2] It may not only have been Oldcastle's name that went. At i. 2. 181 of Part i, Prince Henry's thieving companions are 'Falstaffe, Haruey, Rossill, and Gadshil', and at ii. 4. 193, 195, 199, are speech-prefixes for *Ross*. F here eliminates him by a conjectural redistribution of speeches, but it is clear from other parts of this scene and from ii. 2 that Bardolph and Peto were among the thieves. In *Eliz. Stage*, iii. 196, I took Rossill and Harvey for actors' names; wrongly I think, since *2 Hen. IV*, ii. 2. 1, has the stage-direction 'Enter the Prince, Poynes, sir Iohn Russel, with others'. F substitutes 'Enter Prince Henry, Pointz, Bardolfe, and Page'. This cannot be right, since Bardolph and the Page enter later at 75. But apparently Peto has replaced Sir John Russell and Bardolph Harvey, with the awkward result of having two Bardolphs in the plays. Both Russell and Harvey were familiar names at the Elizabethan court.

Possibly a desire to advertise the purging of the offence led to the publication of *1 Henry IV* unusually soon after its production. This can hardly have been earlier than

---

[1] Cf. App. D.   [2] *Ibid.* i. 224.

1597. A few historical allusions, which have been held to a date later than 1596, are indeed unconvincing. But obviously the play was later than *Richard II*, and its relative maturity of style makes it reasonable to put it after *John*. And I think that Part 2 must have followed pretty quickly. It is true that Meres' notice in the autumn of 1598 might cover either one or two parts, but Justice Silence is named in Jonson's *E.M.O.* of 1599,[1] and the survivals of Oldcastle and Russell suggest that the writing had begun before these names were censored. Cowl's derivation of Pistol's 'Cannibal' for 'Hannibal' (ii. 4. 180) from a passage in Brandon's *Virtuous Octavia* of 1598[2] has not much weight against this. It may well be originally Pistol's, and echoed both by Brandon and by Jonson in *E.M.I.* (1598) iii. 4. 53. If I am right as to date, the offended Cobham was probably Henry Brooke, the eighth lord, whose susceptibilities had perhaps also to be consulted in *Merry Wives* (q.v.), and not his father William, the seventh lord, who was Lord Chamberlain from 8 August 1596 to his death on 5 March 1597. Court revivals of one or other or both parts of the play are traceable (App. D) in 1612–13, c. 1619, 1625, and 1638.

The historical source of *Henry IV* was Holinshed's *Chronicle*. This only touches lightly upon the Prince's youthful wantonness, and for an elaboration of the theme, the introduction of Oldcastle, and the naming of a minor character Gadshill after the scene of his exploits, Shakespeare probably drew upon *The Famous Victories of Henry the Fifth*, an old play of the Queen's men. This was registered on 14 May 1594, but the first extant edition is dated 1598.[3] The text, wholly in prose, is probably an abridged one, perhaps from a two-part play. But there is little ground for Morgan's theory that the original was in verse, that it passed to the Admiral's men and was produced by them in a revised form, as their *Henry V* of 1595–6, and that it was then transferred by them to the Chamberlain's, and became Shakespeare's source for *Henry IV*

[1] *Ibid.* iii. 360.   [2] *Ibid.* iii. 236.   [3] *Ibid.* iv. 17.

and *Henry V.* Conjecture for conjecture, it is much more likely that an edition of the *Famous Victories,* as we now know it, was issued about 1594, but is now lost, and that this was used as a source by Shakespeare, and perhaps independently by a writer for the Admiral's. There is no evidence, and little probability, that the Chamberlain's and the Admiral's ever interchanged play-books. I have considered the possible Gloucestershire local colouring of Part 1 in ch. i. Oldys (App. C, no. xxxiv) has a tradition that Falstaff was drawn by Shakespeare from a Stratford neighbour. Dawtrey would find in him a ruffianly and portly Captain Nicholas Dawtrey, who served in Ireland, and was later a persistent suitor at court. But if Shakespeare wanted a model for his elaboration of a familiar stage type, there must have been many out-at-elbows soldiers of fortune available.

XVII. MUCH ADO ABOUT NOTHING

[S.R. 1600?]

4 Augusti

. . . . The Commedie of muche A doo about nothing a booke } to be staied (Arber, iii. 37).

[On the significance of this entry cf. p. 145.]

[S.R. 1600.] 23 Augusti. Andrew Wyse William Aspley. Entred for their copies vnder the handes of the wardens Two bookes, the one called Muche a Doo about nothinge ... Wrytten by master Shakespere. xij^d. (Arber, iii. 170).

[Q. 1600.] [Ornament] Much adoe about Nothing. As it hath been sundrie times publikely acted by the right honourable, the Lord Chamberlaine his seruants. Written by William Shakespeare. [Ornament] London Printed by V⟨alentine⟩ S⟨immes⟩ for Andrew Wise, and William Aspley. 1600. [*Head- and Running-titles*] Much adoe about Nothing.

Facsimile. C. Praetorius (1886, *Sh. Q.* xiv, ed. P. A. Daniel).

[F1. 1623.] [*Catalogue*] Much adoo about Nothing.

[*Comedies*, pp. 101–21, sign. I 3–L 1, *Head- and Running-titles*] Much adoe about Nothing.

[Acts i, sc. 1, ii–v marked.]

Parallel-Text. W. H. Fleming (1889, *Bankside*).

Modern Editions. H. H. Furness (1899, *New Variorum*); F. S. Boas (1916); F. Tucker Brooke (1917, *Yale*); A. T. Quiller-Couch and J. D. Wilson (1923, *C.U.P.*); G. R. Trenery (1924, *Arden*); A. G. Newcomer (1929).

Dissertations. J. P. Collier, *Dogberry and his Associates* (1844, *Sh. Soc. Papers*, i. 1); A. E. Brae, *Collier, Coleridge and Sh.* (1860); J. Bolte, *Deutsche Verwandte von Shs M.A.* (1886, *J.* xxi. 310); K. Weichberger, *Die Urquelle von Shs M.A.* (1898, *J.* xxxiv. 339); G. Sarrazin, *Die Abfassungszeit von M.A.* (1899, *J.* xxxv. 127); M. A. Scott, *The Book of the Courtyer: a Possible Source for Benedick and Beatrice* (1901, *P.M.L.A.* xvi. 475); F. Holleck-Weithmann, *Zur Quellenfrage von Shs Lustspiel M.A.*(1901); J. Le G. Brereton, *M.A. iv. 1. 145–60* (1928, *R.E.S.* iv. 84).

Q is a good text, with a few abnormal spellings and light punctuation, especially in the prose scenes. A passage (iv. 1. 157–60), originally omitted by the compositor and added with difficulty, has crowded the foot of a page. The stage-directions and speech-prefixes are more than usually casual, although the relations of the characters are often indicated. A good many entries and exits are unmarked. Characters are introduced who do not speak (i. 1. 1, 96, 206; ii. 2. 1), and one of these, Innogen, Leonato's wife, occurs twice. Other characters appear with generic instead of personal names; Don John as 'Bastard', Anthonio as 'Old' or 'Brother'. The irregularity is greatest with Dogberry and Verges. They are so named in iii. 3, and Dogberry is called 'maister Constable'. In iii. 5 they enter as 'the Constable, and the Headborough', and in some of the speech-prefixes Dogberry is 'Const. Dog' or 'Con. Do.'. In v. 1 they both enter as 'Constables' and are respectively 'Const' and 'Con 2' in speech-prefixes. These scenes remain intelligible. In iv. 2 they also enter as 'the Constables'; in the speech-prefixes Dogberry is variously Andrew (i.e. Clown), 'Kemp', 'Kem', 'Ke', 'Keeper' (a mere misprint), and only once 'Constable'; Verges is 'Cowley', 'Couley', 'Const'. Obviously the names of actors have been substituted for those of their parts. Wilson thinks that this was done by Shakespeare who in revising (cf. *infra*) could not remember the names of his characters. These, however, he must have invented with some pains, and it is more plausible to suppose that he wrote 'Con 1' and 'Con 2', and that the book-keeper, finding that in iv. 2 'Con' also stood for Conrade, indicated the actors' names for clarity. He may also have made some additions to the speech-prefixes, notably at ii. 1. 89, where a scribbled 'and Balthaser, Bor⟨achio⟩ dun Iohn' has been read by the printer as 'and Balthaser, or dumb Iohn'.

F was set up from Q, with a few corrections and more misprints and sophistications, well analysed by Wilson. The example followed must have been used as, or corrected by, a prompt-copy, since at ii. 3. 39 the name of a singer 'Iacke Wilson' replaces the 'Musicke' of Q. Musical notes have been added at ii. 1. 89, 161, and there has been an inadequate and sometimes incorrect revision of stage-directions and speech-prefixes. The elimination of profanity is exceptionally perfunctory; one passage only (iv. 2. 19–22) has gone. The removal of a hit at German and Spanish costume (iii. 2. 34–7) suggests censorship, perhaps at the time (cf. *infra*) of the Palsgrave's visit in 1612–13.

Much of the stage-direction and speech-prefix confusion can be cleared up by realizing that the singer Balthaser is also Anthonio's son and Leonato's 'cousin' and kinsman (i. 2. 1; ii. 1. 1 s.-d.), and at i. 1. 96 enters, properly enough, as a mute; and that in ii. 1 Don Pedro dances with Hero, Benedick with Beatrice, Balthaser with Margaret, and Claudio, otherwise unpartnered, with Ursula, while Don John and Borachio look on. But Wilson supposes that old inappropriate stage-directions have survived from an earlier version from Shakespeare's hand, which he has revised by abridging the verse scenes and turning the Benedick and Beatrice matter from verse into prose. This theory, which I cannot accept, is supported by pointing to short lines, which are in fact few and not markedly abrupt; to a very few only of the many decasyllabic rhythms which the prose, as in all Shakespeare's plays of about this date (cf. p. 233), contains; to two possible but not certain traces of alteration in particular passages (iv. 1. 157–60; v. 1. 106–8); to features of style, such as quatrains, 'reminiscent of' *Romeo and Juliet* and *Two Gentlemen of Verona*, which need mean no more than that Shakespeare had not quite abandoned his 'lyrical' manner in comedy; and to some obscurities as to the assignation of Borachio and Margaret, which are in part entailed by the use of a conventional plot-motive, and after all, as Wilson himself says, leave the business 'sufficient for the purpose' of the stage, although it provokes inquiry in the study.

The date of *Much Ado about Nothing* is pretty closely fixed to the winter of 1598–9, by Kempe's disappearance from the Chamberlain's company (cf. p. 79) early in 1599, and the absence of the play from Meres' list (App. B, no. xiii), unless indeed, which is not likely (cf. p. 272), it is *Love Labours Won*. With this date the evidence of the style is consistent; it seems to me to be nearest to that of *Merchant of Venice*. There is little else to take account of. Sarrazin's suggestion that the love-stories reflect those of the Earls of Southampton and Rutland may safely be disregarded. The passage (iii. 1. 9) on—

> favourites
> Made proud by princes, that advance their pride
> Against that power that bred it:

has been compared with the arrogance of the Earl of Essex to Elizabeth about July 1598; but such a topical allusion would be very dangerous, and the observation may be quite general. There was a Jacobean revival in 1612–13 (App. D), and an allusion by Digges (App. B, no. lii) shows that the play still held the stage about 1640.

The main theme, of a lover deceived by an impersonation of his mistress, has been traced back to the Greek *Chaereas and Kallirrhoe* of Chariton (c. 400). Less remote sources were available in the story of Timbreo and Fenicia, as given in Matteo Bandello's *Novelle* (1554), xxii, and translated therefrom in F. de Belleforest's *Histoires Tra-*

giques, iii (1569), and in that of Ariodante and Genevra in Ariosto's *Orlando Furioso* (1516), canto v. Probably both were drawn upon, since Belleforest has the names of Peter of Arragon and Leonato and Messina as the locality, but does not, like Ariosto, make the heroine's waiting-maid the decoy. The *Orlando* was translated by Sir John Harington in 1591, but there had been earlier versions of the Ariodante story, which was used by Spenser in the *Faerie Queene* (1590), ii. 4, and presumably in the *Ariodante and Genevora* given at court by the Merchant Taylors' boys in 1583.[1] It has been thought that the title *Panecia* of a play, rehearsed and probably given by Leicester's men in 1574, may be an error for *Fenicia*, and that Bandello's story may have then been dramatized.[2] Bandello was also the main source of Jacob Ayrer's *Die Schöne Phänicia* (c. 1595), printed in his *Opus Theatricum* (1618). Ayrer was not uninfluenced by the plays of English travelling companies, but no dramatic link between this piece and Shakespeare's has been established. It has been suggested that the wit-combats of Benedick and Beatrice may have been inspired by those of Gaspare Pallavicino and Emilia Pia in Baldassare Castiglione's *Il Cortegiano* (1528), translated by Sir Thomas Hoby in 1561. Aubrey (App. C, no. xiii) says that Shakespeare picked up the humour of the constables in journeying from Stratford to London through Grendon in Bucks, although this is a little off the direct road.

XVIII. HENRY THE FIFTH

[S.R. 1600?]
      4 Augusti

Henry the ffift, a booke } to be staied (Arber, iii. 37).

[On the significance of this entry, cf. p. 145.]

[Q1. 1600.] The Chronicle History of Henry the fift,

---

[1] *Eliz. Stage*, iv. 159.   [2] *Ibid.* iv. 149.

With his battel fought at Agin Court in France. Togither
with Auntient Pistoll.   As it hath bene sundry times
playd by the Right honorable the Lord Chamberlaine his
seruants.   [Creede's device (McKerrow 299)]   London
Printed by Thomas Creede, for Tho. Millington, and
Iohn Busby.   And are to be sold at his house in Carter
Lane, next the Powle head. 1600. [*Head-title*] The
Chronicle Historie of Henry the fift : with his battel fought
at Agin Court in France. Togither with Auncient Pistoll.
[*Running-title*] The Chronicle Historie of Henry the fift.

Facsimile. C. Praetorius (1886, *Sh. Q.* xxvii, ed. A. Symons).

Reprints. B. Nicholson (1875, *N.S.S.*); W. A. Wright (1893,
Cambridge Sh. ix. 461).

[S.R. 1600.] 14 Augusti. Thomas Pavyer. Entred for his
Copyes by Direction of master White warden vnder his
hand wrytinge. These Copyes followinge beinge thinges
formerlye printed and sett over to the sayd Thomas
Pavyer. viz. . . . The historye of Henry the Vth with the
battell of Agencourt vj^{d} . . . (Arber, iii. 169).

[Q2. 1602.] The Chronicle History of Henry the fift,
With his battell fought at Agin Court in France. Together with Auntient Pistoll. As it hath bene sundry times
playd by the Right honorable the Lord Chamberlaine his
seruants. [Creede's device (McKerrow 299)] London
Printed by Thomas Creede, for Thomas Pauier, and are
to be sold at his shop in Cornhill, at the signe of the Cat
and Parrets neare the Exchange. 1602. [*Head-title*] The
Chronicle Historie of Henry the fift : with his battel fought
at Agin Court in France. Togither with Ancient Pistoll.
[*Running-title*] The Chronicle Historie of Henry the fift.

[Q3. 1619.] [Ornament] The Chronicle History of
Henry the fift, with his battell fought at Agin Court in
France. Together with ancient Pistoll. As it hath bene
sundry times playd by the Right Honourable the Lord
Chamberlaine his Seruants. [William Jaggard's device
(McKerrow 283)] Printed for T⟨homas⟩ P⟨avier⟩ 1608.
[*Head-title*] The Chronicle Historie of Henry the fift : with
his battell fought at Agin Court in France. Togither with

Ancient Pistoll. [*Running-title*] The Chronicle History of Henry the fift.

[On the misdating, cf. p. 133.]

Facsimile. C. Praetorius (1886, *Sh. Q.* xxviii, ed. A. Symons).

[F1. 1623.] [*Catalogue*] The Life of King Henry the Fift. [*Histories,* pp. 69 *bis*–95 *bis,* sign. h–k 2. *Head- and Running-titles*] The Life of Henry the Fift.

[Acts i, sc. i, ii–v marked (altered in modern eds.).]

Parallel-Texts. B. Nicholson and P. A. Daniel (1877, *N.S.S.*); H. P. Stokes (1892, *Bankside*); E. Roman (1908).

Modern Editions. W. G. Boswell-Stone (1880, *N.S.S.*); G. C. Moore Smith (1896, *Warwick*); H. A. Evans (1903, *Arden*); R. D. French (1918, *Yale*).

Dissertations. B. Nicholson, *The Relation of the Q to the F of Hen. V* (1879, *N.S.S. Trans.* 77); G. Sarrazin, *Nym und Ben Jonson* (1904, *J.* xl. 212); J. D. Wilson, *Martin Marprelate and Sh.'s Fluellen* (1912, *3 Library,* iii. 113, 241); J. Le G. Brereton, *Sh.'s Wild Irishman* (1917, *M.L.R.* xii. 350); A. W. Pollard and J. D. Wilson, *The 'Stolne and Surreptitious' Shn. Texts: Hen. V* (1919, Mar. 13, *T.L.S.*); H. T. Price, *The Text of Hen. V* (1920); J. M. Robertson, *The Origination of Hen. V* (1922, *Sh. Canon,* i. 1); H. Craig, *The Relation of Q1 to F1 of Sh.'s Hen. V* (1927, *P.Q.* vi. 225); E. M. Albright, *The F Version of Hen. V in Relation to Sh.'s Times* (1928, *P.M.L.A.* xliii. 722).

F1 is a fairly regular text, with few mislineations, except that Pistol's bombastic verse, occurring in prose scenes, is printed as prose. Editors have adopted a good many emendations; in the French and dialectic passages it is not always clear whether an error is a misprint or an intended blunder by a speaker. The stage-directions are normal. There are some summarized entries for crowded scenes, and some musical notes. They may represent prompt-copy, contributed to by author and book-keeper.

Q2 and Q3 were probably set up independently from Q1, since Q3 reverts to many Q1 readings altered by Q2. The common divergences of Q2 and Q3 from Q1 are limited to corrections of obvious misprints, with one or two possible exceptions which may be accidental agreements in conjectural amendment. Greg, *Emendation,* 41, 45, notes that Q3, like the *Contention* of 1619, seems occasionally to anticipate a reading of F1.

If Q1 is read side by side with F1, it is impossible to regard it as anything but a continual perversion of the same text. Some of the verse-lines are truly rendered; others contain words related to those of F1 as variants of inflexion or indifferent alternatives, or words which read like mishearings. Many phrases are omitted, resulting in mislineations. Line after line is bungled metrically, by a writer incapable of handling blank verse. Larger omissions cause *lacunae* in the sense. Sometimes Q gives a mere paraphrase of the substance of F. The prose scenes are even more fragmentary, and are throughout in lines of irregular length and capitalized as verse. As a paradoxical result, Pistol's speeches resume verse form. There are some transpositions in the order of the dialogue, especially in the prose scenes. Two scenes (iv. 4, 5) change places. One passage, at the end of iii. 7, appears in F at iv. 2. 62–3. There is at least one phrase, at the end of ii. 3, of indecent 'gag'. This corruption is far beyond what can be attributed to errors of transcription and printing, and can only be explained by some process of reporting. It in certain respects differs from that to be observed in *Henry VI*, *Romeo and Juliet*, and *Hamlet*. There is no introduction of un-Shakespearean verse; practically everything is related to F. Price has argued for the use of shorthand, but mainly on grounds, such as the mishearings and alternatives, which do not (cf. p. 157) exclude memorization. Some unevenness of demerit suggests that the reporter may have been an actor. The best-rendered scenes are those in which Exeter, Gower, and the Governor of Harfleur appear. Conceivably the 'part' of one or more of these may have been available, and conceivably a 'plot', since a few marginal notes for action (ii. 1. 103; iv. 8. 9; v. 1. 30) are common to Q1 and F. But if so it was a very skeleton one. The Q stage-directions are even slighter than those of F. There are no long descriptive stage-directions comparable to those in Q1 of *Romeo and Juliet*.

On the other hand, the omissions of Q point to a performance for which much of the F text had been 'cut'. It is hardly possible to distinguish short cuts from the

reporter's lapses, but there is no representation at all in
Q of the prologue, the four other choruses, and the epilogue; or of three scenes (i. 1; iii. 1; iv. 2); or of substantial passages (e.g. i. 2. 115–35; ii. 2. 105–42; iii. 2.
69–153, iii. 3. 11–41; iii. 5. 27–68; iii. 7. 140–69; iv. 1.
1–34, 118–39, 247–301; v. 2. 307–58, 387–400) in
others. Cutting may be estimated to have reduced the
3,381 lines of the play by about 1,000, making a performance in two instead of three hours possible. Eleven
speaking parts are saved by the process, and this may point
to a provincial performance. Some good Shakespearean
matter goes, but it is of poetic rather than dramatic value.
In any case compression in the basis of the Q text is more
plausible than expansion for that of F, and there are analogies in the theatrical treatment of other long plays (cf.
p. 229). The attempts of Nicholson and Craig to trace
a literary revision fail to appreciate sufficiently the extent
and nature of the Q corruption. As in other reported texts
it entails vulgarization. And the historical corrections
attributed to Q by Daniel are also illusory. It is true that,
while F is in general closer to Holinshed than Q, its introduction of the Dauphin at Agincourt is a departure,
inconsistent with the King's order (iii. 5. 64) for him
to stay at Rouen, whereas Q leaves him out at Agincourt
and gives his speeches there to Bourbon. But the inconsistency is nothing to Shakespeare; the Dauphin must
come into dramatic conflict with Henry; and I can only
suppose that the reporter has failed to disentangle the
French lords. He also brings in among them (iii. 7; iv. 5),
apparently for the Rambures of F, a Gebon, possibly an
actor's name. Price suggests a corruption of that of
Samuel Gilburne, or less plausibly a Thomas Gibborne,
only known as a Fortune 'housekeeper' in 1624.[1] Probably the only change in F from the original text was the
very incomplete excision of profanity. That it is un-
abashed in the rather pointless episode (iii. 2. 69–153) of
the English, Scottish, Irish, and Welsh captains, which is
not in Q, tells against the suggestion that this is an inter-

[1] Murray, i. 214.

polation motived by the Jacobean policy of a union of kingdoms. But although it is not altogether appropriate to Elizabethan conditions, Holinshed does in fact give Henry Scottish mercenaries. Moreover, while Captain Jamy is not unsympathetically drawn, would the king have altogether approved the selection of the name for a comic character? An alternative and perhaps more plausible conjecture is that the passage was censored in 1599, because of earlier offence given to James by theatrical references to Scotland.[1] If so, we cannot suppose that it was restored when he saw the play on 7 January 1605 (App. D), but the F printer may, quite properly, have ignored a deletion mark.

The omission of the choric matter from Q may be only part of the abridgement, but it is also possible that the performances reported took place after the unsuccessful return of Essex from Ireland on 28 September 1599 made the reference to him in the chorus before Act v unsuitable. The last two lines of that to Act ii must be an afterthought, intended to correct the suggestion of 34–5 that the locality at once shifted to Southampton. This may be due to the Folio editor, who may have had the choruses on loose scrolls, and should have inserted this one and begun Act ii a scene later. In fact his supplementary lines probably replaced an act heading already set up, and he then put in Acts ii and iii where Acts iii and iv should be, and an Act iv, for which he had no chorus left, at random. 'Topical' speculation reaches its maximum of absurdity in Miss Albright's suggestion that the choruses belong to a special performance given at the Globe to further the interests of the Essex conspiracy and that the phrase 'bringing rebellion broached on his sword' was meant to foretell a return to broach the cask of rebellion.

A double Shakespearean handling is an element in Pollard and Wilson's interpretation of Q1 as one of a group of old plays (cf. p. 226), partly revised by Shakespeare, and then transcribed in an abridged form for provincial use in 1593, and finally printed partly from this transcript and partly from an actor's report of a performance of the

[1] *Eliz. Stage,* i. 323.

play as further revised by Shakespeare on the original manuscript. As in other plays of the group, a meticulous substitution of colourless equivalents is entailed. Pollard and Wilson's study is based mainly upon an examination of Act ii. In the verse scenes they take the metrical lines as derived from the transcript and the bungled lines as attempts of the reporter to fill the gaps. The metrical or tolerably metrical lines amount, so far as I can judge, to about 500 for the whole play, and would give a very sketchy outline of the plot, with many solutions of continuity in the dialogue. But I suppose that Pollard and Wilson think that this would be good enough for a provincial audience. Surely, however, they give an obviously illiterate reporter an impossible task, in going through an apparently complete manuscript and determining, as he must have done with considerable accuracy, the exact points at which expansion from a very imperfect memory of the later version was required. There must of course have been more than 500 lines in the provincial play, but I understand the theory to be that for certain scenes the transcript was entirely abandoned and a report of Shakespeare's later prose scenes substituted. It is suggested that in these scenes the reporter played either Bardolph or Mrs. Quickly, but surely neither part is consistently well reproduced. The original play rehandled by Shakespeare is taken to have been itself a revision of the *Famous Victories* (cf. s.v. *Hen. IV*), and to have left traces in the choruses and historical scenes of the F text.

This 'intermediate' *Henry V* is also assumed by Robertson, as a play written about 1590 by Marlowe, probably with the collaboration of Peele and Greene, if not also of Kyd; revised for the Admiral's in 1595, probably by Peele, although Munday, Chettle, Heywood, Drayton, and Dekker are also conceivable; revived with comic relief by Chapman; transferred by the Admiral's to the Chamberlain's; and finally revised by Shakespeare and perhaps Chettle. Such a string of hypotheses, involving the possible interaction of about a dozen writers at five stages is of course incapable of demonstration and would not repay systematic refutation. An example of Robertson's method is to be found in the suggestion that the reference to Essex may in an earlier version have been to some other episode in his career, such as his expedition to France in 1591. So far as Marlowe is concerned, the attempt to find his hand here is less plausible even than Robertson's attempt to find him in *Richard II*; and the 'clues' of supposed un-Shakespearean words and phrases are extraordinarily thin.

Shakespeare's historical source is again mainly Holinshed, and for anything borrowed from the later scenes of *Famous Victories* it is not necessary to look further than the version left to us, which had become available in the 1598 edition, even if there was (cf. p. 383) no earlier one. I think we must take the 'Ireland' of the chorus as meaning 'Ireland', and therefore as datable between Essex's departure thither on 27 March 1599 and his return on September 28. Nor do I see sufficient reason for supposing the choruses to be of different date to the play as a whole. They are naturally written in a somewhat artificial and old-fashioned manner. The metrical tests, for what they are worth, consist well enough with 1599, and the play must of course follow the promise in the epilogue to *2 Henry IV* to 'continue the story, with Sir John in it, and make you merry with fair Katharine of France: where, for any thing I know, Falstaff shall die of a sweat'. It is true that the general literary quality does not show any marked advance upon *Henry IV* itself. One may even trace a reversion, in spite of some fine rhetorical passages, to a more traditional way of handling chronicle matter, there less conspicuous. Perhaps Shakespeare was again, as in *Richard II*, imperfectly interested in epic themes. Nor are the added 'humorists' quite on the level of their predecessors. Wilson has made a fair case for finding traits of the Welsh soldier Sir Roger Williams in Fluellen; and Sarrazin for regarding Nym, with his jerky style and constant repetition of the word 'humour', as a satire of Ben Jonson's early dramatic manner; although I do not think (cf. p. 72) that it is the 'purge' which Shakespeare is said to have given him. Jonson's prologue to *E.M.I.* (App. B, no. xxii), probably of later date than the play itself, in turn satirizes the chorus wafting the action overseas. The names of William Fluellen and George Bardolfe appear as those of fellow recusants (cf. p. 25) with John Shakespeare in 1592. Those of Bate, Court, and Williams are also found (French 327) in Stratford records.

XIX. JULIUS CAESAR

[F1. 1623.] [*Catalogue*] The Life and death of Julius Cæsar. [*Tragedies*, pp. 109–30, sign. kk–ll 5ᵛ. *Head-and Running-Titles*] The Tragedie of Julius Cæsar.
[Acts i, sc. 1, ii–v marked.]

Facsimile. J. D. Wilson (1929).

Modern Editions. A. D. Innes (1893, *Warwick*); M. Hunter (1900); F. H. Sykes (1909); M. Macmillan (1902, *Arden*); H. H. Furness (1913, *New Variorum*); L. Mason (1919, *Yale*).

Dissertations. F. G. Fleay, *J.C.* (1874, *N.S.S. Trans.* 357; *Sh. Manual*, 262); N. Delius, *Shs J.C. und seine Quellen in Plutarch* (1882, *J.* xvii. 67; *Abl.* ii. 153); P. Simpson, *The Date of Sh.'s J.C.* (1899, 9 *N.Q.* iii. 105, 216); E. Koeppel, *Shs J.C. und die Entstehungszeit des anonymen Dramen The Wisdom of Dr. Dodypoll* (1907, *J.* xliii. 210); P. Kannen-giesser, *Eine Doppelredaktion in Shs J.C.* (1908, *J.* xliv. 51); W. Keller, *Zwei Bemerkungen zu J.C.* (1909, *J.* xlv. 219); M. W. MacCallum, *Sh.'s Roman Plays and their Background* (1910); H. M. Ayres, *Sh.'s J.C. in the Light of Some Other Versions* (1910, *P.M.L.A.* xxv. 183); H. C. Bartlett, *Quarto Editions of J.C.* (1913, 3 *Library*, iv. 122); G. Sarrazin, *Sh. und Orlando Pescetti* (1913, *E.S.* xlvi. 347); A. Boecker, *A Probable Italian Source of Sh.'s J.C.* (1913); A. Kerrl, *Die metrischen Unterschiede von Shs K.J. und J.C.* (1913); A. de V. Tassin, *J.C.* (1916, *Columbia Studies*, 255); J. M. Robertson, *The Origination of J.C.* (1922, *Sh. Canon*, i. 66); W. Wells, *The Authorship of J.C.* (1923); M. H. Shackford, *J.C. and Ovid* (1926, *M.L.N.* xli. 172); F. Wölcken, *Shs J.C. und Mar-lowes Massacre at Paris* (1927, *J.* lxiii. 192); E. H. C. Oliphant, *J.C.* (1927, *The Plays of Beaumont and Fletcher*, 316), *B. and F.* (1928, Feb. 23, *T.L.S.*).

Julius Caesar is one of the best printed of the F additions, with only trifling dislocations. The stage-directions are normal. The spellings Antony, and occasionally in early scenes Antonio, diverge from the Anthony regularly used by Shakespeare elsewhere. There is a trace of a revision in iv. 3, not necessarily more than an afterthought at the

time of composition. Brutus and Cassius discuss (143–
58, 166) Portia's death. Thereafter (181–95) Messala
announces that death to Brutus, who is apparently ignorant
of it. Probably the first passage is an insertion, and the
second has been left undeleted or imperfectly deleted in
the manuscript. The play is a very short one, and a few
abrupt short lines may be evidence of cuts.

The date of production can be fairly definitely fixed by
Platter's visit (App. D) to a Julius Caesar play on 21
September 1599. He does not name the Globe, but the
theatre was south of the river, and the Swan was probably
not in regular use.[1] The Rose no doubt was, but as the
Admiral's had new Caesar plays (cf. *infra*) in 1594–5 and
again in 1602, they are not very likely to have been staging
one in 1599. Platter's 'at least fifteen characters' agrees
fairly with *Julius Caesar*, on the assumption that he disregarded a number of inconspicuous parts. The date of
1599 fits in well with other evidence. Weever clearly
refers to the play in his *Mirror of Martyrs* (App. B, no.
xix), which he says was fit for the print two years before
1601, even though it may have been added to in the interval. There is an obvious quotation of iii. 2. 109 in Jonson's *E.M.O.* (1599), (iii. 4. 33), 'Reason long since is
fled to animals, you know', as well as a less indicative
repetition (v. 6. 79) of 'Et tu Brute' (iii. 1. 77). *The Wisdom of Dr. Dodipoll*, printed in 1600,[2] also quotes iii. 2. 109,
and 'Et tu Brute' is in S. Nicholson's *Acolastus his Afterwit*
(1600). On the other hand, if there are echoes in iii. 1.
113 of Daniel's *Musophilus* and in i. 2. 52 of Sir John
Davies's *Nosce Teipsum*, these were registered on 9 January
and 14 April 1599 respectively. The play held the stage
in the seventeenth century. Court performances are
recorded (App. D) in 1612–13, 1636, and 1638.

Jonson tells us (App. B, no. xxii) that iii. 1. 47 originally ran—

   Cæsar did never wrong, but with just cause,

and glances at the same passage in *Staple of News* (1626),
ind. 36, '*Cry you mercy*, you neuer did wrong, but with iust

<hr/>

[1] Cf. *Eliz. Stage*, ii. 413.   [2] *Ibid.* iv. 54.

cause'. Incidentally Jonson gives testimony, if that were needed, to Shakespeare's authorship of the play; and so does Digges (App. B, no. lii) in 1640. Yet in no play of the canon have recent critics more persistently sought other hands. Fleay regarded it as an abridgement of Shakespeare's work, due to Jonson himself. Abridged it may be, but the evidence produced for any incorporation of Jonsonian matter, unless he suggested an alternative for iii. 1. 47, is negligible. Robertson, Wells, and Oliphant all find a considerable substratum of Marlowe. Thereafter they diverge. Robertson supposes that Marlowe, perhaps with Kyd, although he only hints (i. 115) at this, wrote a play in three parts, dealing successively with the struggle of Caesar and Pompey, with Caesar's death, and with Philippi. Part 1 was revived by the Admiral's as *Caesar and Pompey* in 1594,[1] and Part 2, revised by Chapman and Drayton and perhaps (i. 142) Heywood, as the second part of *Caesar* in 1595.[2] Part 3 was revised as *Caesar's Fall or The Two Shapes*, also for the Admiral's, by Drayton, Dekker, Middleton, Munday, and Webster in 1602, although of this Robertson does not seem very certain, and he makes no attempt to trace any of these writers except Drayton in *Julius Caesar* as we have it.[3] However, Part 1 was then laid aside, until Chapman handled it in his *Caesar and Pompey*,[4] while Parts ii and iii were transferred by the Admiral's to the Chamberlain's, and revised by Shakespeare about 1603. It may be noted that such a transference between rival companies is far from plausible, and also that Robertson is not accurate in stating that Henslowe does not record the plays of 1594 and 1595 as 'ne'. The writers of 1602 also got full value for a new play. Finally, according to Robertson, Jonson compressed Parts 2 and 3 into the present form of *Julius Caesar* either about 1607 or after Shakespeare's death. Wells thinks that a play, apparently a single play, by Marlowe was given for revision to Shakespeare, who abandoned it after completing the first 57 lines, and that

---

[1] *Eliz. Stage*, ii. 143.
[2] *Ibid*. ii. 144.
[3] *Ibid*. ii. 179.
[4] *Ibid*. iii. 259.

the rest of *Julius Caesar* is a revision by Beaumont, who disregarded Shakespeare's opening, slid the triumph into the feast of· *Lupercalia*, and made no further use of the tribunes and their mob. Oliphant is surprised that Wells should find Beaumont's hand continuously throughout the play, and would reduce his share, if any, to little more than portions of iv. 3, regarding the rest as the work of an early writer, probably Marlowe, revised by Shakespeare. These conflicting theories may perhaps be left to cancel each other out. I believe them to be all equally misconceived, and to rest partly upon characteristic Shakespearean inconsistencies in the handling of detail, and partly upon two special features of the play. One is that, while Shakespeare's later tragedies move in a single curve to a catastrophe in the death of the title-character, the action of *Julius Caesar* has two peaks, one in the Capitol and the other at Philippi, and the psychological interest is at least as much in Brutus as in Caesar. The effect of a double theme is therefore given. The other is that Shakespeare is deliberately experimenting in a classical manner, with an extreme simplicity both of vocabulary and of phrasing. This has already been noted by Bradley, *Shakespearean Tragedy*, 85. It is often admirably telling, but sometimes it leads to a stiffness, perhaps even a baldness, of diction, which may awake reminiscences of pre-Shakespearean plays. I do not see any special resemblance to Marlowe; the constant use of mid-line speech endings and mid-line pauses is not pre-Shakespearean at all. As for Beaumont, it is merely a matter of verbal parallels, and the derivation of Beaumont's diction from Shakespeare's has long been recognized. The element of simple dignity in the style of *Julius Caesar*, although we have no particular reason to suppose that he knew it otherwise than on the stage, seems to have made a special appeal to him.

Of course there were Elizabethan plays on the Caesar story before Shakespeare's, and before those which Henslowe records. It was a favourite Renaissance subject. Marc Antoine Muret's Latin *Julius Caesar* (1544) had been followed by Jacques Grévin's *César* (1561) and

Robert Garnier's *Cornélie* (1574), of which a translation by
Kyd appeared in 1594.[1] An entry in Machyn's *Diary*,
which may record an English play as early as 1562, seems
to be in part a forgery.[2] The Paul's boys played a
Pompey at court in 1581,[3] and Gosson notes a *Caesar and
Pompey*, possibly, although his words are not quite clear,
at the Theatre, in his *Plays Confuted* of 1582.[4] Richard
Edes produced a Latin *Caesar Interfectus* at Christ Church
in 1582, of which the epilogue alone survives.[5] On these
or others many early literary allusions, some of which lay
special stress on Caesar's triumph, may rest, although by
themselves they would prove no more than a knowledge of
the classical story. They are particularly numerous in
Shakespeare's own early plays, continue to *Hamlet*, where
there are three, *All's Well that Ends Well*, *Measure for
Measure*, and *Othello*, and then disappear, except in *Coriolanus* and *Cymbeline*, where Caesar is historically appropriate. Shakespeare had purged his imagination of the
theme. There are several also in Marlowe. But I find
nothing to indicate that Marlowe ever wrote a Caesar
play. Wells quotes Greene, *Orlando Furioso*, 457, where
Sacrepant—

> (like to Cassius)
> Sits sadly dumping, ayming Cæsars death,
> Yet crying Ave to his Maiestie,

combines it with Greene's *Francescos Fortunes*, where
Cicero says to Roscius, 'if the Cobler hath taught thee to
say Aue Caesar, disdain not thy tutor',[6] and decides that the
cobbler must be Marlowe, and that the 'Aue Caesar' is not
from *Edward III*, i. 1. 164, but from a play by Marlowe
with Cassius in it. But I hope to have shown [7] that the
cobbler and his crow who cried 'Ave Caesar', not to Julius
but Augustus Caesar, came, like Roscius, from Macrobius.
More interesting are the passages in Marlowe's *Massacre
at Paris*, 1220, 1246, where the Guise before his death says

[1] *Eliz. Stage*, iii. 397.
[2] Cf. vol. ii, p. 386.
[3] *Eliz. Stage*, iv. 158.
[4] *Ibid.* iv. 216.
[5] *Ibid.* iii. 309.
[6] *Ibid.* iv. 236.
[7] *Ibid.* i. 377.

of himself, 'Yet Cæsar shall goe forth', and again, 'Thus Cæsar did go foorth, and thus he dyed'. The first phrase repeats *Jul. Caes.* ii. 2. 28. Here it is in place, and Shakespeare's Caesar habitually speaks of himself in the third person. The *Massacre*, although written in 1593, only exists in an undated edition, possibly as late as 1599. It is corrupt and may have an element of 'reporting' in it. Perhaps this brought the phrases in. But even if Marlowe wrote them, and took them from an earlier play, it would not prove that the play was his, still less that, as Wells thinks, he meant Caesar for a covert representation of the Guise, about whom, indeed, he showed no hesitation in writing openly.

Shakespeare mainly derived his material from Plutarch's *Lives* of Brutus, Caesar, and Antony, as translated by Sir Thomas North (1579) from the French (1559) of Jacques Amyot. He often borrows North's actual wording. Individual passages have been compared with others in Lucan's *Pharsalia*, Cicero's *Letters*, Pliny's *Natural History*, Appian's *Civil Wars*, Dion Cassius's *Annals*, Suetonius's *Lives of the Caesars*, and Orlando Pescetti's *Il Cesare* (1594), but how far he drew directly upon these, it is difficult, in view of the lost earlier English plays, to say. The famous 'Et tu Brute' is probably in its origin an adaptation of the καὶ σὺ, τέκνον of Suetonius. It has only been traced once in English literature before *Julius Caesar*, in the *True Tragedy*, xxi. 53; it is not in *3 Hen. VI*, v. 1. 77–80, of which the passage in the *True Tragedy* is a corruption. A play of *Julius Caesar* was given by John Green's company at Dresden in 1626.[1] It may or may not have been Shakespeare's.

XX. AS YOU LIKE IT
[S.R. 1600?]
         4 Augusti
As you like yᵗ, a booke ⎫ to be staid
.   .   .   .   . ⎭ (Arber, iii. 37).
[On the significance of this entry, cf. p. 145.]

[1] *Ibid.* ii. 286.

[F1. 1623.] [*Catalogue*] As you Like it. [*Comedies*, pp. 185–207, sign. Q 3–S 2. *Head-title*] As you Like it. [*Running-title*] As you like it.

[Acts and scc. marked.]

Facsimile. J. D. Wilson (1929).

Modern Editions. H. H. Furness (1890, *New Variorum*); J. W. Holme (1914, *Arden*); J. R. Crawford (1919, *Yale*); A. T. Quiller-Couch and J. D. Wilson (1926, *C.U.P.*).

Dissertations. N. Delius, *Lodges Rosalynde und Shs A.Y.L.* (1871, *J*. vi. 226; *Abl*.i. 206); W. G. Boswell-Stone, *Sh.'s A.Y.L. and Lodge's Rosalynde Compared* (1882, *N.S.S. Trans.* 277); J. Zupitza, *Die mittelenglische Vorstufe zu Shs A.Y.L.* (1886, *J*. xxi, 69); C. H. Herford, *Sh.'s Masters and A.Y.L.* (1890); A. H. Thorndike, *The Relation of A.Y.L. to Robin Hood Plays* (1902, *J.E.G.P.* iv. 59); W. W. Greg, *Lodge's Rosalynde: being the Original of Sh.'s A.Y.L.* (1907, *Sh. Classics*); H. Conrad, *Die Erzählung von Gamelyn als Quelle zu Shs A.Y.L.* (1910, *J*. xlvi, 120); A. Gray, *How Sh. 'Purged' Jonson* (1928); B. H. Newdigate, *Harington, Jaques and Touchstone* (1929, Jan. 3, 10, *T.L.S.*).

F is a fair text, with only small typographical disturbances, chiefly due to rapid transitions between verse and prose. The stage-directions are slight, and only occasionally suggest the hands of the author (ii. 1. 1; ii. 4. 1; iii. 2. 131) and the book-keeper (i. 2. 158, 224, 227; ii. 4. 1; ii. 5. 40; iv. 2. 11; v. 5. 114). Wilson suggests, without elaborating the point, that the copy may have been assembled from 'parts'.

The entry in the Stationers' Register and the absence of the play from Meres' list of 1598 give limits of date, within which it is difficult to be more precise. On grounds of style a grouping with *Twelfth Night*, a little after *Much Ado about Nothing*, in 1599 seems reasonable. The 'lover and his lass' song (v. 3. 17) is probably original here, as it echoes one at the same point in the source. There is a setting in Thomas Morley's *First Book of Airs, or Little Short Songs* (1600), of which the only known copy is in the collection of H. C. Folger. The forest theme may have been selected in rivalry with the Admiral's Robin Hood plays of 1598.[1] The quotation (iii. 5. 81) of a line from Marlowe's *Hero and Leander* would come most naturally

[1] *Eliz. Stage*, iii. 446.

after the publication of that poem in 1598. Some other historical and literary echoes which have been suggested are too vague or too remote in date. If 'Diana in the fountain' (iv. 1. 154) was the image in Cheapside, that was set up in 1596.[1] One cannot seriously, with Chalmers, relate the antithesis of court and country to the troubles of the Earl of Essex in 1599, or, with Aldis Wright, Rosalind's chaff about 'pretty oaths that are not dangerous' (iv. 1. 193) and a magician who tenders life dearly (v. 2. 77), to the Act against witchcraft in 1603 or that against abuses of players in 1606. Of the earlier parallels, Wilson stresses a close one at iii. 2. 103, 119, and one less striking at ii. 2. 8, to passages in Nashe's *Strange News of the Intercepting of Certain Letters* of 1592 or 1593,[2] and thinks this unlikely to have been read by Shakespeare in 1599. He also supposes that Shakespeare knew *Hero and Leander* in manuscript before it was published, which is of course possible, and that a reference to the death of Marlowe in a quarrel about a tavern bill, as well as to the 'Infinite riches in a little room' of *Jew of Malta*, i. 1. 72, is to be found in Touchstone's complaint (iii. 3. 14) that a lack of understanding 'strikes a man more dead than a great reckoning in a little room'. Such an allusion, which would surely have been rather heartless, does not seem to me plausible, and Wilson's points cannot of course weigh against the general evidence for 1598–1600. Indeed, he accepts this date, but only for a revision of an earlier version of 1593, which largely took the form of rewriting verse scenes in prose. For this he finds evidence, partly in textual inconsistencies as to the relative heights of Rosalind and Celia (i. 2. 284; i. 3. 117; iv. 3. 88) and as to the nomenclature of the Dukes (i. 2. 87, 246; v. 4. 160), both of which are more easily explained by misprints, and as to the period of the elder Duke's sojourn in the forest (i. 1. 120; i. 3. 73; ii. 1. 2), which is too Shakespearean to need explanation at all; but mainly upon a theory, suggested to him by Pollard, that certain prose passages, unusually full of scannable lines (cf. p. 233), had originally

---

[1] Stowe, *Survey*, i. 266.   [2] *Works*, i. 275, 324.

been written as verse. They make very good prose, how-ever, and in fact it is just as easy (cf. my criticism in *Year's Work* for 1926) to rewrite as verse, with what Wilson calls 'a little innocent faking', passages which he does not believe to have been revised.

As You Like It has been claimed, on the authority of a document not now verifiable (App. D), as the play given by the King's men at Wilton on 2 December 1603. Nothing else is known of its after-history. It is quite possible, how-ever, that the verses of Hymen in v. 4. 114–52, markedly inferior in style to the rest of the play, may be a specta-cular interpolation not due to Shakespeare. There is no textual disturbance in F, but the scene would run well enough without them. A stage tradition (App. C. nos. xxxiv, xliv) represents Shakespeare himself as playing the part of Adam.

The source is Thomas Lodge's prose novel of *Rosalynde, or Euphues' Golden Legacy* (1590), which itself owes some-thing to the *Tale of Gamelyn*, found, although not Chaucer-ian, in some manuscripts of the *Canterbury Tales*. It is pos-sible, although not very probable, that a further reference to this motived some small departures by Shakespeare from *Rosalynde*. But it was not in print until 1721. On A. Gray's theory that Jaques was Shakespeare's 'purge' to Jonson, cf. p. 72. Newdigate's suggestion that he stands for Sir John Harington is even less plausible. Harington was not that sort of man.

XXI. TWELFTH NIGHT

MS. H:P., *Reliques*, 115, describes a copy from F2 appar-ently made for a seventeenth-century performance, and marked with the names of characters at their points of entry. It was afterwards at Warwick Castle.

[F1. 1623.] [*Catalogue*] Twelfe-Night, or what you will. [*Comedies*, pp. 255–75, sign. Y 2–Z 6. *Head-title*] Twelfe Night, Or what you will. [*Running-title*] Twelfe Night, or, What you will.

[Acts and scc. marked.]

Facsimile. J. D. Wilson (1928).

Modern Editions. H. H. Furness (1901, *New Variorum*); A. D. Innes (1895, *Warwick*); M. Luce (1906, 1929, *Arden*); G. H. Nettleton (1922, *Yale*); A. T. Quiller-Couch and J. D. Wilson (1930, *C.U.P.*)

Dissertations. F. G. Fleay, *On the Date and Composition of T.N.* (1874, *N.S.S. Trans.* 298; *Sh. Manual,* 227); C. H. Coote, *Sh.'s 'New Map'* (1878, *N.S.S. Trans.* 88) and in *Voyages and Works of John Davis,* lxxxv (1880, *Hakluyt Soc.* lix); H. Conrad, *Über die Entstehungszeit von T.N.* (1895, *J.* xxxi, 177), *Zu den Quellen von Shs T.N.* (1912, *E.S.* xlvi. 73); H. Meissner, *Die Quellen zu Shs T.N.* (1895); H. Logemann, *Johannes de Witt's Visit to the Swan Theatre* (1897, *Anglia,* xix. 117); J. de Perott, *Noch eine eventuelle Quelle zum T.N.* (1910, *J.* xlvi. 118); I. Gollancz, *Malvolio* (1916, *Sh. Homage,* 177); J. D. Wilson, *T.N. and the Gunpowder Plot* (1929, June 13, *T.L.S.*).

F is a good text, with normal stage-directions, including notes for the introduction of music and a misnaming (i. 5. 177) of Viola as Violenta; it may rest on prompt-copy.

The earliest notice of the play is John Manningham's record (App. B, no. xxiv) of a performance in the Middle Temple on 2 February 1602. It was evidently then new to him. But it is so akin in style and temper to *As You Like It* that a somewhat earlier date appears probable; and if this is put in 1600–1, it is fairly consistent with such literary and historical clues as are not too tenuous to deserve consideration. We must, however, assume that if the song at ii. 3. 40 is Shakespeare's, which it may well be, it may not have been originally written for the play, since music for an air called 'O mistress mine' appears, without words, in Thomas Morley's *First Book of Consort Lessons* (1599). It is, however, not clear (Noble 81) that this setting was for Shakespeare's song, and one of *Mistress Mine* in Morley's *Short Book of Airs* (1600), now in the Folger collection, is said to be distinct from his. But the song-scraps in ii. 3. 109–21 are from Robert Jones's *First Book of Songs and Airs* (1600). Logemann's identification of the scene (iii. 4) where Malvolio appears cross-gartered with the action represented in De Witt's Swan drawing of 1596 must in any case be rejected; *Twelfth Night* can hardly have been played at the Swan. The satire of 'cross-wooing' in *E.M.O.*

(1599), iii. 6. 195, is too general to carry a special application to the play. On the other hand, the 'fat fool', who will
'rore out his barren bold iests, with a tormenting laughter,
betweene drunke, and drie' in *Poetaster* (1601), iii. 4. 345,
sounds very much like an echo of Sir Toby Belch. Sir
Robert Shirley, returning enriched from Persia in 1599,
perhaps inspired the allusion (ii. 5. 197) to 'a pension of
thousands to be paid by the Sophy'; and the 'new map
with the augmentation of the Indies' (iii. 2. 85) was
probably the 'Hydrographical Description' prepared
about 1598–9 by Emerie Molyneux. Examples are
sometimes bound up with Hakluyt's *Principall Navi-
gations* (1598–1600). Orsino, Duke of Bracciano, visited
London during the winter of 1600–1.[1] The rather vague
reference discovered by Wilson in iii. 1. 24–35 to the
Jesuit doctrine of equivocation (cf. s.v. *Macbeth*), already
avowed by Robert Southwell at his trial in 1595, cannot
weigh in favour of a date after the Gunpowder Plot
against the evidence for one in or before 1602.

Fleay thought that the Viola-Orsino-Olivia plot, fairly
detachable from that of Malvolio, was a revision of earlier
work, chiefly because i. 2. 57 and ii. 4. 2 suggested to him
that the songs were originally given to Viola; but this is
very slight ground. Conrad found more parallels to early
than to late work in this part of the play, and Sarrazin
showed that this argument was based on inadequate
observation.[2] It is open to any one to produce a fresh case
for revision on the basis of the many scannable lines (cf.
p. 233) in the prose scenes.

The play was revived at court in 1618 and again under the
title *Malvolio* in 1623 (App. D), and Digges (App. B, no. lii)
records its popularity in 1640. The mildness of Sir Toby
Belch's profanity may be due to Jacobean expurgation.

The motive of a lady disguised as a page to the man she
loves is widespread, and had been combined before *Twelfth
Night* with that of the resembling twins and their separation by a shipwreck. Shakespeare had already used one in
Two Gentlemen of Verona and the other in *Comedy of Errors*.

---

[1] Chamberlain, *Eliz.* 99.   [2] *J.* xxxii. 164.

Manningham compared the play to the Italian *Inganni*. Perhaps he meant the *Inganni* of Nicolo Secchi (1562); perhaps that of Curzio Gonzaga (1592), which has the name Cesare; perhaps the earlier *Ingannati* (1537) of the academy of Intronati, which comes nearer to Shakespeare's handling, and has in the induction a Fabio, a Malevolti, and a mention of 'la notte di Beffana' (Epiphany). This was perhaps the source of a story in Matteo Bandello's *Novelle* (1554), ii. 36, translated in P. de Belleforest's *Histoires Tragiques*, iv (1571) 59; and this in its turn the source of the story of *Apolonius and Silla* in Barnabe Riche's *Farewell to the Military Profession* (1581). Shakespeare probably used this, as it adds the shipwreck theme, but his debt was not very great. He may also have read of the disguised lady in Giraldi Cintio's *Ecatommiti*, v. 8, or Sidney's *Arcadia* (1590), or the play of *Sir Clyomon and Clamydes* (1599), or Emanuel Forde's *Parismus* (1598), which also has a shipwreck and the names Olivia and Violetta.

Riche's story became also the source of the German play *Tugend- und Liebes-Streit* (1677), of which an earlier form may have been the *King of Cyprus and Duke of Venice*, played by Green's company of travelling English actors at Gräz in 1608 and Dresden in 1626.[1] Creizenach, who prints *Tugend- und Liebesstreit* in *Schauspiele der Englischen Komödianten* (1889), 53, thinks that some common divergences from Riche here and in *Twelfth Night* may point to a lost English play as an intermediary. Riche says that some of his stories had been 'presented on a stage'.

There is no clear source for the Malvolio episodes. Gollancz[2] has suggested an analogue to the misrule of ii. 3 in a quarrel at court between the Earl of Southampton and Ambrose Willoughby, and I have suggested another in a story told of Sir William Knollys and Elizabeth's maids of honour.[3]

[1] *Eliz. Stage*, ii. 281, 286.   [3] *Sh. : A Survey*, 178.
[2] *Sh. Homage*, 177.

XXII. HAMLET

[S.R. 1602.] xxvj^{to} Julij. James Robertes. Entred for his Copie vnder the handes of master Pasfield and master Waterson warden A booke called the Revenge of Hamlett Prince Denmarke as yt was latelie Acted by the Lord Chamberleyne his servantes. vj^{d}. (Arber, iii. 212).

[Q1. 1603.] The Tragicall Historie of Hamlet Prince of Denmarke By William Shake-speare. As it hath beene diuerse times acted by his Highnesse seruants in the Cittie of London: as also in the two Vniuersities of Cambridge and Oxford, and else-where [Nicholas Ling's device (McKerrow 301)] At London printed ⟨by Valentine Simmes⟩ for N⟨icholas⟩ L⟨ing⟩ and Iohn Trundell. 1603. [*Head-title*] The Tragicall Historie of Hamlet Prince of Denmarke. [*Running-title*] The Tragedie of Hamlet Prince of Denmarke.

Facsimile. W. Griggs (1880, *Sh. Q.* i, ed. F. J. Furnivall).

Reprints. W. A. Wright (1893, *Cambridge Sh.* ix. 697); G. B. Harrison (1923).

Edition. F. G. Hubbard (1920).

[Q2. 1604.] The Tragicall Historie of Hamlet, Prince of Denmarke. By William Shakespeare. Newly imprinted and enlarged to almost as much againe as it was, according to the true and perfect Coppie. [Nicholas Ling's device (McKerrow 301)] At London, Printed by I⟨ames⟩ R⟨oberts⟩ for N⟨icholas⟩ L⟨ing⟩ and are to be sold at his shoppe vnder Saint Dunstons Church in Fleet-street. 1604. [*Head-title*, under ornament with royal arms, *and Running-title*] The Tragedie of Hamlet Prince of Denmarke.

[In some copies the t.p. is dated 1605.]

Facsimile. W. Griggs (1880, *Sh. Q.* ii, ed. F. J. Furnivall).

[S.R. 1607.] 19 Novembris. John Smythick. Entred for his copies vnder thandes of the wardens. these bookes followinge Whiche dyd belonge to Nicholas Lynge. viz. . . . 6 A booke called Hamlett . . . (Arber, iii. 365).

[Q3. 1611.] The Tragedy of Hamlet Prince of Denmarke.

By William Shakespeare. Newly imprinted and enlarged
to almost as much againe as it was according to the true
and perfect Coppy. [Smethwick's device (McKerrow 376)]
At London, Printed for Iohn Smethwick, and are to be
sold at his shoppe in Saint Dunstons Church yeard in
Fleetstreet. Vnder the Diall. 1611. [*Head-title*] The
Tragedie of Hamlet Prince of Denmarke. [*Running-title*]
The Tragedy of Hamlet Prince of Denmarke.

[F1. 1623.] [*Catalogue*] The Tragedy of Hamlet
[*Tragedies*, pp. 152–6, 257–80, sign. nn 4ᵛ–qqᵛ. *Head-
title*] The Tragedie of Hamlet, Prince of Denmarke.
[*Running-title*] The Tragedie of Hamlet.
[Acts and scc. marked to ii. 2.]

[Q4. n.d. (1611⟨⟩1637)] W⟨illiam⟩ S⟨tansby⟩ for Iohn
Smethwicke.

[Q5. 1637.] R. Young for John Smethwicke.

Parallel-texts. E. P. Vining (1890, *Bankside*, Q1+F1); W.
Vietor (1891, Q1+Q2+F1).

German Version. MS. Library of Gotha, with title *Tragoedia Der
bestrafte Bruder-mord oder: Prinz Hamlet aus Dännemark,* dated
'Pretz ⟨Preetz in Holstein⟩, den 27 October 1710'.

Editions. H. A. O. Reichard (1781, *Olla Potrida,* ii. 18); A. Cohn
(1865, *Sh. in Germany*); W. Creizenach (1889, *Schauspiele der
Englischen Komödianten,* 125).

Translations. G. Archer (with Cohn's ed., under title *Fratricide
Punished*); H. H. Furness (1877, *Hamlet,* ii. 121).

Modern Editions. H. H. Furness (1877, *New Variorum*); E. K.
Chambers (1894, *Warwick*); E. Dowden (1899, 1928, *Arden*).

Dissertations. T. Mommsen, *Beurtheilung über den Delius'schen H.* (1855,
Neue Jahrbuch f. Philologie und Pädagogik, lxxii. 57, 107, 159); R. G.
Latham, *Two Dissertations on the H. of Saxo Grammaticus* (1872); F. A.
Marshall, *A Study of H.* (1875); K. Silberschag, *Shs H., seine Quellen und
politischen Beziehungen* (1877, *J.* xii. 261); B. Nicholson, *Kemp and the
Play of H.—Yorick and Tarlton* (1880, *N.S.S. Trans.* 57); C. H. Herford
and W. H. Widgery, *The Q1 of H.* (1880); G. Tanger, *The Q1 and Q2
and F1 of H.* (1880, *N.S.S. Trans.* 109), *H. nach Shs Manuscript* (1881,
Anglia, iv. 211), *Der B.B. und sein Verhältniss zu Shs H.* (1888, *J.* xxiii.
224); H. Conrad (Isaac), *Hs Familie* (1881, *J.* xvi. 274), *Die H.-Periode*

in Shs Leben (1885–6, *Archiv*, lxxiii. 163, 371; lxxiv. 45; lxxv. 1. 269), H. *und sein Urbild* (1897, *Shs Selbst-bekenntnisse*); F. G. Fleay, *Neglected Facts on H.* (1884, *E.S.* vii. 87); W. Creizenach, *Die Tragödie B.B. und ihre Bedeutung für die Kritik des Sh'schen H.* (1887, *Berichte der Phil.- Hist. Classe der Sachsischen Gesellschaft der Wissenschaften*), *B.B. and its Relation to Sh.'s H.* (1904, *M.P.* ii. 249), *H.-Fragen* (1906, *J.* xlii. 76); G. Sarrazin, *Die Entstehung der H. Tragödie* (1889–91, *Anglia*, xii. 143; xiii. 117; xiv. 322), *Thomas Kyd und sein Kreis* (1892), *Das Personal von Shs H. und der Hof Friedrichs II von Dänemark* (1895, *E.S.* xxi. 330), *Der Name Ophelia* (1895, *E.S.* xxi. 443); F. A. Leo, *Rosenkrantz und Guldenstern* (1890–1, *J.* xxv. 281; xxvi. 325); R. Loening, *Die H.- Tragödie Shs* (1892); O. Elton, *Sh.'s H.* (1894, with *Transl. of Saxo Grammaticus*); J. Corbin, *The Elizabethan H.* (1895), *The German H. and the Earlier English Versions* (1896, *Harvard Studies and Notes*, v. 247); I. Gollancz, *Hamlet in Iceland* (1898), *The Name Polonius* (1914, *Archiv*, cxxxii, 141), *Polonius* (1916, *Sh. Homage*, 173); *The Sources of H.* (1926); M. W. MacCallum, *The Authorship of the Early H.* (1901, *Furnivall Misc.*); J. Schick, *Die Entstehung des H.* (1902, *J.* xxxviii. xiii), *Corpus Hamleti- cum* (1906); A. H. Thorndike, *The Relation of H. to Contemporary Revenge Plays* (1902, *P.M.L.A.* xvii. 125); M. B. Evans, *B.B., sein Verhältniss zu Shs H.* (1902, 1910), *B.B. und Shs H.* (1905, *M.P.* ii. 433); A. H. Tolman, *The Views about H.* (1904); H. Logeman, *Sh. te Helsingör* (1904, *Mélanges Paul Fredericy*); F. P. v. Westenholz, *Die H.-Qq* (1904, *E.S.* xxxiv. 337); R. Zenker, *Boeve-Amlethus* (1905); A. E. Jack, *Thomas Kyd and the Ur- H.* (1905, *P.M.L.A.* xx. 729); E. E. Stoll, *Sh., Marston and the Malcontent Type* (1906, *M.P.* iii. 281), *H., a Comparative Study* (1919); J. W. Cun- liffe, *Nash and the Earlier H.* (1906, *P.M.L.A.* xxi. 193); C. M. Lewis, *The Genesis of H.* (1907); T. Eichhoff, *Versuch einer praktischen H.- Kritik* (1907, *Anglia*, xxx. 56); R. B. McKerrow, *Note on Preface to Menaphon* (1908, *Works of Nashe*, iv. 444); J. Allen, *The Lost H. of Kyd* (1908, *Westminster Review*); C. Meier, *Zum Ur-H.* (1909, *Anglia, Beiblatt*, xx. 119); J. D. Fitzgerald, *The Sources of the H. Tragedy* (1909), *Q1 of H.: a Literary Fraud* (1910), *Q1 of H.* (1919, Aug. 7, *T.L.S.*); E. B. Reed, *The College Element in H.* (1909, *M.P.* vi. 453); J. Huizinga, *Rosenkranz und Güldenstern* (1910, *J.* xlvi. 60); W. W. Greg, *The H. Qq* (1910, *M.L.R.* v. 196), *The H. Texts and Recent Work in Sh. Bibliography* (1919, *M.L.R.* xiv. 380), *Principles of Emendation in Sh.* (1928), 23, 54; W. v. Gersdoff, *Vom Ursprung des deutschen H.* (1912, *J.* xlviii. 148); M. J. Wolff, *Zum Ur-H.* (1912, *E.S.* xlv. 9), *Italienisches bei Sh.* (1920, *E.S.* liv. 473); G. G. A. Murray, *H. and Orestes* (1914, 1927, *The Classical Tradition in Poetry*, 205); H. D. Gray, *Q1 of H.* (1915, *M.L.R.* x. 171), *Did Sh. Write a Tragedy of Dido?* (1920, *M.L.R.* xv. 217), *Thomas Kyd and Q1 of H.* (1927, *P.M.L.A.* xlii. 721), *Reconstruction of a Lost Play* (1928, *P.Q.* vii. 254); B. A. P. van Dam, *Are there Interpolations in the Text of H.* (1916, *Sh. Homage*, 473), *The Text of Sh.'s H.* (1924); J. D. Wilson, *The Copy for H. 1603 and the H. Transcript 1593* (1918, from *3 Library*, ix. 153, 217), *Spellings and Misprints in Q2 of H.* (1924, *Essays and Studies*, x. 36);

F. G. Hubbard, *The Marcellus Theory of Q1 of H.* (1918, *M.L.N.* xxxiii. 73), *The Readings of Q1 of H.* (1923, *P.M.L.A.* xxxviii. 792); J. M. Robertson, *The Problem of H.* (1919), *H. Once More* (1923); V. Østerberg, *Studier over H.-Texterne* (1920); L. Winstanley, *H. and the Scottish Succession* (1921), *H. and the Essex Conspiracy* (1924–5, *Aberystwyth Studies*, vi. 47; vii. 37); A. Clutton-Brock, *Sh.'s H.* (1922); W. Poel, *Q1 of H.* (1922, *12 N.Q.* xi. 301); W. S. Fox, *Lucian in the Grave-Scene of H.* (1923, *P.Q.* ii. 132); K. Malone, *The Literary History of H.* (1923), *On the Etymology of H.* (1925, *P.Q.* iv. 158), *Etymologies for H.* (1927, *R.E.S.* iii. 257), *More Etymologies for H.* (1928, *R.E.S.* iv. 257); H. de Groot, *H., its Textual History* (1923), *De Geschiedenis van het Hamletprobleem* (1928, *Neophilologus*, xiii. 282); H. Farr, *Notes on Sh.'s Printers and Publishers* (1923, *4 Library*, iii. 225); E. Seligman and others, *Rosencrantz and Guildenstern* (1926, Jan. 7, 14, 21, 28, *T.L.S.*); W. J. Lawrence, *H. as Sh. Staged It* (1927, *Pre-Restoration Studies*, 102). *The Date of Sh.'s H.* (1928, *Sh.'s Workshop*, 98), *The Mystery of the H. Q1* (1928, *ibid.* 110); J. M. Murry and others, *A Sh. Problem* (1928, July 12, Aug. 2, 16, *T.L.S.*); W. Marschall, *Welchen Dialekt spricht Hamlet?* (1928, *Anglia*, lii. 362); G. F. Bradby, *The Problems of H.* (1928).

A play, not indicated as 'ne', of *Hamlet* was given by the Admiral's or Chamberlain's or both (App. D) for Henslowe at Newington Butts on 11 June 1594. Probably it belonged to the Chamberlain's, and later performances by them are recalled in T. Lodge, *Wit's Miserie* (1596), 56, 'the Visard of yᵉ ghost which cried so miserably at yᵉ Theator, like an oister wife, Hamlet, revenge'. In Dekker, *Satiromastix*, iv. 1. 150, Tucca says, 'my name's Hamlet revenge: thou hast been at Parris garden hast not?'[1] This seems to suggest performance at the Swan in Paris Garden, as well as at the Theatre, but the Chamberlain's men are not known to have used the Swan. The Ghost does not call 'Hamlet, revenge' in the Shakespearean texts, although the demand for revenge is in i. 5. 7. The old play is not likely to have survived Shakespeare's, but is still echoed in S⟨amuel⟩ R⟨owlands⟩ *The Night-Raven* (1620), sign. D 2, 'I will not call Hamlet Revenge my greeves'. It is uncertain whether it is quoted in Robert Armin, *Nest of Ninnies* (1608), 55, 'Ther ar, as Hamlet saies, things cald whips in store'.[2] The passage is not in the earlier editions (1600, 1605) of Armin's work. The phrase 'things called whippes' is found both in

---

[1] Cf. *Eliz. Stage*, iii. 293.   [2] Cf. *ibid.* ii. 300.

2 Hen. VI, ii. 1. 136 and in the additions to *Spanish Tragedy* (1602), 1904, but Armin's version suggests contamination by *Ham*. iii. 1. 70, 'the whips and scorns of time'. Probably the old play already existed in 1589, and is referred to in Nashe's *Epistle* to Greene's *Menaphon* of that year,[1] 'English *Seneca* read by Candlelight yeelds many good sentences, as *Blood is a begger*, and so forth ; and if you intreate him faire in a frostie morning, hee will affoord you whole *Hamlets*, I should say handfuls of Tragicall speeches'. The whole passage is an attack on 'a few of our triuiall translators', who are also imitators of Seneca. Allusions to 'the trade of *Noverint*, whereto they were borne' and to 'the Kidde in Æsop', suggest that one of these was Thomas Kyd, but do not, in view of Nashe's plurals, necessarily carry the inference that he wrote the *Hamlet*.

It will be simplest, before describing the versions, to state my general conclusion, that Q2 substantially represents the original text of the play, as written once and for all by Shakespeare, and that F1, Q1, and *Der bestrafte Brudermord* (B.B.) are all in various ways based upon derivatives from that text. The literature of the play is unwieldy, but the tabulation and analyses of structural and textual variants by Tanger, Wilson, De Groot, and Van Dam provide adequate material for a departure from many of their conclusions.

Q2 is the fullest version, being longer by over 200 lines than F1, and much more than half as long again as Q1, but it omits some 85 lines found in F1. It is a fair text, with little mislineation, light punctuation, and a good many abnormal spellings, and may very possibly be from the author's manuscript, but if so, numerous misprints suggest that this was not very legible. There is no evidence that it had been used as prompt-copy. The stage-directions are normal. There are some variations of nomenclature between 'Queene' and 'Gertrard', 'King' and 'Claudio', and 'Courtier' and 'Ostricke'. The later Qq were set up successively from Q2 and each other.

[1] *Eliz. Stage*, iv. 234.

The greater part of the F text is close enough to that of
Q2 to show a common origin.   But the absence of any
typographical resemblance and of any but trifling and probably accidental concurrence in error does not suggest that
it was set up from that or any Q, even with the aid of
an independent manuscript, such as must have supplied,
not only the substantial passages lacking in Q2, but also
a number of smaller omissions.   Many of these are repetitions of words and phrases.   This is an easy kind of misprint, and a theory that these repetitions were inserted by
the actors, or in particular by Burbadge, is quite superfluous.   They are not confined to one part, and in fact
there are some in Q2, which F in its turn omits.   The
same trick of repetition is found in other plays, notably
Richard III.   Nevertheless, the manuscript underlying F,
presumably in its origin a transcript from that underlying
Q2, had no doubt been used as a prompt-copy.   The
nomenclature has been unified, and the stage-directions,
although still bearing a resemblance to those of Q2, have
been revised, by clearing up indefiniteness, and omitting
or varying the provision for music and properties.   These
changes may be ascribed to the book-keeper; but it is not
obvious that some fresh notes for action, especially in the
graveyard and duel scenes, would be required by him.
Some of the numerous verbal variants in F from Q2 bear
a similar explanation; they are sophistications of vocabulary or grammar, such as we find in other F texts.   Others
are due to misprints on one side, or in the case of F mis-
transcriptions.   The subconscious mind of the transcriber
is probably seen in the substitution of synonyms or other
associated alternatives for Q2 words, and he may have
emended occasionally to make sense of matter he could not
read.   The concurrence of Q1 and F against Q2 points,
on my view (*infra*) of Q1, to the responsibility of the F
transcriber for a variant; that of Q2 and Q1 against F to
the responsibility of the F printer.   There remain a few
variants which it is difficult to explain.   Wilson has shown
that a combination of literal misreadings may lead to some
odd transformations.   Greg thinks that a few deliberate

alterations were introduced into the transcript by or with the authority of Shakespeare.[1] The punctuation of F tends to be heavier than that of Q2.

I come now to the substantial omissions of the two texts. There are only two in Q2 for which a reason other than printing-house carelessness must be sought; ii. 2. 244–76, a depreciatory account of Denmark as a prison, followed by a dialogue on ambition, and ii. 2. 352–79, where the travelling of the players is ascribed (cf. p. 65) to the success of 'an ayrie of children'. Both passages must have been part of the original text; the excision in the first case has left an awkward duplication of 'But' at the beginnings of two consecutive sentences, and in the second has obscured the point of the reference to the King's 'picture in little'. Perhaps the best explanation is that of De Groot, that by 1604 Anne of Denmark was Queen of England, and had taken the criticized company of children under her special protection. If so, we have an unusual example of cutting, not for stage purposes, but as a result of discretion or censorship at the time of printing. One cannot always be sure whether the F omissions are due to accident or to cutting. But I think that the latter is responsible for i. 1. 108–25; i. 4. 17–38, 75–8; iii. 4. 71–6, 161–5, 167–70, 202–10; iv. 1.41–4; iv. 4. 9–66; iv. 7. 69–82, 115–24; v. 2. 110–41, 144–50. One or two of these passages the players may have found obscure or undramatic, but they are mostly digressions, which do not advance the action, and their removal shortens long speeches or long sections of dialogue. They only amount to less than 200 lines and leave the play still a very long one. Probably iv. 1. 4, although only a single line, was also cut, to save the introduction of two actors. There are other traces of similar savings. A lord drops out of v. 2, and one recorder (iii. 2), one sailor (iv. 6), one ambassador (v. 2) were thought sufficient, where the author's stage-directions contemplated more. A little of this cutting (cf. *infra*) may be later than the preparation of the transcript, and possibly F incorporates other slight theatrical modifications. Thus

[1] *Emendation*, 24, 56.

there may be a bit of interpolated clowning ('Get thee to
Yaughan' for 'Get thee in' of Q2) at v. 1. 67.   One would
like to think that the 'O, o, o, o', which follows Hamlet's
dying 'The rest is silence' at v. 2. 369, is another example,
and its recurrence in the reported Q of *Lear*, v. 3. 309, but
not in F, gives some encouragement. Profanity has been
expunged, but only perfunctorily.

   Q1 is a very difficult problem.   It is generally accepted
that many of its features are due to a reporter, introducing,
as in *2, 3 Henry VI, Romeo and Juliet, Henry V*, and *Merry
Wives of Windsor*, 'gross corruption, constant mutilation,
meaningless inversion and clumsy transposition'.   The
attempt of Hubbard to 'edit' it, on the assumption that
the corruption is only a matter of misprinting, leaves a quite
incredible text.   A comparison with Q2 and F, wherever
the substance is the same, is a continuous revelation of
the reporter.   He makes omissions, causing *lacunae* of
sense and grammar.   He gives the beginnings and ends
of speeches without their middles.   He paraphrases.   He
merges distinct speeches.   He makes a mosaic of recollected fragments.   He catches vigorous words without
their context.   He makes double use of phrases.   He
shifts the order of bits of dialogue within their scenes.
Above all he uses or echoes in one scene passages which
really belong to an earlier or later one.   Thus vii. 53 of Q1
is from iii. 2. 354, ix. 211–21 from iv. 2. 12–23, xi. 34–5
from i. 5. 49–50, xi. 46 from iii. 3. 90, xv. 8 from iv. 5.
137; while i. 1. 173 is echoed in ii. 25 of Q1, iii. 2. 138 in
ii. 33, i. 2. 193 in iii. 12, iii. 1. 160 in v. 38, i. 5. 185–7
in viii. 18.   The process entails much vulgarization.
Many lines are unmetrical or bald.   Many words are
represented by weak synonyms; others by words of
similar sound but different sense or no sense, which point
to errors of hearing.   By hearing, too, many 'connective'
words introduced by actors have been incorporated.
These, with omissions and failures to recognize Shakespeare's short lines, have led to much mislineation.
Nearly all the prose is printed in capitalized lines of
irregular length.   A few exceptions may be due to the

occasional realization of the compositor that he is dealing with prose. I do not think that the reporter was
wholly ignorant of blank verse, in spite of his metrical
lapses. He fakes up a good many lines, and when he comes
on a couplet and has forgotten a rhyming word, he is often
capable of substituting another. But he evidently fought
shy of reconstructing imperfectly recollected long speeches,
and left them incoherent. The stage-directions must be
his own; they are of a descriptive character, although not
so elaborate as some in *Romeo and Juliet*. And in two places
(xi. 7, 115) he puts into words what he has merely seen
as dumb action on the stage. Some portions of the play
are better reported than others. The scenes (i. 1; i. 2. 160–
258; i. 4; i. 5. 113–91), in which Marcellus occurs, are
notably good, although not perfect, and it is quite possible
that the reporter was the actor of this part. The single
long speech (ii. 2. 60–80) of Voltimand agrees almost
exactly with F. The reporter can hardly have played this
himself, or he would not have corrupted the name into
Voltemar. It may be that a manuscript of this small part
was available.

Some concurrences between F and Q1 against Q2
suggest that the text of the performances reported in Q1
was derived from the same transcript which underlies F.
Moreover, most of the passages cut in F find no representation in Q1. There are, however, traces in a stage-direction
at xi. 111 and a speech at xviii. 30 of iv. 1. 4 and v. 2. 203–
18. F must, therefore, at these points have diverged from
the transcript. Q1, antedating the *Act of Abuses*, of course
retains some profanity expunged from F. But it also has
diverged. Two important structural changes have been
made. One of these concerns the order of the tests by
which the court endeavours to ascertain the reason of
Hamlet's strangeness. There are three, in interviews
with Rosencrantz and Guildenstern (the Schoolfellow
scene), with Polonius (the Fishmonger scene), with
Ophelia (the Nunnery scene). The sequence in Q2 and
F is as follows. The King plans the Schoolfellow test
(ii. 2. 1–39). Polonius plans the Ophelia test (ii. 2. 85–

167). Hamlet appears reading, and Polonius improvises his own test (ii. 2. 168–223). The Schoolfellow test is carried out (ii. 2. 224–323). Then the arrival of the players intervenes (ii. 2. 324–634). The failure of the Schoolfellow test is reported (iii. 1. 1–28). Finally, the Ophelia test is tried (iii. 1. 28–196). In Q1 on the other hand, the Ophelia test is put much earlier, and immediately follows its planning. We can hardly ascribe the difference to the reporter. He generally gets the succession of his episodes right, and the link-passages in Q1 indicate a careful modification to fit the new order. In particular Ophelia, absent from ii. 2 in Q2 and F, enters with her father at the point (vi. 19) corresponding in Q1 to ii. 2. 40, and is thus available when Hamlet appears reading. Why the change should have been made is not so clear. It abridges the interval between the planning and execution of the Ophelia test, but lengthens the interval before the Schoolfellow test. Possibly it was an attempt to remove an original inconsistency, characteristic enough of Shakespeare, by which Ophelia is bidden to accompany her father to the King in ii. 1, but left out in ii. 2. The second change is towards the end of the play. Here Q1 omits altogether iv. 6, in which Horatio receives Hamlet's letter about his voyage, and v. 2. 1–74, in which Hamlet and Horatio discuss the same matter, and substitutes in the place of iv. 6 a different scene, in which Horatio, after Hamlet's return, tells the story of the voyage to the Queen. Here the original version must be that of Q2 and F, since v. 2. 1–74 is represented in *B.B.*

Two other divergences in Q1 are noteworthy. For the names of Polonius and his servant Reynaldo we get Corambis and Montano. It is impossible that these should, as Tanger thought, be mishearings of the reporter. Many students have assumed that Corambis and Montano were the earlier names, but there is nothing to show this, and if I am right in supposing Q1 dependent on Q2, the chances are that it was the other way round. Shakespeare used the name Corambus in *All's Well*, iv. 3. 185.

There are two rather curious stage-directions in Q2, which may conceivably be relevant. At i. 2. 1 comes 'Enter . . . Counsaile: as Polonius, and his Sonne Laertes', and at ii. 1. 1, 'Enter old Polonius, with his man or two'. These may be mere examples of indefiniteness, although Laertes would make an odd councillor. But it is also possible that, when the change was made in an acting version, the new names were roughly noted in the original manuscript, and were there misread by the compositor. Again the motive for the change is quite obscure. One can only suspect censorship, or the fear of censorship. Gollancz has suggested that Polonius and his worldly maxims may be a reflection of the Polish statesman Laurentius Grimalius Goslicius, whose *De Optimo Senatore* was translated as *The Counsellor* in 1598. If so, this is another reason for regarding Polonius as the original name. It has often been thought that Polonius may glance at Lord Burghley, who wrote *Certaine Preceptes, or Directions* for the use of his son Robert Cecil. These were printed (1618) 'from a more perfect copie, than ordinarily those pocket manuscripts goe warranted by'. Conceivably Shakespeare knew a pocket manuscript, but Laertes is less like Robert Cecil than Burghley's elder son Thomas. And if the Chamberlain's men feared that Polonius would be taken for Burghley and Reynaldo for Robert Cecil, why should a change of name but not of character make a difference. Can 'Polonius' have resembled some nickname of Burghley? I do not profess to solve the mystery. But some theatrical allusion to Polish affairs seemed to me a possible element in the trouble about *The Isle of Dogs* in 1597,[1] and there might have been some reason for avoiding the appearance of another at any time during 1600–3, when negotiations with regard to the Baltic trade were taking place, on the one hand with Denmark and on the other with the Hanseatic towns, in some of which Poland had an interest in 1597.[2] Lastly, there is a passage in Q1 which can

---

[1] *Eliz. Stage*, iii. 455.

[2] N. R. Deardoff, *Early Trade in the Baltic during the Reign of Elizabeth*, *passim*; cf. Dasent, xxx. 195; *Hatfield MSS.* xii. 283, 645.

only be a theatrical interpolation. Hamlet's advice to the players is in the main a report. But this is followed by a series of clownish witticisms which are not in Q2 or F, and two of which Wilson has traced to the 1611 edition of *Tarlton's Jests*, 5, 12. There was probably an earlier edition.[1] But in any case the witticisms were doubtless traditional, and their introduction here of the nature of 'gag'. Rhodes (*Folio*, 79) suggests that, as the reference to Hamlet's fatness (v. 2. 298) is not in Q1, and the interval since Yorick's death is given (v. 1. 190) as a 'dozen' instead of '23' years, the part had been adapted to an actor of nineteen. This is ingenious, but hazardous.

How far, apart from these alterations, does the theory of a report account for Q1, as we have it? I think that it accounts for most of it, and will here quote Greg's comment that his study of *Merry Wives of Windsor* had led him 'to doubt whether any limit can be set to the possible perversion which a text may suffer at the hands of a reporter'.[2] But in *Hamlet*, as in other bad Quartos, we have to reckon with a certain amount of blank verse, which does not rest upon anything in Q2 and F, and is plainly un-Shakespearean. To call these passages 'pre-Shakespearean' is to beg a question, but they are not in Shakespeare's manner, although they might still be in that of others, when he was writing *Hamlet*. They are mostly short passages distributed amongst the reported matter, especially in the latter part of the play. And they are often difficult to distinguish from the reporter's fakings. One is certainly tempted to find patches of an alien hand or hands in the whole or parts of iii. 65–70, ix. 50–6, 100–9, x. 1–12, xi. 37–41, 51–8, 90–5, 104–7, 155–60, xiii. 41–4, xvii, xviii. 109–23, and perhaps in smaller fragments elsewhere. The Horatio-Queen scene (cf. *supra*) may be disregarded. That is no doubt un-Shakespearean, but due to an alteration. It is no doubt arguable that both in this scene and in xi. 90–5, 104–7, the Queen's denial of complicity in the murder and ranging of herself on Hamlet's side put her character in a

---

[1] *Eliz. Stage*, ii. 344.   [2] *M.L.R.* v. 197.

different light to that of Q2 and F. But I doubt whether this is more than an accidental emphasizing of Shakespeare's own intention. There is certainly nothing in Q2 and F to show that she had any part in or knowledge of Claudius's crime. In fact she shows no sign of disturbance in the play-scene, and she was certainly not a Lady Macbeth.

The un-Shakespearean matter in Q1 and the knowledge which we have for *Hamlet*, as we have not in the cases of the other bad Quartos, that an earlier play on the subject has been lost, are the main supports to an alternative reconstruction of the textual history, which has its most elaborate statement in Wilson's papers of 1918. He thinks that the reporter did no more than make additions to an early *Hamlet* text. This was an abridged transcript for provincial use from the old play as partly revised by Shakespeare. The revision 'had not extended much beyond the Ghost-scenes'. The original manuscript remained available for a subsequent further revision by Shakespeare into the *Hamlet* of Q2 and F. In this the reporter acted not only Voltimand and Marcellus, but also other small parts, perhaps a Player, the Second Gravedigger, Reynaldo, the Priest, Fortinbras's Captain, and the English Ambassador; and from his memories of the scenes in which these occur and such other fragments as he could pick up at the stage-door, he attempted to supply the gaps left by abridgement in the manuscript. Of other scenes he knew nothing, and here we get in Q1 bits of the old play not reached by Shakespeare's first revision. This is of course all on the lines of Wilson and Pollard's general theory (cf. p. 155) as to the genesis of the bad Quartos. Apart from the general difficulties which I feel about that theory, I think that the application of it to *Hamlet* is inadequate, in that I find constant traces both of the reporter and of Shakespeare in scenes, such as those of Ophelia's madness, which, according to Wilson, Shakespeare had not yet revised, and the reporter could not get at. Nor do I believe that, what with performances and what with rehearsals, a company could in fact effectively prevent an

actor from seeing any part of a play that he wanted to see.
I have not space to follow here all the details of Wilson's
ingenious argument. But he is clearly right in calling
attention to the typographical resemblance, especially as
regards orthography, between the earlier pages of Q1 and
Q2. I do not find the same cogency in his arguments from
a similar use, but at different points, of quotation-marks
and brackets, or from a concurrence in misprints, which
do not seem to me to be misprints. Wilson explains the
resemblance by a 'meticulous' care in the writer of the
early transcript to follow exactly the copy before him.
But was an Elizabethan transcriber ever 'meticulous'
about spelling? Possibly an attempt to begin the setting-
up of Q2, as in the case of *Romeo and Juliet*, upon an example of Q1, is the more plausible conjecture.   If so, the
attempt was probably very soon abandoned.

I have no desire to be dogmatic upon a very obscure
question, and even if one does not accept Wilson's view as
it stands, some contamination of Q1 by the old play is of
course a possibility. The un-Shakespearean element rather
predominantly affects scenes in which the Queen is present.
I have sometimes thought that the reporter might have
been the Queen, as a boy, in the old play, and helped
himself out with memories of that. Certainly one ought
not to bring in an expensive hack-poet for a surreptitious
enterprise, of which the profits could not be great. But
there is another alternative. The belief that Kyd wrote the
old *Hamlet* has led to much search for Kydian parallels in
Q1, and even in Q2. They do not amount to much,
except in the case of the *Spanish Tragedy*. Those to
I Jeronimo are irrelevant. The searchers have taken it
for Kyd's in error, and the play only exists in a text, itself
probably reported, of 1605.[1] There is only one to
Spanish Tragedy in Q2, and that is not a mere echo. In
iii. 2. 304 Hamlet's

> For if the King like not the Comedie,
> Why then belike he likes it not perdy.

[1] *Eliz. Stage*, iv. 22.

is clearly deliberate burlesque of *Spanish Tragedy*, iv.
1. 196,

> And if the world like not this Tragedie,
> Hard is the hap of olde Hieronimo,

just as iii. 2. 264 'The croaking raven doth bellow for
revenge' is deliberately burlesqued from *True Tragedy of
Richard III*, 1892,

> The screeking Rauen sits croking for reuenge.
> Whole heads of beasts comes bellowing for reuenge.

But in Q1, ix. 111 is comparable to *Sp. Tr.* ii. 1. 26; xi.
106–7 to iv. 1. 46–7; xiii. 122 to ii. 4. 20; xv. 13 to iv.
1. 178; xv. 14–15, 37 to iv. 1. 74, 126; xv. 53 to ii. 5. 23;
xv. 54 to ii. 5. 41; xvi. 164 to iii. 14. 148; xvii. 8–9 to iii. 14.
154–5. These are not all very close, but in bulk they seem
to establish some echoing of *Spanish Tragedy* in Q1.
But other plays, not Kyd's, are also echoed, *Hen. V*, ii. 2.
12, 58 in xi. 156, 159, and Dekker's *Satiromastix*, ii. 2. 29
in xviii. 8, 35. Is not the explanation the same in all these
cases, that the reporter, especially towards the end of the
play, when he was growing tired or impatient, has helped
out his failing memory with scraps from recent pieces
familiar to him on the stage? And if so, of course, he may
also have drawn upon plays not known to us. *Henry V* and
Satiromastix were Chamberlain's plays of 1599 and 1601
respectively. *Spanish Tragedy* was revived by the Admiral's
men in 1602, but also, in all probability (cf. p. 148), by the
Chamberlain's about the same time.

B.B. has only come down in a text of 1710, but it may
be derived from a *Tragoedia von Hamlet einen printzen in
Dennemark*, played by John Green's company at Dresden
in 1626, and possibly at Danzig in 1616.[1] I believe
that it throws no light on the early *Hamlet*, being
founded on an acting version of Shakespeare's play closely
related to that underlying Q1. It cannot be from Q1
itself, since it echoes many passages which are in Q2 and
F, and must have been missed by the Q1 reporter. Its
source had diverged slightly less from the common trans-

---

[1] *Eliz. Stage*, ii. 286; Herz 92.

cript than that of Q1. It had the name Corambus, but it also had still the Hamlet and Horatio episode from v. 2. 1–74 of the original. *B.B.* itself has been much perverted by the introduction of German themes and a farcical wooing of Ophelia by a Phantasmo, who represents Osric. A Senecan prologue has been prefixed, which is inappropriate to the play as it stands, since it introduces a motive of jealousy between the King and Queen not there used. There are only two or three passages on which any reasonable case for a pre-Shakespearean origin could be based. In iii. 10, Hamlet bids the King send him 'to Portugal, so that I may never come back again', and this has been held to be an allusion to the disastrous English expedition of 1589.[1] But it may just as well be of much later origin. Germany had been interested in Portugal, for example, during the war of Portuguese independence in 1661 and that of the Spanish succession in 1704. It has also been suggested that Hamlet's reference (ii. 5) to his father's guards as an obstacle stands nearer to Belleforest (cf. *infra*) than to Shakespeare, and that his 'crocodile's tears' (iii. 5) are Belleforest's 'pleur dissimulé'. But it is not possible to build an argument for a source upon such obvious ideas.

There is not much evidence as to the precise date of *Hamlet*. The reference by Harvey (App. B, no. xvii) justifies putting it after the publication of Speght's *Chaucer* (1598) and almost certainly before the death of Essex in February 1601. Although 'innovation' may mean a political uprising, I do not think (cf. p. 65) that it does in ii. 2. 348, or that there is any allusion here to the Essex revolt. Lawrence [2] may be right in thinking that in 'the humorous man shall end his part in peace' (ii. 2. 335) we have one to the trouble caused by the original ending of Jonson's *E.M.O.* late in 1599.[3] The citation of a phrase in Q1 of *Merry Wives of Windsor* (q.v.) gives us reason to suppose that *Hamlet* preceded that play. To put *Hamlet* in 1600 would not be counter to any indication of style or allusion, and would bring it near *Julius Caesar* as a

[1] Cheyney, i. 153.   [2] *Sh.'s Workshop*, 101.   [3] *Eliz. Stage*, iii. 361.

companion study of tragic idealism. The performances
at Oxford and Cambridge mentioned on the title-page of
Q1 are likely, in view of the date of the S.R. entry, to
have been earlier than 1603–4, when the King's came to
Oxford. An unnamed company came in 1599–1600,
and three in 1600–1. A revival at court seems to have
been contemplated about 1619 and there was another in
1637 (App. D).

A vast deal of erudition has been devoted to the source,
but most of it bears upon the Scandinavian, Irish, and conceivably Greek origins of the story of Hamlet, as found in
the twelfth-century *Historiae Danicae* (pr. 1514) of Saxo
Grammaticus. Thence it came into P. de Belleforest,
Histoires Tragiques, v (1576), and from this version the
play derives. It was translated in *The Hystorie of Hamblet*
(1608), which has a tag or two clearly from the play itself.
No earlier edition is known, but in any case it is likely that
the old play was intermediate between Belleforest and
Shakespeare, and some writers have suspected that an
Italian tragedy may also have intervened. Whether the
old *Hamlet* was by Kyd, it seems to me impossible to say;
Nashe's reference is quite inconclusive and the verbal
parallels are still more so. There are clearly resemblances
of dramatic technique between *Hamlet*, as we have it, and
the *Spanish Tragedy*. Both use a ghost, a play within a play,
madness, a pair of sons seeking revenge for their fathers,
a woman's suicide. This duplication of motives may really
be held to point to the probability either of a single plotter
or of two different plotters, according to taste. Nor can we
say how far the divergences from Belleforest are due to the
old play and how far to Shakespeare. All that we know
about the old play is that there was a ghost in it, who
called 'Hamlet, revenge!' Robertson, who makes little of
the reporter, finds a considerable Kyd element both in
Q1 and Q2, and thinks that Chapman rewrote the interlude and the scene (ii. 1. 1–74) between Polonius and
Reynaldo, and perhaps contributed the Pyrrhus speech
(ii. 2. 474–519) from an early classical tragedy of his own.
This speech has also been claimed both as early work of

Shakespeare's own and as a parody of Marlowe and
Nashe's *Dido*.[1] It is simpler, and equally plausible, to
regard both it and the interlude as written with the rest of
Hamlet, in styles deliberately differentiated from that of
the ordinary dialogue. They are, of course, not completely
serious. It is only by accident (cf. vol. ii, p. 3) that the name
Hamlet coincides with one familiar in Warwickshire, but
of different derivation, but one may fancy (cf. p. 35) that
the setting of Ophelia's death owed something to that of
Katharine Hamlett in the Avon on 17 December 1579.
The names Rosencrantz and Guildenstern have been
much discussed. They are those of well-known sixteenth-
century Danish families, who were connected by marriage.
Both are said to be found in the official documents of the
University of Wittenberg, and both appear, in the forms
Rosenkrans and Guldensteren, among the ancestral
names on a portrait of the astronomer Tycho Brahe, engraved by Jacob de Gheyn at some date earlier than 1602
from a painting of 1586. I cannot verify the statement of
a descendant, that representatives of both families came to
England on a diplomatic mission 'in the last decade of the
sixteenth century'.[2] There seems to have been no such
mission. There was, however, one in 1603 for the coronation [3] and in May and June of that year a Laxman
Gyldenstiern was travelling in England.[4] This, however,
is too late to affect *Hamlet*. Shakespeare may have heard
the names from the players who went to Denmark
in 1586.[5] There is no evidence for the conjecture that he
himself visited Helsingör.

XXIII. THE MERRY WIVES OF WINDSOR

MS. H.P., *Reliques*, 72, described a copy which he believed
to have been written 'during the Commonwealth for some
private playhouse', and possibly to record stage-readings,
not in F1. It was afterwards at Warwick Castle.

[1] *Eliz. Stage*, iii. 426.
[2] *T.L.S.* 28 Jan. 1926.
[3] *V.P.* x. 77.

[4] *R.O. Deputy Keeper's Reports*, xlvi,
App. ii. 69; *V.P.* x. 47.
[5] *Eliz. Stage*, ii. 272; cf. p. 39.

[S.R. 1602.] 18 Januarij. John Busby. Entred for his copie vnder the hand of master Seton, A booke called An excellent and pleasant conceited commedie of Sir John Faulstof and the merry wyues of Windesor vj^d. Arthur Johnson. Entred for his Copye by assignement from John Busbye, A booke Called an excellent and pleasant conceyted Comedie of Sir John Faulstafe and the merye wyues of Windsor. vj^d. (Arber, iii. 199).

[Greg (*4 Library*, vii. 378) notes that the original entry and that of the assignment are written in different hands.]

[Q1. 1602.] A Most pleasaunt and excellent conceited Comedie, of Syr Iohn Falstaffe, and the merrie Wiues of Windsor Entermixed with sundrie variable and pleasing humors, of Syr Hugh the Welch Knight, Iustice Shallow, and his wise Cousin M. Slender. With the swaggering vaine of Auncient Pistoll, and Corporall Nym. By William Shakespeare. As it hath bene diuers times Acted by the right Honorable my Lord Chamberlaines seruants. Both before her Maiestie, and else-where. [Ornament] London Printed by T⟨homas⟩ C⟨reede⟩ for Arthur Iohnson, and are to be sold at his shop in Powles Church-yard, at the signe of the Flower de Leuse and the Crowne. 1602. [*Head-title*] A pleasant conceited Comedie of Syr Iohn Falstaffe, and the merry Wiues of Windsor. [*Running-title*] A pleasant Comedie, of the merry wiues of Windsor.

Facsimile. W. Griggs (1881, *Sh. Q.* vi, ed. P. A. Daniel).

Type-Facsimile. W. W. Greg (1910).

Reprints. J. O. Halliwell-Phillipps (1842, *Sh. Soc.*); W. C. Hazlitt (1875, *Sh. Library*, Pt. ii. ii); W. A. Wright (1893, *Cambridge Sh.* ix. 421).

[Q2. 1619.] A Most pleasant and excellent conceited Comedy, of Sir Iohn Falstaffe, and the merry Wiues of Windsor. With the swaggering vaine of Ancient Pistoll, and Corporall Nym. Written by W. Shakespeare. [William Jaggard's device (McKerrow 283)] Printed for Arthur Johnson, 1619. [*Head-title*] A Pleasant conceited Comedie of Sir John Falstaffe, and the merry Wives of

Windsor. [*Running-title*] A pleasant Comedy, of the
merry Wives of Windsor.

[On the misdating, cf. p. 133.]

Reprint. G. Steevens (1766, *Twenty of the Plays of Shakespeare*).

[F1. 1623.] [*Catalogue*] The Merry Wiues of Windsor.
[*Comedies*, pp. 39–60, sign. D 2–E 6ᵛ. *Head- and Running-titles*] The Merry Wiues of Windsor.

[Acts and scc. marked.]

[S.R. 1630.] 29 Januarii 1629. Master Meighen.
Assigned ouer vnto him by master Johnson and Consent of
Master Purfoote Warden, All the said master Johnsons
estate in the 4 Copies hereafter menconed . . . The merry
Wives of Winsor (Arber iv. 227).

[Q3. 1630.] T. H. for R. Meighen.

Parallel-Text. A. Morgan (1888, *Bankside*).

Modern Editions. H. C. Hart (1904, *Arden*); A. T. Quiller-Couch
and J. D. Wilson (1921, *C.U.P.*); G. van Santvoord (1922, *Yale*).

Dissertations. J. O. Halliwell-Phillipps, *An Account of the only known
Manuscript of Sh.'s Plays* (1843), *The M.W.* (1850, *New Boke*, 82); W.
Vollhardt, *Ein italienischer Falstaff* (1907, *Studien zur vergleichenden
Literaturgeschichte*, vii. 110); J. D. Bruce, *Two Notes on M.W.* (1912,
M.L.R. vii. 239); J. M. Robertson, *The Problem of M.W.* (1917, *Sh. Ass.*);
A. W. Pollard and J. D. Wilson, *The 'Stolne and Surreptitious' Shn. Texts.
M.W.* (1919, Aug. 7, *T.L.S.*); R. S. Forsythe, *A Plautine Source of M.W.*
(1920, *M.P.* xviii. 401).

All discussions of *Merry Wives* relate it to certain
historical incidents which were brought to light in W. B.
Rye, *England as seen by Foreigners* (1865), lv. In 1592
Frederick, Count of Mömpelgart, and heir-presump-
tive to his cousin Lewis, Duke of Württemberg, visited
England. Rye translates the relevant part of his *Baden-
fahrt* as written by his secretary Jacob Rathgeb and
printed in 1602. He was in the country from August 9
to September 5, saw London, spent August 17–19 with
the Queen at Reading and visited among other places
Windsor (Aug. 19–21), Uxbridge (Aug. 25–6), Oxford
(Aug. 26–8), and Cambridge (Aug. 29–30). At Oxford he
was delayed because his post-horses were worn out, and could
not be replaced, even at double the normal cost. When he

finally left London, however, he had a passport from the Lord Admiral, directing that he should be furnished with post-horses and shipping and 'pay nothing for the same'. Apparently the Queen gave him hopes of the Garter, and after his return to Germany he wrote several letters reminding her of this, to which she returned characteristic and evasive answers. On 8 August 1593 he became Duke of Württemberg. In 1595 he sent an ambassador, John Jacob Breuning von Buchenbach, to urge his claim. Rye quotes Breuning's narrative of his mission at second-hand, but it was printed by A. Schlossberger,[1] and is translated in V. von Klarwill, *Queen Elizabeth and Some Foreigners* (1928), 357. Breuning was in England from March 26 to May 23. He was at St. George's Feast on April 23, and visited Windsor and other places during May 6–8. The duke had instructed him to buy some horses, but he found them expensive, and was nearly cheated with a spavined grey. He was much embarrassed by a certain John Henry Stamler, who had been for nearly a year in England, trying to obtain remission of export duty on a thousand bales of cloth. It was thought an unworthy request and had caused much comment. Stamler told Breuning that he was not a regular agent of the duke, but had a special mission. Here the duke notes on the report, 'Put a rope round his neck'. Breuning suspected a fraud, and warned Essex against Stamler. Stamler produced copies of a ducal letter of 20 February 1594 (now in *Cott. Vesp. F.* iii, f. 97) asking for the export, and others of 12 December 1594, naming him as the agent, and offering Burghley (*Lansd. MS.* lxxvi, 68), a gold chain for his support. Essex obtained the original of the letter of February 20 and the date proved to have been altered from 1593 to 1594. Ultimately Stamler admitted that his own commission was only from the ducal paymaster at Emden, and that the letters were not directed by the duke, but written and sealed by his secretary, who hoped himself to profit by the cloth. H.P. ii. 266 says that Stamler was also engaged in 'nefarious equine transactions', but I think this only rests on a state-

---

[1] 1865, Stuttgart, *Bibliothek des Litterarischen Vereins*, lxxxi.

ment by Breuning that, as he heard that Stamler was trying to buy a horse, he suspected that he meant to take
flight, and had him watched. The duke got no satisfaction
from Breuning's mission. He wrote further letters and
did his best to explain the Stamler affair. He was in fact
elected to the Order on 23 April 1597, and sent a second
embassy in 1598 to express his gratitude.[1] But in spite
of a protest in January 1599 and a third embassy in 1600
he still could not get his insignia, and the investiture was
left for James to grant in November 1603.

The relation between Q and F has been minutely
examined in the admirable study by Greg. F is 'a distinctly
good, though demonstrably not perfect text'. There is
nothing to show whether the manuscript used was of a
playhouse or a literary type. The stage-directions are very
slight. Only the final exits of each scene are noted, and
except for a single 'Enter Fairies' (v. 5. 41), all the characters of each scene are listed in initial stage-directions,
according to the order in which they enter, but not that in
which they speak. Greg explains this as an unhappy
application by a 'devil charged with the duty of preparing
the play for press' of 'the Jonsonian method of character
indication to the English method of scene division'.
Wilson regards it as a case of 'assembling' from 'parts'
(cf. p. 153).

Q is obviously a 'garbled and corrupt' text. The most
obvious thing about it is the presence of a reporter. 'The
playhouse thief reveals himself in every scene', bringing
about 'gross corruption, constant mutilation, meaningless
inversion and clumsy transposition'. Scenes iv. 1 and v.
1–4 of F are omitted altogether, and there are considerable omissions in other scenes, some of which cause sense-
lacunae. Scenes iii. 4 and iii. 5 appear in inverted order.
Particularly significant of a reporter are numerous 'anticipations and recollections' (cf. p. 157) of passages from
earlier and later scenes. Moreover, there are similar
transferences from other plays (sc. v. 352 from *1 Hen. IV*,
ii. 4. 366; sc. v. 363 from *2 Hen. IV*, v. 3. 124; sc. xiii.

[1] G. F. Beltz, *Memorials of the Garter*, clxxxiii.

1188 from *Ham.* v. 1. 312 in its Q2 and F form). The report degenerates from iii. 3 onwards and in iii. 4; iv. 4 and v. 5 are passages of un-Shakespearean verse. Daniel thought that the reporter may have been the same who was responsible for *Henry V*, but that is of a rather different type, and the common abnormal spellings cited by Daniel probably point to the press of Thomas Creede. Greg has shown that in *Merry Wives* the reporter was almost certainly an actor who played the Host, and reconstructed the play from memory. He appears in eight scenes, and in six of these not only his own part, although he was evidently not word perfect, but also the parts of others on the stage with him, are in unusual agreement with F. In iv. 5, 6, however, he is (cf. *infra*) less successful. Act v, in which he does not appear, shows the maximum divergence from F. Wilson agrees that the Host had a hand in Q, but thinks that bits of the text must be from a transcript, on account of some typographical resemblances, which he perhaps exaggerates, in punctuation and capitalization to the corresponding bits of F; and that the transcription may have been from 'parts,' because of the repeated, although not invariable appearance of prose in capitalized lines of irregular length. But if 'parts', as is possible (cf. p. 183), were written in this way, the Host would have been familiar with it, and might quite well adopt it in writing out his report. In F Dr. Caius has (i. 4) a room with a closet behind it. In Q this becomes a shop with a counting-house behind and a stall in front. Perhaps it was so represented on the stage. The Q stage-directions are full and often descriptive of action, and do not show the abnormality of those in F.

Greg considers the possibility of cutting and perhaps consequent adaptation for the performance represented by Q, and so far as the greater part of the play is concerned, finds no satisfactory evidence for it. Some of the 'anticipations and recollections' are from scenes omitted by Q, and as there are no obvious reasons why an adapter should transfer the passages, it seems likely that the scenes were in fact played. The parts of Robin in ii. 2 and iii. 2, 3, and of William in iv. 1 may, as Greg thinks, have been deliberately cut out. But Robin's part is very small anyhow, and I think an oblivion of him by the reporter not impossible. The reporter may also have fought shy of William's Latin. But it is quite possible that this scene was only intended for the court performance, where it would please Elizabeth's pedantry. The omissions in i. 1, where Q does not give the bit on the Lucy arms, and at the beginning of Act v are considerable. But these scenes precede or follow the concern of the Host with the play.

On the other hand, Greg finds traces of more than one revision of the play. The most important of these he thinks to have been antecedent to both the Q and the F text, and to have involved two factors. One was an attempt 'to modify and largely to remove' a horse-stealing plot, of which traces remain, and which had some connexion with the Count of Mömpelgart. The motive appears in iv. 3; iv. 5. 64–95; and iv. 6. 1–5. All we learn is that three Germans, who had lodged for a week at the Garter Inn, borrowed three horses from the Host to meet their duke who was coming to court; that subsequently the Host was informed by Bardolph, Evans, and Caius that there was no duke, and that the Germans were cozeners who had run off with his horses, and had also tricked all the hosts of Reading, Maidenhead, and Colebrook; and that he was left with a heavy loss. Here, as elsewhere, Q is a mere perversion of F, with the exception that Evans substitutes (iv. 5. 79) 'cosen garmombles' for the 'Cozen-Iermans' of F. The meaning of 'garmomble' is 'confusion' or in a literal sense 'bruise', but it is reasonable to see a pun on Mömpelgart's name.[1] Greg thinks that there must have been more in it, that the plot must have originally contributed to the *denouement* of v. 5, and that the horses arrested for Falstaff's debt (v. 5. 118) and the 'postmaster's boy' found in the guise of a fairy (v. 5. 199) must have had some connexion with it. A revision left the story in mid-air, and if the actors learnt the altered matter badly, may also explain the comparative breakdown of the Host in reporting iv. 5. I am bound to say that I am very sceptical about this. Falstaff's horses were not the Host's, and it was the wives who plotted (ii. 1..96) to keep him dangling in Windsor until he had pawned them. Windsor must have been full of postmaster's boys. If the censor intervened, why did he allow the Germans and their duke to remain in the play at all? There they are, quite recognizable, and no doubt they added considerably to the amusement of any Garter knights present at the court performance and familiar with the Duke of Württemberg's efforts to get his insignia. 'Garmombles' may be a bit of 'gag' in any case; there are probably others (sc. vii. 704; sc. ix. 819–20; sc. xviii. 1522) in the Q text. Certainly the episode is left in the air. So also is that of Shallow and his stolen deer. The play was written in haste and its structure suffered. Of this haste, or of Shakespeare's carelessness, there are other indications in the time confusion of iii. 5 and in the variant personal names of Thomas (i. 1.46) and George (ii. 1.153; v. 5. 213) for Page. Imaginations less bridled than Greg's have essayed to recover his lost story. Hart thinks that Evans and Caius plotted a revenge on the Host for the mock duel into which he had led them, and that the horse-thieves were really Pistol, Nym, and Rugby. This proves acceptable to Wilson, who adds that it looks as if Ford and Shallow arranged that the loss should ultimately fall upon Falstaff. I cannot imagine why all this should have been suppressed.

The second factor in Greg's supposed revision is that the playwright, obviously not Shakespeare, who carried it out, was instructed to provide two alternative endings, one for the court, the other for the common stage, and that this accounts for the divergence between the Q and F versions of v. 5. This is no doubt substantial. The 'Garter' passage (v. 5. 60–77) of F, particularly appropriate to a court performance, is not in Q, and instead we get a long passage of octosyllabic dialogue, certainly not of Shakespeare's writing. Part of it echoes the F version, but Falstaff is absurdly described as a 'metamorphised youth', and there is a completely irrelevant passage about serjeants and proctors, which reads like a scrap from some popular London poem. But Greg's theory would apparently make the F version also un-Shakespearean, and this I hesitate to accept. The Q has un-Shakespearean verse also in place of iii. 4. 1–21 and iv. 4 of F, and I take it that the explanation is the same in all three cases, namely that the Host had forgotten too much, and that an attempt was made to fill the *lacunae*. If the Host was incapable of faking some verse for himself, some one else was called upon. I find it easier to suppose this, than to believe that the same playwright did both the divergent versions in v. 5, which are of very different degrees of merit.

Greg finds some traces of further alteration in the F text, at later dates. One is of course a partial excision of oaths. A few passages containing minor variants between Q and F, he thinks that Shakespeare may have touched up at random on the theatre copy. The strongest case for this is at ii. 2. 1, where Falstaff says 'I will not lend thee a penny', and Pistol replies in Q, 'I will retort the sum in equipage', but in F—

> Why then the world's mine Oyster,
> Which I with sword will open.

It is just possible that both phrases were in the original, and that Q has omitted one and F the other. But if so, both must also have omitted some intermediate words of Falstaff, probably 'Not a penny', which he repeats in the next line. This would have been an odd combination of coincidence and diversity in error, but Q does seem here and there to retain an original phrase missed by the F printer. In one respect there has clearly been revision at some stage. In Q, the disguised Ford takes the name of Brooke, and the connexion of meaning shows that this was the original name. In F, it is altered consistently to Broome. This is, I think, a bit of cautious censorship. Brooke was the family name of that Lord Cobham to whose intervention the extrusion of Oldcastle from *Henry IV* was probably due. Some writers, and Greg among them, have found allusions to Oldcastle in *Merry Wives* itself. At

iv. 5. 6 the Host says of Falstaff, 'There's his chamber, his house, his castle, his standing-bed and truckle-bed'. This has a good enough meaning, without any such allusion. At i. 3. 2 the Host calls Falstaff 'bully-rook', and no doubt in chess a 'rook' is, and was by the time of Guillim's *Heraldrie* (1611), a 'castle'. But the Host applies the same term successively in ii. 1 to Page, Shallow, and Ford.

If Oldcastle were in *Merry Wives*, we should have to put the date close to that of *Henry IV*, as the Chamberlain's men are not likely to have gone out of their way later to provoke a memory of their indiscretion. But Q contains a transference (cf. *supra*) from *Hamlet*, and at the same time it must rest on a report of some of the earliest performances, since Brooke could hardly have survived the special review of the play by the Revels officers for the court.[1] It seems, therefore, that *Merry Wives* must be later than *Hamlet*, in spite of the difference of its tone from that of the comedies which immediately followed. I put it, therefore, in 1600–1. If the death of Sir Thomas Lucy (7 July 1600) became known about when it was ready, that may be the reason why the 'louses' do not appear in Q. That the play is in any case later than *Henry V* is likely, because the description of Nym as 'corporal' would be meaningless, if he had not already made his appearance on the battle-field. It is of course an irrelevant fact that in the biography of Falstaff the adventures of *Merry Wives* must precede those of *Henry V*, where he dies and Pistol has married Mrs. Quickly. I think we may accept the story of Elizabeth's request, and suppose it motived by Shakespeare's failure to redeem in *Henry V* the promise of a reintroduction of Falstaff suggested by the epilogue to *2 Henry IV*. The Garter passage suggests a performance at Windsor, where a choir of boys would be available for the fairies. Elizabeth does not seem to have been much at Windsor during the later years of her life, although the rather scrappy notices of her movements for some of those years forbid one to be positive. A short

---

[1] Cf. *Eliz. Stage*, i. 223.

visit is recorded in August 1601, but the *Chamber Accounts* show no payment for a play.[1] There was a Garter installation on 26 May 1601, but the Queen was not ordinarily present at such ceremonies.[2] The play was given at court on 4 November 1604 and again in 1638 (App. D).

For Greg, as for me, there is no suggestion of the original version of *Merry Wives* having been by another hand than Shakespeare's. But this is not so for Wilson or for Robertson. They adopt the notion of Fleay that the *Jealous Comedy* produced by the Alleyn company for Henslowe on 5 January 1593 (App. D) may have been an early form of *Merry Wives*. It may, of course, have been any play with jealousy as a prominent motive in it, *Comedy of Errors* (q.v.) or another. But the notion fits in with the general theory of Pollard and Wilson (cf. p. 225) as to a group of early plays abridged in 1593 for provincial use, and contributing, with a pirate actor, to the bad Quartos. The particular application of this theory to *Merry Wives*, so far as I can piece it together from Wilson's edition, which is not very explicit on the point, and the articles of 1919, is as follows. The horse-stealing plot must go back to Mömpelgart's visit of 1592 and a scandal due to his 'trick of commandeering horses under the Queen's warrant'. As to this it must be pointed out that there is no evidence of any such scandal, unless it is to be found in an allusion in Nashe's *Summer's Last Will and Testament* of 1592 to 'the horses lately sworn to be stolne'.[3] This is possible, but Nashe does not connect the matter with Mömpelgart. The count had a difficulty in getting post-horses at Oxford on August 27. He had presumably no warrant for their impressment then, but on September 4 he received one from the Lord Admiral for his return to Gravesend. On the whole, the clue may just as well lie in the horse-dealing transactions of Breuning or Stamler in 1595. In the development of the play, eight stages are suggested: (i) The *Jealous Comedy*, a piece of unknown authorship on London citizen-life, with a befooled lover, who was not a

---

[1] *Ibid.* iv. 114.   [2] G. F. Beltz, *Memorials of the Garter*, clxxxiii.
[3] *Eliz. Stage*, iii. 452.

fat knight, but a 'simpering lady-killer', with the characteristics of Joseph Surface; (ii) a provincial abridgement,
without, in this case, any handling by Shakespeare; (iii)
a possible revision, still not by Shakespeare, into an 'Oldcastle' play; (iv) a further revision by Shakespeare, 'perhaps with help from others', to meet Elizabeth's command;
(v) an abridged playhouse version of this; (vi) a further
revision of (iv), involving alteration of the verse scenes;
(vii) a further revision of (vi) at the time of the command
performance; (viii) a possible abridgement of (vii) for the
Jacobean revival of 1604. This is very elaborate, but I
do not think that stages (iv) to (viii) are meant to differ
essentially from Greg's reconstruction. F was based on
'parts' of (vi), (vii) or (viii), and Q, if I understand Wilson
correctly, upon a report of (v) by an actor, who had 'parts'
of (iii) to fall back upon when his memory gave out. But I
do not quite understand why, if this was so, he speaks (p.
96) of the 'higher authority than has hitherto been suspected' of the Q version. Moreover, one of the passages
(ii. 2. 4–13), upon the typographical character of which
(cf. *supra*) he relies as evidence for the use of 'parts',
contains a reference to Nym, and if so, Nym must have
been in the *Jealous Comedy*, which is hardly consistent
with Wilson's acceptance of the view (cf. s.v. *Hen. V*)
that he is a satire on Ben Jonson. However, the main
issue is that, on Wilson's theory, there are un-Shakespearean elements from the *Jealous Comedy* still surviving
after the revisions in F, and still more, owing to the
reporter's use of the 1593 text, in Q. His 'bibliographical'
evidence of revision in F consists partly of bits of verse
printed as prose, largely, I think, as in *Henry V*, due to the
confusion of the printer by Pistol's verse intrusions into
prose scenes; partly of the familiar feature (cf. p. 233)
of verse-rhythms in prose, which as usual he interprets as
a result of rewriting in a fresh medium; and partly in the
blending in some scenes of prose and verse, on which I
will quote his collaborator, Sir Arthur Quiller-Couch, who
says, 'Shakespeare has everywhere a most delicate sense of
the separate capacities of verse and prose, and alternates

them with an easy tact quite superior to rule'. On literary rather than bibliographical grounds, Wilson ascribes to the *Jealous Comedy* some language (i. 3. 2; ii. 1. 57–62; ii. 2. 186, 247–50; v. 5. 128–35) used by or of Falstaff, which suggests a 'sententious philanderer' and euphuistic scholar, somewhat out of keeping with the main conception of him. This seems to me rather hypercritical, given the haste of the play. Wilson does not, as he might have done, call in aid the 'metamorphised youth' (*supra*) of Q. But presumably the double dose of the *Jealous Comedy* in Q accounts in his mind for those sections of un-Shakespearean verse which I put down to the reporter or his assistant.

Wilson does not attempt to identify his un-Shakespearean author or authors. Robertson is less reticent. He takes *Merry Wives* for the first of the Falstaff plays, on the ground that both Falstaff and Mrs. Quickly seem to him to be comparatively young in Q, and I understand him to identify the version there represented with the *Jealous Comedy* itself. It was probably the work of several collaborators, among them Shakespeare and possibly Chapman. And Chapman had a larger hand than Shakespeare in the revision which produced the F version. This claim for Chapman is mainly based on the frail evidence of vocabulary clues.

On the source of the plot there is not much to be said. The lover concealed in household stuff appears in several Italian stories. In Giovanni Straparola's *Le Tredeci Piacevoli Notte* (1550–3), iv. 4, followed in Richard Tarlton's *Newes Out of Purgatory* (1590) the vehicle is 'a greate driefatte full of feathers'; in Ser Giovanni Fiorentino's *Il Pecorone* (1558) it is 'un monte di panni di bucato', which is nearer to the buck-basket. Henry Julius of Brunswick employs a linen-basket in his *Tragedia Hibeldeha von Einer Ehebrecherin* (1594), the resemblance of which to *Merry Wives* is very slight, although it introduces an English clown (Cohn xliii, xlvii). The names Ford, Page, Evans, Herne, and Brooke have been traced in Elizabethan records of Windsor,[1] but they are mostly common names,

---

[1] R. R. Tighe and J. E. Davis, *Annals of Windsor*, i. 666.

and all but Brooke are noted by French 314 at Stratford. Later Windsor tradition pointed to the houses of Ford and Page, and a Falstaff's oak, which was also that of Herne the Hunter. I have considered the relation of the play to Sir Thomas Lucy and Shakespeare's deer-stealing in Ch. I.

XXIV. TROILUS AND CRESSIDA

[S.R. 1603.] 7 februarii. Master Robertes. Entred for his copie in full Court holden this day to print when he hath gotten sufficient aucthority for yt, The booke of Troilus and Cresseda as yt is acted by my lord Chamberlens Men vj^d (Arber, iii. 226).

[S.R. 1609.] 28^uo Januarii. Richard Bonion Henry Walleys. Entred for their Copy vnder thandes of Master Segar deputy to Sir George Bucke and master warden Lownes a booke called the history of Troylus and Cressida. vj^d (Arber, iii. 400).

[Q (*first issue*) 1609.] The Historie of Troylus and Cresseida. As it was acted by the Kings Maiesties seruants at the Globe. Written by William Shakespeare. [Ornament] London Imprinted by G. Eld for R. Bonian and H. Walley, and are to be sold at the spred Eagle in Paules Church-yeard, ouer against the great North doore. 1609. [*Head- and Running-titles*] The history of Troylus and Cresseida.

[Q (*second issue*) 1609.] The Famous Historie of Troylus and Cresseid. Excellently expressing the beginning of their loues, with the conceited wooing of Pandarus Prince of Licia. Written by William Shakespeare. [Ornament, imprint, and head- and running-titles, as in first issue.]

[For this issue, the original leaf A1 was cut away, and two new leaves substituted; the first unsigned, with the amended title on the r° and the v° blank; the second signed ¶2, with an epistle (App. B, no. xxxii) not in the first issue.]

Facsimile. W. Griggs (1886, *Sh. Q.* xiii, ed. H. P. Stokes).

[F1. 1623.] [*No entry in Catalogue. Between Histories and Tragedies*, pp., two unpaged, 79, 80, twenty-five unpaged,

followed by one blank page; sign. two blank, ¶–¶¶¶2,
Head-title] The Tragedie of Troylus and Cressida.
[*Running-title*] The Tragedie of Troylus and Cressida *on*
pp. 79, 80, thereafter Troylus and Cressida.

[Act i, sc. 1 marked.]

Parallel-Text. A. Morgan (1889, *Bankside*).

Modern Editions. K. Deighton (1906, *Arden*); J. S. P. Tatlock
(1912, *Tudor*); N. B. Paradise (1927, *Yale*).

Dissertations. K. Eitner, *Die Troilus-Fabel in ihrer Literatur-geschicht-*
lichen Entwickelung (1868, *J.* iii. 252); W. Hertzberg, *Die Quellen der*
Troilus-Sage in ihrem Verhältniss zu Shs T.C. (1871, *J.* vi. 169;) F. G.
Fleay, *On the Composition of T.C.* (1874, *N.S.S. Trans.* 304; *Manual*, 232);
H. Ulrici, *Ist T.C. Comedy oder Tragedy oder History?* (1874, *J.* ix. 26);
C. H. Herford, *T.C. and Euphues, his Censure to Philautus* (1888, *N.S.S.*
Trans. 186); E. Stache, *Das Verhältniss von Shs T.C. zu Chaucers gleich-*
namigen Gedicht (1893); R. A. Small, *T.C.* (1899, *Stage-Quarrel*, 139);
R. Boyle, *T.C.* (1901, *E.S.* xxx. 21); A. Acheson, *Sh. and the Rival Poet*
(1903); E. Koeppel, *Studien über Shs Wirkung auf zeitgenössische Drama-*
tiker (1905); J. Q. Adams, *Timon of Athens and the Irregularities in F1*
(1908, *J.E.G.P.* vii. 53); K. Young, *The Origin and Development of the*
Story of Troilus and Criseyde (1908, *Chaucer Soc.*); N. E. Griffin, *Un-*
Homeric Elements in the Story of Troy (1908, *J.E.G.P.* vii. 32); J. S. P.
Tatlock, *The Siege of Troy in English Literature, especially Sh. and Hey-*
wood (1915, *P.M.L.A.* xxx. 673), *The Welsh T.C. and its Relation to the*
Elizabethan Drama (1915, *M.L.R.* x. 265); *The Chief Problem in Sh.*
(1916, *Sewanee Review*); W. W. Lawrence, *The Love Story in T.C.* (1916,
Columbia Studies, 187); H. E. Rollins, *The T.C. Story from Chaucer to*
Sh. (1917, *P.M.L.A.* xxxii. 383); J. M. Robertson, *T.C.* (1917, *Sh. and*
Chapman, 193); P. K. Guha, *The Problem of Sh.'s T.C.* (1926, *Dacca*
Univ. Bull. ix. 23); P. Alexander, *T.C. 1609* (1928, *4 Library*, ix. 267).

Q and F represent substantially the same text. Q is certainly a good Quarto. Pollard, *F.Q.*, 58, says that it
was not used by the Folio editors. But I am inclined to
think that F was set up from a copy of Q, not so much
because of a few misreadings and abnormal spellings which
they have in common, since these might be derived from
a common original, as because of a traceable resemblance in orthography and the like, of which ii. 2. 163–193
afford a good illustration. Greg, *Emendation*, 12, and
Alexander have independently criticized the view adopted
by Pollard. The example of Q used must of course have
been corrected from a manuscript. F has many better

readings, although some worse, and it restores several passages omitted by Q. Most of these omissions (i. 3. 315; ii. 3. 59–65, 96; iii. 1. 124; iv. 4. 79, 146–50; iv. 5. 206; v. 2. 68; v. 3. 20–2, 58; v. 10. 21–2) are probably mere printer's errors; thus in ii. 3 the repeated phrase 'Patroclus is a fool' caught the printer's eye at 65 instead of 58. On the other hand, i. 3. 354–6 and iii. 3. 161–3, both of which are accompanied by corruption in the neighbouring text, and possibly also iv. 5. 132, 165–70, rather look like deliberate excisions of, or bungling attempts to emend, passages found unintelligible in a manuscript. I think that i. 3. 70–4, including the line 'When rank Thersites opes his mastic jaws' was probably also an accidental omission; it has also been explained both as a dropped personal allusion (cf. *infra*) in Q, and as an addition in F. Finally, there is ii. 3. 80–2, with its characteristic reference by Thersites to 'the dry serpigo'. The only reason for not regarding this as an error is that F in its turn abbreviates Thersites' medical details, as given by Q, in v. 1. 20–8, but why Q should bowdlerize one passage and F another is not clear. Either passage might be a gag, but two independent stage-versions of this play do not (cf. *infra*) seem likely. F, like Q, makes some minor omissions (i. 2. 300; ii. 1. 31–3; iii. 1. 95; iii. 3. 105–6; iv. 5. 29), which must be accidental; at iii. 3. 105–6, the occurrence of lines with identical endings is again the cause. At iv. 5. 96, F inserts unmetrically the words 'they call him Troylus'. These recur at 108, where they are metrical and Q has them. I can only suppose that Shakespeare originally wrote them at 96, then reserved them for a point later in the speech, replacing them by 'a true knight', and made a mark of deletion, which the printer failed to observe. A repetition at v. 10. 33–5 of three lines already used at v. 3. 113, where modern editors omit them, looks at first sight like a similar case, but here (cf. *infra*) the real explanation may be different. If I am right as to iv. 5. 96, the manuscript used for F was probably the author's original, and the variations between Q and F are intelligible on the assumption that this was so and that Q was printed from a transcript, perhaps made for a private owner. The epistle implies that it was not obtained from 'the grand possessors'; that is, the King's men. There are a good many verbal variants between the two versions, but given two printers, and for F the usual sophisticating editor, and for Q a scribe, less expert at reading manuscript and more inclined to cut or emend what he did not understand than a printer, they do not make it necessary to resort to Furnivall's hypothesis that F incorporates some trivial alterations by Shakespeare of later date than the Q text. I do not agree with Alexander that Q is shown, by abnormal spellings, 'rhetorical' stops, and misprints which the *S.T.M.* script might explain, to rest directly on copy in Shakespeare's hand. In so far as he had a monopoly in such things, they might show through a transcript as well as a print. And some of the stops which Alexander cites are palpable errors. The alternative possibilities of divergence in both Q and F from the original inevitably entail some eclecticism in the adoption of readings. The F editor seems to have revised the Q punctuation and made it heavier. The stage-directions evidently have a common basis, but Q abbreviates the names in a way not usual, and lacks some entries and musical notes found in F. This might be due either to omission or to addition, but there is nothing which points clearly to a book-keeper rather than an author, and one cannot be sure from the texts alone that either rests on stage-copy.

The bibliographical record of the play presents several difficulties. There is the double entry in S.R. That to Roberts in 1603, given with the formality of 'a full Court', suggests that some matter of doubt had required discussion, presumably the need for 'sufficient aucthority' required by the entry itself. Pollard, *F. Q.* 66, suggests that it may have been a 'provisional' or 'cautionary' entry as an obstacle (cf. p. 146) against piracy. But for whatever reason, perhaps the lapse of time without printing, it does not in fact seem to have afforded any obstacle to the later entry and subsequent publication by Bonian and Walley in 1609. The preservation of a cancelled leaf in two examples of F1 (cf. p. 341) seems to show that a start was made with setting-up the play after *Romeo and Juliet*; that then a hitch arose, possibly, as Pollard suggests, owing to trouble with Bonian and Walley over the copyright, and *Timon of Athens* took its place; and that finally, after the *Catalogue* had been printed without it, it was thrust in, partly on single leaves and partly on unpaged sheets with special signatures, in a new place. This is a more plausible explanation than any doubt whether it could be properly classed as a tragedy, even although the description of it as such was left out of the running-titles on most of its pages. It might have been classed as a comedy, but certainly not as one of the English histories, and in its new place it can still have been regarded as a tragedy. It is in fact a tragedy, having no kindly ending, as all the comedies have. Then there is the conflict between the entry of 1603, which records performance by the Chamberlain's men, and the confirmation of this, with a merely formal change of the description to King's men, in the first title-page of 1609, and on the other hand the omission of any such record from the revised title-page and the definite declaration in the epistle that the piece was 'neuer stal'd with the Stage'. We are bound to assume that Bonian and Walley had come to this belief. It does not follow that they were right. On the face of it a statement of 1603 is better evidence, as nearer to the date, than one of 1609. But it is just possible that the only performance had been at court, or as Alexander suggests, at an Inn of Court, and that this was not thought to amount to staling with the stage. It is possible, to cite Pollard again, that Roberts made his entry in anticipation of an intended performance which, for whatever reason, never came off. But I think there is sufficient, although not much, evidence to indicate that *Troilus and Cressida* was known by about 1604, and if known, it must have been performed. Mere allusions to the Troilus-Cressida-Pandar story, such as that in Dekker and Webster's *Westward Ho* (c. 1604), of course prove nothing, in view (cf. *infra*) of the Admiral's play. Marston, *Dutch Courtesan* (c. 1603–4), ii. 1. 154, 'Much o' your worship's brain lies in your calves', and iv. 1. 93, 'Sometimes a falling out proves falling in', may echo ii. 1. 108 and iii. 1.112, respectively. More convincing are the lines in I. C. *Saint Marie Magdalens Conversion* (1603), A 3—

> Of Helens rape and Troyes beseiged Towne,
> Of Troylus faith, and Cressids falsitie,
> Of Rychards stratagems for the English crowne,
> Of Tarquins lust, and Lucrece chastitie,
> Of these, of none of these my muse nowe treates.

Here both of the *Troilus and Cressida* themes are touched, and linked with two others, both Shakespearean.

The S.R. entry gives one limit of date for *Troilus and Cressida*. The other is less clear. The story of the fool and the ice, alluded to in iii. 3. 215, is probably that in Armin's *Foole vpon Foole* (1600).[1] This Shakespeare may have heard personally from Armin. But the 'prologue arm'd' of *Troilus and Cressida* clearly refers to that of Jonson's *Poetaster*, produced in 1601.[2] Such a reference would have little point after an interval, and I incline to put the play in 1602. Of course the prologue might be later than *Troilus and Cressida* itself, and a date as early as 1599 has been inferred from the play-scrap on Troilus and Cressida, recited by Sir Oliver Owlet's men in *Histriomastix*, ii. 269, with its reference to the knight who 'shakes his furious Speare'. *Histriomastix* was very likely revised in 1599, perhaps by Marston, although I am not sure that this passage belongs to the revision.[3] In any case, although the coincidence with Shakespeare's name may be an odd one, it is not really necessary to assume that there is an allusion to him. The phrase 'shake a spear' is common in Elizabethan poetry. Robertson has collected a number of examples from Spenser onwards. And if any real play is mocked in the *Histriomastix* passage, it may well be that written for the Admiral's by Dekker and Chettle about April 1599, of which a fragmentary 'plot' survives.[4] The temper of *Troilus and Cressida*, in so far as it is humorous, does not at

---

[1] H.P. i. 321.
[2] *Eliz. Stage*, iii. 365.
[3] Cf. *ibid*. iv. 19.
[4] *Ibid*. ii. 169; iv. 51.

all suggest 1599. Even in 1602, although it is consonant with that of the comedies *All's Well* and *Measure for Measure* which follow, it represents a great break away from that of the earlier series which ends with *Merry Wives*. But if the play is thought of as tragedy rather than comedy, it falls into place as a development of the critical attitude to life already apparent in *Hamlet*. The formal tests of style are not inconsistent with 1602. But Shakespeare's thought is becoming more analytic and his expression of it more involved. And there are some stylistic qualities, which, in degree rather than in kind, give *Troilus and Cressida* a place apart. The language is highly Latinized, and there is a marked tendency to the use of out-of-the-way words, and in particular to the replacement of ordinary words by variant forms with terminations, themselves sometimes showing a Latin influence, such as *-ion*, *-ure*, *-ive*, *-ate*, *-ance*. These features can of course be paralleled to a less extent from other plays, especially plays of near date. In *Troilus and Cressida* they are most frequent in the argumentative discourse of Ulysses and his fellows. But they pervade the play throughout, and must, I think, be held to indicate something of a deliberate stylistic experiment. It remains to add that the entry of 1603 does not in itself preclude the possibility of alteration between 1602 and 1609. One cannot tell whence Shakespeare got the statement (ii. 2. 165) that Aristotle thought young men unfit to hear moral philosophy. It is found in Bacon's *Advancement of Learning* (1605), bk. ii, but rests (Lee 653) on a common and quite justifiable Renaissance rendering of τῆς πολιτικῆς ἀκροατής in *Nic. Eth.* i. 3. 5. In ii. 3. 22, Thersites says, 'I have said my prayers and devil Envy say Amen'. This is generally taken as a second reference to *Poetaster*, in which Envy is crushed by the Prologue. But it comes much nearer to *Mucedorus*, epil. 79, where Envy does in fact say 'Amen' to the praise of James. This is not in the 1598 and 1606 editions, where it is Comedie who calls upon the audience to 'saie amen'; it is in the 1610 edition, representing a recent revival. The date of this cannot be exactly fixed, especially

as an edition of 1609, although not now known, is cited
by Collier.[1] But it is more likely to have followed than
preceded the publication of *Troilus and Cressida*. Much
weight cannot, therefore, be attached to either of these
points. To me *Troilus and Cressida* seems in the main to
be all of one piece, with the probable exception of the
epilogue. This may very well not be Shakespearean at all,
and to speak it Pandarus, over and done with at the end of
v. 3, is incongruously brought back, on to the battle-field
of all places, and introduced with the lines borrowed
(cf. *supra*) from v. 3. 113–15. The Q transcriber must have
spotted the duplication, and cut out the first appearance of
the passage.

    Troilus and Cressida has, however, been the happy
hunting-ground of disintegrators, who have dwelt upon
the slight connexion—surely not unlike Shakespeare—
between the Trojan and camp plots, and the inconsistency
—due, I think, to the use of different sources—between
the continuous warfare of the former and the truce of the
latter; and have attempted to trace corresponding differences of style, pointing to different dates or to different
hands. Fleay in 1874 thought that Shakespeare wrote the
Troilus-Cressida scenes in 1594–6, added the Hector-
Ajax combat and death of Hector a little later, and the
plan of Ulysses to substitute Ajax for Achilles as late as
1606–7; and that parts of the last act were made up of
débris from the Dekker-Chettle play. It is difficult to see
how a play can be built up like this, or how the Ajax story
in particular can be so split up. Fleay seems to have
recognized these points, and in 1886 produced a new
theory, according to which a complete play was written
by Shakespeare and an unknown coadjutor at a date now
put back with *Romeo and Juliet* to about 1593. Most of
the coadjutor's work was replaced by Shakespeare about
1602, but the prologue and v. 4–10 are still his. There is
now no addition of 1606–7. This, however, still rules
with Boyle, for whom Shakespeare wrote an early play
on the love-story at the time of *Romeo and Juliet*, began to

---

[1] Cf. *Eliz. Stage*, iv. 34.

recast it about 1606 by introducing the Ulysses story, but did not get beyond Act iii, and left the completion to Marston, who added the Hector story, and the prologue and epilogue. Small contented himself with regarding v. 7–10 as un-Shakespearean and the prologue and v. 4–6 as only partly Shakespearean. Robertson breaks new ground. Dekker and Chettle's play was rehandled successively by Chapman and Shakespeare, and to Chapman much of the vocabulary and the 'ratiocinative discussions', but not the present versification, are due. As usual, these conflicting theories may largely be left to cut each other's throats. They all seem to me to raise more difficulties than they solve. There is no evidence that Shakespeare ever rewrote the work of a coadjutor or that an Admiral's play was ever transferred to the Chamberlain's. No doubt Chapman made much use of far-fetched and invented words and of Latinisms in his poems and prefaces; but not to any great extent in his plays. Nor can the attitude of *Troilus and Cressida* to the Homeric heroes conceivably be Chapman's. Marston, too, liked out-of-the-way words, and Boyle finds his bluster in the speeches of Hector and Aeneas and Diomede, and his coarseness in Thersites. But the arrogance of the heroes belongs to the temper of the play, and if, as Boyle thinks, Shakespeare wrote the earlier Thersites scenes, why not all of them? Nor do I find anything in the style which need be early. The echoes to and from other plays reach back to *Romeo and Juliet* and forward at least to *Lear*. The use of rhymed couplets does not tell against Shakespeare in 1602; there are a good many still in *Macbeth*. It is not unnatural, in view of the similarity of theme in the love-story, that a passage here and there should recall the manner of *Romeo and Juliet* and *Merchant of Venice*. That most relied upon is i. 1. 101–7. There is not much to back it up, and the Shakespeare of 1595–7 certainly never wrote the speech of Troilus in iv. 4. 35–50. I do not even think that Small is right, except as regards the epilogue, when he finds a second hand in v. 4–10. The double-ending test, on which he largely relies, cannot properly be applied to a group of scenes, in which the blank verse amounts to no more than 42 lines. These are huddled scenes, with some poor work in them, but Shakespeare did sometimes scamp his work, especially at the end of a play. And the Margarelon bit and v. 10. 22—'Hector is dead; there is no more to say'—are surely his. On this point Small has no doubt supporters, even outside the ranks of professed disintegrators. I believe them to have been misled by the notion that the first occurrence of the repeated lines (cf. *supra*) marks the original end of the play. It does not; it only marks the end of Pandarus. The other story must always have involved the death of Hector, which is already foreshadowed in v. 3. Nor can one easily suppose that a collaborator was brought in for the first time at the tag-end of the play. As to the prologue, I see nothing to exclude Shakespeare. Some differentiation between the style of a prologue and that of its play is usual enough. And the specialized *Troilus and Cressida* vocabulary is there. I have dealt elsewhere (cf. p. 72) with the possible relations of *Troilus and Cressida* to the 'stage-quarrel', and need only add here that if Marston was Thersites, he certainly was not also the author.

Directly or indirectly, *Troilus and Cressida* draws upon four sources. The first is Chaucer's *Troilus and Criseyde*, itself derived ultimately, not from Homer, but from two Latin pseudo-Homeric narratives, the *Ephemeris Belli Troiani* of Dictys Cretensis (4th cent. A.D.) and the *De Excidio Troiae Historia* of Dares Phrygius. On these were based the *Roman de Troie* (c. 1160) of Benoit de Saint-Maure; on Benoit the *Historia Troiana* (1287) of Guido delle Colonne; and on both Benoit and Guido, with borrowings from his own *Filocolo* and from medieval romance, the *Filostrato* (c. 1339) of Boccaccio. Chaucer in his turn followed the *Filostrato*, and added something direct from Benoit, Guido, and the *Filocolo*. Secondly, material for the camp-scenes, which mostly lie outside the Chaucerian story, come from one of two derivatives from Guido, either Lydgate's *Sege of Troye* (c. 1412–20) or Caxton's

Recuyell of the Historyes of Troye (1475); probably the latter, to which the spelling of names in *Troilus and Cressida* is closer than to the *Sege*. Thirdly, although not much use is made of it in the play, the Elizabethans were familiar with the tragic development of Cressida's story to an end in a lazar-house, as given to it in Robert Henryson's Scottish *Testament of Cresseid*, printed as Chaucer's in the edition of 1532. And fourthly there was Homer, to whom much of the presentation of the Greek heroes, as well as the introduction of Thersites, must be due. Chapman's Homeric translations began with *Seaven Bookes of the Iliades* (i, ii, and vii–xi) and *Achilles Shield* (xviii) both in 1598, and probably suggested the theme of *Troilus and Cressida*. The other books came too late for use in the play. Arthur Hall's *Ten Bookes of Homers Iliades* (i–x) was of 1581. These selections would not have told Shakespeare that it was not Troilus, as in the pseudo-Homeric versions, but Hector, who was dragged at the heels of the horse of Achilles. He may have known the full French translation of Hugues Salel and Amadis Jamyn (1584, 1597). But such questions are hardly worth pursuing, since a general contemporary knowledge both of the Homeric story and of the Sophoclean presentation of Ajax may be assumed. An outline of the latter, for example, was given in Peele's *Tale of Troy* (1589). The earlier Shakespearean plays contain many references to the classical personages, as well as to Troilus and Cressida themselves. Moreover, there was already a stage-tradition. A 'story of Troylous and Pandar' was played by the Chapel as far back as 1516.[1] Bale records a *comoedia* of 'Troilum ex Chaucero' by Nicholas Grimald about 1540–7.[2] The Windsor Chapel gave an *Aiax and Vlisses* at court in 1572[3] and Oxford's boys an *Agamemnon & Vlisses* in 1584.[4] The Admiral's produced a *Troy* on 25 June 1596 as well as Dekker and Chettle's play (cf. *supra*) of 1602.[5] *Troy* has sometimes been regarded as an early form of Heywood's

---

[1] *Med. Stage*, ii. 205; Brewer, ii. 2. 1205.
[2] *Med. Stage*, ii. 450.
[3] *Eliz. Stage*, iv. 146.
[4] *Ibid.* iv. 160.
[5] *Ibid.* ii. 144.

Iron Age, printed in two parts in 1632. This is, of course, a mere conjecture. But Tatlock has argued that the *Iron Age* was written before Heywood's narrative *Troia-Britannica* of 1609, and explains some passages, which are too close to *Troilus and Cressida* to be altogether independent of it, as due to the use by Heywood and Shakespeare of a common dramatic source. His main ground is that *Iron Age* repeats lines from two poetical epistles between Paris and Helen which are in a different metre to the rest of *Troia-Britannica* and may be of earlier date, and makes no similar use of the rest of *Troia-Britannica*, which he therefore thinks not to have been yet in existence. This is ingenious, but it can hardly stand against the clear inference from the epistles to Heywood's earlier *Ages* that the *Iron Age*, whether based upon earlier work or not, had not yet 'aduentured the Stage' in 1611, although it was contemplated 'by Gods grace' in 1613.[1] And I think we must ascribe the parallels with *Troilus and Cressida* to borrowings by Heywood from Shakespeare.

XXV. ALL'S WELL THAT ENDS WELL

[F1. 1623.] [*Catalogue*] All is well, that Ends well. [*Comedies*, pp. 230–54, sign. V1ᵛ–Yᵛ. *Head- and Running-titles*] All's (Alls) Well, that Ends (ends) Well. [Acts i, sc. 1, ii–v marked.]

Modern Editions. W. O. Brigstocke (1904, 1929, *Arden*); A. E. Case (1926, *Yale*); A. T. Quiller-Couch and J. D. Wilson (1929, *C.U.P.*).

Dissertations. H. v. Friesen *A.W.* (1867, *J*. ii. 48); F. G. Fleay, *On A.W.* (1874, *N.S.S. Trans.* 285; *Manual*, 224); H. v. d. Hagen, *Über die altfranzösische Vorstufe des Shs A.W.* (1879); N. Delius, *Sh.'s A.W. and Paynter's Giletta of Narbonne* (1887, *J*. xxii. 27; *Abl.* ii. 283); R. Boyle, *A.W. and Love's Labour's Won* (1890, *E.S.* xiv. 408); L. Frankel, *Zu A.W.* (1892, *Anglia*, xiv. 457); W. W. Lawrence, *The Meaning of A.W.* (1922, *P.M.L.A.* xxxvii. 418); J. M. Robertson, *A.W.* (1925, *Sh. Canon*, iii. 28).

F is not a satisfactory text, and requires a good deal of emendation. The mislineations are not extensive, and seem mainly due to the transitions between verse and

---

[1] *Ibid.* iii. 345.

prose. The stage-directions are mainly normal, but a few (ii. 1. 1; ii. 3. 191; iv. 1. 1) indicate the nature of the scenes they introduce. There is much variation of nomenclature, especially for the Countess and for Bertram, and the F editor can have made no attempt at unification. These features suggest nearness to the author's copy. But the book-keeper has probably added the letters G. and E. to the 1. and 2. by which the author discriminated the brothers Dumain, who are indifferently described (i. 2; ii. 1; iii. 1, 6; iv. 1, 3; v. 1) as Lords, Captains, or Frenchmen, and are apparently also the Gentlemen of iii. 2. The letters may indicate the names of actors; Gough and Ecclestone have been guessed at. The 'Enter a gentle Astringer' of v. 1. 7 is a well-known crux. An astringer was an officer of falconry, and probably F so interpreted the stage-direction. But such an officer would be out of place in the scene, and I have a suspicion that Shakespeare wrote 'Gentle⟨man⟩ Usher', and that again the book-keeper added over it the initial 'T' of an actor.[1] There may be some indication of cutting in the long dashes printed at i. 1. 61 and i. 3. 159, the two successive short lines at iii. 5. 42, the abrupt change of subject at i. 1. 179. Violenta is a mute in iii. 5. A statement is ascribed to Diana at v. 3. 199, which she has not made, as the text stands.

There is little external evidence on the date of the play. There was an earthquake (i. 3. 91) on 24 December 1601.[2] Parolles is chaffed for his exploit with the drum, as 'Tom Drum' (v. 3. 322) and as getting 'John Drum's entertainment' (iii. 6. 40). But the phrase 'Tom Drum's entertainment' is cited in a proverbial sense by Holinshed, and one cannot therefore be sure of an allusion to the Paul's play, probably written by Marston in 1600, of *Jack Drum's Entertainment*, and printed in 1601.[3] But Lafeu's 'Lustique, as the Dutchman saies' (ii. 3. 47) must clearly come from Jacob van Smelt's repeated 'lustick' in *The Weakest Goeth to the Wall*, 943–6, and there is no reason

---

[1] Prof. Wilson tells me that a slovenly 'usscher' might become 'astrĩger' without the 'T'.

[2] Chamberlain, *Eliz.* 124; Stowe, *Annales*, 1412.

[3] *Eliz. Stage*, iv. 21.

to regard this play as much older than its publication in 1600.[1] There are no very clear early references to *All's Well* itself; the title may be echoed in Marston's *Dutch Courtesan*, iv. 1. 16; iv. 2. 48; iv. 4. 1–4; v. 3. 150, 170. This is a play of about 1603–4.[2] There are some fairly close echoes in *All's Well* of *Hamlet* (i. 1. 170), *Troilus and Cressida* (ii. 1. 100), and *As You Like It* (iv. 1. 45), and the names Corambus, Jaques, Sebastian, Violenta are used in *Hamlet*, *As You Like It*, and *Twelfth Night*, although Capilet and Dumain point back to *Romeo and Juliet* and *Love's Labour's Lost*. Such faint indications are at least consistent with a date in 1601–4, and I put *All's Well* tentatively in 1602–3, between *Troilus and Cressida* and *Measure for Measure*. These are the plays to which it has the closest affinity in temper, and on the whole in style. The Latinized vocabulary of *Troilus and Cressida* does not recur to any marked extent. Throughout the play one gets the impression that Shakespeare's mind and pen are not moving easily, and there is a rather more considerable use of rhyme for substantial sections of dialogue than is typical of his work at this period. Explanations have been given which seem to me to raise more difficulties than they solve. Boyle thinks that the rhyme and some of the prose have survived from earlier work, and argues, with the help of some slight Shakespearean inconsistencies in the plot, that *All's Well* is a revision of *Love Labours Won*, and cites Helena's 'Will you be mine, now you are doubly won?' (v. 3. 315) as an echo of that inconclusive title. I do not, however, believe that the rhyme is early at all. The passages in which it occurs do not in other respects differ much from the neighbouring blank verse; like that, they are broken up by internal pauses and run-on lines. Sometimes, although not always, they can be read as having a dramatic intention; to mark a change of mood (i. 1. 231–44), to convey sententious comment (i. 3. 135–41; ii. 3. 132–51), to create an atmosphere of exaltation in preparation for a miraculous cure (ii. 1. 133–213). Robertson, perturbed by the comparative weakness,

---

[1] *Ibid*. iv. 52.　　　　　　[2] *Ibid*. iii. 430.

which must be admitted, of the play as a whole, boldly claims that it is substantially by Chapman, possibly revising work of Greene, and only slightly worked over in his turn by Shakespeare. The suggestion of Greene seems to me quite ill-founded. Nor do I agree that the episode of Parolles and his drum is quite so irrelevant and inane as to require attribution to Chapman, or that the patches of continuous rhyme are in his manner, or that (cf. p. 222) Robertson's clues to his vocabulary will bear analysis. On the other hand, I think that in certain passages of the blank verse (e.g. i. 2. 24–48; i. 3. 226–36; ii. 1. 106–31; ii. 5. 59–76), which are stiffly written and seem struggling to express more than is there to be expressed, there does emerge a quality which for whatever reason approximates to that of the blank verse of Chapman. But to read the play as a whole in the light of Robertson's theory is, for me, at once to be confirmed in the conviction that, however much it may be unlike Shakespeare's more normal manner, it is even more unlike any of the ingenious but empty comedies of Chapman. On the whole, therefore, I do not see that any other assumption helps to make this difficult play more intelligible than the assumption of Shakespeare working in an abnormal mood.

The source is Boccaccio's tale of *Giglietta di Nerbona*,[1] as translated in William Painter's *Palace of Pleasure*, i (1566), 38. Shakespeare uses Painter's 'Senois' for 'Siennese'. There is no reason to suppose that he knew Bernardo Accolti's *Virginia* (1513, 1535), also based on Boccaccio's story. The substitution of one woman for another in bed, common to *All's Well* and *Measure for Measure*, is, of course, a commonplace of romantic literature.

XXVI. MEASURE FOR MEASURE

[F1. 1623.] [*Catalogue*] Measure for Measure. [*Comedies*, pp. 61–84, sign. F–G 6ᵛ. *Head-title*] Measure, For Measure. [*Running-title*] Measure for Measure.

[Acts and scc. marked. 'The Scene Vienna' and 'The names of all the Actors' at end.]

---

[1] *Decameron*, iii. 9.

Modern Editions. H. C. Hart (1905, 1925, *Arden*); A. T. Quiller-Couch and J. D. Wilson (1922, *C.U.P.*); W. H. Durham (1926, *Yale*). *Dissertations.* K. Foth, *Shs M.M. und die Geschichte von Promos und Cassandra* (1878, *J.* xiii. 163); L. L. K. *The Plot of M.M.* (1893, 8 *N.Q.* iv. 83); G. Sarrazin, *Herzog Vincentio in M.M. und sein Urbild* (1895, *J.* xxxi. 165); E. Law, *The First-Night Performance of M.M.* (1910, Dec. 26, *Times*); J. M. Robertson, *The Problem of M.M.* (1923, *Sh. Canon*, ii. 158).

The textual confusions and mislineations of F are so frequent as to give plausibility to the conclusion of Wilson that a transcriber has intervened between the original copy and the printer; and the extreme slightness of the stage-directions, which often omit entries and exits, lead him to think that the transcriber was, at least to some extent, 'assembling' (cf. p. 153) from 'parts'.

The play was given at court on 26 December 1604 (App. D). Allusions (i. 1. 68; ii. 4. 26) to a royal dislike of crowds may reflect an idiosyncrasy of James, but the proclamations of 29 May and 6 July 1603 restraining access to London and the court,[1] which are sometimes cited in confirmation of this, were merely normal precautions against the spread of plague. Fleay[2] cites other possible indications of 1604, some of which are rather thin, while one, the supposed allusion in 'Like doth quit like' (v. 1. 416) to the name of a play by Heywood and Chettle rests on a forgery by Collier.[3] Wilson finds in the black masks (ii. 4. 79), which proclaim an 'enshelled' (F. 'en-shield') beauty, an allusion to Jonson's coming *Mask of Blackness* on 6 January 1605.[4] It may be so, but although the maskers entered in a shell, they were painted black and wore no masks. The style of the play is not inconsistent with 1604, and the temper is consonant with that of *Troilus and Cressida* and *All's Well*. There is better poetry than in *All's Well*, but, as in that, a good deal of ineffective verse and humourless prose, while the structure still indicates the same uncertainty of dramatic intention. The only marked early echo, which has been traced, is of ii. 4. 24–6 in William Barksted's *Mirrha* (1607).

Wilson scents a later date than 1604 in the reference

[1] *Procl.* 951, 961.
[2] *L. and W.* 234.
[3] Henslowe, i. xliii.
[4] *Eliz. Stage*, iii. 375.

(i. 2. 5) to the King of Hungary's peace. This he takes to be a disgraceful peace made against the will of the Emperor by the Archduke Matthias, King of Hungary, with the Turks at Zsitva-Torok on 11 November 1606. But surely it may as well be the peace made and treacherously broken by Sigismund of Hungary in *2 Tamburlaine*, i. 2; ii. 1. 2. However, the double date so arrived at serves Wilson as the starting-point for an elaborate and even statistical reconstruction of a complicated stage-history for *Measure for Measure*. It may have been originally a sixteenth-century play, perhaps with a long history behind it, going back to *Promos and Cassandra* (cf. *infra*), and only revised by Shakespeare. In any case the text used in the performance of 1604, for which Shakespeare 'scribbled' the topical court passages, was a drastic abridgement in some 2,000 lines, carried out, not by him but by a 'second-rate collaborator', on the 'parts'. Later than 11 November 1606, a longer version was required for the public stage. But the original copy was lost. Somebody therefore, again not Shakespeare, took the parts, hastily transcribed 1,604 blank verse, 20 rhymed, and 241 prose lines of Shakespeare's work as cut, scrapped 135 more lines of blank verse and expanded their material into 430 lines of prose, added on his own account 364 more lines of prose and 46 of iambic and trochaic rhyme, and thus produced the extant text, amounting, in the numeration of Wilson's edition, to 2,705 lines. It takes a brave man to produce so precise a result from an admittedly corrupt text. It is quite possible that there may be some cutting in *Measure for Measure* as we have it. The total number of short lines is not out of the way for a play of this period, and many of them are normal. A few, however, read awkwardly, and may indicate gaps. Moreover, although Shakespeare does (cf. p. 231) introduce mute or almost mute personages, there are several in this play; a Friar Thomas, if he is not the same as Friar Peter, in i. 3; a Francisca in i. 4; a Justice, if he is not the same as the Provost, in ii. 1; a Varrius in iv. 5, where also a Flavius, who never appears, is sent for. It is possible that some of these parts may once have been longer. Varrius and Flavius, in particular, occur in one of two very scrappy scenes at the end of Act iv, where they are involved in some rather unintelligible manœuvring by the Duke. It is less easy to be sure that the Duke's reflections in iv. 1. 60–5 have been transferred, as Wilson thinks, from an original place contiguous to those in iii. 2. 196–200, in order to cover a textual gap. If they stood together, there would be a very awkward repetition of the word 'greatness'. However this may be, the analogy of other plays shows us that cuts often came far short of a 'drastic abridgement'. Nor do I think that Wilson is safe in resting upon the length of *Tempest* a theory that court performances were normally limited to some 2,000 lines. Some on record lasted late enough to allow for three hours, or about 3,000 lines.[1] If there has been any cutting, then it need not have been extensive, and need not have been as early as 1604. And if there has also been any interpolation, that may have accompanied the cutting itself. The song at iv. 1. 1 is good enough for any one. If not Shakespeare's, one could fancy it Campion's. The statement in Munro, i. 202, that Isaac Walton ascribed it to Marlowe is an error. But it recurs, with a less good second verse, more clearly within Fletcher's compass, in *The Bloody Brother*, which several experts on Beaumont and Fletcher place before 1623; and in this form it is reproduced in the 1640 volume of Shakespeare's *Poems* (cf. p. 557). A musical interpolation in a Jacobean revival is always possible. Certainly, the Duke's unusual trochaic rhymes at iii. 2. 275, not unlike those in the Gower choruses of *Pericles*, are not much like Shakespeare. But I feel little confidence in Wilson's stylistic reasons for assigning 24 decasyllabic rhymed lines, and 794 lines of prose to a reviser. There is no continuous rhyme, as in *All's Well*. The 24 decasyllables are couplets of dismissal, mostly in the mouth of the Duke, who is choric, like the old folk in *All's Well*, and they do not seem to me markedly inferior to some at least of those which Wilson leaves to Shakespeare. As for the prose,

---

[1] *Eliz. Stage*, i. 225; iv. 122.

Wilson's strongest point is on i. 2, in one section of which Mrs. Overdone knows of Claudio's offence, while a few lines later she seems to receive it as news. Either Shakespeare has been unusually careless, even for him, or there has been some alteration. But in the literary quality of this and other ribald scenes of Pompey and his fellows, I cannot see any marked difference between the 'sheer mud, dreary, dead' of what Wilson gives to the reviser and the 'full Shakespearean flavour' of what he spares. Of course he has picked out the best bits (i. 2. 83–118; ii. 1. 41–201; iv. 3. 1–59) for Shakespeare. But there is little of that full flavour anywhere, and even in the muddiest passages an occasional sniff of it may be caught. The reviser is credited also with some scraps of prose alternating with verse, mainly from the mouth of Lucio, whose part Wilson thinks that he considerably expanded. Such transitions from one medium to another are common enough (cf. p. 182) in the plays, and it is hardly justifiable to assume a second hand, merely because they are carried to an extreme here and the reason for a change of mood is not always obvious. So far I have been dealing with supposed additions of the reviser's own. The rest of the prose, much of it colourless and merely concerned with the machinery of the plot, is on Wilson's theory an expansion of 135 lines of lost Shakespearean verse. Here the evidence offered is different. There are numerous circumlocutory phrases, such as 'Let me desire to know', or 'This I can let you understand', which 'seem absurd in prose', but 'would be quite natural in verse'. And there are 'verse-fossils' embedded in the prose. I think that a glance at the concordance, where the word 'desire', for example, occupies more than three columns, would have shown Wilson that the complimentary circumlocutions are very common indeed in Shakespeare's prose. He burlesques them himself in *Merry Wives*, i. 2. 9, where Evans says, 'The letter is, to desire and require her to solicit your master's desires to Mistress Anne Page'. And of course the 'verse-fossils' are (cf. p. 233) an equally common feature. Moreover, in *Measure for Measure* they are not confined, as the theory requires, to the passages where it suspects an expansion of verse, but are found also in the original prose ascribed to Shakespeare and to the reviser respectively.

Robertson, with Wilson's theory before him, produces his inevitable alternative. *Measure for Measure* is 'a working recast by Shakespeare of a play drafted by Chapman on the basis of the older play of Whetstone, or perhaps of an earlier condensation of that two-part drama into a single one'. Greene is only slightly hinted at as a possible predecessor of Chapman. I need not discuss Robertson's case in detail. It is closely analogous to that for *All's Well*, although I think even less plausible. Those who accept the one are likely to accept the other.

The substantial source of *Measure for Measure* was George Whetstone's *Promos and Cassandra* (1578). This was apparently designed for the stage, but had not, when Whetstone published his *Heptameron* in 1582, been performed.[1] It was itself based upon Giraldi Cintio's *Ecatommiti* (1565), viii. 5, and this perhaps in its turn upon an historical incident of 1547 near Milan, in which the course of the Duke was taken by Fernando Gonzaga, the governor of the province. Sarrazin finds analogies between Shakespeare's Duke and a later Vincentio Gonzaga, Duke of Mantua from 1587 to 1612.

XXVII. OTHELLO

[S.R. 1621.]   6° Octobris, 1621.   Thomas Walkley. Entred for his copie vnder the handes of Sir George Buck, and Master Swinhoe warden, The Tragedie of Othello, the moore of Venice. vj^d (Arber, iv. 59).

[Q1. 1622.] The Tragœdy of Othello, The Moore of Venice. As it hath beene diuerse times acted at the Globe, and at the Black-Friers, by his Maiesties Seruants. Written by William Shakespeare. [Okes's device (McKerrow 316)] London, Printed by N⟨icholas⟩ O⟨kes⟩ for Thomas Walkley, and are to be sold at his shop, at the Eagle and Child, in Brittans Bursse. 1622. [*Head-title*] The Tragedy

---

[1] *Eliz. Stage*, iii. 512.

of Othello the Moore of Venice [*Running-title*] The
Tragedy of Othello The Moore of Venice.

[Epistle (App. B, no. xlix) headed 'The Stationer to the Reader',
signed 'Thomas Walkley'. Acts ii. 1, iv, v marked.]

Facsimile. C. Praetorius (1885, *Sh. Q.* xxxi, ed. H. A. Evans).

[F1. 1623.] [*Catalogue*] Othello, the Moore of Venice.
[*Tragedies*, pp. 310–39, sign. ss 3ᵛ–vv 6ʳ. *Head-title*] The
Tragedie of Othello, the Moore of Venice. [*Running-title*]
The Tragedie of Othello the Moore of Venice.

[Acts and scc. marked. 'The Names of the Actors' at end.]

[S.R. 1628.] 1ᵐᵒ Marti 1627. Master Richard Hawkins.
Assigned ouer vnto him by Thomas Walkley, and Con-
sent of a Court holden this Day all the estate right title and
Interest which he hath in these Copies following .. vizᵗ ..
Orthello the more of Venice. (Arber, iv. 194.)

[Q 2. 1630.] The Tragœdy of Othello, The Moore of
Venice. As it hath beene diuerse times acted at the Globe,
and at the Black Friers, by his Maiesties Seruants.
Written by William Shakespeare. [Mathewes's device
(McKerrow 188ᵇ)] London, Printed by A⟨ugustine⟩
M⟨athewes⟩ for Richard Hawkins, and are to be sold at his
shoppe in Chancery-Lane, neere Sergeants-Inne. 1630.
[*Head- and Running-titles*] The Tragedy of Othello the
Moore of Venice.

[ii. 1; iii. 1; iv. 1; v. 1 marked.]

Facsimile. C. Praetorius (1885, *Sh. Q.* xxxii, ed. H. A. Evans).

[S.R. 1638.] 29° Maij 1638. Master Mead and Master
Meredith. Entred for their Copies by order of a full
Court held the fifth day of June Last ⟨1637⟩ according to
the request of Vrsula Hawkins widdow (late wife of
Richard Hawkins deceased) then present in Court All
these Copies and parts of Copies following which did
belong vnto her said husband as followeth ... Orthello the
More of Venice a play ... (Arber, iv. 420).

[S.R. 1639.] 25ᵗʰ of Januarij 1638 Master William
Leake. Assigned ouer vnto him by vertue of a warrant
vnder the hands and seales of Master Mead and Master

Meredith and with the Consent of a full Court of Assistants holden this day. All the Estate Right Title and Interest which the said Master Mead and Master Meredith haue in these Copies and partes of Copies following which were Entred vnto them from Mistris Hawkins the 29th of May last . . . vizt . . . Orthello the More of Venice a Play . . . (Arber, iv. 452).

[Q3. 1655.] . . . The fourth Edition . . . Printed for William Leak . . . 1655.

Parallel-Texts. T. R. Price (1890, *Bankside*); M. M. A. Schröer (1909).

Modern Editions. H. H. Furness (1886, *New Variorum*); H. C. Hart (1903, 1928, *Arden*); L. Mason (1918, *Yale*); C. H. Herford (1920, *Warwick*).

Dissertations. R. O'Connell, *Desdemona in the Flesh* (1885, 6 *N.Q.* xi. 147); W. R. Turnbull, O., *A Critical Study* (1892); E. Engel, *Zur Urgeschichte des O.* (1899, *J.* xxxv. 271); A. C. Bradley, *The Additions in the Folio Text of O.* (1904, *Sh. Tragedy*, 429); E. Law, *O. on All Hallows Day, 1604* (1910, Oct. 31, *Times*); C. Nolte, *Die Überlieferung von Shs O.* (1923); L. Winstanley, *O. as the Tragedy of Italy* (1924); A. H. Krappe, *A Byzantine Source of Sh.'s O.* (1924, *M.L.N.* xxxix, 156); W. A. Bullock, *The Sources of O.* (1925, *M.L.N.* xl. 226).

Q and F are both good and fairly well-printed texts; and they clearly rest substantially upon the same original. A feature of this seems to have been the occasional writing of lines of verse, perhaps (cf. p. 184) for emphasis, as two separate half-lines. Q and F have generally preserved this at different points, but at i. 1. 53–4 they concur. The variations between the texts throw some light on their origins. F has eliminated, more rigorously than usual, profanities which stand in Q. Each text contains passages not found in the other. The F omissions are trifling and doubtless due to error. So are many of those in Q. Twice (i. 3. 194; iv. 2. 73–6) the cause is obvious, in taking off from the second instead of the first of two lines with identical last words. Twice (i. 2. 65; i. 3. 63) Q seems to have regarded parenthesis brackets in the original as marks for deletion. Some longer omissions in Q require to be explained otherwise. Some of these passages have been taken for later Shakespearean additions in F. There is, however, no example in which this can be proved to be so, and on the other hand in most cases (i. 1. 122–38; i. 2. 72–7; i. 3. 24–30; iii. 3. 383–90; iv. 3. 31–53, 55–7, 60–3, 87–104; v. 2. 246–8, 266–72) the omission is accompanied by alteration in neighbouring lines, or leaves the sense of the context abrupt or inadequate. Q is pretty clearly cut here. It is true that the omissions in iv. 3 include the *Willow Song*, and that a song forms a natural interpolation. But an interpolator would not have added the scraps of dialogue with which Desdemona's is broken, or the reference back to it in v. 2. 246–8. There is no reason why the other longer Q omissions (iii. 3. 453–60; iv. 1. 38–44; iv. 2. 151–64; v. 2. 151–4, 185–93) should not be cuts also. If so, the cutting amounts to 125 lines; and, as usual, it mainly affects long speeches or sections of dialogues. Of course the song may have been omitted, not to shorten a performance, but because the actor could not sing. The purely verbal variants between Q and F are very numerous. The great majority are due to different readings of the same word in the original, and generally, although by no means always, F has the better. But sometimes the divergence is greater than mere misreading will explain. There are some 'equivalents' probably due (cf. p. 180) to subconscious substitution. There are some traces of sophistication by the F editor. But I think there must be perversion in Q. There are a good many passages in which more than one word is varied, and here Q often seems to have attempted an emendation of language or metre, or of a phrase found unintelligible, or to have started (iii. 4. 74–5; v. 1. 86) with a misreading and altered the context to suit it. These features suggest a transcriber rather than a printer, and the relation becomes intelligible if we regard F as printed from the original and Q from a not very faithful transcript, without a few passages cut in representation. It must have been an early transcript, in view of the profanities. Whether it was made for stage purposes or for a private collector one can hardly say. The F stage-directions seem to have been altered from those in

Q, which are normal. They tend to be shorter; they have fewer notes for properties and the like; the order of the names in entries differs. The only notable addition is at v. 2. 1 where, for the 'Enter Othello with a light' of Q, F has 'Enter Othello, and Desdemona in her bed'. But the bed is elsewhere (v. 2. 198) in Q. The Q stage-directions may well be the author's, but the transcriber might have added some marginal notes for action, not in F. It is perhaps noteworthy that Q regularly spells Emillia, Roderigo, Montanio, for the Æmilia, Rodorigo, Montano of F. Q2 seems to have been set-up from Q1, but corrected and the omissions supplied, either from F, or as the Cambridge editors, perhaps unnecessarily, suggest, from a manuscript closely resembling that used by F.

I do not think there are any cuts common to Q and F. A few short lines seem abrupt, but short lines have become very common in plays of this period. There is an odd patch of prose at i. 3. 221–9, probably deliberate, to introduce a change of subject and tone, and led up to by the last line of the foregoing speech, which is prose, although Q turns it into verse. Similarly, the rhyme of i. 3. 202–19, which Robertson [1] claims as an interpolation by Chapman, is appropriate to the sententious comments which it conveys; the Duke calls his contribution 'a sentence'. Gildon (App. C, no. xxi) had been told that Shakespeare put some words and expressions 'perhaps not so agreeable to his Character' into the part of Iago, for the benefit of a comedian who played it. This may refer to the ribald rhymes of Iago's discourse with Desdemona of ii. 1. 101–61, which Hart, who finds parallels with Nicholas Breton's *Choice, Chance and Change* (1606), would like to regard as an interpolation. But it is in both texts, and Breton probably borrowed. The passage, like the dull Clown in iii. 1, 4, reads like a survival of the manner of *All's Well* and *Measure for Measure* from which Shakespeare has for the most part purged himself in *Othello*.

A court performance on 1 November 1604 (App. D) gives one limit of date, and this was no doubt the 'indis-

---

[1] *Sh. and Ch.* 216.

putable evidence' which led Malone, who formerly thought
Othello one of the latest plays, to put it in 1604.[1] A later
date has been claimed for iii. 4. 47, 'our new heraldry is
hands, not hearts,' on the ground that it alludes to the
adoption of 'the bloody hand of Ulster' as a badge for the
new order of baronets in 1611. But the antithesis of hands
and hearts is widespread, and there are close parallels to
Shakespeare's use of it in Peele, *Polyhymnia* (1590), 190,
where also it takes an heraldic form, and Sir William Corn-
wallis, *Essayes* (1600–1), xxviii. Collier (App. F, xi, *c*, *e*)
forged entries in Egerton and Dulwich manuscripts to
support earlier dating. A production in 1604 is consonant
with the stylistic evidence, and would give time for an
apparent echo of the Moor's murder in Dekker and
Middleton's *1 Honest Whore*, i. 1. 37, of that year.[2] *Othello*
held the stage well; performances are traceable in 1610,
at court in 1612–13, in 1629, in 1635, and at court on
8 December 1636 (App. D). Burbadge and Swanston
played Othello and Taylor Iago.[3] Collier has an epigram,
of doubtful authenticity, ascribing Othello also to Field
(App. F, xi, *h*).

The source is Giraldi Cintio's *Ecatommiti* (1565), iii. 7,
but here the Moor and the Ensign have no names. Iago is
the ordinary Italian form of James; it is not known where
Othello came from. A ballad on the story cited by Collier
is (App. F, xi, *c*) a forgery. O'Connell cites from P. G.
Molmenti, *Vecchie Storie* (1882), 77, a case of an actual
wife-murder by a Venetian noble in 1602. The Willow
Song (iv. 3. 41) may be borrowed. A text with musical
notation is printed in Noble 152 from *Addl. MS.* 15117,
f. 18 (c. 1615), and the music by itself is in a lute-book by
Thomas Dallis of Cambridge, dated 1583.[4] A play given
before James, just after a treaty with Spain, obviously
cannot be, as Miss Winstanley thinks, a symbolical allegory, at once of the domination of Italy by Spain, and of
the relations of Philip II (Othello) with his wife and his

---

[1] *Var.* ii. 404; Edition (1800) of
Dryden's *Grounds of Criticism*, 258.
[2] *Eliz. Stage*, iii. 294.
[3] *Ibid.* ii. 309; iv. 371.
[4] *T.C.D. MS.* 410.

minister Antonio Perez (Iago). If such an intention had been intelligible, the censor would not have passed the play; if not, it would have been pointless.

XXVIII. KING LEAR

[S.R. 1607.] 26 Novembris. Nathanael Butter John Busby. Entred for their Copie under thandes of Sir George Buck knight and Thwardens A booke called. Master William Shakespeare his historye of Kinge Lear, as yt was played before the Kinges maiestie at Whitehall vppon Sainct Stephens night at Christmas Last, by his maiesties servantes playinge vsually at the Globe on the Banksyde vj^d (Arber, iii. 366).

[Q1. 1608.] M. William Shak-speare: His True Chronicle Historie of the life and death of King Lear and his three Daughters. With the vnfortunate life of Edgar, sonne and heire to the Earle of Gloster, and his sullen and assumed humor of Tom of Bedlam: As it was played before the Kings Maiestie at Whitehall vpon S. Stephans night in Christmas Hollidayes. By his Maiesties seruants playing vsually at the Gloabe on the Bancke-side. [George and Lionel Snowden's or Nicholas Okes's device (McKerrow 316)] London, Printed for Nathaniel Butter, and are to be sold at his shop in Pauls Church-yard at the signe of the Pide Bull neere S^t. Austins Gate. 1608 [*Head-title*] M William Shak-speare His Historie, of King Lear. [*Running-title*] The Historie of King Lear.
[Sheets D, E, F, G, K are found in corrected and uncorrected forms (cf. p. 174). There is a note on the variants by W. W. Greg in *R.E.S.* i. 469.]
Facsimile. C. Praetorius (1885, *Sh. Q.* xxxiii, ed. P. A. Daniel).

[Q2. 1619.] M. William Shake-speare, His True Chronicle History of the life and death of King Lear, and his three Daughters. With the vnfortunate life of Edgar, sonne and heire to the Earle of Glocester, and his sullen and assumed humour of Tom of Bedlam. As it was plaid before the Kings Maiesty at White-Hall, vppon S. Stephens night, in Christmas Hollidaies. By his Maiesties Seruants, playing vsually at the Globe on the Banck-side. [William Jaggard's device (McKerrow 283)] Printed for Nathaniel Butter. 1608. [*Head-title*, under ornament with royal arms, used by John Roberts and William Jaggard] M. William Shake-speare His History, of King Lear. [*Running-title*] The History of King Lear.

[On the misdating, cf. p. 133.]

Facsimile. C. Praetorius (1885, *Sh. Q.* xxxiv, ed. P. A. Daniel).

[F1. 1623.] [*Catalogue*] King Lear. [*Tragedies*, pp. 283–309, sign. qq 2–ss 3ʳ. *Head- and Running-titles*] The Tragedie of King Lear.

[Acts and scc. marked.]

[Q3. 1655.] . . . Printed by Jane Bell, and are to be sold at the East-end of Christ-Church. 1655.

Parallel-Texts. A. A. Adee (1890, *Bankside*); W. Vietor (1892).

Modern Editions. H. H. Furness (1880, *New Variorum*); W. J. Craig (1901, 1927, *Arden*); D. Nichol Smith (1902, *Warwick*); W. L. Phelps (1917, *Yale*).

Dissertations. N. Delius, *Über die ursprünglichen Text des K.L.* (1875, *J.* x. 50; tr. 1875, *N.S.S. Trans.* 125); H. von Friesen, *Über Shs Quellen zu K.L.* (1877, *J.* xii. 169); R. Koppel, *Textkritische Studien über Shs R. III und K.L.* (1877); F. G. Fleay, *The Date and the Text of K.L.* (1879, Aug. 1, *Robinson's Epitome of Literature*); A. Schmidt, *Zur Text-kritik des K.L.* (1880, *Anglia*, iii. 1); E. Richter, *Eine Altportugiesische Version der K.L.-Sage* (1901, *E.S.* xxix. 208); M. W. Sampson, *On the Date of K.L.* (1902, *M.L.Q.* v. 71); A. C. Bradley, *Notes on K.L.* (1904, *Sh'n. Tragedy*, 443); E. Bode, *Die Learsage vor Sh.* (1904); W. Perrett, *The Story of K.L. from Geoffrey of Monmouth to Sh.* (1904); R. A. Law, *On the Date of K.L.* (1906, *P.M.L.A.* xxi, 462); R. B. Merriman, *On the Date of K.L.* (1908, May 23, *Athen.*); R. H. Cunnington, *The Revision of K.L.* (1910, *M.L.R.* v. 445); W. D. Moriarty, *The Bearing on Dramatic Sequence of the Varia in R. III and K.L.* (1913, *M.P.* x. 451); R. Fischer, *Quellen zu K.L.* (1914); L. Winstanley, *Macbeth, K.L. and Contemporary History* (1922); E. Sievers, *Shs Anteil am K.L.* (1925, *Anglica*, ii. 173).

Most of the sheets of Q1 are found both in corrected and uncorrected states, variously combined in the existing examples; sheet C is in three states. Some of the corrections suggest further reference to copy; others are clearly due to erroneous conjecture; and it is possible that in carrying them out some further blunders were made by the compositor. Q2 was set-up from a Q1 containing uncorrected sheets D, G, H, with some further conjectural corrections. F1 mainly rests upon an independent manuscript, but it too is shown by a continuance of errors and a general orthographic resemblance to have been set up from a Q1 containing uncorrected sheets E, H, K. The stage-directions like the text, have been revised. They are normal, in both cases. But F omits a good many Q notes for properties and action, and adds a few, together with many 'noises'. The texts are substantially derived from the same original. There are a good many verbal variants, and where one is clearly wrong, the better reading, except for a dozen or score of cases, is in F. Subject, therefore, to its usual sophistications, F must have the preference where the variants are indifferent. Q seems to contain some 'connective' phrases by actors, and many of its misreadings might well be due either to actors' blunders or to mishearing. There is not a great deal of mislineation in F, and most of what there is may be explained by the setting-up from Q, or by the rapid transitions in several scenes between verse and prose. On the other hand, mislineation is a constant feature in Q. The verse is often put wrong by an initial error, and runs from central pause to central pause, until another error or the end of a speech recovers it. Occasionally it is altogether unmetrical. Prose is printed as verse. Still more often is verse printed as prose, throughout long passages, in a way which cannot be explained either by errors of composition or by marginal insertions in copy. Moreover, Q has practically no punctuation except commas, even in places where both logic and enunciation require heavier stops and these are supplied by F. I think that the characteristics of Q point to a reported text. It is, of course, a much better version than the bad Quartos of *2, 3 Henry VI, Romeo and Juliet, Henry V, Merry Wives*, and *Hamlet*. In particular it does not misplace bits of dialogue within a scene, or bring in bits from other scenes or other plays. Possibly it was produced (cf. p. 161) by shorthand and not memorization. The reporter, except for subconscious substitutions by himself or the actors, has not got his words badly. The failure is in putting his continuous notes into metre, and in punctuating them. And these tasks he seems to have largely shirked. If reported, the Q text was presumably surreptitious. There is nothing irregular about the registration of the play, but it is worth noting that it was Nathaniel Butter who published the first part of Heywood's *If You Know Not Me, You Know Nobody* (1605), which the author complained of as drawn 'by Stenography'.[1] This text, however, although corrupt enough, has not the long passages of prose for verse or the peculiar punctuation of *Lear*.

Apart from stray words and phrases, Q omits about 100 lines found in F, and F omits about 300 lines, including the whole of iv. 3, found in Q. These differences have been much discussed, and several writers have regarded them as due to deliberate revision of the play. Thus Koppel argues that the passages special to Q represent a series of added touches, as a result of which the play became too long, and required the abridgement shown by the F omissions. The arguments used carry no conviction to me. No doubt the play is better with the special Q passages than without them, but so it would be on any reasonable hypothesis of their nature. Similarly the reasons given for regarding some of the F omissions as improvements in the interests of dramatic clarity and directness seem to me highly subjective. The play, as pointed out by Bradley, is in any case unusually full, even for Shakespeare, of inconsistencies and obscurities of action, and it is impossible to stress the resultant effect of an addition or an omission upon some one of these. I take it that, both in Q and in F, more than one cause has operated. Practically all the special passages I believe to be part of the original text. The only exception I should make is F's Merlin prophecy by the Fool in iii. 2. 79–95, which is generally, and I think rightly, taken as an incongruous theatrical interpolation. I see no sufficient reason for regarding the Fool's couplet at i. 5. 55–6 as another, since

---

[1] *Eliz. Stage*, iii. 342.

it is in both texts. And Edgar's rhymed couplets in iii. 6.
109–22, omitted by F, contain sententious matter, such
as Shakespeare still rhymes even in late plays. Apart from
iii. 2. 79–95, most of the Q omissions might well be errors.
They leave *lacunae* of sense or action at i. 1. 41–6, i. 2.
118–24, ii. 4. 142–7, iv. 1. 6–9, iv. 6. 169–74. In a
reported text, actors, reporter, and printer may all have
contributed. Identical line-ends have led to mistakes at
i. 1. 90 and iii. 4. 18. Probably the reporter's lapses of
attention are mainly responsible, and some linked omissions (ii. 4. 99–100, 104; iii. 4. 26–7, 37–8) and small
contextual alterations suggest that he was sometimes aware
of these, and attempted to cover them up. On the other
hand, there is some political and social criticism in the
play, and it is conceivable that the omission of i. 2. 118–
24 and iv. 6. 169–74 and also of iii. 1. 22–9 may have
been directed by a censor. F omissions in turn leave
lacunae at i. 4. 154–69, i. 4. 252–6, iv. 2. 31–50, v. 3.
204–21. Here also there are probably some printer's
errors, while a censor may have operated on i. 2. 157–66,
i. 4. 153–69, iii. 6. 18–59. But in the main we probably have to do with ordinary theatrical cutting. It is
not unintelligent, affecting chiefly narratives of episodes in
France and elsewhere away from the main action (iii. 1.
30–42; iv. 2. 53–9; iv. 3; v. 1. 23–8; v. 3. 204–21),
some dialogue between servants (iii. 7. 99–107; iv. 7.
85–98), a bit of poetic description (iii. 1. 7–15), Edgar's
sententious rhymes (iii. 6. 109–22), some interchanges of
amenities between Albany and Goneril (iv. 2. 31–50, 62–
9). The chief loss is in iv. 3, where the introduction, if
only in narrative, of Cordelia is important to bridge the
interval between her earlier and later appearances. It is
idle to ask whether Shakespeare himself or a colleague
made these cuts. They point, of course, to the use of
stage-copy for F. I can make nothing of the attempt of
Sievers to distribute the play between three authors by
the method of '*Schallanalyse*'.

It is difficult to fix the date of *Lear* with precision. The
probable borrowing of the devil names (iv. 1. 62) from

Samuel Harsnett's *Declaration of Popish Impostures* (1603) and the use (iii. 4. 189) of 'British' for 'English' may perhaps confirm, if that is needed, the stylistic evidence that it is a Jacobean play. It was performed at court on 26 December 1606, and the natural, if not absolutely imperative, inference from the particularity of that record would be that this was the first court performance of a new play. The eclipses referred to in i. 2. 112 must be the nearly total eclipse of the sun on 2 October 1605 and the partial eclipse of the moon on 27 September 1605; and although it is true that these had been anticipated as far back as John Harvey's *Discoursive Probleme concerning Prophesies* (1588), they are spoken of by Gloucester as 'these late eclipses'. The reference to 'machinations, hollowness, treachery and all ruinous disorders' (i. 2. 122) is hardly specific enough to bear pressing as a reminiscence of the Gunpowder Plot of 5 November 1605. There is a fairly palpable imitation of i. 4. 9–42 in Edward Sharpham's *The Fleir*, i, *ad fin*. This was probably produced after 30 January 1606, registered on May 13, and printed in 1607.[1] So far a date of production in the earlier part of 1606 would fit best for *Lear*. Aldis Wright's suggestion that the colouring of ii and iv points to composition in winter and summer respectively and the storm of iii to that of March 1606 seems to limit the poet's imagination rather unduly by climatic conditions. The difficulty about 1606 is that the earlier part of 1606 seems also to fit best for *Macbeth*, and that the time-table left available by plagues (cf. p. 78) makes it unlikely that two Shakespearean plays appeared almost concurrently at this date and none at all in 1605, which was clearer from sickness. On the whole, perhaps *Lear* is the easier play to put back to 1605. Bradley has argued strongly for its priority to *Macbeth* on the basis of metrical tests, and no doubt the statistics of these give him support, although I doubt whether much reliance can be placed upon them in determining the sequence of contiguous plays, especially when the text of one of them, like that of *Macbeth*, may only be before us

[1] *Eliz. Stage*, iii. 490.

in a much abridged form. Bradley also thought he saw signs of the influence of *Lear* on Marston's *Dutch Courtesan* (1605). I cannot find any very plausible parallel except a bit (iii. 2. 44) about taking butter'd shrimps from horses, which recalls *Lear*, ii. 4. 126. It may be doubted whether the jest was original in either play. Moreover, the *Dutch Courtesan*, although registered on 26 June 1605, probably goes back to 1603–4.[1]

The matter is complicated by the relation of the play to the old *Leir*. The history of this is obscure, but it probably remained unprinted until 1605, when it was registered for a second time on May 8, apparently in disregard of an existing copyright, and issued as 'lately acted'.[2] A facsimile of the entry given in H.P., *Folio*, xiv. 354, shows, as Arber (iii. 289) does not, that it was originally entered as a 'tragedy' and the description altered to 'tragecall historie'. On the title-page it is 'chronicle history'. There is not much in this; the action is tragic, although it has not a tragic ending. But it has been suggested that Shakespeare's play was already on the stage, and that the publication was an attempt to pass off the old play as his. This rather disregards the fairly obvious use made by Shakespeare of the old play. It is true that the story of Lear, originally due to the inventive genius of Geoffrey of Monmouth, was available for him in several other versions; in Holinshed, in a contribution by John Higgins (1574) to the *Mirrour for Magistrates*, in Spenser's *Faerie Queene*, ii. 10. 27–32. All these he may have consulted, as well as a variant of the story, attributed to the Saxon Ina, in Camden's *Remaines* (1605). A ballad in Richard Johnson's *Golden Garland* (1620) is likely to be later than *Lear*. Spenser probably gave him the form of the name Cordelia. Whatever his sources he handled them very freely. But certainly *Lear* bears a closer resemblance to *Leir* than to any of the other versions. It is not so much discernible in echoes of phrase and situation, although there are some of these, as in the foreshadowing of the characters of Kent and Oswald by the Perillus and

Ibid. iii. 430.   *Ibid.* iv. 25.

less markedly the Messenger of *Leir*. On the whole I think it is likely that *Leir* had been 'lately acted' shortly before *Lear* was written, and gave suggestions for it. There is no great probability that the King's men themselves possessed a manuscript of *Leir*, and any reminiscences of the 1594 performances (cf. p. 53) would be rather remote. On the other hand, the resemblances are not such as to make it necessary to suppose that the printed *Leir* itself was before Shakespeare. Indeed, it is conceivable that the play as 'lately acted' may not have been quite in the form of the printed book. H.P. ii. 338 inferred from the mention of 'Kentes woden leage' in an Admiral's inventory of 1598, that they had a play on the Lear theme with Kent and his stocks in it.[1] There is no wooden leg in Munday's *John a Kent and John a Cumber*,[2] as we have it, and although there is a mutilation near the end of the manuscript it cannot have held such an episode.[3] It is, of course, not very likely that the King's would use as a source an unprinted play belonging to another company.

Tentatively I conclude that *Lear* was written in 1605, possibly not finished before the eclipses of the autumn, and for some reason, conceivably the need for censorship, not performed at court until 1606. Of course the theory of Miss Winstanley that *Lear* is symbolical mythology, representing at once the Darnley murder and the massacre of St. Bartholomew, is not worth serious examination. Such a play could never have been performed at court at all. The Gloucester story is not in *Leir* or in any other of the early versions. It was based on that of a Paphlagonian king in Sidney's *Arcadia* (1590), ii. 10. A *Tragoedia von Lear König von Engelandt* in John Green's Dresden repertory of 1626 may have been derived either from *Lear* or from *Leir*.[4]

---

[1] *Henslowe Papers*, 117.
[2] *Eliz. Stage*, iii. 446; cf. p. 108.
[3] Cf. M. St. C. Byrne in *M.S.R.*
[4] *Eliz. Stage*, ii. 286.

XXIX. MACBETH

[F1. 1623.] [*Catalogue*] The Tragedy of Macbeth. [*Tragedies*, pp. 131–51, sign. ll 6–nn 4. *Head- and Running-titles*] The Tragedie of Macbeth. [Acts and scc. marked.]

Facsimile. J. D. Wilson (1928).

Modern Editions. W. G. Clark and W. A. Wright (1869, *O.U.P.*); H. H. Furness (1873, *New Variorum*); E. K. Chambers (1893, *Warwick*); J. M. Manly (1896); M. H. Liddell (1903); H. Conrad (1907); H. Cunningham (1912, 1928, *Arden*); C. M. Lewis (1918, *Yale*).

Dissertations. N. Delius, *M.* (1841); J. W. Hales, *On the Porter in M.* (1874, *N.S.S. Trans.* 255; *Notes and Essays*, 273); F. G. Fleay, *M.* (1874, *N.S.S. Trans.* 339; *Manual*, 245), *Davenant's M. and Sh.'s Witches* (1884, *Anglia*, vii. 128); G. Sarrazin, *Shs M. und Kyds Sp. Tr.* (1895, *E.S.* xxi. 328); C. C. Stopes, *Sh.'s Materials for M.* (1896, *Alten.* ii. 138), *The Scottish and English Macbeth* (1897, *Sh.'s Industry*, 78); D. L. Chambers, *The Metre of M.* (1903); A. C. Bradley, *Notes on M.* (1904, *Shn. Tragedy*, 466); E. Kröger, *Die Sage von M. bis zu Sh.* (1904); A. Brandl, *Zur Vorgeschichte der Weird Sisters in M.* (1921, *Liebermann Festgabe*, 252); L. Winstanley, *M., King Lear, and Contemporary History* (1922); W. J. Lawrence, *The Mystery of M.* (1928, *Sh.'s Workshop*, 24); R. C. Bald, *M. and the 'Short' Plays* (1928, *R.E.S.* iv. 429).

Macbeth is doubtless printed from a prompt-copy. The stage-directions are a little fuller than usual. A bookkeeper's 'Ring the bell', noted for his own use, has got into the text at ii. 3. 85. I am not so sure of some other cases brought forward by Bald.

The text is unsatisfactory, not so much on account of verbal corruption, as of a rehandling to which it bears evidence. This seems to have been most obviously a matter of abridgement. The play, as it stands, is shorter than any other except *Comedy of Errors*, and its 2,106 lines, even if allowance is made for the spectacular scenes, would furnish little more than a two-hours' performance. Moreover, although many of its short lines are otherwise explicable, a few (i. 2. 20, 51; ii. 3. 109; iii. 2. 32, 51; iii. 4. 4; iv. 3. 28, 44) are abrupt or accompanied by obscurities, and may indicate cuts. Any substantial cutting may have involved partial transcription, and this may, as Wilson thinks, explain the mislineated passages, which are rather numerous in i–iii, although rare thereafter. There seems also to have been some manipulation of the rather scrappy final battle-scene (v. 7, 8). Here the present action gives no opportunity for the removal of the dead Siward, recited at v. 8. 44, and the stage-direction 'Enter Fighting, and Macbeth slaine', placed between two others at 34, is inconsistent with the more dramatic 'Enter Macduffe; with Macbeths head' at 53. Cutting and some consequential adaptation may perhaps also explain the inconsistency which has troubled editors in the accounts of Cawdor in i. 2, 3, the apparent reference at i. 7. 47 to an episode in which Macbeth breaks the enterprise of murder to his wife, and the mysterious Third Murderer (may-be Macbeth himself) of iii. 3.

Probably there has also been some interpolation. I believe this to be confined to three passages (iii. 5; iv. 1. 39–43, 125–32) in the witch-scenes, which can be distinguished from the genuine text by the introduction of Hecate, by the use of an iambic instead of a trochaic metre, and by prettinesses of lyrical fancy alien to the main conception of the witches. Songs are introduced at iii. 5. 34 and iv. 1. 43, but their content is only indicated by the opening words in the stage-directions. But the full texts occur at iii. 3. 39 and v. 2. 60 of Thomas Middleton's *The Witch*. This has some echoes of genuine passages in *Macbeth*, and it is not unreasonable to suppose that its author was also the interpolator of the Shakespearean text. Many writers have carried the theory of interpolations in *Macbeth* much farther than I am prepared to do. Coleridge held the Porter scene (ii. 3. 1–47) not to be authentic, and probably now has few adherents. Others— Clark and Wright, Fleay (although he hesitated in 1876), Conrad, and Cunningham—have doubted the whole or parts of i. 1; i. 2; i. 3. 1–37; iii. 4. 130–44; iv. 1; iv. 3. 140–59; v. 2; v. 5. 47–50; v. 6; v. 8. I have given reasons for rejecting such views in the Warwick edition, and am not convinced by anything which has been written since. Conrad's attempt to isolate v. 6 and arbitrarily chosen sections of i. 2 and v. 8 by metrical analysis is particularly futile (cf. p. 266), since he has only about 100 lines upon which to base an induction. *The Witch* has only come down to us in manuscript and is of uncertain date. Lawrence would put it as early as the autumn of 1608. Probably he meant to write 1609, as he thinks that Middleton was utilizing the vogue of the witch-dances in Jonson's *Mask of Queens* on 2 February 1609.[1] And he supposes the interpolated version of *Macbeth* to have been that which Simon Forman saw at the Globe in April 1610. Forman's visit was, however, pretty clearly on 20 April 1611 (cf. App. D). I do not find Lawrence very convincing, since Shakespeare himself had furnished the witch motive. Forman gives an outline of the plot, much as we have it, except that there is nothing in the text or stage-directions to confirm or refute his statement that Macbeth and Banquo came riding through a wood in i. 3. The play was not, of course, new in 1611, even if it was new to Forman. The style and metre are not so late as this, and there is a good deal of cumulative evidence for an earlier date. There are topics of special interest to King James; it is, of course, merely a fancy that the royal letter to the poet, said (App. C, nos. xxvii, xxxiv) to have been once in the possession of Sir William Davenant, was in return for *Macbeth*. Some of these allusions would have been appropriate from the beginning of the reign. The King's interest in witchcraft was of old standing. The 'two-fold balls and treble sceptres' of iv. 1. 121 can have nothing to do, as suggested by some commentators, with the triple style of King of Great Britain, France, and Ireland, adopted by *Procl.* 1003 of 20 October 1604. The earlier English style was triple, and there were no sceptres for France and Ireland. The 'two-fold' balls must be the 'mounds' borne on the English and Scottish crowns, and the 'treble sceptres' the two used for investment in the English coronation and the one used in the Scottish coronation. James was 'touching' for the 'king's evil' (iv. 3. 141) as early as 6 November 1604.[2] The bestowal of

---

[1] *Eliz. Stage*, iii. 382.   [2] *Venetian Papers*, x. 193.

Cawdor's honours upon Macbeth is in Holinshed, and can hardly have been inspired, as Hunter thought, by the investiture of Sir David Murray, who had for some years held the lands and honours of the attainted Gowrie family, as Lord Scone on 1 April 1605. It is true that the King's men got into trouble through a play on the Gowrie conspiracy in December 1604,[1] but *Macbeth* cannot very plausibly be regarded as an apology for this. On the other hand, it is likely enough that a hint for the witches came from Matthew Gwinne's show of 'tres Sibyllae', with which James was greeted, when he visited Oxford on 27 August 1605.[2] Subject to the doubts as to the authenticity of ii. 3 1–47, a slightly later date is probably given by the 'equivocator, that could swear in both the scales against either scale; who committed treason enough for God's sake, yet could not equivocate to heaven'. No doubt the Jesuit doctrine of equivocation had been familiar, at least since the trial of Robert Southwell in 1595. But here it is associated with treason, as it was at the trial of Father Henry Garnet for complicity with the Gunpowder Plot on 28 March 1606. The passage does not, however, oblige us to put the play quite as late as this, since an exposure of equivocation by Lord Salisbury is said to have been 'greedily read' before 5 February 1606.[3] The reference is to his *Answer to Certain Scandalous Papers* (1606), which deals *inter alia* with equivocation and cites St. Augustine's disallowance of it. Two other allusions in the same episode do not help very much. A tailor is damned 'for stealing out of a French hose'. This suggests some temporary fashion of wearing tight instead of round hose. But this cannot be dated. A passage often cited from A. Nixon's *Black Year*, registered on 9 May 1606, seems only to refer to a new fashion of wearing lace on hose. A farmer is damned because he 'hang'd himself on the expectation of plenty'. But Malone's evidence for the low price of corn in 1606 is good also for 1605 and 1607, when it was only a little higher, and in fact the suicide of a disappointed engrosser of corn was an old notion, and had

[1] *Eliz. Stage*, i. 327.   [2] *Ibid.* i. 130; iii. 332.   [3] *S.P.D. Jac. I*, xviii. 66.

been staged by Ben Jonson in *E.M.O.*, i. 3; iii. 7, 8, originally produced in 1599 and revived at court on 8 January
1605.[1] A date late in 1605 or early in 1606 would be
consistent with some echoes, not individually conclusive,
in other plays. The prick of ambition's spur (i. 7. 25–8) is
in the anonymous *Caesar's Revenge*, 1468–9, but this,
although registered on 5 June 1606, may very likely be
Elizabethan.[2] In *The Puritan*, iv. 3. 89, registered on
6 August 1607, but probably a play of 1606, comes 'in
stead of a Iester, weele ha the ghost ith white sheete sit at
vpper end a'th Table'.[3] The 'ghost' is a personage in the
play, but an allusion to iii. 4 may none the less be possible.
Another may be in *Knight of the Burning Pestle*, v. 1. 20–
30, almost certainly a play of 1607.[4] It may not be a mere
accident that William Warner put an account of Macbeth
into his *Continuance of Albion's England* (1606). Some
still earlier echoes are traced by Bradley 471 in Marston's
Sophonisba (1606). They are slight, but taken together
suggest a knowledge of *Macbeth*. *Sophonisba* was registered
on 17 March 1606,[5] and we must therefore suppose that
the equivocation passage, if it forms part of the original
text, was written earlier than the actual trial of Garnet.
The matter is complicated by the corresponding uncertainty as to the date of *Lear* (q.v.) and as to the time-
relation of its metre to that of *Macbeth*. It is, therefore,
only tentatively that I put *Macbeth* early in 1606.

Shakespeare's source was the *Chronicle* of Holinshed,
itself based, for the Scottish matter, upon the *Scotorum
Historiae* (1527) of Hector Boece; and this in turn, with
much imaginative elaboration, upon the *Scotichronicon*
(c. 1384) of John Fordun and the *Orygynale Cronykil of
Scotland* (c. 1424) of Andrew Wyntown. Holinshed probably used a translation of Boece by John Bellenden
(1536). Another, by William Stewart (1535) remained
in manuscript to 1858. There is not much substance in
the suggestions that some of Shakespeare's departures from

---

[1] *Eliz. Stage*, iii. 360; cf. App. D.   [4] *Ibid.* iii. 220.
[2] *Ibid.* iv. 4.   [5] *Ibid.* iii. 433.
[3] *Ibid.* iv. 41.

Holinshed are due to this or to Wyntown. We do not know whether Macbeth was the theme of a tragedy of *The Kinge of Scottes* given at court [1] in 1567–8, or of a *Malcolm King of Scots* bought by the Admiral's men from Charles Massey in 1602.[2] A 'ballad of Macedbeth' seems to have been before the Stationers' Company in 1596, but Greg rejects the genuineness of the record, which was published by Collier (cf. App. F, xi, *l*). William Kempe, however, in *Nine Daies Wonder* (1600), 21, speaks of 'a penny Poet, whose first making was the miserable stolne story of Macdoel, or Macdobeth, or Macsomewhat, for I am sure a Mac it was, though I neuer had the maw to see it'. It is unlikely that Shakespeare ever visited Scotland,[3] and no importance need be attached to Miss Winstanley's theory (cf. p. 67) that *Macbeth* is a symbolical allegory, based upon the Gunpowder Plot, St. Bartholomew's Day, the Darnley murder, and the relations of James with Francis Hepburn, fifth Earl of Bothwell.

XXX. ANTONY AND CLEOPATRA

[S.R. 1608.] 20 Maij. Edward Blount. Entred for his copie under thandes of Sir George Buck knight and Master Warden Seton A booke called. The booke of Pericles prynce of Tyre. vj[d].

Edward Blount. Entred also for his copie by the like Aucthoritie. A booke Called Anthony. and Cleopatra. vj[d]. (Arber, iii. 378).

[S.R. 1623, with other plays for F1: cf. p. 138.] The Tragedie of Anthonie, and Cleopatra.

[F1. 1623.] [*Catalogue*] Anthony and Cleopater. [*Tragedies*, pp. 340–68, sign. v v 6^v–z z 2^v. *Head-title*] The Tragedie of Anthonie, and Cleopatra. [*Running-title*] The Tragedy of Anthony and Cleopatra.

[Act i, sc. 1 marked.]

Facsimile. J. D. Wilson (1929).

---

[1] *Eliz. Stage*, iv. 144.
[2] *Ibid.* ii. 179; iii. 435.
[3] *Ibid.* ii. 269.

Modern Editions. R. H. Case (1906, 1930, *Arden*): H. H. Furness (1907, *New Variorum*): H. S. Canby (1921, *Yale*).

Dissertations. T. Vatke, *A.C. und Plutarchs Biographie des Antonius* (1868, *J*. iii. 301); F. Adler, *Das Verhältniss von Shs A.C. zu Plutarchs Biographie des Antonius* (1895, *J*. xxxi. 262) A. C. Bradley, *A.C.* (1909, *Oxford Lectures on Poetry*); M. W. MacCallum, *Sh.'s Roman Plays and their Background* (1910).

F gives a fair text, so far as verbal corruption goes, although there are a good many literal misprints. But there is also a good deal of mislineation, perhaps especially in the first half of the play. This chiefly affects short speeches and the beginnings and ends of long ones. Several short speeches are printed in prose instead of verse throughout. The trouble often starts with a failure to keep distinct an initial half-line of a speech. Similarly a final half-line is sometimes printed continuously with the last full line of a speech. Probably these features derive from the copy, and Shakespeare did in fact, in this play, merge his numerous half-lines, and wrote his shorter speeches, or some of them, continuously. At the same time, he often split a line, to indicate a long pause, and this feature also the compositor reproduced. The interior of the longer speeches is generally free from mislineation. The stage-directions are not markedly full, but there are occasional notes for action or for the grouping and attitude of personages.

There is no reason to doubt that the S.R. entry of 20 May 1608 relates to the play, although Blount appears to have forgotten it when the entry for F1 was made. This gives a limit of date. But there is reason for putting *Antony and Cleopatra* earlier than 1608. In 1607 Samuel Daniel issued a new edition of his *Certain Small Workes*, and herein made considerable changes in his *Cleopatra* of 1594.[1] These, as carefully analysed by Case, seem to me clearly to show the influence of Shakespeare's play. There are some parallels of idea and phrase. Dialogue often replaces narrative or soliloquy. Dircetus and Diomedes are introduced for the first time. Charmian, Iras,

[1] *Eliz. Stage*, iii. 275.

and Gallus are elaborated. A new scene relates, through the mouth of Dircetus, events leading up to the death of Antony, as given by Shakespeare. One may recall a probable similar use by Daniel of *Richard II* (cf. *supra*). The metrical character of *Antony and Cleopatra* forbids us to put it before *Macbeth* or *Lear*. But it may have been produced early in 1607, and of this there is confirmation in Barnes's *Devil's Charter* (1607), 2546–69, where Alexander Borgia uses asps, which he calls 'Cleopatraes birds', to poison two boys. *Devil's Charter* was given at court as early as 2 February 1607, but thereafter 'reuewed, corrected and augmented' for the reader, and registered on October 16.[1] Parallels to iv. 14. 2 in Chapman's *Bussy d'Ambois*, iii. 1. 23 and to i. 4. 20 in the anonymous *Nobody and Somebody*, 36, may be left out of account. Probably both plays are earlier than *Antony and Cleopatra* and the ideas are in both cases of still older standing.[2]

The main source is Plutarch's life of Antony. Possibly Appian's *Bella Civilia* was also used; and Shakespeare may have read Daniel's *Cleopatra* in its earlier form, or Lady Pembroke's *Antonius* of 1592,[3] or Samuel Brandon's *Virtuous Octavia* of 1598,[4] but hardly Lord Brooke's *Antonie and Cleopatra*, which he burnt.[5]

XXXI. CORIOLANUS

[F1. 1623.] [*Catalogue*] The Tragedy of Coriolanus. [*Tragedies*, pp. 1–30, sign. a a–c c 3ᵛ. *Head-title*] The Tragedy of Coriolanus. [*Running-title*] The Tragedie of Coriolanus.

[Acts i, sc. 1, ii–v marked.]

Facsimile. J. D. Wilson (1928).

Modern Editions. E. K. Chambers (1898, *Warwick*); G. Gordon (1912, *O.U.P.*); W. J. Craig and R. H. Case (1922, *Arden*); C. F. Tucker Brooke (1924, *Yale*); H. H. Furness (1928, *New Variorum*).

Dissertations. J. O. Halliwell-Phillipps, *A Hint on the Date of Cor.* (1874,

[1] *Eliz. Stage*, iii. 214.
[2] *Ibid.* iii. 253; iv. 37.
[3] *Ibid.* iii. 337.
[4] *Ibid.* iii. 236.
[5] *Life of Sidney*, 155.

N.S.S. Trans. 367); N. Delius, *Shs Cor. in seinem Verhältniss zum Corio-lanus des Plutarch* (1876, *J.* xi. 32; *Abl.* i. 388); R. Büttner, *Zu Cor. und seiner Quelle* (1905, *J.* xli. 45); M.W. MacCallum, *Sh.'s Roman Plays and their Background* (1910); A. C. Bradley, *Cor.* (1912, *British Academy*).

F is again not a satisfactory text, less on account of verbal corruptions, as of frequent mislineations. These are very similar in character to those in *Antony and Cleopatra*, and probably the explanation is the same in both cases. The stage-directions to *Coriolanus* are more elaborate than those to *Antony and Cleopatra* and give many notes for position, movement, and even gesture on the stage. They suggest the author's hand. Wilson also finds Shakespearean spelling.

There is practically no concrete evidence as to date, and the attempts to find some have been far-fetched. Mulberries (iii. 2. 79) were known to Shakespeare [1] before James issued instructions to encourage the growth of them on 19 January 1609.[2] There was a dearth of corn (i. 1. 69) in 1608 and 1609, but Plutarch gives the Roman dearth. There is no reason to suppose that Volumnia was inspired by Shakespeare's mother, who was buried on 9 September 1608. The character of Raleigh has been traced in that of Coriolanus, and the struggles of James with his Parliaments in the politics of the play. Both views are highly speculative, and neither would yield a precise date. Rather more plausible is the suggestion that 'the coal of fire upon the ice' (i. 1. 177) derives from the great frost of 1607–8, described in a contemporary pamphlet.[3] The Thames was frozen over, for the first time since 1564–5, and on January 8 'pans of coals' were burning on it. Shakespeare may, of course, have seen the same thing before, on a smaller river. There may be an echo of ii. 2. 105 in Jonson, *Epicoene*, v. 4. 227, 'you haue lurch'd your friends of the better halfe of the garland'. This is a play of late 1609 or early 1610.[4] The evidence of style and metre puts *Coriolanus* between *Antony and Cleo-*

---

[1] *Mid. N. Dr.* iii. 1. 170; v. 1. 149; *Ven. & Ad.* 1103.

[2] *Harleian Misc.* ii. 218.

[3] A. Lang, *Social England*, 163; cf.

Stowe, *Annales*, 891; Birch, *James*, i. 70, 71; Lodge, iii. 224.

[4] *Eliz. Stage*, iii. 370.

patra and *Pericles*. It may have been produced early in 1608.

The source of the play was Plutarch's life of Coriolanus. Shakespeare may also have known the version of the fable of the belly and the members (i. 1. 99) in Camden's *Remaines* (1605) or that in Livy, ii. 32. It has been argued that he used the 1612 edition of North's *Plutarch*, on the ground that it could give him 'unfortunate', instead of the 'unfortunately' of earlier editions, for v. 3. 97. But the metre would in any case dictate 'unfortunate', and that *Coriolanus* should be as late as 1612 is inconceivable.

XXXII. TIMON OF ATHENS

[F1. 1623.] [*Catalogue*] Timon of Athens. [*Tragedies*, pp. 80–2, 81 *bis*–98+one unnumbered page, sign. G g^v– h h 6. *Head-title*] The Life of Tymon of Athens. [*Running-title*] Timon of Athens.

[Act i, sc. 1 marked. 'The Actors Names' at end.]

Modern Edition. K. Deighton (1905, 1929, *Arden*).

Dissertations. N. Delius, *Ueber Shs Tim.* (1867, *J.* ii. 335; *Abl.* i. 46); B. Tschischwitz, *Tim. Ein kritischer Versuch* (1869, *J.* iv. 160); A. Müller, *Über die Quellen aus denen Sh. Tim. entnommen hat* (1873); F. G. Fleay, *On the Authorship of Tim.* (1874, *N.S.S. Trans.* 130, 242, with discussion by F. J. Furnivall and B. Nicholson; *Manual*, 187); G. Kullmann, *Shs Antheil an dem unter seinem Namen veröffentlichten Trauerspiel Tim.* (1882, *Arch. f. Litteraturgeschichte*, xi); W. Wendtlandt, *Shs Tim.* (1888, *J.* xxiii. 109); H. Conrad, *Shs und Bulthaupts Tim.* (1894, *J.* xxix. 110); A. C. Bradley, *King Lear and Tim.* (1904, *Shn. Tragedy*, 443, 477); W. H. Clemons, *The Sources of Tim.* (1904, *Princeton Univ. Bull.* xv); J. Q. Adams, *Tim. and the Irregularities in F1* (1908, *J.E.G.P.* vii. 53), *The Timon Plays* (1910, *J.E.G.P.* ix. 506); H. Conrad, *Shs Tim. Urheberschaft, Abfassungszeit, und Enstehung* (1909, *Z. f. Vergleichende Litteraturgeschichte*, N.F. xvii. 337); E. H. Wright, *The Authorship of Tim.* (1910); J. M. Robertson, *Tim.* (1917, *Sh. and Chapman*, 121); W. Wells, *Tim.* (1920, *12 N.Q.* vi. 266); T. M. Parrott, *The Problem of Tim.* (1923, *Sh. Ass.*); H. D. Sykes, *The Problem of Tim.* (1923, *13 N.Q.* i. 83, sqq; *Sidelights on Eliz. Drama*, 1); D. Wecker, *Sh.'s Purpose in Tim.* (1928, *P.M.L.A.* xliii. 701).

Timon was placed in F between *Romeo and Juliet* and *Julius Caesar* to fill the gap left (cf. p. 442) by the temporary withdrawal of *Troilus and Cressida* and does not completely do so. There is much mislineation in the text. Lines are irregularly divided; prose speeches are printed as verse, and verse speeches as prose. The passages affected are mostly short. Many verse lines are split, and the splitting is often not explicable as due to considerations of space or a desire to indicate major pauses. It is very likely that there were frequent marginal insertions in the copy. There are some elaborate stage-directions resembling those in *Coriolanus*. Occasionally (i. 2. 1; iii. 1. 1, 3. 1, 4. 1; v. 3. 1) a touch seems superfluous for theatrical purposes, but in the main there is nothing which an author, wishing to give careful directions for the ordering of his groups, might not write. Two entries (i. 1. 173; i. 2. 120), in anticipation of the intervention of the entrants in the dialogue, show practical knowledge of the stage.

The literary quality of the play is somewhat unusual.[1] There is much fine Shakespearean poetry and the general conception is clearly Shakespeare's, in a mood of highly strained tragic exaltation resembling that of *Lear*. On the other hand, there are dull business scenes and humourless comic scenes, which in their turn recall the uninterested manner of *All's Well*. And there are several scenes (i. 2; iii. 1, 2, 3, 4. 1–79, 5; iv. 2. 30–50; iv. 3. 1–47, 464–543; v. 1. 1–118) in which the verse at least cannot be the complete and jointed work of Shakespeare. This is particularly noticeable in the longer speeches. These contain Shakespearean ideas, sometimes inchoate, and scattered Shakespearean phrases. But they are not constructed as articulated paragraphs at all. They consist of juxtaposed sentences, now in blank verse, now in rhyme, now in wording which can most easily be read as prose. There are many short lines, occasionally successive, for which no rhythmic or dramatic justification is apparent. There are unmetrical long lines. It must be added that the structure of *Timon* as a whole is incoherent. There are many small confusions and inconsistencies. The

---

[1] Cf. *Sh. a Survey*, 268.

dramatic relation of some of the characters to Timon and his tragedy is obscure. Even the identity of some of the subordinate personages becomes uncertain. The nomenclature shows much orthographic variation.

These features have naturally evoked theories, whose chief common element lies in the assumption of a second hand. They differ as to the extent of the work regarded as un-Shakespearean, and as to whether Shakespeare was the originator or a reviser of the play. And they differ as to their selection of a second hand. Thus a draft or fragmentary play by Shakespeare is held to have been rehandled by Heywood (Verplanck), Tourneur (Fleay in 1874), Wilkins (Fleay in 1886), Chapman and perhaps Field (Parrott), Middleton (Wells). And again Shakespeare is held to have rehandled the work of Wilkins (Delius), Chapman (Robertson), Day and Middleton (Sykes). Some of the writers are discreet enough to leave the second hand anonymous. None of the theories seem to me convincing in detail, and their very multiplicity suggests that their exponents are on the wrong tack. Moreover, most of these are compelled to admit that the revision, by whomsoever accomplished, was itself blundering or incomplete. One does not see why the King's men should have dealt with their plays in this way. Fleay, indeed, was driven to conjecture that the revision was undertaken, not for theatrical purposes, but to enable *Timon* to be printed in F1. I do not doubt that it was left unfinished by Shakespeare, and I believe that the real solution of its 'problem', indicated long ago by Ulrici and others, is that it is unfinished still. The passages of chaotic verse, in particular, look very much like rough notes, hastily jotted down to be worked up later. I do not think that any reputable playwright, such as the King's men would have employed, wrote like this, or that the 'cutting' contemplated in Parrott's theory could have produced quite this result. Other Shakespearean plays were certainly more intelligently cut. Shakespeare seems to have worked chiefly on the beginning and end of the play, and to have left the middle acts in a very imperfect state.

Timon, as it stands, is of course very short, and it may be that some scenes are lacking altogether. One may reasonably guess that ultimately some at least of the inconsistencies would have been removed, and Alcibiades and the whores more definitely linked with Timon's fortunes. I do not suggest that *Timon* throws much light upon Shakespeare's normal methods of working. It is, perhaps, a subjective view that he dealt with it under conditions of mental and perhaps physical stress, which led to a breakdown. In any case he seems to have abandoned it, and never to have taken it up again.

Timon clearly belongs to the tragic period, but there is little to fix its exact date. No Jacobean representation is recorded. There almost certainly was none. The only possible contemporary allusion, noted by Sykes, is in iv. 3 of John Day's *Humour out of Breath*, a play of 1607–8,[1] where one is as mad 'as the lord that gave all to his followers, and begged more for himself'. But this is far from conclusive. Jacobean extravagance could easily furnish prototypes from real life. Bradley argues, on the basis of metrical tests and the points of contact between *Timon* and *Lear*, for placing it between that play and *Macbeth*. But the time-table of 1605 and 1606 leaves little room for it, and the metrical tests cannot be applied with much confidence to a play of which no part may be quite in its final form. On the whole, I incline to put the work on *Timon* between *Coriolanus* and *Pericles* in 1608.

The story of Timon is told briefly in Plutarch's life of Antony, and referred to again in that of Alcibiades, and from Plutarch the version in Painter's *Palace of Pleasure* (1566), i. 28, is taken. It is told again, with greater detail, in Lucian's *Misanthropos*, which was the main source, direct or indirect, of the anonymous *Timon* preserved in *Dyce MS. 52*.[2] Shakespeare certainly used Plutarch, but he has also some points, which are in Lucian and the Dyce *Timon*, but not in Plutarch, and two, the faithful steward and the mock banquet, which are in the Dyce *Timon*, but not in either Lucian or Plutarch. Deighton cites some

[1] *Eliz. Stage*, iii. 287.   [2] *Ibid.* iv. 49.

passages, in which Shakespeare seems to follow the actual
wording of Lucian pretty closely. There was no English
translation of the dialogue available, but there were
Italian ones, and a French one by Filbert Bretin (1582).
The Dyce *Timon* also is not very likely to have been
accessible to Shakespeare, since it reads like an academic
play, and has only been preserved in manuscript. It is
not an improbable conjecture that one or more unknown
versions may have mediated between Lucian and both the
Dyce *Timon* and Shakespeare's. Possibly the stage-direction (iv. 3. 399) 'Enter the Bandetti' may indicate an
Italian source. It does not appear to be the *Timone* of
Matteo Boiardo or that of Galeotto del Caretto, both of
which are plays of the late fifteenth century. The spectacular *Triumph of Time* in Beaumont and Fletcher's *Four
Plays in One* is also based on the Lucianic dialogue, but
this has little of Shakespeare's detail and its date is uncertain.[1] Most students of the Beaumont and Fletcher
plays make it later than *Timon*.

XXXIII. CYMBELINE

[F1. 1623.] [*Catalogue*] Cymbeline King of Britaine.
[*Tragedies*, pp. 369–99, sign. z z 3–b b b 6. *Head-title*]
The Tragedie of Cymbeline. [*Running-title*] The Tra-
gedie [or Tragedy] of Cymbeline.
[Acts and scc. marked.]

Reprint. W. J. Craig (1883, *N.S.S.*)

Modern Editions. A. J. Wyatt (1897, *Warwick*); C. M. Ingleby
(1886); E. Dowden, 1903, *Arden*); H. H. Furness (1913, *New
Variorum*); S. B. Hemingway (1924, *Yale*).

Dissertations. K. Schenkl (1864, *Germania*, ix. 458); B. Leonhardt, *Über
die Quellen Cys* (1883, *Anglia*, vi. 1), *Schlusswort zu Cy.* (1885, *Anglia*,
viii. 455); S. Levy, *Eine neue Quelle zu Shs Cy.* (1884, *Anglia*, vii. 120),
Noch Einmal die Quellen Cys (1885, *Anglia*, viii. 197); K. Elge, *A Letter
to C. M. Ingleby on Sh.'s Cy.* (1885); B. ten Brink, *Zu Cy.* (1886, *Anglia*,
ix. 267); R. W. Boodle, *The Original of Cy.* (1887, 7 *N.Q.* iv. 404); E.
Yardley, *Sh. and Calderon* (1889, 7 *N.Q.* viii. 26); R. Ohle, *Shs Cy. und*

---

[1] *Eliz. Stage*, iii. 231.

seine romanischen Verläufer (1890); H. Reich, *Zu Quelle des Cy.* (1905, *J*. xli. 177); F. Brie, *Eine neue Quelle zum Cy.* (1908, *J*. xliv. 167); J.de Perott, *Der Prinzenraub aus Rache* (1909, *J*. xlv. 228); J. M. Robertson, *The Interlude in Cy.* (1917, *Sh. and Chapman*, 218); W. W. Lawrence, *The Wager in Cy.* (1920, *P.M.L.A.* xxxv. 391); P. Reyher, *The Date of Cy.* (1925, June, *Rev. Anglo-Américaine*); L. Kellner, *Cy. Eine text-kritische Studie* (1925, *Anglica*, ii. 150).

The F text is regularly lined, but leaves some room for emendation. The stage-directions are as a rule slighter than in *Coriolanus*.

Forman (App. D) saw *Cymbeline*, probably between 20 and 30 April 1611, and in any case before his death on 12 September 1611. A date of production in 1609–10 would fit the evidence of metre and style, which links the play with *Winter's Tale* and *Tempest*. The source of *Cymbeline* also yielded a passage (iv. 4. 812) in *Winter's Tale*. Reyher finds a parallel in the relations of Posthumus and Imogen to those which brought William Seymour and Arabella Stuart to imprisonment in July 1610. Obviously the motive in *Cymbeline* need have no such origin, and in so far as there is an analogy, it tells in favour of a date before July, since discretion would have avoided it just afterwards. The plot has a close resemblance to that of Beaumont and Fletcher's *Philaster*, but it is impossible to say with which play the priority rests. *Philaster* cannot be shown to have existed before 8 October 1610, when John Davies of Hereford's *Scourge of Folly*, which contains a mention of it, was registered.[1] The theory that Shakespeare was inspired to write romantic tragi-comedy by the example of Beaumont and Fletcher can hardly be substantiated. The name Belarius recalls the Bellario of *Philaster*, but Shakespeare may well have adapted it from Bellaria, the prototype of Hermione in *Pandosto*, his source for *Winter's Tale*, and if so, it is in favour of his priority. Fleay thought that the historical scenes (iii. 5; iv. 2–v. 3) were written earlier than the rest, about 1606, because Shakespeare was then using Holinshed, because the scenes contain some parallels to *Macbeth*, and because he thought that the character of Cloten, as a brave prince

---

[1] *Ibid.* iii. 222.

and counsellor to his father, was inconsistent with that shown in the more romantic episodes. Ingleby accepted the same date for v. 2–5, and also for iii. 1, and for ii. 2 which belongs to the romantic plot, but in which he also found *Macbeth* parallels. Oliphant[1] has withdrawn a suggestion[2] that Beaumont and Massinger successively revised the play, although he still believes in the double date. Robertson has adumbrated a theory that Chapman had a share in recasting a pre-Shakespearean play, perhaps partly by Peele. This can wait until it is expounded. I see no grounds for a double date. Parallels do not necessarily mean proximity of date. A brave prince may none the less prove a boor in love. The questioned scenes have their fair share of the light and weak endings characteristic of Shakespeare's latest work. The separate writing of detached scenes, apart from the framework to which they belong, is *a priori* most unlikely. On the other hand, the vision in v. 4 is generally, and I think rightly, regarded as a spectacular theatrical interpolation. Dowden would limit the extent of this to 30–92, leaving the dumb-show, with 97–126, and possibly 93–6 as genuine. But it seems to me that the whole passage must stand or fall together. And with it must of course go the reference to the vision in v. 5. 425–59. The song in iv. 2. 258–81 has also been questioned, partly because it does not name Fidele, which is thought inconsistent with 237—

> use like note and words
> Save that Euriphile must be Fidele.

No doubt songs lend themselves to interpolation, but this is an exquisite one. Staunton distinguished himself by finding the last couplet of each stanza inferior to the rest. God knows why! Disintegration is a constant itch in some minds. *Cymbeline* was performed at court in 1634 (App. D).

The wager theme is widespread in romantic literature. Stray coincidences of detail are insufficient to show that Shakespeare used any other version of it than the story of

---

[1] *B. and F.* 101.   [2] *M.L.R.* iii. 349.

Bernabo of Genoa in Boccaccio's *Decameron*, ii. 9. They are closest in a story called *Westward for Smelts*, but this, although dated by Steevens in 1603, was not registered until 15 January 1620.[1] Boccaccio's story was translated into English as *Frederick of Jennen*, and printed by Jan van Doesborgh at Antwerp in 1518. The cave-life of Belarius and Imogen has also, of course, many analogues. Shakespeare is less likely to have got hints from a German tale of *Sneewitchen* or a second novel of Boccaccio (ii. 8) than from Fairfax's translation of Tasso's *Gerusalemme Liberata* in *Godfrey of Boulogne* (1600) or *The Mirrour of Knighthood* (1601) or the old play (1589) of *The Rare Triumphs of Love and Fortune*, which has the name Fidelia, as well as that used in *Winter's Tale* of Hermione.[2] The substitution of a sleeping-draught for poison might come from the *Golden Ass* of Apuleius or Richard Johnson's *Tom of Lincoln* or elsewhere. The historical material is in Holinshed, and here too most of the other names could be picked up. It is curious that Forman calls the heroine Innogen and not Imogen. Shakespeare had an Innogen as a mute in *Much Ado about Nothing*. Lawrence says that he found it in *Locrine*.[3] As a matter of fact, unless he saw that in manuscript (cf. p. 537), he could only have found (l. 240) Iunoger, since the printer thought that he knew more Latin than the writer. Holinshed has Innogen, which is the normal form of Geoffrey of Monmouth, who makes her wife of Brutus, not daughter of Cymbeline. Are we to infer that the name Imogen is only due to persistent minim misprinting in F1?

XXXIV   THE WINTER'S TALE

[F1. 1623.] [*Catalogue.*] The Winters Tale. [*Comedies*, pp. 277 [304 in *Cat.*]–303, sign. A a–C c 2, *Head- and Running-titles*] The Winters Tale.

[Acts and scc. marked. 'The Names of the Actors' at end.]
Facsimile. J. D. Wilson (1929).

---

[1] *Var.* xiii. 2.   [2] *Eliz. Stage*, iv. 28.   [3] *Shakespeare's Workshop*, 44.

Modern Editions. H. H. Furness (1898, *New Variorum*); F. W. Moorman (1912, *Arden*); F. E. Pierce (1918, *Yale*).

Dissertations. J. Caro, *Die historischen Elemente in Shs Tp. und W.T.* (1879, *E.S.* ii. 141); N. Delius, *Greenes Pandosto und Shs W.T.* (1880, *J.* xv. 22; *Abl.* ii. 68); R. Boyle, *Shs W.T. und Tp.* (1885); J. Bolte, *Zur Schlusscene des W.T.* (1891, *J.* xxvi. 87); C. D. Mount, *Sir Philip Sidney and Sh.* (1893, *8 N.Q.* iii. 305); K. Fries, *Quellenstudien zu Shs W.T.* (1900, *Neue Jahrbücher für Pädagogik*, vi. 557); P. G. Thomas, *Greene's Pandosto* (1907, *Sh. Classics*); J. J. Jusserand, *W.T.* (1907, 1924, *School for Ambassadors*, 229); S. A. Tannenbaum, *Textual and other Notes on W.T.* (1928, *S.P.* vii. 358).

Herbert (App. D) allowed a fresh copy for the play on 19 August 1623, because 'the allowed booke was missinge'. This may have been in view of the court performance (*ibid.*) on 18 January 1624. As there had been a similar performance in 1618 and probably another about 1619 (*ibid.*), we cannot suppose that the old book perished in the Globe fire of 1613. It may have been mislaid during the printing of F1. But it is more likely that F1 itself rests on the fresh copy. The text is remarkably clean typographically, and has peculiarities of its own in the great number of its parentheses and in the occasional (e.g. ii. 3. 148; iv. 4. 592, 731) meticulous use of apostrophes to supply the place of ellipsed words. A blank page precedes it, and it has a special set of signatures. It seems probable that there was some delay in obtaining the copy and that it was not set-up until some progress had already been made with the Histories, which follow it.[1] R. C. Rhodes, *Shakespeare's First Folio*, 99, regards the text as 'assembled' (cf. p. 153) from 'parts', and no doubt Herbert's entry gives some plausibility to this view. But Rhodes gives a very inexact and incomplete account of the stage-directions. These contain little more than entries and exits, and the latter are often omitted. The entries are normally given in iv. 3 and v. 2, but for the other scenes all the characters taking part, whether they are present from the beginning or not, are grouped in an initial entry. This follows the order of their appearance, and in ii. 1, iii. 2, v. 1, 3, but not elsewhere, the successively appearing characters or

[1] Pollard, *F.Q.* 135; E. E. Willoughby in *R.E.S.* iv. 326.

groups of characters are marked off by colons in the stage-directions. These stage-directions might come from a plot. The case differs from that of *Two Gentlemen of Verona* in that some of the entries are given again in i. 2, ii. 3, iii. 3, and iv. 4 at their proper places in the text, and here too the dancers at iv. 4. 165, 352, who are not in the initial stage-directions, and some of the exits are noted. The text itself would generally indicate these.

The play was seen by Forman on 15 May 1611 and given at court on 5 November 1611 and in 1612–13. Besides the later Jacobean court performances already cited, there was a Caroline one in 1634 (App. D).

The style and metre group *Winter's Tale* with *Cymbeline* and *Tempest*, and it may reasonably be placed between them. A date early in 1611 is suggested by the probability that the bear of iii. 3 and the dance of satyrs at iv. 4. 352 were both inspired by those in Jonson's mask of *Oberon* on 1 January 1611.[1] The bear perhaps came originally from *Mucedorus*. I once suggested that this also followed *Oberon*. But this was an error.[2] The bear is in the original edition of 1598, although he gets an additional scene in that of 1610, and I was probably wrong (cf. p. 175) in thinking that the Shrove Sunday court performance, for which that scene was written, can have been in 1611. The reference in i. 2. 357 to the fate of those who 'struck anointed kings' is too general to bear pressing as an allusion to the murder of Henri IV by Ravaillac on 14 May 1610. Jonson glances at *Winter's Tale* with *Tempest* in his *Bartholomew Fair* of 1614 and at its sea-coast for Bohemia in his *Conversations* of 1619 (App. B, no. xxii).

The main source was Greene's novel of *Pandosto or The Triumph of Time*, (1588) reprinted (1607) as *Dorastus and Fawnia*. Greene himself may have drawn, directly or indirectly, upon an incident of the fourteenth-century history of Poland and Bohemia, as well as upon motives, such as the oracle, derived from Greek erotic romance. There is not much to suggest that Shakespeare used a derivative from Greene in Francis Sabie's *Fisherman's Tale*

---

[1] *Eliz. Stage*, iii. 385.   [2] *Ibid.* iv. 35.

(1595). He took some names from Sidney's *Arcadia*, Florizel probably from *Amadis de Gaule*, bk. ix, and Autolycus from *Odyssey*, xix. 394. The episode of the living statue, which is not in Greene, may have been suggested by Lyly's *Woman in the Moon* (1597) or Marston's *Pygmalion's Image* (1598). A resemblance of the return of Hermione to that of Alcestis is surely remote, and Shakespeare is not likely to have known the fifteenth-century Dutch play of *Esmoreit*, as thought by Fries. 'Recognition' themes are of course widespread in romantic literature.

XXXV. THE TEMPEST

[F1. 1623.] [*Catalogue*] The Tempest [*Comedies*, pp. 1–19, sign. A–B4^r. *Head- and Running-titles*] The Tempest. [Acts and scc. marked. 'The Scene, an vn-inhabited Island' and 'Names of the Actors' at end.]

Facsimile. J. D. Wilson (1928).

Modern Editions. H. H. Furness (1892, *New Variorum*); F. S. Boas (1897, *Warwick*); M. Luce (1902, 1926, *Arden*); C. B. Tinker (1918, *Yale*); W. Vickery (1911, *Rowfant Club*); A. T. Quiller-Couch and J. D. Wilson (1921, *C.U.P.*).

Dissertations. E. Malone, *An Account of the Incidents from which the Title and Part of Sh.'s Tp. were Derived, and its True Date Ascertained* (1808; *Var.* xv. 377); G. Chalmers, *Another Account of the Incidents from which the Title and Part of Sh.'s Tp. were Derived* (1815); J. Hunter, *A Disquisition on the Scene, Origin, Date, etc. of Sh.'s Tp.* (1839); J. Meissner, *Untersuchungen über Shs Tp.* (1872); A. E. Brae, *Prospero's Clothes-Line* (1874, *Trans. Royal Soc. of Lit.* N.S. x); M. Landau, *Le Fonti della Tp. di Sh.* (1878, *Nuova Antologia*, ii); J. Caro, *Die historischen Elemente in Shs Tp. und W.T.* (1879, *E.S.* ii. 141); R. Boyle, *Shs W.T. und Tp.* (1885); R. W. Boodle, *The Original of Cy. and possibly of Tp.* (1887, 7 *N.Q.* iv. 404); R. Garnett, *The Date and Occasion of Tp.* (1889, *Universal Review*, iii. 556); A. E. H. Swaen, *Caliban* (1895, *E.S.* xxi. 326); W. W. Newell, *The Sources of Sh.'s Tp.* (1903, *Journ. American Folk-Lore*, xvi. 234); J. de Perott, *The Probable Sources of the Plot of Sh.'s Tp.* (1905, *Publ. of Clark Univ. Library*, i. 209), *Die Magelönen- und die Sturmfabel* (1911, *J.* xlvii. 128); G. Sarrazin, *Die Vertreibung des Herzogs Prospero* (1906, *J.* xlii. 179); G. Becker, *Zur Quellenfrage von Shs Tp.* (1907, *J.* xliii. 155); S. Lee, *The Call of the West* (1907, *Scribner's Mag.*), *The American Indian in Elizabethan England* (1907, *Scribner's Mag.* xlii. 313), *Caliban's Visits to England* (1913, *Cornhill Mag.* 338); F. Neri, *Scenari delle Maschere in*

Arcadia (1913); R. M. Kelsey, *Indian Dances in Tp.* (1914, *J.E.G.P.* xiii. 98); C. M. Gayley, *Sh. and the Founders of Liberty in America* (1917); J. M. Robertson, *The Masque in Tp.* (1917, *Sh. and Chapman*, 210), *The Masque in Tp.* (1921, Mar. 31, *T.L.S.*); J. D. Rea, *A Source for the Storm in Tp.* (1919, *M.P.* xvii. 279), *A Note on Tp.* (1920, *M.L.N.* xxxv. 313); A. W. Ward, *Sh. and the Makers of Virginia* (1919, *Proc. of British Academy*, 141); W. J. Lawrence, *The Masque in Tp.* (1920, *Fortnightly*, cxiii. 941), *Sh. avrebbe tratto il soggetto di La Tempesta da Scenari Italiani* (1923, *La Lettere*, ii. 3); H. D. Gray, *The Sources of Tp.* (1920, *M.L.N.* xxxv. 321), *Some Indications that Tp. was Revised* (1921, *S.P.* xviii. 129); C. Still, *Sh.'s Mystery Play* (1921); A Lefranc, *L'Origine d'Ariel* (1921, *Cinquantenaire de l'École Pratique des Hautes Études*); E. Law, *Sh.'s Tp. as Originally Produced at Court* (1922, *Sh. Assn.*); E. K. Chambers, *The Integrity of Tp.* (1925, *R.E.S.* i. 129); M. Longworth-Chambrun, *Influences Françaises dans la Tp. de Sh.* (1925, *Rev. de Litt. Comparée*); A. Eichler, *Shs Tp. als Hofaufführung* (1925, *Die Neueren Sprachen*, Beiheft 6); R. R. Cawley, *Sh.'s Use of the Voyagers* (1926, *P.M.L.A.* xli. 688).

F is a very fair text, with careful punctuation. The stage-directions, especially for the spectacular episodes, are more elaborate than in any other play. They may be, in the main, the author's.

The play was given at court (App. D) on 1 November 1611 and again during the winter of 1612–13. Malone's statement that it 'had a being and a name in the autumn of 1611' probably rests only on a knowledge of the November date.[1] His promise to show in a revision of his Chronological Order that it was performed before the middle of 1611 was never carried out.[2] That it cannot have been written much earlier than 1611 is clear from the use made of the narratives describing the wreck of Sir George Somers at the Bermudas during a voyage to Virginia on 25 July 1609. With Somers were, among others, Sir Thomas Gates, William Strachey, Sylvester Jourdan, and Richard Rich. They escaped from the island and reached James Town in Virginia on 23 May 1610. On July 15 Gates, Jourdan, and Rich started for England with a dispatch of July 7 from the Governor of Virginia, Lord Delawarr, and a narrative dated July 15 by Strachey. A ballad of *News from Virginia* (1610) by Rich was registered on October 1. But the first full description of

[1] *Var.* xv. 423.   [2] *Ibid.* 414.

the island life to be issued seems to have been Jourdan's
A Discovery of the Barmudas (1610). The dedication of
this is dated October 13. It was followed by an official
publication of the London Council of Virginia, *A True
Declaration of the Estate of the Colonie in Virginia* (1610),
registered on November 8. Strachey's narrative was cir-
culated to the Council, but is not known to have been
printed before 1625, when it appeared as *A True Reportory of the Wracke and Redemption of Sir Thomas Gates,
Knight* in Samuel Purchas's *Hakluytus Posthumus or Purchas
his Pilgrimes*, iv. 1734. Strachey himself returned to England late in 1611 and was in the Blackfriars on December 13. Shakespeare doubtless used the prints of 1610, but
numerous verbal parallels make it clear that his main
authority was the *True Reportory*, and this it seems that he
can only have seen in manuscript. Malone's date of 1611
for *Tempest* remains reasonable. It has been suggested
that the play was revised in 1612–13 and the mask in iv. 1
inserted, to make it more appropriate to the celebrations
attending the wedding of the Elector Palatine and the
Princess Elizabeth on 14 February 1613; and the mask
has been claimed by Fleay for Beaumont and by Robertson
for Chapman or Heywood. Wilson has a more elaborate
theory, which involves an early rhymed or partly rhymed
play by Shakespeare, two distinct recasts, and at least one
and possibly two abridgements, as well as the introduction
of the mask. I will not repeat here my detailed criticism
of these views in *R.E.S.* i. 129. The play is short, but
the songs and dumb-shows would eke it out. The long
passages of exposition, which Wilson regards as replacing
matter originally shown in action, are due to an attempt,
unusual with Shakespeare, to secure unity of time. The
rest of the supposed evidence for recasting and abridgement consists mainly of very small points, such as incoher-
encies and obscurities, the presence of mutes, broken lines,
misdivided lines, accidental rhymes, a scrap of doggerel,
transitions between verse and prose, for most of which
alternative explanations seem to me more plausible.
At two places, however, i. 2. 298–304, 317 and ii. 1. 297–

305, it is just possible that there may have been some theatrical expansion of the spectacular and musical elements. Conceivably the song of Juno and Ceres (iv. 1. 106–17) in the mask may be another example; the rest of the mask is, I think, fully Shakespearean.

The notion of an early date for *Tempest* in some form has been encouraged by its analogies to the play of *Die Schöne Sidea*, which forms part of the *Opus Theatricum* (1618) of Jacob Ayrer of Nuremberg, who died in 1605. Here, too, are a prince and magician, with a familiar spirit, a fair daughter, and an enemy's son, whose sword is held in thrall by the magician's art, who must bear logs for the lady, and who wins release through her love. Use of a common source is a more plausible explanation than borrowing on either hand. But it has not been found. A play of *Celinde and Sedea* was given in 1604 and 1613 by English actors in Germany, but Ayrer has no Celinde.[1] William Collins, the poet, told Thomas Warton that he had found the *Tempest* story in the *Aurelio and Isabella* of Juan de Flores, of which there is an English translation (1556), but it is not there.[2] *Die Schöne Sidea* has no storm and no enchanted island. Some analogues to these have been found in various novels of Spanish and Italian origin, but in no case does a direct relation to *Tempest* seem likely. Probably we get nearer in the *scenari* for *commedie dell'arte* printed by Neri from *Casanatense MS.* 1212 at Rome. Of these there are four; *La Pazzia di Filandro, Gran Mago, La Nave, Li Tre Satiri*. In all of these shipwrecked crews land upon an island, and there are love-intrigues between the nobles and the native girls, and comic business in the hunger and greed of the sailors. These are complicated by the action of a Mago who controls the island. The resemblances to *Tempest* are closest in *Li Tre Satiri*, where the foreigners are taken for gods, as Trinculo is by Caliban, and the Pantalone and Zanni steal the Mago's book, as Trinculo and Stephano plot to steal Prospero's. The Mago appears also in other *scenari* not printed, and in one of these,

---

[1] *Eliz. Stage*, ii. 284, 289.   [2] *Var.* xv. 2.

Pantaloncino, he abandons his arts at the end, as Prospero does. The *scenari* are from the second of two manuscript volumes dated in 1618 and 1622 respectively. They were prepared for the press and for acting by Basilio Locatelli, but it is clear from the preface that his is merely a *rifacimento.* How old the *scenari* themes may be, one can hardly say, but Neri points to a very similar plot of a shipwreck and a Mago in Bartolomeo Rossi's fully written pastoral comedy of *Fiammella* (1584). Rossi performed in Paris during the same year. He is not known to have come to England. And of course we cannot assume that the *scenari* were used for performances there, although, since writing *Eliz. Stage,* ii. 261–5, I have found a trace of the presence of an Italian comedian, possibly Daniell by name, in 1610.[1] An historical basis for Prospero's political fortunes has been suggested in those of a fourteenth-century Lithuanian Witold, which got into English chronicles, and with those of a fifteenth-century Prospero Adorno, whose deposition from his duchy of Genoa is told of in William Thomas's *Historie of Italie* (1549, 1561). But neither parallel is at all close. A Ferdinand II succeeded his father Alfonso as King of Naples in 1495. Whatever Shakespeare's romantic source, if any, was, he worked into it the details of the Bermudas adventure, and he has probably used earlier travel-books, particularly Richard Eden's *History of Travayle* (1577), which would have given him Setebos, as the name of a Patagonian god. Caliban appears to be derived from the Gipsy *cauliban,* 'blackness'. Ariel is a Hebrew name, variously used in magical writings for one of the spirits who control the elements or the planets. Gonzalo's Utopian disquisition (ii. 1. 143–68) is borrowed from the essay *Of the Canibales* in Florio's *Montaigne,* ch. xxx. A ballad of *The Inchanted Island* is (App. F, no. xi, *d*) one of Collier's forgeries.

[1] *R.E.S.* i. 133.

XXXVI. HENRY THE EIGHTH

[F1. 1623.] [*Catalogue*] The Life of King Henry the Eight. [*Histories*, pp. 205–32, sign. t 3–x 4^v. *Head-title*] The Famous History of the Life of King Henry the Eight. [*Running-title*] The Life of King Henry the Eight. [Acts and scc. marked.]

Modern Editions. D. Nichol Smith (1899, *Warwick*); C. K. Pooler (1915, *Arden*); J. M. Berdan and T. Brooke (1925, *Yale*).

Dissertations. R. Roderick, *On the Metre of Hen. VIII* (c. 1756, T. Edwards, *Canons of Criticism*[6]; 1874, *N.S.S. Trans.*66*); J. Spedding, *On the Several Shares of Sh. and Fletcher in the Play of Hen. VIII* (1850, *Gent. Mag.* 115; 1874, *N.S.S. Trans.* 1*); S. Hickson, *A Confirmation of Mr. Spedding's Paper on the Authorship of Hen. VIII* (1850, 1 *N.Q.* ii. 198; 1874, *N.S.S. Trans.* 18*); N. Delius, *Fletchers angebliche Betheiligung an Shs Hen. VIII* (1879, *J.* xiv. 180; *Abl.* ii. 35); W. Zeitlin, *Shs Hen. VIII und Rowleys When You See Me, You Know Me* (1881, *Anglia*, iv. 73); R. Boyle, *Beaumont, Fletcher, and Massinger* (1887, *E.S.* x. 393), *Hen. VIII, An Investigation into the Origin and Authorship of the Play* (1885, *N.S.S. Trans.* 443); F. G. Fleay, *Mr. Boyle's Theory as to Hen. VIII* (1885, *Ath.* i. 355); E. H. C. Oliphant, *The Works of B. and F.* (1891, *E.S.* xv. 326), *Hen. VIII* (1927, *B.F.* 302); A. H. Thorndike, *Hen. VIII* (1901, *Influence of B. and F. on Sh.* 35); H. Conrad, *Hen. VIII. Fletchers Werk, überarbeitet von Sh.* (1918, *E.S.* lii. 204); H. D. Sykes, *King Hen. VIII* (1919, *Sidelights on Sh.* 18); K. Ege, *Shs Anteil an Hen. VIII* (1922, *J.* lviii. 99); M. H. Nicolson, *The Authorship of Hen. VIII* (1922, *P.M.L.A.* xxxvii. 484); B. Maxwell, *Fletcher and Hen. VIII* (1923, *Manly Studies*, 104), *Review* of Sykes (1926, *M.P.* xxiii. 365).

The text is a good one, with unusually elaborate stage-directions for the spectacular episodes. A clear date is given by the notices of the Globe fire of 29 June 1613 during a performance of the play.[1] It is called by Howes and Lorkin 'the play of Henry the Eighth'. Wotton gives an alternative title *All is True*, which is echoed by three references to truth in the prologue. But he also says that 'some principal pieces of the reign of Henry VIII' were represented, and specifies the mask scene, from the discharge of chambers in which (i. 4. 49) the fire arose. And he calls the play a 'new' one. There is no reason to suppose that it differed in any way from the extant version,

[1] App. D; *Eliz. Stage*, ii. 419.

merely because a ballad mentions 'the Foole' among the actors in the house. He was a familiar member of the company, even if he had no part in *Henry VIII*. Nor need the references in the prologue to 'the first and happiest hearers of the town' and to a shilling admission fee point to a performance at the Blackfriars. There were shilling seats in the public theatres during the seventeenth century, and probably increased prices for new plays.[1]

Modern scholarship has generally adopted the view of Spedding that there are two hands in *Henry VIII*, of which the first only wrote i. 1, 2; ii. 3, 4; iii. 2. 1–203; v. 1. Spedding took the first hand to be Shakespeare's and the second Fletcher's; and I see no reason to dissent. A general impression of stylistic difference is confirmed by the tests of double endings, overflows, and speech-endings, and, for what it is worth, by Thorndike's test of the variant uses of *'em* and *them*, although the possible intervention of printers must be borne in mind here. Conrad has shown that the proportion of parallels to Shakespeare's diction elsewhere is considerable in the scenes ascribed to him, and slight elsewhere. Boyle and Sykes have attempted to substitute Massinger for Shakespeare, again mainly on the basis of parallels, but those to Massinger certainly do not outweigh the Shakespearean ones. Moreover, Massinger is full of Shakespearean echoes. Maxwell points out that he has as many to *Hamlet*, *Othello*, and *Coriolanus* as to *Henry VIII*, and also, which is significant, that such echoes are most frequent in the plays which he wrote after the appearance of F1. I doubt whether Boyle and Sykes are on any stronger ground in also finding sections of Massinger in the non-Shakespearean scenes. The occasional discernment of him by Oliphant as touching-up both parts here and there seems to me quite subjective. It is, I think, easier to make out a case against Fletcher than against Shakespeare. Maxwell shows that the second hand keeps closer to his sources, and uses more overflows, parentheses, and sententious maxims, and fewer repetitions of words than are usual in Fletcher's work, and concludes that, if he

[1] *Eliz. Stage*, ii. 532.

was the second hand, 'either he was revising another's work, or the peculiarities of his style and method were modified by a collaborator'. I should agree that *Henry VIII* is not very characteristic Fletcher, and should add that it is not very characteristic Shakespeare either. Shakespeare must have been writing in a tired vein and with some loss of concentration. Fletcher is clearest in the lighter scenes, i. 3 and v. 4, and here the superabundance of double endings, often with stressed final syllables, and the linking of contiguous or nearly contiguous words by cheap alliteration must be his. I think that the revels scene (i. 4), the comparatively colourless state scenes (ii. 2 ; iv. 1 ; v. 2, 3), the final rhetoric (v. 5) and the pathetic scenes (ii. 1 ; iii. 1 ; iii. 2. 203—end; iv. 2) may be his also. There is some very good writing for him in the pathetic scenes, and the play as a whole is a little out of his ordinary line. He may well have been working under the influence of Shakespeare. Some kind of collaboration, even if Shakespeare was at a distance, is more plausible than revision, for which there is no clear evidence. The other indications of collaboration between Shakespeare and Fletcher about 1613, in *T.N.K.* and perhaps the lost *Cardenio* (cf. p. 539), cannot be left altogether out of account. Shakespeare starts most of the themes. He deals pretty fully in i. 1, 2 with Wolsey's greatness and the ruin of his opponent Buckingham. He introduces Anne (ii. 3). He does the trial of Katharine, evidently leaving a gap, as there has been nothing to lead up to it. He begins the fall of Wolsey and leaves its ending to Fletcher. He introduces Cranmer, Cromwell, and Gardiner. He does the birth of Elizabeth. It is an epic, rather than a tragic scheme. Perhaps Fletcher upset the intended balance, by stressing the pathos of Katharine and Wolsey. Obviously in a Jacobean play there must be something of James, to follow Elizabeth. The reversion to the epic chronicle at the very end of Shakespeare's career is odd. I have sometimes thought that an earlier plot may have been adapted. Sussex's men played a *Buckingham* in 1593–4, although, if this is one of Henslowe's loose titles for a Shakespearean play, it is perhaps more likely to be *Richard III* than an early *Henry VIII*. There is no early language, of course, in *Henry VIII*. Downes says that Lowin played Henry, and was instructed in the part by Shakespeare himself.[1] According to the comedy of *Knavery in All Trades* (1664), Taylor and Pollard acted with Lowin in the play.[2] They were not King's men in Shakespeare's lifetime, but there was a revival (App. D) in 1628. The historical incidents are pieced together from Holinshed and Foxe's *Book of Martyrs*. Possibly the writers had also Samuel Rowley's *When You See Me, You Know Me* (1605) before them.[3] A reprint of 1613 may have been due to the production of *Henry VIII*. We may fancy, if we like, that it was the 'merry bawdy play' of the prologue.

[1] *Eliz. Stage*, ii. 329.   [2] H.P. ii. 295.   [3] *Eliz. Stage*, iii. 472.

CHAPTER X
PLAYS OUTSIDE THE FIRST FOLIO

[*Bibliographical Note. Pericles*, but not as a rule *Two Noble Kinsmen*, forms a part of most recent editions of Shakespeare. The most convenient collection of other plays ascribed to him in the Third Folio or elsewhere is C. T. Tucker Brooke, *The Shakespeare Apocrypha* (1908). Others are by N. Delius (1854–74); K. Warnke and L. Proescholdt (1883–8); A. F. Hopkinson (1891–1914). A fuller and more detailed list is in *Eliz. Stage*, iii. 204. Dissertations are R. Sachs, *Die Sh. zugeschriebenen zweifelhaften Stücke* (1892, *J*. xxvii. 135; A. F. Hopkinson, *Essays on Sh.'s Doubtful Plays* (1900).]

I. SIR THOMAS MORE

[*Bibliographical Note*. The play is preserved in *Harl. MS.* 7368. It must have passed into the Harleian library from that of John Murray, who lent it to Thomas Hearne (*Collections*, ix. 393) in 1727. Editions were published by A. Dyce (1844, *Sh. Soc.*), A. F. Hopkinson (1902), and C. F. Tucker Brooke (1908, *Sh. Apocrypha*), and a photographic facsimile by J. S. Farmer (1910, *T.F.T.*). The foundation of modern study is W. W. Greg's type-facsimile edition (1911, *M.S.R.*). Shakespeare's participation in the play was first suggested by R. Simpson, *Are there any extant MSS. in Sh.'s Handwriting* (1871, 4 *N.Q.* viii. 1) and J. Spedding, *Sh.'s Handwriting* (1872, 4 *N.Q.* x. 227), *On a Question concerning a Supposed Specimen of Sh.'s Handwriting* (1879, *Reviews and Discussions*). The theory was revived with great palaeographical learning by Sir E. M. Thompson, *Sh.'s Handwriting* (1916), and supported in *Sh.'s Hand in the Play of S.T.M.* (1923), with contributions by A. W. Pollard, W. W. Greg, E. M. Thompson, J. D. Wilson, and R. W. Chambers. Much controversy followed, and its later stages require a reconsideration of the case as stated in *Eliz. Stage*, iv. 32. The palaeographical issue has been summed up by W. W. Greg in *Sh.'s Hand Once More* (1927, Nov. 24, Dec. 1, *T.L.S.*). Other discussions are: B. Nicholson, *The Plays of S.T.M. and Ham.* (1884, 6 *N.Q.* x. 423); A. Hall, *Sh.'s Handwriting* (1899); C. R. Baskervill, *Some Parallels to Bartholomew Fair* (1908, *M.P.* vi. 109); W. W. Greg, *Autograph Plays by A. Munday* (1913, *M.L.R.* viii. 89), *T. Goodal in S.T.M.* (1929, *P.M.L.A.* xliv. 633); L. L. Schücking, *Das Datum des pseudo-Sh. S.T.M.* (1913, *E.S.* xlvi. 228), *Sh. and S.T.M.* (1925, *R.E.S.* i. 40); P. Simpson, *The Play of S.T.M. and Sh.'s Hand in It* (1917, 3 *Library*, viii. 79), A. Green, *The Apocryphal S.T.M. and the Sh. Holograph* (1918, *Am. J. Philology*, xxxix. 229); E. H. C. Oliphant, *S.T.M.* (1919, *J.E.G.P.* xviii. 226); W. H. Stevenson, *Sh.'s Schoolmaster and Handwriting* (1920, Jan. 8, *T.L.S.*); M. St. C. Byrne, *A. Munday and his Books* (1921, 4 *Library*,

i. 225); G. G. Greenwood, *The Sh. Signatures and S.T.M.* (1924); B. A. P. van Dam, *The Text of Sh.'s Ham.* (1924), 369; S. A. Tannenbaum, *Sh.'s Unquestioned Autographs and the Addition to S.T.M.* (1925, *S.P.* xxii. 133; *Problems*, 179); *The Booke of S.T.M.* (1927, p.p., reviewed by R. B. McKerrow in *R.E.S.* iv. 237 and W.W. Greg in *4 Library*, ix. 202), *More About the Booke of S.T.M.* (1928, *P.M.L.A.* xliii. 767); E. Sievers, *S.T.M.* (1925, *Anglica*, ii. 173); G. B. Harrison, *The Date of S.T.M.* (1925, *R.E.S.* i. 337); A. W. Pollard, *Verse Tests and the Date of S.T.M.* (1925, *R.E.S.* i. 441); A. Acheson, *Sh., Chapman and S.T.M.* (1926, *Rev. Anglo-Américaine*, iii. 428, 514); T. W. Baldwin, *The Organisation and Personnel of the Shn. Company* (1927), 131; E. M. Albright, *Dramatic Publication in England* (1927), 128; W. Marschall, *Das S.T.M. Manuskript und die englische Commedia dell' Arte* (1928, *Anglia*, lii. 193); S. R. Golding, *Robert Wilson and S.T.M.* (1928, *N.Q.* cliv. 237, 259; clv. 237).

There has also been much correspondence, to which many of the above writers, with M. A. Bayfield, J. A. Fort, and W. J. Lawrence, have contributed, in *T.L.S.* (1919, Apr. 24–June 19, Nov. 6, Dec. 18; 1920, May 27–July 1, Aug. 12, 19; 1921, June 30, Aug. 4, 18; 1922, Nov. 23, 30; 1923, Oct. 18–Dec. 20; 1924, Aug. 24–Nov. 6; 1925, Jan. 15–29, Aug. 27–Nov. 12).

Much of the discussion on *S.T.M.* covers Shakespeare's handwriting as shown in his signatures. Other dissertations are: F. Madden, *Observations on an Autograph of Sh.* (1838, from *Arch.* xxvii. 113); W. D. Macray, *Annals of the Bodleian* (1868, 1890), 379; A. P. Paton, *North's Plutarch: Notes as to a Copy Supposed to have been Sh.'s* (1871); W. W. Skeat, *Sh.'s Plutarch* (1875), xii; F. A. Leo, *Sh.'s Ovid in the Bodleian* (1881, *J.* xvi. 367); J. F. Nisbet, *The Insanity of Genius* (1891); F. J. Furnivall, *On Sh.'s Signatures* (1895); S. Lee, *Sh.'s Handwriting* (1899); E. M. Thompson, *An Analysis of Sh.'s Signatures* (1917, 1926, *Sh.'s England*, i. 299), *Two Pretended Autographs of Sh.* (1917, *3 Library*, viii. 193); F. Madan, *A Supposed Sh. Autograph* (1918, *3 Library*, ix. 97); G. G. Greenwood, *Sh.'s Handwriting* (1920), *Sh.'s Handwriting and the Northumberland Manuscript* (1925); R. W. Leftwich, *Sh.'s Handwriting and Other Papers* (1921); W. Thompson, *Sh.'s Handwriting* (1925, *Quarterly*, ccxliii. 209); C. L. Dana, *The Handwriting in Nervous Diseases, with Special Reference to the Signatures of William Sh.* (1925, *Essays for M. Prince*); S. A. Tannenbaum, *Reclaiming one of Sh.'s Signatures* (1925, *S.P.* xxii. 392), *A New Study of Sh.'s Will* (1926, *S.P.* xxiii. 117); *Problems in Sh.'s Penmanship* (1927); G. C. Taylor, *The Date of Edward Capell's Notes and Various Readings* (1929, *R.E.S.* v. 317). I give facsimiles (Plate XII) of the accepted signatures. Others are in the books of E. M. Thompson and S. A. Tannenbaum. For general treatises on Elizabethan handwriting, cf. p. 168.]

THE title of the play is given on a vellum wrapper, inscribed 'The Booke of Sir Thomas Moore'. It has no divisions, but the original text, in so far as it is now pre-

served, makes seventeen scenes, which can be grouped
into three sections, dealing respectively with the Rise,
Greatness, and Fall of More. The first section (Scc. i–vii)
was devoted, except for the description of an isolated
early prank of More in Sc. ii, to the events of 'Ill May-
Day', 1517. More was represented as taking a leading
part (Sc. vi) in quelling the riot against the Lombard and
French aliens in London. The second section (Scc. viii and
ix) was mainly occupied with a visit of Erasmus to More,
and with a play, in which More took an impromptu part.
The third gave the closing episodes of his life, from his
resignation of the Chancellorship (Sc. x) to his execution
(Sc. xvii). The manuscript has undergone alteration.
There are two *lacunae* in the original text. Probably one
leaf, containing the end of Sc. v and beginning of Sc. vi,
has been removed, and the whole of Sc. iv and beginning of
Sc. v on the verso of the preceding leaf, with a few lines of
Sc. vi on the following leaf, have been marked for deletion.
Into this *lacuna* have been inserted four leaves, of which
the first contains a passage (Addition I) clearly intended
for the third section and here misplaced, and the others
(Addition II) contain (a) a revised Sc. iv, (b) a new scene to
replace Sc. v, (c) a new beginning for Sc. vi. Probably two
leaves, containing the central part of Sc. viii, have also been
removed, and the beginning and end of that scene on the
preceding and following leaves marked for deletion. This
second *lacuna* has been filled by two inserted leaves
(Addition IV) containing a revised Sc. viii. Further, a
slip (Addition III) bearing a single speech, probably
intended as an introduction to this scene, has been pasted
over part of the deleted matter on the leaf preceding the
lacuna. Some additions have also been made to the later
scenes. Another slip (Addition V), pasted over deleted
matter on the leaf following the second *lacuna*, bears an
introductory speech to Sc. ix, and this introduction has
itself been expanded by lines written partly on the slip and
partly on the leaf which holds it. A leaf (Addition VI) has
been inserted before that containing the original end of
Sc. ix, and contains a new episode to be appended to that

scene. And at the end of this inserted leaf is found a draft for the expanding lines in Addition V. Finally, a reference sign against a speech by More marked for deletion in Sc. xiii indicates that the misplaced Addition I was meant to come in here.

The original matter is written throughout in a single hand. The Additions are in five other hands, known as A, B, C, D, and E. The contributions of A, D, and E are confined to single scenes. A wrote Addition I. D wrote Addition II(c), the revised part of Sc. vi, in which More's oratory quells the riot. E wrote the last 31 lines of Addition IV. Hands B and C range more widely. B wrote Additions II(a) and VI. He also added a few speeches for the Clown in the margins of the latter and original part of Sc. vi and of Sc. vii. And he is possibly responsible for the marginal words 'This must be newe written', at the opening of the deleted Sc. viii. C wrote Additions II(b), III, IV (except E's 31 lines), and V. He also made many alterations in the speech-prefixes and a few in the text of D's contribution, similarly but more slightly corrected B's II(a), added stage-directions to his VI, and revised some of the directions in those parts of the original text which were to be retained, partly to adapt them to the Additions, and partly, it would seem, to get important directions in the left margin.[1] Dr. Greg reasonably conjectures that B and C shared the general responsibility for the revision of the play. Moreover, while it is reasonable to suppose that A, B, D, and E were themselves the authors of what they wrote, C was clearly copying in part of V the draft by B at the end of VI, and it is therefore possible that he was nothing but a copyist elsewhere. In fact, his services seem to be those of a book-keeper; and of this there is confirmation in the facts that his hand reappears on the wrappers, both of *Sir Thomas More* itself and of *John a Kent*, for which the same piece of vellum was used, in some stage-directions added to *John a Kent*, and in the 'plots' of *2 Seven Deadly Sins* and *2 Fortune's Tennis*.[2]

The play has been submitted for censorship to Edmund

Tilney, as Master of the Revels. He has written no 'allowance' upon it, but he has made some 'reformations' and given instructions for others. His main attention was directed to the 'Ill May-Day' scenes in the first section. Here, in Scc. i and iii he has marked long passages for deletion, put crosses against individual lines, and altered several words, apparently with the idea of suggesting that the aliens concerned were only Lombards and not of any other nation. Even the non-committal word 'straunger' has to go. Against a passage referring to 'daungerous times' and 'the displeased commons of the Cittie', he has written 'Mend y^{is}'. With Sc. iii the 'reformations' stop, and although Tilney's ink seems to be rather blacker than that of Hand C or that of the main scribe, the difference does not make it possible to assign the marks for the deletion of the original Sc. iv and the remnant of Sc. v. My impression is that when Tilney had finished with Sc. iii he realized that piecemeal reformation of this section of the play was hopeless, and that he then turned back to the first page, and wrote the note 'Leaue out y^e insurrection wholy & y^e Cause ther off & begin w^t Sr Tho: Moore att y^e mayors sessions ⟨ = Sc. ii⟩ w^t a reportt afterwardes off his good service don beinge Shriue off London vppon a mutiny Agaynst y^e Lumbardes only by A shortt reportt & nott otherwise att your own perrilles E. Tyllney'. He did not interfere with the harmless second section of the play, but in Sc. x he crossed out the episode of More's resignation, and wrote in the margin what appears to be All Altr'.

Dr. Greg has identified the original hand with Anthony Munday's and Hand E with Thomas Dekker's, accepts Dr. Tannenbaum's identification of Hand A with Henry Chettle's, but decisively rejects that of Hand C with Thomas Kyd's. Nothing indeed that we know of Kyd's life, except perhaps that his father was a scrivener, suggests that he is likely to have been a book-keeper as well as a dramatist; and there is a high probability that the plot of *2 Fortune's Tennis*, which C wrote, belongs to 1597 or 1598, when Kyd was long dead. Hand B may possibly be

Thomas Heywood's, but that is far from certain. Presumably Munday was himself the author of at least part of the original play. The substitution in his hand of an alternative ending for that first written to the last scene looks like the work of an author. So do some of the *currente calamo* corrections in the text. Others, however, might be those of a scribe. Attempts have been made to trace original work by Chettle, Heywood, Dekker, and even Chapman, on literary grounds, and similarly to distribute responsibility for the additions in C's hand. These lie outside the scope of the present study. But the question of Shakespeare's participation must be faced. Hand D is claimed as his, and if the claim is sound, it is difficult to resist the conclusion that he was also the author of Addition II(c), in that hand. Both palaeographical and literary considerations are relevant. But the discussion starts with palaeography, in the theory of Sir E. Maunde Thompson that the hand is the same as that found in the few undisputed fragments of Shakespeare's script. Of these there are six, all, with one small exception, limited to signatures. The earliest (Plate XII, fig. *a*) is attached to the *Deposition* of 11 May 1612 in the case of *Belott* v. *Mountjoy* (App. A, no. x). It is abbreviated in the form

Wiłłm Shaksp

Conceivably the baptismal name reads 'Wiłm'; if not, the 'm' has not its three minims and is little more than a flourish. The 'p' has been read as an Italian long 's'. More probably it is the contraction for 'per', with a crossbar joined by a left-hand loop to the foot of the letter. Here it may serve as a more general contraction for 'sper' or 'spere'. The 'k' is badly blotted. There is an ornamental dot in the final loop of the W, which can be paralleled from other lay hands, as well as those of scriveners. Next come the signatures to the *Conveyance* (Fig. *b*) of 10 March and *Mortgage* (Fig. *c*) of 11 March 1613 (cf. App. A, no. xxiii). They are both on parchment strips passed through slits in the parchment of the deeds. That to the *Conveyance* is in two lines, which is again not

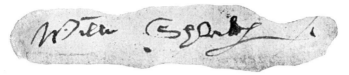

(a) DEPOSITION

(b) CONVEYANCE

(c) MORTGAGE

SHAKESPEARE'S SIGNATURES

PLATE XII B

(*d*) WILL (1)

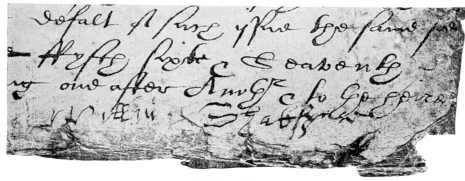

(*e*) WILL (2)

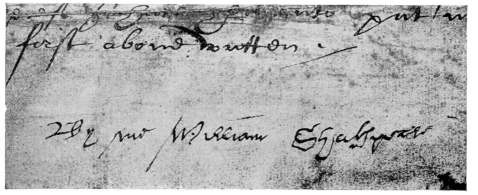

(*f*) WILL (3)

SHAKESPEARE'S SIGNATURES

unusual in Elizabethan writing. It is also abbreviated, and reads

William
Shakspẽ

The writing is close to the right-hand edge of the strip, and there are some supplementary ink marks on this edge and on the body of the deed which suggest to Sir E. M. Thompson an attempt to add an 'r', which would presumably have left the contraction mark to stand for a final 'e' only. The 'W' is blotted and has the ornamental dot. The *Mortgage* signature is again abbreviated, reading

Wᵐ Shakspẽ

It is disjointedly written, probably because the parchment was greasy. There is no dot in the 'W'. The contraction mark is angularly shaped and apparently blotted in the centre. It has been read as a superscribed 'a', but that would leave the name incomplete. Dr. Tannenbaum conjectures that Shakespeare was not present at the legal completion of the purchase transactions, that he signed the strips before they were inserted in the deed, and that, in trimming them to fit the slits, the scrivener mutilated the ends of the signatures. This does not sound plausible as legal procedure. Moreover, there was plenty of room for trimming on the left-hand side of the slips. It is surely a lame suggestion that 'the clerk may have had a "superstition" against widening a prepared slit or trimming a label on the left side'. Finally, there are the signatures (Figs. *d–f*) on the three sheets of the *Will* of 25 March 1616 (App. A, no. xxiv). That on the first sheet is again in two lines. It is now much worn and faded, and the surname is undecipherable without the aid of old facsimiles, which justify the reading

William
Shakspere

The signature on the second sheet is legible enough as

Willm̃ Shakspere

But the descending bow of an 'h' in the line above has led

to the supposition that the first 'e' was followed by an 'a', and to the erroneous reading 'Shakspeare'. The 'W' in these two signatures has no dot, but this recurs in the final and legally the most important signature on the third sheet of the *Will*. Here, too, the spelling differs. The reading is

By me William Shakspeare

Sir E. M. Thompson thinks that the signature originally ended with a contraction, and that the last three letters were then added. They are, in any case, worse written than the rest.

Innumerable other examples of Shakespeare's handwriting, mostly inscriptions in books, have been brought forward, and practically all of them are unauthentic. Dr. Tannenbaum has collected facsimiles of 108, including 79 Ireland forgeries.[1] A recent attempt to ascribe to Shakespeare the jotting on the *Northumberland MS.* (App. B, no. xvi), in which his name and the titles of some of his plays occur, is negligible. A copy of Ovid's *Metamorphoses* (1502, Aldus, Venice) in the Bodleian has the inscription 'W^m Sh^r' or 'W^m Sh^{re}' on the title-page, and opposite it on the front cover 'This little Booke of Ovid was given to me by W. Hall who sayd it was once Will Shakesperes. T. N. 1682'. A copy of John Florio's translation (1603) of Montaigne's *Essayes*, now in the British Museum, has and already had before 1780 the inscription 'Willm̃ Shakspere' on a fly-leaf, since used as a lining paper to the cover. Thompson rejects both of these. Madan states some points in favour of the Ovid. Tannenbaum argues for the authenticity of the Montaigne, and Taylor adds that there would be no motive for a forgery before Capell had called attention for the first time in 1780 to Shakespeare's use of Montaigne.

Only the six legal signatures can be regarded as available for comparison with the Hand D in *Sir Thomas More*. They can be relied upon, in spite of some rather amateur attempts to suggest that some of them may have been

---

[1] Some are reproduced in his *Problems*.

written by the scriveners concerned. The nature of the
documents makes this most improbable *a priori*, except
perhaps as regards the 'By me' on the will, which, however,
is not in the hand of the main scribe, or of Francis Collins.
It has every appearance of continuity with the signature.
And the six signatures themselves, although differing in
some details, present sufficient common features to justify,
if that were needed, ascription to the same hand. They
are not the work of an illiterate writer, although they may
seem so to those unfamiliar with the 'English' type of
hand in which, with some admixture of 'Italian' letters and
notably the long medial 's', they are written. Sir E. M.
Thompson accepted the theory that they show signs of
writer's cramp or some other nervous disorder. This is
repudiated by Dr. Tannenbaum, who is, I believe, an
expert in such disorders. No doubt Shakespeare may have
shared the usual uncertainty of a layman, when called upon
to execute a legal document. The will, in particular, he
may have signed in a condition of physical infirmity, and
exhaustion may account for the comparative badness of
the second signature and the close of the third. It is not
possible to be certain in what order these signatures were
made. Later legal practice would suggest that the operative signature on the last sheet was given first, and that
afterwards the testator turned back to the first and second
sheets and signed them for identification. It must be
added that signatures are not always fully typical of a
man's ordinary script, that a good many years must have
intervened between *Sir Thomas More* and the earliest
signature, and that the Shakespearean examples only give
eleven out of the twenty-six minuscule letters of the
alphabet and only three majuscules. The basis for comparison with Hand D (Plate XIII) is therefore slight.
Moreover, both hands are of a very normal kind. Hand
D was indeed at first taken to be identical with Hand C.
Sir E. M. Thompson, however, was able to discern certain
minor peculiarities distinctive alike of Shakespeare and of
Hand D, which confirmed his general impression that the
two hands were the same. He found them using similar

abnormal forms of 'a', 'k', 'p', 's', and other letters, of which one at least, the so-called 'spurred a', does not seem to have been exactly paralleled elsewhere. He found them also using the same two normal varieties of 'e', 'h', and 'p', and the same three of 'a' and 'k'. And they have in common the dotted 'W', the looped *per* symbol, and a habit of beginning certain initial letters with a long, fine upstroke, to the similar formation of which an example in each hand of a needle-like eye at the base bears witness. The most elaborate criticism of Sir E. M. Thompson's theory has come from Dr. Tannenbaum, who questions the validity of some of his points, and calls attention to dissimilarities, not only in individual letter-forms, but also in general features, such as the distribution of light and heavy strokes, the shaping of contractions, and the linking of letter to letter. Shakespeare's pen, he thinks, moved stiffly, and D's with facility. D, again, generally dots his 'i's'; Shakespeare, in his signatures, never does. I am no palaeographer, but so far as a layman can judge, I am content to adopt the cautious conclusions of Dr. Greg, who thinks that, while some of the specific tests are doubtful, weight must be attached to the effect of 'numerous hardly definable traits of resemblance' on the mind of so experienced a student as Sir E. M. Thompson at the end of an exhaustive investigation; that the case for Shakespeare's authorship must rest on 'the convergence of a number of independent lines of argument—palæographic, orthographic, linguistic, stylistic, psychological—and not on any one alone'; and that although the palæographic case does not approach complete proof, it may be sufficient, in the absence of any more plausible candidate for D among dramatists whose hands are known, to 'incline the balance of probability in favour of identification'.

The problem has, of course, been approached along the other lines indicated by Dr. Greg. I do not think it can be said that the quality of the scene is such as to make an ascription of it to Shakespeare imperative on purely literary grounds. On the other hand, I think that it might have passed well enough as his in any Elizabethan play of

PLATE XIII

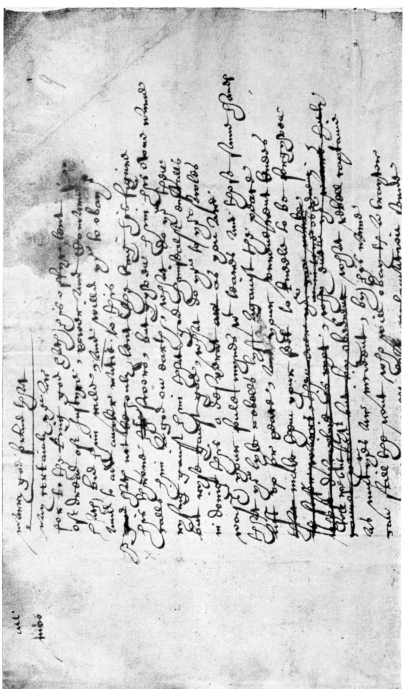

the canon. Professor R. W. Chambers has shown that its combination of sympathy for the psychology of the mob with a strong sense of order and degree, as maintainers of the social system against anarchy, is consonant with the political temper, not only of the early Cade scenes, but also of *Julius Caesar*, *Troilus and Cressida*, and *Coriolanus*. Technical considerations of style, again, certainly do not rule out Shakespeare. Professor J. D. Wilson has listed 'abnormal' spellings analogous to those which seem (cf. i, p. 187) in some of the Quartos to have escaped the vigilance of the compositors. The vocabulary and diction justify themselves, on comparison with the concordance, as quite reasonably Shakespearean, in spite of the strictures of Professor Schücking. There are, no doubt, words and uses of words which do not precisely recur, but that is so in every one of the plays. I find nothing obviously rebellious to Shakespeare's manner.[1] The same is true of the metre. A statistical comparison with a single scene is, of course, valueless, but More's long speech shows a good deal of internal pausation and other variation from the early blank-verse norm.[2] What one does not find is that absence of 'blots' for which Heminges and Condell especially lauded Shakespeare. There are a score of places which show alterations made either *currente calamo* or as afterthoughts. And even then there were some oversights left for Hand C to correct. Perhaps the writer did not take the play he was tinkering very seriously. I do not take the statement of Heminges and Condell very seriously. If the scene is Shakespeare's, we get some useful hints towards the interpretation of the Quarto and Folio texts. We should expect to find there a writer who used very little

[1] Schücking suggests Heywood as a possible alternative, and Pollard (*Sh.'s Hand*, 14) would agree, were not Heywood 'ruled out by his handwriting'.

[2] The 77 lines of More's speech, not quite continuous, from 'Look what you do offend' to 'momtanish inhumanyty', as we may conceive that the author meant them to read, with two lines misunderstood by C restored, yield 22 double endings (including runs of 5 and 4), 4 extra mid-line syllables, 16 trochees in the first foot, 6 in the third, 3 in the fourth, 8 trisyllabic feet (of which one is harsh), 6 run-on lines, 16 strong internal pauses. This, for what it is worth, does not suggest the earliest Shakespeare.

punctuation and attached his speech-prefixes—perhaps, as Dr. Greg thinks, after completing the texts,—carelessly and with many abbreviations.[1]   D's pages run to 46, 50, and 52 script-lines respectively.   At the foot of the second page, he runs four verse-lines into two script-lines.   Similarly, he merges a final half line with a full one at the foot of the third. Professor Wilson regards a knowledge of D's hand as helpful in detecting the causes of misprints in Shakespearean plays.   But it is, after all, a fairly ordinary 'English' hand, and play manuscripts seem to have been usually written in 'English' hands.

The clues to date and to the company concerned with the play are very uncertain.   The changes in Munday's script put the original text earlier than his *Heaven of the Mynde* (1602) and later than *John a Kent*, but as the '1596' on the *John a Kent* manuscript is not held to be his, and therefore does not necessarily date the play, this may be early.   Munday may quite well have been writing by 1580, although it is not necessary to go so far back as this.[2] The relation, if any, of *John a Kent* to the Admiral's *Wise Man of West Chester* in 1594 is obscure.   Tilney was Master of the Revels from 1579 to 1610; Buck cannot be shown to have deputized for him before 1603.   The mention of 'Mason among the Kings players' (1151) is inconclusive; none is known in the companies of Henry VIII or James.   So are those (1006, 1148) of Ogle as a theatrical furnisher; Ogles were so occupied from 1571 to 1585[3] and in 1600.[4]   So is that to the scouring of Moorditch, which is, moreover, in an Addition (IV, 215).   It was scoured in 1595, but the allusion would have been as much in place while it wanted scouring.   The back-sword men Garret and George Philpots (458) are unknown.   More is to be learnt from Tilney's dealings with the play, which show that he was nervous of references to the question of aliens.

---

[1] In the 77 lines cited above, the MS. has only 25 commas and 2 semi-colons, none of either at line-ends. There are 4 full-stops, 3 at line-ends. There are no colons. Interruptions have no stops. Many necessary pauses are unstopped.

Of the 16 strong internal ones, 1 has a full-stop, 2 semi-colons and 9 commas; 4 are unstopped.

[2] *Eliz. Stage*, iii. 444.

[3] Feuillerat, *Eliz. passim.*

[4] Henslowe, i. 118.

This had become a subject for agitation in London, as a result of the competition with native handicraftsmen of Dutch and Flemish immigrants since 1561 and of French Huguenots since 1580. It is noticeable that, while only Lombards and French were concerned in More's day, both Munday (420, 687) and the writers of Additions (II, 19, 40, 55, 250) bring in the Dutch and Flemish. Tilney does not seem to mind much about the Lombards, but dislikes mention of the French or of 'strangers' generally. The agitation was more or less chronic, but active in 1586, when there were mutterings of another 'Yll May Daye', in 1592–3, and in 1595.[1] Any one of these dates would fit the original play. The theatrical conditions were not, however, favourable (cf. ch. ii) for new productions between 23 June 1592 and April 1594; nor is there any sign of *Sir Thomas More* in Henslowe's lists of performances by Strange's and Sussex's men during that period. The Additions have, of course, to be considered, as well as the original. It is unfortunate that we cannot say with certainty whether they were made before or after the submission of the manuscript for censorship. Dr. Greg thinks that they must have been made before, on the ground that most of the alterations are of a literary character, and that nobody could have seriously supposed that those in the riot scenes in any way carried out Tilney's instructions. The argument is a strong one. On the other hand, it obliges us to suppose that the play was sent to Tilney in a most untidy and in places almost unintelligible condition; in a variety of hands; with long passages only marked for deletion by marginal lines; with Addition I fitted into the wrong scene; with Addition VI so fitted in as to break the continuity of Sc. ix, and still containing a draft of part of Addition V. If Tilney was prepared to stand this, he must have been very easygoing. Moreover, why should a play just written have been subjected to so much literary revision? I think it is just possible that *Sir Thomas More* was laid aside when

---

[1] Documents are in Dasent, *P.C. Acts*, xxii. 506 (2 June 1592) and *Sh.'s Hand*, 33 (1586, 1593, 1595); cf. Cheyney, ii. 256; J. S. Burn, *Hist. of Foreign Protestant Refugees* (1846), 10, 12.

Tilney sent it back, and taken up later by new writers, with different literary notions from Munday's, in the hope that the political cloud had blown by and that Tilney might now be persuaded to allow the main original structure to stand. If so, probably the hope proved fallacious and the revision was never completed. I do not pretend to decide between the alternatives. The matter would be set at rest if Tilney's hand or ink could be identified in the Additions. But it is not so, and although Dr. Greg thinks that a passage (II, 68–75) introducing Sir John Munday has been scored out on political grounds, and therefore by Tilney, my own impression is that this was done to save a once-speaking character by persons less interested than Anthony Munday in his namesake, whom he had probably introduced in the original Sc. iv. As it stands, the manuscript seems inadequate for prompt-copy. Besides perfecting the insertions, the book-keeper has still to supply a few missing entries and speech-prefixes. Many exits are unmarked, but about these book-keepers do not appear (cf. p. 120) to have troubled much. In the text itself, many ragged edges left by deletions have still to be joined. The name of an actor, T. Goodal, written against the entry of a Messenger in Addition V suggests that at least the casting had been done. It is true that there are many very small parts in the play, and one would expect a book-keeper, if he wanted a reminder (cf. p. 122) for one of these, to want it for others. But there is equally sparse casting in other plays. Dr. Tannenbaum treats the name as a forgery by Collier, and links it with what looks like a marginal 'Laneham' (111) in apparently modern ink. Dr. Greg, however, is clear that, while 'Laneham' is to be suspected as Collier's, a forgery of the Goodal note is out of the question.[1] He tells me that the hand is doubtless C's, and that tests of the ink have disclosed no difference. Collier did in fact state, as early as 1835, that a Goodale acted with Laneham in *Sir Thomas More*.[2] He called him Baptiste Goodale, and included him in

---

[1] *P.M.L.A.* xliv. 63. Tannenbaum defends his view (*ibid.* 934).
[2] *New Facts*, 12.

a forged list of Queen's men at the Blackfriars in 1589.[1]
Thomas Goodale had been one of Lord Berkeley's men
in 1581.[2] He played in 2 *Seven Deadly Sins* (cf.
p. 44) for Strange's, or the Admiral's, or the combined
Alleyn company about 1590. He was a mercer and
had a business transaction with John Alleyn and Robert
Lee, who had both also been connected with those companies, in 1593.[3] He was alive and a player in 1598
and perhaps 1599, but we do not know what company
he was then of.[4] Hand C was book-keeper to the 2 *Deadly
Sins* company about 1590, and to the later Admiral's
in 1597 or 1598 (cf. p. 124). We do not know
when he joined them or how long he stayed with
them. If Shakespeare wrote the Addition, these facts
would perhaps fit best with a date in 1592–3. But we
are first certain of Heywood (born, as Professor Sisson
kindly tells me, in 1573) as a playwright in 1596,
and of Dekker (born c. 1572) in 1598; and 1592–3
would be rather early for either of them. On the hypothesis of a second attempt to produce *Sir Thomas More*, the
recrudescence of anti-alien agitation in 1595 might explain
a second abandonment. On grounds of style and parallels,
this or even a later date for Shakespeare's intervention
would not particularly surprise me. Schücking would
group *Sir Thomas More* as a whole with the Chamberlain's *Thomas Lord Cromwell* (cf. p. 534), 'lately acted' in
1602 and the Admiral's Wolsey plays of 1601–2,[5] but
that seems too late for the stage of development reached by
Munday's script. I am afraid that the date, or dates,
must remain undetermined. Some evidence tending to
suggest that the play did ultimately get performed is not
very conclusive. Baskerville cites parallels which make
him think that Jonson borrowed from Sc. ii for the purse-
cutting scene (ii. 6) in *Bartholomew Fair*, but the source,
whatever it was, may have been open to Jonson. Golding,
perhaps more pertinently, notes a double echo in Munday

[1] App. F. xi (*b*).   [4] *P.M.L.A.* xli. 100.
[2] *Ibid.* ii. 103.   [5] *Eliz. Stage*, ii. 178; iv. 8.
[3] Warner, *Dulwich MSS.* iv. 29.

and Chettle's *Death of Robert, Earl of Huntingdon* (1598),
iv. 1, of the long-haired ruffian and the Lady Vanity in
S.T.M. 797, 1080. But obviously Munday, if not also
Chettle, was familiar with the play, whether it was performed or not. Of course, it might have been further
revised and licensed on a fair copy, but why then should
the rough copy be carefully wrappered and preserved as
'The Booke of Sir Thomas Moore'?

One more point. If Shakespeare wrote Addition II(c),
is it not possible that he also wrote Addition III, although
it is in C's hand?

It is in heaven that I am thus and thus
And that wch we prophanlie terme o^r fortuns
Is the provision of the power aboue
fitted and shapte Iust to that strength of nature
wch we are borne ⟨?withal;⟩ good god good god
that I from such an humble bench of birth
should stepp as twere vp to my Countries head
And give the law out ther ⟨;⟩ I in my fathers lif
to take prerogative and tyth of knees
from elder kinsmen and him bynd by my place
to give the smooth and dexter way to me
that owe it him by nature, sure thes things
not phisickt by respecte might turne o^r bloud
to much Coruption. but moore. the more thou hast
ether of honor office wealth and calling
wch might accite thee to embrace and hugg them
the more doe thou in serpents natures thinke them⟨,⟩
feare ther gay skinns wth thought of ther sharpe state
And lett this be thy maxime, to be greate
Is when the thred of hazard is once Spuñ
A bottom great woond vpp greatly vndonn.

My attention was first called to the passage by the parallel
in the first line to *Oth.* i. 3. 322:

'tis in ourselves that we are thus or thus.

But the whole is at least as good as anything in Addition II(c). The vocabulary is consistent with Shake-

speare's.[1] The coupling of words, especially of the English 'smooth' with the Latin 'dexter' is like him. Even the pun in the fourteenth line is characteristic.

II. EDWARD THE THIRD

[S.R. 1595.] primo die Decembris Cutbert Burby Entred for his copie vnder the handes of the wardens A booke Intitled Edward the Third and the Blacke Prince their warres with kinge John of Fraunce vj^d. (Arber, iii. 55).

[Q1. 1596.] The Raigne of King Edward the third: As it hath bin sundrie times plaied about the Citie of London. [Ornament] London, Printed for Cuthbert Burby. 1596. [Head- and Running-titles] The Raigne of K. Edward The Third.

[Q2. 1599.] [Ornament] The Raigne of King Edward the Third. As it hath bene sundry times played about the Citie of London [Stafford's device (McKerrow 281)] Imprinted at London by Simon Stafford, for Cuthbert Burby: And are to be sold at his shop neere the Royall Exchange. 1599. [Head- and Running-titles] The Raigne of King Edward the third.

[S.R.] Transfers by Mrs. Burby to William Welby on 16 October 1609, Welby to Thomas Snodham on 2 March 1618, Mrs. Snodham to William Stansby on 23 February 1626. Mrs. Stansby to George Bishop on 4 March 1639 (Arber, iii. 420, 621; iv. 152, 459).

Modern Editions. E. Capell (1759–60, *Prolusions*); K. Warnke and L. Proescholdt (1886); G. C. Moore Smith (1897); C. F. Tucker Brooke (1908, *Sh. Apocrypha*, 67).

---

[1] *W.T.* i. 2. 313, 'whom I from meaner form Have bench'd and rear'd to worship'; *T.C.* i. 3. 106,'The primogenitive and due of birth, Prerogative of age'. Shakespeare is rather fond of 'prerogative', 'physic' (vb.), 'hazard', and the 'thread' of life, which is 'spun' in *2 Hen. VI*, iv. 2. 31. He has the 'bottom' of thread (*T.S.*, *T.G.*, *M.N.D.*), 'corrupt' blood (*K.J.*, *2 Hen.* *IV*, *T.N.*, *Lear*), 'dexter' of a cheek (*T.C.* iv. 5. 128), 'accite' in this sense (*2 Hen. IV*, ii. 2. 64), as well as that of 'summon' (*2 Hen. IV*, v. 2. 141; *T.A.* i. 1. 27). 'Respect' has many shades of meaning; that of 'reflection' is not uncommon; e.g. *Ham.* iii. 1. 68, 'There 's the respect, That makes calamity of so long life'. I do not find 'tithe' in the general sense of 'tribute'.

Dissertations. H. v. Friesen, *Ed. III, angeblich ein Stück von Sh.* (1867, *J.* ii. 64); J. P. Collier, *Ed. III, A Historical Play by Sh.* (1874); A. Teetgen, *Sh.'s Ed. III* (1875); A. C. Swinburne, *On the Historical Play of Ed. III* (1879, *Gent. Mag.*; 1880, &c., *Study of Sh.*); E. Phipson, *Ed. III* (1889, *N.S.S. Trans.* 58*); G. Liebau, *K. Ed. III von England und die Gräfin von Salisbury* (1900, 1901), *K. Ed. III von England im Lichte Europäischer Poesie* (1901); R. M. Smith, *Ed. III* (1911, *J.E.G.P.* x. 90); A. Platt, *Ed. III and Sh.'s Sonnets* (1911, *M.L.R.* vi. 511); S. R. Golding, *The Authorship of Ed. III* (1928, *N.Q.* cliv. 313).

There is no external evidence for ascribing any part of *Edward III* to Shakespeare, since we can hardly account as such its inclusion with *Edward II* and *Edward IV* as his in Rogers and Ley's play-list of 1656.[1] Capell's claim for Shakespeare on internal grounds was blessed by the poetic judgement of Tennyson and condemned by that of Swinburne. As a whole the play continues, if only as a belated survivor, the manner of the early school, and stylistic discrimination is therefore (cf. p. 223) difficult. But probably modern criticism is right in finding two hands, of which one only requires serious consideration as Shakespeare's. This begins in i. 2, not I think before l. 94, and goes on to the end of Act ii, taking a complete episode of the wooing of the Countess of Salisbury by Edward, which delays the main progress of the chronicle history. Its literary quality is higher than that of the bulk of the play, and it makes a comparatively free use, about 12 per cent., of feminine endings. This alone would not be conclusive, since feminine endings are much affected (cf. p. 261) by differences of subject-matter. But these scenes are also marked by a constant habit of ringing the changes on individual words, which often run through longish speeches or sections of dialogue. This feature is not apparent in the rest of the play, except in iv. 4, and as this scene is also of better quality than the rest and again has a fairly large number of feminine endings, it may possibly be due to the hand of Act ii. Confidence in dealing with work of this character, when we do not know either its precise date or the company for which it is done, would be absurd. But it is quite possible that these scenes may be Shake-

---

[1] Greg, *Masques*, lxiv.

speare's. The ringing of changes is like him, and the light handling in ii. 1 of Lodwick's love-poetry. Moore Smith notes his 'battledore play of thought'. Some weight, moreover, must be given to the appearance of the line

> Lilies that fester smell far worse than weeds

both as ii. 1. 451 and in *Sonn.* xciv. 14, and in a less degree to the use of 'scarlet ornaments' for blushes in ii. 1. 10 and for sealing lips in *Sonn.* cxlii. 6. I am not much impressed by the arguments which would find these phrases more appropriate in one or the other connexion. But the repetition of the first at least is something more than an echo, and on the whole it seems less plausible to suppose that Shakespeare borrowed from another man's play, than that he made a double use, once in public and once in poems for which he probably did not, when writing them, contemplate publicity. If the *Edward III* scenes are Shakespeare's, the relation to the *Sonnets*, and possibly also the allusion (ii. 2. 153) to Hero and Leander may suggest a date in 1594–5. So does a comparison of the Countess (ii. 2. 193) to Lucrece as

> her, whose ransacked treasury hath task'd
> The vain endeavour of so many pens.

This allusion might, of course, have come either from Shakespeare himself, or from another. The proportion of feminine endings is not too low for that period, outside comedy. Shakespeare had more in *Richard III*, but about as many in *2, 3 Henry VI*, if those are his, and as a whole the play rather recalls that early period. I do not feel able to attempt any serious identification of the second hand. Peele, much given to patriotic writing, was available at any likely date. But we do not know by what writers the tradition of the old school may have been continued after 1593. If, however, the play is of earlier date, Greene may be also a possibility. Robertson is confident that Marlowe was the original writer, and that there was rehandling, especially of the Countess episode, by Greene; and thinks that he can trace contributions by both Peele and Kyd. If there is any such amalgam, we have no tests sufficient to dissolve it.

But I do not see any evidence of revision. The Countess episode is linked to the rest by references at iii. 3. 155 and iii. 5. 100, and R. M. Smith points out that both writers use Froissart for incidents not in Holinshed. For the Countess episode Painter, who repeats additions made to Froissart by Bandello, is also drawn upon. Robertson's treatment does not sufficiently keep apart the problems of the two sections. In that claimed for Shakespeare, the feminine endings are dead against both Marlowe and Greene. Robertson attempts to get over this by assuming that in plays later than those known to be theirs, they both increased their use of this metrical variation. But this is merely *a priori*.

III. PERICLES

[S.R. 1608.] 20 Maij. Edward Blount. Entred for his copie vnder thandes of Sir George Buck knight and Master Warden Seton A booke called. the booke of Pericles prynce of Tyre (Arber, iii. 378).

[Q1. 1609.] The Late, And much admired Play, Called Pericles, Prince of Tyre. With the true Relation of the whole Historie, aduentures, and fortunes of the said Prince: As also, The no lesse strange, and worthy accidents, in the Birth and Life, of his Daughter Mariana. As it hath been diuers and sundry times acted by his Maiesties Seruants, at the Globe on the Banck-side. By William Shakespeare. [*Ornament*] Imprinted at London ⟨by William White⟩ for Henry Gosson, and are to be sold at the signe of the Sunne in Pater-noster row, &c. 1609. [*Head-title*] The Play of Pericles Prince of Tyre, &c. [*Running-title*] Pericles Prince of Tyre. [*or*] The Play of Pericles Prince of Tyre.

[Rules before Gower speeches introducing Acts ii, iii.]

Facsimiles. C. Praetorius (1886, *Sh. Q.* xxi, ed. P. Z. Round; S. Lee (1905).

[Q2. 1609.] [*Title-page and Head-title*] As in Q1. [*Running-title*] The Play of Pericles Prince of Tyre.

[Differentiated from Q1 by 'Eneer Gower' for 'Enter Gower' on sign. A 2 and other variant readings.]

Facsimile. C. Praetorius (1886, *Sh. Q.* xxii, ed. P. Z. Round).

[Q3. 1611.] The Late And much admired Play, Called Pericles, Prince of Tyre. With the true Relation of the whole History, aduentures, and fortunes of the sayd Prince: As also, The no lesse strange and worthy accidents, in the Birth and Life, of his Daughter Mariana. As it hath beene diuers and sundry times acted by his Maiestyes Seruants, at the Globe on the Banck-side. By William Shakespeare. [Ornaments] Printed at London by S⟨imon⟩ S⟨tafford⟩. 1611. [*Head-title*] The Play of Pericles Prince of Tyre, &c. [*Running-title*] The Play of Pericles Prince of Tyre.

[Q4. 1619.] The Late, And much admired Play, Called Pericles, Prince of Tyre. With the true Relation of the whole History, aduentures, and fortunes of the saide Prince. Written by W. Shakespeare. [Jaggard's device (McKerrow 283)] Printed for T⟨homas⟩ P⟨avier⟩ 1619. [*Head-title*] The History of Pericles Prince of Tyre. [*Running-title*] Pericles Prince of Tyre.

[One of the Jaggard reprints (cf. p. 133). The signatures continue those of Q3 of 2, 3 *Hen. VI.*]

[S.R. 1626.] 4° August 1626. Edward Brewster Robert Birde Assigned ouer vnto them by Mistris Pavier and Consent of a full Court of Assistantes all the Estate right title and Interest which Master Thomas Pavier her late husband had in the Copies here after mencioned. xxviij⁵ vizt . . . Master Pavier's right in Shakesperes plaies or any of them . . . (Arber, iv. 164).

[Q5. 1630.] I⟨ohn⟩ N⟨orton⟩ for R. B.
[Two issues.]

[S.R. 1630.] 8° Nouembris 1630 Richard Cotes. Assigned ouer vnto him by master Bird and Consent of a full Court holden this day All his estate right and interest in the Copies hereafter menconed. iiij⁵ . . . Pericles (Arber, iv. 242).

[Arber's 'Persiles' is a misreading; cf. W. W. Greg, *Emendation*, 32.]

[Q6. 1635.] By Thomas Cotes.

[F3, 2nd issue, 1664.] . . . And unto this Impression is added seven Playes, never before Printed in Folio. viz. Pericles Prince of Tyre. . . . [*Additional plays*, pp. 1–20] The much admired Play, called Pericles, Prince of Tyre. With the true Relation of the whole History, Adventures, and Fortunes of the said Prince. Written by W. Shakespeare, and published in his life time.

Parallel-Text. A. Morgan (1891, *Bankside*, xiv).

Modern Editions. K. Deighton (1907, 1925, *Arden*); A. R. Bellinger (1925, *Yale*).

Prose Version.

[1608.] The Painfull Aduentures of Pericles Prince of Tyre. Being the true History of the Play of Pericles, as it was lately presented by the worthy and ancient Poet Iohn Gower. [Woodcut of Gower] At London Printed by T. P⟨urfoot⟩ for Nat. Butter, 1608.

[Only examples known in B.M. and in Zurich Stadtbibliothek. Epistle to Henry Fermor, J.P. of Middlesex, signed George Wilkins.]

Edition. T. Mommsen (1857).

Dissertations. N. Delius, *Über Shs P.* (1868, *J.* iii. 175; *Abl.* i. 77); F. G. Fleay, *On the Play of P.* (1874, *N.S.S. Trans.* 195; *Manual*, 209); R. Boyle, *P.* (1882, *E.S.* v. 363), *On Wilkins's Share in the Play called Sh.'s P.* (1882, *N.S.S. Trans.* 323); A. H. Smyth, *Sh.'s P. and Apollonius of Tyre* (1898); H. T. Baker, *The Authorship of P. v. 1. 1–101* (1907, *M.L.N.* xxii. 222), *The Relation of Sh.'s P. to George Wilkins's Novel* (1908, *P.M.L.A.* xxiii. 100); D. L. Thomas, *On the Play P.* (1908, *E.S.* xxxix. 210); R. M. Garrett, *Gower in P.* (1912, *J.* xlviii. 13); T. S. Graves, *On the Date and Significance of P.* (1916, *M.P.* xiii. 545); K. Steinhaüser, *Die Neueren Anschauungen über die Echtheit von Shs P.* (1918); H. D. Sykes, *Wilkins and Sh.'s P.* (1919, *Sidelights on Sh.* 143); G. Crosse, *P. on the Stage* (1921, *12 N.Q.* viii. 361); H. D. Gray, *Heywood's P. Revised by Sh.* (1925, *P.M.L.A.* xl. 507); V. Østerberg, *Grevinden af Salisbury og Marina af Sh.* (1926); R. P. Cowl, *The Authorship of P.* (1927); P. Allen, *Sh., Jonson and Wilkins as Borrowers* (1928).

The priority of Q1 to Q2 is determined on small typographical points. A misprint of *Eneer* for *Enter* in the first stage-direction serves to distinguish Q2. The text is extremely corrupt and even in the free rearrangement of modern editions many lines remain unrhythmical. Long sections of verse, especially in Acts iii–v, are printed as prose, or are irregularly divided. This prose is not quite like that in *Lear*, because it has more punctuation, but it suggests a report, possibly with the aid of shorthand. There may have been some omissions. This condition of the text complicates both the problem of authorship and that of date. The most obvious thing about the play is that, as it stands, it cannot all be by one writer. It may be divided into (*a*) the main substance of Acts i–ii, (*b*) that of iii–v, (*c*) the brothel scenes, iv. 2, 5, 6, chiefly in prose, (*d*) the prologues and epilogue spoken by Gower, with their dumb-shows. These include iv. 4 and v. 2, which divide the last two acts into sections. There is an unmistakable difference of style between (*a*) and (*b*). The latter is clearly Shakespeare's in the temper and manner of his late romances, and the best passages are sufficient to dispose of Cowl's suggestion that a deliberate imitator has been at work. On the other hand (*a*) does not read like Shakespeare at any stage of development. It is fairly competent verse, but without distinction. Many rhymed couplets are awkwardly interspersed, and there are only two-thirds as many feminine endings as in (*b*). One might be tempted to ascribe to Shakespeare i. 1. 100:

> The blind mole casts
> Copp'd hills towards heaven, to tell the earth is throng'd
> By man's oppression; and the poor worm doth die for't.

No weight, however, can be attached to such an isolated passage. Attempts have been made to ascribe (*c*) to a third hand, but in view of the similar scenes in *Measure for Measure*, there is no reason why they should not go with (*b*), and several phrases seem very Shakespearean. Of the Gower passages (*d*) those before the first four acts and also v. 2 are in octosyllabic couplets of intended archaism. This quality is not so obvious in the decasyllabic couplets of the others, but they are probably by the same hand and not Shakespeare's.

In some form the play must have existed before Blount's

registration entry of 20 May 1608. This is clearly for a
play, as Buck was the licenser. We do not know why
Blount never published a Quarto, or why he did not take
the play into F1. It is of course possible that he made an
unregistered transfer to Gosson, but he is not very likely
to have been concerned with surreptitious copy. Pollard
(cf. p. 146) suggests that his was a 'blocking' entry, but
if so it was singularly futile, since, so far as we know,
he did not intervene when Gosson published. A performance of *Pericles* was seen (cf. App. D) by the Venetian ambassador Zorzi Giustinian at some date between
5 January 1606 and 23 November 1608. The prose
novel by Wilkins was printed in 1608, and it is safest
(cf. p. 175) to regard this as a calendar-year date. The
relation of the novel to the play is obscure. Wilkins, in the
epistle, offers 'a poore infant of my braine' and this does
not necessarily refer to anything but the novel itself. In
an 'Argument', he entreats the reader 'to receiue this
Historie in the same maner as it was vnder the habite of
ancient *Gower* the famous English Poet, by the Kings
Maiesties Players excellently presented'. He makes no
other reference to Gower except on the title-page and in
a heading to ch. i. The incidents narrated by Gower as
presenter of the play come in the ordinary run of the
novel. But in the novel as in the play the names of the
characters are substantially from Gower's *Confessio Aman-
tis*, although in both much use is made of Laurence
Twine's *The Patterne of Paynfull Adventures*, the title of
which that of the novel echoes. This was registered in
1576.[1] A later undated edition and one of 1607 are extant.
The names Pericles and Marina, neither in Gower nor
in Twine, are also common to the novel and the play.
It has often been held that the second hand of the play is
that of Wilkins himself. The case is most fully put by
Sykes, on the basis of a stylistic comparison with other
work of Wilkins. There is, however, little to go upon.
Beyond the novel itself and a prose pamphlet on *The
Miseries of Barbary* (1603) the recorded and independent

[1] Arber, ii. 301.

writing of Wilkins is limited to his *Miseries of Enforced Marriage* (1607), for the King's men.[1] He shared with Day and William Rowley in *The Travels of Three English Brothers* (1607) for the Queen's,[2] and with Dekker in the pamphlet *Jests to Make You Merrie* (1607). Conjecture has assigned to him *A Yorkshire Tragedy* (cf. p. 535), and shares in *Timon of Athens* and Day's *Law Tricks* (1608), probably produced in 1604.[3] The often repeated statement of Fleay, *L.W.* 302, that he 'left the King's company for the Queen's in 1607' means nothing. He was not an actor or tied to any company. I do not myself feel any very strong conviction for or against a common style between *Pericles* i, ii on the one hand, and the *Miseries* and *Travels* on the other. It is part of Sykes's case that the novel was written before the play and formed its basis. I do not think that there is anything in the title-page or the prefatory matter to disprove or to prove this. Structurally the two follow much the same lines. There are some differences in the detail of incidents, and some inversions of order. These are most marked in iii–v. Two episodes, a musical performance by Pericles at Pentapolis and a blow given by him to Marina at Mitylene, are fully dealt with in the novel, but only obscurely alluded to in ii. 5. 25 and v. 1. 101, 127. Both belong to the traditional story. It must be remembered that we do not know what the reporter of the play may have omitted. Verbally the novel is much less close to the play than one would expect if the writer were merely paraphrasing, and especially if he were paraphrasing his own dramatic work. Here and there throughout, and rather more in i–ii than in iii–v, there are small equivalences of expression, often no more than a single word or pair of words, but enough to testify to some connexion. On the other hand, the greater part of the play dialogue, even where it is striking, is not reflected at all in the novel, but is represented by something much more commonplace. The novel, again, makes far more use than the play of Twine, and reproduces con-

[1] Cf. *Eliz. Stage*, iii. 513.   [3] *Ibid.* iii. 285.
[2] *Ibid.* iii. 286.

siderable passages *verbatim*. So far one would gladly think that it stood intermediate between Twine and the play, and that the dramatists, whether Wilkins·was one of them or not, used it as their source, and picked up from it a stray phrase here and there. The difficulty is that some of the common phrases, as well as some other phrases in the novel, read like blank verse. No doubt Wilkins, like Shakespeare himself (cf. p. 233), might let his prose run into verse rhythms. Some of the bits in question may be of this type. But such an explanation can hardly cover those which do in fact occur in the same or almost the same form in the play. One cannot suppose that two distinct playwrights followed the practice of incorporating these. They are not many, but have to be accounted for. I will give them.

> (1) A gentleman of Tyre; my name Pericles;
>   My education been in arts and arms;
>   Who, looking for adventures in the world,
>   Was by the rough seas reft of ships and men
>   And after shipwreck driven upon this shore   (ii. 3. 81–5).

Pericles . . . thus returneth what hee is, that hee was a Gentleman of Tyre, his name Pericles, his education beene in Artes and Armes, who looking for aduentures in the world, was by the rough and vnconstant Seas, most vnfortunately bereft both of shippes and men, and after shipwrecke, throwen vpon that shoare (Mommsen 32).

> (2) I came unto your court for honour's cause,
>   And not to be a rebel to her state   (ii. 5. 61–2).

Pericles . . . replyed, That . . . euen in his bosom he would write the lie: affirming, that he came into his Court in search of honour, and not to be a rebell to his State (Mommsen 39).

> (3) Thou art the rudeliest welcome to this world
>   That ever was princess' child. Happy what follows!
>   Thou hast as chiding a nativity,
>   As fire, air, water, earth and heaven can make,
>   To herald thee from the womb:
>   Even at the first, thy loss is more than can
>   Thy portage quit, with all thou canst find here:
>   Now the good gods throw their best eyes upon't. (iii. 1. 30–7).

Poore inch of Nature (quoth he) thou arte as rudely welcome to the worlde, as euer Princesse Babe was, and hast as chiding a natiuitie, as fire, ayre, earth, and water can affoord thee (Mommsen 44).

Here the reporter may have omitted 'Poore inch of Nature' from the play. It would fit well enough into the fifth line, the incompleteness of which is obscured by rearrangement in the Globe text. Sykes thinks that it might be Wilkins's phrase, but surely in its setting it is Shakespearean, and there are analogous uses of 'inch' in *Ant. & Cleo.* i. 2. 59 *Wint. Tale*, ii. 1. 137; iv. 4. 460. It is difficult to resist the conviction that, in these passages at least, the novel rests on the play, and on the play with Shakespeare's contribution in it. Of this last point, there is confirmation in the following:

> Her eyelids, cases to those heavenly jewels
> Which Pericles hath lost,
> Begin to part their fringes of bright gold;
> The diamonds of a most praised water
> Do appear, to make the world twice rich. (iii. 2. 99–103).

Hee perceiued . . . the golden fringes of her eyes alitle to part . . . lifting vp those now againe pricelesse diamonds of her eyes (Mommsen 48).

Here the 'now againe' can only be a clumsy rendering of Shakespeare's 'twice rich'. Given a borrowing of verse from the play in the examples already cited, one may legitimately suspect it in one or two other places. Perhaps the most notable are:

(1) I traytour, quoth the king, that thus disguised, art stolne into my Court, with the witchcraft of thy actions to bewitch, the yeelding spirit of my tender Childe (Mommsen 38).

(2) A stragling Theseus borne we know not where (Mommsen 39).

(3) But daughter (quoth Simonides) equalles to equalles, good to good is ioyned, this not being so, the bauine of your minde in rashnesse kindled, must againe be quenched, or purchase our displeasure. And for you sir (speaking to prince Pericles) first learne to know, I banish you my Court (Mommsen 40).

(4) It shall become you still to be euen as you are, a peece of good-

ness, the best wrought vppe, that euer Nature made, and if that any shall inforce you ill, if you but send to me, I am your friend (Mommsen 67).

The rhythms of (1) (2) (4) are not from the corresponding passages at ii. 5. 49, 78; iv. 6. 118–23, and there is no passage corresponding to (3). Again we must keep the reporter and his perversions in mind. It is, however, conceivable that the writer of the novel was here quoting a version of the play which is not quite ours. A rather elaborate theory is required to reconcile the evidence of the verse snippets with the structural resemblance of play and novel, their general remoteness from each other in wording, and their increasing divergence in Acts iii–v. And where all is dark, I incline to find a solution in the view that there was an earlier play, that a new version was written by Shakespeare and another, and that the novel was not the source of the play, but was put together by Wilkins, not directly from any dramatic text, but from reminiscences of both versions, with the help of a liberal resort to Twine. I do not think it is inconceivable that Wilkins was Shakespeare's collaborator, although the textual remoteness of the novel from the play is rather against it. But I see no reason to suppose that he had anything to do with iii–v, unless he supplied the Gower passages, or that any part of the older version survives in our text. An analogy for the complete Jacobean rehandling of an old dramatic theme is afforded by *Lear*, and the addition of scenes to the old *Mucedorus* about 1610 may also be noted. The hypothesis here adopted is helpful chronologically, because it enables Shakespeare's work to be put late in 1608, instead of before Blount's entry in the previous May. It would be difficult to find room for it earlier, since it must be later than *Coriolanus* and *Timon of Athens*, for both of which we seem driven to 1607–8. On the other hand, we have nothing else for 1608–9. I take it that the old play had been revived, that it proved sufficiently popular in topic to justify a rewriting, and that Blount meant to print it, but desisted on learning that rewriting was contemplated. The reprinting of Twine's story in 1607 possibly dates the

revival. Giustinian may have seen either the old or the
new version. Little importance, however, can be attached
to the attempt of Graves to find 1606 by analogies, in i. 1 to
the alleged plot to shoot James I, and in i. 4 to Giustinian's negotiations for the export of grain to Venice.
The incidents in the play come from the traditional story.
Marina need not be the Princess Mary (1605–7) and the
success of Pericles in the tourney would be an imperfect
consolation to James for his failure against Christian of
Denmark.[1] Perhaps some hints of antiquity may be found
in the linking of *Pericles* with *Shore*[2] in the *Pimlyco* of 1609
(App. B, no. xxxiii), although the writer has also a 'new
play' in mind; in Jonson's scoff at the 'mouldy tale' (App.
B, no. xxii); and even in Dryden's obviously mistaken
notion that *Pericles* was Shakespeare's first play (App. C,
no. xii). Collier forged an entry to suggest a performance
at the Rose about 1598 (App. F, no. xi, *e*). Baker conjectured that two early English plays might underlie two
seventeenth-century Dutch ones which he had not seen.
But the description of these, which were by Pieter Bor
Christiaenz, in Smyth 35 does not suggest an English
origin. Some relation between Twine's *Patterne of Paynfull Adventures* and the *Paynfull Pilgrimage* played at
court in 1567–8 has also been conjectured.[3] *Pericles* itself
was revived in 1619 and 1631 (App. D).

The evolution of the story is admirably traced by Smyth.
It is that of Apollonius of Tyre, probably of Greek origin,
but first known in a fifth- or sixth-century Latin form, of
which manuscripts are widespread. It got into all the
European tongues. Gower took it from the *Pantheon* (c.
1186) of Godfrey of Viterbo, and Twine from the *Gesta
Romanorum*. The name Pericles, as a substitute for Apollonius, is generally regarded as derived from the Pyrocles of
Sidney's *Arcadia* and not from the Athenian statesman. But
Smyth points out (69) that Perillie is in a fifteenth-century
French version, and Philemon, as the name of Cerimon's
servant, seems (71) only to be paralleled by the Philominus
of Heinrich von Neustadt's fourteenth-century *Apollonius*

---

[1] *Eliz. Stage*, i. 146.   [2] *Ibid.* iv. 10.   [3] *Ibid.* iv. 144.

von Tyrland. Unless these are mere coincidences, there may
have been some unrecorded channel of transmission. An
Apolonius and Camilla was registered by John Perrin on
9 October 1587.[1]

IV. THE TWO NOBLE KINSMEN

[S.R. 1634.] 8° Aprilis Master John Waterson Entred
for his Copy vnder the hands of Sir Henry Herbert and
master Aspley warden a Tragi Comedy called the two
noble kinsmen by John ffletcher and William Shakespeare.
vj^d. (Arber, iv. 316).

[Q. 1634.] The Two Noble Kinsmen: Presented at the
Blackfriers by the Kings Maiesties servants, with great
applause: Written by the memorable Worthies of their
time;

> { M^r. John Fletcher, and ⎫ Gent.
> { M^r. William Shakspeare. ⎭

[Cotes's device, formerly Jaggard's (McKerrow 283)]
Printed at London by Tho. Cotes, for Iohn Waterson:
and are to be sold at the signe of the Crowne in Pauls
Church-yard. 1634.

[Prologue and epilogue.]

Facsimile. J. S. Farmer (1910, *T.F.T.*).

Reprint. H. Littledale (1876, *N.S.S.*).

[S.R. 1646.] The 31th of October 1646. Master Moseley.
Assigned over unto him by vertue of a note under the
hand & seale of Master Waterson and both the wardens,
all the Estate, right, title & interest which the said M^r
Waterson hath in these Playes following (vizt)

> The Elder Brother, his parte. ⎫ by M^r
> Mounsieur Thomas.   ⎬ Flesher.
> The Noble kinsman.   ⎭

(Eyre, i. 250).

[Moseley advertised the play in 1653 and 1654 (Greg, *Masques*,
xxvi, xxviii), and was perhaps selling Waterson's stock. I cannot
find a transfer from him or his estate to the F 2 publishers.]

---

[1] Arber, ii. 476.

[F2. 1679.] Fifty Comedies and Tragedies. Written by Francis Beaumont and John Fletcher, Gentlemen. All in one Volume. Published by the Authors Original Copies, the Songs to each Play being added. [Motto] London, Printed by J. Macock, for John Martyn, Henry Herringman, Richard Marriot, M.D.CLXXIX.

Modern Editions. W. W. Skeat (1875); H. Littledale (1876–85, *N.S.S.*); W. J. Rolfe (1891); C. H. Herford (1897); C. F. Tucker Brooke (1908, *Sh. Apocrypha*).

Dissertations. W. Spalding, *A Letter on Sh.'s Authorship of T.N.K.* (1833; 1876, *N.S.S.*); S. Hickson, *The Shares of Sh. and F. in T.N.K.* (1847, *Westminster Review*, xcii. 59; 1874, *N.S.S. Trans.* 25*, with additions by F. G. Fleay and F. J. Furnivall); N. Delius, *Die angebliche Sh.-F. Autorschaft des Dramas T.N.K.* (1878, *J.* xiii. 16; *Abl.* ii. 1); R. Boyle, *Sh. und T.N.K.* (1881, *E.S.* iv. 34), *On Massinger and T.N.K.* (1882, *N.S.S. Trans.* 371); L. C. T. Bierfreund, *Palemon og Arcite* (1891); E. H. C. Oliphant, *T.N.K.* (1891, *E.S.* xv. 323), *T.N.K.* (1927, *B.F.* 325); A. H. Thorndike, *T.N.K.* (1901, *Influence of B. and F. on Sh.* 44); W. Y. Durand, *Notes on Richard Edwardes* (1902, *J.G.P.* iv. 348); B. Leuschner, *Über das Verhältniss von T.N.K. zu Chaucers Knightes Tale* (1903); O. Petersen, *T.N.K.* (1914, *Anglia*, xxxviii. 213); H. D. Sykes, *T.N.K.* (1916, *M.L.R.* xi. 136; *Sidelights on Sh.* 1); W. J. Lawrence, *New Light on T.N.K.* (1921, July 14, *T.L.S.*, followed by correspondence); A. H. Cruickshank, *Massinger and T.N.K.* (1922); H. D. Gray, *Beaumont and T.N.K.* (1923, *P.Q.* ii. 112); K. Ege, *Der Anteil Shs an T.N.K.* (1924, *J.* lix. 62).

The Q text is a good one, requiring little emendation. Most of the prose (ii. 2; iv. 3) is in capitalized lines of irregular length, and occasionally a passage of verse is printed as prose. The known examples show some variants. The stage-directions are elaborate for the spectacular episodes. Evidently the manuscript had been used as prompt-copy, since some book-keeper's notes, printed in roman type and generally (cf. p. 121) in the left margin, are distinguishable from the italicized stage-directions. Some are additional stage-directions; others notes to have actors and properties ready in advance. Thus '2. Hearses ready, with Palamon: and Arcite: the 3. Queenes. Theseus: and his Lordes ready' (i. 3. 58) is for i. 4; '3. Hearses ready' (i. 4. 26) is for i. 5; 'Chaire and stooles out' (iii. 5. 66) is for iii. 5.

102. A book-keeper must have also added *Curtis* after *Messengers* in the stage-direction to iv. 2. 71, and *T. Tucke: Curtis* after *Attendants* in that to v. 3. 1. The F text is reprinted from Q with many conjectural alterations.

The clearest indication of date is the use in the morris-dance (iii. 5) of characters from one of the anti-masks in Beaumont's *Inner Temple and Gray's Inn Mask* of 20 February 1613.[1] There may be a confirmation of 1613 in Jonson, *Bartholomew Fair* (1614), iv. 3:

> *Quarlous.* Well my word is out of the *Arcadia,* then: *Argalus.*
> *Win-wife.* And mine out of the play, *Palemon.*

The *Arcadia* here is Sidney's. A Palaemon, however, is also in Daniel's play of *The Queen's Arcadia* (1606). A parallel between i. 1. 118 and *The Honest Man's Fortune* of 1613, iii. 1. 151, is perhaps too much of a commonplace to be indicative.[2]   There is certainly no reason to accept the suggestion that the Doctor's cures for love-melancholy (iv. 3; v. 2) come from Burton's very derivative *Anatomy* (1621), ii. 3. 5. The Globe fire of 1613 need not, of course, be the explanation of prol. 30:

> If this play doe not keepe
> A little dull time from us, we perceave
> Our losses fall so thicke, we must needs leave.

In fact the prologue is probably of later date than the play, since it speaks of 'a writer', although there are clearly two. There was probably a court performance about 1619 (App. D). But Littledale's inquiry for a date at which the King's men's losses fell so thick as in 1613 may perhaps point us to 1625, when the death of James was followed by a heavy plague, and the theatres were closed.[3] The actor names in the stage-directions point to a revival of about 1625–6. Curtis Greville left the Lady Elizabeth's men for the Palsgrave's in 1622 and was of the King's by 11 October 1626. Thomas Tuckfield is only known as a hired man of the King's in 1624.[4]

[1] *Eliz. Stage*, iii. 233.   London, 170.
[2] *Ibid.* iii. 227.   [4] Murray, i. 172, 214, 216; Herbert
[3] F. P. Wilson, *Plague in Sh.'s*   74.

The categorical ascription of the play on its title-page to Fletcher and Shakespeare is not much affected by Moseley's later treatment of it as Fletcher's. A 'tradition' that it was Shakespeare's, mentioned by Pope, may only rest on the title-page.[1] Clearly there are at least two hands in the play. Fletcher's is unmistakable in the verse of ii. 3–6, iii. 3–6; iv. 1–2; v. 2. Most of that in i. 1–3; iii. 1; v. 1, 3, 4 cannot possibly be his. The short Scc. i. 4, 5 and iii. 2 may be a little more doubtful. Metrically, the non-Fletcherian verse agrees with that of Shakespeare, in its latest stage, and most precisely with that of the scenes generally ascribed to him in *Henry VIII*, and the converging evidence for the two plays, with the slighter indication for the lost *Cardenio* (cf. p. 539), all pointing to 1613, is strong for some collaboration between Shakespeare and Fletcher in that year. Stylistic features, other than metrical, are confirmatory; the constant use of coined words, of archaistic words, of vigorous unliterary words; the characteristic involutions of the sentence-structure. This is perhaps less noticeable in Act v than in Act i, and I have sometimes thought that a distinction might be made. But probably the impression of style in v is affected by the formal character of the great invocations. Moreover, no other than Shakespeare, certainly not Tourneur, Rowley, or Chapman, who have been loosely talked of, can be supposed capable of these invocations, except possibly Beaumont, and Beaumont is excluded by the metre. They are quite outside the imaginative range of Massinger, whom Boyle and Sykes, regardless of the title-page, would substitute for Shakespeare on the ground of parallels. These, as in *Henry VIII*, are poor evidence for such a derivative writer as Massinger; and even on their merits they are not so strong as those to Shakespeare's own work collected by Littledale. It is noticeable that while these are naturally closest to his late plays, there are also several to *Midsummer-Night's Dream*, associations with which the resumed handling of Theseus may well have evoked. Part of the scepticism as to Shakespeare's presence

[1] *Var.* i. 9.

rests upon the inadequate characterization, especially of Emilia and of the Gaoler's Daughter. But here it is Fletcher, rather than Shakespeare, who is at fault, and Fletcher, especially if he was collaborating with Shakespeare at a distance, may well have failed to hold the pitch. The distribution of the Shakespearean matter shows that it is a case of collaboration and not of the completion by Fletcher of a Shakespearean fragment. In fitting the scenes together, Fletcher may possibly have added a few lines to Shakespeare's. The most likely are i. 1. 25–8; i. 4. 32–8; v. 1. 1–17; v. 4. 23–38. I incline to give i. 5 and iii. 2 to Fletcher and i. 4 on the whole to Shakespeare. Either might have written the song in i. 1. But on these minor points there can be no certainty. Both Littledale and Oliphant think that Beaumont might have helped Fletcher a little. Oliphant suggests that the burlesque at the end of iii. 5 is more in his vein than Fletcher's, and of course it is his mask that is drawn upon. It is not clear that he was still writing in 1613. There is not much room for him in the play, but if he is there at all, the prose of ii. 1 and iv. 3 might be his, rather than Shakespeare's. Either is more likely than Fletcher, who did not make much use of prose. I do not find any evidence of revision.

The source is, of course, Chaucer's *Knightes Tale*. An academic play of *Palamon and Arcite* by Richard Edwardes in 1566 is only known by description.[1] It had some characters and episodes other than those of *Two Noble Kinsmen*. A *Palamon and Arcite* was also produced, not as Oliphant says by the Chamberlain's, but by the Admiral's, in 1594.[2] Petersen would link both the early plays with *Two Noble Kinsmen* in a wonderful and fearful stage history involving five revisions.

V. PLAYS ASCRIBED IN THE THIRD FOLIO

The four plays already discussed are the only ones, outside F1, which can be seriously thought of as, in whole or in part, the work of Shakespeare. Philip Chetwinde, who

---

[1] *Eliz. Stage*, iii. 311.   [2] *Ibid.* ii. 143.

added *Pericles* to the second issue (cf. p. 520) of the Third Folio in 1664, accompanied it with six others. Shakespeare's authorship of them all had already been asserted or suggested in Quartos, and in bookseller's lists, which may, as Pollard, *F.Q.* 162, thinks, have influenced Chetwinde. The record of the Quartos is as follows:

(*a*) *Locrine.*

[S.R. 1594.] xx° die Iulij. Thomas Creede. Entred for his Copie vnder thandes of the Wardens. The lamentable Tragedie of Locrine, the eldest sonne of Kinge Brutus, discoursinge the warres of the Brittans &c vjᵈ. (Arber, ii. 656).

[Q. 1595.] The Lamentable Tragedie of Locrine, the eldest sonne of King Brutus, discoursing the warres of the Britaines, and Hunnes, with their discomfiture: The Britaines victorie with their Accidents, and the death of Albanact. No lesse pleasant then profitable. Newly set foorth, ouerseene and corrected, By W. S. [Creede's device (McKerrow 299)] London Printed by Thomas Creede. 1595.

(*b*) *1 Sir John Oldcastle.*

[S.R. 1600.] 11 Augusti. Thomas Pavier. Entred for his copies vnder the handes of master Vicars and the wardens. These iij copies viz. . . . The first parte of the history of the life of Sir John Oldcastell lord Cobham. (Arber, iii. 169).

[Q1. 1600.] The first part Of the true and honorable historie, of the life of Sir John Old-castle, the good Lord Cobham. As it hath been lately acted by the right honorable the Earle of Notingham Lord high Admirall of England his seruants [Simmes's device (McKerrow 142)] London Printed by V. S. for Thomas Pauier, and are to be solde at his shop at the signe of the Catte and Parrots neere the Exchange. 1600.

[Q2. 1619.] The first part Of the true & honorable history, of the Life of Sir Iohn Old-castle, the good Lord

Cobham. As it hath bene lately acted by the Right honorable the Earle of Notingham Lord High Admirall of England, his Seruants. Written by William Shakespeare. [Jaggard's device (McKerrow 283)] London printed for T. P. 1600.

[On the misdating, cf. p. 133.]

(c) Thomas Lord Cromwell.

[S.R. 1602.] 11° Augusti. William Cotton. Entred for his Copie vnder thandes of master Jackson and master Waterson warden A booke called the lyfe and Deathe of the Lord Cromwell, as yt was lately Acted by the Lord Chamberleyn his servantes vj^d. (Arber, iii. 214).

[Q1. 1602.] The True Chronicle Historie of the whole life and death of Thomas Lord Cromwell. As it hath beene sundrie times publikely Acted by the Right Honorable the Lord Chamberlaine his Seruants. Written by W. S. [Richard Read's (?) device (McKerrow 320, without initials)] Imprinted at London for William Iones, and are to be solde at his house neere Holburne conduict, at the signe of the Gunne. 1602.

[S.R. 1611.] 16to Decembris. John Browne. Entred for his Copyes by assignement from William Jones and vnder master warden Lownes his hand . . . and one other booke called, the lyfe and death of the Lord Cromwell, by W: S. xij^d. (Arber, iii. 474).

[Q2. 1613.] The True Chronicle Historie of the whole life and death of Thomas Lord Cromwell. As it hath beene sundry times publikely Acted by the Kings Maiesties Seruants. Written by W. S. [Snodham's device (McKerrow 227)] London: Printed by Thomas Snodham. 1613.

(d) The London Prodigal.

[Q. 1605.] The London Prodigall. As it was plaide by the Kings Maiesties seruants. By William Shakespeare, [Creede's device (McKerrow 299)] London. Printed by T. C. for Nathaniel Butter, and are to be sold neere S Austins gate, at the signe of the pyde Bull. 1605.

(e) *The Puritan*.

[S.R. 1607.] 6 Augusti. George Elde Entred for his copie vnder thandes of Sir George Bucke knight and the wardens a book called the comedie of the Puritan Widowe vj^d (Arber, iii. 358).

[Q. 1607.] The Puritaine Or The Widdow of Watling-streete. Acted by the Children of Paules. Written by W. S. [Eld's device (McKerrow 320, without initials)] Imprinted at London by G. Eld. 1607. [*Head- and Running-titles*] The Puritaine Widdow.

(f) *A Yorkshire Tragedy*.

[S.R. 1608.] 2do die Maij. Master Pavyer Entered for his Copie vnder the handes of master Wilson and master Warden Seton A booke Called A Yorkshire Tragedy written by Wylliam Shakespere vj^d. (Arber, iii. 377).

[Q1. 1608.] A Yorkshire Tragedy. Not so New as Lamentable and true. Acted by his Maiesties Players at the Globe. Written by W. Shakspeare. [Bradock's device (McKerrow 280)] At London Printed by R. B. for Thomas Pauier and are to bee sold at his shop on Cornhill, neere to the exchange. 1608. [*Head-title*] All's One, Or, One Of The Four Plaies In One, Called A York-shire Tragedy As It Was Plaid by the Kings Maiesties Plaiers. [*Running-title*] All's One, or A Yorkshire Tragedy.

[Q2. 1619.] A Yorkshire Tragedie. Not so New, as Lamentable and True. Written by W. Shakespeare. [Jaggard's device (McKerrow 283)] Printed for T. P. 1619: [One of the Jaggard reprints; cf. p. 133.]

These six plays are conveniently reprinted in C. F. Tucker Brooke, *The Shakespeare Apocrypha* (1908). I will not repeat my notices of them from *Eliz. Stage*, iii. 306; iv. 8, 26, 27, 41, 54. The ascriptions now receive no critical support, except that Ward, ii. 231, finds Shakespeare's hand in a few passages of *A Yorkshire Tragedy*. I do not concur. This is claimed as Shakespeare's throughout its bibliographical history. But Pavier's name does not inspire confidence (cf. p. 135), and even if

Henry IV was sometimes (cf. p. 382) called *Sir John Oldcastle*, it can hardly have been through a legitimate confusion that he allowed a second edition of the Admiral's play by Drayton and others to be reprinted with *A Yorkshire Tragedy* as Shakespeare's in Jaggard's enterprise of 1619. Nor does anything we know (cf. pp. 133, 147) of Nathaniel Butter encourage belief in his *bona fides*, when he printed *The London Prodigal* without registration. In these three cases Shakespeare's name was used in full. A charitable construction would find in the W. S. of *The Puritan*, again not even a Chamberlain's play, and of *Thomas Lord Cromwell* some other writer than Shakespeare; a Wentworth or more dubious William Smith,[1] or in the case of *Thomas Lord Cromwell* William Sly. But it looks as if Shakespeare's reputation had 'publicity' value. The playlists of Archer (1656) and Kirkman (1661, 1671) expand both sets of initials into his name (Greg, *Masques*, lx, c). The W. S. of *Locrine* stands on a different footing. Here the only claim is that the play was 'newly set foorth, ouerseene and corrected' by him. I must add to *Eliz. Stage*, iv. 26, that the example with a marginal note by Sir George Buck, there discredited, exists, and is now in the possession of Mr. A. S. W. Rosenbach. It is recorded in the catalogues of E. D. Church (1909) and J. L. Clawson (1924), and attention was called to it by T. S. Graves in *T.L.S.* for 8 January 1925. A facsimile is given by S. A. Tannenbaum, *Sh. Forgeries*, 77, 79, 94. Greg would read the note, which is slightly clipped at the edge:

> Char. Tilney wrot⟨e a⟩
> Tragedy of this mattr ⟨w^ch⟩
> hee named Estrild: ⟨& w^ch⟩
> I think is this. it was ⟨lost?⟩
> by his death. & now(?) ⟨some⟩
> fellow hath published ⟨it⟩
> I made dūbe shewes for it.
> wch I yet have.   G. B⟨ ⟩

Tannenbaum thinks this a forgery. But according to Greg it is probably genuine, and in the rough scribble used

---

[1] *Eliz. Stage*, iii. 493.

by Buck for his annotations on *Barnavelt*.[1] The last two lines were inserted after signature. The play might well, if not written for the public stage, be as early as Tilney's death in September 1586, and it has clearly been 'ouerseene and corrected' before publication, at least to the extent of inserting a reference to Elizabeth's thirty-eighth regnal year, ending on 16 November 1596. If the author was dead, it is not inconceivable that Shakespeare or some other W. S. may have been asked to 'oversee' the printing.

VI. OTHER ASCRIBED PLAYS

Chetwinde did not take into F3 all the plays which had been ascribed to Shakespeare on title-pages. As he had *King John*, he was not likely also to print *The Troublesome Reign*, to Q2 (1611) of which John Helme had added 'Written by W. Sh.'.[2] Perhaps he could not obtain *Two Noble Kinsmen* or the following:—

[Q. 1662.] The Birth Of Merlin: Or, The Childe hath Found his Father. As it hath been several times Acted with great Applause. Written by William Shakespear, and William Rowley. Tho. Johnson for Francis Kirkman and Henry Marsh. 1662.

Rowley is generally accepted as author or reviser,[3] and although Oliphant, *Beaumont and Fletcher*, 410, claims to detect 'one or two lines that seem of a Shakespearean coinage', the suggestion need not be taken seriously.

If Chetwinde had recourse to the booksellers' play-lists,[4] he did not use the anonymous *Edward III*, *Edward IV*, *1 Jeronimo*, *Leir*, *Merry Devil of Edmonton*, and *Mucedorus*, or the Beaumont and Fletcher *Chances*, or Chettle's *Hoffman*, or Kyd's *Spanish Tragedy*, or Marlowe's *Edward II*, or Massinger's *Roman Actor*, or Middleton's *Trick to Catch the Old One*, or Peele's *Arraignment of Paris*; all of which were attributed to Shakespeare either in that of Richard Rogers and William Ley (1656) or in that of Edward Archer (1656), or in those of Francis Kirkman

---

[1] *Eng. Lit. Autographs*, I. xxx, and R.E.S. v. 351.   [2] Cf. p. 364.   [3] *Eliz. Stage*, iii. 474.   [4] Greg, *Masques*, xli, sqq.

(1661, 1671), or in more than one of these. *The Merry Devil of Edmonton*, although it had been in print since 1608, was registered as Shakespeare's by Humphrey Moseley on 9 September 1653. No edition from him is extant. Examples of this play, and of *Mucedorus* and the anonymous *Fair Em*, now separately preserved in the British Museum, were once bound up together in the library of Charles II, and lettered 'Shakespeare, Vol. I'.[1] Speculative criticism has occasionally attempted to find Shakespeare's hand in these three plays, or parts of them, and in others, particularly *Arden of Faversham*, selected by conjecture. But these views now receive little support, and deserve none. Moseley, alone or in co-operation with Humphrey Robinson, was active in collecting plays during the Commonwealth. His more important entries are printed in Greg's *Bakings of Betsy*.[2] Many never got into print, and are now lost. At the Restoration he seems to have claimed the acting rights for his collection.[3] Among the lost plays which he registered on 9 September 1653[4] are

The History of Cardennio, by M[r]. Fletcher. & Shakespeare.
and
Henry y[e]. first, & Hen: y[e] 2[d]. by Shakespeare, & Dauenport.

Others of 29 June 1600[5] include:

The History of King Stephen.
Duke Humphrey, a Tragedy.   } by Will:
Iphis & Iantha, or a marriage } Shakespeare.
   without a man, a Comedy.

John Warburton (1682–1759) left a list of play-manu-scripts, most accurately printed from *Lansdowne MS*. 807 by Greg,[6] which he says were 'unluckely burnd or put under Pye bottoms' by a servant, after he had been many years collecting them. Here recur, among many other of Moseley's titles,

Henry y[e] 1st by Will. Shakespear & Rob. Davenport.
Duke Humphery Will. Shakespear.

---

[1] *Var.* ii. 682; Lee 264.
[2] *3 Library*, ii. 225.
[3] Herbert 90.
[4] Eyre, i. 428.
[5] *Ibid.* ii. 271.
[6] *3 Library*, ii. 230.

The list also has—

A Play by Will Shakespear.

This last entry may be the source of the attribution of *The Second Maiden's Tragedy* (cf. p. 109) to Shakespeare, in a writing later than Warburton's time. That play is a survivor from his collection, but his list assigns it to Chapman. Greg is inclined to doubt whether Warburton really ever had the bulk of Moseley's unprinted plays, and thinks that he may have forgotten the nature of a list of titles which he had compiled from the *Stationers' Register*. However this may be, nothing further is known of *King Stephen*, *Duke Humphrey* (a subject, one would think, sufficiently treated in *Henry VI*), or *Iphis and Iantha*. Obviously no reliance can be placed on Moseley. Robert Davenport's *History of Henry the First* was licensed (Herbert 27) for performance by the King's men on 10 April 1624. An *Iphis* by Henry Bellamy (*c.* 1623) survives in MS. (Hazlitt, *Manual* 116).

Cardennio is another matter. A play of *Cardenno* or *Cardenna* was given by the King's men at court in the winter of 1612–13, and again on 8 June 1613.[1] The source was probably the story of Cardenio and Lucinda, as given in Thomas Shelton's translation (1612, *S.R.* 19 January 1611) of *Don Quixote*; and this, although with altered names, was in fact the source of *Double Falsehood*, produced at Drury Lane on 13 December 1727 by Lewis Theobald as an adaptation from Shakespeare. The career of Theobald may be studied in J. C. Collins, *The Porson of Shakespearean Criticism*;[2] T. R. Lounsbury, *The First Editors of Shakespeare* (1906); R. F. Jones, *Lewis Theobald: His Contribution to English Scholarship* (1919); E. B. Koster, *Lewis Theobald*.[3] A not very successful dramatist, he had already adapted *Richard II* in 1719. His power as a textual scholar had been shown in his *Shakespeare Restored* (1726) and he had made enemies by his criticism of Pope's edition of the plays. His own was to follow in 1734. Doubts were thrown upon the *bona fides*

---

[1] *Eliz. Stage*, iv. 128, 180.   [3] 1922, *English Studies*, iv. 20, 49.
[2] 1895, *Essays and Studies*, 263.

of *Double Falsehood*. It was printed in 1728 with the following title-page:

Double Falshood; Or, The Distrest Lovers. A Play, As it is Acted at the Theatre-Royal in Drury-Lane. Written Originally by W. Shakespeare; And now Revised and Adapted to the Stage By Mr. Theobald, the Author of Shakespeare Restor'd. Quod optanti Divûm promittere nemo Auderet, volvenda Dies, en! attulit ultrò. Virg. London: Printed by J. Watts, at the Printing-Office in Wild-Court near Lincolns-Inn Fields. MDCCXXVIII.

A preface contained the following statement.

It has been alledg'd as incredible, that such a Curiosity should be stifled and lost to the World for above a Century. To This my Answer is short; that tho' it never till now made its Appearance on the Stage, yet one of the Manuscript Copies, which I have, is of above Sixty Years Standing, in the Handwriting of Mr. *Downes*, the famous Old Prompter; and, as I am credibly inform'd, was early in the Possession of the celebrated Mr. *Betterton*, and by Him design'd to have been usher'd into the World. What Accident prevented This Purpose of his, I do not pretend to know: Or thro' what hands it had successively pass'd before that Period of Time. There is a Tradition (which I have from the Noble Person, who supply'd me with One of my Copies) that it was given by our Author, as a Present of Value, to a Natural Daughter of his, for whose Sake he wrote it, in the Time of his Retirement from the Stage. Two other Copies I have (one of which I was glad to purchase at a very good Rate), which may not, perhaps, be quite so old as the Former; but One of Them is much more perfect, and has fewer Flaws and Interruptions in the Sense . . . Others again, to depreciate the Affair, as they thought, have been pleased to urge, that tho' the Play may have some resemblances of *Shakespeare*, yet the *Colouring*, *Diction*, and *Characters* come nearer to the Style and Manner of *Fletcher*. This, I think, is far from deserving any Answer.

The explanation did not quell scepticism; and while some students have been content to take the play as of old, but non-Shakespearean origin, others have treated it as a fabrication, for which the phrase 'ironical mystification' seems inadequate.[1] Recent studies by G. Bradford, *The History of Cardenio, by Mr. Fletcher and Shakespeare*,[2] R. Schevill, *Theobald's Double Falsehood*,[3] W. Graham, *The*

[1] Lee 439.   [2] 1910, *M.L.N.* xxv. 51.   [3] 1911, *M.P.* ix. 269.

Cardenio-Double Falsehood Problem,[1] E. H. C. Oliphant, *Double Falsehood: Shakespeare, Fletcher and Theobald*,[2] show on balance a tendency to rehabilitate the theory of Shakespearean authorship at least in part, which is most clearly expressed by Oliphant in his *Beaumont and Fletcher* (1927), 282. He finds, much overlaid by Theobald's, two original hands, with habits as regards metrical variation, which differ alike from each other's and from those of Theobald in his admitted plays. One of these he takes to be undisputably Fletcher's, and the other, 'a firmer, stronger hand', he accepts as Shakespeare's. He finds it in i. 1, 2; ii. 1, 2, 3; iii. 1, 2; iv. 1; v. 2, but only free from Theobaldian admixture in parts of iv. 1 and v. 2. The view is founded partly on thoughts and phrases which seem to him Shakespearean, partly on the statement of Moseley, partly on the evidence for other collaboration of Fletcher and Shakespeare in 1613, when *Cardenio*, which he supposes to be the original play, appeared. He admits that the divergence of metrical habit between his two hands does not correspond very closely to that between the parts ascribed to Shakespeare and Fletcher respectively in *Henry VIII* and *Two Noble Kinsmen*, but this he ascribes to the levelling effect of Theobald's adaptation. I do not myself think that much can be made of the metrical evidence in such conditions. It is, of course, most unlikely that Theobald knew anything of the *Cardenio* record, and to some extent, therefore, that supports his story. Similarly, he cannot have known of Moseley's entry, since he repudiates Fletcher. There are many queer points about Theobald's own account of the matter. One can hardly find a support for the tradition of the natural daughter in Rowe's unexplained statement (cf. App. C, no. xxv) that Shakespeare left three daughters; and indeed it is absurd, not so much because of any great improbability in Shakespeare's having a natural daughter, as because he did not write his plays under conditions which left him any property in them to transmit, and in any case a play would have been an inadequate provision

[1] 1916, *M.P.* xiv. 269, 568.   [2] 1919, *12 N.Q.* v. 30, 60, 86.

for the poor girl. It is odd that nobody else appears to have seen the three (or was it four?) manuscripts which Theobald claimed to possess, and that they should all have disappeared at or before his death. There is no item which looks at all like them in his sale catalogue of 23 October 1744. It is odd that, if Betterton contemplated a production, there should be no signs of the play in Restoration theatrical records or in the writings of Downes. It is perhaps oddest of all that Theobald, as a Shakespearean scholar, although he still asserted the poet's authorship in his edition of 1734 (iv. 287), made no attempt to publish the unadapted text. But, on the whole, with the *Cardenio* record and Moseley's statement to go upon, it seems to me less likely that Theobald was responsible for a fabrication, than that he had an old play of some sort and a stage tradition about it varying from Moseley's own. It does not follow that Shakespeare had anything to do with the play. I cannot share Oliphant's confidence in Moseley on this point. The play itself, as it stands, is a very poor one. And while I can see traces that may well be Fletcher's, I cannot find a single passage which compels a belief in Shakespeare. Here and there are lines which might be his in no inspired mood. But what possible criterion can distinguish, through the veil of adaptation, second- or third-rate work of Shakespeare from that of a contemporary disciple, or even from what Theobald himself, with his mind steeped in Shakespeare, might write. I will not go into the possibility of alternatives. Malone seems to have thought of Massinger, Farmer of Shirley. Oliphant himself hints at Beaumont.

CHAPTER XI

THE POEMS AND SONNETS

[A full treatment of the problems raised by Shakespeare's non-dramatic writings does not fall within the scope of this work. I have confined myself in the main to points bearing on the biography and the plays. Fuller bibliographical *data* will be found in H. Farr, *Notes on Shakespeare's Printers and Publishers* (1923, *4 Library*, iii. 225), R. Sachs, *Shakespeares Gedichte* (1890, *J.* xxv. 132), and for the *Sonnets* in the editions of Dowden and Alden.]

I. VENUS AND ADONIS

[S.R. 1593.] xviii° Aprilis. Richard Feild Assigned ouer to master Harrison senior 25 Junii 1594. Entred for his copie under thandes of the Archbisshop of Canterbury and master warden Stirrop, a booke intituled, Venus and Adonis, vj^d S. (Arber, ii. 630).

[Q1. 1593.] [Ornament] Venus and Adonis Vilia miretur vulgus: mihi flauus Apollo Pocula Castalia plena ministret aqua. [Field's device (McKerrow 192)] London Imprinted by Richard Field, and are to be sold at the signe of the white Greyhound in Paules Church-yard. 1593.

[A 2 has

To the Right Honorable Henrie Wriothesley, Earle of Southampton, and Baron of Titchfield.

Right Honourable, I know not how I shall offend in dedicating my vnpolisht lines to your Lordship, nor how the worlde will censure mee for choosing so strong a proppe to support so weake a burthen, onelye if your Honour seeme but pleased, I account my selfe highly praised, and vowe to take aduantage of all idle houres, till I haue honoured you with some grauer labour. But if the first heire of my inuention proue deformed, I shall be sorie it had so noble a god-father: and neuer after eare so barren a land, for feare it yeeld me still so bad a haruest, I leaue it to your Honourable suruey, and your Honor to your hearts content which I wish may alwaies answere your owne wish, and the worlds hopefull expectation.

Your Honors in all dutie,

William Shakespeare.]

Facsimiles. W. Griggs (1886, *Sh. Q.* xii, ed. A. Symons); Clarendon Press (1905, ed. S. Lee).

[Q2. 1594.] R. Field.

[S.R. 1594, June 25.] Transfer to John Harrison (Arber, ii. 655).

[Octavo 1. 1595?] R. Field for J. Harrison? [fragment].

[O2. 1596.] Field for Harrison.

[S.R. 1596, June 25.] Transfer to William Leake (Arber, iii. 65).

[O3. 1599.] ⟨Peter Short⟩ for Leake.
Type-Facsimile. C. Edmonds (1870).

[O4. 1599.] ⟨Richard Bradocke⟩ for Leake.

[O5. 1602?] ⟨Bradocke for Leake⟩.
[T.p. missing.]

[O6. 1602.] ⟨Robert Raworth⟩ for Leake.

[O7. 1602.] ⟨Humphrey Lownes⟩ for Leake.

[O8. 1602.] for Leake.
[T.p. only known.]

[S.R. 1617, Feb. 16.] Transfer to William Barrett (Arber, iii. 603).

[O9. 1617.] ⟨William Stansby⟩ for Barrett.

[Five other editions were printed before 1640, including one at Edinburgh in 1627. H. Farr, who identified the unnamed printers in 4 *Library*, iii. 225, called attention to the apparent absence of editions between 1602 and 1617, and suggested that *Venus and Adonis* was in disfavour as licentious, and that as a result some of the editions dated in 1602 were really printed later with unaltered dates. Raworth in fact only took up his freedom as a stationer in 1606 and ceased printing in 1608. According to one statement in the notes on London printing collected by Sir John Lambe in 1635 he was 'supprest for printing another's copy'; according to another he 'forfeited for Venus and Adonis'. Lambe calls him 'an Arrant

Knave' (Arber, iii. 701, 703; iv. 528). I do not see any very clear evidence here of a belated treatment of *Venus and Adonis* as licentious.]

Modern Editions. G. Wyndham (1898); C. K. Pooler (1911, 1927, *Arden*); A. Feuillerat (1927, *Yale*).

Dissertations. J. P. Reardon, *Sh.'s V.A. and Lodge's Scilla's Metamorphosis* (1847, *Sh. Soc. Papers*, iii. 143); A. Morgan, *V.A. a Study of Warwickshire Dialect* (1885, 1900); A. Wuerzner, *Die Orthographie der ersten Q Ausgabe von V.A. und L.* (1887); M. Dürnhofer, *Shs V.A. im Verhältnis zu Ovids Metamorphosen und Constables Schäfergesang* (1890); G. Sarrazin, *Die Abfassungszeit von Shs V.A.* (1894, *E.S.* xix. 352); W. Marschall, *Shs Orthographie* (1927, *Anglia*, li. 307).

A fancy that Shakespeare came from Stratford-on-Avon with *Venus and Adonis* in his pocket still lingers, and rests mainly on the abundance of rural imagery in the poem. This is, of course, readily to be paralleled in *Lucrece* and the earlier plays, and indeed throughout the work of a writer, whose imagination, while it assimilated town life, never became oblivious of the country. It is more natural to refer *Venus and Adonis* to the 'idle hours' of its epistle, which the plague year of 1592 would afford. The writer is in the full literary tide of Renaissance narrative poetry initiated by Spenser, and even if Marlowe's *Hero and Leander* was not yet known to him, not improbably owed at least his metre to Thomas Lodge's *Scillaes Metamorphosis* (1589). In calling *Venus and Adonis* 'the first heir of my inuention', he need mean no more than that it was his first published work. No inference can reasonably be drawn as to whether he had or had not previously written for the stage. Lee 142, however, finds in these words 'reason to believe that the first draft lay in the author's desk through four or five summers and underwent some retouching before it emerged from the press in its final shape'.

II. THE RAPE OF LUCRECE

[S.R. 1594.] 9 Maij Master Harrison Senior Entred for his copie vnder thand of Master Cawood Warden, a booke intituled the Ravyshement of Lucrece vi^d C (Arber, ii. 648).

[Q. 1594.] [Ornament] Lucrece [Field's device (Mc-Kerrow 222)] London. Printed by Richard Field, for Iohn Harrison, and are to be sold at the signe of the white Greyhound in Paules Churh-yard ⟨sic⟩. 1594. [Head-and Running-titles] The Rape Of Lucrece.

[A 2 has

To the Right Honourable, Henry Wriothesley, Earle of Southhampton, and Baron of Titchfield.
The loue I dedicate to your Lordship is without end: wherof this Pamphlet without beginning is but a superfluous Moity. The warrant I haue of your Honourable disposition, not the worth of my vntutored Lines makes it assured of acceptance. What I haue done is yours, what I haue to doe is yours, being part in all I haue, deuoted yours. Were my worth greater, my duety would shew greater, meane time, as it is, it is bound to your Lordship; To whom I wish long life still lengthned with all happinesse.

Your Lordships in all duety.
William Shakespeare.]

Facsimiles. C. Praetorius (1886, *Sh. Q.* xxxv, ed. F. J. Furnivall); Clarendon Press (1905, ed. S. Lee).

[Octavo 1. 1598.] P⟨eter⟩ S⟨hort⟩ for Harrison.

[O2. 1600.] 'London,' I⟨ohn⟩ H⟨arrison⟩ for Harrison.

[O3. 1600.] 'London.' I⟨ohn⟩ H⟨arrison⟩ for Harrison.

[O4. 1607.] N⟨icholas⟩ O⟨kes⟩ for Harrison.

[S.R. 1614, March 1.] Transfer to Roger Jackson (Arber, iii. 542).

[O5. 1616.] T⟨homas⟩ S⟨nodham⟩ for Jackson.
[Two other editions were printed before 1640.]

Modern Editions. G. Wyndham (1898); C. K. Pooler (1911, 1927, *Arden*).

Dissertations. A. Wuerzner, *Die Orthographie der ersten Q Ausgabe von V.A. und L.* (1887); W. Ewig. *Shs L.* (1899, *Anglia*, xxii. 1, 343, 393); W. Marschall, *Shs Orthographie* (1927, *Anglia*, li. 307).

Lucrece may reasonably be taken to be the 'graver labour'

of 'idle hours' promised to Lord Southampton in the epistle to *Venus and Adonis* and can safely be dated in 1593–4.

III. THE PASSIONATE PILGRIM

[Octavo 1. 1599.] The Passionate Pilgrime. By W. Shakespeare. [Ornament] At London Printed ⟨by Thomas Judson⟩ for W. Iaggard, and are to be sold by W. Leake, at the Greyhound in Paules Churchyard. 1599. [*Second title on C 3*] Sonnets To sundry notes of Musicke. [Same imprint].

Facsimile. W. Griggs (1883, *Sh. Q.* x, ed. E. Dowden); Clarendon Press (1905, ed. S. Lee).

[O2. ? date.] A fragment, bound up with one of O1 in the Folger collection, may belong to a second edition.

[O3. 1612.] The Passionate Pilgrime Or Certaine Amorous Sonnets, betweene Venus and Adonis, newly corrected and augmented. By W. Shakespeare. The third Edition. Where-unto is newly added two Loue-Epistles, the first from Paris to Hellen, and Hellens answere backe againe to Paris. Printed by W. Iaggard. 1612.

[The Bodleian copy (Malone 328) contains two t.ps., one of which omits the ascription to Shakespeare.]

Modern Edition. C. K. Pooler (1911, 1927, *Arden*).

Dissertations. A. Hoehner, *Shs P.P.* (1867); J. O. Halliwell-Phillipps, *The P.P.* (1890, *Outlines*, i. 401); E. P. Kuhl, *Sh. and the P.P.* (1919, *M.L.N.* xxxiv. 313).

There are twenty short poems in *The Passionate Pilgrim* since those usually numbered as xiv and xv are continuous. The double title might suggest an intention to attribute i–xv but not xvi–xxi to Shakespeare. In fact there is a little of his work in both sections; i and ii are versions of *Sonnets* cxxxviii and cxliv; iii, v, and xvii are the poetic missives of *Love's Lab. Lost*, iv. 2. 108–22; 3. 60–73, 101–20. There are textual variants, and those in i are so considerable as to indicate either a different form or a loose memorization. It is very doubtful whether any of the other items are by Shakespeare. Richard Barnfield's *Poems in Divers Humours* (1598) had already included viii and xxi, and xviii is assigned to the same Ignoto as xxi in *England's Helicon* (1600). Part of xviii had appeared in Thomas Weelkes, *Madrigals* (1597), but Weelkes did not necessarily write the words as well as the music. *England's Helicon* also has xx as Marlowe's, with the reply, usually ascribed to Raleigh, from which the *Passionate Pilgrim* takes its last quatrain. Bartholomew Griffin's *Fidessa* (1596) had included xi, and the use of the same Venus and Adonis theme in iv, vi, and ix suggests that these may be his, although they have sometimes been accepted as Shakespearean variations on *Venus and Adonis*. A longer version of 'Crabbed age and Youth' (xii) is in Thomas Deloney's *Garland of Goodwill* (1631). This was registered in 1629 as 'the new garland of Goodwill' [1], and perhaps this phrasing may give some support to the very dubious evidence, set out in F. O. Mann, *Works of Deloney*, 562, for an earlier edition. But if it existed, we do not know that 'Crabbed age' was in it. There must at least have been a good deal of new matter to make a fresh registration desirable in 1629, and there can be no assurance that this was all by Deloney, who died about 1600. Perhaps xii is the only doubtful item in the *Passionate Pilgrim* that one would much care to salve as Shakespeare's. Of the rest, xvi cannot be his, and those who think that vii, x, xiii, xiv–xv, and xix may be do not express themselves with much confidence.

The two epistles noted as 'added' on the 1612 title-page are from Thomas Heywood's *Troia Britanica*, 197, 215. This was printed by W. Jaggard in 1609. Heywood (App. B, no. xxxvi) tells us of his annoyance at the use of them, and says that it was shared by Shakespeare. Possibly, therefore, a protest led to the alteration in the 1612 title-page. Malone notes in his copy that, besides the two epistles, there are six other 'added' pieces on D 5–H 7 from *Troia Britanica*, 113, 152, 239, 254, 328. Lee, *P.P.* 49, has missed this. All the borrowings from Heywood seem to be Ovidian translations or adaptations.

---

[1] Arber, iv. 221.

IV. THE PHOENIX AND TURTLE

[Q1. 1601.] Loves Martyr: Or, Rosalins Complaint. Allegorically shadowing the truth of Loue, in the constant Fate of the Phoenix and Turtle. A Poeme . . . by Robert Chester. . . . To these are added some new compositions of seuerall moderne Writers whose names are subscribed to their seuerall workes, vpon the first subiect: viz. the Phoenix and Turtle. . . . London Imprinted ⟨by Richard Field⟩ for E⟨dward⟩ B⟨lount⟩. 1601. [*Second title on Z*] Hereafter Follow Diuerse Poeticall Essaies on the former Subiect; viz: the Turtle and Phœnix. Done by the best and chiefest of our moderne writers, with their names subscribed to their particular workes: neuer before extant. And (now first) consecrated by them all generally, to the loue and merite of the true-noble Knight, Sir Iohn Salisburie . . . [*Ornament*, with Field's motto] MDCI.

[Z 3ᵛ has verses without title, beginning 'Let the bird of lowdest lay', and introducing a *Threnos*, signed 'William Shake-speare'.]

Reprint. A. B. Grosart (1878, *N.S.S.*).

[Q2. 1611.] The Anuals of great Brittaine . . . [Allde's device (McKerrow 310)] London Printed for Mathew Lownes. 1611

Dissertations. J. O. Halliwell-Phillipps, *Some Account of Chester's Love's Martyr* (1865); A. H. R. Fairchild, *The P. and T.* (1904, *E.S.* xxxiii. 337); C. Brown, *Sir John Salusbury and Robert Chester: Poems* (1914).

Love's Martyr is a rambling collection of poems by Robert Chester which, so far as they have any unifying theme, find it in the celebration, under the symbols of the phoenix (Love) and the turtle (Constancy), of the wedded love of his patron, Sir John Salisbury or Salusbury of Lleweni, Denbighshire, himself a poet and Esquire of the Body, and his wife Ursula, illegitimate daughter of Henry 4th Earl of Derby, and its culmination in their daughter Jane. He seems (Brown xxii) to have been an adherent of Cecil, and unfriendly to Essex. The added poems by Shakespeare, Jonson, Chapman, Marston, Vatum Chorus, and Ignoto mostly pay some compliment to the phoenix theme. That of Shakespeare cannot rest upon any deep study of Chester's work, since it laments the childless death of the phoenix and turtle. A son or other relative of Salisbury wrote verses on the First Folio (App. B, no. liv).

V. A LOVER'S COMPLAINT

[For Bibliographical History, see *Sonnets.*]

Modern Edition. G. Wyndham (1898).

Dissertations. N. Delius, *A.L.C.* (1885, *J.* xx. 41; *Abl.* ii. 223); G. Sarrazin, *Über Shs Klage der Liebenden* (1902, *Kleine Sh. Studien*); J. W. Mackail, *A.L.C.* (1912, *Essays and Studies* of *English Assn.* iii. 51); J. M. Robertson, *A.L.C.* (1917, *Sh. and Chapman*, 7).

The Shakespearean authorship of *A Lover's Complaint* is open to much doubt. Mackail points to many features of diction, syntax, and phrasing which, in their cumulative effect tell against him, and finds 'a certain laboriousness, a certain cramped, gritty, discontinuous quality' in the writing as a whole. He rejects the idea that the poem is the work of a beginner, and thinks that the echoes of Shakespeare may be due to imitation, perhaps by the Rival Poet of the *Sonnets.* Robertson argues at length for the authorship of Chapman, and perhaps this is more plausible than some of his other ascriptions to that writer.

VI. ASCRIBED VERSES

The manuscript anthologies and commonplace books of the seventeenth century sometimes contain, not only extracts from Shakespeare, but also miscellaneous poems under his name or initials. Little reliance can be placed on such ascriptions. A few are noted in *Var.* ii. 481, 507; W. J. Thoms, *Anecdotes and Traditions* (1839, *C.S.*), 49; H.P. *Marriage of Wit and Wisdom*, 93, *Rarities*, 52, 237. There is no complete collection and I will not attempt one. A special group is studied in J. Q. Adams, *Sh. as a Writer of Epitaphs.*[1] I discuss elsewhere the 'tombstone' verses (App. A, no. xxv) and the epigrams on Combe (App. A,

[1] 1923, *Manly Studies*, 78.

no. xviii) and Jonson (App. B, no. xxii), and will here note
two others.

(*a*) *Epitaph on Elias James.*

An
Epitaph
When god was pleas'd ye world vnwilling yet
Elias James to nature payd his debt
And here reposeth; as he liv'd he dyde
The saying in him strongly verefi'de
Such life such death y^{en} ye known truth to tell
He liv'd a godly life and dy'de as well.

W^m: Shakespeare.

This is from *Bodl. Rawlinson Poet. MS.* 160, f. 41. It is
dated in the *Cat.* 'about 1640', and I note poems of 1630
(f. 30ᵛ) and 1633 (f. 55).

(*b*) *Epitaphs on the Stanleys.*

Shakspeare   An Epitaph on Sr Edward Standly.
          Ingraven on his Toombe in Tong Church.
    Not monumentall stones preserves our Fame;
    Nor sky-aspiring Piramides our name;
    The memory of him for whom this standes
    Shall out live marble and defacers hands
       When all to times consumption shall bee given,
       Standly for whom this stands shall stand in Heaven.

          On Sr Thomas Standly
    Idem, ibidem
    Ask who lies heere but doe not wheepe;
    Hee is not deade; Hee doth but sleepe;
    This stony Register is for his bones,
    His Fame is more perpetuall, then these stones,
       And his owne goodnesse wth him selfe being gone,
       Shall live when Earthly monument is nonne.

This is given in facsimile by H.P. *Folio,* i (1853), 162,
from a manuscript which is more fully described in H.P.
Reliques, 32, and was later at Warwick Castle. H.P. ascribes the hand to the early part of the reign of Charles I.

If he is right, the manuscript is a much earlier authority than Sir William Dugdale, who copied the epitaphs, with slightly different spelling and punctuation, in a collection appended to his *Visitation of Shropshire* in 1664.[1] Hence it was communicated by Sir Isaac Heard, Garter, to Malone who printed it.[2] It was again given from the manuscript by Mrs. Esdaile in *The Times* for 22 April 1929, with a discussion of the date and authenticity, which was supplemented by Mr. C. G. O. Bridgeman in a letter of May 22. Dugdale heads his copy 'Shakespeare. These following Verses were made by William Shakespeare, the late famous Tragedian', and notes the 'Ask' set as 'Written upon the East end of this Tombe' and the 'Not' set as 'Written upon the West end thereof'. The tomb is still at Tong. It originally stood on the north side of the chancel, but is now at the east end of the south aisle. Descriptions are in G. Griffiths, *History of Tong* (1894), and D. H. S. Cranage, *Architectural Account of Churches in Shropshire*, i (1901), 42. Four arches bear a canopy, and on this lie, rather cramped between four pyramids at its corners, a man in heavy plate-armour and a woman, and beneath it another man wearing, according to Mrs. Esdaile, 'lighter armour of a later type'. On the south face of the tomb is the inscription:

Thomas Stanley Knight second soone of Edward Earle of Derbie Lord Stanley and Strange desended from the familie of the Stanleys married Margaret Vernon one of the daughters and cohaires of Sir George Vernon of Nether Haddon in the countie of Derbie Knighte By whom he had issue two soons Henri and Edw. Henry died an infant and Edw survived to whom thos Lordshipes desended and married The La. Lucie Percie second daughter to Thomas Earl of Northumberland by her he had issue seaven daughters and one soone shee and her 4 daughters 18 Arabella 16 Maie 15 Alis and 13 Priscilla are interred under a monument in ye church of Waltham in ye countie of Essex. Thomas his soone died in his infancie and is buried in ye parishe churche of Winwicke in ye countie of Lanca: ye other three Petronella Francis and Venesie are yet Livinge. Beati mortui qui in Domino moriuntur.

---

[1] *College of Arms MS.* C. 35, f. 20.   [2] 1790, i. 1. 130; *Var.* ii. 507.

The Stanley pedigree, so far as relevant, is as follows:

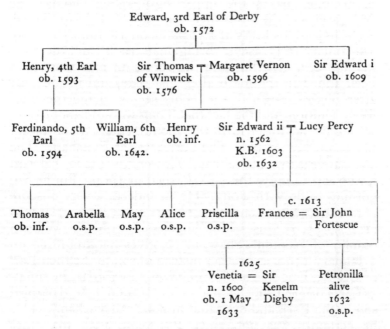

The monument bears no record of its own date, and the only direct indication is an unsupported statement in Every, *Etchings of Tong Church* (1841), that this was 1612. Such a date would be consistent with Mrs. Esdaile's opinion that the style 'suggests the developed Jacobean work of 1610–25', and with Mr. Bridgeman's observation that the inscription would probably have given the marriage (c. 1613) of Frances Stanley, if it had taken place. On the other hand, 1612 would be rather late to put up a monument to persons who died in 1576 and 1596 respectively, and the absence of any description of Sir Edward ii as a knight would of itself suggest that the inscription fell between 1603 and Venetia's birth in 1600. The deaths of his wife and children, to which it refers, have not been dated. But then, again, on what Sir Edward was the verse epitaph written, and whose is the lower figure, which clearly occupies the chief place on the monument?

Mrs. Esdaile, probably influenced by the different types of armour, makes the upper figures Sir Thomas and Margaret, and the lower their son. But Sir Edward ii died, according to his brass at Eynsham, on 18 June 1632 (not 18 January 1633, as Mr. Bridgeman has it), and therefore his figure, if it is his, and the verses on him must have been added to the tomb after that date, and incidentally after Shakespeare's death. This seems to me the most likely solution, and the fact that Tong was sold about 1623 would be no obstacle if the monument, with a vacant place, already existed. The burial was at Eynsham. The alternative is to suppose that the lower figure is Sir Edward i, who according to the *D.N.B.* died in 1609. But he had nothing to do with Tong. He is, indeed, a very obscure personage. The anonymous *History of the House of Stanley* (1767), 51, confuses him hopelessly with Sir William Stanley of Hooton. Shaw, ii. 70, gives his knighting on 2 January 1560, as brother instead of son to the then Earl of Derby. Dugdale in his *Visitation of Lancashire* in 1664–5 (*Chetham Soc.*), iii. 282, makes him second instead of third son to the Earl, and describes him as 'of Eynsham'. This he certainly was not, since Eynsham, with the other Stanley manors in Oxfordshire, were settled (Seacome 52) upon Sir Thomas and his son, afterwards Sir Edward ii, in 1562. Mrs. Esdaile, I fear, rates Dugdale's accuracy, considerable antiquary though he was, altogether too highly, and if the case for Shakespeare's authorship of the verses rested on him, it would not be worth much. Certainly it was no part of his heraldic duty, as she thinks, to record church monuments. The case does not really rest upon him, in view of H.P.'s manuscript, and it was probably from some similar source, directly or indirectly, that the ascription reached him. But such a manuscript is in itself far from being a good authority. It is clear that one set of the verses cannot be Shakespeare's, if it relates to the Sir Edward who owned Tong, and on internal evidence there is no temptation to accept either of them as his. Malone, however, thought them 'of a better leer' (not, as Mrs. Esdaile says, 'better beer') than the James epitaph.

(c) *The Phaethon Sonnet.*

Some anonymous poems have also been attributed to Shakespeare on mere conjecture. The only one worth consideration is a sonnet prefixed to John Florio's *Second Fruits* (1591, S.R. 30 April 1591), which was put forward by W. Minto, *Characteristics of English Poets* (1885), 371.

Phaethon to his Friend Florio.

Sweet friend, whose name agrees with thy increase,
    How fit a rival art thou of the Spring!
    For when each branch hath left his flourishing,
And green-locked Summer's shady pleasures cease,
She makes the Winter's storms repose in peace
    And spends her franchise on each living thing:
    The daisies sprout, the little birds do sing;
Herbs, gums, and plants do vaunt of their release.
So that when all our English wits lay dead
    (Except the Laurel that is ever green),
Thou with thy fruits our barrenness o'erspread
    And set thy flowery pleasance to be seen.
Such fruits, such flow'rets of morality,
Were ne'er before brought out of Italy.

I do not find the conjecture very convincing, although the sonnet has merit. And we are rather in the dark as to the possibilities of any association between Shakespeare and Florio as early as April 1591.

VII. THE SONNETS

[S.R. 1600.] 3 Januarij. Eleazar Edgar Entred for his copye vnder the handes of the Wardens. A booke called *Amours* by J D. with certen oy^r sonnetes by W S. vj^d (Arber, iii. 153).

[The book and its authorship are unknown. Lee 672 says that the *Amours* were 'doubtless' sonnets by Sir John Davies, and that it is 'probable' that the *Sonnets* were by William Smith, who published some as *Chloris* (1596). But this is very confident guessing, where there is nothing but commonplace initials to go upon.]

[S.R. 1609.] 20 Maij Thomas Thorpe Entred for his copie vnder thandes of master Wilson and master

Lownes Warden a Booke called Shakespeares sonnettes vj^d. (Arber, iii. 410).

[Q. 1609.] [Ornament] Shake-speares Sonnets. Neuer before Imprinted. At London By G. Eld for T. T. and are to be solde by Iohn Wright, dwelling at Christ Church gate. 1609. [*Head-title*] Shake-speares, Sonnets. [*Running-title* to K1] Shake-speares Sonnets. [*Head-title* on K1^v] A Louers complaint. By William Shake-speare. [*Running-title* from K2] A Lovers Complaint.

[Some copies of the t.p. end 'and are to be solde by William Aspley. 1609'. On A2 is

TO . THE . ONLIE . BEGETTER . OF.
THESE . INSVING . SONNETS.
M^r. W. H. ALL . HAPPINESSE.
AND . THAT . ETERNITIE.
PROMISED.
BY.
OVR . EVER-LIVING . POET.
WISHETH.
THE . WELL-WISHING.
ADVENTURER . IN.
SETTING.
FORTH.
T. T.   ]

Facsimiles. C. Praetorius (1886, *Sh. Q.* xxx, from *B. M.* C. 21, c. 44, ed. T. Tyler); Clarendon Press (1905, from *Bodl. Malone*, 34, ed. S. Lee); Jonathan Cape (1925, from *B.M.* G. 11181); Noel Douglas (1926).

[S.R. 1639.] 4° Nouembris 1639 . . . John Benson Entred for his Copie vnder the hands of doctor Wykes and Master Fetherston warden An Addicion of some excellent Poems to Shakespeares Poems by other gentlemen. vizt. His mistris drawne. and her mind by Beniamin: Johnson. An Epistle to Beniamin Johnson by Francis Beaumont. His Mistris shade. by R: Herrick. &c. vj^d. (Arber, iv. 487).

[1640.] Poems: Written by Wil. Shake-speare. Gent. [Cotes's device (McKerrow 283)] Printed at London by

Tho. Cotes, and are to be sold by Iohn Benson, dwelling
in S^t. Dunstans Church-yard. 1640.

[Sign. ✱ 2 has

To the Reader.

I Here presume (under favour) to present to your view, some excellent and sweetely composed Poems, of Master William Shakespeare,
Which in themselves appeare of the same purity, the Authour himselfe then living avouched; they had not the fortune by reason of
their Infancie in his death, to have the due accommodation of pro-
portionable glory, with the rest of his everliving Workes, yet the
lines of themselves will afford you a more authentick approbation
than my assurance any way can, to invite your allowance, in your
perusall you shall finde them *Seren*, cleere and eligantly plaine, such
gentle straines as shall recreate and not perplexe your braine, no
intricate or cloudy stuffe to puzzell intellect, but perfect eloquence;
such as will raise your admiration to his praise: this assurance I
know will not differ from your acknowledgement. And certaine
I am, my opinion will be seconded by the sufficiency of these
ensuing Lines; I have beene somewhat solicitus to bring this forth
to the perfect view of all men; and in so doing, glad to be serviceable
for the continuance of glory to the deserved Author in these his
Poems.   I. B.

This is followed by verses on Shakespeare by Leonard Digges
(App. B no. lii) and John Warren. Besides the *Sonnets*, the text
contains (*a*) the full contents of the *Passionate Pilgrim* of 1612,
partly interspersed among the *Sonnets*; (*b*) *A Lover's Complaint*;
(*c*) the *Replies* by Raleigh (now in full) and Ignoto to Marlowe's
lines (*P.P.* xx) from *England's Helicon* (1600); (*d*) the *Song* from
M.M. iv. 1. 1, in the longer version found in Beaumont and
Fletcher's *Bloody Brother* (1639); (*e*) The *Phoenix and Turtle*; (*f*)
Orlando's verses from *A.Y.L.* iii. 2. 133; (*g*) Milton's *Elegy* (App.
B, no. lv); (*h*) Basse's *Elegy* (App. B, no. xlvi); (*i*) an anonymous
Elegy, beginning 'I dare not do thy memory that wrong'. Sign. L 2
is headed 'An Addition of some Excellent Poems, to those precedent,
of Renowned *Shakespeare*, By other Gentlemen'. I have not
attempted to trace these fully, as they are not claimed for Shake-
speare. But they include poems by, or elsewhere ascribed to, Ben
Jonson, Francis Beaumont, Carew, Herrick, Strode, Richard
Clarke, and one I. G.]

Reprint. A. R. Smith (1885).

Modern Editions. E. Dowden (1881), T. Tyler (1890, 1899), G. Wyndham (1898, with *Poems*), S. Butler (1899), C. C. Stopes (1904), H. C. Beeching (1904), A. H. Bullen (1905), W. H. Hadow (1907), C. M. Walsh (1908), R. M. Alden (1916, *Variorum* ed.), C. K. Pooler (1918, *Arden*), E. B. Reed (1923, *Yale*), T. G. Tucker (1924).

Dissertations (selection). J. Boaden, *On the S. of Sh.* (1832, *Gent. Mag.*; 1837); C. A. Brown, *Sh.'s Autobiographical Poems* (1838); N. Delius, *Ueber Shs S.* (1865, *J.* i. 18; *Abl.* i. 1); G. Massey, *Sh.'s S. Never Before Interpreted* (1866), *The Secret Drama of Sh.'s S.* (1872, 1888); H. v. Friesen, *Ueber Shs S.* (1869, *J.* iv. 94); H. Brown, *The S. of Sh. Solved* (1870); K. Goedeke, *Ueber die S. Shs.* (1877, *Deutsche Rundschau*, 386); W. Hertzberg, *Eine griechische Quelle zu Shs S.* (1878, *J.* xiii. 158); T. A. Spalding, *Shs. S.* (1878, *Gent. Mag.*); H. Conrad (formerly Isaac), *Zu den S. Shs* (1878–9, *Archiv*, lix. 155, 241; lx. 33; lxi. 177, 393; lxii. 1, 129), *Wie weit geht die Abhängigkeit Shs von Daniel als Lyriker?* (1882, *J.* xvii. 165), *Die S.-Periode in Shs Leben* (1884, *J.* xix. 176), *Shs Selbstbekenntnisse* (1897); E. Stengel, *Bilden die ersten 126 S. Shs einen Sonettencyclus?* (1881, *E.S.* iv. 1); F. Krauss, *Die schwarze Schöne der Sh-S.* (1881, *J.* xvi. 144); C. C. Stopes, *Sh'.s S.* (1890, *J.* xxv. 185), *The Date of Sh.'s S.* (1898, March 19, 26, *Athenæum*), Mr. *W. H.* (1900, Aug. 4, *Ath.*); G. Sarrazin, *Die Entstehung von Shs L.L.L.* (1895, *J.* xxxi. 200), *Wortechos bei Sh.* (1897, 1898, *J.* xxxiii. 120; xxxiv. 119), *Die Jugend-S.* (1897, *W.S.L.* 149), *Zu S. civ* (1898, *J.* xxxiv. 368), *Die Freundschaftssonette* (1906, *A.S.M.* 75); W. Archer, *Sh.'s S.* (1897, *Fortnightly*, lxii. 817); Lady Newdigate Newdegate, *Gossip from a Muniment-Room* (1897, 1898); T. Tyler, *The Herbert-Fitton Theory of Sh.'s S.* (1898); C. F. McClumpha, *Sh.'s S. and L.L.L.* (1900, *M.L.N.* xv. 335), *Sh.'s S. and M.N.D.* (1901, *M.L.N.* xvi. 328), *Sh.'s S. and R.J.* (1904, *J.* xl. 187); A. Acheson, *Sh. and the Rival Poet* (1903), *Mistress Davenant, The Dark Lady of Sh.'s S.* (1913), *Sh.'s S. Story* (1922); C. Hughes, *Willobie his Avisa* (1904); E. S. Bates, *The Sincerity of Sh.'s S.* (1910, *M.P.* viii. 87); A. Platt, *Ed. III and Sh.'s S.* (1911, *M.L.R.* vi. 511); J. W. Mackail, *Sh.'s S.* (1911, *Lectures on Poetry*, 179); R. M. Alden, *The Q Arrangement of Sh.'s S.* (1913, *Kittredge Anniversary Papers*), *The 1640 Text of Sh.'s S.* (1916, *M.P.* xiv. 17); H. D. Gray, *The Arrangement and Date of Sh.'s S.* (1915, *P.M.L.A.* xxx. 629); M. J. Wolff, *Petrarkismus und Antipetrarkismus in Shs S.* (1916, *E.S.* xlix. 161); H. Ord, *Chaucer and the Rival Poet in Sh.'s S.* (1921); W. Poel and others, *Sh. and the Davenants* (1921, June 2–Aug. 4, *T.L.S.*); O. F. Emerson, *Sh.'s Sonnetteering* (1923, *S.P.* xx. 111); H. T. S. Forrest, *The Five Authors of Sh.'s Sonnets* (1923); J. A. Fort, *The Two Dated S. of Sh.* (1924), *Thorpe's Text of the S.* (1926, *R.E.S.* ii. 439), *The Story Contained in the Second Series of Sh.'s S.* (1927, *R.E.S.* iii. 406), *Further Notes on Sh.'s S.* (1928, 4 *Library*, ix. 305), *The Date of Sh.'s 107th S.* 1929, 4 *Library*, ix. 381), *A Time Scheme for Sh.'s S.* (1929); Sir D. Bray, *The Original Order of Sh.'s S.* (1925), *The Art-Form of the Elizabethan S.*

Sequence and Sh.'s S. (1927, *J.* lxiii. 159); R. Fischer, *Shs S.* (1925); G. B.
Harrison, *Willobie his Avisa* (1926), *The Mortal Moon* (1928, Nov. 29,
T.L.S.); J. M. Robertson, *The Problems of the Sh.S.* (1926); W. Marschall,
Aus Shs poetischen Briefwechsel (1926), *Das Zentralproblem der Sh. S.*
(1927, *Anglia,* li. 31); E. Beckwith, *The Chronology of Sh.'s S.* (1926,
J.E.G.P. xxv. 227).

The 1609 text of the *Sonnets* is not a very good one.
It may rest upon a fairly authoritative manuscript, but
there are sufficient misprints, including misprints of
punctuation not explicable upon any theory (cf. p. 195)
of rhetorical punctuation, to make it clear that the
volume cannot have been 'overseen', as *Venus and Adonis*
and *Lucrece* may have been, by Shakespeare. The absence
of any author's epistle is a further indication of this. The
1640 text does not rest upon any fresh reference to a
manuscript, although the sonnets, of which eight are
omitted, have been regrouped in a new order under
fancy headings, and the pronouns altered so as to suggest
that those really written to a man were written to a woman.
In this respect at least they cannot be, as Benson claimed,
'of the same purity, the Authour himselfe then living
avouched'. For what it is worth, however, the phrase
seems to imply a belief that the original publication was
not contrary to Shakespeare's desire, and perhaps the
same inference might be drawn from William Drummond's statement about 1614 (App. B, no. xl) that Shakespeare had lately published his works. Drummond may
not have been in a position to know much about it.

Shakespeare was known to Meres (App. B, no. xiii)
as a writer of 'sugred Sonnets among his private friends'
in 1598, and versions of two (cxxxviii, cxliv) of those in the
1609 volume had already appeared in the *Passionate
Pilgrim* (1599). It does not follow that all those now
extant were already written. A traditional interpretation,
from the days of Malone, has taken the arrangement of
the 1609 volume at its face value, and treated the bulk
of its contents (i–cxxvi) as forming a single continuous
series, written to a single recipient. If so, this recipient
was a man, since the pronouns show that some of the

sonnets were certainly written to a man. He was a 'lovely boy', whose hair recalled buds of marjoram and his face the lovely April of his mother's prime; and he was of higher social position than the poet's own. The earliest sonnets (i–xvii) urge him to marriage and progeny. The rest take on a more personal note. The boy is at once a patron, to be immortalized by the poet's verse, and an object of close affection, to be spoken of in language which, but for the pronouns, one would have taken to be addressed to a woman. In some of the sonnets he is called 'You'; in others the more intimate 'Thou' is used. I do not think that there is any significance in this. There are many fluctuations of mood. Sometimes the boy is reproached for scandal and wantonness. Sometimes the poet is conscious of his own unworthiness, his 'tann'd antiquity', his 'disgrace with fortune and men's eyes', his 'bewailed guilt', a 'brand' upon his name, due to 'public means which public manners breeds'. He is lame; a literal criticism takes this for autobiography. He is tired of life and obsessed with thoughts of death. There are estrangements and neglects on both sides. Some of these themes are dropped and recur again. At an early stage the friend steals the poet's mistress and is forgiven. Other poets compete in praising the boy. One in particular is a serious rival. The remaining sonnets (cxxvii–cliv) are less homogeneous. They have been called 'a disordered appendix'. But several of them record the poet's love for a dark beauty, who is faithless to him, and who is not unreasonably supposed to be the stolen mistress of the main series. It is in favour of the traditional theory that there is evidently some grouping in the sonnets, and that, if they are read in the light of the theory, there is no obvious lack of coherence. It is certainly not imperative to accept the theory as a whole. The unity of the sonnets is one of atmosphere. The thread of incident is a frail one. Each sonnet is generally self-contained. A few are linked. On the other hand, there is occasionally a jar in the continuity, which may suggest misplacement. There is room for subjective interpretations; and the licence has been freely used. It has been held that the sonnets of the main series were not all written to the same person; that some of them were after all to a woman, Elizabeth or Anne Hathaway or another; that they were written for another man to give to a woman, or for a woman to give to a man; that their intention is dramatic and not personal; that they are a dialogue between 'You' and 'Thou'; that they are allegorical; that they are mere literary exercises in the Petrarchan convention. There is much absurdity in many of these views. More folly has been written about the sonnets than about any other Shakespearean topic. No doubt there is a convention. The attitudes and language of the sonnets can be abundantly paralleled from other Renaissance poems, Italian, French, and English. But the use of a convention is not inconsistent with the expression of personal feeling. The level of poetic value is far from even. It has been thought that the work of other men has been intermingled with Shakespeare's. Mackail rejects or doubts, perhaps justifiably, seven sonnets (cxxviii, cxxxv, cxxxvi, cxliii, cxlv, cliii, cliv) in the second series. Robertson regards about fifty throughout as spurious, and offers as alternative writers Barnes and Chapman. Forrest thinks that Barnes, Warner, Daniel, and Donne all contributed. A claim has been made for Raleigh, who was no doubt at one time lame from a wound. Again, Thorpe's order has been doubted, and attempts made to revise it. Here, too, subjectivity has had full swing. But an objective criterion is proposed by Bray, who thinks that an original order can be determined by rhyme-links between sonnet and sonnet. These are sometimes the same words and sometimes merely words that rhyme together, and they may come in any line of a sonnet. According to the theory, the 'Thou' sonnets were written first on this principle, and the 'You' sonnets dovetailed in later by similar links. It is difficult to think of Shakespeare as occupying himself through a span of years with an exercise of such profitless ingenuity. Moreover, there are many recurrent rhymes in the sonnets, and different arrangements could be worked out on Bray's lines. Much would depend upon the arbitrary selection of this or that sonnet for a starting-point. It is impossible, I think, to be dogmatic on the evidence available. But on the whole, it does not seem to me likely, in view of the character of some of the sonnets in the second series, that the whole collection can have been kept together by any one but Shakespeare himself. And if so, it is most likely that the arrangement of 1609 was his. It does not, of course, follow that in putting them together he made no departure from the chronological order of composition. One might suppose, for example, that cxxvi, which now ends the first series, originally ended the group i–xvii. But clearly, if it was so, the strict chronological order is irrecoverable. Nor does it much matter, so far as the very slight indications of external biography are concerned. And indeed these would remain unaltered, even if it could be shown that some of the sonnets were not Shakespeare's, and that some of the first series were written to a woman. The boy would still be there, and the stolen mistress, and the rival poet. And we should still know little more about them than that they existed, and for a time counted for much in Shakespeare's personal life. It is not surprising that great pains have been spent upon attempts to identify them. The date of the sonnets is, of course, material. Their wording does not give us much help. In xxvii–xxviii, and again in xlviii and l–li the poet is travelling. It is rather futile to relate these absences to the known provincial tours of the Chamberlain's men. Shakespeare may have had many other opportunities of leaving London. In lxvi he speaks of 'art made tongue-tied by authority'. If the reference is to theatrical art, the troubles of 1596 or 1597 (cf. p. 64) are more likely to be in point than those of 1600, by which the Chamberlain's men at least did not stand to lose much. In c we learn that there has been some interval in the sonnetteering; in civ that three years have elapsed since the 'fair friend' was first met. In cxxiv is a very vague allusion to

> thralled discontent,
> Whereto the inviting time our fashion calls.

There should be something more specific in cvii.

> Not mine own fears, nor the prophetic soul
> Of the wide world dreaming on things to come,
> Can yet the lease of my true love control,
> Supposed as forfeit to a confined doom.
> The mortal moon hath her eclipse endured,
> And the sad augurs mock their own presage;
> Incertainties now crown themselves assured
> And peace proclaims olives of endless age.
> Now with the drops of this most balmy time
> My love looks fresh, and Death to me subscribes,
> Since, spite of him, I'll live in this poor rime,
> While he insults o'er dull and speechless tribes:
> > And thou in this shalt find thy monument,
> > When tyrants' crests and tombs of brass are spent.

But even this proves difficult to date. There can be no reference, as has been thought, to anybody's imprisonment. The 'confined doom' can only be the limited duration to which a lease is subject. The 'mortal moon' is doubtless Elizabeth, and the sonnet has been placed in 1603, when James succeeded to the throne, without the opposition which had been anticipated, in the balmy days of spring, and a prospect of peace with Spain opened. Apart from the lateness of the date, an objection to this is that, while death may be called an eclipse, it is not so easy to think that to 'endure' an eclipse can mean to die. G. B. Harrison suggests 1596 when an illness of Elizabeth, in the year of her 'grand climacteric', had caused some alarm at court, which seems to have soon been dispelled, and when a fresh alliance with Henri IV was ratified at Rouen in October, with a royal entry in which Henri was presented by an angel with a sword of peace. He may have been, but the whole object of the alliance was to avoid peace and keep Henri at war with Spain.[1] The augurs, no doubt, had been busy at the end of 1595, and a *Prognostication* printed by Abel Jeffes was suppressed. It seems to have foretold a sea-battle, rather than any special danger to Elizabeth's life.[2] Nor can we suppose that the 'peace' of the sonnet was the Peace of Vervins, made between France and Spain in 1598,

[1] Cheyney, ii. 148, 157.   [2] Cf. E. F. Bosanquet in *4 Library*, viii. 460.

since this when it came was still contrary to English interests.[1] A more plausible date is 1599–1600. In August 1599 there was an alarm of Spanish invasion. Elizabeth was again ill, and the gathering of troops led to 'wilde conjectures' that her life was in danger and even that she was dead.[2] Negotiations for peace had already been opened. They soon became matter of public knowledge, and continued to 28 July 1600, when they broke down at Boulogne.[3] This sonnet cvii comes late in the first series, and for the dating as a whole we are thrown back upon internal evidence. This mainly consists of a large accumulation of parallels. Many of these, of course, are individually slight; it is the mass effect (cf. p. 254) which is relied upon. Alden 447 reduces to statistics the studies of Conrad and H. Davis. Averaged out, these find the greatest number of parallels to the sonnets to be in *Venus and Adonis* and *Lucrece*. Each has about 50. Of the plays, it is naturally only those with a strong love-interest which are relevant. But it seems significant that *Two Gentlemen*, *Love's Labour's Lost*, *Romeo and Juliet*, and *Midsummer-Night's Dream* account between them for about 150, and *Merchant of Venice*, *Much Ado*, *As You Like It*, and *Twelfth Night* for only about 50. McClumpha's examination of *Love's Labour's Lost*, *Romeo and Juliet*, and *Midsummer-Night's Dream* confirms these results. Unfortunately Davis's list remains in manuscript and Conrad's is not fully given. I have an impression that the parallels to the second group of comedies and to *Hamlet*, *Troilus and Cressida*, and other later plays increase in number towards the end of the first sonnet series. The chronological inferences appear to be that the sonnets began as a continuation of the lyrical impulse represented by *Venus and Adonis* and *Lucrece*, in the former of which the invitation to marriage theme is already, rather inappropriately, found; that the three-

---

[1] Cheyney, ii. 447.
[2] Chamberlain, *Eliz.* 62; *Sydney Papers*, ii. 114; *Hatfield MSS.* ix. 277, 302, 428; *H.M.C.* xv, App. v, 88, 94.

[3] Cheyney, ii. 448, 559, citing N. G. Goodman, *Efforts for Peace between England and Spain, 1597–1603* (1925).

years' range of civ was probably 1593–6; that the bulk of
the sonnets belong to this period; and that others were
added more sparsely up to 1599 or so. Some reflection
of the sentiments which occupied the poet's mind may be
traceable in the structure of the plays of 1595 and 1596.
It has been generally assumed that the boy-friend was
some young noble to whom Shakespeare was devoted.
Robert Devereux, Earl of Essex, Henry Wriothesley,
Earl of Southampton, William Lord Herbert, from 1601
Earl of Pembroke, have had their champions. Essex, born
in 1566 and married in 1590, is chronologically impossible.
The careers of Southampton and Herbert show curious
analogies. Both are known (pp. 62, 68; vol. ii, p. 228) to
have shown favour to Shakespeare. Both were good-looking
and had beautiful mothers. Both were much in the public
eye. Both were the subjects of early negotiations for
marriages which came to nothing. Both had amorous relations with ladies of Elizabeth's court and suffered disgrace
and imprisonment as a result, although Southampton
married his Elizabeth Vernon in 1598, whereas Herbert
declined to marry his Mary Fitton in 1601. Neither of
these can, of course, be the Dark Lady, a married woman,
who broke her bed-vow (clii) to take first Shakespeare and
then his friend. Southampton, born in 1573, was perhaps young enough to be called a 'boy' by Shakespeare in
1593–6, and to him *Venus and Adonis* and *Lucrece* were
dedicated. The case for him as the friend of the sonnets
is now very generally accepted, and has been well put
recently by Fort. I do not think it a convincing one. If it
were sound, one would expect to find some hints in the
sonnets of the major interests of Southampton's early life;
his military ambitions, his comradeship with Essex, the
romance of his marriage. There are none. It has, of course,
been apparent that the volume of 1609 is dedicated to 'Mr
W. H.', and that Southampton's initials were H. W.
Attempts have been made to turn this issue by suggesting
that, since 'begetter' in Elizabethan English may mean
'procurer' as well as 'inspirer', the dedication is not to the
friend but to the person who furnished Thorpe with copy.

If so, perhaps the best guess which has been made at a 'Mr W. H.' by the believers in Southampton is Sir William Harvey, who married his mother in 1598. Lee 681 offered William Hall. He found a W. H. who wrote a dedication to the *Foure-fold Meditation* printed as Robert Southwell's in 1606, assumed that both were the William Hall, who was a printer in 1609, but did not print the *Sonnets*, and gave a blessing to a further assumption that this was also a William Hall who married at Hackney in 1608 and might therefore be congratulated on the birth of a child in 1609. He did not go so far as to suggest with Fort and others that 'M^r. W. H. ALL . HAPPINESSE' might be read in a double sense by the omission of a full stop. But all his equations seem to me quite unwarrantable, in view of the commonness of the initials W. H. and the name Hall. And there is some unconscious humour in the notion of Thorpe's dedicating the volume to a printer whom he had not employed. To me it seems more difficult, every time I read the dedication, to believe that, even in Thorpe's affected phrasing, the person to whom he wished eternity was any other than the person to whom the 'ever-living poet' promised eternity. Nor do I feel that in such a document there would be anything very out of the way either in the inversion of initials or in the suppression of an actual or courtesy title. If Southampton was meant by 'Mr W. H.' both these things have been done; if Herbert, one only. The case for Herbert was elaborately argued by Thomas Tyler and others thirty years ago, and I think that it was mishandled. Obsessed by Mary Fitton, they put the bulk of the sonnets in 1598–1601, after Herbert had come to live in London, and related the early group, urging marriage upon the friend, to an abortive match between him and Lady Bridget Vere, which was under discussion in 1597. If the sonnets are of 1593–6, it might well be thought that Herbert, born in 1580, was too young to be their subject, even though he was more naturally to be called a 'boy' at that time than Southampton. But oddly enough, although Tyler used the *Sydney Papers*, he failed, so far as

PLATE XIV

WILLIAM EARL OF PEMBROKE

I can discover, to notice the evidence which they contain that an attempt, probably due to his father's failing health, had already been made as early as 1595 to betroth Herbert at the tender age of 15. On October 8 Rowland Whyte writes to Sir Robert Sydney (i. 353):

> My Lord ⟨Pembroke⟩ hymself, with my Lord *Harbart*, ⟨is⟩ come vp to see the Queen, and (as I heare) to deale in the Matter of a Marriage with Sir *George Careys* Daughter.

The visit was in fact put off, but had taken place, probably by October 29 and certainly by November 3 (i. 355, 356, 357, 361), and on December 5 Whyte reports (i. 372):

> Sir *George Carey* takes it very unkindly, that my Lord of *Pembroke* broke of the Match intended between my Lord *Herbart* and his Daughter, and told the Queen it was becawse he wold not assure him 1000ˡ· a Yeare, which comes to his Daughter, as next a Kinne to Queen *Ann Bullen*. He hath now concluded a Marriage between his Daughter and my Lord *Barkleys* Sonne and Heire.

I will not lay stress upon the doubtful possibilities of an earlier connexion between Shakespeare and Lord Pembroke through the company of 1592–3 (cf. p. 46) or through Fulke Greville, who served under the Earl in his Presidency of Wales (App. C, no. x), or on Shakespeare's alleged visit to Wilton in 1603 (App. D). But it is, I think, relevant that Sir George Carey was son to the patron of the Chamberlain's men in 1595, and that the ultimate marriage of Elizabeth Carey to Thomas Berkeley is perhaps at least as likely as any other to have been honoured by the production of *Midsummer-Night's Dream*. And I am rather struck by the fact that, although Southampton was still alive, it was not to him, but to Herbert and his brother, that F1 was dedicated. On the whole, therefore, I think that, if we are to look in the ranks of the higher nobility, it is Herbert, rather than Southampton, who affords the most plausible identification for Shakespeare's friend. I am not clear that the conditions might not be satisfied by some young man of good birth and breeding, but of less degree than an earl. But I have no candidate to propose. The Rival Poet, from whom we

should desire light, only adds to the obscurity. The
'precious phrase by all the Muses filed' (lxxxv) and 'the
proud full sail of his great verse' (lxxxvi) ought to mean
Spenser, or failing him, Daniel or perhaps Drayton.
Marlowe's death in 1593 probably puts him out of question. Daniel, who was Herbert's tutor at Wilton, dedicated more than one book to his mother Lady Pembroke,
but nothing to Herbert himself before his *Defence of
Rhyme* of 1603. He is perhaps as likely as any one to have
praised him in unpublished verse. His *Epistles* of 1603
include one to Southampton. There are no extant poems
by Spenser or Drayton either to Herbert or to Southampton. Indeed, Southampton was not a great mark for dedications until he came into favour under James. There are
sonnets, in which he is only ranked with others, by
Barnabe Barnes (1593), Gervase Markham (1595),
Henry Lok (1597), and John Florio (1598). It is difficult
to agree with Lee 201 that 'all the conditions of the problem are satisfied' by Barnes. Nashe addresses to Southampton his prose tale of *The Unfortunate Traveller* (1594).
The same writer's indecent *Choise of Valentines* were for a
'Lord S', but Southampton had no claim to be addressed
as the 'fairest bud the red rose euer bare'.[1] W. Minto,
Characteristics of English Poets (1885), 221, suggested an
identification of the rival with Chapman, and his *Shadow
of Night* (1594) has phrases about his inspiration which
might be echoed, although not very closely, in the rival's
'affable familiar ghost' and 'compeers by night' (lxxxvi).
Only the courtesy of a rival, however, could represent the
uncouth manner of his 'hymns' as a 'proud full sail'. Some
hint of Chapman there may also be in *Love's Labour's
Lost* (cf. p. 337), but Acheson's attempts to find traces
of a standing feud between Shakespeare and Chapman
throughout both the sonnets and Chapman's poems
are very far-fetched. And Chapman again dedicated
nothing Elizabethan to Herbert, or to Southampton, or
to a 'Mr W. H.'. One other clue proves equally elusive.
A poem called *Willobie his Avisa* was registered on

[1] McKerrow, iii. 403.

PLATE XV

HENRY EARL OF SOUTHAMPTON

3 September 1594 and printed in the same year. In fluent but undistinguished verse it describes the successive and fruitless assaults upon the virtue of Avisa by 'a Nobleman' before her marriage, and after by 'a Caveleiro', by 'D. B. a French man', by 'Dydimus Harco, Anglo-Germanus', and finally by 'Henrico Willobego, Italo-Hispalensis'. The last of these has (cf. App. B, no. viii) a 'familiar friend W. S. who not long before had tryed the curtesy of the like passion, and was now newly recouered of the like infection', and who 'vewing afar off the course of this louing Comedy, determined to see whether it would sort to a happier end for this new actor than it did for the old player'. The 'like passion' does not, I think, mean a passion for Avisa herself. There is a dialogue between W. S. and H. W. in which W. S. says (cf. *Sonn.* xli; 1 *Hen. VI*, v. 3. 78; *Tit. Andr.* ii. 1. 83; *Rich. III*, i. 2. 229):

> She is no Saynt, She is no Nonne,
> I thinke in tyme she may be wonne.

It seems natural to see some sort of allusion to Shakespeare's love affair here; the more as his *Lucrece* is cited (cf. App. B, no. ix) in a set of commendatory verses, mysteriously subscribed 'Contraria Contrarijs: Vigilantius: Dormitanus'. Another set by Abell Emet tells us nothing. Henry Willobie is said in an epistle, subscribed 'Hadrian Dorrell', and dated at Oxford on an October 1, to be himself the author of the poem. I will not draw any inference from the fact that his inverted initials would make W. H. We know very little about him. Dorrell says that he was his 'chamber fellow' and 'a scholler of very good hope', who had 'departed voluntarily to her Maiesties service' to see other countries. Dorrell had found the poem in his friend's study. He thinks Avisa 'a fained name', but one A. D. in the west of England can rival her virtues. Presumably A. D. is Dorrell's own wife. There are later editions of the poem in 1605 ('The fourth time corrected and augmented'), 1609, and 1635 ('The fifth time corrected'). Obviously some have been lost, probably because, when the High Commission were condemning satirical books in

1599, they directed 'Willobies *Adviso* to be Called in'.[1] One of these may have been in 1596, as the edition of 1635 has a fresh epistle by Dorrell, again from Oxford, but evidently misdated as '30. of *June*. 1569'. Here he seems to imply that Avisa was only an imaginary personage. A statement that the poem was written 'thirtie and fiue yeeres since' cannot, however, date from 1596. The 1635 edition has an added poem in which one Rogero judges a contention on chastity. It is subscribed 'Thomas Willoby Frater Henrici Willoby nuper defuncti'. Finally, it may be noted that Dorrell's later epistle refers to the poem of one P. C. This is *Penelope's Complaint* (1596), which has an epistle by Peter Colse to Edith, wife of Sir Ralph Horsey, and verses by S. D. to Colse, discrediting Avisa's virtue in comparison with Penelope's, and calling her 'conjux cauponis, filia pandochei'. I see no reason to reject Willobie's authorship of *Avisa*. Hughes pointed out that Henry Willobie of Wilts. and not Hadrian, but Thomas Darell of Berks., matriculated together, the former from St. John's and the latter from B.N.C. on 19 December 1591. Willobie migrated to Exeter, whence he took his degree, presumably on his return from abroad, in February 1595. With his brother Thomas he is in the pedigree of the Willoughbys of West Knoyle, Wilts.[2] There are some topographical indications in the poem itself which Harrison has satisfactorily interpreted as showing that Avisa was born at Cerne Abbas in Dorset, 'where Austine pitcht his Monkish tent', and dwelt after marriage at an inn of St. George in the neighbouring town of Sherborne, 'where hanges the badge of England's Saint'. Both places are within reasonable reach of West Knoyle. The belated condemnation of 1599 shows that there was some element of scandal in the poem. Probably it is beyond recovery. The suitors, other than Willobie, as yet throw no light, although Harco should stand for Harcourt. I do not think that Harrison is justified in transferring the authorship of the poem from Willobie to Matthew Roydon, the friend of Chapman, and

[1] Arber, iii. 678.   [2] G. W. Marshall, *Visitation of Wilts*, 58.

treating it as an attack on the morals of Southampton in the interests of Raleigh. It is true that in 1592 Raleigh had acquired the estate of Sherborne, and that in March 1594 Cerne Abbas was the scene of an inquiry into charges of atheism against him, held by Viscount Howard of Bindon, Sir Ralph Horsey, and others at the direction of the High Commission. It is not known that anything came of it, or that Southampton was in any way concerned. No doubt, as a friend of Essex, he may not have been on good terms with Raleigh. Peter Colse's lucubration may imply some interest of the Horsey family in Avisa. One of the three extant poems ascribed to Roydon uses the same stanza-form as *Avisa*. It is, I think, more pedantic and cumbrous in style. Roydon was with the King of Scotland in the autumn of 1593, and it is not known when he returned. Even more tenuous are the speculations of Acheson, by whom the claim for Roydon as the author of *Avisa* was originally made. Avis or Avice is a known Christian name, of which Hughes found several examples at Mere, close to West Knoyle. Acheson treats it as standing for a surname Bird, assumes that Avisa's Christian name was Anne, and identifies her, certainly in error, with the A. D. of Dorrell's epistle. At Bristol, connected, like Cerne Abbas, by tradition with St. Augustine, he finds a William Bird, who was mayor in 1576 and died in 1590. He left five 'natural' children. A daughter Mary married Miles Jackson and a daughter Anne married John Dowle. This Anne will not do for Acheson. Bird also left legacies to Anne and Mary, daughter of one William Sachfeilde, mercer. These Acheson conjectures to have really been Bird's own 'natural' children, taking the term not in its normal Elizabethan sense of children by blood, but in its later one of 'bastards', of which the first *O.E.D.* example, and that a quibbling one, is of 1586. In 1616 Miles Jackson left a legacy to 'my sister Hatton'. She is put down as Mary Sachfeilde. And now, by an astonishing leap, Anne Sachfeilde is transferred to Oxford, and becomes a hypothetical first wife of John Davenant, who is assumed to have lived, although he did not, at the sign of St. George. And according to Acheson, it was with this wife that Shakespeare had an amour, which tradition has transferred to Davenant's blameless second wife Jane. The link is in Davenant's will of 1622, in which he makes a John Bird overseer, and invites 'my sister Hatton' to live with his daughters.[1] I have only set out this romance, because it gives a convenient opportunity of stating what is known of John Davenant. The facts are mainly collected from the documents in A. Acheson, *Shakespeare's Sonnet Story* (1922), especially the valuable *excursus* by E. T. Leeds on the Crown Inn and Tavern, contributions by W. H. Hutton and E. T. Leeds to the *Catalogue of the Bodleian Shakespeare Exhibition* (1916), and H. E. Salter, *Oxford City Properties* (1926, *O.H.S.*), *Oxford Council Acts* (1928, *O.H.S.*). G. Matcham's pedigree in *The Hundred of Frustfield*, 85, contributed to R. C. Hoare, *Modern History of South Wilts* (1844), v, does not seem to be quite correct. John Davenant's will shows an interest in the Merchant Taylors of London, at whose school three of his sons, but not William, were educated.[2] It is reasonable to identify him with the son of a John Davenett who became free of the Merchant Taylors in 1563, was warden of the company in 1592,[3] and was probably of an Essex family, from which also came John (1576–1641), Bishop of Salisbury. His son John was born in 1565, himself went to the Merchant Taylors' School in 1575, was apprenticed in 1581, and became free of the Merchant Taylors in 1589.[4] Thereafter he disappears from London; there is nothing to connect him with Bristol. At Oxford, 'Mr John Davenauntt vintener' took out his freedom by purchase and obtained a city licence to sell wine on 4 June 1604.[5] He passed through the various stages of the municipal hierarchy, became mayor in 1621, and died during his mayoralty on 19 April 1622.[6] The earliest

[1] H.P. ii. 46, from *P.C.C. Saville*, 113.

[2] C. J. Robinson, *Register of Merchant Taylors' School*, i. 85, 97, 98.

[3] Acheson 611; C. M. Clode, *Early History of the Merchant Taylors*, ii. 343.

[4] Robinson, i. 23.

[5] *O.C.A.* 160.

[6] *Ibid.* 308.

traces of him in Oxford are the christenings in St. Martin's church of his children Jane (11 Feb. 1602), Robert (14 March 1603), Alice (30 Dec. 1604), William (3 March 1606). Here the name is Dennant, Devenet, and Davenannt, and in the entry of 1603 John is already a vintner. His wife, buried a few days before him, was a Jane. Matcham calls her Jane Shepherd of Durham. Verses, once preserved at Warwick Castle, call her 'a vertuous wife', and bid the pair 'Sleepe ondisturb'ed as in your marriagebed'.[1] Their second son, William, became the well-known playwright and theatrical manager of Caroline and Restoration days. It is not necessary to go to Bristol for the John Bird and 'sister Hatton' of Davenant's will. A John Bird, mercer, was his colleague on the city council, and had himself been mayor in 1615–16. He is traceable from 1601 to 1625, and therefore survived Davenant.[2] A Timothy Hatton, embroiderer, was also of the council. He took a lease of a house at Eynsham, which the city had recently purchased, on 29 February 1616 and was buried on 5 November 1616.[3] His widow may well have been Davenant's 'sister Hatton'. The tradition of Shakespeare's relations with the Davenants is given in 1681 by Aubrey (App. C, no. xiii), in part at least from Robert Davenant and Samuel Butler, and in 1692 by Wood (App. C, no. xvii), and later by Hearne (App. C, no. xxvi), who got it at Oxford, and by Spence, Oldys, and Wight (App. C, nos. xxx, xxxiv, xxxv), who got it through Pope from Betterton. Rowe does not mention it. Wood is discreet, but the rest all know the rumour that William Davenant was the natural son of Shakespeare, which was first put in print by Chetwood (App. C, no. xxxvii) in 1749. The scandal, whether there was any ground for it or not, includes, from Hearne onwards, a jest, which is first found in John Taylor's *Wit and Mirth* (1629). Here it is anonymous, but according to Oldys Taylor picked up other jests in his collection at Oxford.

A boy, whose mother was noted to be one not overloden with

---

[1] H.P. ii. 48.
[2] *O.C.A.* 139, 148, 170, 212, 247, 335.
[3] *Ibid.* 179, 196, 222, 233, 252, 263; Wood, *City of Oxford*, iii. 231.

honesty, went to seeke his godfather, and enquiring for him, quoth one to him, Who is thy godfather? The boy repli'd, his name is goodman Digland the gardiner. Oh, said the man, if he be thy godfather, he is at the next alehouse, but I fear thou takest God's name in vain.

It is likely enough that Shakespeare sojourned with the Davenants on his way between London and Stratford, and that William was his godson. And it is, one fears, not unlikely that William, desirous to be thought Shakespeare's poetic son, was tolerant to the ascription of a more literal paternity. But the story, such as it is, is a seventeenth-century one, and can have nothing to do with *Willobie his Avisa* in 1594. John Davenant certainly lived at some time in the house known in Wood's day as the Crown Tavern, the history of which has been traced by E. T. Leeds. It survives, refronted, as 3 Cornmarket St., Oxford, and here, in an upper room, probably once a bed-chamber, was discovered in 1927[1] the interesting mural decoration of flowers and vines and pious utterance, reproduced as Plate XVI. The house stood in St. Martin's parish, and seems to have been contiguous at the back to the Cross (now Golden Cross) Inn, from which a small intervening tenement separated it on the street front. It was the property of New College, in whose books a series of leases of it are recorded. There were, however, evidently sub-leases from time to time to actual occupiers. Vintry in Oxford was subject to licence, and the jurisdiction was disputed between the university and the city, each of which appears to have issued three licences.[2] One John Tattleton had a college lease of No. 3 from 1564 to his death in 1581. He may have been a vintner, but no licence is on record. In 1583 John Underhill had a lease, but Elizabeth Tattleton was still occupier. In 1592 William Hough junior had a lease, and William Hough, furrier, was resident. A William Hough died about 1596, and his son, also a William, about 1606. The elder William had college leases of the Cross Inn in 1574, 1583, and 1592, but the actual occupier here up to 1583

---

[1] *Oxford Times* for 6 July 1928.   [2] *O.C.P.* 347.

was John Waklin. Hough's widow Joan remarried with
John Staunton and still occupied No. 3 in 1601. She was
then for the second time a widow, but her husband had
conveyed the Cross Inn to her brother Pearse Underhill,
who died as innholder there in 1604, and in 1605 Andrew
Leigh had a college lease of the inn. Pearse Underhill had
obtained university licences both for an inn and a wine-shop
in 1596. At an earlier date (1583–92) he had held a
college lease of the small tenement between No. 3 and the
Cross. Joan Staunton bought a garden behind No. 3 in
1601 and was still alive in 1622, when she gave it to her
son Daniel. But she cannot then have been still resident
at No. 3, since on 1 August 1613 a college lease had
been granted to Walter Payne, and in this the house is
described as in the occupation of 'John Davenett, vintner,
late Elizabeth Tattleton widow'. Davenant was still in
'my house, the taverne' at the time of his death in 1622,
and his lease had then another five or six years to run.

He left the house to his son Robert, but with a right to his
apprentice Thomas Hallom, in the event of his marrying
one of his daughters, to use the wine-shop. There is a little
puzzle about this, since provision is made for the payment of a rent to 'Mr Huffe', and the New College leases
suggest that the Houghs had no interest at this time in
No. 3, although Daniel Hough obtained such a lease in
1627. Conceivably a rent was due to him in 1622 for the
garden, which was not the property of New College until
1638 when he sold it to them. But one would expect also
to find a rent due for the house to some inheritor of Walter
Payne, who died in 1619.[1] Conceivably, again, Daniel
Hough acquired Payne's interest. In any case Thomas
Hallom did marry Jane Davenant in 1622, and they
remained as occupiers and vintners at least to 1636. Up
to this date the house seems to have had no sign but a
bush. It is still called 'Tattleton's' in 1627. By 1648 it
was the Salutation and by 1675 the Crown. A Crown
from which a burial is noted in 1622 was presumably
another house.[2] John Davenant's tenancy of No. 3 from

[1] A. Wood, *City of Oxford*, iii. 231.   [2] C. J. H. Fletcher, *St. Martin's, Oxford*, 136.

1613 overlaps with Shakespeare's lifetime. It is not so clear that it existed earlier and covered the date of William Davenant's birth in 1606. Walter Payne had a city wine licence in 1595, with a proviso that he was not to appoint a substitute without consent. He also held a city inn or victualling licence in 1596, and is still described as an innholder in 1617.[1] He was, however, also a cordwainer, and long acted as scrutator of leather for the city.[2] Salter suggests that he surrendered his wine licence, and that it is this which was granted to Davenant in 1604.[3] It may be so, but this would not bring Davenant to No. 3 Cornmarket St. Moreover, holders of city licences had to be freemen,[4] and John was already a vintner by 1603. Probably, therefore, he then held a university licence, and apparently he still had one in 1611–12, and probably in 1620 when he surrendered his city one. If this was that granted to Pearse Underhill in 1596, Davenant might have obtained with it the occupation of No. 3 at some time after 1601. I must leave it at that, but it is necessary to add that a wine-shop was not a place of accommodation for travellers, and that if Shakespeare stayed there, it was presumably as a private guest of the Davenants. On the other hand, a Christ Church lease of property adjoining the Cross Inn in 1619 is said by Acheson, 655, on the authority of Salter, to show John Davenant, vintner, as then occupying the inn under Walter Payne. This, of course, suggests that Shakespeare may have sojourned there, but not before 1605. There is no reference to the inn in Davenant's will.

---

[1] Wood, *City of Oxford*, iii. 35.   [3] *O.C.P.* 349.
[2] *O.C.A.* 1, 92, 105, 106, 114, 152.   [4] *O.C.A.* 84.

PRINTED IN GREAT BRITAIN AT THE UNIVERSITY PRESS, OXFORD
BY VIVIAN RIDLER, PRINTER TO THE UNIVERSITY